the Unofficial Guide® to Paris

2nd Edition

David Applefield

& Bob Sehlinger

Hungry Minds™

Best-Selling Books • Digital Downloads • e-Books • Answer Networks • e-Newsletters
Branded Web Sites • e-Learning

New York, NY ♦ Cleveland, OH ♦ Indianapolis, IN

Also available from Hungry Minds

Beyond Disney: The Unofficial Guide to Universal,
Sea World, and the Best of Central Florida

Inside Disney: The Incredible Story of Walt Disney World
and the Man Behind the Mouse

Mini Las Vegas: The Pocket-Sized Unofficial Guide

Mini-Mickey: The Pocket-Sized Unofficial Guide to Walt Disney World

The Unofficial Guide to Bed & Breakfasts in California

The Unofficial Guide to Bed & Breakfasts in New England

The Unofficial Guide to Bed & Breakfasts in the Northwest

The Unofficial Guide to Bed & Breakfasts in the Southeast

The Unofficial Guide to Branson, Missouri

The Unofficial Guide to California with Kids

The Unofficial Guide to Chicago

The Unofficial Guide to Cruises

The Unofficial Guide to Disneyland

The Unofficial Guide to Disneyland Paris

The Unofficial Guide to Florida with Kids

The Unofficial Guide to Golf Vacations in the Eastern U.S.

The Unofficial Guide to the Great Smoky and Blue Ridge Region

The Unofficial Guide to Hawaii

The Unofficial Guide to Las Vegas

The Unofficial Guide to London

The Unofficial Guide to the Mid-Atlantic with Kids

The Unofficial Guide to New England and New York with Kids

The Unofficial Guide to New York City

The Unofficial Guide to New Orleans

The Unofficial Guide to San Francisco

The Unofficial Guide to Skiing in the West

The Unofficial Guide to South Florida

The Unofficial Guide to the Southeast with Kids

The Unofficial Guide to Walt Disney World

The Unofficial Guide to Walt Disney World for Grown-Ups

The Unofficial Guide to Walt Disney World with Kids

The Unofficial Guide to Washington, D.C.

The Unofficial Guide to the World's Best Diving Vacations

For Julia, Alexandre, Anna, and Ernesto

Please note that prices fluctuate in the course of time, and travel information changes under the impact of many factors that influence the travel industry. We therefore suggest that you write or call ahead for confirmation when making your travel plans. Every effort has been made to ensure the accuracy of information throughout this book and the contents of this publication are believed correct at the time of printing. Nevertheless, the publishers cannot accept responsibility for errors or omissions or for changes in details given in this guide or for the consequences of any reliance on the information provided by the same. Assessments of attractions and so forth are based upon the author's own experience and therefore, descriptions given in this guide necessarily contain an element of subjective opinion, which may not reflect the publisher's opinion or dictate a reader's own experience on another occasion. Readers are invited to write to the publisher with ideas, comments, and suggestions for future editions

Your safety is important to us, so we encourage you to stay alert and be aware of your surroundings. Keep a close eye on cameras, purses, and wallets, all favorite targets of thieves and pickpockets.

Hungry Minds, Inc.
909 Third Avenue
New York, NY 10022

Produced by Menasha Ridge Press
COVER DESIGN BY MICHAEL J. FREELAND
INTERIOR DESIGN BY MICHELE LASEAU

Unofficial Guide is a registered trademark of Hungry Minds, Inc.

ISBN 0-7645-6445-5

ISSN 1521-4915

Manufactured in the United States of America

10 9 8 7 6 5 4 3 2 1

Contents

List of Maps

Introduction

Welcome to the City of Light

Bonjour (bohn-**jzoor**), you're a lucky person. You're going to Paris, one of the most enchanting spots on earth. As experienced lovers of the French capital ourselves, trust us when we tell you that when it comes to feeling the vibrancy of being alive, there is nothing like a visit to Paris. Adrenaline runs high in the City of Light, as Paris is popularly called, and its magical ability to ignite the passions of its visitors awaits you. No wonder why the terms *bon vivant* and *savoir vivre* are French!

Brace yourself for that glorious feeling of freedom that accompanies you as you lose yourself (or find yourself) in the anonymity of the place. Truly, you do not need a highly programmed schedule to indulge in the riches of Paris. Simple things like strolling along the banks of the Seine river or wasting away an hour or two in a picturesque café with a glass of red wine, for example, produce genuine and original delight no matter the time of year or hour of day (or night). Alone, with a friend or spouse, or even with the whole family, the experience of being in Paris is always singular and personal. It's as if the city marks you on the forehead and you become one of its children, destined to come back to redo the things you loved doing and seeing the last time. So, in essence, much of the myth becomes real and the clichés are rooted in fact—when you know what you're doing. Which, of course, is where *The Unofficial Guide to Paris* comes in.

Although it only takes a moment to fall in love with Paris, you need to be energetic, curious, well informed, well prepared, poised in psychic elegance, and yet wholly spontaneous to really know her. And if you can't be all of these things? Well then, you'll have to settle for simply being in love.

Paris is not only the capital of France, it is the northern capital of the Latin spirit. It's where the soul meets the body and the mind meets the heart. It's where you lovingly do the "wrong" things for the right reasons.

Like eating sinfully rich and expensive desserts, buying silk, kissing in public, learning to drink Calvados, and ignoring the clock. Paris is not a city to be overly rational in. And yet it's also the hub of high intellect and culture, where matters of theory consume people in cafés and style and form take on greater importance than practicality and price. Be forewarned, Paris is going to be on the expensive side, but this won't bother you except in contemplation. Once in Paris, your billfold will disengage from your conscience and attach itself to your spirit. You won't give another thought to what you are spending until you arrive home and have to pay off your credit card. Of course, we will scrupulously try to protect your pocketbook at each turn of your visit, but in the end, don't be surprised to discover that you've reevaluated the relationship between money and value.

Although a Catholic country (although not too Catholic; Church and State were officially separated in 1905), the French don't live for tomorrow. There may be an afterlife, but what really counts is dinner this evening and that concert tomorrow night, sexy shoes, and strong coffee. In Paris, let your motto be carpe diem!

Even as a visitor to this city, you will walk a tightrope between the finest relics of the past and the sophistication of the moment. When you approach your stay with the openness needed to become a surrogate Parisian, the city reveals its curious ability to seduce you and you'll suddenly find yourself on one of Paris's gilded bridges asking yourself if you shouldn't give up your job back home and become a watercolorist on the Left Bank. Or a chef or poet, or write that novel. The question is perfect to rejuvenate the soul! But don't panic; there's no need to decide right away. Duck into a bistro for a glass of Beaujolais. And dream a bit. Being a traveler in Paris is a never-ending odyssey; actually, you don't visit Paris, you end up having a relationship with it over the course of your life. And this is by far the best way to enjoy the city, as a visitor like yourself. Although you're not a Parisian, we urge you to feel like one. Paris belongs to its visitors during the days they are here and beyond. You're not a stranger. You become part of your host city, and you will come back to revisit those special feelings as often as you can. This is the Paris we encourage you to discover. The real Paris—and its culture, which lies richly embedded in the art and architecture, the cuisine and wine, the perfume and fashions, the language and music, and, of course, the gestures of the people.

But like all good things, Paris is also complex, and Parisians can be complicated. The truth remains that, although Paris is one of the world's most visited places, it is also one of its most misunderstood cities. A rapid wave of crass commercialism, indicative of corporate globalization everywhere, has not spared the French capital, and the frenzy of contemporary life encroaches on the city's deep, indigenous charm. The impatience of a people consumed by a deeply reserved public self often translates wrongly as rudeness. The sense of independence and national pride, characteristic of the French, is often felt as arrogance or intolerance. Most often you'll think you're witnessing cool indifference, but in reality there is lots going on beneath that disinterested glare that Parisians often show tourists. The insistence on local ways being combined with a love of form and an obsession with procedure can be particularly difficult for Anglo-Saxons to comprehend. In the street or at the dinner table, in a taxi or at your hotel, you may find that the way things are done in Paris is disorienting or, worse, defies logic. Yes, but it's your logic, not theirs. You'll not understand why you can't have lunch at 3 p.m. or dinner at 6 p.m. You'll question why that Right Bank gift shop won't give you a refund, and you'll want to pull your hair out wondering why the bank won't put out another teller when there are 13 people waiting in line to change money. In the larger realm of a Paris visit, these are small things that can be deflected with elegance and calm by simply knowing in advance and planning around the cultural sticking points. This "knowing,"—the key to the *Unofficial Guide to Paris*—will be your ticket to understanding, and let's face it, along with accurate expectations, understanding your destination is the magic potion to a satisfying visit anywhere. Making you feel at home from the moment you set foot on French soil, while packing your mental luggage with a treasure chest of otherwise unavailable tips, inside information, and smart little tricks of the Paris trade, has been both our *raison d'être* and pleasure. So, *bienvenue à Paris* (welcome to Paris) and *on y va*—let's get going. We have lots to see and do.

About This Guide

Why Unofficial?

Welcome to the *Unofficial Guide to Paris*. Along with London, this guide marks the maiden voyage for the popular *Unofficial* series overseas. The internal structure and organization of this guide has been specifically conceived for Paris while maintaining the same orientation as all the other *Unofficial Guides*. We have made a special effort to turn over every stone in your path, to open doors, to anticipate the questions and obstacles that foreign travel to Paris may present. Like usual, this guide sets out to represent your interests and save you time, money, and effort so that in the three, five, or seven days you have in Paris you won't waste half of them in just figuring out how things work. Above all, we have attempted to bring you close to the best and most authentic aspects of a mythic place. Paris is not New York or Tokyo, and we want you to find the most Parisian parts of Paris.

Much of the information in this guide is not found elsewhere. When possible we've included details tailored to your needs and expectations. We've thought in advance what Paris is like if you're traveling with children, if you're on a limited budget, if you're a single woman, if you're gay, if your French is dreadful . . . The inside track of experiencing Paris is the product of 20 years of hands-on, on-site research. Having said that, the needs of international travelers change and vary. As do the conditions of hotels, the quality of restaurants, and the prices of everything. With humility and curiosity we invite you to tell us what you have found most helpful, what we might want to include in subsequent editions, and where—if any—our recommendations need to be reexamined. Thank you/*Merci* (**mair**-see).

About *Unofficial* Guides

Readers care about the authors' opinions. The authors, after all, are supposed to know what they are talking about. This, coupled with the fact that the traveler wants quick answers (as opposed to endless alternatives), dictates that authors should be explicit, prescriptive, and above all, direct. The authors of the *Unofficial Guide* try to do just that. They spell out alternatives and recommend specific courses of action. They simplify complicated destinations and attractions and allow the traveler to feel in control in the most unfamiliar environments. The objective of the *Unofficial Guide* authors is not to give the most information or all of the information, but to offer the most accessible, useful information. Of course, in a city like Paris there are many hotels, restaurants, and attractions that are so closely woven into the fabric of the city that to omit them from our guide because we can't recommend them would be a disservice to our readers. We have included all the famous haunts, giving our opinion and experience of them, in the hope that you will approach (or avoid) these institutions armed with the necessary intelligence.

An *Unofficial Guide* is a critical reference work; it focuses on a travel destination that appears to be especially complex. Our authors and research team are completely independent from the attractions, restaurants, and hotels we describe. The *Unofficial Guide to Paris* is designed for individuals and families traveling for the fun of it, as well as for business, and will be especially helpful to those hopping across the pond for the first time. The guide is directed at value-conscious, consumer-oriented adults who seek a cost-effective, though not spartan, travel style.

Special Features

- Handy pronunciation key for essential French words.
- Friendly introductions to key Paris neighborhoods.

- "Best of" listings giving our well-qualified opinions on everything from croissants to trips on the Seine.

- Listings that are keyed to your interests, so you can pick and choose.

- Advice to sightseers on how to avoid the worst crowds; advice to business travelers on how to avoid traffic and excessive costs.

- Recommendations for lesser-known sights that are off the well-beaten tourist path, but no less worthwhile.

- A district (arrondissement) system and maps to make it easy to find places you want to go and avoid places you don't.

- A hotel section that helps you narrow down your choices quickly, according to your needs and preferences.

- Shorter listings that include only those restaurants, clubs, and hotels we think are worth considering.

- A district section that tells you what you can do in a particular area, with "rain dates" to cover any need to make a quick change in plans.

- A table of contents and detailed index to help you find things fast.

- Insider advice on best times of day (or night) to go places.

About This Updated Second Edition

With this edition, we introduce the arrival of the new European currency, the euro, which in France replaces the French franc. All prices are now listed in euros only (€). There are other significant trends worth noting. The price of hotel rooms has risen substantially in Paris over the last two years in the three- and four-star categories. Count on 20–25-percent increases. The role of the Internet in Paris has increased dramatically, and now you can reach most hotels and businesses by e-mail. Additionally, although this guide is self-sufficient, there are two excellent websites that are particularly helpful as a companion—www.viamichelin.com, which allows you to trace an itinerary from any street address in Paris (or elsewhere in Europe) to any other street address, and www.pagesjaunes.fr, which is your online telephone directory for all Paris area listings and detailed street maps. There is no excuse for picking a location for a hotel, restaurant, etc., blindly anymore.

How This Guide Was Researched and Written

In preparing this work, we've taken little for granted. We try to regain the innocence of a first-time visitor and anticipate every area of surprise, confusion, and curiosity. Each hotel, restaurant, shop, and attraction has been visited by trained observers who conducted detailed evaluations and rated each according to formal criteria. We've conducted hundreds of informal interviews with tourists of all ages and backgrounds to determine what they enjoyed most and least during their Paris visit.

While our observers are independent and impartial, they are "ordinary" travelers. Like you, they visited Paris as tourists or business travelers, noting their satisfaction or dissatisfaction.

The primary difference between the average tourist and the trained evaluator is the evaluator's skills in organization, preparation, and observation. The trained evaluator is responsible for much more than simply observing and cataloging. Observer teams use detailed checklists to analyze hotel rooms, restaurants, nightclubs, and attractions. Finally, evaluator ratings and observations are integrated with tourist reactions and the opinions of patrons for a comprehensive quality profile of each feature and service.

In compiling this guide, we recognize that a tourist's age, background, and interests will strongly influence his or her taste in Paris's wide array of attractions and will account for a preference for one sight or museum over another. Our sole objective is to provide the reader with sufficient description, critical evaluation, and pertinent data to make knowledgeable decisions according to individual tastes.

Letters, Comments, and Questions from Readers

We expect to learn from our mistakes, as well as from the input of our readers, and to improve with each new book and edition. Many of those who use the *Unofficial Guides* write to us asking questions, making comments, or sharing their own discoveries or lessons learned on their trips. We appreciate all such input, both positive and critical, and encourage our readers to continue writing. Readers' comments and observations will frequently be incorporated into revised editions of the *Unofficial Guide* and will contribute immeasurably to its improvement.

How to Write the Author:

David Applefield
The Unofficial Guide to Paris
P.O. Box 43673
Birmingham, AL 35243
E-mail: david@paris-anglo.com

When you write, be sure to put your return address on your letter as well as on the envelope; sometimes envelopes and letters get separated. And remember, our work takes us out of the office for long periods of time, so forgive us if our response is delayed.

Reader Survey

At the back of the guide you will find a short questionnaire that you can use to express opinions about your Paris visit. Clip out the questionnaire along the dotted lines and mail it to this same address.

How This Guide Is Organized: By Subject and Geographic Districts *(Arrondissements)*

We have organized this guide in the order in which you will need it. Thus, Part One, **Understanding Paris,** gives a quick tutorial on the French language, explains how numbers and prices are handled, and gives a brief history of the city. Part Two provides an in-depth discussion for **Planning Your Visit to Paris**—essentially, all you can do before leaving home. Part Three covers in fastidious detail your first major decision: which of the Paris **Hotels** to stay in. Part Four, **Arriving, Getting Oriented, and Departing,** walks you through your first and last days, two of the most stressful travel days of any trip. Part Four also investigates all your special needs for the journey—doctors, baby-sitters, disabled facilities, telephone and e-mail services, and so on. The next section, Part Five, is your guide to **Getting Around Paris** and its environs, whereas in Part Six, **Sightseeing and Tours,** we'll show you how to plan your days, and we offer detailed profiles of Paris's most important attractions. Of course, you must eat, so Part Seven, **Dining in Paris,** takes you on a gourmet tour of some of the best restaurant choices. Since shopping is the second most favorite activity of many travelers, Part Eight, **Shopping in Paris,** takes you by the arm into the best boutiques and suggests what gifts your friends back home will love. Part Nine tells you how to stay in shape and relax via **Exercise and Recreation.** Lastly, Part Ten anticipates your evening activities, outlines the major cultural and entertainment options, and key nightlife under the heading **Entertainment and Nightlife.**

Paris has the built-in convenience of being organized into 20 districts, called *arrondissements,* each with its own mayor and municipal council. Every Paris address indicates the *arrondissement* in which the establishment is found, so we've preserved these geographic borders as a way of organizing this guide. However, note that Paris also has several neighborhoods and regions dating back hundreds of years in some cases, and these may overlap several different *arrondissements.* Detailed explanations of both the neighborhoods and *arrondissement* system follow below. If you can keep the organization of arrondissements in mind while remembering the general locations of the neighborhoods, you'll have no problem navigating the City of Light. *Voila!* And *bon voyage!*

Hotels

There are hundreds of decent hotels in Paris, and yet the criteria you use to choose a hotel in Paris is different than North American criteria. Size of hotel, size of room, star ratings, location, price, aesthetics, convenience to public transportation, organization of the bathroom (does the room have a shower?), breakfast, service, credit cards, view, and more all need to figure in to your decision. We've explained most of the nuances for you to proceed with confidence.

Attractions (Museums, Monuments, Parks, Churches, Landmarks)

Here, instead of long and drawn-out histories, you'll find concise overviews highlighting the key things to see and the best ways to see them. Our fundamental goal is for you to be able to figure out what there is to see and then decide if and when you'll be adding this to your itinerary. Additionally, if you pass by a huge and impressive building or monument, we want to make sure you'll be able to find a handy explanation in this guide.

Restaurants (Bistros, Brasseries, Cafés)

Not only do we provide a bouquet of choice restaurants in Paris, cuisine is such an integral part of experiencing Paris that we've also treated the entire culture of food and drink with great detail. Since you will probably eat a dozen or more restaurant meals during your stay, and since not even you can predict what you might be in the mood for on Saturday night, you can browse through our detailed profiles of some of the best restaurants and some of the best-valued places to eat in the city. There's an abundance of restaurants, so knowledge is the key to eating well at fair prices.

Entertainment and Nightlife (Clubs, Bars, Cabarets)

The Paris nightlife scene is vibrant, varied, and constantly rejuvenating itself. With only a limited number of evenings, it's important to select well what you do and where you go after dinner. Cultural events that happen at night have been included here in the bar and club scene. Other cultural events are found in Part Six, Sightseeing and Tours. Since clubs or night-spots, like restaurants, are usually selected spontaneously after arriving in Paris, we believe detailed descriptions are warranted and helpful. Our selections include the famous and celebrated as well as the latest and trendy, for both the young and immortal and the less-than-young and mortal.

Neighborhoods and *Arrondissements*

Once you've decided where you're going, getting there becomes the issue. To help you do that, we have presented Paris in terms of its historic neighborhoods (and which *arrondissments* they encompass), which we have briefly described here to give you a quick idea of what they're about.

Fortunately, Paris is a very condensed city, and you'll find that whereas London is spread out and distances between areas are great, in Paris it's easy to walk from the Marais to Châtelet and from the Latin Quarter or Saint-

Germain-des-Prés to Montparnasse. Then, we've provided an overview of Paris's main sections or areas worth exploring. They often cross over into more than one *arrondissement.*

Latin Quarter (5th arrondissement)
(Central Paris, Left Bank, from the Seine to Port Royal, Boulevard Saint-Michel to Jardin des Plantes)

This is Paris's spiritual center. The fountain at Saint-Michel is Paris's best-known meeting spot. The area is cluttered with bookstores, students, cafés, boutiques, churches, and small hotels. Intellectual life finds its roots here, with the Sorbonne at the symbolic center. The narrow pedestrian streets are especially lively at night, cluttered now with inexpensive Greek and North African restaurants. The Luxembourg Gardens require at least an hour of your leisure time. If you're not staying in this area, plan to spend some time walking around both during the day and in the evening.

The Marais (3rd arrondissement)
(Central Paris, Right Bank, from the Seine at Hôtel de Ville to République, the Bastille to rue Beaubourg)

Probably Paris's most quaint and charming area, the Marais is steeped in character and history. *Marais* means low land or swamp, and this is in keeping with the area, which is flat and extends from the Seine on the Right Bank. Home of the traditional Jewish community, the Marais has also emerged as the seat of Gay Paris. Filled with wonderful, small streets with lovely facades and doorways, the area hosts some of Paris's best museums, hotels, and shops. Place de Vosges cannot be missed.

Châtelet–Les Halles (1st and 2nd arrondissements)
(Central Paris, Right Bank, from the place du Châtelet to Réamur-Sébastopol, between the Louvre and Hôtel de Ville)

The traditional market area for the city, today Châtelet–Les Halles represents the commercial core of the city. Busy and loud, this area hosts the Pompidou Center, Hôtel de Ville, and the Halles shopping mall. Filled with cafés, shops, movie houses, restaurants, galleries, and hotels, this is also the transportation hub for subway and RER transfers.

Île Saint Louis/Île de la Cité (1st and 4th arrondissements)
(Central Paris, the Two Islands, Notre-Dame and Environs)

Paris's two islands in the center of the city afford visitors a taste of medieval Paris, mixed with both 17th-century mansions and contemporary sophistication. Visits to Notre-Dame and Sainte-Chapelle are musts. Ice cream at Berthillon on the Île Saint Louis shouldn't be overlooked.

Saint-Germain-des-Prés (6th arrondissement)
(Central Paris, Left Bank, Boulevard Saint-Germain-des-Prés, between Saint-Michel and Musée d'Orsay, from the Seine to Jardin du Luxembourg and Sèvres-Babylone)

Chic shopping meets the best of Parisian literary and artistic elements. The famous cafés Les Deux Magots and La Hune nourished many of the last century's greatest writers and thinkers, such as Jean-Paul Sartre and Simone de Beauvoir. Explore the back streets between Boulevard Saint Germain and the Seine for a sampling of avant garde galleries and bookstores. La Palette is the area's best watering hole for the culturally inclined. There are scores of excellent and charming hotels and restaurants here, but be prepared to pay for quality and style.

Bastille/République (11th arrondissement)
(Place de la Bastille, Gare de Lyon, Nation, République, Oberkampf)

Centered around the new Bastille Opéra, this once-poor and bohemian area is now the pulse of Paris nightlife. The rue de Lappe and rue de la Roquette reflect the tone and tempo of the city's music and bar scene. Artists and craftspeople have their workshops in the many alleys and courtyards of the area. Oberkampf is the latest area to explode with hopping nightlife.

Champs-Elysées/Concorde (1st and 8th arrondissements)
(from the Louvre to the Arc de Triomphe, Place de la Concorde, Madeleine, Place Vendôme)

Much of Paris's reputation comes from the aristocratic splendor and the chic grandeur of the world's most famous avenue. It's worth a stroll, but not too much more. The area is expensive and somewhat ruined by the arrival of international clothing and fast-food chains. The walk between the Arc de Triomphe at Etoile and Place de la Concorde, where Marie-Antoinette lost her head, will be memorable, day or night. The Louvre and the Tuileries Gardens, included in this area, are essential stops for all Paris visitors.

Invalides/Eiffel Tower (7th arrondissement)
(Right Bank from Musée d'Orsay to Eiffel Tower, Trocadéro on the Left Bank, Assemblée Nationale to Duroc)

Highly characterized by officialdom, government ministries, and upper-class respectability, this area nonetheless houses the world's most famous landmark, the Eiffel Tower. Les Invalides is Napoléon's resting place, and the Orsay Museum is the place to visit the Impressionists and the best examples of art deco. The area is quiet at night and sometimes a bit too sedate for visitors wishing to be in the throes of street life.

Montparnasse (14th arrondissement)
(Left Bank between Denfert-Rochereau and Jardin du Luxembourg and Port-Royal)

Famous for its large and brassy brasseries—La Coupole, Le Dôme, Le Sélect, La Closerie des Lilas—Montparnasse provided shelter for artists, writers, and bohemians after the First World War. Although upscale and pricey today, these cafés continue to attract the cultural crowd and are worth visiting. The area is filled with small hotels, regional restaurants (Breton crêpes shops), and stores. Go up the Tour Montparnasse, Paris's only skyscraper. The view is breathtaking. Also visit Sartre, Beauvoir, and Beckett in the Montparnasse Cemetery.

Grands Boulevards (10th arrondissement)
(Right Bank between Strasbourg-Saint-Denis and Miromesnil, Opéra, la Bourse, and Covered Arcades)

Once the showcase of Haussmann's 19th-century renovated Paris, today the area is alive with a mixture of financial institutions, old theaters, seedy backstreets, wonderful arcades with tea salons and antiques, and large immigrant communities. Behind the Opéra Garnier you'll find Paris's leading department stores, Les Galeries Lafayette and Le Printemps.

Montmartre (18th arrondissement)
(between the Grands Boulevards and Sacré Coeur, Pigalle, Clichy)

At the northern edge (or top) of the city lies Montmartre. Once a village to itself, today it attracts both Parisians and visitors for its charming little streets around the striking Sacré Coeur Basilica, its tiny restaurants, and art-lined Place du Tertre. Down below, you'll find the Moulin Rouge and other venues of cabaret and burlesque. Pigalle is dotted with porn shops and sex shows. Place Blanche is celebrated for its prostitutes and transvestites. It's safe to walk around day or night, but hang on to your purses and wallets. In the summer, the area is overrun with busloads of tourists from Germany, England, and Holland.

Outer Arrondissements

Here we have grouped other hotels, restaurants, attractions, and nightlife worth visiting that fall outside the inner *arrondissements*. Since this covers a large area that even extends outside Paris at times, note that there is no map of this area.

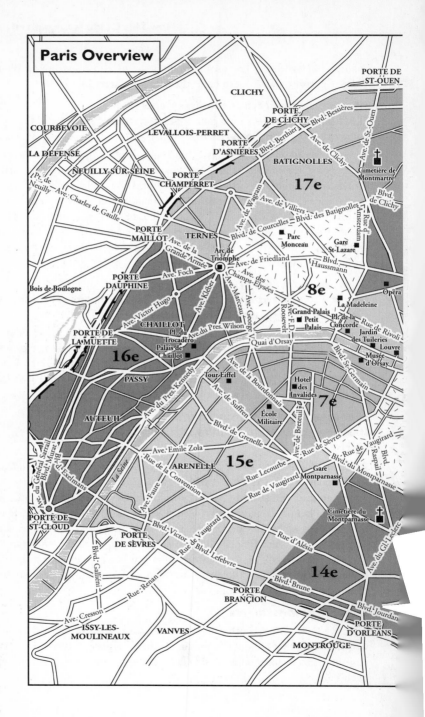

Paris Overview

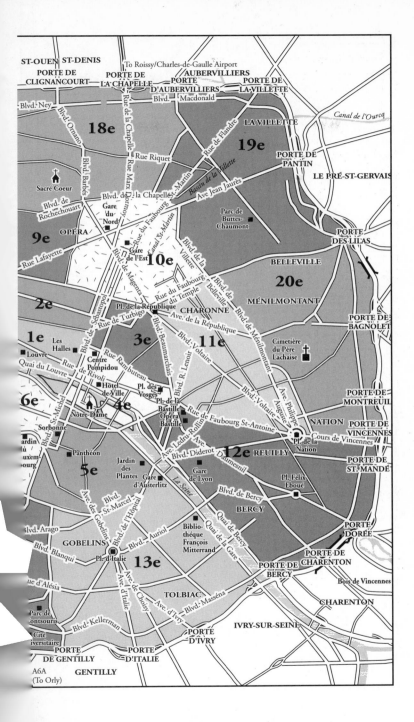

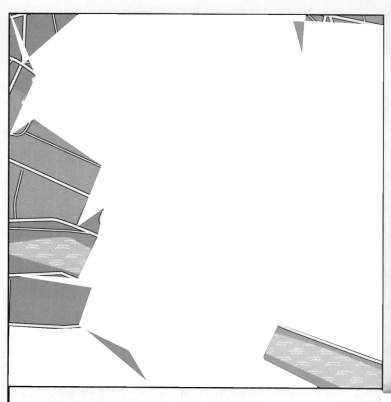

■ *1ST ARRONDISSEMENT*

HOTELS

1. Hôtel Brighton
2. Hôtel Britannique
3. Hôtel Clarion Saint-James & Albany
4. Hôtel des Tuileries
5. Hôtel du Cygne
6. Hôtel Regina

ATTRACTIONS

7. Eglise St. Eustache
8. La Conciergerie
9. Le Louvre
10. Les Tuileries
11. Musée de l'Orangerie
12. Musée des Arts Décoratifs
13. Palais Royal
14. Place Dauphine
15. Place des Victoires
16. Place Vendôme
17. Saint-Chapelle

RESTAURANTS

18. Au Chien Qui Fume
19. Café Véry
20. Chez La Vieille
21. L'Ami Léon
22. Le Grand Vefour
23. L'Escargot Montorgueil
24. Toupary

NIGHTCLUBS

25. Au Duc des Lombards
26. Petit Opportun
27. Taverne Henri-IV

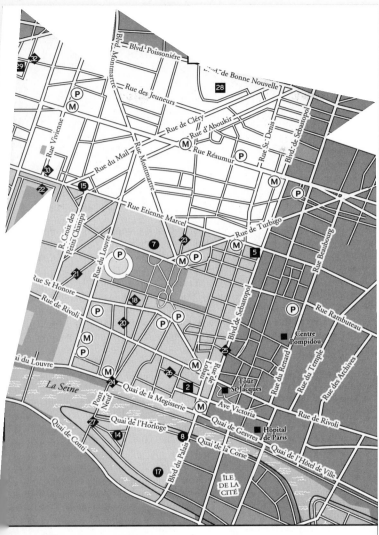

☐ **2nd ARRONDISSEMENT**

HOTELS

28 Hôtel Bonne Nouvelle
29 Hôtel Favart

ATTRACTIONS

30 Musée Grévin

RESTAURANTS

31 Café Drouant
32 Café Runtz
33 Le Grand Colbert

NIGHTCLUBS

34 Harry's New York Bar

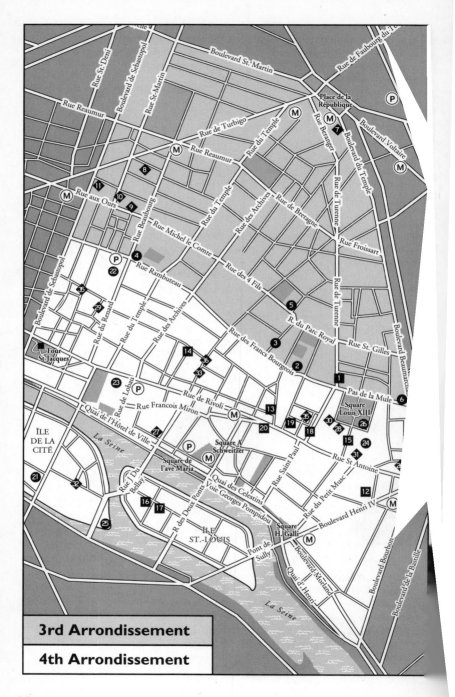

3rd Arrondissement

4th Arrondissement

3RD ARRONDISSEMENT

HOTELS

1 Hôtel des Chevaliers

ATTRACTIONS

2 Musée Carnavalet
3 Musée Cognacq-Jay
4 Musée d'Art et d'Histoire du Judaïsme
5 Musée Picasso
6 Places des Vosges

RESTAURANTS

7 Chez Jenny
8 404
9 L'Ambassade d'Auvergne
10 L'Auberge Nicolas Flamel

NIGHTCLUBS

11 Les Bains Douches

4TH ARRONDISSEMENT

HOTELS

12 Castex Hôtel
13 Grand Hôtel Malher
14 Hôtel de La Bretonnerie
15 Hôtel de La Place Des Vosges
16 Hôtel de Lutèce
17 Hôtel des Deux-Iles
18 Hôtel Libertel Grand Turenne
19 Hôtel Saint-Paul Le Marais
20 Hôtel Sévigné

ATTRACTIONS

21 Cathedrale de Notre-Dame
22 Centre George-Pompidou (Musée National d'Art Moderne)
23 Hôtel de Ville
24 Maison Victor Hugo
25 Mémorial de la Déportation

RESTAURANTS

26 Bofinger
27 Chez Julien
28 Coconnas
29 Dame Tartine
30 L'Ambroisie
31 L'Impasse
32 Le Vieux Bistro
33 Les Philosophes
34 Pitchi Poï

NIGHTCLUBS

35 Café Beaubourg
36 Le Petit Fer à Cheval

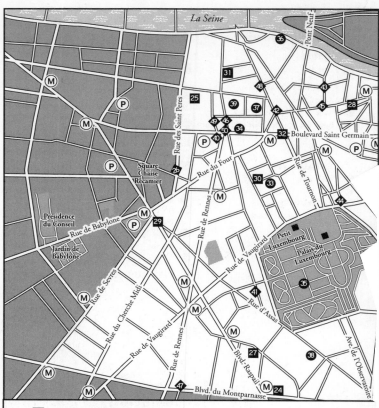

6TH ARRONDISSEMENT

HOTELS

24 A La Villa des Artistes
25 Hôtel d'Angleterre
26 Hôtel des Saints-Pères
27 Hôtel du Danemark
28 Hôtel Eugénie
29 Hôtel Lutétia
30 Hôtel Récamier
31 L'Hôtel
32 Welcome Hôtel

ATTRACTIONS

33 Eglise de St. Sulpice
34 Eglise St-Germain-des-Prés
35 Jardin du Luxembourg
36 Musée de la Monnaie
37 Musée Eugène Delacroix
38 Musée Zadkine
39 Place de Fürstemberg

RESTAURANTS

40 Brasserie Lipp
41 Chez Jean-Claude Gramond
42 Fish!
43 Jacques Cagna
44 La Bastide Odéon
45 Roger la Grenouille

NIGHTCLUBS

46 Café de Flore
47 Closerie des Lilas
48 La Palette
49 Le Bilboquet
50 Les Deux Magots

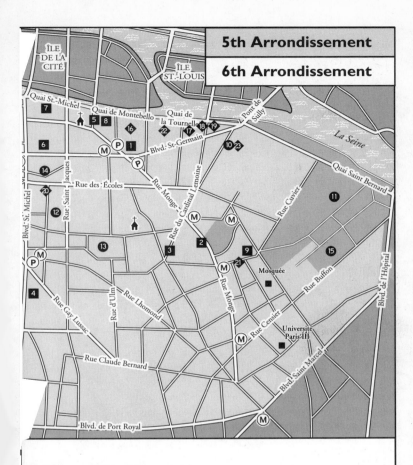

5th Arrondissement

6th Arrondissement

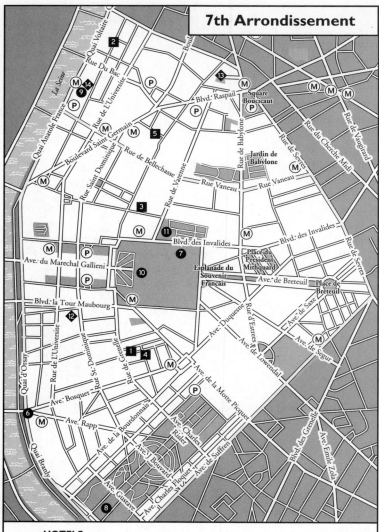

7th Arrondissement

HOTELS

1. Grand Hôtel Lévêque
2. Hôtel Bersoly's
3. Hôtel de Varenne
4. Hôtel du Champ-de-Mars
5. Hôtel Duc de Saint-Simon

ATTRACTIONS

6. Egouts de Paris (sewers)
7. Hôtel National des Invalides

8. La Tour Eiffel
9. Musée d'Orsay
10. Musée de l'Armée
11. Musée Rodin

RESTAURANTS

12. Le Bellecour
13. Le Récamier
14. Restaurant du Musée d'Orsay

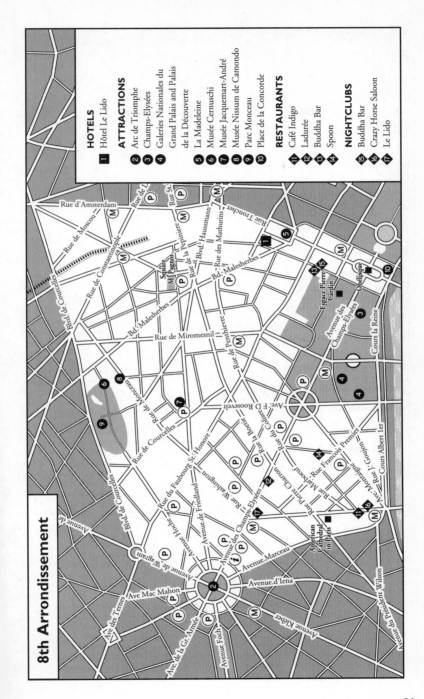

8th Arrondissement

HOTELS
1 Hôtel Le Lido

ATTRACTIONS
2 Arc de Triomphe
3 Champs-Elysées
4 Galeries Nationales du Grand Palais and Palais de la Découverte
5 La Madeleine
6 Musée Cernuschi
7 Musée Jacquemart-André
8 Musée Nissum de Camondo
9 Parc Monceau
10 Place de la Concorde

RESTAURANTS
11 Café Indigo
12 Ladurée
13 Buddha Bar
14 Spoon

NIGHTCLUBS
15 Buddha Bar
16 Crazy Horse Saloon
17 Le Lido

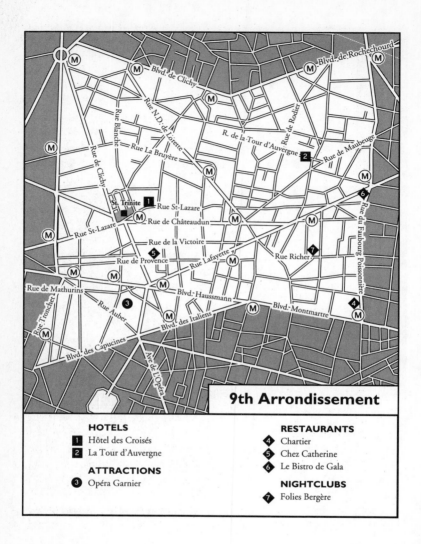

9th Arrondissement

HOTELS
1 Hôtel des Croisés
2 La Tour d'Auvergne

ATTRACTIONS
3 Opéra Garnier

RESTAURANTS
4 Chartier
5 Chez Catherine
6 Le Bistro de Gala

NIGHTCLUBS
7 Folies Bergère

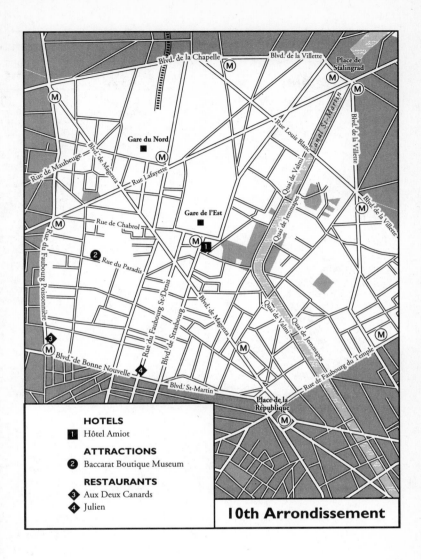

HOTELS

1 Hôtel Amiot

ATTRACTIONS

2 Baccarat Boutique Museum

RESTAURANTS

3 Aux Deux Canards

4 Julien

10th Arrondissement

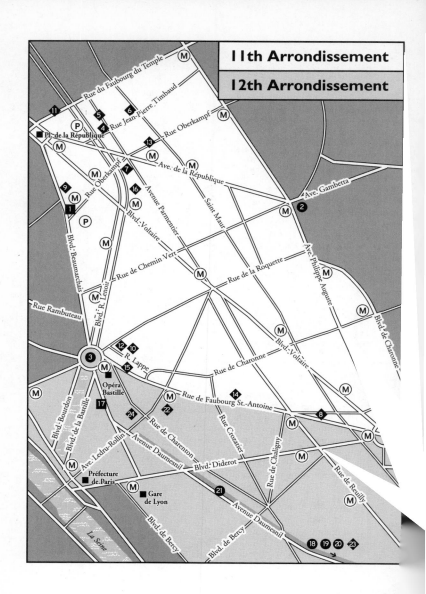

11th Arrondissement

12th Arrondissement

□ 11TH ARRONDISSEMENT

HOTELS
1. Hôtel Beaumarchais

ATTRACTIONS
2. Cimetière du Père-Lachaise
3. Place de la Bastille

RESTAURANTS
4. Astier
5. Au Trou Normand
6. Haiku
7. Le Villaret
8. Les Amognes

NIGHTCLUBS
9. Clown Bar
10. La Chapelle des Lombards
11. La Favela Chic
12. Le Balajo
13. Le Mécano Bar
14. The Reservoir
15. Sans-Sanz
16. Satellit' Café

■ 12TH ARRONDISSEMENT

HOTELS
17. Le Pavillon Bastille

ATTRACTIONS
18. Bois de Vincennes
19. Musée des Arts d'Afrique et d'Océanie
20. Parc Zoologique de Vincennes
21. Promenade Plantée and Viaduc des Arts

RESTAURANTS
22. Le Square Trousseau
23. Les Zygomates

NIGHTCLUBS
24. China Club

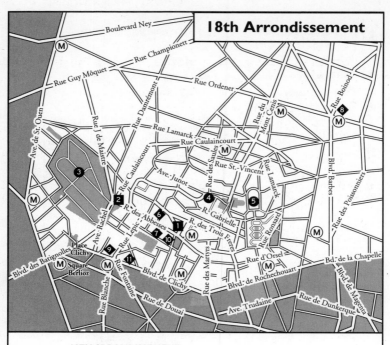

18TH ARRONDISSEMENT

HOTELS

1 Hôtel le Bouquet le Montmartre
2 Terrass Hôtel

ATTRACTIONS

3 Cimetière de Montmartre
4 Espace Montmartre-Salvador Dali
5 La Basillique du Sacré-Coeur

RESTAURANTS

6 Le Moulin à Vins
7 Le Restaurant
8 Rendez-Vous des Chauffeurs

NIGHTCLUBS

9 La Locomotive
10 Le Sancerre
11 Moulin Rouge

The Arrondissements

To find a Paris address, you need to know that the city of Paris is organized into 20 districts called *arrondissements* (ahron-dees **mohn**). Each *arrondissement* is its own political entity, with a mayor and district government. The *arrondissement* is built into every Paris address, much like zip codes. Every Paris postal code address begins with 75, the number of the state or department, followed by the *arrondissement* number. So, it's easy to know the general area in which a hotel or restaurant is located by simply paying attention to the postal code. For example, 75001 indicates the first *arrondissement* of Paris, and 75020 is the 20th *arrondissement* of Paris. Easy!

The *arrondissements* are organized starting in the middle of the city and circling like a whirlpool clockwise. With a simple map, you'll be able to situate yourself easily.

A quick tip on French addresses: Street numbers running north-south begin at the Seine and increase as they move away from it. Odd and even numbers on a street do not always fall opposite or even very near each other. If you see a street address with the letters *bis* or *ter* after the number, the address is located next to that number or before the next number. Finally, the French are accustomed to adding a comma after the number in the street address. Example: 23, rue de Rivoli.

Okay, so Paris has *arrondissements,* but how are they different? Well, it's hard to characterize the *arrondissements* in simple terms, and it's especially dangerous to overgeneralize about what you'll find in which. There are extremely charming spots in almost every area of Paris, and every *arrondissement* enjoys subway (Métro) access. Unlike London, where the scale of the city is large, Paris is very dense and the distances are not overwhelming. Whereas it would be difficult to walk between two subway stops in London, the distance between subway stops in Paris represents a five- to ten-minute walk. The scale of Paris permits active visitors to cross most of the city by foot.

Left Bank/Right Bank

You may have heard of Paris's Left Bank (Rive Gauche—say reeve **gowsh**) and Right Bank (Rive Droite—say reeve **dwaht**), but you haven't a clue as to the difference between them or which is a better address. Let's start here. In short, the Seine River cuts Paris in half, along an east-west axis. The southern side of the river is the Left Bank (Rive Gauche), whereas the northern side is the Right Bank (Rive Droite). Although traditionally the Left Bank was more bohemian and proletariat, housing the famous Latin Quarter (Quartier Latin—say car**tee-yay** lah**tahn**) area, so called because of its student population who studied Latin, today it's impossible to generalize or identify major differences. The Left Bank today can be as upscale as the traditionally more bourgeois Right Bank. You may decide to stay on the Left Bank, but there are equally attractive offerings on the Right Bank. So, although some people religiously prefer one over the other, there are great locations to be found on both sides of the river.

On Being a "Tourist"

Although we've tried to avoid referring to our readers as "tourists," we do use the term throughout the book. There is no shame in being a tourist. A tourist is simply a person who travels for pleasure, and we assume that that's what you are. In fact, the best way to visit Paris is as a tourist. The negative images the word conjures come from the early days of mass, group travel, when Europe became accessible to culturally insensitive mobs. Hence, the term "ugly tourist." Today, you won't be confused with one of them, and we're bringing the word back into fashion.

Understanding Les Bises (lay bees)

For some unexplained reason the French are world-renowned for their kiss, the open-mouthed version that humans everywhere find so pleasurable. Parisians find the anglicized nomenclature very curious though in that any other kind of kiss, well, just ain't a kiss. *Les bises*, however, that funny but tender ritual of planting a succession of tiny kiss-like gestures on the right and then left cheek of the man or woman you are greeting, is paramount for Parisians to the Anglo-Saxon handshake or backslap. Getting this banal but endearing form of hello and goodbye down pat isn't quite as easy as it looks. Each Parisian has his or her habit, style, and number, ranging between two and four. Most true Parisians practice the even number two and start on the recipient's right cheek, not too close to the mouth. Remember, *les bises* are not kisses; these greeting-pecks signify only a polite affection that's reserved for friends, close acquaintances, familiar colleagues, family, and extended family. Parisians who have migrated from the south of France or other provinces may tend to use the more loquacious and elaborate succession of three or four kisses. This varies according to culture, region, or individual preference and personality, and it'll take you plenty of time to coordinate the habit of, let's say, your two *left-right* combo, with your good neighbor's *left-right-left* trilogy. Come into a room with 11 cousins and three sets of close friends and their flock of kids, and be prepared to buckle down for a good ten minutes of facial gymnastics. Just do it, or you'll never get to the *apéritifs*. As you'll quickly see, a Parisian instantly learns that his wife's friend Camille from Avignon always plants three quick ones, while her husband Jean-Claude, who rarely leaves his native 16th *arrondissement,* never exceeds two rather-indifferent cheek-graces while steering his lips up and away à la Chirac like any good bourgeois. Form, as you know, is everything in Paris, and so much of French form—language, gestures, attitudes, responses, even politics—begins poutfully with the lips. Don't forget, there is nothing ambiguous about *les bises,* and certainly nothing sexual about the practice, so don't assume someone has a crush on you, wants to take you to bed, is giving you a gay message, or is trying to get you excited with his or her sweet *eau de cologne,* by simply gracing your cheeks with *les bises.* You'll know when *that* happens. What's interesting to note here is that the French are simply used to and comfortable with close personal contact. They are not bothered by human proximity or touching. They don't require the same distance Anglo Americans insist upon when talking. So take it from someone who has dished out at least 21,000 pairs of *bises* and has shaken hands 390,000 times (often with the exact same Parisians) in 15-odd years in the French capital—practice *les bises* before arriving. Toss your head, convey confidence, steer your lips noiselessly in the direction of the ears, and for heaven's sake, keep it dry!

A final word to the wise: when in doubt, keep shaking hands. Don't start shelling out these friendly doses of "non-kisses" until you get the greenlight feeling from the initiating Parisian acquaintance. Otherwise, you risk being perceived as too familiar too quick, which can be a real turn-off in Paris. When the *bises* time is right, however, be consistent and repeat the ritual every time you come and go; otherwise, you'll offend. And that, *mes amis,* is a whole other lesson.

Commas vs. Decimal Points

In this guidebook, numbers are expressed in the fashion familiar to you, where one hundred dollars and fifty cents is written $100.50, and so on. However, in writing numbers and prices, the French use commas where you use decimal points. So, in French, $100.50 would be written $100,50. The euro maintains this style. So be careful with numbers, especially when it's time to pay.

FAST FACTS ABOUT FRANCE AND PARIS

- Capital of France: Paris. The country is a republic, divided into 22 regions of which the Île de France is one with Paris at its center. Within these 22 regions there are 96 states or départements.

- Population of France: 58,520,688 (1999 census).

- Population of Paris: 2.1 million in Paris, nearly 11 million in the greater Paris area (Île de France).

- French national independence day: 14 July, dating back to 1789 when the Bastille was stormed and independence was won from the monarchy.
- Voting age: 18. Driving age: 18. Drinking age: 18 (16 for beer and wine).
- Chief of State: President, elected by popular vote for a seven-year term. Mandate may be reduced to five-year term.
- Religion: 81% Roman Catholic, 2% Protestant, 2% Jewish, 7% Muslim, 8% nonaffiliated.
- Store hours: Generally 9 a.m. to 7 p.m., with many closing during the lunch hours.
- Banking hours: Although these vary from bank to bank, hours are most often 9 a.m. to 4 or 5 p.m. Monday through Friday. Some branches are closed from noon or 12:30 to 1:30 or 2 p.m., and others are open on Saturdays or Saturday mornings.
- Time: Paris is on GMT + 1. So 6 p.m. in Paris is noon in New York and 9 a.m. in Los Angeles. (Caution: clocks are not pushed ahead and set back on the same days as in North America, so each year there are a few weeks in which Paris time is either 5 or 7 hours ahead of the U.S. east coast.)
- Electric current: 220 W.
- Official Language: French. (English spoken in large hotels, many businesses, tourist trade. There are over 100,000 permanent Anglo-American residents in Paris.)
- Currency: French franc (extinct as of January 2002), replaced by the euro (6.55 francs to the euro).
- Geographic location: 48°58' N latitude, 2°27' E longitude.
- Size of country: Approximately the size of Texas.

OTHER PUBLIC HOLIDAYS

January 1—New Year's Day (Jour de l'an)

Easter (Pâques)

Easter Monday (Lundi de Pâques)

May 1—Labor Day (May Day) (Fête du Travail)

May 8—VE Day

Ascension Day (Ascension) (sixth Thursday after Easter)

Pentacost (Pentecôte)

Whit Monday (second Monday after Ascension) (Lundi de Pentecôte)

July 14—Bastille Day (Fête Nationale)

August 15—Assumption (Assomption)

November 1—All Saints' Day (Toussaint)

November 11—Remembrance Day (Armistice 1918)

December 25—Christmas Day (Noël)

Part One

Understanding Paris

A Brief History of Paris

One of the great advantages of visiting Paris is the closeness to history that the experience offers you. Everywhere you look you're reminded of what transpired here at an earlier epoch, from the Romans and the Gauls through the Prussians and the Germans. As a basic crutch for orienting yourself to the city and its traditions, here is an overview of Paris's colorful history. According to the travel writer Robert Cole, the Parisian view of its own history is the reverse of "all roads lead to Rome." Everything great in France began in Paris and spread outward.

Les Parisii and the Romans

The first settlers on the largest island in the Seine (now Île de la Cité) were the Parisii, a community of Celtic fishermen and boatpeople governed by Druidic religious practices. Soon after, in the year 52 A.D., the Romans arrived and began constructing the first buildings on the Left Bank of the river up the hill that consists of today's Montagne Sainte-Geneviève, in the fifth arrondissement. Here, as well, were the ruins of the Cluny Baths and the Arènes de Lutèce, where Julien was proclaimed emperor in 360 A.D. The Romans named their settlement Lutetia Parisiorum, which lent itself to the legend that the city was founded by Helen of Troy's lover, Paris. After refusing to send delegates to Julius Caesar's Assembly of Gaul, the Celts revolted against Roman domination and set fire to the city and bridges, but were ultimately crushed by Caesar's legion, which camped at the site of today's Louvre. Lutetia spread to the Left Bank, which took on the name the Latin Quarter.

Barbarian Invasions

Threatened by Attila the Hun (and subsequently saved by the visionary Christian Geneviève, who was made patroness of the city) and the warring

Francs, the town began to take on wings as the Frank King Clovis declared it his capital and his official residence in 508. It is believed that the site of present-day Paris was a stopping-off point between Marseilles and Britain along an ancient trading route. Abbeys and chapels flourished on the Right Bank as well as the Left, as witnessed by Saint Germain L'Auxerrois and Saint Germain des Prés, and the city took on a unique religious importance. The western Frank kingdom of Neustria was referred to by the end of the ninth century as Francia, which became France. Over time, the residents of Francia looked to the governors of this kingdom for political direction. Hugh Capet emerged as ostensibly the first king of Francia and the founding monarch to rule France.

Charlemagne

Over the next four centuries, Paris was occupied and deserted by the Merovingians and by Charlemagne, and raided by the Normands. It wasn't until near the end of the first millennium, under the Capetian dynasty, that Paris gained importance as a royal capital and urban economic center. Under the reign of Philippe Auguste, a wall was erected around the city. The principal streets were paved in cobblestone (*pavé* in French) and the first bridges joining the Right and Left Banks were built. Notre-Dame was erected on Île de la Cité in 1163 and the university sector on the Left Bank was conceived in 1215, with the Université de Paris becoming the primary theological and philosophical center in medieval Christianity. Here was where Bonaventure, Thomas Aquinas, and others taught. The Palais Royal functioned as the political core of the capital. Flourishing due to its floating merchants (from which Paris's coat of shields is derived) and a vibrant silver market, Paris grew to over 100,000 inhabitants by the 13th century, making it the largest city in the western Christian world.

Renaissance and the Reformation

Insurrections followed and the 1300s were marred by massacres and invasions by regional tribes. Joan of Arc besieged the city in 1429 while Paris was under the rule of the English, and in 1438 the legitimate monarch Charles VII took control.

It wasn't until François I, known as a Renaissance prince and patron of the arts, that Paris became the official residence of the king. Renaissance structures replaced medieval ones, and Paris witnessed the construction of its Hôtel de Ville, the Tuileries, and the Pont Neuf, Paris's first stone bridge.

The 1500s were bloodied by religious wars (the Protestant Reformation, Huguenots) and a devastating famine (1589), forcing King Henri III, who was later assassinated, to flee. Henri of Navarre proclaimed himself Henri IV (1589–1610) and assumed the reins of the city; under Henri IV major architectural additions were commissioned: the Place de Vosges, place Dauphine, l'Horloge. Under Louis XIII the city experienced the construction of new areas—the Marais, the Bastille, and Saint Honoré—walled in along a periphery that vaguely followed today's Grands Boulevards. The Île St. Louis was refurbished, and new communities sprung up on the Left Bank, especially near the Luxembourg Gardens, which were built by Marie de Médicis.

Louis XIII and Louis XIV

Paris's importance as a cultural center grew as the Royal Imprimerie was built and the Academie Française was established. The powerful Cardinal Richelieu left his administrative mark on the style and form of government under Louis XIII. He's buried in the chapel of the Sorbonne. Nonetheless, Louis XIV (the Sun King), known for his maxim "The State Is Me," preferred his château in Versailles. But to glorify the monarchy, under the auspices of the famed Colbert, great additions were made to Paris: the colonnade of the Louvre, Les Invalides, the arches at the Portes Saint Denis and Saint Martin, the Place Vendôme, and many other points of great architectural beauty.

The arts and music flourished in the city, and the logical next step in urban development was the creation of the café, a place for intellectuals, writers, and artists to meet. The 18th century enjoyed the opening of the first restaurants, le Procope, la Régence, and the first theaters, l'Odéon and the Comédie Française. Business, banking, and commerce gained an increasingly important foothold, and property prices rose steadily. Interest and development of the law as a discipline mounted. A group of thinkers called the Encyclopedists met and gained influence, contending that all knowledge was finite and could be catalogued and distributed. The city expanded to the west and north, and by the time of the French Revolution in 1784, the population had risen to 650,000 within the city walls.

The French Revolution

King Louis XVI and his famous wife, the Austrian-born Marie-Antoinette (of "Let them eat cake" fame), ascended the throne in 1774. At first popular, the couple made rather condemning public-relations errors, and those combined with harsh conditions, food shortages, and inept governing, sparked public revolts and riots. Inspired by the American Revolution and the ideological concept of the Universal Declaration of Human Rights, revolution broke out. Louis XVI and Marie-Antoinette were guillotined at the Place de la Concorde, renamed the Place de la Révolution. *"Liberté, Egalité, Fraternité"* became the motto of the Republic.

The Bastille prison was stormed on July 14th, 1789, the start of the French Revolution and the *Fête nationale* to this day. The First Republic dates from 1791 to 1799, followed by the reign of Napoléon Bonaparte, under a regime called the Consulat (echoing the Romans). The monarchy returned to power between 1815 and 1848 with the Bourbons. From 1848 until 1852 France entered its Second Republic, with Louis-Napoléon Bonaparte (the nephew) at the helm. The next 20 years are called the Second Empire. Then in 1871, France installed the Third Republic, and ended the monarchy for good.

Napoléon I (Napoléon Bonaparte)

Napoléon's vision was to make Paris the capital of Europe, and he proceeded to build the Arc de Triomphe and the column at Place de la Vendôme, and opened the Ourcq canal, bringing drinking water into the city. The markets, public high schools *(lycées)*, and slaughterhouses were developed. The Madeleine and the Pantheon were built, and the sewer system was installed. Napoléon's reign marked the First Empire. This popular general as emperor profoundly modified the legal code and administrative structure of France. After an eventful rise and fall from power, Napoléon regained power in 1815 only to be defeated the same year at the Battle of Waterloo. He abdicated and was sent by the British to the island of Saint-Hélène where he died in 1821. His son, Napoléon II, succeeded him.

It was the Second Empire under Napoléon III (Louis Napoléon Bonaparte, the brother of Napoléon I) that gave Paris its new look, with the creation of a centralized administration and economic, social, and cultural services. The period was characterized by the writings of Honoré de Balzac and Victor Hugo, as well as Alexandre Dumas, Musset, and Nerval, and the music of Rossini, Chopin, Liszt, Wagner, and Offenbach.

Haussmann and the New Paris

In 1860 Paris was organized into 20 *arrondissements,* each with its own mayor and city government. Preoccupied with urban development and questions of security, the urban planning of the city was overhauled and remodeled by the celebrated architect Haussmann, who conceived the wide boulevards (rue de Rivoli, avenue de l'Opéra) and the wide sidewalks in the upper-class areas, driving the hordes of working-class poor into the outer districts, primarily to the east. Vast parks on both sides of the city were erected, Bois de Vincennes (for the poor) and Bois de Boulogne (for the rich), as well as numerous new bridges and the Opéra Garnier.

FRENCH PERIODS AND RULERS

The Gallo-Roman Period 3rd century BC to 360
Gallo-Romans build the City of Lutetia in 1 AD.

Early Middle Ages 450–885
Clovis makes Paris his captial. Charlemagne abandons Paris.

The Capetians 12th century to 1300
Notre Dame is built. Sorbonne is built.

The Valois 1337–1590
Charles V builds the Bastille and a wall around Paris. Henri VI is crowned king of France.

The Bourbons 1590–1790
Henri IV converts to Catholicism. Île de St. Louis is developed. Treaty of Versailles is signed.

The French Revolution and First Empire July 14, 1789 to 1814
Louis XVI adopts red, white, and blue as the colors of France. Louis XVI is executed. Napoleon Bonaparte creates the police system. Napoleon is coronated at Notre-Dame.

The Restoration 1815–1848
Battle of Waterloo. The Fall of Louis-Philippe.

The Second Republic 1848–1870
World Exhibitions in 1855 and 1867.
Town planning is undertaken by Baron Haussmann.

The Third Republic 1870–1950
Napoleon III goes into exile. The Paris Commune is supressed. World Exhibition at the new Eiffel Tower. First Métro line opens in 1900. Paris is occupied by the Germans in June 1940. Liberation of Paris August 25, 1944.

The Fifth Republic 1958 to the present
General strikes in 1968. Building of the Périphérique in 1973. Pompidou Center opens in 1977. Socialist president Mitterrand wins in 1982. Jacques Chirac elected in 1995.

Commune de Paris

Rapid growth of industrial activity helped contribute to the city's mounting population of 1.8 million inhabitants by the year 1871. An imbalance of the social and economic classes ensued, and in 1830 and 1848 popular uprisings ripped through the capital, culminating in the celebrated and dramatic revolution, between March and May 1871, of the Commune de Paris, immortalized by Hugo's *Les Miserables*. The Prussians then besieged the city.

The Third Republic

The Third Republic (1870–1940) followed this time of unrest, and prosperity and economic stability retook the city, as marked by the Exposition of 1889 and the construction of the Eiffel Tower. The construction of the Grand and Petit Palais followed, as did the building of the Alexandre III bridge. In 1886 Bartoldi's Statue of Liberty, a gift from the people of France to the people of the United States, was transported and installed in New York harbor. In 1889 the Moulin Rouge opened in Clichy.

The Impressionist painters Renoir, Monet, Sisley, and Pisarro portrayed the day in attractive and gay colors and scenes, and by the beginning of the 20th century, Paris had established itself as the international capital of art, attracting painters from around the world to such noted centers of cultural life as Toulouse-Lautrec's Montmartre, the Bateau Lavoir, and La Ruche. Cabarets opened and the Sacré Coeur Basilica was erected.

World War I

The Battle of the Marne, in which Paris taxis carried troops to the battlefield for lack of transport, saved Paris in the early days of World War I. The peace treaty to end the war was signed in Paris. Following World War I, the city's geographic boundaries moved outward as the new building material, concrete, was introduced. With the Russian Revolution, Paris was inundated with eastern aristocratic expatriates, who contributed to the rapid growth of bistros (the Russian word for "rapid," thereby meaning fast food).

Between the Wars

New cafés opened on the boulevards, and the area of Montparnasse became a magnet for artistic and literary life, with disillusioned souls settling in Paris to write, paint, and drink. The city became the studio for André Breton, Jean Cocteau, Aragon, Eluard, Picasso, and the writers James Joyce, Ernest Hemingway, and Gertrude Stein, the core of expatriates that came to be known as the Lost Generation. Art deco flourished and the Paris Métro expanded.

World War II

Right-wing extremists began gaining attention as fascism grew in Europe, generating the need for the creation of the workers party, the *Front Populaire*, in 1936.

In June 1940, the German *Wermacht* marched through the Arc de Triomphe and began the Occupation of Paris. France was partitioned, and Philippe Pétain led the Vichy Government. By July 1942, large numbers of French Jews had been gathered up and deported to Nazi concentration camps, and France experienced a political and social rift between German collaborators and the Resistance fighters, a wound from which France has never fully healed. In August 1944, General Charles de Gaulle and his army marched down the Champs-Elysées, marking the Liberation of Paris.

The Fourth Republic

The Fourth Republic was created when Charles de Gaulle formed a provisional government. Paris stabilized and regained its position as the capital of fashion, style, and art. A second wave of expatriate writers and artists settled in the City of Light, repelled by the repressiveness and conservative mood in postwar America. In the late 1950s and 1960s the Saint-Germain-des-Prés area of Paris became the headquarters of leading French intellectuals, led by existentialist Jean Paul Sartre and Simone de Beauvoir.

Handicapped by its colonial past, especially in North Africa, France was violently confronted with the Algerian war for independence. This conflict brutally divided the country and led to the collapse of the Fourth Republic and popular demand that Charles de Gaulle restructure the government.

The Fifth Republic

Charles de Gaulle was called upon to form the Fifth Republic of France. In 1965 de Gaulle pulled France out of NATO. In May 1968, general strikes and student protests against the outdated administration of President de Gaulle crippled the country; rioting broke out in the Latin Quarter and the country came to a halt. De Gaulle was forced to step down and was succeeded by Georges Pompidou.

The Socialist Years

In 1982, Socialist leader François Mitterrand was elected president of France, the beginning of a 14-year period of socialist domination of French politics. Selected French industries were nationalized. Mitterrand launched his great spending spree on major architectural legacies. I. M. Pei was commissioned to renovate the Louvre, and his controversial Pyramid was inaugurated for the bicentennial of the French Revolution in 1989; the new Bastille Opéra opened as well. The Grande Arche at La Defence was inaugurated.

In 1994, the Eurotunnel connecting France and England began commercial service. France signed the Treaty of Maastricht, an important commitment toward the goal of a unified Europe. In 1996, Mitterrand died in office. In 2001, a 20-year retrospective of the Mitterrand years was marked by events and publications.

End of the Millennium

Jacques Chirac, the mayor of Paris and the leader of the conservative Right Wing RPR Party, was elected president of France after Mitterrand's death.

The euro, the single currency of the European Union, was adopted as the official money of France and ten other European countries. In 1997, Chirac called for new elections and ended up in a coalition government, with Socialist Lionel Jospin as prime minister. In 1999, France participated in the NATO war on Yugoslavia while attempting to maintain a sense of political and economic sovereignty from the United States and its American model for globalization. The Right Wing was weakened by scandals and infighting, and the political future of French government is uncertain. In 2002, the euro replaces French banknotes and coins. Jospin is positioned to run for president in the next presidential elections.

The Language: Français

In Paris one speaks French (*Français* [frahn-say]). So much of your experience will be flavored by your ability to communicate. If you speak some French, so much the better; your linguistic abilities will be applauded. If you have a notion of French, use it. Abandon all fears of seeming ridiculous. You'll be commended for your effort and respected by Parisians for not automatically assuming that everyone on earth must speak English. If your French is as clumsy as a six-pack of Coke falling down the stairs, try anyway, and use your hands. Point. Smile. Shrug your shoulders. Anything but fall into the "get me some ketchup, *garçon*" mind-set. The worse attitudinal error you can make in Paris is to convey either ignorance or arrogance when it comes to the language. It's okay that you don't speak French, but look apologetic about it.

The French take their language and culture seriously and are constantly reminded of their dwindling influence in the world. It wasn't all that long ago that French was the official diplomatic language on earth. Ever wonder why the text in your passport is bilingual with French as the second language? Fortunately, both the tourists and the Parisians have made major headway over the last generation in gaining language skills. More of you handle yourself well in French today than was true twenty years ago. And, similarly, more Parisians can get by in English today, recognizing the international need for a universal language (and understanding that it is no longer French), and enjoy doing so.

At the bare minimum, arrive with a few humble, rehearsed phrases proving that your French at least starts and stops with *bonjour, au revoir, merci, rendez-vous,* and *combien.*

Getting Linguistically Equipped: *Parlez-vous Français?*

You might know some French, or are willing to give it a try, but knowing a word and being able to say it are two different things. French pronunciation can be daunting in that letters are silent and lots of words are not pronounced like they appear. The worst is when words in French are the same as in English but you can't make them sound right. Try pronouncing the French for hospital, *hôpital.* Wrong, it's pronounced "ooh-peetal." How *beaucoup* ends up sounding like "bowkew" is beyond most tourists' imaginations. The toilet becomes "twalet," instead of the English "toylit." Many guidebooks offer travelers lists of terms and phrases, but without the articles that precede them, and more importantly, easy-to-use phonetic transcriptions, you might as well give up before you contort your mouth and lips into incomprehensible sounds. It won't come out as recognizable French!

So—for those who need it—we have included next to each French word in italics a transcription of the sound that's not scientific or difficult to wrap your tongue around. The syllable that is in bold is the one that you stress. *D'accord?* (**dac**-core?) All right? We just want you to be able to look at a cluster of letters, pronounce it, and find that someone is rushing off to fetch you another towel or bringing you the salt and pepper. (**Note: we have only added a pronunciation guide to words that you might need to pronounce.**) Just read these transcriptions out loud as if they were in English. Purse your lips, raise your shoulders, and let the music and passion take over. You're speaking French.

Survival French

Start out by being able to ask in French whether the person in front of you speaks English. To be safe, start every sentence with either *pardon* (pahr-**doh**n) or *excusez-moi* (**ex**-cuzay **mwa**). *Parlez-vous anglais?* You'll get as an answer either *oui, un peu* or *non, pas de tout* (yes, a little, or no, not at all). If you get the latter, you'll want to set the record straight right away that you also do not speak French. *Moi non plus. Je ne parle pas français.* Or, *je parle un peu* (I speak a little bit). *Merci,* of course, is thank you, and *merci beaucoup* is thank you very much.

Get in the habit quickly of greeting your hotel concierge or the chamber maid with *Bonjour, monsieur* or *Bonjour, madame.* On your second day try adding *Comment allez-vous?* (**co**mo-tah**lay vous**) or *Comment ça va?* (**co**mo sah-**vah**), which means how are you? They'll be impressed. But be warned: do not ask people on the street that you have not already met, *Comment ça va?* They'll probably ignore you anyway, thinking you're weird. Strangers usually do not talk to each other. Yes, you can err on the friendly side.

Remember that French is far more formal than English, and the rules of language need to be respected. A basic difference between English and French is that French uses the *tu* and *vous* form for you. When addressing anyone other than a close friend, family member, or child, you should only use the *vous* form. French people who work together in the same office for years do not change over to the *tu* form. So don't initiate familiarity; let the French person do it. In any case, most Parisians understand that Americans and their language are naturally casual and familiar, so tourists usually are excused for their innocent murder of French formalities.

When greeting and/or taking leave of someone, don't be surprised if you are extended a hand. Shake it. You may repeat this formal act with the same person several times in the same day. For a note on *les bises,* that charming succession of little kisses that Parisians are always giving each other, see the Introduction.

Saying Hello and Goodbye

Bonjour madame. (bohn-**jzoor** ma**dahm**).
Au revoir madame. (oh rev**war** ma**dahm**).
Bonjour monsieur. (bohn-**jzoor** miss**yiuh**).
Au revoir monsieur. (oh rev**war** miss**yiuh**).
(These days, when you don't know the marital status of a woman, use *madame* instead of *madamoiselle.*)
A more casual greeting is simply *Salut* (sah-**loo**).

Other Useful Phrases

Enchantez (on-**shahntay**), which means pleased to meet you.
Je suis ravi de faire votre connaissance (dzjuh **swee** ra**vee** duh **fair voh**tra ko**ness sahnz**) which means pleased to make your acquaintance (very formal). You'll either impress them or make them laugh.
Combien ça coûte? (**comb**-bee-**yen** sah **coot**). How much does it cost?
Ooh la la! (yes, people do say this when impressed or surprised).

MISNOMERS

- French fries are really Belgian in origin and are simply called *les frites* in French. The way of cutting thin strips was originally French.

- The French have no idea what French dressing is. The most common salad dressing is called *vinaigrette,* resembling your idea of Italian.

- The French don't think of French bread as particularly French. It's just a *baguette* or stick of bread.

- French cuffs don't mean a thing in France. They're *manchette.*

- There is no such thing in France as the French kiss. Open-mouthed tongue kissing has no national boundaries.

- French windows are just normal windows for the French.

- Don't look for a French harp. It doesn't exist in France. The same is true for the French knot or French omelet.

- French pastry in France is just *pâtisserie*.

- Of course, French toast, having nothing to do with France, is logically called *pain perdu* (lost bread).

However, the French have their own misnomers for you:

- A *café américain* is a full cup of weak coffee, like Americans are used to drinking. (We agree, Starbucks has improved the item a lot. Note that Starbucks is planning a French invasion!)

- A *bar américain* is the kind of bar you stand up and drink at.

- A *cuisine américaine* is a kitchen with a center counter or bar, open and roomy; in other words, a kitchen.

- A *voiture américaine* is a big and sporty car like a Cadillac.

- *Homard à l'américaine* is lobster cooked with tomatoes and shallots, as is never done in America.

- And, novels that are *traduit de l'américain* means that they are translated from American (as opposed to English), as if American were its own language.

Numbers and Prices: The Euro!

As is always true, numbers change—phone and fax numbers, opening and closing times, and especially prices. To complicate matters, the French franc has been replaced. In the spirit of being the most accurate and helpful, we have decided to list all prices in this guide in euros (€) only. Where we describe pre-travel purchases or services and products with U.S. list prices, we have included U.S. dollar prices. Everything else is in euros.

To make conversion easy for you, we have included a handy chart indicating equivalent prices in U.S. dollars, British pounds, and the euro. The euro has been pegged at 6.55957 (rounded out to 6.55) francs and has remained between 10–15 percent weaker than the U.S. dollar, although you should expect fluctuations.

For example: a baguette used to be 4F; now it is 61 eurocents, 56 American cents, or 38 pence. A hotel room was 750F; now it's €114.33, $104.89 US or £71.91. Caution: exchange rates fluctuate; make sure you check rates before making reservations and purchases!

CURRENCY CONVERSION TABLE

(Based on €1.09 to the U.S.$, and €1.59 to the U.K.£)

Euros	U.S. Dollars	British Pounds
1c =	$0.01	£0.01
2c =	$0.02	£0.01
5c =	$0.05	£0.03
10c =	$0.09	£0.06
20c =	$0.18	£0.13
50c =	$0.46	£0.31
€1 =	$0.92	£0.63
€2 =	$1.83	£1.26
€5 =	$4.59	£3.14
€10 =	$9.17	£6.29
€20 =	$18.35	£12.58
€50 =	$45.87	£31.45
€100 =	$91.74	£62.89
€200 =	$183.49	£125.79
€500 =	$458.72	£314.47

Quick Currency Conversion

To get a quick idea if something in Euros is expensive, think of the conversion as one-to-one, one U.S. dollar is one euro, then fine tune according to the exchange rate.

Part Two

Planning Your Visit to Paris

How Far in Advance Should You Plan?

Well, it depends. The earlier you get started and pick your dates, the better. In general, trips should be organized and booked at least three to four months before the departure date; however, spontaneous and flexible travelers have the advantage of landing great, last-minute deals. United Airlines, for example, offered a springtime special, Los Angeles–Paris roundtrip for $349, but travelers only had three weeks to make a reservation and pay. If you hope to travel at peak times—holiday seasons, Christmas, Easter, or during school vacations—you should reserve your airline tickets at least six months in advance, or as soon as you know your dates.

France is divided into three school regions, each setting its own scholastic calendar. Dates change from year to year and are often only announced at the beginning of each September. For exact dates, inquire with your closest French consulate or travel office, and indicate that it is the Paris region that concerns you.

The highways, train stations, airports, and ski slopes are jammed with vacationing families during the school breaks. Paris proper can actually be less congested. Reserved train seats between Paris, the mountain areas, and the south of France get snapped up quickly for these periods, so be forewarned if you plan on heading out of Paris or hope to get into the city then. The primary dates are Toussaint (the last weekend in October and first week in November), Christmas (December 18 or so until January 4), winter break (February 19 or so till about March 8), spring break (mid-April to about March 3), and of course during summer vacation (end of June to early September). Avoid arrivals and departures on the first and last days of the school holidays.

We recommend visiting Paris in the off-season, but this requires a different mental outlook since the weather can often be dark, chilly, and/or wet.

Otherwise, Paris is glorious in April, May, June, and September to mid-October, but the prices are highest. There are mixed opinions on visiting Paris in August, but we tend to like it. The pace is slower and the city is less congested. The weather can be uncomfortably hot, but usually it is manageable, and good deals can be had on hotel rooms.

Try to avoid traveling on the first and last few days of July and August, when a massive exodus of excited Parisians flee the city for their annual summer vacations. Although less so than before, most Parisians still leave the city at the same time, and, should you travel on these dates, you're certain to be caught up in a hectic cross-current of agitated travelers excited about leaving or irritated about returning. July 15 and August 15 are also very busy travel days in France and should be avoided when possible. If you can't avoid these heavy traffic days, keep in mind that the crowds will be heavy.

Making early plane and hotel reservations will guarantee you seats on the dates you've chosen and rooms in your hotel of choice. Although travel professionals specializing in cut-rate trips warn that booking too early precludes your getting the best deals and bargains, we feel that as soon as you know your dates, you should start your research for either a package tour or for an affordable airfare. And book it. Your time and peace of mind are worth a lot. Airlines will usually hold seats on that date and at that price for several days. This buys you time without obliging you to commit immediately. Usually you can extend the holding date by a few days by simply asking, but this depends on the restrictions attached to the special fare and the cooperative spirit of the salesperson. Your travel agent will be better at making and holding a reservation in your name than you may be yourself. You can hold several reservations at the same time, which will enable you to continue your search for the best dates, prices, and conditions. Be careful not to lose an attractive deal by forgetting to confirm the reservation before the expiration date (and hour, usually midnight). The best deals often require that you commit immediately and pay with a credit card. Cancellations and changes are subject to penalties.

When to Go

You should consider the price, the weather, and your mental outlook. The first two are absolutes, but the last is a bit harder to judge. As mentioned above, seasoned travelers who wish to spend lots of time inside great museums, theaters, restaurants, cafés, and hotels may truly find off-season Paris trips more enjoyable. The weather may be grim, but your experience may remain untainted by wind and clouds, so November through March may make sense. There are great airfare deals and lower hotel rates for the courageous or romantic who visit Paris during these months. Even so, first-time visitors are advised to opt for summer months, when Paris puts on its prettiest face.

Price

High season in Paris runs from April 1 or Easter Sunday through June 30, September 1 through October 31, and the week between Christmas and New Year's Day. This is when prices are at their highest and availability is at its lowest. Low season runs from November 1 through March 31, with a slight rise between early July and August 31. The "TOs" (tour operators) call this summer variation the shoulder season.

Don't forget that prices soar during international trade shows and conferences like the Prêt-à-Porter fashion extravaganza and the International Aeronautics Show at Le Bourget. Hotels fill up qickly. The www.ccip.com website lists all trade shows and their dates. There are ways to defend yourself during high season and peak weeks, so don't only use "season" as your guide for travel dates. One tourist tells us that he prefers the off-season because it's very affordable, "plus you don't sweat climbing the stairs at the Notre-Dame and Sacré Coeur! The spring and fall in Paris are particularly pleasant, and the Champs-Elysées and other noted shopping areas are beautifully illuminated around Christmas. And the competition for sidewalk-café table space is purely Parisian." What you lose in climate, you'll gain in atmosphere.

Weather

The pleasures of Paris transcend its meteorological conditions. There's a lot to say about Paris's weather and seasons, and it's not all great news. It's wholly possible to have a great time in the grayest months. Knowing what to expect in advance is the key.

PARIS AVERAGE TEMPERATURE

January	2°–6° C	35°–43° F
February	2°–8° C	35°–46° F
March	4°–11° C	39°–52° F
April	7°–15° C	45°–59° F
May	10°–19° C	50°–66° F
June	13°–22° C	55°–72° F
July	15°–24° C	59°–75° F
August	15°–23° C	59°–73° F
September	12°–21° C	54°–70° F
October	9°–16° C	48°–61° F
November	5°–10° C	41°–50° F
December	3°–7° C	37°–45° F

PARIS RAINFALL

Month	# Rainy Days	Monthly Rainfall	Average Hours of Sunshine per Day
January	10	55mm (2.2 in.)	2
February	9	45mm (1.8 in.)	3
March	7	30mm (1.2 in.)	5
April	6	40mm (1.6 in.)	6
May	8	50mm (2 in.)	7
June	9	50mm (2 in.)	8
July	8	55mm (2.2 in.)	8
August	8	60mm (2.4 in.)	7
September	8	50mm (2 in.)	6
October	8	50mm (2 in.)	4
November	8	50mm (2 in.)	2
December	9	50mm (2 in.)	1

The summers are hot but bearable, the winters are long and gray, cold and wet, but usually not freezing. September and October, like April through June, can be divine. In August, many Parisians clear out for the long summer holiday, which makes the city less congested and more manageable for a visit. Some guidebooks will tell you that all you see in Paris in August is other tourists; this is not our experience. True, there are fewer Parisians in Paris, but there are also fewer people in general, and the city is calmer. And, although there are fewer Parisians, there actually are lots of French tourists, so you'll be sharing restaurants and cafés with French people, who are not all Parisians. There are fewer restaurants open, but there still are many. August can be hot, but the quality of the daylight and the shade on the sidewalk cafés are sources of great comfort. Paris in August can be surprisingly pleasant.

It's the grayness *(grisaille* [greez-**eye**]*)* of winter that tends to haunt the moods of the locals. It takes a cheery outlook, a decent pair of waterproof walking shoes, a handy umbrella, and an interesting itinerary to claim victory over the Parisian weather between the late fall and early spring. One tip is to wear wool and silk to resist Paris's particularly penetrating winter chill. Clearly, the Paris you visit in June will not feel like the Paris of January. One of the great advantages to off-season travel is that the city feels more authentic; there are fewer visitors, the lines are shorter, and of course, hotel prices are reduced. As odd as it sounds, the food in the colder months tends to be particularly savory. French onion soup *au gratin* (oh-gra**tah**n) is always good, but it's even better in the heart of winter. The same goes for hot chocolate.

Check weather conditions in Paris before leaving for your trip at www. meteo.fr (an excellent source, but all in French) on the web, or www.cnn.com

for their five-day forecast. Also try www.excite.com/travel/countries/france, which provides reliable weather information. You can also call Paris for weather conditions (in French): from the United States, call 011 33 8 36 68 02 75.

It rarely snows in Paris, but the city does get flurries that stick for a few hours once or twice each winter. Parisians get all excited by the white flakes, and the inexperienced Parisian drivers slide around the roads like foolish seals. More often there is rain or sleet. Each summer a hot-weather hail hits the city for an hour or so and ice balls create a strange cacophony on the metal roofs of the city. The heat in the summer can build, and Paris air gets heavy and diesel-laden. We'll tell you later how to avoid urban heat waves.

Note that the preferred month for visiting Paris is August for the Brits, June for the Americans, and May for the Germans. September and October and May and June have the most foreign visitors in Paris.

Package Deals and Travel Agents

Everyone wants to pay as little as possible, have as few hassles as possible, and have the most authentic experience possible. But to get all this, should you leave the planning to someone else and buy a packaged deal to Paris or should you piece it together yourself? Unfortunately, according to knowledgeable insiders, three-fourths of all the agents and packagers selling trips to France today do *not* really know enough about Paris or what they are selling. We met a poor couple who had been sold a Mont Saint-Michel road trip as an add-on to their three-day Paris stay. Thirty minutes out of Paris they asked their driver if they were almost there. Mont Saint-Michel is in Normandy, a four-hour drive each way. They spent eight hours in a car and two hours at the scenic coastal monastery. With only three days in Paris, a third of their time was sacrificed for this interesting but misplaced excursion. They couldn't have known. Their travel agent back home blindly bought the wonderful-sounding trip from a packager.

These kinds of things happen with Paris plans too. The travel market to France is so large that all sorts of packages at all sorts of prices are sold, and the results are at best unpredictable. The success of your packaged deal depends greatly on the quality and size of the tour operator, your own sense of self-confidence, and your degree of experience in international travel. In the packet of brochures sent out by the Maison de la France, you'll find a brochure for Jet Vacations, subtitled "Sourcebook for today's independent traveler." There are eight different "packages" for Paris offered here, beginning with "Affordable Paris" at $898 for *five* nights at a three-star hotel, airfare from New York included; the final package is "Paris in Style" at $1,498 for *three* nights at a four-star hotel. There are so many variables involved, like the price of the room, the location of hotel, the number of stars, the number of nights, excursions included, airport transfers, and whether or not passes and meals are included, that it's really difficult to know if you're getting good value or, more importantly, what you want. We noticed that the photos do not always correspond with the actual hotels being advertised, and that the photos that are used are misleading. The tour operator gives itself the option to place you in "a similar hotel" to the one mentioned in the catalog, and there are plenty of black-out periods, plus weekend surcharges and other fine print. You really have no control over what you'll end up with.

Knowledge is power. When selecting a package from a brochure, be aware of the pitfalls. The tour operator will not be available to answer specific questions once you're in Paris. The hotel you'll end up in, in any case, depends on available inventory just before your travel dates.

If you are pitched a package deal by a travel agent, aside from the obvious questions—"What's included in the package?" "How much free time do we have?" and "How large are the groups?"— ask specific questions:

- Which is the nearest Métro station to the hotel?
- Which restaurants near the hotel can you recommend?
- How far is the hotel from the Louvre?
- How many others will be on the bus? How long does it take to get to our destination?
- How many people have you booked on this trip in the past year? Could I talk to some of them?

If you draw blank looks to any of these, move on. These are not the right people for you. If you do need others to help make your Paris plans, consider this: unless you're extremely budget sensitive and you find a real all-inclusive steal, work with a small, personalized tour operator who has a love affair with France—or do it yourself. You'll enjoy greater freedom and mobility, you'll eat whatever and wherever you choose, you'll increase your chances of staying in a charming spot, and you'll be pleased with yourself for opting for greater adventure. If you are already an expert on Paris and you don't mind staying in a more commercial hotel, check out the packages.

Whether you like package tours or not, they can offer hotel accommodations, meals, and airport transfer, along with airfare, for not much more (and sometimes less) than you'd otherwise pay for the airfare alone. However, don't be lazy. Do the math. The package price may not cheaper than if you pieced it together yourself. Often, however, it is, and the savings may be worth losing some charm. Admittedly, the greatest attraction is the ease of not having to make the arrangements yourself. If savings are more motivating than location, you don't have the time or energy to make a few calls, and you don't mind being in a large, touristy hotel, you may choose the packaged trip and be quite satisfied.

At the minimum, you can learn a lot from examining the packages and then deciding to book on your own or opting for a smaller, specialized tour operator. Otherwise, use one of the recommended tour operators we mention or one who comes highly recommended by friends who have been to Paris and with whom you share similar tastes. Note that there are escorted tours and individual or self-driven tours; choose according to the level of independence you require or prefer.

To conclude, we suggest avoiding the huge packagers that sell volume, not quality. Your trip to Paris has to be special—you want every moment to be a treasure. You want to feel immersed in the local culture and seduced by its style and beauty, so don't be too quick to sacrifice splendor and control for a few dollars or a few hours of research. Many of us frequent travelers firmly believe that planning the trip is half the fun!

If your local travel agent is particularly knowledgeable about Paris, by all means work with him or her. If he regularly sends customers to a favorite little hotel in the Latin Quarter that he has been to himself, fine, do it, follow his lead. If he works with a great tour operator and can get you an attractive deal in a charming two- or three-star hotel, certainly consider it. But chances are, although travel agents book a lot of people to Paris, they often do not know the ins and outs of Parisian tourism. Local travel agents buy trips from big packagers with lots of marketing muscle and a lot of "product" to push. This is not likely to lead you to a delightful excursion. If you end up in a high-rise hotel in the 15th arrondissement or near the *périphérique,* you will have missed the real charm that Paris has to offer—and although you might enjoy a view of the Seine, you may not realize that you could have done a lot better. Many travelers come back and teach their travel agents a thing or two. So, if the travel agent doesn't have special Parisian knowledge, experience, and contacts, research and reserve the trip yourself.

A compromise is to have your travel agent book the trip that you have researched yourself. Try one of the hotels that we profile and let the professionals do their job. That way you know what you're getting, but you don't have the hassle of making reservations and confirmations.

For more details on Paris lodging, see Part Three, Hotels.

Finding a Package Tour, Tour Operator, or Consolidator

Packages are put together in a variety of ways by their vendors. Wholesalers tend to purchase blocks of airfares, hotel rooms, or tour slots in advance with the intention of assembling them into various package configurations, sometimes with an eye toward particular dates, events, or groups. They may start bulk buying the various package components a year in advance of their use, which allows them to get good prices to pass along to the customer. Consolidators, on the other hand, work a much narrower margin of time. These operators purchase airplane seats or other travel products that are in danger of going unsold, negotiating discounted rates with the airlines (or hotels, etc.) based on the perishability of the product. Both approaches have their advantages, and many companies use both to some degree.

Consult the Maison de la France's Brochure, Easy Reference Guide France

This supplement to the French government tourist office (Maison de la France) publication, *Focus on France,* includes everything from U.S. tour operators, charter-flight companies, bed-and-breakfasts, château stays, villa rentals, and youth hostels, to ski trips, barging, canal cruises, guide services, festival tours, bike tours, golf tours, horseback-riding trips, and even ballooning excursions. To request a free copy of the *Easy Reference Guide to France,* call (202) 659-7779.

Check the Travel Section of Your Local Newspaper

Do this regularly to see who's offering specials to Paris. Wholesalers, charter companies, and the major airlines dangle Paris teasers to attract attention. Also, be on the lookout for travel and tourism trade shows in your area.

Surf the Web

The Internet, as cybernauts already know, is a jungle in which all things are found. But the tangle of information can be overbearing, confusing, and unreliable, as well as incredibly helpful. If you're inclined to explore, here is a presifted list of web addresses at which package tours to Paris may be found and examined:

Paris Package Tours on the Web

www.paris-anglo.com	www.paris-tourism.com
www.travnav.com	www.francetourism.com
www.travnet.com	www.travel-in-france.com
www.thetrip.com	www.lowestfare.com
www.france.com	www.frenchexperience.com
www.repmark.com/europevacationpackages.html	

Suggested Tour Operators

In the spirit of saving you time, energy, and money as well as sparing you any feelings of disappointment, we have assembled a group of highly reliable and top-quality outfits offering travel services and trips to Paris. Again, we believe that it's better to insist on quality from the start if you want a truly memorable experience in a particularly Parisian way.

Tour operators specializing in Paris and France include the following. We've selected them for the quality of tours they propose, not by price. In general, these suggestions do not provide "low-end" budget travel.

D'Tours   P.O. Box 2, Newtown Square, PA 19073; (610) 356-9900. E-mail: Rosemarie@Dtoursfrance.com. Excellent culinary programs in Brittany and Provençe, with an especially wonderful trip to the Dordogne.

EC Tours, Inc.   12500 Riverside Drive, Suite 210, Valley Village, CA 91607; (818) 755-9333 or (800) 388-0877. Fax (818) 755-0999 or visit www.ectours.com. Particularly good organizers of small, personalized, and individual itineraries around France.

The French Experience   370 Lexington Avenue, New York, NY 10017; (212) 986-1115 or (800) 283-7262. Fax (212) 986-3808 or visit www. frenchexperience.com. Quality trips for individuals and groups to Paris and the provinces, 4- to 7-day self-drive tours with stays in private château.

Insightful Travelers   57 Rutland Square, Boston, MA 02118; (617) 859-0720. Fax (617) 267-4794 or e-mail: rhugel@tiac.net. Highly personalized Paris travel consultants Susan Fox and Richard Hill can help you find short-term apartments and organize your itinerary. Very knowledgeable and accommodating.

Progressive Travels   224 W. Galer, Suite C, Seattle, WA 98119; (206) 285-1987or (800) 245-2229. Fax (206) 285-1988 or visit www.progressive travels.com. They have excellent self-guided bicycling tours in Burgundy, Alsace, Dordogne, and the Basque country. A great combination with your Paris stay.

Tour de France   P.O. Box 379, Franklin Lakes, NJ 07417; (201) 891-0076 or (800) 261-2891. Fax (201) 891-4551 or visit www.francetourisme.com. Specialists in Paris and the provinces with custom château stays and tours.

Finding Airfare Deals and Making Reservations

If you're planning your own trip, start by securing your airline reservations. With your travel dates in place, you can then proceed to plan the rest of your trip.

Start with Your Local Travel Agent

If he or she can land you a nonstop or direct flight to Paris on your selected dates at a fare that is within your budget, take it. Tell your travel agent in advance what you're looking for.

Give your travel agent a range of possible dates and an idea of your top dollar. Tell him or her if you're willing to fly on a charter flight, if you'd consider changing planes in another city, what frequent-flyer programs you use, and anything else that might give your schedule and itinerary more flexibility. Lastly, give your travel agent a deadline, like "I need to hear back from you by Friday." Good travel agents are like magicians. Unfortunately, today many only know how to write tickets.

Skim the Travel Section of Your Local Paper

This is where specials emerge, but you have to move quickly. Often, there are only a few tickets available at the price offered and they're snapped up even before the paper comes out. Jockeying for great deals, especially during the peak season, can be nightmarish. Airline restrictions, black-out dates, and other airline rules can be enough to spoil the journey before you leave.

KEY WEB SITES FOR AIR TRAVEL RESERVATIONS

www.bemextours.com	www.bestfares.com
www.budgetfares.com	www.etn.nl/frq/fusfrpar.htm
www.cheapertravel.com/menueurope.htm	www.frenchexperience.com
www.economytravel.com	www.mapquest.com
www.expedia.com	www.previewtravel.com
www.lowestfare.com	www.thetrip.com
www.nos.net/airtravel	www.travelocity.com
www.priceline.com	www.travnet.com

Surfing for Inexpensive Airfare

The Internet today is so rich in travel offers that we're unable to predict what you'll find. On the exotic side, an online travel agent in Bombay, India, was recently offering New York–Paris round-trip tickets for $299! You pay with your credit card, and the tickets are sent to you by Federal Express. These offers occur because different travel outfits obtain negotiated prices on certain airlines for certain periods for certain flights. You might get lucky. But don't make yourself crazy by becoming obsessive about the prices—they change very quickly. Try the popular website www.last minutetravel.com or the French site www.ebookers.com for good deals.

Remember, as a security measure when buying online, always use secure websites (signified by a closed "lock" in the bottom corner of your web browser or "https://"—the "s" is for secure—in the address), and buy your tickets with a credit card. Double check to make sure that the name you submit for each ticket matches the name on each passenger's passport exactly. When making long-distance purchases, it is difficult to make changes after you've received your tickets. We recommend that you always request a paper ticket rather than an e-ticket. So if you prefer to shop online, be sure to call customer service to make the reservation so that you can receive a paper ticket by mail. And give yourself plenty of time to receive tickets, vouchers, etc., by mail well before your departure date.

Closer to home, many travelers recommend Microsoft's www.expedia. com as an excellent means of at least pricing fares. Expedia also has a "fare alert" feature that e-mails you if fares drop below a designated price. Travelocity and others do this too, and it is a very useful feature. One Paris-loving American reports: "I've heard of New York–based 'Moment's Notice' which has a recording of reduced, last-minute fares for the next weekend." Leave no stones unturned.

New services are cropping up all the time. Priceline advertises nationally, both online and by calling (800) PRICELINE. You submit a price that you're willing to pay for a given destination, with a credit card number. If Priceline can get the tickets at your price, they do, and they'll debit your credit card immediately. It's a great concept, but be very careful. There are all sorts of conditions and disclaimers to this type of sale—not least of which is that you may have to make numerous stopovers to reach your destination (a flight to Paris via New York, Reykjavik, and London may not be what you had in mind!). Much of the pleasure of traveling to Paris is the expectation and period of preparation. If there is a risk that your plans are going to get wiped out, or that you'll spend 18 hours on multiple flights to get there, then the potential savings are hardly worth it. If you need personal, good old-fashioned hand-holding, this won't be the best route for you.

Bestfares.com and an affiliate called World Travel boast of cut-rate fares to Paris. We found $205 round-trip tickets, from Boston to Paris, on their website, but when we tried to buy them we were led to a page that obliges users to become members first. To become a member you need to subscribe to their magazine for $53 a year. Admittedly, there were lots of perks connected to the membership, and lots of savings on hotels and cars and meals and other things, but you might not feel like becoming a subscriber, and you certainly can't rely on any one-to-one human contact and advice. We e-mailed Bestfares' customer services numerous times, but we got no reply, which is typical of online travel services. The prices may be attractive, but service is either nonexistent or spotty. A number of readers have raved about great fares on www.previewtravel.com ($430 round-trip Los Angeles–Paris). Give it a whirl. We discussed a London-based outfit called Dial-a-Flight which offers excellent service and remarkable fares. Start at their website, www.dialaflight.com and then pick up phone numbers to reserve. Reliable service.

Call the Airlines Directly

Be ready to be put on hold for intolerable lengths of time. If your travel dates are inflexible you'll be limited to the normally expensive published fares. If you are flexible, insist on hearing about all their specials. The airlines put up promotional offers all the time. These deals change frequently and are often very limited and carry contorted restrictions, blackout dates, minimum-stay requirements, and the like. Ask, ask, ask. One option is to consider other cities of arrival, like Brussels or Geneva, or other cities of departure. Keep asking. If you hit a dud salesperson, thank them, hang up, and call back—someone else with the same airline might be savvier. This happens all the time. Don't wait for the airline to be creative. Ask: "If I were to fly from Philadelphia do you have any specials?" "If we leave on a Saturday instead of Monday, isn't the fare lower?" "Do you have any senior-citizen discounts?" Determination and a proactive attitude can often lead to new options and fare reductions.

If you get a particularly helpful and knowledgeable sales representative on the phone, ask if he or she has a direct number or an alternative number so you don't have to hold again for them for another 20 minutes when you call them back. In this era of not-so-great customer service, you have to defend yourself!

Note: If you see two flights listed for the exact same time and destination, for example, Air France and Continental or Delta, don't get confused. This is the same plane, but it takes two flight numbers (code sharing) and is sold separately by both companies. Ask if you're flying on the airline that is selling you the ticket. Frequent-flyer miles are applied to the company that issues the ticket.

Air Canada	(800) 776-3000 (U.S.)
	(800) 268-7240 (Canada)
Air France	(800) 237-2747
American Airlines	(800) 433-7300
AOM French Airlines	(800) 892-9136
Canadian Airlines	(800) 665-1177
Continental	(800) 525-0280
Delta Air Lines	(800) 221-1212
Egyptair	(800) 334-6787
Icelandair	(800) 223-5500
Northwest Airlines	(800) 225-2525
Tower Air	(800) 348-6937
TWA	(800) 221-2000
United Airlines	(800) 241-6522
US Air	(800) 428-4322

Note: It is wise to sign up for the airlines' online newsletters. The airlines are actively attempting to lure passengers into buying tickets online and are offering good deals to help change consumer habits. Register on the airlines' websites, and you'll systematically receive the latest offers by e-mail. Paris is often on the list of destinations.

Gateways in North America   The following cities have nonstop service to and from Paris:

Atlanta	Los Angeles	Phoenix
Boston	Miami	Pittsburgh
Charlotte, N.C.	Minneapolis/	San Diego
Chicago	St. Paul	San Francisco
Cincinnati	Montreal	San Jose
Dallas	New York	St. Louis
Detroit	Newark	Toronto
Houston	Philadelphia	Washington, D.C

Tricks for Cheap Airfare

Alternative Destinations: Connecting to Paris

You can investigate flying via another European city, either to save money or to simply find a flight when all the nonstop flights are booked solid. There are advantageous fares to Paris on regularly scheduled flights on major airlines if you are willing to change planes and spend a few extra hours in transit. Your baggage gets checked straight through to Paris. Examples of alternative destinations include British Airways via London, KLM via Amsterdam, Lufthansa via Frankfurt, Swissair via Geneva or Zurich, Aer Lingus via Shannon, Sabena via Brussels, TAP via Lisbon, Iberia via Madrid, SAS via Copenhagen, and Icelandair via Luxembourg and Reykjavik. A stopover and plane change at some obscenely early morning hour will translate into a few extra hours of travel time and even redder eyes, but the savings may be worth it. Some people get a kick out of at least seeing the airport in a new country, and use the time to peruse the airport shops. Amsterdam's Schiphol Airport and Brussels Airport offer good shopping.

Couriers

Call the international courier companies in your city and ask if they are taking volunteers. (Check yellow pages for couriers.) Some offer a two-week round-trip ticket for next to nothing. The hitch is that you cannot take any check-in luggage with you, since you will be checking in baggage for the courier company. But if you're a savvy packer, this can be a very inexpensive way to get to Europe.

Consider London

With the Eurostar train and the Eurotunnel connecting the U.K. and the continent, it's an easy three-hour ride to Paris's Gare du Nord from London's Waterloo Station. This means that if all else fails, or if you'd like to spend a few days in London on either side of your Paris visit, you could consider flying into London's Heathrow or Gatwick airports from North America, and make the easy train commute to London's Waterloo Station and then on to Paris. British Airways has a flight nearly every hour between New York's JFK and London. The direct line for bilingual Eurostar information and reservations is Tel. 011 33 8 36 35 35 39. You can also call the Eurostar office in London at Tel. 011 44 12 33 61 75 75. In Paris, call Tel. 08 36 35 35 39. Dial 1 on the voice options to hear about special discounts.

Little-Known Paris Stopovers

With a bit of research, you'll discover that other major airlines make stops in Paris en route to other destinations, which not all travel agents think to check on, and seats on these flights can be very economical. Egypt Air's Cairo–New York run stops at Orly airport in Paris in both directions. Pakistan International's Karachi–Frankfurt–New York flight stops in Paris too. Cathay Pacific's Hong Kong–London trek touches down in Paris, as does Qantas's London–Sydney flight. The schedules change, and these flights run only on certain days and at odd hours, so check with the airlines directly.

The Paris Airfare Game

The range of airfares is all over the map these days, but to give you a ballpark figure of a round-trip ticket from the east coast of the United States to Paris, expect to pay between $350 and $500 in off-peak periods and up to $900 per person in economy class during the summer and high-season, peak periods. Availability, special offers, frequent-flyer miles, and advance reservations and payment will all affect the fares you'll be quoted. Remember, there are often no two people on the same plane who paid the exact same price for their ticket! If you're being quoted only the expensive fares in this range, keep looking. Use the web. Call tour operators. Ask more than one travel agent. Again, we repeat, if you have the flexibility to travel off-season, you'll be able to land better fares then.

Although the Concorde crash in Paris in 2000 spoiled an otherwise perfect record and left people uneasy for months, the ultimate high-end flight is still the three-and-a-half-hour supersonic trip between New York and Paris on Air France's Concorde. It costs about $5,000 one-way, $8,000 round-trip. Air France now offers a special half-price second ticket when you travel as a couple and stay for at least four nights, including Saturday— $12,000 for two! Note that Concorde tickets are about 25% pricier when purchased in the United States (about $10,000 for a round-trip fare).

Ticket Consolidators

There are plenty of outfits offering cut-rate plane tickets to every city on earth. If you are accustomed to using one and have had positive experiences, by all means continue to rely on this service when buying your Paris tickets.

Otherwise, be careful. Consolidators buy up blocks of tickets to resell at cut prices. This helps airlines reduce the number of empty seats. Sometimes, you are asked to pay before you receive your tickets, or you are issued vouchers which you exchange for your tickets at the airport. Inquire about the reliability of the outfit before you commit, and only use credit cards to pay. Smart travelers call airlines directly to re-confirm their reservations.

Charter Flights

The French tour operator Nouvelles Frontières has a U.S. division called New Frontiers offering consistently excellent charter fares between the United States and Paris on its own aircraft. For example: Oakland–Paris round-trip is offered at roughly $400, year-round. Note that you may save on your fare but charter flights may leave less frequently and maintain less convenient hours.

New Frontiers (Nouvelles Frontières)   (800) 366-6387; Fax: (212) 779-1007; www.newfrontiers.com

Jet Vacations   (800) JET-0999; www.jetvacations.com; e-mail: jetvacations @worldnet.att.net

Paris Travel Agents

Although you may be originating on the other side of the world, Paris-based travel agents often can provide better fares and better service than you are finding at home. New Frontiers/Nouvelles Frontières (described above) is one such agency to check out, and so is Non Stop USA:

Non Stop USA   7 rue Berryer, 75008; Tel. 01 53 93 75 00; fax 01 45 62 02 10; www.non-stop-usa.com; director: Mario Cassuto.

Choosing an Airline

If you have a choice of airlines, try to fly Air France. Why? As soon as you step onto an Air France flight you'll feel the cultural difference. You'll be in a tiny piece of France, served by a French crew that's dressed in French tailored suits and silk scarves, wearing French haircuts and eau de cologne, and offering flutes of French champagne and wine (on Air France the champagne is offered for free). The in-flight entertainment and menu will be bilingual, and the style and quality of the food will clearly be French. This is a great way to start getting into the atmospheric mood of Paris even before you arrive.

Choosing an Airport: Roissy/Charles de Gaulle or Orly

Paris has two international airports. Unlike cities like London, Washington, D.C., or New York, where the choice of airport can make a huge difference in your travel time, comfort, and expense, Paris's two airports are both close to the city and easily accessible by public transportation and taxi. It really does not matter which you arrive at. More important than the airport are the airfares and the arrival times. We prefer the Air France flights from Newark and Boston because they leave the United States around 10 p.m. and arrive mid-morning Paris time. If you do have a choice of airport, remember that Orly is a bit closer to central Paris than Roissy/Charles de Gaulle, although the difference is negligible.

If you know where you'll be staying at the time you make your plane reservations, you may choose the airport that's more convenient to your hotel. One reader tells us that she always flies into Roissy/Charles de Gaulle and stays in a small hotel near Les Invalides, because the Air France airport bus stops there and she can easily walk to her hotel. Airlines are known to change their arrivals and departures from one airport to the other, so be sure to note at which airport you'll be arriving. In 1999, for instance, American Airlines moved operations from Orly to Roissy/Charles de Gaulle.

Other Things to Consider before Leaving Home

- Renting a car. If you decide to rent a car, make sure you reserve one *before* leaving home—U.S. rates are substantially lower than those in France. See details in Part Five, Getting Around Paris.

- Buying train passes or making train reservations. See details in Part Five, Getting Around Paris.

- Pre-purchasing a *Paris Visite* public transportation pass for 1, 2, 3, or 5 consecutive days. See details in Part Five, Getting Around Paris.

- Pre-purchasing a Paris Museum and Monument pass for 1, 2, or 5 days. See details in Part Six, Sightseeing and Tours.

- Pre-purchasing theater, music, opera, or sporting-event tickets before leaving home. Ticket Avenue (www.ticketavenue.com) offers this service.

- To preorder passes, consult www.ticketsto.com or contact "Tickets To . . ." at 10 East 21st Street, New York, NY 10010; (212) 529-9069; fax (212) 529-4838.

- Prepurchasing Paris and France maps from Michelin. (Call (800) 223-0987; ask for operator 28.)

- Reserving a cell phone for use in France. You can do this online at www.paris-anglo.com/cellphone or by sending a fax to 011 33 1 56 24 35 92.

- Reserving a babysitter in advance. Consult the listings in Part Four, Arriving, Getting Oriented, and Departing.

Reducing the Confusion of Choice

It's easy obtaining travel information on Paris. In fact, you may suffer the opposite problem; there is so much written on Paris that it is hard to determine what's helpful and, in the case of conflicting information, who's right. By scanning the travel section of your local bookstore or surfing the web, you'll certainly notice that Paris information is wildly abundant. We found 2 million references to Paris on the Alta Vista search engine alone! You don't need or want 130 hotel rooms; you want a few reliable suggestions and tips that correspond to your needs and interests. Ultimately, all you really want is help making sure that you'll have a great time. We've attempted to sort this out for you, to weed back the "confusion of choice" and spare you from the glut of less-than-useful and often contradictory information and advice littering the market.

Maison de la France (French Government Tourist Office)

The most complete and thorough source of basic travel information on Paris is the French Government Tourist Office, known as the Maison de la France. As of 1998, a phone center in Washington, D.C. fields your questions and requests for brochures and has replaced the more personalized service travelers used to get. In addition, we've found that receiving printed information can take up to a month, so start inquiring early. The direct line in the United States is (202) 659-7779. If you have a hard time getting through or cannot seem to get the information you need, try the Travel Agents' designated number at (202) 293-6173. Although their free booklet, *Easy Reference Guide France,* is a great collection of tour operators and travel agents in the United States specializing in France, the booklet mixes the small and personalized operators with the huge and impersonal ones, the highly reputable with the unproven, and you'll end up not knowing who to contact. See "Suggested Tour Operators" earlier in this chapter for a few tested suggestions from this list. If you're accessing the Internet to gather information, it's worth visiting www.fgtousa.org, www.francetourism.com, and www.paris-touristoffice.com for general information on France.

OTHER MAISON DE LA FRANCE ADDRESSES:

In the United States

- **Chicago**
  676 N. Michigan Avenue, Chicago, IL 60611-2819
  (312) 751-7800; fax (312) 337-6339

- **Los Angeles**
  9454 Wilshire Boulevard, Suite 715, Beverly Hills, CA 90212-2967
  (310) 271-6665; fax (310) 276-2835

- **Miami**
  1 Biscayne Tower, Suite 1750, 2 South Biscayne Boulevard, Miami, FL 33131
  (305) 373-8177; fax (305) 373-5828

- **New York**
  444 Madison Avenue, 16th Floor (between 49th and 50th Streets)
  New York, NY 10022-6903

(212) 838-7029; fax (212) 838-7855
Director: Jean-Pierre Couteau

In Canada

- 1981 Ave. MacGill University, Suite 490, Montreal, Quebec H3A 2W9
(514) 288-4295; fax (514) 845-4868

In the United Kingdom

- 178 Piccadilly, London W1J 9AL
0171 399 35 00; fax 0171 399 35 40

The Alliance Française

The Alliance Française is a great source of cultural and linguistic information and overall support for Paris-bound travelers. It's also a sure way of
both propelling you into the world of French culture before your Paris journey and maintaining your contact with your Parisian experience after your
return. This century-old worldwide network is, according to its brochure,
"dedicated to promoting awareness, understanding, and appreciation of the
French language and culture."

Go to www.afusa.org for a list of its 144 chapters and French schools
throughout the United States (sometimes this may be just a contact person
giving French classes in a small town). Or call or write to get on the
Alliance Française mailing list: 2819 Ordway St. NW, Washington, D.C.
20008; (202) 966-9740; fax (202) 362-1587; www.info-france-usa.org.

Franco-American Chambers of Commerce

If your interest in Paris goes beyond simple tourism and you're on your way
to Paris for professional or commercial reasons, you may have a variety of
specific questions relating to your mission. The Franco-American Chambers of Commerce, founded in 1896 to promote sound, strong relations
between the United States and France (with 16 chapters in the United
States), could be a key source of pretravel information.

United States Franco-American Chambers of Commerce

- **Atlanta**
999 Peachtree Street, NE, Suite 2095, Atlanta, GA 30309
(404) 874-2602; fax (404) 875-9452

- **Boston**
15 Court Square, Suite 320, Boston, MA 02108
(617) 523-4438; fax (617) 523-4461

- **Chicago**
55 East Monroe Street, Suite 3418, Chicago, IL 60603
(312) 263-7668/7858; fax (312) 263-7860

■ **Dallas**
4835 LBJ Freeway, Suite 640, Dallas, TX 75244
(214) 991-4888; fax (214) 991-4887

■ **Detroit**
100 Renaissance Center, Suite 2210, Detroit, MI 48243-1100
(313) 567-6010; fax (313) 567-0142

■ **Houston**
1770 St. James, Suite 425, Houston, TX 77056
(713) 960-0575; fax (713) 960-0495

■ **Los Angeles**
6380 Wilshire Boulevard, Suite 1608, Los Angeles, CA 90048
(213) 651-4741; fax (213) 651-2547

■ **New Orleans**
World Trade Center, #2938, 2 Canal Street, New Orleans, LA 70130
 (504) 524-2042; fax (504) 522-4003 or 561-6560

■ **Miami**
Associates, Inc., 141 Sevilla Avenue, Coral Gables, FL 33134
(305) 443-3223; fax (305) 444-1587

■ **Minneapolis**
Foshay Tower, Suite 904, 821 Marquette Avenue, Minneapolis, MN 55402
(612) 338-7750; fax (612) 338-7750

■ **New York**
1350 Avenue of the Americas, 6th Floor, New York, NY 10019
(212) 765-4460; fax (212) 765-4650

■ **Philadelphia**
4000 Bell Atlantic Tower, 1717 Arch Street, Philadelphia, PA 19103-2713
(215) 994-5373; fax (215) 994-5366

■ **Pittsburgh**
435 Sixth Avenue, Pittsburgh, PA 15219
(412) 288-4174; fax (412) 288-3063

■ **San Francisco**
425 Bush Street, Suite 401, San Francisco, CA 94108
(415) 398-2449, fax (415) 398-8912

■ **Seattle**
2101 Fourth Avenue, Suite 2330, Seattle, WA 98121
(206) 443-4703; fax (206) 448-4218

■ **Washington, D.C.**
1730 Rhode Island Avenue, NW, Suite 711, Washington, D.C. 20036
(202) 775-0256; fax (202) 785-4604

What to Pack

The best piece of advice is: "Bring less!" Travelers have a terrible tendency to overpack. Some visitors fear that they won't be able to find Tylenol or corn flakes in Europe and decide to bring 'em along. Please, only bring the essentials.

Some savvy travelers go so far as to carry just one suitcase that is small enough to fit into the overhead compartments inside the plane; this saves lots of time on both ends. However, be certain that your bag does fit international size and weight restrictions—and on fully booked flights, you may find your carry-on luggage being checked anyway.

Airline restrictions from the United States limit you to either two checked-in bags per person or a 40-pound weight limit. Check with your travel agent or carrier for specifics. Some people like to travel with one bag and pack an empty nylon or duffel bag in order to have space for gifts and other purchases for the return flight. This is a great idea—you will definitely have some treasures you will want to lug home from Paris. Otherwise, you can buy throwaway, soft zip-around bags made of indestructible red, white, and blue nylon cord in all the flea markets and cut-rate shops— you've probably seen them at airports before; they're fairly ubiquitous. This might be your best value purchase. They cost less than $5 and are perfect for lugging back your great finds *(trouvailles* [troo-**vye**]*)*.

We always advise international travelers to avoid heavy suitcases that do not roll. Bags with shoulder straps and rollers will give you much needed mobility and will also help you save on taxi fares. If you have one or two bags with rollers, you may opt to get to your hotel via public transportation rather than a taxi, and pay around €8 instead of €40 each way!

For some people, packing is an obsessive science. The most amusing tip we've heard in a long time comes from an American woman who writes: "Call me a wasteful American, but I do take older undergarments and socks along and pitch them at the end. This is a great way to clean out your drawer, create suitcase room along the way, and avoid a pile of laundry upon return." But if there is any city in the world in which you'll feel like wearing your fanciest or most risqué underwear, it'll be Paris!

Other packing tips: Take along photocopies of your passports, credit cards, and other important papers, to be left in your hotel room in case you lose the originals (also leave copies of this information at home or with a family member). Avoid taking along anything electric, unless it's dual-voltage or adaptable; otherwise you'll have problems with the current. You'll also risk delays at security checkpoints in the airports, and most hotels (even one-stars) provide hair dryers.

Cordless shavers are handy. Bring a small solar calculator for quick currency conversions while shopping. Note that all of France uses 220–230 volts AC (not the North American 110 volts). Electrical current alternates at 50 cycles, not the 60 in use in America. If you are bringing shavers, travel irons, hair dryers, or whatever, make sure that they are adapted for European current. Otherwise, you'll need a voltage transformer, which is bulky and heavy and not worth the trouble to carry. Remember, too, that the outlet prongs are shaped differently, and your appliances won't fit into French wall outlets without adapters. You'll need an adapter plug, which costs only about $3 and is easily found in Radio Shacks, appliance and travel shops, and even in the luggage sections of all-purpose stores like K-Mart and Wal-Mart. You'll also need one if you're planning on plugging in a laptop computer or charging the batteries of your video camera.

Bring along a few extra identity photos of yourself. These come in handy when you need to get a train pass, a senior-citizens reduction card, a permit to fish in the Seine, or whatever else crops up.

Many travelers carry an extra pair of eyeglasses, medication (with prescription and generic name), and valuables on their person instead of checking this through in luggage. Smart.

If you need some quick extra-baggage capacity, the duty-free liquor shops at both Roissy–Charles de Gaulle and Orly airports sell an excellent, blue tote bag marked "Aeroboutique Duty Free Paris" for six euros. It's strong, insulated, and not too ugly.

With the more stringent security enforced for carry-on luggage, you must be careful to put the following items in your check-in luggage: scissors, nail files, nail clippers, pen knives, razors or razor blades, or any other sharp object that could conceivably be used as a weapon.

Cell Phones

Check with your phone company to find out if your cell phone will work in France. Most won't. France uses a GSM system.

Passports and Visas

As is true with all international travel, when visiting France you must be in possession of a valid passport. Note that the date of expiration should not fall shorter than three months after the date of your expected return. Citizens of the United States, Canada, Britain, and other European Union countries do *not* need a visa for France. Upon entry into France, your passport will be stamped, enabling you to stay in the country for up to three months. If you hold a passport from another country, make sure to inquire about visa requirements at the closest French consulate. It is always a good idea to leave a copy of the information page of your passport at home and put a second one in your luggage. That way, in case your passport is lost or stolen, you will facilitate its replacement by showing this photocopy at your consulate in Paris.

You do not need an International Health Certificate to enter France from the United States, although if you plan to continue your journey to another country, you should inquire with that country's consulate before leaving home.

French Consular Offices

For all other administrative, commercial, and legal issues concerning your travels to France, contact the French Consular office nearest to you. Note that the French government posts travel and administrative information on its official website at www.info-france-usa.org.

French consular offices in the United States

- **Atlanta**
  285 Peachtree Street, NE, Suite 2800, Atlanta, GA 30303
  (404) 522-4226; fax (404) 880-9408

- **Boston**
  Park Square Building, 31 St. James Avenue, Suite 750, Boston, MA 02116
  (617) 542-7374; fax (617) 542-8054

- **Chicago**
  Olympic Center, 737 N. Michigan Ave., Suite 2020, Chicago, IL 60611
  (312) 787-5359; fax (312) 664-4196
  e-mail: fsltchic@ix.netcom.com

- **Houston**
  2777 Allen Parkway, Suite 650, Houston, TX 77019
  (713) 528-2181; fax (713) 528-1933

- **Los Angeles**
  French Consulate, One Westwood Building, 10990 Wilshire Boulevard,
  Suite 300, Los Angeles, CA 90024
  (310) 235-3200; fax (310) 312-0704

- **Miami**
  1 Biscayne Tower, 2 S. Biscayne Boulevard, Suite 1710, Miami, FL 33131
  (305) 372-9798; fax (305) 372-9549; visas: (305) 372-9798

- **New Orleans**
  Lykes Building, 300 Poydras Street, Suite 2105, New Orleans, LA 70130
  (504) 523-5774; fax (504) 523-5725
  e-mail: consulatnola@webtv.net

- **New York**
  934 Fifth Avenue, New York, NY 10021
  (212) 606-3688,; fax (212) 606-3260; visas (212) 606-3614

- **San Francisco**
  540 Bush Street, San Francisco, CA 94108
  (415) 397-4330; fax (415) 433-8375
  e-mail: cgsfo@best.com
- **San Juan**
  Ponce De Leon Avenue, Suite 720, Hato Rey
  Puerto Rico 00918
  (809) 753-1700
- **Washington, D.C.**
  French Chancery, 4101 Reservoir Road, NW, Washington, D.C. 20007
  (202) 944-6000 or (202) 944-6195; fax (202) 944-6148; visas (202) 944-6212

In Canada

- **Moncton/Halifax**
  Consulate, 250 Lutz Street, CP 1109, Moncton NB, E1C 8P6
  (506) 857-4191 (and 92); fax (506) 858-8169
- **Montreal**
  General Consulate, 1 place Ville Marie, Suite 2601, Montreal, QC H3
  (514) 878-4385; fax (514) 878-3981
  www.consulfrancemontreal.org
- **Toronto**
  General Consulate, 130 rue Bloor ouest # 400, Toronto, ON M5S 1N
  (416) 925-8041; fax (416) 925-3076
  www.consulfrance-toronto.org
- **Vancouver**
  General Consulate, 1201/736 Granville Street, Vancouver BC V6Z 1H9
  (604) 681-4345; fax (604) 681 42 87

In the United Kingdom

- **London**
  General Consulate, 21 Cromwell Road, London SW7 2EN
  (0207) 838-2000; fax (0207) 838-2001
  www.ambafrance.org
- **Edinburgh/Glasgow**
  General Consulate, 11 Randolph Crescent, Edinburgh EH3 7TT
  (0131) 225-7954; fax (0131) 225-8975

Travel Restrictions

If you're wondering whether France has any restrictions as to what you can bring into the country as a tourist, you can relax. France has comparatively few travel restrictions. You can strut past customs inspectors with a pair of Irish setters and not be questioned (although you do need health certificates for bringing pets into the country). As long as your passport is valid and you're not carrying massive amounts of electronic equipment, customs and immigrations inspectors at Paris's two main airports are relatively lax. For absolute assurance, you may want to stick photocopies of any invoices or receipts for expensive video, photographic, or computer equipment that you are traveling with into your carry-on luggage. There are no restrictions on cameras or film you bring in, as long as they are for your own use. You may bring with you any reasonable gifts, and like in the United States, up to the equivalent of $10,000 in cash or negotiable instruments without having to declare it. You're limited to 200 cigarettes or 50 cigars or 100 cigarillos or 250 grams of tobacco, and one liter of alcohol and two liters of wine (but no one brings wine to France!). Legally, you cannot import gold other than your own personal jewelry.

How to Dress

Parisians tend to dress nicely and more formally than their North American counterparts, so when in doubt, err on the dressy side. The line between being dressed up and being simple and elegant, as Parisians often are, is a fine one. The French way of dressing includes subtleties and nuances that are hard for visitors to grasp quickly. The choice of broach, the tasteful belt, the shoes, the fabric of your vest, the shape of buttons, and a pair of unique earrings all make a difference. Elegance in France is not necessarily eye-catching; it's often the opposite, the art of the understatement. To be comfortable, don't overdress in formal evening wear when going to a Paris restaurant. We do suggest that you find for yourself a balance between looking good and being looked at.

In the summer months, you'll rarely see Parisians bopping around town in shorts, although women often wear short skirts. There are no stigmas to wearing shorts when it's 90° F and you're sightseeing, but as a rule the French don't look favorably on irreverent casualness or sloppiness. They have their own casual look called *decontracté* (relaxed), but it is always stylish. So if blending in is important to you, here are some tips on style. In the winter months, you probably won't want to wear a ski jacket or down parka in the city unless you're going skiing. An overcoat or leather jacket with some warm but not too bulky sweaters is best. The French wear scarves and shawls religiously, and you may even want to buy yourself something French and silky while you're here. A portable umbrella is always a good idea, and chances are that you'll be using it if you're traveling in the fall, winter, or early spring.

Gentlemen, you may decide to throw a tie and jacket into your luggage, but you should note that French elegance and proper dress does not usually oblige you to wear a tie and jacket. Even French commentators on television do not wear ties. The fanciest restaurants will shun jeans, but usually do not require ties.

Jeans are worn frequently, and women even wear them to the office, but they are not accepted in clubs and discos.

Bring your favorite toiletries with you. Although you'll find everything you need in Paris, American products tend to be more costly, and it's a shame to have to pay $8 for shaving cream when you could bring yours along for $2. In the hot months, a great item to pick up is an aerosol can of Evian water, sold in pharmacies. Not only will this keep you cool, it helps keep you from dehydrating on the airplane ride back home.

A Word on Tourist Garb

Although Americans love to wear sneakers, if you want to feel less conspicuous as a visitor, try bringing along very comfortable walking shoes instead of Nikes and Reeboks (unless you plan to jog). Since Paris gets a fair amount of rain, shoes that keep water out are advisable.

Flashy waistline "fanny-packs" and baseball caps both single you out as a tourist. If that's your preference, go ahead—fanny-packs, in particular, are good at keeping your valuables safe (though it's good to wear an open shirt or windbreaker over the bag, as some purse snatchers are very adept at unfastening the clasps of fanny-packs' belts). Small daypacks are equally useful and more discreet. Women should opt for an oversized tote bag to use instead of a purse. These are ideal for storing all the necessities you might need for a day on the town—an umbrella, water bottle, map, sunglasses, and the small purchases you're likely to make throughout the day.

Savvy travelers like black clothing. Black goes with everything and hides dirt. Black shoes are always appropriate and are easy to clean. One smart tourist admits that she's "a true shoe hound, but can go an entire week on one pair of black shoes in Paris!"

For those of you traveling in the winter months, listen up. If you have a tendency to get cold walking outside in the winter but hate it when you roast in department stores, be sure to dress in layers.

Estimating Your Budget: A Ballpark Idea

To budget your trip, use the following information as a rough indicator for the basics, *per person*, noting that there are great variations in the costs of hotel rooms, dining and wining, and shopping preferences. Estimates are based on two people traveling for a week. Airfare and airport transfers are not included as part of the total per day per person.

Airline tickets	$600
Airport transfers	$40

Hotel room	$75
(based on a modern and comfortable three-star hotel, per person, per night)	
Meals	$50
(lunch and dinner, good but not starred restaurants)	
Métro/museum passes	$20
Miscellaneous	$30
Total	$175/per day per person

How Much Cash to Carry?

As much as you can! No, really, the amount of cash you bring is totally subjective, depending on how much you tend to spend and what you plan to buy. Since your airplane tickets, hotel room, and much of your wining, dining, and entertainment can be paid by credit card, you won't need large amounts of cash. A mix of euros and U.S. cash, a major credit card, and perhaps major travelers checks in small denominations in either U.S. dollars or euros is preferable. (Note that the French franc continues to exist only until 2002; subsequently, the euro becomes the local currency in the European Union.)

It is relatively easy to get cash out of Cirrus- and Plus-affiliated ATMs in Paris by using your VISA or MasterCard, or your bank's ATM card. American Express also has a limited number of its own ATMs. Most Paris banks are on the Cirrus or Plus system and even offer instructions in English. You must remember to bring your PIN (four digit number) with you—your PIN for international-banking access may be different than the one you use every day at home, so ask your bank for this information before leaving the country. Some banks are slow in processing these requests, so plan on asking about this at least a month prior to your departure. We advise having a second card with you in case a Paris machine eats one card and you cannot recover it right away. You may want to request a second copy of the same card and keep one in a safe place in case the magnetic strip on the other card becomes defective.

When possible, after January 2002, you'll want to show up in Paris with at least €200 in cash in your pocket in case you need to pay a taxi or get something to eat before you can change money. Ask your local bank if they can get you some euros before you leave—as a service, they usually will. But don't buy too much. U.S. exchange rates on foreign funds are usually lower, and unless you have easy access to a major foreign-currency dealer in a large American city, you'll do a lot better waiting to change most of your money in Paris. Call a foreign-currency dealer in the city nearest you to inquire about rates and commissions. You can check prevalent exchange rates in the business section of most newspapers, but note that these are the bank-to-bank rates. Expect to get about 10% less.

If you can't get a hold of euros before you arrive in Paris, do change a small amount of currency into euros at the airport—you'll need it for the taxi, bus, or other small items on your way into Paris.

Exchange rates at ATMs tend to be better than those offered at Parisian banks. When using a debit card, your bank at home will charge you between two and five dollars per transaction or a small percentage of the amount withdrawn. Inquire first with your bank or credit-card company what the fees are for withdrawing funds from an ATM abroad. Most credit card companies consider overseas ATM withdrawals as "cash advances" and start charging you a steep interest rate from the day of withdrawal until the day the next statement is paid. Be sure you know what these often hidden fees are before you use them, so that you're not surprised by the costs on your statement when you get home. To avoid these interest fees, consider simply prepaying a sum of money to your credit card company and traveling with a credit balance. Then your cash advances won't cost you a cent in interest.

One little trick that we have shared with our readers in the past is the purchase of French franc coins (as opposed to paper currency) at the airport or at an exchange office before traveling. You can often buy coins at a much better exchange rate simply by asking for them. It's a bit inconvenient to carry a packet of coins, but the savings in the exchange rate may be enough to buy you a sandwich or drink, and you may need the coins upon arriving for tips, Métro tickets, telephone cards, and small items like newspapers, candy, or water. Ten-franc coins are your best bet. You may not be able to find euro coins, but French francs will still be exchanged in French banks for full value until 2004.

When returning home, we recommend that you either save your coins in one of those little black plastic film containers and keep them for your next visit or, if you have the option, leave them for the World Wildlife Fund or UNICEF at the airport or on your plane (your flight attendant will have envelopes available for these on-board donations).

Bring some U.S. cash with you, preferably in crisp $20 or $100 denominations. Fifties are often confused for other denominations. There are a number of 24-hour cash machines in Paris that convert foreign bank notes into local currency. This can be a real life-saver late at night when you need taxi money or cash to pay for a late round of cognacs.

Part Three

Hotels

Understanding Your Options

Later in this chapter, you'll find a broad selection of profiled hotels from which to choose. But before you make a reservation, you need to get a handle on where in Paris you want to stay and how much you're willing to pay. A basic understanding of the Paris hotel scene and the various types of lodging available will also be helpful. We understand that your choice of lodging is perhaps the single most important detail of your trip. Your hotel room, after all, will be your point of contact with the city, your base camp, and your home away from home.

By North American standards, many Paris hotel rooms are generally small, sometimes painfully so. You may find yourself in an elegantly decorated room in the Latin Quarter where you can barely walk around the outside of your bed. The closet might be cramped, and the shower may demand a gymnast's flexibility to maneuver inside. Also, in France, bigger does not necessarily mean better. So, what you give up in space, you might gain in decor or view or taste. The key to being satisfied is not to settle for less but to think differently. A small room can often be especially cozy and secure-feeling.

Bath towels may seem like washcloths, and you may have to crane your neck to see the little TV suspended in the corner of the room. Of course, if you're really claustrophobic or unhappy with your lodging, ask if there is another room available. The hotel manager may have put you in a room with the best view, while you may prefer a larger room with a nondescript view or with a shower in the hall. Just ask.

Often the largest rooms are not the best rooms. Sometimes they are on the top floor and there is no elevator. Sometimes they are on the ground floor and open out into a small courtyard. Sometimes they are designed for three people and have three twin beds. Decide what's most important to you.

The Hotel Scene

The good news is that Paris enjoys a wealth of wonderful hotels of immense charm and enchantment at relatively affordable rates, and you're on your way to staying in one! The wealth of choices, in fact, is overwhelming, and your key to ending up in the right place depends mostly on you and your priorities—location, style, needs, and, of course, price.

The fact that the city is so old and dense and is bound by strict building codes has protected Paris from the development of numerous large hotels inside the city, which has protected the smaller hotels. Most Paris hotels have less than 60 rooms and are independently owned or family-run, even the ones that belong to a group or network. And it is the attitude of independence that characterizes many Parisian hotels. There is no reason at all to settle for accommodations that do not charm and delight you, that do not meet your needs, and in which you don't feel like a special person.

The little independent hotels with character offer you personality and originality. What you don't get is the predictability of chains or the consistency of standards and generic tastes. For this reason, it's hard to judge hotels according to North American standards. A lovely hotel with 16 rooms in the Marais, built in the 17th century and decorated in Louis XIV–style original furniture, may not have an elevator, and most likely does not have air-conditioned rooms, ice machines, or even a bellboy. It's the perfect spot for one couple, but cramped and impractical for another.

When North American travelers are asked about their hotel, most begin by saying, "It's clean." Rest assured, most Paris hotels are clean, well kept, and safe. The plainest and cheapest ones, even the few shabby ones, are by and large clean and safe. So you can base your criteria on other things, like location, aesthetics, and price.

Location

Visualize the city as an egg laying on its side, with the Seine river flowing east-west (like a crack in the egg), starting in the southeast, heading through central Paris, and then sloping down and out of the city to the southwest. An inner ring-road called the PC or *petite ceinture* encircles the city, and a fast-moving and often congested beltway called the *Périphérique* encapsulates Paris, dividing the city from the encroaching suburbs *(les banlieues proches)*. Major highways *(autoroutes)* feed into the *Périphérique* from all directions at various ports of entry *(les portes de Paris)* or gateways into the city. The A1 and A3 lead north to Roissy/Charles de Gaulle Airport and onward to the north of France, the English Channel, and Brussels. The A4 leads east to Disneyland Paris (30 miles from Paris) and onward to the east of France and then Germany. The A6 leads south to Orly Airport, and then southward to Lyon and the south of France. The A13 runs through the Bois de Boulogne, west toward Versailles, and then out toward Normandy and Brittany.

All road signs in France list distances in kilometers, and distances to Paris are measured from the heart of the city, Notre-Dame Cathedral, also known as *kilometer zero*. France is a highly centralized country, with Paris located at the geographic and administrative center of the whole.

Most visitors who book their own trip to Paris prefer to stay in one of the more central neighborhoods known for their liveliness and individual character: the Latin Quarter, the Marais, Châtelet–Les Halles, Île St. Louis/Île de la Cité, Saint-Germain-des-Prés, Bastille/République, Opéra, Champs-Elysées/Concorde, Invalides/Eiffel Tower, or Montparnasse.

While there are scores of perfectly comfortable hotels that may offer excellent values outside these areas, the great advantage to being here is that you know in advance that you'll find charming restaurants, shops, and animated street life within a short walk.

Seasoned travelers or affirmed Paris aficionados may opt for a small hotel out in the 20th *arrondissement* and use the savings to splurge on good restaurants. We like the ones around Père Lachaise cemetery. Far from the center. But it all depends on you!

Prime Areas

The most centrally located *arrondissements* are the 1st, 2nd, 3rd, 4th, 5th, 6th, and 7th, with the 4th, 5th, and 6th probably being the choicest. But, being quaint comes with its price. Again, these generalizations are too broad to be wholly fair. Simply put, if you find a package tour offering seven nights at a hotel in, say, the 15th *arrondissement,* don't expect to be centrally located or in a small and charming hotel. Since the Eiffel Tower borders the 7th and the 15th *arrondissements,* a hotel brochure may boast of rooms with a view of the Tower. This may seduce you, but a view of the Eiffel Tower is not the only, or most important, criterion for selecting your hotel. In fact, if you'd like to be in an area with the sounds and smells of Parisian street life, don't be motivated by famous monuments. Similarly, the Champs-Elysées area is world-famous and glitzy and certainly worth a good, long stroll, but it's ultimately a rather boring and overpriced area to stay in. Again, there are exceptions to the rule. On the whole, beware of flashy offerings near easily recognizable sights. Think of atmosphere instead of tourist attractions.

Smart travelers who are not loaded down with luggage can save time and money by selecting hotels that are an easy walk from either an RER stop or an Air France Airport bus stop. Staying near RER stations while being in central Paris affords you easy access to the Eurostar to and from London and the Thalys fast trains for Brussels, as well as to and from both airports.

See the hotel profiles later in this chapter for hotels situated within walking distance of Gare du Nord, Châtelet–Les Halles, Luxembourg, Port-Royal, or Denfert-Rochereau.

Types of Lodging

Once you have at least a general idea of location, you should determine what kind of lodging best suits your needs and budget. Alternatives include large and small hotels (either part of a recognizable chain or an independent), furnished apartments, or hostels.

Small vs. Large Hotels

We love the small Parisian hotels that have charm, character, style, and ambience, and represent the essence of Paris. Some larger hotels, like the Lutétia, the Crillon, and the Raphaël, also capture Parisian authenticity along with grandeur, but at memorable prices! In any event, there's nothing worse than finding yourself in a nondescript hotel room that could be anywhere from Indianapolis to Singapore. You want to feel Paris in the style and decor of your hotel from the moment you walk into the lobby.

Hotel Chains vs. Independents

The international chains that you are familiar with—Holiday Inn, Best Western, Hilton, Sheraton, to name a few—are available in Paris and may afford you some preliminary comfort. You'll be able to reserve with an 800 number and you'll recognize their logo as your taxi approaches, but often the overseas versions of the chain differ markedly from their domestic cousins, and you may be in for a big surprise. This, incidentally, cuts both ways. Best Westerns in Paris are sometimes upscale establishments in swanky neighborhoods and sometimes simpler hotels on quiet back streets. The Holiday Inns in Paris command greater status than their North American counterparts and tend to be more expensive. Often, the hotel chain buys or franchises the name and reservation system to independent Paris hotels. Thus travelers expecting the consistency of a known brand are often amazed by the diversity found among the chain's Paris locations. An exception is the Hilton, which complies with Hilton standards worldwide but is in a location that isn't too convenient.

Even with the diversity and charm characteristic of some Paris chain hotels, we remain partial to the independents, including more of them than chain hotels in our detailed hotel profiles later in this section. If, however, you want to check out the Paris rates and availability at the chain hotels, here are the 800 numbers in North America:

Best Western	(800) 528-1234
Hilton Hotels	(800) 445-8667
Hyatt Hotels	(800) 228-9000
Ritz-Carlton	(800) 223-6800
Sheraton	(800) 325-3635
Westin Hotels	(800) 228-3000

About French Hotel Chains

There are a handful of French chains found all over France that you might not have heard of.

Accor   This French mega-chain owns five major chains—Les Jardins de Paris, Ibis, Mercure Hotels, Novotel, and the more upscale Hotel Sofitel—totaling some 3,000 hotels. In the United States, they own Motel 6. Accor's International Reservations and Information number is (888) 422-2332, and their website is www.hotelweb.fr.

Concorde Hotels   Definitely the chain of prestige, Concorde has six renowned hotels ranging from $230 to $625 a night. Call (800) 888-4747.

Relais & Châteaux   These famed hotels and restaurants, some of the most exclusive properties in the world, have an elegant website on which you can request their catalog (www.relaischateaux.fr) and a toll-free number in the United States: (800) 860-4930.

Timhôtel   This and other chains like the Libertel have brought a number of small and decent hotels under one standardized umbrella and given a face-lift to smaller hotels that merit greater attention. Timhôtel has 14 hotels, all within Paris, and all typically Parisian. All are two- and three-star hotels and have on average 50 rooms, ranging from about €85 to €120 a night for two people. These represent a good compromise between the big chains and the independents. You can reserve a room or request a catalog by calling 011 33 1 53 38 40 00.

Other major French chains include Hotel Formule 1, Etap Hotel, Balladins, Bonsaï, Liberté, and Première Classe, which you'll find primarily at exits on the large, interstate-type freeways around Paris.

Some Have Stars, Some Have None upon Thars

Dr. Seuss's star-bellied sneetches aren't the only ones obsessed with stars (Seuss even spent time in Paris, in the 1920s, mingling with the likes of Ernest Hemingway and Gertrude Stein). The stars you see posted on Paris hotels are assigned according to fixed minimum criteria set by legislation. One hotel owner explained that the "stars are a classification system but are not a reference of quality." It is interesting to note that the **official** criteria include:

1. Number of rooms

2. Size of the reception area

3. Number of entrances

4. Number of elevators

5. Heating and air-conditioning

6. Round-the-clock hot water

7. Public telephones

8. Switchboard and in-room telephones

9. Blinds or shutters on windows

10. Soundproofing

11. Size of rooms (for example, a room in a two-star hotel must be at least nine square meters—99 square feet—while in a four-star the minimum is 12 square meters—132 square feet)

12. Number of suites

13. Cooking facilities

14. Percentage of rooms with in-room sinks and bathrooms

15. Number of out-of-room bathrooms

16. In-room lamps

17. Electrical outlets

18. Hall lighting

19. Linguistic abilities of receptionists

20. In-room breakfast service

21. Disabled access

Note: One square meter equals about 11 square feet; thus, to convert square meters into square feet, multiply the number of square meters by eleven. Example: 10 square meters equals approximately 110 square feet.

Tourist hotels are approved and examined by the French government. There are five official categories determined according to the facilities, the area, and the services provided. The categories are one-star, two-star, three-star, four-star, and, for hotels of great comfort, four-star L (luxury). If you spot an NN after the stars, pay no attention; this is just an old marking for National Norm and is no longer used.

Interestingly, there is only one four-star L hotel in Paris today, Le Scribe. Under the Socialist government in the 1980s and 1990s, the sales tax (TVA) on 4-L star hotel rooms was 18.6%, while all other rooms were taxed at 5.5%. As a result, the 4-L star hotels applied to be demoted to 4-stars in order to be able to offer their rooms at more competitive prices and pay less tax to the state. Today, a sales tax of 5.5% applies to all rooms, but the super deluxe hotels have yet to request the reinstatement of the L rating.

Alain-Philippe Feutré, president of the French Hotels Syndicate, suggests that many Americans are ill-informed about hotel standards in France. "The star system does not take into account such important things as service and *accueil* (hospitality), which are very important to American guests. The stars are awarded on the basis of square meters and other technical aspects of the facilities. You can find a four-star today that's a veritable 17th-century palace, and you can end up in a four-star cell-block like the Hotel Niko, which was put up to serve the large Japanese package tours. In essence, the stars do not correspond to anything anymore. Don't base your choice on stars," he contends.

Two- and Three-Star Hotels

Paris actually has 1,800 *hôtels classés* (one, two, three, and four stars) totaling over 100,000 rooms within the city limits. Nine hundred fifty of these are two- and three-star hotels, the ones best-adapted for most travelers' needs and desires. The occupancy rate for Paris hotels ranges between 55% and 65%, although many of our favorite hotels are full *(complet)* most of the year and require reservations at least several months in advance.

One-Stars, Inexpensive Choices, and Hostels

If you'd like to spend as little on accommodations as possible in order to make your trip economically feasible, or if you want to free up money for fine dining or gifts, you'll be pleased to know that Paris has several hundred small hotels with one or no stars, offering clean and simple rooms, with and without showers and toilets in the room. In general, however, be cautious, especially with those hotels situated in the expensive areas. Although all are safe and most are clean, standards are variable, comfort is minimal, and some are not too charming.

There are still 400–600 *hôtels non classés* (without stars) and one-star hotels, although they are disappearing rapidly. The ones we profile later in this chapter are some of the best economical choices in the city.

Students and low-budget travelers have lots of choices in Paris. There are a number of fine hostels in Paris, as well as student residences. See the section, "Alternative Lodging Options," below.

Alternative Lodging Options

Furnished Apartments

For stays of a week or longer you can have your own furnished apartment in central Paris for less than you would pay at many hotels. This choice is particularly attractive when traveling with a family, a small group of friends, or two or more couples. Reserve as far in advance as possible.

A number of small companies in Paris offer quality apartments for rent by the week. This is a sure way of living like a Parisian while feeling at home. This may not be the best solution for inexperienced travelers, but it certainly is an interesting housing option.

"If you've stayed in your own apartment in Paris, you'll have a hard time going back to a hotel," claims British co-director of RothRay, Ray Lampard, whose small but top-rate collection of elegant apartments in central Paris is said to be the best in town.

The West Coast newsletter, *Paris Notes,* published an interesting feature on short-term apartment rentals, weighing the pros and cons of this lodging option. According to them, if you are staying less than a week, go to a hotel. For two weeks or a month or longer, keep reading. If your main motivation is to save money, proceed carefully, because savings depends on the number of people in your party and whether you plan on cooking at home. If you never cook, think again. On the other hand, if you're a family of four or five, two or more couples, or a small group of friends, the prospect of sharing a large 17th-century apartment with beamed ceilings and a view of Notre-Dame can be very tempting, and ultimately more comfortable and economical than taking hotel rooms. If you fear that the scale and aesthetics of old Paris buildings, kitchens, bathrooms, and the like may be too alienating or too much of a hassle—or you've decided not to have any dishes to wash in Paris—you might consider this option for another trip.

RothRay's 20 or so centrally located apartments are both well selected and impeccably maintained. Chosen for both business travelers and discriminating tourists, RothRay focuses only on the "heart of Paris," the Marais and the Châtelet–Les Halles area, from where you can walk to almost everything. With limited inventory, a highly loyal following, and a seven-day minimum, RothRay's only downside is that they fill up quickly. They require only a 25% refundable deposit, and payment can be made by personal check in your own currency. Daily rates range from $90 to $200, but if you consider that their top-priced apartment located on the rue Saint-Germain l'Auxerrois is an 18th-century 5th-floor duplex with two double bedrooms, a large living room, kitchen, full bathroom, washing machine, and terrace, you see that the economics make sense. Reserve as far in advance as possible.

RothRay
10, rue Nicolas Flamel, 75004

Tel. 01 48 87 13 37; Fax 01 42 78 17 72
e-mail: lampard@worldnet.fr

Other reliable apartment rental agencies include:

A.B.M. Rent a Flat Tel. 01 45 67 04 04; Fax 01 45 67 90 15; www.abmrentaflat.com
At Home in Paris Tel. 01 42 12 40 40; Fax 01 42 12 40 48
France Appartements Tel. 01 56 89 31 00; Fax 01 56 89 31 01; www.apartments-of-france.com
Gérald de Conclois's Apartment Living in Paris Tel. 01 45 67 27 90; Fax 01 45 66 60 90; www.apartment-living.com
Paris Appartements Services Tel. 01 40 28 01 28; Fax 01 40 28 92 01; www.pariserve.tm.fr
Servissimo Tel. 01 43 29 03 23; Fax 01 43 29 53 43; www.servissimo.com

For longer-term apartment rentals (three months minimum) of the highest quality, many professionals consult De Circourt Associates: Tel. 01 43 12 98 00; fax 01 44 94 08 30; circourt@easynet.fr.

For short- or long-term aparment rentals (a week or up to several months), here are two recommended options:

Cooper Paris Flats
Attn: Mr. Glenn Cooper
7, rue Bridaine, 75017
Tel. 06 87 74 01 08; Fax 01 43 57 06 21
glenn@paris-flats.com, www.paris-flats.com
They offer a small number of well-furnished upscale one-bedroom apartments located in the 3rd, 5th, 6th, 16th, and 17th *arrondissements*. Rates are $850–950 per week and $2,500–3,000 per month.

Rentals in Paris
Attn: Mr. Abby Cooper
160 Brookville Lane, Old Brookville, NY 11545
Tel. (516) 671-1744; Fax (516) 674-2384
abby@rentals-paris.com, www.rentals-paris.com
They offer a nice selection of upscale apartments including studios, one bedrooms, and two bedrooms, all located in the prime areas for Paris tourism and business travel (1st, 3rd, 4th, 5th, 6th, 7th, 11th, 14th, 15th, 16th, 17th, and 18th *arrondissements*). Rates are $800–1,500 per week and $2,500–4,500 per month.

U.S. Apartment Rental Services for Paris

Paris Notes named Chez Vous the "Best American-based Paris Specialists" and recognized Paris Séjour Réservation for their supply of large apartments.

Chez Vous 1001 Bridgeway, Suite 245, Sausalito, CA 94965; Tel. (415) 331-2535; fax (415) 331-5296

Paris Séjour Réservation (PSR) 645 North Michigan Avenue, Suite 638, Chicago, IL 60611;Tel. (312) 587-7707; fax (312) 587-9887
Their website (www.qconline.com/parispsr) will allow you to visualize what a Paris apartment looks like.

These two companies manage their own Paris properties:
France Homestyle:Tel. (206) 325-0132; fax (206) 328-3673
Paris Connection:Tel. (954) 475-0615

The Paris-Anglophone website (www.paris-anglo.com) offers a housing section, Housing in France, from its home page, and an online classified section, PICS, commonly used by people looking to rent or trade apartments. A Paris chat forum at www.delphi.com offers Francophiles a chance to exchange ideas and contacts on where to stay in Paris.

Hostels in Paris

Young travelers, students, and budget travelers may opt to stay in one of Paris's hostels *(auberge de jeunesse)*. This is another way of experiencing Paris, and a totally worthwhile option if you have to do Paris on the cheap. MIJE hostels are all centrally located and filled with historic atmosphere. Here is where to find them.

BVJ Louvre
20, rue Jean-Jacques Rousseau, 75001
Tel. 01 53 00 90 90
Métro: Louvre

BVJ Quartier Latin
44, rue des Bernardins, 75005
Tel. 01 43 29 34 80
Métro: Maubert-Mutualité

Comité National des Unions Chrétiennes de Jeunes Gens, (YMCA)
Résidence Sienne
5, place de Vénétie, 75013
Tel. 01 45 83 62 63
Métro: Porte de Choisy

Fédération Unie des Auberges de Jeunesse
9, rue Brantôme, 75003
Tel. 01 48 04 70 40
Métro: Chatelet–Les Halles

Ligue Française des Auberges de Jeunesse
67, rue Vergniaud, 75013

Tel. 01 44 16 78 78
Métro: Corvisart

MIJE Fauconnier
11, rue du Fauconnier, 75004
Tel. 01 42 74 23 45
Métro: St. Paul

MIJE Fourcy
6, rue Fourcy, 75004
Tel. 01 42 74 23 45
Métro: St. Paul

MIJE Maubisson
12, rue des Barres, 75004
Tel. 01 42 74 23 45
Métro: Hôtel-de-Ville

Three Ducks Hostel
6, place Etienne-Pernet, 75015
Tel. 01 48 42 04 05
Métro: Félix-Faure

Young & Happy Hostel
80, rue Mouffetard, 75005
Tel. 01 45 35 09 53
Métro: Monge

WEB ADDRESSES FOR PARIS LODGING

Hotel Sites

www.economytravel.com	www.pageszoom.com
www.france.com	www.paris-anglo.com
www.france-hotel-guide.com	www.tenonline.com
www.frenchexperience.com	www.travel-in-france.com
www.hotelnetdiscount.com/	www.travnet.com
directory/city/paris	www.ViaMichelin.com
www.hotelsparis.fr	www.virtually-there.com
www.hotelsupermarket.com/europa	

Apartment Sites

www.france-apartment.com	www.locaflat.com
www.guestapartment.fr	www.paris-anglo.com
www.homerental.fr	www.paris-appartements-services.fr
www.lamaison.fr	

Hostel Sites

www.3ducks.fr	www.woodstock.fr
www.villagehostel.fr	www.youngandhappy.fr

Specialized and Unusual Accommodations

Here are some types of lesser known accommodations that allow you to see France from a different perspective. Note: these mostly apply to areas outside of Paris.

Châteaux-Hôtels   For the adventurous, try independent châteaux, manors, and mills, in classic architectural style or full of individual character. You can see the many options at the website: www.chatotel.com, or, in Paris, call: 01 45 72 96 50. In the United States, call: (212) 856-0115; fax (800) 860-4930.

Country Residences/Gîtes   The French love *gîtes* (zheet), over 40,000 individually owned, fully equipped accommodations in rural villages and in the countryside. Classified according to standards of comfort ranging from one to four *épis* (stalks of wheat), *gîtes* can be rented for weekends, by the week, or by the month. A detailed directory guide is published every November and is available at the Maison des Gîtes at Paris, at Tel. 01 49 70 75 75, in local bookshops, or online at www.gîtes-de-france.fr.

Efficiency Apartments/Résidence de Tourisme   A tourist residence is a block of fully equipped apartments available for rent by the week or month, offering the services of a hotel and the privacy and price of an apartment. For information, contact the Syndicat National des Résidences de Tourisme at Tel. 01 53 81 01 12. The advantage of an efficiency apartment is that you have a full apartment to yourselves. At times, though, these *résidences* feel a bit like dolled-up dorms or classy retirement homes.

One firm called Parissimo rents individual apartments in wonderful, old buildings. Stay in an edifice erected by the famous architect and city planner Haussmann or in a 120-square-meter apartment with a 50-square-meter terrace with a Jacuzzi! It's large enough for the whole family or for two or three couples. The €122–135 daily range is often in the same ballpark as a three-star hotel. Contact Voyages à Paris at Tel. 01 55 35 38 00.

Other choices: Citadines—on the web at www.citadines.com; Flatotel International (Paris only)—at Tel. 01 45 75 62 20, fax 01 53 95 20 39; Home Plaza (Paris only)—at Tel. 01 40 21 22 23, fax 01 47 00 82 40; and Orion—on the web at www.apartmenthotels.com.

For rooms in French households, call 01 34 25 44 44 or visit www.tchvoyage.fr.

Camping   There is essentially no camping in Paris proper, although some travelers have admitted to pitching a tent in the Bois de Vincennes and Bois de Boulogne. We do not advise this. There are a few caravan (RV) campsites on the edges of Paris. Camping is forbidden on beaches, beside roads, on listed sites, and in reserves and natural parks, except in special areas set up for the purpose. An official guide to campsites is published by the *Fédération Française de Camping-Caravaning* (Tel. 01 42 72 84 08).

Staying in a Private Home or with Parisian Friends

If you have friends who live in Paris or have the opportunity to stay in the apartment or house of Parisians, you'll want to know something about local habits, customs, and practices. Of course, like in any city and culture, your experience will depend on the kind of people you stay with, their personalities, their economic bracket, their age, and their general openness. On the whole, be warned that Parisians tend to be more formal than you may be used to, and they certainly will take longer to "warm up" or joke around than perhaps you would if receiving French people at your home. This is not being unfriendly; it is being reserved, respectful, and tastefully timid. Don't count on Parisians to be gregarious backslappers. However, when they get comfortable with you, you'll find many locals to be natural *bon vivants*, and you just might end up friends for life. Parisians often find that Americans are too friendly too quickly, and that ultimately this kind of chummy contact is superficial.

If you're renting a room in an apartment shared with the host family, you'll want to remember a few simple rules.

■ Don't expect large bath towels.

- If you're invited for dinner, always bring something, usually a nicely wrapped bouquet of flowers (tell the florist that they're "*pour offrir*" (pour off-**reer**)—flowers for personal consumption are wrapped in plain paper, and flowers that are being given to someone as a gift are dolled up for the same price). A decent bottle of wine or champagne is standard. By decent, we mean that you should spend at least €8. Don't bring a bottle of table wine *(vin de table)* or any bottle with a plastic cork or with blue metal wrapping over the cork. Trust us. Even simple, unpretentious, and modest Parisians know a thing or two about wine. Small gifts from home are highly appreciated, and if you happen to think of it in advance, a bottle of California wine will be greeted with pleasant curiosity.

- After dinner, you may offer to help with the dishes, but there is a good chance that you will not be encouraged to enter the kitchen or be invited to help out, so although you'll want to be polite, don't be overly insistent.

- Be prepared to spend a lot more time sitting around the table at the end of the meal, drinking coffee, eating clementines, sipping cognac or calvados, smoking, and talking than you'd ever think of doing back home. This is one of the great pleasures of being in Paris—eating, drinking, and talking.

- In French, the bathroom sink and the kitchen sink, the *lavabo* and *évier*, respectively, should not be confused.

- Don't take really long showers; be conscious of water consumption and hot water quantities, especially in the colder months, and try not to create puddles on the floor even though shower curtains are either absent or skimpy. Laundry is not done as often or as easily as back home. Lots of people do not have automatic dryers and still hang laundry in the bathroom.

Hotels for Business Travelers

Business travelers want to be near airports, train stations, business centers, commercial districts, convention halls, or conference centers. Business travelers want comfort and convenience, business amenities like computer connections, fax and e-mail facilities, and meeting rooms. Paris, which is well equipped for the business traveler, has the wonderful ability to meet both your professional and personal needs without compromising either.

Hotel prices sometimes double during major trade shows or salons like the Prêt-à-Porter fashion week and the aeronautics show at Le Bourget Airport, which attracts big rollers from the world's rich industries. You may be surprised to see that not only is it harder getting a room, but that room rates jump on these selected days. If you haven't been alerted to rate changes, do not agree to pay the higher rate. Check your bill. Using the housing services offered by a convention center or trade show may also result in higher-than-necessary room rates. Inflated prices are often tacked onto standard rack rates during conferences or shows. Unsuspecting travelers, often on expense accounts, bear the brunt.

Paris's Major Conference Centers

For a list of Paris trade shows, contact the Franco-American Chambre of Commerce (see list in Part Two, Planning Your Visit to Paris) at www.birp.com or www.comite-expo-paris.asso.fr/englishcep/index.html.

For business services provided by the Chambre, visit "Doing Business in France" at www.paris-anglo.com or www.ccip.fr. Almost all major trade shows in Paris are organized by Reed OIP, Tel. 01 41 90 47 47, fax 01 41 90 47 00. Their website is found at www.salon.reed-oip.fr.

CNIT   2, Place La Defense; Tel. 01 46 92 15 15 (rental of offices and show rooms); Tel. 01 46 92 24 24 (short-term rental of business services and commercial space); Métro: Grande-Arche-de-la-Défense. Organization of exhibitions, expositions, trade shows, fairs, seminars, and congresses, and rental of business equipment and services. Visit www.cnit.com for more information.

Parc d'Exposition de Paris   Nord Villepinte BP 60004 95970 Roissy CDG Cedex; Tel. 01 48 63 30 30; fax 01 48 63 33 70. Major site for large international commercial fairs and business events. For more information, consult their website at www.expoparisnord.com.

Hotels at the Airports

Not only professionals prefer to stay at or near the airport. Conservative tourists unfamiliar with Paris may feel more secure staying within eyesight of the runway and their returning flight. Unless you're only in Paris for an overnight stay or a quick transfer, we advise travelers to venture into the city rather than staying at or near either airport. The city is not prohibitively far, and access is relatively easy and affordable. The areas around both airports are not pretty, and the hotels are not particularly impressive or economical.

If you still want to sleep at the airport and commute into town, here is a list of airport hotels. Pay special attention to our comments on obtaining the best possible rates. If you arrive at either Roissy–Charles de Gaulle or Orly without hotel reservations, proceed to the ADP Information Stand. Their reservation service for same-day hotel reservations will obtain significant discounts for you. We discovered that by picking up the direct airport hotel phone we were quoted a rate that was only about €8 more than when we had the information stand book the room for us, and 50% lower than if we had just walked into the Sofitel Roissy Hotel ourselves ten minutes later without a reservation. So give yourself a few minutes to figure out how to get the same thing for the least amount of money.

Roissy–Charles de Gaulle Airport Hotels

★★★★	Hilton	01 49 19 77 77
★★★★	Sheraton	01 49 19 70 70
★★★★	Sofitel	01 49 19 29 29
★★★	Novotel	01 49 19 27 27
★★	Ibis	01 49 19 19 19

Orly Airport Hotels

★★★★	Holiday Inn	01 49 78 42 00
★★	Ibis Orly	01 56 70 50 60
★★	Citotel La Rotonde	01 69 38 97 78
	Climat de France	01 60 48 77 00
	Hôtel de L'Escale	01 69 38 60 56
	Novotel Orly	01 45 12 44 12

Rates, Rules, and Recommendations

As a rough approximation, you can spend as little as €45 for a double room with a shower in a modest hotel, not necessarily centrally located but certainly 10–20 minutes from the center of Paris. In the center of town, a very comfortable, newly renovated hotel room with a good dose of charm and style will cost you between €70 and €165. There is a lot of diversity in this range. Larger, more elegant hotels offer double rooms from about €165, whereas spacious, top-of-the-luxury-line hotel rooms or suites can easily run €410 to €835 a night. Ouch!

The hotel industry in Paris, as everywhere, is driven by a commercial need to fill available rooms. Only since the early 1990s have hotel owners been free to set prices at will. With the invention of what insiders call "yield management," many hotels are constantly manipulating prices to do just that. Even the smaller, family-run establishments are obliged to play this game in order to survive—especially during the low season. Consequently, room rates are known to fluctuate like stock market prices. So beware; you may be quoted different prices for the same room at the same or different times of the year. If you've entrusted your travel agent or have reserved via one of the knowledgeable and quality-oriented tour operators serving Paris, you can sleep comfortably.

The published "rack rates," the ones hung on the board behind the front desk, are the highest possible rates you can be charged. French law stipulates that hotels cannot announce a price and then charge a higher one, so to protect themselves hotels announce the maximum, but are prepared in most cases to sell rooms for less. If you book way ahead, you'll avoid headaches and stress, but you'll get booked at the highest published price.

Late reservations yield the possibility of a better rate but present the stress of finding your first choice fully booked *(complet* [comb-**play**]*)*. Last-minute reservations are not only subject to availability, but require a bit of finesse to negotiate. The unsuspecting traveler with a naive look (or telephone voice) will be quoted one price, while the savvy traveler poses a succession of key questions and ends up saving $30 to $50 per night on a room in a three- or four-star hotel. You can walk into a hotel and be quoted $100 a night or call ten minutes before arriving and obtain the same room for $60 or $70, if there is availability. It's that wild. According to the hotel booking service at Roissy–Charles de Gaulle Airport, for example, the Sheraton Hotel quotes different rates every hour!

We don't think you should spend endless hours jockeying to save a few bucks, but we do want you to be able to obtain the best quality room that meets all your needs for the best possible price. A $40 savings a night amounts to $280 per week; that's enough to buy you a very memorable meal, an extra night in a château, or a great pair of French shoes.

In addition to displaying the highest rates, there are a number of other "rules" that French hotels must abide by, and a few that you must follow also:

- Prices displayed outside the hotel and in bedrooms must be inclusive of all charges and taxes. A surcharge can be levied for an extra bed or for breakfast.

- Rooms must usually be left by noon on the day of departure, but this can be flexible.

- Rates are usually quoted for a double room (two people).

- Rates include service and value added tax (VAT), but not always the *taxe de séjour* (hotel tax), which is only a euro or two per night per person.

- Guests are expected to arrive at their hotel no later than 8 p.m. But after 7 p.m. the hotel is not obliged to hold the room. So call ahead if you are going to be later than you indicated. To avoid misunderstandings from the start, it is best to let the hotel keeper know your approximate arrival time, especially if you expect to arrive after 7 p.m. If you have only a telephone reservation without a deposit, the hotel is not required to hold the room after 7 p.m.

- If guests arrive before 7 p.m. on the day of confirmed reservation and find that no rooms are available, a hotel is obligated to find them a room at a comparable price.

- Paris hotels are increasing their use of e-mail and the Internet. Many are letting online companies handle reservations, referrals, and payment. It's advisable that you bring paper copies of your e-mail confirmations with you, just in case.

Alain-Philippe Feutré, president of the French Hotels Syndicate, vice president of the Paris Office of Tourism, and the only special adviser on hotel accommodations to the Ministry of Culture, is devoted to increasing the quality of service afforded to tourists and helping inform visitors about the hotel conditions in Paris. Monsieur Feutré offers the following insights and advice.

Americans and Britains make up the largest part of the Paris hotel clientele and thus are very important to hotel owners who are in general eager to please. Don't select a hotel just because you like the sound of the name, or a descriptor affixed to the name. "Everyone [for example] is using the term *hôtel de charme* these days. Insist on seeing photos or reading a detailed description of the hotel you're considering. Ask how many rooms the hotel has. If there are 150 rooms, it is not a *hôtel de charme!*" Locations can be misleading as well. A hotel called Notre-Dame or Tour Eiffel may not be near Notre-Dame or the Eiffel Tower at all.

In terms of size, you should be clear that almost any hotel with character and charm in central Paris will have small rooms. "This is a matter of history and architecture," Monsieur Feutré explains. "It's better that people know this in advance. I prefer that guests who need a large room go to the Hilton and maintain their positive attitude about Paris than end up in a small room and be unhappy."

When asked about the amount of English that is spoken in Paris hotels, he replied, "*Ça vient!*" (We're getting there!). "In the luxury hotels there's no problem with language. And in almost all the smaller ones, at least the receptionist speaks some English. We recognize the need. But one point that disappoints us is that very few Americans make an effort to communicate in French. Isn't one of the reasons people travel is to try to understand something about the place they are visiting? It's appreciated when you arrive with at least a few words of our language."

Regarding special services, no-smoking rooms, disabled access, and the like, Monsieur Feutré advises that you clearly request your needs in advance. Small hotels usually do not have designated rooms for nonsmokers, but they don't always admit this. The Paris Tourism Office's website (www.paris-touristoffice.com) lists 678 hotels adapted for the disabled. Monsieur Feutré warns, though, that there are lots of different sets of needs that have not yet been addressed. "There are no hotels in Paris that are adequate for the blind," he admits.

Commenting on recent trends, Monsieur Feutré says that "travelers are more prone to negotiate the rate. They tend to reserve at the last minute. Clients treat hotels today like the airlines. We experience no-shows without cancellations. We need both clients and hotels to act responsibly in order to preserve quality service."

With regard to reservations and deposits, there are plenty of interesting ambiguities that need to be spelled out. Legally, in France, holding a reservation with a credit card number is not a true guarantee for either the hotel or the client. The only way to make sure that a reservation is guaranteed is for the client to instruct the hotel in writing to debit the card (usually the price of one night). With the authorization to debit the card, and the transaction going through, the hotel is obliged by law to respect its commitment. If the hotel doesn't debit the card, it can't know if the card is valid and is not bound to respect the reservation. The same is true if a hotel holds your check until arrival. If your check is not cashed, the deposit is considered *les ahrres* (a refundable deposit), which is not binding. You should stipulate when you reserve by fax or e-mail that you are sending an *accompte* (deposit), which will not be refunded unless you cancel by a certain date. "I advise guests to put in writing the cancellation date. Otherwise, a reservation held by an uncashed check or undebited credit card could be cancelled at the last minute by the hotel. Imagine if a hotel has 20 free rooms and a tour operator comes around and offers to buy 25. The hotel will sacrifice yours to sell all the empty rooms in a group. When you arrive, he may say, 'I'm sorry, but there has been a flood.'"

Making Reservations from Home

Having considered the type of accommodation, location, and price, you're ready to choose a specific lodging property and reserve. Review our profiles later in this chapter for detailed suggestions.

The most efficient means of reserving is by sending a fax. Simply state your dates of arrival and departure, the number of guests, and any special needs or requests; for example, one large bed, two single beds, with bath or shower, if you prefer lower floors or upper floors, and so on. The smaller French hotels do not distinguish between queen- and king-size beds. If you want a big bed for yourself or are sharing a bed, just use the term *un grand lit* (ah gran **lee**). Don't offer your credit card number until after you obtain the information you've requested.

Note that the French write dates differently than you may be used to: day/month/year. So, 3/5/2002 is May 3, 2002, not March 5, 2002!

If you are reserving a hotel room on your own by telephone or fax, make sure to ask for the best room rate available and be sure that the rate you've been quoted includes all taxes and services (as required by French law). Ask if the breakfast *(petit déjeuner)* is also included or not. If not, ask if the breakfast can be included for the same price. Chances are, if the hotel is not full, you'll win on this point. Specify if you want a full bathroom *(salle de bain)* with shower *(douche)* or bath *(bains)*. There's a little trick here, since rooms with showers tend to be between €8 and €20 cheaper than those with bathtubs, so if you prefer a shower in any case, you'll save a bit. Watch out, though. Showers, mostly with hand-held nozzles, are quaint but may not be up to your standards. The point here is to inquire on all your room options. In the smaller hotels, sometimes a room that is quieter, but less-scenic, is cheaper, which may suit you fine. You will most likely be quoted prices in euros, so note the prevailing exchange rate. If you're planning to pay by credit card, ask for a euro rate, because your card will be charged in euros but debited in dollars.

If the hotel has a lot of empty rooms, you may obtain a better rate by simply asking for one. (One Paris concierge tells us that he regularly offers a deep discount of up to 50% off the posted rate when he has empty rooms.) Before being quoted a price, you will often be asked how many nights you'll be staying. The longer you stay, the greater the chance for a discount off the rack rate. If you're not sure, intimate that you *may* want to stay for a longer number of nights. To persuade you or entice you, you may be quoted a reduced rate. On the other hand, in high season you'll probably get a "take it or leave it" response.

You have other options, though. Your local travel agent may be able to obtain a better rate for you. You may manage to have the breakfast included in the rate when normally it is not. Ask. You may be able to have parking thrown in if you're driving. You may be able to obtain an extra bed without charge, or not be charged for your children. You must ask, and ask again. Parisians tend to be gun-shy when it comes to asking for discounts or advantages. It's not in their culture, but it is in yours, and hotel reservation people and sales agents know this. So ask, always ending with *s'il vous plaît* and *merci beaucoup*, and *c'est gentil* when you've obtained something. "C'est gentil" means "that's nice," and it conveys that you are appreciative of the effort that has been made to please you. Form is important!

Never get angry or huffy when dealing with Parisians in the service sector. You will not help your cause. Don't try to go over someone's head or ask for a supervisor. This, likewise, will not bring you greater satisfaction and can easily make matters worse. No one fears for his job in France, and supervisors almost always defend their own hierarchy. Furthermore, you may be speaking to the owner or manager already. Take on a rather apologetic tone and start again. Parisians need to be stroked and seduced, or else they don't seem to care or respond. Small, charming hotels usually provide charming personnel but are also proud of their independence. You may not be used to having to adopt an apologetic tone when you are the paying customers, but it's like that in Paris. In France, like elsewhere, the customer's money is king, but the customer himself, well, he's only a high-ranking serf holding a wallet. Also note that the French are not as telephone-oriented as North Americans; you may find the telephone service or manners of people on the phone to be inadequate. Often this is just a cultural difference and not rudeness.

So let's recap the reservations process. If your travel agent handles this for you, he or she should be no less thorough.

1. Reservations should be in writing (letter, fax, or e-mail). Usually, hotels will ask that you either send a deposit to hold the reservation or give a credit card number. Most of the time, personal checks will not be cashed nor card numbers debited until your arrival. A hotel may ask for a 25% deposit, but usually all you need to send or agree to is the cost of the first night as the deposit. With some hotels you may send a U.S. dollar check with instructions that the hotel hold this for your arrival. As per Monsieur Feutré's advice, make sure you have a clear written understanding about when the hotel should debit your credit card or cash your deposit check.

2. Make sure your reservation, room rate, receipt of deposit, and conditions for cancellations are confirmed in writing by the hotel management. Bring the confirmation with you.

3. If you do not show up or do not cancel in advance, the deposit will not be refunded. Legally, you could be held responsible for the cost of your entire stay, but this never happens. Out of consideration, call to cancel once you know for sure you're not coming. If the hotel cancels your reservation or does not hold your room (after debiting your credit card or cashing your deposit check), the law states that the hotel must pay you double the amount of the deposit.

Arriving without Reservations

Sure, you can do it. Plenty of travelers do. But be aware that there are five distinct disadvantages and one great advantage.

Disadvantages

1. You may arrive on a day in which the city is packed due to a trade show or sports event.

2. You'll lose time tracking down a hotel, making phone calls, figuring out how to find the hotel, and so on.

3. You'll have less bargaining power in terms of choice and price by reserving on the day you arrive.

4. You may arrive early in the morning or late at night and have difficulty connecting with a hotel of your choice.

5. You may be too tired to deal with the hassle and end up checking into a hotel at the airport, overpaying, and missing the charm of your first night in Paris. If you change hotels you'll have to settle in twice. Not fun.

Advantage

A little-known tip for the more flexible, spontaneous traveler: You can pick up excellent deals on hotel rooms by booking at the well-marked Information Stands operated by Aéroport de Paris (ADP) at both airports and in all terminals. There is no sign indicating that hotel reservations are made here, and the ADP makes no attempt to publicize this or the amazing fact that between 100 and 200 excellent hotels fax the airport each morning offering their available rooms at savings that can run up to 50%! Reservations must be made for one or more nights beginning on the day you reserve (arrive). The Information Stand staff will make the call for you, give you a confirmation voucher, and instruct you on how to get to your hotel. You pay 12% of the first night's rate as a deposit on the spot (cash or credit card), which the ADP keeps as its commission. The 12% is deducted from your hotel bill.

It's better to have an idea of where you'd like to stay and the type of hotel before you ask, but the staff here is very friendly and helpful and speaks good English, if you need advice. We called the Sofitel airport hotel for a room for two and were quoted €15 more than if the Information Stand, ten feet away, made the reservation for us! Try both, and take the best offer. Although the Information Stand is co-branded with the Office de Tourisme de Paris and ADP, the relationship between the two is ambiguous, and the ADP, curiously, offers a much more dynamic and advantageous hotel service than the Paris Tourism Office.

The main Paris Tourism Office in the city is located at 127, avenue des Champs-Elysées in the 8th *arrondissement* at Métro Charles-de-Gaulle-Etoile. A word of warning: Although they distribute lots of pamphlets and brochures, we've been told that their staff has been instructed not to spend more than two minutes per tourist inquiry. They also do not make reservations for you, but they can lead you in the right direction. Their website (www.paris-touristoffice.com) lists all Paris hotels that have one, two, three, or four stars.

The Parisian Hotel Room

First of all, in France the ground floor of a building is called the *Rez-de-Chaussée* (RC) (**ray**ch-show**say**) and not the first floor. What you think of as the second floor is in France the first floor, the *premier étage* (preh-mee**ay**-ay**tadj**). So if your hotel room is on the fourth floor, be prepared to go to the fifth floor, not a problem when there is an elevator, but a bit tough on the thighs and calves when there is not. Most hotels are equipped with elevators, but the smaller and more modest ones may still rely on the good old stairs, something to consider if you have a back problem or suffer from asthma.

Don't be disturbed if you are asked for your passport when you check in. This is a common, legal formality. You'll get your passport returned either right away or a little while later. There is no stigma whatsoever about unmarried couples checking into hotels together. In fact, Parisians are not at all judgmental when it comes to questions of the heart or body. Public affection is widespread and is discreetly applauded.

Elevators/Ascenseurs (ah-sohn-sir)

In small hotels to reach the upper floors you'll either have to walk or squeeze into an elevator that may be reminiscent of the marvels of Houdini. These devices were adapted to the small spaces available in the stairwells of old buildings. Luggage goes up by itself or piece by piece. Claustrophobes might opt for the stairs.

Both in hotels and apartments, don't be alarmed when the lights go off on the stairway as you're in the corridor or climbing up arching steps. All Paris buildings are on electric timers. Most Europeans have been energy-conscious since electric power was invented.

Beds

French bedding on the whole is very comfortable, although there are a few details that will seem unusual, like the shape of the pillows—square instead of rectangular. Made beds often have long sausage-like pillows maintaining a neat round form. These are great when sitting up and reading, but when it's time to catch some Zs, substitute the soft and square pillow (often feather-stuffed) you'll find in the closet to avoid getting a stiff neck.

Many European hotel beds are equipped with a duvet (a sort of down comforter) instead of the more traditional sheets and blankets. If you find a duvet too hot to sleep under, you have three alternatives. First, you can ask the hotel to provide sheets and blankets (sometimes available, sometimes not); second, you can take the duvet out of its lightweight case and use the case for a sheet; or three, you can bring a sheet or two from home.

Other than in the expensive luxury hotels, double beds will not be as large as king size. Double rooms come with either a double bed or two twin beds, so state your preference when you reserve. Single rooms often come with single beds, unlike in American hotels, where you pay for a single but get a big bed anyway.

Bathrooms/Salle de Bains (sahl-duh-bahn)

Hotel bathrooms in Paris are full of surprises. You may be enthralled or you may burst into fits of laughter. One travel editor stayed in a modest but tasteful older hotel in the 9th *arrondissement* and found his bathroom "large enough to play racquetball in." At the other extreme, a woman from Boston got stuck in the narrow tub of her hotel bathroom in the Latin Quarter.

Most newly renovated hotels have redone the plumbing and opted for international standards including big mirrors, recessed lighting, built-in hair dryers (or at least the right electrical plugs), and Formica or stone countertops. In many hotels these concessions to style are meant to compensate for lack of space. Hotel rooms with bathtubs are slightly more expensive than those with showers.

Showers vs. Bathtubs

One of the most culturally conflicted details in the Anglo-Franco worlds revolves around *la douche*, the shower.

It's rather amusing how humorless and inflexible North Americans can be when it comes to their morning shower. You may relish every variation of goose liver, but when it comes to that wet, morning ritual there's little room for experimentation. You want to turn on the hot water and stand blissfully and unthinkingly beneath a pulsating shower head until life comes back into your body. The French see the shower as a hygienic, practical event attached to contemporary life; North Americans approach their ritual as a daily renaissance.

In essence, the Parisian bathroom, *salle de bain*, is what it says, a "bath" room, and the shower part is a historical add-on, a bastardization of the source. Anyone who has showered in France knows just how much dexterity one needs—and the naked gymnastics required—to hang onto the nozzle *(pommeau de douche)* with one hand and lather up with the other, while keeping the water inside the confines of the often short and squatty bathtub *(baignoire)*. The shower head, as an object, virtually does not exist in French households, and the stall shower *(cabine de douche)* is not commonly found. Considering that many buildings were first constructed in the 16th and 17th centuries, bathroom plumbing itself is an afterthought.

So approach your Parisian hotel visit with some forewarning. Your *salle de bain* will include a sink, a *bidet* (but that's another story), and a bathtub—which in most cases, but not all, will be equipped with the hand-held shower nozzle and a moderately effective shower curtain. The shower curtain rod often poses a major architectural problem with the high ceiling and round-shouldered tubs. Some Parisians will tell you that you should first wet yourself down, then turn off the water and replace the nozzle, then lather yourself up, and finally turn the water back on, grab the nozzle, and rinse yourself with the shower spray. Clearly, they missed the point—but you do save water. Plus, in the winter you freeze.

Additionally, although most Parisian hotels have resolved problems of water pressure, you may not find the water supply abundant enough for your taste. Remember, you can always take a leisurely bath, if there's enough length of tub to stretch out. The larger, newer, and more costly hotels provide perfectly adequate bathtubs . . . usually. The older ones have tried to keep up. To reassure you, though, most four-star hotels have also installed stall showers. Ask for a room with a *douche séparée*. You should note that even these will have the removable, hand-held nozzles that hang on a hook. And, more importantly, rooms with stall showers often do not have bathtubs and are the smaller, less desirable, and cheaper rooms. So beware, you may be sacrificing your lovely view of the Seine or your splendid terrace for the sake of a few vertical drops of H_2O. Wasn't it Marie-Antoinette who said "let them take showers; kings and queens take baths"?

The tub itself is prone to many interesting variations, since many were installed to fit into a nonstandardized, prearranged space. In older and more modest hotels, you may still find the sitting tub *(sabot,* meaning clog*)* to be a short porcelain tub with a large inner step on which you are obliged to sit. Although excellent for washing your feet, you neither get a real shower nor a real bath. But they're fun!

If fun is not your thing and you are a stickler for your shower-like-home, ask your hotel when reserving if they have rooms with a *cabine de douche* (stall shower) or if the *bain* comes only with a *pommeau de douche.*

One travel writer recently pointed out that Americans should be forewarned about the high calcium levels in Parisian water and the dehydrating results to visitors' skin. Come equipped with skin creams to replenish the epidermal injuries caused by Parisian showers, she suggests.

Last, before hosing yourself down in your Parisian *douche*, don't get confused: the **F** is for *froid* (cold) and the **C** is for *chaud* (hot).

The Bidet (bid-ay)

You may be perplexed on your first trip to a French bathroom to find a curious porcelain structure (with funky plumbing) situated between the sink and the shower. Welcome to the *bidet*, one of the great icons of French culture.

Historically designed to serve aristocratic women as a hygienic aid, especially after sex, today the bidet can be used for lots of things, from relieving the pain of hemorrhoids, hand-washing delicate clothing, or soaking your feet. Fresh water enters the fixture through a vertical spray in the center of the bowl, through a flushing rim or integral filler or through a pivotal spout that delivers a horizontal stream of water. A pop-up drain allows you to fill it with water. It's surprising, but you'll still find these in even newly renovated hotel bathrooms.

The Toilet

Les toilettes (lay twalet) in France are also called the WC (**doub**la vay **say**, or just say vay **say)** meaning "water closet," and that's what it is, a closet-sized space with a toilet. The WC (also called *le water*, pronounced as if the word were French, wah-**tair**) is very often a separate room. Although this may seem odd at first, it's rather practical, and some hotel rooms are still organized this way. Newer ones usually aren't, though. It's always a great travel joy discovering the culturally diverse methods of flushing. For a tour of the all-inviting "Turkish toilet" see "Cafés and Café Tabac" in Part Seven, Dining in Paris. The good news is that Parisian toilet paper has joined the 21st century and is no longer known for its abrasive quality.

Closets

A closet is known in France as a *penderie* (pon-**dree**), *armoire* (arm-**wahr**), or *placard* (plah-**cahr**). If closet space and drawer space are important to you, state this when you reserve. The built-in closet was not yet conceived in the 17th century. In older and smaller hotels, it hasn't always been possible to create built-in closets or have enough room for a vestibule. Rooms in smaller hotels may not have closets at all. Rooms without closets generally offer some sort of wardrobe for hanging clothes.

Hotel Clocks and Time

For most of the world, a hotel room is a hotel room, but there are nonetheless interesting nuances in each country worth noting. If you're used to a clock on the night table, you may not find one in Paris. So bring a travel clock. Almost all the larger hotels are automatically equipped with wake-up call technology, but the smaller ones still use the manual phone call or a knock on the door. To avoid confusion and to avoid missing a train, don't forget that time is counted on the 24-hour clock in France, so 1 p.m. is 13h and 9 p.m. is 21h.

Automated Wake-Up Calls

If you have a direct-dial telephone in your room, you may be able to automatically program an electronically monitored wake-up call from France Telecom by calling Automated Call Alarm (*Mémo appel*), a service provided by France Telecom for under a dollar. Simply dial 55 and then the hour (using the French, 24-hour clock) you wish to be awakened, followed by the # sign on your telephone. (For example: dial 55 and then 0715 plus # to be called at 7:15 a.m.) To cancel or change the wake-up call, repeat these steps and punch in the corrected time. This works from any private telephone in France. Ask at your hotel.

Radios

If you're used to waking up with the radio or love to roam the air waves late at night, you may have to bring your own radio, since your Parisian hotel room may not be equipped with one. If it is, though, here are the locations of a few key stations you might find interesting or useful:

RADIO STATIONS

Radio Station	Frequency	Category
France Inter	87.8 MHz	News, Talk
Nostalgie	90.4	Oldies, Top 40, Club
Chérie FM	91.3	Rock, Top 40
France Culture	93.5–93.9	Talk, Classical, News
BFM	96.4	News, sometimes in English
Radio Latina	99	Latin American, Salsa
Radio Nova	101.5	Top 40, Rap, Club
Fun Radio	101.9	Shock ShockDJ, Top 40
Oui FM	102.3	Top 40, Club
RMC	103.1	Folk, French, Easy
FIP	105.1	Eclectic, great to wake up to
France Info	105.5	News, Talk

No Bible in the Drawer

Church and state officially separated in France in 1905. Despite the fact that France is predominantly Roman Catholic, there are no prayers in the local schools and few references to God in public life. Your hotel room will not be equipped with a Gideons Bible in the night table top drawer (though sometimes you'll find a four-language New Testament or the like). For a short list of local religious congregations and the times of masses and services in English, see "Religion and Houses of Worship" in Part Four.

A Word on Noise (Yours and Others)

Paris is lively, and with the liveliness comes noise. Especially on weekends, Parisians go out in hordes and stay out late. Even at 1 a.m. the streets around the Bastille or in the Latin Quarter will be swamped with Parisians out on the town, eating, drinking, coming from the cinemas, and congregating in the cafés. On Friday nights between 11 p.m. and midnight an astonishing roar may be heard along the Grands Boulevards starting at the Place de la Bastille and heading west. Thousands of motorcyclists on everything from Harleys to mopeds drive en masse around the city, a tradition that dates back several decades. This may be amusing, but it may also be annoying if your hotel room looks out over the street. Some older hotels still do not have noise-proof windows, but this is slowly changing. If you're sensitive to high decibels, ask for a room that looks out onto a courtyard or garden (i.e., a room in the back). The view may not be inspiring, but you'll preserve your ability to sleep. To check if a hotel room has been sound-proofed or has double-glazed windows, ask if the room is *insonorisée* or if the windows are *double-vitrage* (**doob**la vee**traj**).

French law stipulates that no one can make loud noises in the street or in their homes after 10 p.m., and on the whole Parisians within apartment houses are cautious about not disturbing their neighbors, so if you're the rowdy one, observe the law and be sensitive to your neighbors.

Heating and Air-Conditioning

Although more and more hotels are adding air-conditioning *(climatisation* [clee-mah-tee-zah-**seeyown**]*)* when they renovate, do not automatically count on air-conditioned rooms. In fact, you should generally assume that there is no air-conditioning. The summer heat may be hard to take in small hotel rooms, but even in the hot days of August an open window often does the trick. The only inconvenience is when your room faces onto a noisy street. So if you're sensitive either to the heat or noise, pick either an air-conditioned room or a quiet one. In any case, there are only 20 or 30 days in the entire year when air-conditioning would be needed in Paris. Many smaller hotels, even the top-quality ones, can't justify the expense of installing such systems, especially in 17th- and 18th-century buildings.

Heat is rarely a problem in Parisian hotel rooms, although some travelers complain about rooms being too warm. Heating in French is *chauffage* (show-**fahj**). Radiator is pronounced rah-dee-a-**tur**.

Mini-Bar

Three-star hotels and above almost always provide a mini-bar in the room. This is convenient not only for finding a Perrier to quench your thirst but also for storing your own drinks and snacks. The prices of items are item-ized and will be 30–40% higher than in a grocery store, but about the same price as in a café. In the summer, it's a good idea to chill a bottle of water the night before to take with you on your excursion the next day.

Making Calls from Your Hotel Room

Finding the best way to call home from a foreign hotel room has always been a tricky deal, and one open to lots of theories and interpretations. Ask the receptionist at your hotel how much you'll be charged to call the United States and you'll see what we mean. No one really knows for sure. Most hotel computers do the calculating automatically, and the personnel don't have a clue. At the Hotel Westminster we were told to make our call first and we'd see the cost on our bill. At one hotel you'll be told €0.50 per impulsion, but no one can tell you how long an impulsion. Another will tell you €2.50 a minute . . . they think. To clear this up, see "Calling Home from Your Hotel" in Part Four, Arriving, Getting Oriented, and Departing. The best advice is to avoid calling from your room, and to use your local or international calling card. You'll only have to pay for the local calls.

Watching French Television

Although we suggest that you spend little time in your hotel room and maximum time out and about in Paris, you will savor those cozy moments when resting in the afternoon or lounging late at night on your bed in your hotel room. Aside from reading or writing postcards, you may find it amusing or enlightening to zap on the television and soak up some of the local programming. You'll note right away several major differences. There are far fewer stations in France than in North America—in fact, only five free stations: TF1, France 2, France 3, La Cinq (5), and M6; plus one subscription cable station, Canal + (channel 4), which serves up a strong offering of films and international live sporting events like the U.S. Super Bowl and NBA basketball. If you're up at 7 a.m., you can pick up the previous night's ABC Nightly News in English with Peter Jennings on Canal +.

The larger hotels receive other stations via satellite, so if you're in the Crillon or Intercontinental or Plaza Athénée you're certain to be able to tune into CNN, CNBC, TNT Classics, and Sky Channel. Otherwise, it'll be the French stations, which to our thinking are more interesting for Parisian visitors anyway.

You'll also note that there are fewer commercials polluting the airwaves than on U.S. television. And in France the commercials are placed between the programs, instead of interrupting them. You'll enjoy the ads though; here, the aesthetics and style are as important as the sales message. You'll also see unabashed nudity in everything from a shampoo ad to a movie made for television. The French don't share American sensibilities on this subject and are quick to ridicule Anglo-Saxon Puritanism.

The other difference is the amount of cultural programming in prime-time slots. The French have a fathomless respect for culture. They support and encourage it in many ways, not the least of which is through the increasingly ubiquitous influence of television. In France you can expect to see theater, opera, or ballet on one of five publicly broadcast television stations, even during prime-time scheduling. Arté (Ahr-**tay**) is a Franco-Germanic state-funded station broadcast on channel 5 after 7 p.m. until, depending on the programming, 2 or 3 a.m. It often shows English language movies, documentaries, and performances that are subtitled rather than dubbed in French. Most foreign language French television, however, from American sitcoms like *Friends* to the English comedy of Rowan

Atkinson, is dubbed, and unless you speak French or read lips, you'll find your familiar programs from home have become incomprehensible. For those who speak a little French or are eager to learn, we suggest the following full-immersion French TV programs:

Nulle part ailleurs (Canal+, 7:15 p.m. to 9:15 p.m. Monday through Friday). Irreverent presentation of the latest in Parisian entertainment, news, and weather, with guests, comic sketches, music, and *les guignols* (satirical puppets).

Culture pub (M6, 5 p.m. Sunday) explores the world of advertising (mostly commercials from around the world) through a humorous, intelligent, and socio-critical perspective.

Métropolis (*Arte*, 9:40 p.m. Saturday and rebroadcast at various times during the week) is a European guide to "what's on" in culture, art, and entertainment (with a bias toward France and Germany).

Keys and Outer Doors

Smaller hotels may not stay open all night long. You'll be told to take the key (*clé* [clay]) with you if you plan on returning after midnight. Some hotels have a key for the outer door to the street. Others will provide you with a door code to get in.

La Cour vs. La Rue

Rooms usually face the street or a courtyard or small garden called *la cour*. Street-side rooms are usually noisier but may be more scenic. To ask if the room looks out onto the street or courtyard, ask: *Est ce que la chambre donne sur la rue ou la cour?* (Es-kuh lah **shahm** dun **soo**wer la **roo** oow lah **coor**?)

The Lobby

In the lobby of many Parisian hotels you'll find racks of pamphlets aimed at tourists. Although some of this information may interest you, we find most of it distracting. Be careful with appeals from restaurants and nightclubs that are mass-marketing the tourist industry. Your time and dollars in Paris are precious and you don't want to waste either.

Most reception areas will have a public telephone and a Paris telephone book, called the *annuaire* (an-nyew-**air**) or *botin* (bow-**tahn**). The Yellow Pages are called the *Pages Jaunes* (pahj-**joan**). Travel agents are listed under *Agents de voyages*. Airlines are *compagnies aériennes*.

To Breakfast or Not to Breakfast

Whereas dinners are almost always long, Parisian breakfasts tend to be concise, rarely consisting of more than a coffee with milk *(café au lait)*, tea, hot chocolate, bread *(baguette* [bah-**get**]*)*, butter *(beurre* [buhr]*)*, and jam *(confiture* [con-fee-**tur**]*).* You may be offered orange juice or cereal, but these are American add-ons that have only made it onto the Parisian break-fast table in the last decade or so. To this, you may add yogurt, a *croissant* (kwa-**sohn**), or *petit pain au chocolat* (peh-tee-**pahn**-oh show-ko-**lah**).

You should know that Parisians are used to what Anglo Americans call the "Continental Breakfast." In people's homes you may be served your cof-fee in a bowl instead of a cup. This is a tradition in the countryside, which many Parisians embrace, and a habit you'll see practiced in French movies.

Only in the last few years have Parisians started to understand the con-cept of brunch, and a number of local restaurants now offer Sunday brunch specials. Not very French, but part of contemporary Paris these days. The larger hotels are offering buffet breakfasts too; they are easier to serve.

As for the structure of a French meal, see Part Seven, Dining in Paris. For a detailed look at coffee and drinks, see the "Café and Café Tabac" section also in Part Seven.

If breakfast is not included, you can decide if you want to have your con-tinental or buffet breakfast in your hotel or not. And you can decide from day to day. Some guidebooks advise budget-conscious travelers never to take the hotel breakfast unless it's already included in the room rate, but we generally advise travelers to take the breakfast, especially in small hotels—but look at its cost first. Generally, for the extra €5 to €10 you'll spend you can enjoy a leisurely morning in the breakfast room, drinking a pot of good coffee while munching your morning croissants with raspberry *confiture.* You can get yourself calmly organized for the day, you can easily use the bathrooms, and the croissants you'll be eating come from the same neigh-borhood *boulangerie* anyway. If you take your breakfast in a local *café*, be prepared to spend at least the same amount, if not more, especially if you are sitting at a sidewalk table where the prices are up to twice the price than at the counter inside. The advantage to the breakfast in large hotels is that the buffet-style breakfasts with fruit juice, eggs, bacon, sausage, or cereal allow you to load up and start a full day of sightseeing or business well nourished. Large hotels will often include the buffet breakfast in the room price. If not, try to get it included.

A Word on the Hotel Concierge

At three- and four-star hotels your hotel *concierge* or receptionist may become your best ally in Paris. He (they're almost always men) can and will answer almost any of your questions, and when he does not know he'll know how to find out for you. This is a source of great pride. Your hotel concierge, especially in the bigger and more expensive hotels, should be able to arrange for any of your special needs or desires as well. We've even heard of concierges being able to rent helicopters, racing cars, and acupuncture sessions on demand. Most likely your requests will be contained to restaurant reservations, opera tickets, nightclub recommendations, and tour guides, but it's good to know that a good concierge is worth every euro of tip you give him. (No need to tip on small and easy requests, but a €5 or €10 bill will be appreciated when the concierge tracks down court-side tickets to the French Open Tennis match at Rolland Garros or gets you a table by the window at the Jules Verne restaurant on the Eiffel Tower.) Hotels with one or no stars don't usually have concierges, but the owner or manager should be helpful to you in any case.

Apartment Concierges

The live-in guardians or superintendents of all Parisian apartment houses are also called concierges. They, however, are usually women, or a husband-and-wife team. They clean the building, distribute the daily mail, gossip profusely, and end up being either your buddy or enemy. If you're staying in an apartment, always be extra nice to concierges. You'll depend on them often, and if you create a good relationship with them your life will run a lot more smoothly. If you annoy them, watch out.

The Staff

It's always dangerous to generalize. But it is generally true, especially with small hotels, that the night staff may be less capable to answer questions and to make flawless reservations. When calling to make reservations, remember that you will probably receive the most efficient and competent service from the day staff. The best time to get anything administrative done in Paris is between 10 a.m. and noon and 3 and 5 p.m.

Paris Hotels Rated and Ranked

In the *Unofficial* tradition, we have rated Parisian hotels according to relative quality, convenience of location, tastefulness, state of repair, cleanliness, size of standard rooms, and overall value. We have leaned toward the charming and small rather than the impersonal and large, while including some larger hotels that have a lot of style and, although expensive, represent good value. Paris possesses many quaint yet sophisticated establishments often referred to as *hôtels de charme*. Today, as the demographic profile of travelers has risen in terms of age and affluence, a good many of the popular guidebooks focus primarily on these excellent and "charming" places, which despite their proven quality tend to be expensive. You would expect a Hilton or Hyatt to be $150 a night, but you're shocked to find a little hotel with 25 rooms to be the same price, regardless of its charm and history. Many international travelers today are wholly accustomed to and willing to pay between $100 and $150 a night for a good hotel. We have supplied lots of choices that fulfill these expectations. However, we've compiled an original composite of simpler and more economical choices too, that nonetheless represents quintessential Paris for more modest budgets. You may consider scaling down or adapting your hotel expectations and using the savings for your culinary exploits.

Star System and Price Ranges

Our system of awarding stars is based on overall quality of the hotel and has not been aligned or influenced by the stars assigned officially by the Paris Office of Tourism.

★★★★★   **Superior Rooms**, very high class, de luxe   €400–550

Tasteful and luxurious. Be prepared to feel like royalty. And insist on it. Hotels in this category are generally not profiled in this guide, but listed as Crème de la Crème.

★★★★   **Extremely nice rooms**, high class   €150–400

What you'd expect at a luxury chain hotel, but with added touches of European elegance. We've profiled a number of these that offer the best value for the high price. For your information only, we include one- and two-star descriptions, although we recommend the three-, four-, and five-star hotels we highlight.

★★★   **Very comfortable rooms**   €100–250

What you'd expect at a mid-range chain hotel but with more style and charm. We focus on numerous hotels in this category.

★★   **Adequate rooms**   €70–100

Clean, comfortable, and functional without any frills, but in some cases, a surprising amount of character and overall quality. The less interesting two-stars are not mentioned here.

★   **Super budget**, rooms of basic comfort   under €70

Simple rooms with or without toilets or showers in rooms. Often less central, but not necessarily. Safe and clean, though. The ones profiled here represent good value.

European Criteria

Our star ratings have been applied in a European context. Being able to have your breakfast in a quaint garden, for us, is more seductive than in-room mini-bars. Lovely watercolor paintings in your room or Louis XVI chairs in the lobby get higher marks from us than the presence of an ice machine. Elsewhere, the ice machine or laundry service may be more important, but not in Paris. So here's a big clue to Parisian happiness: Do not perpetually compare what you find in Paris with what you're used to in San Francisco or Orlando. Things are older in Europe, style is revered more than functionality, and in order to maintain original charm and historically authentic details, modern comforts have been added afterward to catch up to contemporary needs. As mentioned earlier, many luxury Parisian apartments were initially built before indoor plumbing existed. Elevators in many cases have had to be custom-built to fit into 17th-century stairwells. Bathtubs are often molded into the spaces below mansard ceilings. It's a whole new ball game, and understanding the ratings relies on your appreciating the Parisian culture. In Paris, you're paying for not only the amenities and comfort, but also for the elegance or authenticity.

Overall Ratings We have distinguished properties according to relative quality, tastefulness, state of repair, cleanliness, and size of standard rooms, grouping them into classifications denoted by stars. Overall star ratings in this guide apply to Paris properties only and do not correspond to ratings awarded by the department of tourism, automobile clubs, or other travel critics. Overall ratings are presented to show the difference we perceive between one property and another. They are assigned without regard to location or to whether a property has restaurants, recreational facilities, entertainment, or other extras.

★★★★★	Superior	Tasteful and luxurious by any standard
★★★★	Extremely Nice	Above average in appointments and design; very comfortable
★★★	Nice	Average but quite comfortable
★★	Adequate	Plain but meets all essential needs
★	Budget	Spartan, not aesthetically pleasing, but clean

Quality Ratings In addition to overall ratings (which delineate broad categories), we also employ quality ratings. They apply to room quality only and describe the property's standard accommodations. In addition to standard accommodations, many hotels offer luxury rooms and special suites that are not rated in this guide. Our rating scale is ★–★★★★★, with ★★★★★ as the best possible rating and ★ as the worst.

Value Ratings We also provide a value rating to give you some sense of the quality of a room in relation to its cost. As before, the ratings are based on the quality of room for the money and do not take into account location, services, or amenities.

Our scale is as follows:

- ★★★★★ An exceptional bargain
- ★★★★ A good deal
- ★★★ Fairly priced (you get exactly what you pay for)
- ★★ Somewhat overpriced
- ★ Significantly overpriced

A ★★½ room at €100 may have the same value rating as a ★★★★ room at €200, but that does not mean that the rooms will be of comparable quality. Regardless of whether it's a good deal or not, a ★★½ room is still a ★★½ room.

For each hotel we also provide the Paris *arrondissement* where the property is located.

For travelers who feel that too much of a travel budget is consumed by the cost of a hotel room (which you don't plan to spend all that much time in, anyway), we include a number of well-situated, clean, safe, modest, independent, and small, no-star, one-star *(hôtels de préfecture)*, and two-star hotels. These are nothing fancy but are wholly reliable for very little money. The last remaining one-star hotels, although inconsistent and risky, are perhaps the unsung heroes of the Paris hotel scene. (It's remarkable that two people can sleep in a safe and clean, admittedly spartan, hotel room, with a shower in the room, in central Paris, for under $60.) Each year there are fewer and fewer of these cost-conscious gems, as they either close for good or get bought up, renovated, and gain stars. Some are undoubtedly run-down and funky. Others are fine yet remain unknown or overlooked by the travel agents and travel writers. Without frills, they offer not only the essentials but also their own kind of low-brow Parisian charm. Plus, a one-star or no-star may be as much as $50 cheaper than the two- and three-star haunts! You'll witness this proletariat style—known in French as *populaire* (**pohp-you-laihr**), as opposed to *bourgeois* (bore **jwah**)—in the flowered wallpaper, the bedspreads, the crisp but worn hand towels, the house dress that the patron of the hotel is wearing, and the handwritten notes behind the bathroom door giving you instructions for not flooding the perfectly clean but comically cramped bathtub or shower. It's all up to you. We just want you to have a range of choices. If the no-stars and one-stars scare you off, consider the two stars, often as good as the three-stars but considerably cheaper. We found a two-star hotel that didn't qualify for a third star only because it didn't have a separate toilet for men and women in the lobby. The two-stars are the most enigmatic category. You can find dull and ugly joints with two-stars and absolutely enchanting two-stars with 17th-century decor. Some of the best housing deals in Paris are the two-stars that are elegantly designed and decorated but don't qualify for three stars and have maintained two-star prices so as not to scare off customers.

Prices in Profiled Listings

Cost estimates are based on the hotel's published rack rates for standard rooms for two people with full bathroom (usually shower, not bath). Generally, in Paris, you pay by the amount of people staying and not simply by the room. (Some hotels have designated "single" rooms that are often smaller.) A general price range appears at the top of each profile, with more detailed information listed under "Pricing."

How Paris Room Rates Are Organized

Most Paris hotels organize their rates in the following way. We've added sample prices. Some maintain the same rack rate year-round. Others use high-season and low-season rack rates.

Example:

Room	Low Season	High Season
Single (one person)	€85	€100
Double with twin beds	€100	€115
Double with *"grand lit"*	€135	€160
(double or king-size bed,		
often a better room)		
Triple	supplement of €15	
Suites or apartments	€140–225	€260
Buffet breakfast	€10 (Some include breakfast)	
Hotel tax	€1 per person	

A Word on Paris Hotel Prices

Although Paris is an expensive city, hotel rates tend to be significantly cheaper than those in London or New York. Spending $100 a night for a decent hotel room these days seems like a bargain. For $100 a night in Paris, you can not only expect a hotel room of quality in a desirable area, you can demand one. For $120–150 a night you can stay in one of Paris's numerous small but very comfortable and utterly charming hotels. In some of the areas highlighted here, it's even difficult to spend more. Likewise, for as little as $50 a night you can stay in a perfectly clean and safe, small and modest hotel. For students, backpackers, and travelers with very tight budgets, we've included some of these in the list at the end but have not profiled them.

On the high-end, Paris's luxury hotels can be wildly extravagant, running $350–800 a night. Most of these are located in the chic 8th and 16th *arrondissements*. Other than on one occasion—the Lutétia, which is particularly beautiful—these ultra-chic establishments have simply been mentioned under "Crème de la Crème" below but have not been profiled.

Independence

In order to remain independent and impartial, this guide has not attempted to negotiate special discounts for its readers. However, some French guidebooks have. Although a bit sly, ask the hotel concierge if his hotel offers a discount to readers of any guides, for example, the *Guide du Routard.* If the answer is yes, well, you know what to do next. Ask for the same discount. Hôtel Lévêque in the 7th *arrondissement* offers free breakfast for readers of Rick Steve's travel guides. You should insist on the free breakfast too. Some of the larger chains offer free miles on frequent flyer programs, so don't forget to ask for them.

Crème de la Crème

Below is a quick survey of Paris's most luxurious hotels. Rates in these 15 establishments run between $350 and $900 a night.

Bristol   (156 rooms) 112, rue Fbg. Saint-Honoré, 75008, Tel. 01 53 43 43 00, fax 01 53 43 43 01, Restaurant: Bristol

Le Crillon   (120 rooms) Place de la Concorde, 75008, Tel. 01 44 71 15 00, fax 01 44 71 15 02, Restaurant: Les Ambassadeurs

Grand Hôtel Inter-Continental   (488 rooms) 2, rue Scribe, 75009, Tel. 01 40 07 32 32, fax 01 40 07 33 86, Restaurant: Café de la Paix

Hilton   (453 rooms) 18, av. Suffren, 75015, Tel. 01 44 38 56 00, fax 01 44 38 56 10, Restaurant: Pacific Eiffel

Inter-Continental   (443 rooms) 3, rue Castiglione, 75001, Tel. 01 44 77 11 11, fax 01 44 77 14 60, Restaurant: Brasserie 234 Rivoli

Hôtel Lutétia   (220 rooms) (see Hotel Profiles) 45, bd. Raspail, 75007, Tel. 01 49 54 46 46, fax 01 49 54 46 00, Restaurant: Paris

Meurice   (48 rooms/46 suites) 228, rue de Rivoli, 75001, Tel. 01 44 58 10 10, fax 01 44 58 10 15, Restaurant: Le Meurice

Parc   (116 rooms) 55, av. Raymond Poincaré, 75116, Tel. 01 44 05 66 66, fax 01 44 05 66 00, Restaurant: 59 Poincaré

Plaza Athénée   (143 rooms) 25, av. Montaigne, 75008, Tel. 01 53 67 66 65, fax 01 53 67 66 66, Restaurant: Plaza Athénée

Prince de Galles   (138 rooms) 33, av. George V, 75008, Tel. 01 53 23 77 77, fax 01 53 23 78 78, Restaurant: Jardins des Cygnes

Raphaël   (62 rooms) 17, av. Kléber , 75116, Tel. 01 53 64 32 00, fax 01 53 64 32 01

Le Ritz   (187 rooms) 15, place Vendôme, 75001, Tel. 01 43 16 30 30, fax 01 43 16 31 78, Restaurant: Espadon

Royal Monceau   (142 rooms) 387 av. Hoche, 75008, Tel. 01 42 99 88 00, fax 01 42 99 89 90, Restaurant: Le Jardin

Saint-James Paris   (20 rooms) 43, av. Bugeaud, 75116, Tel. 01 44 05 81 81, fax 01 44 05 81 82

Scribe (206 rooms) 1, rue Scribe, 75009, Tel. 01 44 71 24 24, fax 01 42 65 39 97, Restaurant: Les Muses

Notable Places to Sleep

Best Location
Delhy's Hôtel
Hôtel Colbert
Hôtel de la Place des Vosges
Hôtel Studia
Les Rives de Notre-Dame

Best for Bohemians
Castex Hôtel
Delhy's Hôtel
Hôtel de la Place des Vosges
Hôtel des Croisés
Hôtel Studia

Class Acts
Hôtel Colbert
Hôtel Lutétia
Hôtel Clarion Saint-James & Albany
Hôtel Regina
Hôtel Lotti
L'Hôtel

Super Charm
Hôtel de la Bretonnerie
Hôtel des Marronniers
Hôtel des Saints-Pères
Hôtel du Champs-de-Mars
Hôtel Duc de Saint-Simon
Hôtel Parc Saint-Séverin
Les Rives de Notre-Dame

Most Romantic
Hôtel Regina
Hôtel Saint-Louis Marais
L'Hôtel
The rooms above the fourth floor on the street side of rue Joseph-de-Maître at **Terrass Hôtel** at the top of Montmartre offer lovers a sublime experience, marrying an exquisite panorama with total privacy. Here, you're in Paris and you're in heaven.

Most Unusual
L'Hôtel on the rue des Beaux Arts offers you the chance to sleep in the room that Oscar Wilde died in. The decor has been left in the same style it was when our talented bohemian lived here.

Best View
Hôtel Lutétia's Eiffel Tower Suite not only gives you a view of the world's greatest monument, it affords you a bird's-eye glance from every room in the suite, the bathtub included!

Best Air
Hôtel des Grandes Ecoles has an exquisite garden that transforms an urban setting into the countryside.

HOW THE HOTELS COMPARE

Hotel	Overall Rating	Quality Rating	Value Rating	Price	Arrondisse-ment
Hôtel Lutétia	★★★★½	★★★★★	★★★	€350–760	6
L'Hôtel	★★★★½	★★★★★	★★★	€235–685	6
Hôtel Clarion Saint-James & Albany	★★★★½	★★★★½	★★★★	€168–579	1
Hôtel Duc de Saint-Simon	★★★★½	★★★★½	★★★	€195–310	7
Hôtel Regina	★★★★½	★★★★½	★★	€270–640	1
Hôtel Britannique	★★★★	★★★★½	★★★	€120–165	1
Hôtel d'Angleterre	★★★★	★★★★½	★★★	€90–260	6
Hôtel de La Bretonnerie	★★★★	★★★★½	★★★★	€105–170	4
Hôtel des Saints-Pères	★★★★	★★★★½	★★★★	€105–275	6
Hôtel Saint-Paul Le Marais	★★★★	★★★★½	★★★★	€95–285	4
Les Rives de Notre-Dame	★★★★	★★★★½	★★★	€170–380	5
Melia Colbert Boutique Hôtel	★★★★	★★★★½	★★★	€290–560	5
Terrass Hôtel	★★★★	★★★★½	★★★	€180–290	18
Hôtel de La Place des Vosges	★★★★	★★★★	★★★★★	€75–105	4
Hôtel de Notre-Dame	★★★★	★★★★	★★★★	€125–135	5
Hôtel des Grandes Ecoles	★★★★	★★★★	★★★★★	€90–130	5
Hôtel du Champ-de-Mars	★★★★	★★★★	★★★★★	€60–85	7
Hôtel Istria	★★★★	★★★★	★★★★	€90–100	14
Hôtel Parc Saint-Séverin	★★★★	★★★★	★★★	€85–245	5
Hôtel de Varenne	★★★½	★★★★	★★★★	€100–120	7
Hôtel des Croisés	★★★½	★★★★	★★★★★	€65–105	9
Hôtel des Tuileries	★★★½	★★★★	★★★★	€120–335	1
Hôtel Récamier	★★★½	★★★★	★★★★	€80–190	6
Timhôtel Jardin des Plantes	★★★½	★★★★	★★★★	€105–120	5
Welcome Hôtel	★★★½	★★★★	★★★★	€70–110	6
Grand Hôtel Lévéque	★★★½	★★★½	★★★★★	€60–90	7
Hôtel Le Lido	★★★½	★★★½	★★★★	€125–170	8
A La Villa des Artistes	★★★	★★★★	★★★★	€115–145	6
Grand Hôtel Malher	★★★	★★★★	★★★★	€80–160	4
Hôtel de Lutèce	★★★	★★★★	★★★	€115–155	4

HOW THE HOTELS COMPARE (continued)

Hotel	Overall Rating	Quality Rating	Value Rating	Price	Arrondisse- ment
Hôtel des Deux-Îles	★★★	★★★★	★★★	€115–140	4
Le Pavillon Bastille	★★★	★★★★	★★★	€130–210	12
Hôtel Beaumarchais	★★★	★★★½	★★★★	€60–130	11
Hôtel Bersoly's	★★★	★★★½	★★★	€100–120	7
Hôtel des Arènes	★★★	★★★½	★★★★	€100–145	5
Hôtel des Chevaliers	★★★	★★★½	★★★★	€104–125	3
Hôtel des Jardins du Luxembourg	★★★	★★★½	★★★	€125–135	5
Hôtel du Cygne	★★★	★★★½	★★★★★	€65–100	1
Hôtel du Danemark	★★★	★★★½	★★★	€110–135	6
Hôtel Favart	★★★	★★★½	★★★★	€85–105	2
Hôtel Eugénie	★★★	★★★	★★★★	€90–120	6
Hôtel Brighton	★★★	★★★	★★★½	€109–220	1
Hôtel Libertel Grand Turenne	★★★	★★★	★★★★	€133–183	4
Castex Hôtel	★★½	★★★½	★★★★★	€45–75	4
Hôtel Amiot	★★½	★★★½	★★★★★	€41–81	10
Hôtel Esméralda	★★½	★★★½	★★★★★	€30–90	5
La Tour d'Auvergne	★★½	★★★½	★★★★	€115–130	9
Hôtel Bonne Nouvelle	★★½	★★★	★★★★★	€55–115	2
Hôtel Le Bouquet de Montmartre	★★½	★★★	★★★★★	€60	18
Hôtel Sévigné	★★½	★★★	★★★★	€55–80	4

PARIS HOTELS BY ARRONDISSEMENT

Hotel	Overall Rating	Quality Rating	Value Rating	Price
1st arrondissement				
Hôtel Clarion Saint-James & Albany	★★★★½	★★★★½	★★★★	€168–579
Hôtel Regina	★★★★½	★★★★½	★★	€270–640
Hôtel Britannique	★★★★	★★★★½	★★★	€120–165
Hôtel des Tuileries	★★★½	★★★★	★★★★	€120–335

PARIS HOTELS BY ARRONDISSEMENT (continued)

Hotel	Overall Rating	Quality Rating	Value Rating	Price
1st arrondissement (continued)				
Hôtel du Cygne	★★★	★★★½	★★★★★	€65–100
Hôtel Brighton	★★★	★★★	★★★½	€109–220
2nd arrondissement				
Hôtel des Chevaliers	★★★	★★★½	★★★★	€104–125
Hôtel Favart	★★★	★★★½	★★★★	€85–105
Hôtel Bonne Nouvelle	★★½	★★★	★★★★★	€55–115
4th arrondissement				
Hôtel de La Bretonnerie	★★★★	★★★★½	★★★★	€105–170
Hôtel Saint-Paul Le Marais	★★★★	★★★★½	★★★★	€95–285
Hôtel de La Place Des Vosges	★★★★	★★★★	★★★★★	€75–105
Grand Hôtel Malher	★★★	★★★★	★★★★	€80–160
Hôtel de Lutèce	★★★	★★★★	★★★	€115–155
Hôtel des Deux-Îles	★★★	★★★★	★★★	€115–140
Hôtel Libertel Grand Turenne	★★★	★★★	★★★★	€133–183
Castex Hôtel	★★½	★★★½	★★★★★	€45–75
Hôtel Sévigné	★★½	★★★	★★★★	€55–80
5th arrondissement				
Les Rives de Notre-Dame	★★★★	★★★★½	★★★	€170–380
Melia Colbert Boutique Hôtel	★★★★	★★★★½	★★★	€290–560
Hôtel de Notre-Dame	★★★★	★★★★	★★★★	€125–135
Hôtel des Grandes Ecoles	★★★★	★★★★	★★★★★	€90–130
Hôtel Parc Saint-Séverin	★★★★	★★★★	★★★	€85–245
Timhôtel Jardin des Plantes	★★★½	★★★★	★★★★	€105–120
Hôtel des Arènes	★★★	★★★½	★★★★	€100–145
Hôtel des Jardins du Luxembourg	★★★	★★★½	★★★	€125–135
Hôtel Esméralda	★★½	★★★½	★★★★★	€30–90
6th arrondissement				
Hôtel Lutétia	★★★★½	★★★★★	★★★	€350–760
L'Hôtel	★★★★½	★★★★★	★★★	€235–685
Hôtel d'Angleterre	★★★★	★★★★½	★★★	€90–260
Hôtel des Saints-Pères	★★★★	★★★★½	★★★★	€105–275
Hôtel Récamier	★★★½	★★★★	★★★★	€80–190
Welcome Hôtel	★★★½	★★★★	★★★★	€70–110
A La Villa des Artistes	★★★	★★★★	★★★★	€115–145
Hôtel du Danemark	★★★	★★★½	★★★	€110–135
Hôtel Eugénie	★★★	★★★	★★★★	€90–120

PARIS HOTELS BY ARRONDISSEMENT (continued)

Hotel	Overall Rating	Quality Rating	Value Rating	Price
7th arrondissement				
Hôtel Duc de Saint-Simon	★★★★½	★★★★½	★★★	€195–310
Hôtel du Champ-de-Mars	★★★★	★★★★	★★★★★	€60–85
Hôtel de Varenne	★★★½	★★★★	★★★★	€100–120
Grand Hôtel Lévéque	★★★½	★★★½	★★★★★	€60–90
Hôtel Bersoly's	★★★	★★★½	★★★	€100–120
8th arrondissement				
Hôtel Le Lido	★★★½	★★★½	★★★★	€125–170
9th arrondissement				
Hôtel des Croisés	★★★½	★★★★	★★★★★	€65–105
La Tour d'Auvergne	★★½	★★★½	★★★★	€115–130
10th arrondissement				
Hôtel Amiot	★★½	★★★½	★★★★★	€41–81
11th arrondissement				
Hôtel Beaumarchais	★★★	★★★½	★★★★	€60–130
12th arrondissement				
Le Pavillon Bastille	★★★	★★★★	★★★	€130–210
14th arrondissement				
Hôtel Istria	★★★★	★★★★	★★★★	€90–100
18th arrondissement				
Terrass Hôtel	★★★★	★★★★½	★★★	€180–290
Hôtel Le Bouquet de Montmartre	★★½	★★★	★★★★★	€60

Hotel Profiles

We have carefully selected a wide variety of hotels by choosing several from each price range, attempting to offer a choice of styles and sizes as well.

You'll find in most areas at least one profiled hotel that is inexpensive (under €70), two that are moderately priced (€80–130), two that are expensive (€130–230), and one that is very expensive (€230 and up).

Profiled hotels are listed in alphabetical order.

REMINDER ON DEPOSITS

Most Parisian hotels do not require that you send them a deposit. Instead, most ask that you fax them your request for reservations along with a credit card number and expiration date. Your number will be held for your arrival as a deposit. If you do not show up, usually you will be debited for one night's stay. If you cancel your reservations at least a day in advance your card should not be debited.

A LA VILLA DES ARTISTES €115–145

OVERALL ★★★ | QUALITY ★★★★ | VALUE ★★★★ | 6TH *ARRONDISSEMENT*

9, rue de la Grande-Chaumière, 75006; 01 43 26 60 86; fax 01 43 54 73 70; hotel@villa-artistes.com; www.villa-artistes.com

On a relatively quiet street, the hotel is extremely well named given that it's not far from the Montparnasse cafés where myths were made: La Coupole, Le Dôme, Le Sélect, and La Rotande—and of course La Closerie des Lilas up the street. Though for the most part the modern decor prevents you from realizing that the building is from the 18th century, the stone corridor walls give you a glimpse of the building's history. On the ground floor there seems no end to places to sit, converse, relax, ingest: the salon's intimately lit comfy armchairs; the small bar's closely grouped stools; the breakfast room's informal tables and chairs; the little garden/courtyard's white wrought-iron furniture, where breakfast can be taken as well. A plus is the wonderfully welcoming, attentive, and professional staff, starting with the director herself.

SETTING & FACILITIES

Location Montparnasse. **Nearest Métro Station** Vavin. **Quietness Rating** A on courtyard and B on street. **Dining** €7.50 buffet breakfast. **Amenities** Parking nearby. **Services** Laundry.

ACCOMMODATIONS

Rooms 59. **All** TV with satellite, direct-dial phone, individual safety box, hair dryer, mini-bar. **Bathrooms** Bright and functional. **Comfort & Decor** If you're lucky enough to get room 3—right on the garden—you'll have a tendency to think you've gone to the country for a bit of bucolic tranquility (as opposed to being in one of the most "animated," as the French say, areas of the city!). The room's glistening, warm colors and comfortable appointments (good closet space, mini-bar, TV) add to the atmosphere of simple luxury.

RATES, RESERVATIONS, & RESTRICTIONS
Pricing: Single or double €115, club room €145 (air-conditioned). **Credit Cards** All major credit cards. **Check-In/Out** 3 p.m./noon. **Not Allowed** Pets. **Elevator** Yes. **English Spoken** Yes.

CASTEX HÔTEL   €45–75

OVERALL ★★½ | QUALITY ★★★½ | VALUE ★★★★★ | 4TH ARRONDISSEMENT

5, rue Castex, 75004; 01 42 72 31 52; fax 01 42 72 57 91; info@castexhotel.com; www. castexhotel.com

This small, family-run hotel, entirely renovated in 2001, is an excellent choice for those who wish to be in the Marais but don't want to shell out a fortune. The style and aesthetics are plain, functional, and not much more, but the hotel is very clean and perfectly managed. The reception area is tiny with an alcove filled with travel information. This is one of those great addresses where you sleep, you have your breakfast, and off you go into the wonders of the city. Most of their guests have stayed here before, a great testimony. The rue Castex has the advantage of being on the quiet side of the Bastille, sparing you much of the late-night noise, and yet it is close enough that you can do all of your explorations of the area by foot. What impressed us was the friendliness of the Perdigao sons, Vasco and Hervé, who run the hotel. There is a cute but tiny courtyard on which room 4 looks out, a good choice in the summer months. There is no elevator, but this does not detract from the overall value of this address. The hotel's front door locks at midnight, so late-nighters need to take the key with them. The République Hôtel (31, rue Albert Thomas, 75010, phone 01 42 39 19 03) is run by the same family.

SETTING & FACILITIES
Location The Marais. **Nearest Métro Station** Bastille, Sully-Morland. **Quietness Rating** B. **Dining** €5.50 continental breakfast (7:30–10 a.m.). **Amenities** Beverage machine in lobby.

ACCOMMODATIONS
Rooms 27. **All** Phone, WC, bath or shower. **Bathrooms** Simple. **Comfort & Decor** Room 22 is a triple, whereas 12, 27, and 34 are the largest doubles.

RATES, RESERVATIONS, & RESTRICTIONS
Pricing Single (shower) €45, single (shower, TV) €50, double (shower) €55, double (bathtub) €60, triple (shower) €75, extra bed €10, baby bed €4.50. **Credit Cards** AMEX, CB, VISA, EUROCARD, MC. **Check-In/Out** Noon. **Elevator** No. **English Spoken** Yes.

GRAND HÔTEL LÉVÊQUE   €60–90

OVERALL ★★★½ | QUALITY ★★★½ | VALUE ★★★★★ | 7TH *ARRONDISSEMENT*

29, rue Cler, 75007; 01 47 05 49 15; fax 01 45 50 49 36; leveque@hotellerie.net; www.inter-resa.com/hotel/leveque/

Though the entryway of this newly renovated hotel is unremarkable, you'll be attracted by the sitting area's charming furnishings, including a ceiling fan. By the time you reach the large, neighboring breakfast room, you think you've mistakenly wandered into a Parisian café—woven-straw chair seats and all! The corridors provide a nice background for the little pictures on the walls. You'll appreciate the service-oriented attitude of the staff.

SETTING & FACILITIES
Location Invalides. **Nearest Métro Station** Ecole-Militaire. **Quietness Rating** B in the back and C on the street during market hours. **Dining** €6 continental breakfast.

ACCOMMODATIONS
Rooms 50. **All** TV with cable, direct-dial phone, hair dryer, individual safe. **Comfort & Decor** Room 50, street-side, is bright and sunny though small; from its balcony you can glimpse the top of the Eiffel Tower. Ceiling fans function as an effective substitute for air-conditioning.

RATES, RESERVATIONS, & RESTRICTIONS
Pricing Double or twin €60–70, triple €90. **Deposit** Required. **Credit Cards** All major credit cards. **Check-In/Out** 3 p.m./noon. **Not Allowed** Pets. **Elevator** Yes. **English Spoken** Yes.

GRAND HÔTEL MALHER   €80–160

OVERALL ★★★ | QUALITY ★★★★ | VALUE ★★★★ | 4TH *ARRONDISSEMENT*

5, rue Malher, 75004; 01 42 72 60 92; fax 01 42 72 25 37; ghmalher@yahoo.fr

Staying in the Marais is always a treat, and within a short period of time you'll start to feel like this is your neighborhood. Several small hotels are clustered near each other on the rue Malher, but the Grand Hôtel Malher is the most comfortable and most cheerful. Mr. and Ms. Fossiez are the third generation of Fossiezes operating this establishment, and they're pleased to be the ones bringing the hotel into the next millennium. It's perfectly renovated in the Marais style, as evidenced by the exposed stone in the lobby, vaulted ceilings in the medieval breakfast room, and polished stone floors. Of course the location is ideal, in the Marais close to the Bastille and an easy walk to Châtelet and the Latin Quarter. An all-around great address.

SETTING & FACILITIES
Location The Marais. **Nearest Métro Station** St-Paul-Le Marais. **Quietness Rating** B. **Dining** €7.50 breakfast. **Amenities** Hair dryers.

ACCOMMODATIONS

Rooms 31. **All** TV, phone, mini-bar, WC. **Bathrooms** Small but immaculate. **Comfort & Decor** We visited room 30, which is typical of the hotel; it's smallish (which is typical of the Marais) but impeccably clean and perfectly comfortable and quiet, although the quietest rooms face the courtyard. Room 64 is a mini-suite, well suited for three adults or a couple with a child.

RATES, RESERVATIONS, & RESTRICTIONS

Pricing Single (standard room) €80 off-season, €95 high season; single (superior room) €90 off-season, €100 high season; double (standard room) €95 off-season, €110 high season; double (superior room) €100 off-season, €120 high season; junior suite €145 off-season, €160 high season. **Credit Cards** VISA, MC, DC. **Check-In/Out** After noon/noon. **Elevator** Yes. **English Spoken** Yes.

HÔTEL AMIOT   €41–81

OVERALL ★★½ | QUALITY ★★★½ | VALUE ★★★★★ | 10TH ARRONDISSEMENT

76, boulevard de Strasbourg, 75010; 01 44 89 88 89; fax 01 44 89 88 90; www.hotel amiot.com

Right at the Gare de l'Est Métro station, the hotel is done in light tones (except for the deep turquoise room doors), with a predominance of blues and greens. Rare for France: certain main-floor common areas are no-smoking zones. Corridors are lined with paintings.

SETTING & FACILITIES

Location Grands Boulevards. **Nearest Métro Station** Gare de l'Est. **Quietness Rating** B (windows closed) or C. **Dining** €5 (avg.) breakfast 7–10 a.m. **Amenities** Safe. **Services** Room service, bar, laundry, reservations for shows, taxi.

ACCOMMODATIONS

Rooms 68. **All** TV with satellite, direct-dial phone, shower or bath, and WC. **Comfort & Decor** Room 23 is a triple (the placement of the single bed right next to the double makes what looks like a mega-king!) whose simple, comfortably large bathroom offers sink, bathtub, bidet, and WC. A painting of a woman playing a guitar adds a pleasant touch to this room.

RATES, RESERVATIONS, & RESTRICTIONS

Pricing Single €41–54, double €51–60, triple €60–81 (varies according to week or weekend, number of people, and whether you take breakfast). **Credit Cards** All major cards except AMEX. **Check-In/Out** Noon. **Not Allowed** Pets. **Elevator** Yes. **English Spoken** Yes.

HÔTEL BEAUMARCHAIS   €60–130

OVERALL ★★★ | QUALITY ★★★½ | VALUE ★★★★ | 11TH ARRONDISSEMENT

3, rue Oberkampf, 75011; 01 53 36 86 86; fax 01 43 38 32 86; hotel.beaumarchais@ libertysurf.fr; www.hotelbeaumarchais.com

One of the first things you notice is the soft, summery color scheme (much yellow and salmon) of this 30-year-old hotel, not far from the Cirque d'Hiver, tastefully redone with attention to comfort. The effect of the salon's impressive winding metal staircase (actually usable from the second floor up) is a bit undone by the plastic furniture in the nearby breakfast room, but all looks quite accommodating. Artwork tends to be contemporary. You'll find a customer-oriented staff. The hotel was recently upgraded to three stars.

SETTING & FACILITIES

Location Bastille/République. **Nearest Métro Station** Oberkampf, Filles-du-Calvaire. **Quietness Rating** B. **Dining** €6 continental breakfast, €7.50 in the room. **Amenities** Parking nearby. **Services** Room service 24 hours (no alcohol served).

ACCOMMODATIONS

Rooms 31. **All** TV, direct-dial phone, hair dryer, air-conditioning, safe. **Comfort & Decor** Room 2, overlooking the garden, often doubles as the "bridal room"; its mirrored closet doors give the illusion of more space.

RATES, RESERVATIONS, & RESTRICTIONS

Pricing Single €60–85, double €90–100, suite €120–130 (depending on season). **Credit Cards** AMEX, VISA, EUROCARD, MC. **Check-In/Out** 1 p.m./noon. **Elevator** Yes. **English Spoken** Some.

HÔTEL BERSOLY'S   €100–120

OVERALL ★★★ | QUALITY ★★★½ | VALUE ★★★ | 7TH *ARRONDISSEMENT*

28, rue de Lille, 75007; 01 42 60 73 79; fax 01 49 27 05 55; bersolys@wanadoo.fr; www.bersolyshotel.com

A hotel since the 1970s, this 17th-century building still has its exposed beams and period wrought-iron staircase. Guests often gravitate to the sitting area, where they relax and read in period and flower-print furniture. Reproductions of well-known paintings line the white corridor walls.

SETTING & FACILITIES

Location Invalides. **Nearest Métro Station** Rue du Bac. **Quietness Rating** B (sound-proof windows). **Dining** €8.50 continental or buffet breakfast at any time you choose (breakfast included in room rates in February). **Amenities** Parking rue Verneuil (€15 a day), bar.

ACCOMMODATIONS

Rooms 16. **All** TV, direct-dial phone, hair dryer, safety box, air-conditioning. **Comfort & Decor** Each room is named for a famous painter (Gaugin, Van Gogh, Monet, and so on) and displays corresponding reproductions. (To see some of the real things, hop over to the Musée d'Orsay, not too far away.) Coffee- and tea-making facilities in rooms and good closet space. The bathrooms are comfy though not especially large.

RATES, RESERVATIONS, & RESTRICTIONS
Pricing Single (shower) €100, single (bath) €110, double (shower) €105, double (bath) €120, extra bed €25, per dog €15. **Credit Cards** AMEX, MC, VISA. **Check-In/Out** Noon/11 a.m. **Elevator** Yes. **English Spoken** Yes.

HÔTEL BONNE NOUVELLE   €55–115

OVERALL ★★½ | QUALITY ★★★ | VALUE ★★★★★ | 2ND ARRONDISSEMENT

17, rue Beauregard, 75002; 01 45 08 42 42; fax 01 40 26 05 81; info@hotel-bonne-nouvelle.com; www.hotel-bonne-nouvelle.com

Quiet in a busy area, old-style 19th-century charm, great furniture, and a variety of rooms and suites are featured here. In an area of Paris whose glory days were the mid-to-late 19th century, this 1887 hotel has the unmistakable atmosphere of a Balzac novel. The sensation starts as you pass through the ocher- and multi-colored blown-glass front door and continues as you settle into the ground floor's deep, dark colors that, far from being oppressive, make you feel warmly protected from a cold, cold world! The salon's street-side windows, leather furniture, and real armoire remind you of a sitting area in a private home. The guest-floor corridors' interesting touches include brown fabric on the walls, large posters of turn-of-the-century snow scenes, and a table. Though the hotel is on a busy street, the rooms (especially on top floors) are calm—but don't expect total silence.

SETTING & FACILITIES
Location Grands Boulevards. **Nearest Métro Station** Bonne-Nouvelle. **Quietness Rating** B (no sound-proof windows). **Dining** Breakfast €4.50 in the breakfast room, €5.50 in your room; continental, but you also can order eggs. **Amenities** Parking nearby. **Services** Room service 7 a.m.–noon, 7–11 p.m.

ACCOMMODATIONS
Rooms 20. **All** TV, mini-bar, phone, hair dryer, modem jacks. **Bathrooms** Some toilet bowls have a rather dirty appearance due to years of mineral build-up in the water. **Comfort & Decor** Behind room 19's dark wooden door you'll find variegated upholstery, a yellow carpet, and a distinctively turn-of-the-century painting of a nude. The maroon-tiled bathroom (with a red shower curtain) is in perfect condition, except for a bit of rust.

RATES, RESERVATIONS, & RESTRICTIONS
Pricing Single €55–60, double €55–75, triple €80–100, suite €75–115. **Deposit:** Credit card. **Credit Cards** All except AMEX. **Check-In/Out** Noon. **Elevator** Yes. **English Spoken** Yes.

HÔTEL BRIGHTON   €109–220

OVERALL ★★★ | QUALITY ★★★ | VALUE ★★★½ | 1ST ARRONDISSEMENT

218, rue de Rivoli, 75001; 01 47 03 61 61; fax 01 42 60 41 78; hotel.brighton@wanadoo.fr; www.esprit-de-france.com

Check-in personnel are very service-oriented and "friendly" in a way you
expect in only smaller, more intimate establishments. The entrance area is
bright, but the reception desk is small for a hotel of this size. A plus is the
tea/breakfast salon, to the left of the check-in area, lit by chandeliers, graced
by marble columns, furnished with charming little square tables, and protected by curtains from any indiscreet gawking by rue de Rivoli passersby.
Work to enlarge certain rooms is planned for the near future. Still no air-
conditioning but planned for 2002.

SETTING & FACILITIES
Location Concorde/Champs-Elysées. **Nearest Métro Station** Tuileries. **Quietness
Rating** A with windows closed and rooms on the courtyard, C otherwise. **Dining** Con-
tinental breakfast, 7–11 a.m., €7.50. **Services** Room service 7 a.m.–7 p.m.

ACCOMMODATIONS
Rooms 65. **All** TV with cable, direct-dial phone, hair dryer, air-conditioning, mini-bar.
Favorites Rooms with view of the Tuileries garden. Junior suites and standard double or
deluxe double. **Comfort & Decor** Old-world style, turn-of-the-century lamps, and
carved wooden wall panels. Imagine Somerset Maugham staying here.

RATES, RESERVATIONS, & RESTRICTIONS
Pricing Single €109, double €109–215, others €220, €24 per extra person. **Deposit:**
Credit card. **Credit Cards** AMEX, VISA, MC, JCB. **Check-In/Out** Noon/11 a.m. **Not
Allowed** Dogs **Elevator** Yes. **English Spoken** Yes. **Special Tips** Reserve minimum
1 month in advance; during the high season or fairs reserve 3 months in advance.

HÔTEL BRITANNIQUE   €120–165

OVERALL ★★★★ | QUALITY ★★★★½ | VALUE ★★★ | 1ST *ARRONDISSEMENT*

20, avenue Victoria, 75001; 01 42 33 74 59; fax 01 42 33 82 65; mailbox@hotel-britannique.fr;
www.hotel-britannic.com (English); www.hotel-britannique.fr (French)

You'll find remarkably customer service–oriented personnel (maybe
because the hotel was the World War I refuge of the Quakers). No air-
conditioning, and a rather small (three-person) elevator, but some great
touches, like the three clocks in the entryway indicating time in New York,
London, and Victoria.

SETTING & FACILITIES
Location Châtelet–Les Halles. **Nearest Métro Station** Châtelet. **Quietness Rat-
ing** A (when windows are closed). **Dining** €10 for a generous breakfast. **Amenities**
Public parking nearby (Hôtel de Ville). **Services** Room service (breakfast).

ACCOMMODATIONS
Rooms 40. **All** TV with satellite, direct-dial phone, mini-bar, safe deposit box, hair dryer,
sound-proof windows. **Comfort & Decor** Decor tends toward the British, with

wooden furniture whose cushions nicely match the red carpets in hallways and well-lit rooms. Bathrooms are generally large. Some rooms (usually the doubles) overlook the courtyard.

RATES, RESERVATIONS, & RESTRICTIONS
Pricing Single €120, double €145–165, extra bed €20. You can get major discounts if you call and ask for them. Discounts can reach 20 to 30%, but it depends on availability and season. **Credit Cards** VISA, MC, AMEX, DC. **Check-In/Out** 2 p.m./noon. **Elevator** Yes. **English Spoken** Yes.

HÔTEL CLARION SAINT-JAMES & ALBANY   €168–579

OVERALL ★★★★½ | QUALITY ★★★★½ | VALUE ★★★★ | 1ST ARRONDISSEMENT

202, rue de Rivoli, 75001; 01 44 58 43 21; reservations (800) 228-3323; fax 01 44 58 43 11; stjames_albany@compuserve.com; www.clarionsaintjames.com

Now part of the Clarion/Comfort/Quality chain, this lovely mansion was once the home of the Ducs de Noailles, in-laws of Marquis de La Fayette who in 1779 hosted Marie-Antoinette within its walls. You'll get a good taste of the Paris of dukes and duchesses in this stylish yet accessible institution. The large check-in area is adjacent to an interior courtyard and several salons—some rather spacious and all with their own mood: mirrors and beige armchairs in one, for instance, chandeliers and black-leather chairs in another. Pleasingly though not remarkably decorated, with pictures on the walls and often double closets. The rooms are all well designed and decorated although a bit stiff and formulaic. The dining room and the gardens convey the former high society social life for which they were once used. To live like this for a few days on the rue de Rivoli is a treat. News: indoor pool planned for summer 2002.

SETTING & FACILITIES
Location Concorde/Champs-Elysées. **Nearest Métro Station** Tuileries. **Quietness Rating** A with windows closed for rooms with view on the rue de Rivoli. **Dining** Restaurant Le Noailles; €18 American breakfast. **Amenities** Parking, bar Saint-James, meeting and ball rooms. **Services** Room service 24/7.

ACCOMMODATIONS
Rooms 202. **All** TV with cable, direct-dial phone, hair dryer, mini-bar, safe deposit box, air-conditioning. **Bathrooms** All. **Comfort & Decor** Regal, royal, aristocratic, and filled with antiques.

RATES, RESERVATIONS, & RESTRICTIONS
Pricing Standard double €299, "superior" room €335, junior suite €396, suites €533–914. **Deposit** Fax credit card number to hold reservation. **Credit Cards** All major credit cards. **Check In/Out** 3 p.m./noon. **Elevator** Yes. **English Spoken** Yes. **Special Tips** Reserve 2 weeks in advance during the off-season and 6 months during the high season.

HÔTEL D'ANGLETERRE   €90–260

OVERALL ★★★★ | QUALITY ★★★★½ | VALUE ★★★ | 6TH *ARRONDISSEMENT*

44, rue Jacob, 75006; 01 42 60 34 72; fax 01 42 60 16 93; anglotel@wanadoo.fr

Ernest Hemingway once lived in this former British embassy, among the high, wainscoted ceilings, the exposed beams, the period furniture, and the canopy beds. You'll enjoy being on the rue Jacob in the heart of the Saint-Germain-des-Prés area, with an easy walk to the Seine, the city's best galleries, and the most famous cafés.

SETTING & FACILITIES
Location Saint-Germain-des-Prés. **Nearest Métro Station** Saint-Germain-des-Prés. **Quietness Rating** A (rooms on the courtyard, all with windows closed). **Dining** €9 for breakfast (continental or à la carte). **Services** Room service (7 a.m.–8 p.m.); reservations for theaters, restaurants, shows.

ACCOMMODATIONS
Rooms 27. **All** TV with cable, direct-dial phone, safe deposit box, hair dryer. **Some** View of garden. **Comfort & Decor** Each room is spacious, and no two are alike. The best rooms overlook the garden.

RATES, RESERVATIONS, & RESTRICTIONS
Pricing Single €90, double €120–205, suite €260, extra person €40 in certain rooms. **Deposit** First night deposit requested. **Credit Cards** AMEX, DC, MC, VISA, JCB. **Check-In/Out** 3 p.m./noon. **Not Allowed** Pets. **Elevator** Yes. **English Spoken** Yes.

HÔTEL DE LA BRETONNERIE   €105–170

OVERALL ★★★★ | QUALITY ★★★★½ | VALUE ★★★★ | 4TH *ARRONDISSEMENT*

22, rue Ste-Croix-de-la-Bretonnerie, 75004; 01 48 87 77 63; fax 01 42 77 26 78; hotel@bretonnerie.com; www.bretonnerie.com

This favorite hotel of North Americans is in the heart of the Marais. Discreet from the outside, this 17th-century building surprises you as you enter. The delightfully decorated lobby is bathed in warm light streaming through yellow glass panes. Exposed beams and a brand new decor in raspberry tones. The breakfast room is in the vaulted cellar furnished with low chairs and cushions. Very medieval and quaint. The labyrinth-like hallways are covered in stretched fabric in a delightful old rose hue. Color is clearly important to Mademoiselle Sagot, the owner, who knows precisely how to make her guests feel welcomed. This hotel is closed for the month of August.

SETTING & FACILITIES
Location The Marais. **Nearest Métro Station** Hôtel de Ville. **Quietness Rating** A. **Dining** €9 for breakfast.

ACCOMMODATIONS
Rooms 22, 7 suites. **All** TV with satellite, direct-dial phone, mini-bar, hair dryer. **Some** Duplex. **Bathrooms** Perfectly modern. **Comfort & Decor** Four rooms are furnished with very impressive "baldaquin" canopy-covered beds, perfectly in line with the 17th-century motif. All rooms are very inviting, cozy, and country-style. There are three rooms set up as duplexes. Dark wooden stairs and beams, with the sleeping space upstairs, make these feel like small apartments. Ask for the room called "Route du thé," which is decorated in warm rust tones.

RATES, RESERVATIONS, & RESTRICTIONS
Pricing Double (bath, WC) €105, double (duplex or charming rooms) €130, suite €170. **Credit Cards** VISA, MC. **Check-In/Out** Noon/11 a.m. **English Spoken** Yes.

HÔTEL DE LA PLACE DES VOSGES   €75–105

OVERALL ★★★★ | QUALITY ★★★★ | VALUE ★★★★★ | 4TH ARRONDISSEMENT

12, rue de Birague, 75004; 01 42 72 60 46; fax 01 42 72 02 64; hotel.place.des.vosges@gofornet.com

Probably our favorite little hotel in Paris, the Hôtel de la Place des Vosges exudes charm and quality; it is no wonder that the hotel enjoys an occupancy rate of 97% year-round. Americans (primarily from California) make up a large majority of the guests, and the marketing works mostly by word of mouth. The hotel sits on the quiet rue de Birague, which dead-ends into the Place de la Vosges. Decorated in Louis XIII epoch furniture and covered in regal tapestries, the exposed-beam lobby feels more like a salon than a hotel. The proprietor's calm and intelligent approach to innkeeping carries over into the relaxed elegance of her place. "Our guests feel like they're at home. And that's how we like it." The building dates back to the end of the 16th century, when it was a stable set up for the rental of mules. The other point of historical interest is that the novelist Georges Simenon lived here while writing his crime story, *The Outlaw.* The prices are very reasonable for the location and comfort. Reserve well in advance.

SETTING & FACILITIES
Location The Marais. **Nearest Métro Station** St-Paul-Le Marais, Bastille. **Quietness Rating** A. **Dining** Breakfast included in room rates.

ACCOMMODATIONS
Rooms 16. **All** TV with satellite, direct-dial phone, mini-bar, hair dryer. **Comfort & Decor** Each room is a bit different, both in decor and size, but all are bright and carefully decorated, right down to the great beds with firm mattresses.

RATES, RESERVATIONS, & RESTRICTIONS
Pricing Single €75, double €100–105. **Credit Cards** All major credit cards. **Check-In/Out** Noon. **Elevator** Yes. **English Spoken** Yes.

HÔTEL DE LUTÈCE   €115–155

OVERALL ★★★ | QUALITY ★★★★ | VALUE ★★★ | 4TH *ARRONDISSEMENT*

65, rue St-Louis en l'Île, 75004; 01 43 26 23 52; fax 01 43 29 60 25; hotel.lutece@free.fr

The reception desk is just that—a desk, small and simple—chosen expressly so as not to scream "hotel" and to help guests feel that they have entered a very warm, welcoming private home. The service, on the other hand, is huge, and screams, "We want to cater to your every wish!" In keeping with the noble ancientness of the Île St-Louis—around which all of Paris grew out and up—the wood-beamed downstairs is reminiscent of a château in winter, its colors whispering warmth and comfort, its green plants (actually, there are plants all over the hotel) bringing nature in through the front door. Try to take the period staircase (with wrought-iron banister) instead of the elevator to stay within the mood of the hotel and of the Île in general. And be sure not to leave the neighborhood without a stop (or several) at the legendary—and we do mean legendary!—Bertillon ice cream parlor down the street at number 31.

SETTING & FACILITIES
Location Islands. **Nearest Métro Station** Pont-Marie. **Quietness Rating** B. **Dining** €9 continental breakfast. **Services** Reservations for theaters, trains, and so on.

ACCOMMODATIONS
Rooms 23. **All** TV with cable, direct-dial phone, hair dryer, air-conditioning, safe. **Comfort & Decor** Many rooms have exposed beams (the top floor is mansard-roofed), and all are alike in most features; though rather dark (especially courtyard-side), they're not depressing. To save space, armoires have been sacrificed for simple white closets. Interestingly, curtains and bedspreads are in a loud, flower-patterned yellow, which tends to detract from the atmosphere.

RATES, RESERVATIONS, & RESTRICTIONS
Pricing Single €115, double €140, triple €155. **Cancellation Policy** 1 week before arrival without charge. **Credit Cards** AMEX, VISA. **Check-In/Out** Noon/11 a.m. **Not Allowed** Dogs. **Elevator** Yes. **English Spoken** Yes. **Special Tips** Reserve 6 months in advance.

HÔTEL DE NOTRE-DAME   €125–135

OVERALL ★★★★ | QUALITY ★★★★ | VALUE ★★★★ | 5TH *ARRONDISSEMENT*

19, rue Maître-Albert, 75005; 01 43 26 79 00; fax 01 46 33 50 11; hotel.denotredame@libertysurf.fr. www.123France.com

This is one of our favorite little streets in the Latin Quarter. It's close to everything yet so private and tucked away. At the bend in the rue Maître Albert, which cuts from the Place Maubert to the Seine, this renovated medieval structure houses a classy little hotel. The street contains a number of antique shops, plus the Auberge Maître Albert restaurant at the end of the street near the Seine. The lobby captures the style of the establishment with a statue of the duchess of Richelieu, who is often mistaken for Marie Antoinette. The large tapestry hanging on the wall is a favorite possession of the owner, Mr. Fouhety. The exposed stone and earth-tone stone floors set the flavor. The comfort, style, and location make this a prime choice.

SETTING & FACILITIES
Location Latin Quarter. **Nearest Métro Station** St-Michel, Maubert-Mutualité. **Quietness Rating** B. **Dining** €6 breakfast. **Amenities** Parking facilities.

ACCOMMODATIONS
Rooms 34. **All** TV, direct-dial phone, hair dryer, safe, mini-bar. **Comfort & Decor** The rooms are tastefully decorated in bright hues from the south of France, period furniture, and new fabrics. Number 50, at the top of the house, affords a great view of nearby Notre-Dame. Try to stay in room 30, 31, 50, or 54, all of which are a bit more money but larger.

RATES, RESERVATIONS, & RESTRICTIONS
Pricing Double €125–135. **Credit Cards** All major credit cards. **Check-In/Out** Noon. **Elevator** Yes. **English Spoken** Yes.

HÔTEL DE VARENNE   €100–120

OVERALL ★★★½ | QUALITY ★★★★ | VALUE ★★★★ | 7TH *ARRONDISSEMENT*

44, rue de Bourgogne, 75007; 01 45 51 45 55; fax 01 45 51 86 63; www.webscapades.com/france/paris/varenne.htm

The highlight of this hotel is its entryway: a little courtyard (the 7th *arrondissement* is informally known as an *arrondissement* of courtyards, though all of Paris has them) with a garden of ivy and flowers, and a set of wrought-iron tables and chairs in which to relax (while realizing that you've just left the noise back out on the street). And all this before you even enter the building itself! Inside it's just as pleasant—all around, a good place to stay if you want to combine the tranquility of a more "residential" neighborhood with the relative proximity of the livelier quarters like Montparnasse and St-Germain.

SETTING & FACILITIES
Location Invalides. **Nearest Métro Station** Varenne. **Quietness Rating** A. **Dining** €8.50 continental breakfast, served in the garden during summer. **Services** Reservations for shows, restaurants, cars.

ACCOMMODATIONS
Rooms 24. **All** TV, direct-dial phone, hair dryer. **Some** Bathtubs. **Comfort & Decor** French country-style dominates the decor of this tasteful and serene *hotel de charme*.

RATES, RESERVATIONS, & RESTRICTIONS
Pricing Double (shower, WC) €100–105, double (bath, WC) €120; extra bed €20, dog €4.50. **Credit Cards** AMEX, VISA. **Check-In/Out** Noon. **Elevator** Yes. **English Spoken** Yes.

HÔTEL DES ARÈNES   €100–145

OVERALL ★★★ | QUALITY ★★★½ | VALUE ★★★★ | 5TH *ARRONDISSEMENT*

51, rue Monge, 75005; 01 43 25 09 26; fax 01 43 25 79 56; hoteldesarenes@wanadoo.fr

The Hôtel des Arènes has the advantage of being close to the Latin Quarter without being stuck in the congestion of central Paris. Its view onto the Arènes, its proximity to the open market at Place Monge, and its easy access to the Métro all speak favorably of this choice of hotel. The hotel brochure says that Notre Dame is "two steps away." Count on a 15-minute walk. The hotel suffers at times from being understaffed. When we stopped by a small group had just arrived and the receptionist was overwhelmed; we had to wait a long time to ask a question. The rooms are all very neat and clean, modern but not sophisticated in design, and well maintained. The rooms in the back have wonderful views of the Roman arena, and you should insist on one of these.

SETTING & FACILITIES
Location Latin Quarter. **Nearest Métro Station** Cardinal Lemoine, Place Monge. **Quietness Rating** B. **Dining** €9 breakfast. **Amenities** Air-conditioned breakfast room. **Services** Nearby parking.

ACCOMMODATIONS
Rooms 52. **All** TV with satellite, direct-dial phone, mini-bar, safe deposit box, hair dryer. **Some** 2 rooms with disabled access, view of Roman arena. **Comfort & Decor** Modern and functional but not very stylish.

RATES, RESERVATIONS, & RESTRICTIONS
Pricing Single €100, double €125, triple €145. **Deposit** Credit card. **Credit Cards** VISA, MC, AMEX, DC. **Check-In/Out** Noon. **Elevator** Yes. **English Spoken** Yes. **Special Tips** Reserve at least 1 week in advance.

HÔTEL DES CHEVALIERS   €104–125

OVERALL ★★★ | QUALITY ★★★½ | VALUE ★★★★ | 4TH *ARRONDISSEMENT*

30, rue de Turenne, 75003; 01 42 72 73 47; fax 01 42 72 54 10; chevalier19@wanadoo.fr; www.parishotel.com

On a noisy street not far from the Place des Vosges, this was, like so many establishments in the neighborhood, a 17th-century *hôtel particulier* (private town house). Fresh flowers seem to gleam amid the yellow walls and ceiling of the bright check-in area. Drinks are available in a small ground-floor salon. Down a wooden staircase, the cellar hosts breakfasting guests in an atmosphere warmed by yellow tablecloths, a "western-style" ceiling fan, and upholstered chairs. The showpiece of this room is the ancient stone well, now of course decorative only. All rooms have fresh-cut flowers, renewed daily, and guests who stay at least several days receive a box of chocolate or a basket of fresh fruit. Staff is very attentive.

SETTING & FACILITIES
Location Bastille/République. **Nearest Métro Station** Chemin Vert, Saint-Paul-Le Marais. **Quietness Rating** A, with windows closed. **Dining** Continental/gourmand breakfast, 7–10 a.m., €9.15. **Services** Laundry, room service 7 a.m.–8 p.m., reservations for shows, restaurants, taxis.

ACCOMMODATIONS
Rooms 24. **All** TV with cable, direct-dial phone, mini-bar, safe deposit box, hair dryer. **Bathrooms** All. **Favorites** Quietest are 10, 11, 16, 21, 25, 31, 35, 41, 45, 51. **Comfort & Decor** Bright and well-lit, this hotel speaks of good manners, and simple elegance. The fresh flowers everywhere set the tone. Room 11, very well lit, is decorated in discrete, stately tones of gray throughout, accented at certain points with bordeaux.

RATES, RESERVATIONS, & RESTRICTIONS
Pricing Single €119–125, double €125. **Deposit** Fax credit card number to hold reservations. **Credit Cards** AMEX, EUROCARD, MC, VISA. **Check-In/Out** 11 a.m. **Elevator** Yes. **English Spoken** Yes. **Special Tips** Reserve 2 weeks in advance.

HÔTEL DES CROISÉS   €65–105

OVERALL ★★★½ | QUALITY ★★★★ | VALUE ★★★★★ | 9TH ARRONDISSEMENT

63, rue St Lazare, 75009; 01 48 74 78 24; fax 01 49 95 04 43; hotel-des-croises@wanadoo.fr

Whether you take the little, two-person elevator (it's the original and still has the small stool where the operator sat) or the carpet-covered staircase, it's not hard to imagine a day in the early life of this 19th-century hotel. One experienced guest remarked that his bathroom was large enough "to play racquetball in." The Hôtel des Croisés is perfect for seasoned travelers who don't mind being in a less chic neighborhood but appreciate the excellent price-quality relationship. Surprisingly, the Croisés is closer to the heart of town than you'd think, and an easy walk brings you to Place de la Madeleine and Concorde. The Métro is a 30-second jump from your front door. This hotel is frequented by French people from the provinces who've been staying here for years and knowledgeable tourists. For a room half the size you'd pay three times as much in the Marais or in Saint-Germain-des-Prés. This is the kind of place you'd have a hard time finding on your own, but once initiated you'll return and send your friends.

SETTING & FACILITIES
Location Grands Boulevards. **Nearest Métro Station** Trinité. **Quietness Rating** B and A (when windows are closed). **Dining** €6 continental breakfast. **Services** Room service 6:30 a.m.–7 p.m.

ACCOMMODATIONS
Rooms 27. **All** TV with satellite, direct-dial phone, hair dryer, air-conditioning, large bathtubs. **Some** Only 1 room with shower. **Comfort & Decor** The ceilings are high and, though no longer used, there's a fireplace in every room. Room 7, overlooking a courtyard, has red carpet, 2 red armchairs, and a well-lit, spacious bathroom whose toilet is separated by a partition from the bathtub and sink. Though its all-white bathroom is a bit smaller, room 8 is basically the same. The street-side room 10, decorated in greens and gray, is a suite with a fireplace in both the salon and bedroom but a relatively small bathroom. However, the upper floors sport rooms with spacious bathrooms with original tiles and massive bathtubs on feet.

RATES, RESERVATIONS, & RESTRICTIONS
Pricing Single €65–80, double €75–90, suite €100–105, extra bed €15 (room prices depend on season). **Credit Cards** VISA, MC, AMEX, DC. **Check-In/Out** 2 p.m./noon. **English Spoken** Yes.

HÔTEL DES DEUX-ÎLES   *€115–140*

OVERALL ★★★ | QUALITY ★★★★ | VALUE ★★★ | 4TH *ARRONDISSEMENT*

59, rue St-Louis-en-l'Île, 75004; 01 43 26 13 35; fax 01 43 29 60 25

You could almost spend your entire Paris stay here and not be bored: from the cellar's main salon, wander off into an adjoining, comfortably furnished, even more intimate room where you can chat in semiprivacy or enjoy some of its mini-library's guidebooks and beautifully bound 19th- and 20th-century works. A highly enjoyable mix of Anglo-Saxon solidity and the exoticism of the unexpected. Pluses include the stone-walled cellar, with its warm greens and browns (also found throughout the hotel's common areas); the very cozy bar area (with hunting-lodgesque pictures of ducks); and private-club atmosphere straight from a 1940s Hollywood film.

SETTING & FACILITIES
Location Islands. **Nearest Métro Station** Pont-Marie. **Quietness Rating** A in the back and B in the front. **Dining** €9 continental breakfast.

ACCOMMODATIONS
Rooms 17. **All** TV with cable, direct-dial phone, hair dryer, air conditioning. **Some:** Bathtubs. **Comfort & Decor** Bright rooms in greens and yellows, but not especially spacious. The little blue tiles in the bathrooms do a great job of reflecting light.

RATES, RESERVATIONS, & RESTRICTIONS
Pricing Ground-floor single/double €115, single (shower, WC) €120, double (bathtub, WC or shower, WC) €140. **Cancellation Policy** 1 week before arrival without any

charge. **Credit Cards** VISA, MC, AMEX. **Check-In/Out** Noon. **Elevator** Yes. **English Spoken** Yes. **Special Tips** Reserve 3–6 months in advance (more for autumn).

HÔTEL DES GRANDES ECOLES   €90–130

OVERALL ★★★★ | QUALITY ★★★★ | VALUE ★★★★★ | 5TH *ARRONDISSEMENT*

75, rue du Cardinal-Lemoine, 75005; 01 43 26 79 23; fax 01 43 25 28 15; hotel.grandes. ecoles@wanadoo.fr; www.hotel-grandes-ecoles.com

This former monastery is astonishingly pleasant. It's easy to miss if you don't know there is a hotel behind the green doors. You enter a little cobblestone driveway and find yourself in a charming park in front of a late-19th-century building. A sublime mixture of country and city, the Hôtel des Grandes Ecoles, with its main building (newly renovated) and two annexes, is one of Paris's best addresses. Breakfast is served in the parqueted salon, complete with piano and freshly cut flowers. Weather permitting, you can have your breakfast in the garden. The service is so friendly, you feel like you belong to the family. Reserve three or four weeks in advance.

SETTING & FACILITIES
Location Latin Quarter. **Nearest Métro Station** Cardinal-Lemoine, Monge. **Quietness Rating** A. **Dining** €7 breakfast. **Amenities** Parking (€20 a day).

ACCOMMODATIONS
Rooms 51, 3 with disabled access. **All** TV, phone, hair dryer, bathtub/shower, WC. **Bathrooms** Spacious, decorated in pastels and white. **Comfort & Decor** Here, you feel like a private guest in a private mansion at the end of the 19th century. Lacework and delicate decor surround you. Classy and rustic. For Paris, the rooms are very spacious.

RATES, RESERVATIONS, & RESTRICTIONS
Pricing Double €90–100 (main building), €100–105 (garden building), €95–130 (right wing, 3 or 4 people). **Credit Cards** VISA, MC. **Check-In/Out** Noon/11 a.m. **Elevator** In 2 of the 3 buildings. **English Spoken** Yes.

HÔTEL DES JARDINS DU LUXEMBOURG   €125–135

OVERALL ★★★ | QUALITY ★★★½ | VALUE ★★★ | 5TH *ARRONDISSEMENT*

5, impasse Royer-Collard, 75005; 01 40 46 08 88; fax 01 40 46 02 28; relaisstsulpice@ wanadoo.fr

For some, the fact that this was the hotel in which Sigmund Freud stayed in 1885 is an added delight. Others are just charmed by the colorful and inviting environment. The lobby, which also serves as an informal lounge for drinks and coffee, is covered in contemporary paintings, wrought-iron furniture, a fireplace, and a stylish mirror and coat rack on which a straw hat is always hanging. A great advantage to this hotel is its proximity to the Jardin du Luxembourg, perfect for jogging, picnicking, and relaxing strolls after a day of sightseeing. Off the lobby is an attractive spiral staircase that is primarily decorative.

SETTING & FACILITIES

Location Latin Quarter. **Nearest Métro Station** RER Luxembourg. **Quietness Rating** B. **Dining** €9.50 continental breakfast in your room, buffet downstairs. **Amenities** Small sauna (5). **Services** Laundry (if you ask for laundry service before 10 a.m. you can have your items back the same day).

ACCOMMODATIONS

Rooms 26, 2 with disabled access. **All** TV with satellite, direct-dial phone, mini-bar, safe deposit box, hair dryer, air-conditioning. **Some** Balconies. **Bathrooms** Tastefully decorated, capturing both contemporary design and turn-of-the-century aesthetics. **Comfort & Decor** Rooms face both the street and a tiny, flowered courtyard. Street-facing rooms come with small balconies. The ground-floor room, number 12, has been equipped for disabled guests.

RATES, RESERVATIONS, & RESTRICTIONS

Pricing Single or double with bathroom €125, deluxe double with bathroom €135. **Credit Cards** VISA, MC, AMEX, DC, JCB. **Check-In/Out** Noon. **Elevator** Yes. **English Spoken** Yes.

HÔTEL DES SAINTS-PÈRES   *€105–275*

OVERALL ★★★★ | QUALITY ★★★★½ | VALUE ★★★★ | 6TH *ARRONDISSEMENT*

65, rue des Sts-Pères, 75006; 01 45 44 50 00; fax 01 45 44 90 83; hotelsts.peres@wanadoo.fr; www.hotel-esprit-de-france.com

This 17th-century private town house belonged to one of Louis XIV's architects, who had the salon decorated by one of the artists from the Château de Versailles. Today this so-called fresco room is a spacious guest room (number 100), understandably much in demand and one of the main reasons many visitors seek out this hotel; charmingly, it is said to be reserved for couples as there is nothing but a simple screen—as opposed to a door—separating the bathroom (it has a round bathtub) from the bedroom. Of further historical note: from first to third floor, the staircase is the original. As is often the case in this neighborhood, the entryway is deceptive, giving the impression from the exterior of a rather small establishment, only to seem to expand as soon as the visitor crosses the threshold. A highlight is the garden, visible through glass walls from the check-in desk and surrounding area, where breakfast is served on rattan furniture from 9:30 a.m. (so as not to disturb the guests in the 32 of 39 rooms that overlook this little treasure) to 11 a.m. A ground-floor bar with comfortable caramel-colored leather furniture is open until 8 p.m. every day except Sunday. Reserve one month in advance.

SETTING & FACILITIES

Location Saint-Germain-des-Prés. **Nearest Métro Station** Saint-Germain-des-Prés, Sèvres Babylone. **Quietness Rating** A (triple-glass windows). **Dining** €10 continental breakfast. **Services** Room service 7:15 a.m.–noon.

ACCOMMODATIONS

Rooms 39. **All** TV with satellite, direct-dial phone, mini-bar, hair dryer. **Some** View of the little garden, air-conditioning. **Comfort & Decor** Although room 114 is the least favorite because of its placement (its view is of the garden's floor tiles rather than the garden itself and its ceiling is somewhat low) it has some unique features: a "raised" bedroom (once in the room, you have to go up several steps), exposed beams, two large windows (the other overlooks the street), and an 18th-century desk and engraving. As in many French houses and apartments, the WC is separate from the rest of what we call the bathroom.

RATES, RESERVATIONS, & RESTRICTIONS

Pricing Double (shower, WC) €105, twin or double (bathroom, WC) €120–185, suite €275. **Credit Cards** AMEX, MC, VISA, CB. **Check-In/Out** 12:30 p.m./noon. **Not Allowed** Dogs. **English Spoken** Yes.

HÔTEL DES TUILERIES   €120–335

OVERALL ★★★½ | QUALITY ★★★★ | VALUE ★★★★ | 1ST ARRONDISSEMENT

10, rue St-Hyacinthe, 75001; 01 42 61 04 17; fax 01 49 27 91 56; htuileri@aol.com; www.hotel-des-tuileries.com

The welcome is warm and family-like (the hotel enjoys a good amount of repeat business), and once you're at the check-in desk the soft light from its big lamp makes you forget the entryway's rather dark appearance. The guest-floor corridors are not well lit either, but they are pleasant nonetheless. There is a breakfast salon and, in the cellar, a sitting room with stone walls and a vaulted ceiling. The lively neighborhood boasts many Paris "musts," including the Louvre. Ask for rooms with a view of the courtyard if you want silence. Rooms on the street are a little noisy during the summer months, but you have a wonderful view on a calm little street.

SETTING & FACILITIES

Location Champs-Elysées/Concorde. **Nearest Métro Station** Tuileries, Pyramides. **Quietness Rating** B. **Dining** €10 breakfast. **Amenities** Parking nearby (open 24 hours). **Services** Laundry, room service.

ACCOMMODATIONS

Rooms 26. **All** TV with cable, phone, mini-bar, safe, hair dryer. **Some** Family-friendly. **Comfort & Decor** The more traditional rooms, whose decor varies according to room size, are generally done in pastels, with paintings above headboards; modern rooms have striped curtains with touches of red and wooden ceilings in the bathroom. Doubles are truly doubles, featuring two bedrooms separated by their own corridors and are usually reserved for families (you can tell which is the designated children's room right away by its lively blue tones).

RATES, RESERVATIONS, & RESTRICTIONS
Pricing Single €120–185, double €135–215, triple €200–230, suite €260–335, dog €4.
Credit Cards VISA, MC, AMEX, DC, JCB. **Check-In/Out** Noon/11 a.m. **Elevator** Yes.
English Spoken Yes.

HÔTEL DU CHAMP-DE-MARS   €60–85

OVERALL ★★★★ | QUALITY ★★★★ | VALUE ★★★★★ | 7TH *ARRONDISSEMENT*

7, rue du Champ-de-Mars, 75007; 01 45 51 52 30; fax 01 45 51 64 36; stg@club-internet.fr; www.hotel-du-champ-de-mars.com

Near a lively, outdoor market/pedestrian street, the hotel's warm, homey atmosphere is best reflected by the sitting area, where magazines are available to guests relaxing in red-and-yellow-striped armchairs. Of course, the absolute main attraction is the hotel's perpetual proximity to the Eiffel Tower, which you come to understand better when you live near it and walk under it often. Reserve early, because this little hotel fills up well in advance.

SETTING & FACILITIES
Location Invalides. **Nearest Métro Station** Ecole-Militaire, RER: Pont de l'Alma Invalides. **Quietness Rating** A and B (sound-proof windows). **Dining** €6 continental breakfast

ACCOMMODATIONS
Rooms 25. **All** TV with cable, direct-dial phone, hair dryer. **Comfort & Decor** While the decor of the small cellar/breakfast room (only 3 tables) is a bit busy and less attractive than that of the rest of the hotel, the comfort factor does not suffer for it—unless you're a smoker: a blackboard reminds you that this is a nonsmoking area!

RATES, RESERVATIONS, & RESTRICTIONS
Pricing Single (shower, WC) €60, single (bath, WC) €65, double (shower, WC) €60, double (bath, WC) €65, twin (bath, WC) €70, triple (bath, WC) €85. **Credit Cards** All major credit cards. **Check-In/Out** Noon. **Not Allowed** Large pets. **Elevator** Yes.
English Spoken Yes.

HÔTEL DU CYGNE   €65–100

OVERALL ★★★ | QUALITY ★★★½ | VALUE ★★★★★ | 1ST *ARRONDISSEMENT*

3, rue du Cygne, 75001; 01 42 60 14 16; fax 01 42 21 37 02; hotel.cygne2freesurf.fr

This is a friendly place. You may not love the old-fashioned aesthetics and the 1950s decor, but you will feel welcome and comfortable. The most pleasant spot in the hotel is the bright and cozy breakfast nook, which feels like a veranda and is filled with plants. From the lobby, a 17th-century staircase with original beams leads up to the five floors. The hallways are covered in coffee-colored fabric, which darkens the atmosphere but goes well with the staircase and is not offensive. This hotel is well run, the service is friendly, and the owner attempts to please her guests. A surprisingly good deal for central Paris.

SETTING & FACILITIES

Location Châtelet–Les Halles. **Nearest Métro Station** Etienne-Marcel, RER Châtelet–Les Halles. **Quietness Rating** B. **Dining** €6 breakfast.

ACCOMMODATIONS

Rooms 20. **All** TV, direct-dial phone, hair dryer. **Some** Safe, shower and WC, 2 with sink only. **Comfort & Decor** The rooms are spacious for Paris. Room 35 is by far the prettiest, and the owner assigns it only to the most "deserving" guests (we have no idea how one becomes deserving). We like the little salon with its red sofa, which folds out into a third bed. Up a step, you'll find the bedroom and another roomy, white bedroom. Room 41, under the eaves, is very pleasant, with a sunroof window. The bathroom, though, only has a swinging barroom door, so privacy is limited.

RATES, RESERVATIONS, & RESTRICTIONS

Pricing Single (sink only) €65, single (shower, WC) €70, double (shower, WC) €85, double (bath, WC) €90, room 35 €100. **Credit Cards** AMEX, MC, VISA, DC. **Check-In/Out** 1 p.m./noon. **Elevator** No. **English Spoken** Yes.

HÔTEL DU DANEMARK   €110–135

OVERALL ★★★ | QUALITY ★★★½ | VALUE ★★★ | 6TH *ARRONDISSEMENT*

21, rue Vavin, 75006; 01 43 26 93 78; fax 01 46 34 66 06; paris@hoteldanemark.com

Like beautiful serving pieces in a Scandinavian tableware shop, the entryway is all in blue. The basement breakfast room features the fun of café-style tables and chairs. Smack in the middle of Lost Generation territory, the hotel boasts a Hemingway sighting—on a visit to Simone de Beauvoir, who lived in the hotel and ate in the restaurant now called Le Vavin (Le Pagès in her day) on the nearby square.

SETTING & FACILITIES

Location Montparnasse. **Nearest Métro Station** Notre-Dame-des-Champs. **Quietness Rating** B (sound-proof windows). **Dining** €8.50 continental breakfast. **Amenities** Parking nearby.

ACCOMMODATIONS

Rooms 15. **All** Satellite TV, direct-dial phone, hair dryer, mini-bar. **Some** Jacuzzi. **Comfort & Decor** An interesting juxtaposition of the old exposed-stone walls and the sleek, modern, all-black check-in area, peppered with plants. Rooms are spotless and freshly renovated. Bright tones, quilted beds, recessed wall fixtures.

RATES, RESERVATIONS, & RESTRICTIONS

Pricing Double or twin €110, room with Jacuzzi €135. **Credit Cards** All major credit cards. **Check-In/Out** Noon. **Elevator** Yes. **English Spoken** Yes.

HÔTEL DUC DE SAINT-SIMON   €195–310

OVERALL ★★★★½ | QUALITY ★★★★½ | VALUE ★★★ | 7TH ARRONDISSEMENT

14, rue St-Simon, 75007; 01 44 39 20 20; fax 01 45 48 68 25; duc.de.saint.simon@wanadoo.fr

In the otherwise nonstop noise section of Saint-Germain-des-Prés, this hotel's quiet street puts you in a vacation mood before you've even set your bags down. You reach the 18th-century building by crossing a large, well-lit, cobblestoned courtyard whose proliferation of plants casts an agreeable green glow. Converted to a hotel in 1905, the establishment was enlarged in 1950 by combining with an even older neighboring structure, then redone 30 years later. Furnishings are a melange of the classics (Louis XIV, XV, XVI, and Napoléon III). Chandeliers (even in the guest rooms) and fresh flowers abound, and the check-in area looks like a room in a private home. Breakfast is served in a huge, colorful, well-lit, vaulted cellar composed of refreshment-specific rooms (drinks, afternoon tea) with stone walls. Though the rooms have no mini-bar, the hotel will provide bottled water and other beverages on request. If you stay more than three days, you receive a box of chocolates from the management. Interestingly, the hotel created its own set of dishes, their decoration designed to go with the curtains and furniture of the common areas. Service is excellent; the English director, characteristically refined and customer-oriented, leaves no doubt in her guests' minds that she is there to make their stay as perfect as possible.

SETTING & FACILITIES

Location Saint-Germain-des-Prés. **Nearest Métro Station** Rue-du-Bac. **Quietness Rating** A. **Dining** Bar where you can order breakfast, tea, or a light snack or enjoy a drink; €12 for breakfast. **Amenities** Parking nearby. **Services** Room service 7:30 a.m.–10:15 p.m.

ACCOMMODATIONS

Rooms 34. **All** Phone, individual safe. **Some** Showers with bath. **Bathrooms** Only 4 rooms have a shower stall in addition to the bathtub. **Comfort & Decor** Specify whether you want a room overlooking the garden (16 of the rooms—no air-conditioning here, as these rooms tend to remain cool) or courtyard (5 of the rooms). All rooms are different: number 7 (in the 17th-century wing) has a king-size bed and spacious closets; number 6—with garden view—a European-style bed, exposed beams, and a towel dryer.

RATES, RESERVATIONS, & RESTRICTIONS

Pricing Double €195–235, twin €230–250, suite €305–310; extra bed for 30%. Rooms not vacated by noon will be charged an extra night; premature departure also will be charged an extra night. **Deposit** First night. Cancellation must be received 48 hours before arrival. **Credit Cards** AMEX, MC, EUROCARD, VISA. **Check-In/Out** 2 p.m./noon. **Not Allowed** Dogs. **Elevator** Yes. **English Spoken** Yes.

HÔTEL ESMÉRALDA   €30–90

OVERALL ★★½ | QUALITY ★★★½ | VALUE ★★★★★ | 5TH ARRONDISSEMENT

4, rue St-Julien le Pauvre, 75005; 01 43 54 19 20; fax 01 40 51 00 68

What's impressive about this spot is its Middle Ages ambience. Dark and gloomy but very authentic with exposed stone, beams, and aged wood everywhere. Informal service may be a plus or a minus for you. Wonderfully situated at the edge of Notre-Dame, this is a perfect spot for poets and bohemians. Shakespeare & Company Bookshop is just around the corner. Some visitors love staying here, but claustrophobes should go elsewhere.

SETTING & FACILITIES
Location Latin Quarter. **Nearest Métro Station** St-Michel. **Quietness Rating** B. **Dining** €6 continental breakfast.

ACCOMMODATIONS
Rooms 19. **Some** 3 have just a sink, 4 have a shower and WC, 12 have a bath, WC. **Bathrooms** Tiny and not well equipped. **Comfort & Decor** Due to the age of the building, the hotel tends to be dusty and poorly aired. The green tapestry in the corridors is sad and a bit tasteless, and the rooms are very cramped. Room decor leaves a lot to be desired. Old and musty. The rooms that look onto Notre-Dame are by far the best, and you'll need to reserve these 3 months in advance.

RATES, RESERVATIONS, & RESTRICTIONS
Pricing Single €30 (no shower, no WC), €49 (shower, WC); double €50 (shower, WC), €64, €69, €75 (bath, WC, view on Notre-Dame); triple €84 (bath, WC, view on Notre-Dame); four people €91 (bath, WC, view on Notre-Dame). **Deposit** Reserve 3 months in advance. **Credit Cards** Not accepted. **Check-In/Out** Noon. **Elevator** No. **English Spoken** Some.

HÔTEL EUGÉNIE   €90–120

OVERALL ★★★ | QUALITY ★★★ | VALUE ★★★★ | 6TH ARRONDISSEMENT

31, St-André-des-Arts, 75006; 01 43 26 29 03; fax 01 43 29 75 60; eugenie-hotel@ wanadoo.fr, www.123france.com

The staff and the decor are bright, warm, and welcoming. A little TV salon makes you feel like you're at home, and a grand stairway makes you feel like you're away. Often ignored by the guides, this address, newly renovated, merits the attention of people who care about feeling comfortable as opposed to being engulfed in material comfort. The great thing about staying here is the location. Two steps from St-Michel, the busy pedestrian street on which this hotel is perched is one of Paris's liveliest, cluttered with bars, restaurants, boutiques, and galleries. Make reservations three weeks in advance.

SETTING & FACILITIES
Location Saint-Germain-des-Prés. **Nearest Métro Station** St-Michel. **Quietness Rating** B. **Dining** €6 breakfast.

ACCOMMODATIONS
Rooms 30. **All** Satellite TV, direct-dial phone, mini-bar, hair dryer, air-conditioning, safe. **Bathrooms** Contemporary. **Comfort & Decor** The caramel-colored wooden furniture adds a pleasant note throughout.

RATES, RESERVATIONS, & RESTRICTIONS
Pricing Single €90, double €110, triple €120. **Credit Cards** VISA, MC, AMEX, DC, JCB. **Check-In/Out** After noon/11 a.m. **Not Allowed** Pets. **Elevator** Yes. **English Spoken** Yes.

HÔTEL FAVART   €85–105

OVERALL ★★★ | QUALITY ★★★½ | VALUE ★★★★ | 2ND *ARRONDISSEMENT*

5, rue Marivaux, 75002; 01 42 97 59 83; fax 01 40 15 95 58; favart.hotel@wanadoo.fr

We love the fact that the Spanish painter Goya stayed here. There is even a room called the *chambre Goya*. The area is characterized by its theatrical past, and you'll enjoy being both in the calm of a small street and the bustle of central Paris. The rue and the hotel were named after the 18th-century playwright by the same name, an author who influenced Voltaire greatly. You are equidistant from the Grands Boulevards and the Palais-Royale, making shopping, theatergoing, and late-night strolls easy and pleasurable. The spacious lobby is studded with marble columns and a stairway that leads to the rooms.

SETTING & FACILITIES
Location Châtelet–Les Halles. **Nearest Métro Station** Châtelet–Les Halles. **Quietness Rating** B. **Dining** Breakfast included in room rates. **Services** Laundry.

ACCOMMODATIONS
Rooms 37. **All** TV, direct-dial phone, mini-bar. **Bathrooms** Modern and comfortable, although a bit oddly decorated with trompe-l'oeil motifs. **Comfort & Decor** Try to get a room higher than the second floor, where the rooms are large and bright.

RATES, RESERVATIONS, & RESTRICTIONS
Pricing Single €85, double €105. **Credit Cards** All major credit cards. **Check-In/Out** Noon/11 a.m. **Elevator** Yes. **English Spoken** Yes.

HÔTEL ISTRIA   €90–100

OVERALL ★★★★ | QUALITY ★★★★ | VALUE ★★★★ | 14TH *ARRONDISSEMENT*

29, rue Campagne-Première, 75014; 01 43 20 91 82; fax 01 43 22 48 45

When you choose a hotel in Montparnasse it's not easy to avoid bumping into the ghosts of its most celebrated denizens. In this case (an establishment mentioned in the Michelin and Hôtels de Charme guides), you'll be rubbing spiritual elbows with some of the best of 'em—Man Ray, Josephine Baker, Erik Satie, all of whom lived here. And as if the guardian angel of them all, a little statue of Charlie Chaplin graces the charming, well-lit salon. Monsieur Cretey and his fine, customer-oriented team keep everything in very good condition.

SETTING & FACILITIES
Location Montparnasse. **Nearest Métro Station** Raspail. **Quietness Rating** A and B (sound-proof windows). **Dining** €7 generous continental breakfast. **Services** Reservations for theaters, restaurants.

ACCOMMODATIONS
Rooms 26. **All** TV, direct-dial phone, hair dryer, individual safe. **Bathrooms** Rather small (triangular shower stalls save space). **Comfort & Decor** Rooms are decorated in a simple, pleasant style.

RATES, RESERVATIONS, & RESTRICTIONS
Pricing Single or double €90, twin €100, dog €7.50. **Deposit** One-night deposit is requested for all reservations. **Credit Cards** All major credit cards. **Check-In/Out** Noon/11 a.m. **Elevator** Yes. **English Spoken** Yes.

HÔTEL LE BOUQUET DE MONTMARTRE   €60

OVERALL ★★½ | QUALITY ★★★ | VALUE ★★★★★ | 18TH *ARRONDISSEMENT*

1, rue Durantin, 75018; 01 46 06 87 54; fax 01 46 06 09 09; www.bouquetdemontmartre. com

As with much else in Montmartre, you have to climb—in this case, a flight of stairs (about ten steps) to get to the front door. Once inside, check out the breakfast room, where a wooden statue of a maître d' holds a tray filled with business cards for the taking. The room's soft colors, green plants, little tables, and upholstered chairs give the salon a turn-of-the-century feel. Not all that impressive from the outside, this hotel grows on you, and you'll enjoy being in Montmartre. Everything is a matter of taste, and here, either you love being immersed in it or you'll be amused by a style you'll see as kitsch. In any case, the rapport between price and quality is exceptional.

SETTING & FACILITIES
Location Montmartre. **Nearest Métro Station** Abbesses. **Quietness Rating** C. **Dining** €4.50 continental breakfast. **Amenities** Safe.

ACCOMMODATIONS
Rooms 36. **All** Phone, WC, bath or shower. **Comfort & Decor** The rooms are a bit dark and overdecorated with tradition, flowered wallpaper, motif bedspreads, and patterned carpet, but this adds up to indulgence in a period. Room 43 has an excellent view of Paris.

RATES, RESERVATIONS, & RESTRICTIONS
Pricing Double €60. **Credit Cards** VISA, MC. **Check-In/Out** 3 p.m./noon. **Elevator** No. **English Spoken** Some.

HÔTEL LE LIDO   €125–170

OVERALL ★★★½ | QUALITY ★★★½ | VALUE ★★★★ | 8TH *ARRONDISSEMENT*

4, passage Madeleine, 75008; 01 42 66 27 37; fax 01 42 66 61 23; lido@paris-hotels-charme.com

Dating from the 19th century, the hotel became a three-star establishment 12 years ago. It's very quiet, as its dead-end street has almost no traffic and little pedestrian noise. A plus is the staff, which does an excellent job of combining cordiality and professionalism. The interior leaves no doubt that you're in the old world, with its tasteful and luxurious salons, some period furniture, old country-scene tapestries, stone walls, exposed beams, and small lamps softly lighting it all. Don't miss the mini-greenhouse in one of the salons and the turn-of-the-century baby carriage transformed into a flowerpot. Breakfast is served in the cellar, whose decorative elements match those of the floors above it. Reserve three weeks in advance.

SETTING & FACILITIES
Location Concorde/Champs-Elysées. **Nearest Métro Station** Madeleine. **Dining** €9 breakfast. **Quietness Rating** A (windows closed) or B. **Amenities** Small parking lot. **Services** Reservations for shows, restaurants.

ACCOMMODATIONS
Rooms 32. **All** TV with cable, direct-dial phone, hair dryer, air-conditioning, mini-bar, individual safe. **Comfort & Decor** Rooms are draped in traditional patterned bedspreads, wallpaper, and curtains, adding to the exposed beam ceilings to create an ambience of old-world quaintness.

RATES, RESERVATIONS, & RESTRICTIONS
Pricing Single €127–149, double €142–168, extra bed €15. **Credit Cards** All major credit cards. **Check-In/Out** 1 p.m./noon. **Not Allowed** Big dogs. **Elevator** Yes. **English Spoken** Yes.

HÔTEL LIBERTEL GRAND TURENNE   €133–183

OVERALL ★★★ | QUALITY ★★★ | VALUE ★★★★ | 4TH *ARRONDISSEMENT*

6, rue de Turenne, 75004; 01 42 78 43 25; fax 01 42 74 10 74; www.libertel-hotels.com

Although the lobby is comfortable, tasteful, and welcoming (receptionists wear name tags), you know you're in a chain. And this was our only reservation about this address. Rooms, all a bit different in blue/white or green/white, make attentive use of old etchings of Paris to remind visitors of the city's historical richness. Depending on the room, you can have a good view of l'Hôtel de Sully or its gardens, or the Dôme de Saint-Paul. Several rooms are set aside for nonsmokers. Rooms are small, but anyone who has been to Paris before is not bothered by the size here; in fact, the drawers and closet make up for the lack of space and are appreciable. Bathrooms are perfectly adapted to international standards and even have towel heaters.

SETTING & FACILITIES
Location The Marais. **Nearest Métro Station** Saint-Paul or Bastille. **Dining** €13 breakfast. **Amenities** Safe. **Services** Laundry, room service.

ACCOMMODATIONS
Rooms 41, 5 suites. **All** TV with cable, phone, double-pane windows. **Some** 6 w/shower, WC. **Bathrooms** 35 rooms w/bath. **Comfort & Decor** Comfortable and modern, the decor leans toward the practical rather than the authentic.

RATES, RESERVATIONS, & RESTRICTIONS
Pricing Single €128–151, double €141–166, junior suite €198–233, extra bed €25. **Deposit** Fax credit card number to hold reservations. **Credit Cards** VISA, MC, AMEX, DC. **Check-In/Out** Noon. **Elevator** Yes. **English Spoken** Yes.

HÔTEL LUTÉTIA   €350–760

OVERALL ★★★★½ | QUALITY ★★★★★ | VALUE ★★★ | 6TH *ARRONDISSEMENT*

45, boulevard Raspail, 75006; 01 49 54 46 46; fax 01 49 54 46 00; lutetia-paris@lutetia-paris.com; www.lutetia-paris.com

Once you've passed under the stately awning and through the gleaming revolving doors of this 90-year-old hotel, the real treat begins. As with all great classic hotel-palaces of Europe, the immense entrance hall, with its high ceiling and grand chandelier, will take your breath away. The word *palace* keeps coming to mind as the glitter from the numerous chandeliers highlights the richness of the red decor (furniture, marble columns, carpets) and the corps of uniformed receptionists busy themselves with your exigencies. Ask for a top-floor room for both quiet (though the insulated windows throughout the hotel take care of that) and view (great rooftops, the Invalides dome if the angle is right). This hotel served as Gestapo headquarters during World War II and, appropriately enough, as a post-Liberation center where families could inquire about and be reunited with loved ones who had been deported. For romantic occasions, ask for the Eiffel Tower suite, which affords a view of the tower from every window.

SETTING & FACILITIES
Location Invalides. **Nearest Métro Station** Sèvres-Babylone. **Quietness Rating** A (windows closed), C (windows opened). **Dining** Restaurant Paris and brasserie; €10 continental breakfast, €15 breakfast buffet, or €20 in room. **Amenities** Health club, business center. **Services** Room service 24 hours.

ACCOMMODATIONS
Rooms 250. **All** TV with cable, direct-dial phone, mini-bar, safe deposit box, hair dryer, air-conditioning. **Some** Fax. **Comfort & Decor** The art deco decor in the rooms is courtesy of Sonia Rykiel (whose workshop and boutique are not too far away). Spaciousness and marble bathrooms add to the allure. In room 611, overlooking boulevard Raspail, there is a little salon with a television.

RATES, RESERVATIONS, & RESTRICTIONS
Pricing Double €350, junior suite €610, suite €760, extra bed €90. **Credit Cards** VISA, MC, AMEX, DC, JCB. **Check-In/Out** 2 p.m./noon. **Elevator** Yes. **English Spoken** Yes.

HÔTEL PARC SAINT-SÉVERIN   €85–245

OVERALL ★★★★ | QUALITY ★★★★ | VALUE ★★★ | 5TH *ARRONDISSEMENT*

22, rue de la Parcheminerie, 75005; 01 43 54 32 17; fax 01 43 54 70 71; hotel.par.severin@wanadoo.fr; www.esprit-de-france.com

Walk in and you enter the decor of an Agatha Christie novel set in the south of France—with a slightly contemporary, efficient touch. The open office area near the reception desk could double as a private library, and the warmth of the red carpet contrasts comfortably with the salon's citrus-colored cushions on airy white furniture and the floors of pastel (mostly orange) corridors. Hallways host paintings, photos, and somewhat modern-looking gray doors. (Try not to notice the praying oriental statue or the curious fruit tree—both near the ground-floor elevator.)

SETTING & FACILITIES
Location Latin Quarter. **Nearest Métro Station** Cluny-La Sorbonne, St-Michel, RER St-Michel. **Quietness Rating** B, A when windows are closed. **Dining** €8.50 continental breakfast in rooms, buffet in the dining room.

ACCOMMODATIONS
Rooms 27. **All** Air-conditioning, TV with satellite, direct-dial phone, mini-bar, safe deposit box, hair dryer. **Bathrooms** Bathrooms are white and spacious, though not disabled-

adapted. **Comfort & Decor** Although the entrance is on the small rue de la Parcheminerie, many of the rooms offer a view of the place de l'Eglise Saint-Sévrin. Sit in the yellow-upholstered white rattan furniture of room 60—bright and unexpectedly spacious for a French hotel—and gaze out at the church itself, or commune with neighborhood rooftops, the St-Séverin cloister, and the Musée de Cluny gardens from a window on the fifth floor and up. Asking for a corner room on the top floor will get you a balcony as well. A plus is the quiet, whether due to the insulated windows or—even with windows wide open—the general calm of the immediate area, all the more surprising given the proximity to the lively boulevard St-Michel and rue St-Jacques.

RATES, RESERVATIONS, & RESTRICTIONS
Pricing Single €85–155 (bathroom, WC), double €100–170, double with large balcony €170–245, extra bed €17. **Credit Cards** AMEX, DC, MC, VISA, JCB. **Check-In/Out** Noon. **Not Allowed** Dogs. **Elevator** Yes. **English Spoken** Yes.

HÔTEL RÉCAMIER €80–190

OVERALL ★★★½ | QUALITY ★★★★ | VALUE ★★★★ | 6TH ARRONDISSEMENT

3 bis, place St-Sulpice, 75006; 01 43 26 04 89; fax 01 46 33 27 73

Reasonable prices, given the area, are small compensation for a mediocre staff attitude. Once inside, though, you'll find it rather bright and garden-like—due to both green plants and floral upholstery. A Parisian guest deemed it *très Parisien*. Its very slight distance from the Place St-Sulpice affords the best of two worlds: the quiet of a side street and the advantages of being so close to shopping and cafés. Reserve two weeks in advance.

SETTING & FACILITIES
Location Saint-Germain-des-Prés. **Nearest Métro Station** St-Sulpice. **Quietness Rating** B (no sound-proof windows). **Dining** Breakfast included in room rates. **Amenities** Parking nearby.

ACCOMMODATIONS
Rooms 30. **Some** 2 have no WC, no shower; 7 have sink, WC, no shower. **Comfort & Decor** Bright and floral, decorated in pastels and antique-style wallpaper.

RATES, RESERVATIONS, & RESTRICTIONS
Pricing Single (sink, WC) €80, single (shower or bath, WC) €95, double (sink, WC) €90, double (shower or bath, WC) €100, twin (shower, WC) €100, twin (shower or bath, WC, view) €115, triple €140, quad €190. **Credit Cards** MC, VISA. **Check-In/Out** Noon. **Not Allowed** Big dogs. **Elevator** Yes. **English Spoken** Some.

HÔTEL REGINA €270–640

OVERALL ★★★★½ | QUALITY ★★★★½ | VALUE ★★ | 1ST ARRONDISSEMENT

2, Place des Pyramides, 75001; 01 42 60 31 10; fax 01 40 15 95 16; sales@regina-hotel.com; www.regina-hotel.com

The location of this absolute jewel of a hotel is ideal—on the Right Bank rue de Rivoli near the Louvre (at the edge of the Jardin des Tuileries), the Opéra Garnier, Châtelet–Les Halles, and Place de la Concorde, but just a short walk to the Left Bank, Saint-Germain-des-Prés, and the Latin Quarter. The turn-of-the-century Regina, with its 120 rooms and suites furnished in original Louis XV, Louis XVI, and Directoire styles, has both the charm of a small hotel and the efficiency and grandeur of a large one. Why stay here? 1. Location 2. Spacious rooms 3. Sumptuous lobby and public spaces 4. Original art nouveau decor 5. Top rate restaurant, the "Pluvinel," and quaint tea room/Bar Anglais.

SETTING & FACILITIES

Location Right Bank. **Nearest Métro Station** Louvre. **Quietness Rating** A. **Dining** Award-winning restaurant "Le Pluvinel" serves classical French cuisine; seats 45. Open 7–10 a.m. for breakfast (€15.25 continental, €23 buffet), noon–2:30 p.m. for lunch, and 7–10 p.m. for dinner. Drinks and snacks in sumptuously decorated Bar Anglais. **Amenities** Air-conditioning, but windows open out to either a non-obstructed view of the Tuileries Gardens or a quiet, landscaped courtyard. **Services** Room service 7 a.m.–10 p.m., 24-hour porter service, baby-sitting, laundry.

ACCOMMODATIONS

Rooms 49 doubles, 3 singles, 53 twins, all with bath. Select triple and quad rooms, 14 suites. **All** Lovely bathrooms, authentic period-piece furniture, TV with satellite, direct-dial phone with dataport, mini-bar. **Some** Disabled access. Entire 2nd floor is nonsmoking. **Bathrooms** Massive, original ceramic sinks. **Favorites** Rooms 118, 218, 318, 418, and 518 have spectacular views of the Tuileries Gardens, and these rooms can open up into the next room to create suites. **Comfort & Decor** Two-tone 1900s marble floors everywhere. Green original ceramic wall tiles on all the floors, plus copper beds, lovely coiffeuse (make-up tables), and tissu broché fabric on walls. Majestic high ceilings in all rooms, except for the 6th floor. The elegance of the age in which this hotel was built has been preserved, and here you feel princely (and princessly)—a rather rare sensation these days, and well worth the money once in a while. We love the abundance of Aubuisson tapestries, ceramic details, gold-plated stucco, the Louis XV chests of drawers, and the original, painted glass "vitrine" in the restaurant. Every room is painted in trompe l'oeil style, with green paint creating knotty grain of fine beech.

RATES, RESERVATIONS, & RESTRICTIONS

Pricing Singles €270–315, doubles, €315–365, junior suites €442–487, suites €594–640, €65 extra bed. **Deposit** Reservation held with credit card. **Credit Cards** AMEX, VISA, MC, JCB. **Check-In/Out** Noon. **Elevator** Yes. **English Spoken** Yes.

HÔTEL SAINT-PAUL LE MARAIS   €95–285

OVERALL ★★★★ | QUALITY ★★★★½ | VALUE ★★★★ | 4TH *ARRONDISSEMENT*

8, rue de Sévigné, 75004; 01 48 04 97 27; fax 01 48 87 37 04; stpaulmarais@hotellerie.net; www.hotel-paris-marais.com

Here is a hotel that has a lot going for it, with a dynamic, service-conscious, and particularly friendly owner, who has run the show for over a decade. A bright, airy interior with contemporary paintings by an excellent local painter named Joulin and black-leather armchairs dominate the lobby, which nonetheless was renovated in 1999. Comfort reigns in this small hôtel du charme, and everything from the vaulted breakfast room downstairs to the flowering courtyard has been conceived to please its visitors. One of the best places we visited in the area at this price level.

SETTING & FACILITIES
Location The Marais. **Nearest Métro Station** St-Paul, Bastille. **Quietness Rating** B. **Dining** €9 buffet breakfast. **Amenities** Beauty institute, parking nearby. **Services** Laundry.

ACCOMMODATIONS
Rooms 27. **All** TV with cable, direct-dial phone, safe deposit box, tea/coffee, sound-proof windows, hair dryer. **Comfort & Decor** Some rooms offer spectacular features such as lots of space, a Jacuzzi, cloth wall covering, high ceilings, and other particularly elegant touches.

RATES, RESERVATIONS, & RESTRICTIONS
Pricing Single, off-season €95, high season €110; double or twin, off-season €110, high season €125; double luxe, off-season €145–160, high season €160–165; mini-suite, off-season €145, high season €160; luxe suite off-season €240, high season €285. **Credit Cards** VISA, MC. **Check-In/Out** 3:15 p.m./noon. **Not Allowed** Dogs (unless well behaved). **Elevator** Yes. **English Spoken** Yes.

HÔTEL SÉVIGNÉ   €55–80

OVERALL ★★½ | QUALITY ★★★ | VALUE ★★★★ | 4TH *ARRONDISSEMENT*

2, rue Malher, 75004; 01 42 72 76 17; fax 01 42 78 68 26; message.le-sevigne@wanadoo.fr; www.le-sevigne.com

It's often difficult finding an available room in the Marais, so it's good to keep a few trustworthy addresses on hand. The Sévigné enjoys an excellent location on the rue Malher near the Fgb. Saint Antoine, a stone's throw from the exquisite facade of the St-Antoine church. This a reliable address at a very reasonable price in one of Paris's most popular areas. The lobby and reception area doubles up in the mornings as the breakfast room, but for €3.50 for breakfast you can't go wrong. The hotel was named after the celebrated Marquise de Sévigné, best known for her stunning letters and journal, which depict Paris under the reign of Louis XIV.

SETTING & FACILITIES
Location The Marais. **Nearest Métro Station** St-Paul, Bastille. **Quietness Rating** B. **Dining** €3.50 breakfast (7:30–9:30 a.m.).

ACCOMMODATIONS

Rooms 29. **All** TV with satellite, direct-dial phone. **Comfort & Decor** The rooms are comfortable and clean but nothing special. The overall feel is functional.

RATES, RESERVATIONS, & RESTRICTIONS

Pricing Single (shower, WC) €55, double (shower, WC) €60, twin (shower, WC) €65, triple (shower, WC) €80. **Credit Cards** VISA, MC. **Check-In/Out** Noon/11:30 a.m. **Elevator** Yes. **English Spoken** Yes.

L'HÔTEL   €235–685

OVERALL ★★★★½ | QUALITY ★★★★★ | VALUE ★★★ | 6TH *ARRONDISSEMENT*

13, rue des Beaux-Arts, 75006, 01 44 41 99 00; fax 01 43 25 64 81; reservation@l-hotel.com; www.l-hotel.com

Both the best-kept and best-known secret among seasoned Paris travelers, this is a veritable institution that relies on word-of-mouth. Long a haven for celebrities looking for peace and quiet. The bell tower of the Eglise de Saint-Germain-des-Prés can be glimpsed from some windows. The most striking feature is the beehive-shaped dome over the ground floor—the building's former courtyard. Oscar Wilde died here. Reserve one month in advance in high season.

SETTING & FACILITIES

Location Saint-Germain-des-Prés. **Nearest Métro Station** Saint-Germain-des-Prés. **Quietness Rating** B. **Dining** €40 continental breakfast. **Amenities** Parking (rue Mazarine), small pool and steam bath, free Internet access. **Services** Room service, laundry.

ACCOMMODATIONS

Rooms 20. **All** TV with satellite, direct-dial phone, mini-bar, safe deposit box, hair dryer, air-conditioning. **Comfort & Decor** Room 16 has been redone in the style in which Oscar Wilde found it in 1900; Robert de Niro's favorite is apartment 62 and its flower-kissed terrasse. Rooms are rather small. Each claims its own distinct style, but all have period furniture.

RATES, RESERVATIONS, & RESTRICTIONS

Pricing Double (shower, WC), off-season €235–260, high season €260–320; twin (WC), off-season €300, high season €345; suite (bathroom, WC), off-season €505, high season €595; large suite (big balcony, view), off-season €595, high season €685. **Credit Cards** VISA, MC, AMEX, DC, JCB. **Check-In/Out** Noon. **Elevator** Yes. **English Spoken** Yes.

LA TOUR D'AUVERGNE   €115–130

OVERALL ★★½ | QUALITY ★★★½ | VALUE ★★★★ | 9TH *ARRONDISSEMENT*

10, rue La Tour d'Auvergne, 75009; 01 48 78 61 60; fax 01 49 95 99 00

Modigliani lived here. Near Métro Cadet, this attractive three-star hotel situated on a quiet street offers a good reception from the staff and many inviting touches, including a particularly well-stocked table full of cultural and historic information useful during your Paris stay. You can have a drink in the small bar or relax in the little salon. Again, this is one of those places that you'd never find on your own, but once you stay here you're certain to return.

SETTING & FACILITIES
Location Grands Boulevards. **Nearest Métro Station** Anvers. **Quietness Rating** B. **Dining** €8 continental, buffet breakfast. **Services** Room service 7–10 a.m.

ACCOMMODATIONS
Rooms 24. **All** TV, phone. **Bathrooms** Modern and well equipped. **Comfort & Decor** Relatively large and lavishly decorated rooms, all decked with canopy beds.

RATES, RESERVATIONS, & RESTRICTIONS
Pricing Single €115, double or twin €130. **Deposit** Credit card. **Credit Cards** VISA, MC, AMEX, DC. **Check-In/Out** Noon. **Not Allowed** Large pets. **Elevator** Yes. **English Spoken** Some.

LE PAVILLON BASTILLE   €130–210

OVERALL ★★★ | QUALITY ★★★★ | VALUE ★★★ | 12TH *ARRONDISSEMENT*

65, rue de Lyon, 75012; 01 43 43 65 65; fax 01 43 43 96 52; U.S. toll-free fax (800) 233-2552; hotel-pavillon@akamail.com; www.france-paris.com (discounts available with online reservations); www.pavillon-bastille.com

Two steps away from the Bastille, this hotel stands behind a gate. The spacious entryway has Greek-style columns, but the rest of the interior is done in a flowered motif, mostly of blues and yellows. The salon's modern furnishings make you think you've just come to visit your cousins in their New York loft. The management and staff are true customer-service artists; they obviously know and love their trade.

SETTING & FACILITIES
Location Bastille/République. **Nearest Métro Station** Bastille. **Quietness Rating** B. **Dining** €11.50 continental, buffet breakfast. **Amenities** Bar, parking nearby. **Services** Laundry (except Sundays and public holidays), room service 24 hours.

ACCOMMODATIONS
Rooms 25. **All** TV with cable, direct-dial phone, hair dryer. **Comfort & Decor** Elegant and contemporary with neoclassical decor.

RATES, RESERVATIONS, & RESTRICTIONS
Pricing Single €130–145, double €130, suite €210. **Credit Cards** VISA, MC, AMEX, DC, JCB. **Check-In/Out** 2 p.m./noon. **Not Allowed** Big dogs. **Elevator** Yes. **English Spoken** Yes.

LES RIVES DE NOTRE-DAME   €170–380

OVERALL ★★★★ | QUALITY ★★★★½ | VALUE ★★★ | 5TH *ARRONDISSEMENT*

15, quai St-Michel, 75005; 01 43 54 81 16; fax 01 43 26 27 09; hotel@rivesdenotredame.com; www.123france.com/notredame

This little gem of a hotel with its Mediterranean decor has a great reputation due to its classy style and incredibly strategic location in the heart of the Latin Quarter with a stunning view of the Conciergerie. With only ten rooms, Les Rives de Notre-Dame is almost always full, so when possible reserve as soon as you know your travel dates (at least two months in advance). As they are oversolicited, they tend to be a bit blasé with new inquiries, and the select clientele of regulars give the impression of being a bit standoffish. Don't be put off. This is a great address. On the far side of the flower and ivy-covered lobby, notice the high, vaulted, hexagonal glass roof. It's not old, but it drenches this hotel with original charm. Ceramic tile in earth tones and exposed stone dominate the decor.

SETTING & FACILITIES
Location Latin Quarter. **Nearest Métro Station** St-Michel. **Quietness Rating** A (with the windows closed). **Dining** €10.50 continental breakfast, €13.50 complete buffet. **Services** Room service 24 hours.

ACCOMMODATIONS
Rooms 10. **All** TV with satellite, direct-dial phone, hair dryer, air-conditioning. **Comfort & Decor** You enter each room through an arched doorway. The rooms are spacious, generally decked in blue tapestry, and are characterized by Provençal decor with a touch of chic. Furniture in wrought iron. Excellent sound-proofing, necessary in this busy neighborhood.

RATES, RESERVATIONS, & RESTRICTIONS
Pricing Single €170, double €170–265, suite €380. **Credit Cards** All major credit cards. **Check-In/Out** 1 p.m./noon. **Elevator** Yes. **English Spoken** Yes.

MELIA COLBERT BOUTIQUE HÔTEL   €290–560

OVERALL ★★★★ | QUALITY ★★★★½ | VALUE ★★★ | 5TH *ARRONDISSEMENT*

7, rue de l'Hôtel Colbert, 75005; 01 56 81 19 00; fax 01 56 81 19 02; melia.colbert@solmelia.com; www.solmelia.com

You'll find better deals in July and August (for example, €185 instead of as much as €335). If you are looking for the utmost in small, discreet Left Bank hotels combined with perfect comfort and old-world elegance, and you don't mind paying dearly for them, don't look further. The Colbert is the only hotel in this category in the Latin Quarter. Tucked in beyond a quaint garden on the tranquil rue de L'Hôtel Colbert, this recently renovated establishment, part of the Sol Meliá group, caters to an international clientele of sophisticated guests. The receptionist may speak not only English but also German, Spanish, or Italian. The breakfast buffet is copious and stylish, but at €20 a person it should be.

SETTING & FACILITIES
Location Latin Quarter. **Nearest Métro Station** St-Michel, Maubert-Mutualité. **Quietness Rating** A. **Dining** €20 breakfast buffet or room service. **Amenities** Bar. **Services** Laundry.

ACCOMMODATIONS
Rooms 39. **All** TV with satellite, direct-dial phone, mini-bar, hair dryer. **Some** Good views. **Bathrooms** Mix of charm and modernity. **Comfort & Decor** Earth tones, marble, and embroidered fabrics. If you desire a view of Notre-Dame from your room, ask for number 12, 13, 21, 22, 31, 32, or 33. If size is more important than a view (you don't need to see Notre-Dame from your room; the cathedral is a 30-second walk from the door!), ask for one of the larger rooms: 5, 7, 8, or 9. There is also a suite, number 54, that will make you feel presidential.

RATES, RESERVATIONS, & RESTRICTIONS
Pricing Single €290, double €335, suite €500–560. **Deposit** Credit card. **Credit Cards** CB, VISA, MC, DC, AMEX, JCB. **Check-In/Out** 2:30 p.m./noon. **Elevator** Yes. **English Spoken** Yes.

TERRASS HÔTEL   €180–290

OVERALL ★★★★ | QUALITY ★★★★½ | VALUE ★★★ | 18TH ARRONDISSEMENT

12–14, rue Joseph-de-Maître, 75018; 01 46 06 72 85; fax 01 42 52 29 11; reservation@terrass-hotel.com; www.terrass-hotel.com

On a quiet street, the hotel lives up to its four-star rating in terms of both service (excellent—there are at least four extremely customer-oriented, English-speaking receptionists on duty) and luxury (quite impressive—everything is large, well lit, and accommodating). A plus: the rooftop restaurant's superb view of Paris, including the Eiffel Tower (there's also a restaurant on the ground floor as well as a big salon for relaxing). We think this hotel is one of Paris's most romantic places to stay. Once you get back to your room, you won't feel like going out again! If the weather is clear, Paris unfolds beneath you and you'll be content to sip Calvados on the terrace in the cool months and pastis in the summers. If the distance from central Paris doesn't bother you, this is an exceptional address for visiting the City of Light. Reserve four months in advance during trade fairs and three weeks during the rest of the year.

SETTING & FACILITIES
Location Montmartre. **Nearest Métro Station** Place-de-Clichy, Abesses, or

Blanche. **Quietness Rating** A. **Dining** 2 restaurants, I is on the roof-top and open in summer only; €11.50 breakfast buffet at the breakfast room, continental breakfast in your room. **Amenities** Parking, safe, conference rooms for rent. **Services** Reservations for shows, cars, tickets desk, laundry.

ACCOMMODATIONS

Rooms 100. **All** TV with satellite, direct-dial phone, hair dryer, mini-bar, minitel (France's online directory computer). **Some** Air-conditioning. **Comfort & Decor** Modern mixed with 19th-century elegance.

RATES, RESERVATIONS, & RESTRICTIONS

Pricing Single €180–205, double €220–240, suite €290; children under age 12 free in parents' room; special rates for online reservations. **Credit Cards** AMEX, DC, JCB, MC, VISA. **Check-In/Out** Noon. **Elevator** Yes. **English Spoken** Yes.

TIMHÔTEL JARDIN DES PLANTES €105–120

OVERALL ★★★½ | QUALITY ★★★★ | VALUE ★★★★ | 5TH *ARRONDISSEMENT*

5, rue Linné, 75005; 01 47 07 06 20; fax 01 47 07 62 74; jardin-plantes@timhotel.fr; www.timhotel.com

This hotel offers two contrasting and equally engaging moods: the modern brightness of the entrance floor—where you check in, have breakfast, and dine amid floor-to-ceiling mirrors, light wood, flowery ceramic tiles, and summery yellow, blue, and orange fabrics—and the classic sobriety of the vaulted cellar, where you relax and read amid a wrought-iron railing, ceiling beams, stone walls, a piano, "café-au-lait"-upholstered sofas, and low wooden tables. The top floor hosts a balcony with several tables and lots of flowers, but unfortunately a view in the wrong direction: of neighboring buildings rather than the glorious Jardin des Plantes. The corridor reflects the open, garden-style mood of the reception area. Though not overly friendly, the personnel do their job well.

SETTING & FACILITIES

Location Latin Quarter. **Nearest Métro Station** Jussieu. **Quietness Rating** B. **Dining** €8 breakfast, self-service or continental. **Amenities** Public parking nearby. **Services** Room service for breakfast, laundry.

ACCOMMODATIONS

Rooms 33. **All** TV with satellite or cable, direct-dial phone, hair dryer. **Some** 4 with shower, WC. **Comfort & Decor** Room 52 is rather spacious and looks even more so due to its mirrored closet doors. Its furniture in light wood and white rattan as well as its greenhouse-colored fabrics give you the feeling of being away from it all. The bathroom is in white tile.

RATES, RESERVATIONS, & RESTRICTIONS

Pricing Single €105, double €120; prices change; discounts are available during trade fairs. **Credit Cards** VISA, MC, AMEX, DC. **Check-In/Out** 1 p.m./noon. **Elevator** Yes. **English Spoken** Yes.

WELCOME HÔTEL   €70–110

OVERALL: ★★★½ | QUALITY ★★★★ | VALUE ★★★★ | 6TH *ARRONDISSEMENT*

66, rue de Seine, 75006; 01 46 34 24 80; fax 01 40 46 81 59

A 17th-century building in the heart of Saint-Germain-des-Prés, not far from the Odéon section with its famous pedestrian streets and markets. Hallways have beamed ceilings. Common-area carpets are green or orange. Reserve two months in advance.

SETTING & FACILITIES
Location Saint-Germain-des-Prés. **Nearest Métro Station** Mabillon. **Quietness Rating** B (windows closed), C otherwise. **Dining** €7.50 continental breakfast. **Services** Room service 7:30–10:30 a.m.

ACCOMMODATIONS
Rooms 30. **All** TV, direct-dial phone. **Comfort & Decor** Decor is pleasant but not remarkable (though the pictures of old Paris scenes are interesting), and bathrooms tend to be small and a bit drab. Room 53 (twin beds), overlooking boulevard St-Germain, gets plenty of light through lots of windows.

RATES, RESERVATIONS, & RESTRICTIONS
Pricing Single €70–80, double or twin €100. **Credit Cards** MC, VISA. **Check-In/Out** Noon/11 a.m. **Not Allowed** Pets. **Elevator** Yes. **English Spoken** Some.

Part Four

Arriving, Getting Oriented, and Departing

Arriving and Departing

Your two most stressful days in Paris will be your date of arrival and date of departure. Most of the stress, however, can be eliminated with some planning and helpful tips, like knowing the best way to get to the airport, how early you should check in, how much luggage you are allowed to carry, and so on. If you read the following pages a few times and familiarize yourself with the process before traveling, you'll find getting in and out of Paris very manageable. You can find information about the Paris airports on the web at www.paris-tourism.com/airports/ and www.paris.org/accueil/airport.

Beating Jet Lag

Paris time is six hours ahead of the east coast of the United States, and nine hours ahead of the west coast. Most flights originating in North America arrive early in the morning, between 8 a.m. and 10 a.m. Thus, for your body it'll feel like the middle of the night. Everyone has their own theories and tips for coping with jet lag. Here are a few time-tested ones:

- Try to sleep at least a few hours on the plane.
- Drink plenty of water or juice, and limit your alcohol consumption to the occasional glass of champagne or wine with dinner.
- Set your clock to Paris time as soon as you take off. Psychologically, you'll be less disoriented when you arrive.
- Try not to go to sleep as soon as you arrive at your hotel. Go for a walk or begin with some lazy sightseeing. If you absolutely have to take a nap during the day, make it a brief one (just long enough to keep you functioning through the rest of your day)—the goal is to keep yourself awake until evening and then have an early night on Paris time.
- Go to sleep a bit earlier than usual, but not too early. You'll be tired when you awake, but functional. Getting a good night of rest on your first night in Paris is

essential and should "jolt" you into the correct time zone, even though it will be several more days until you feel "normal."

■ Some people take melatonin tablets (consult your doctor before using this product).

Arriving: Day One

Those First Minutes

Tired, time-lagged, disoriented, and unfamiliar with the new currency and exchange rate. The best piece of advice is to just relax, get your bearings, pinch yourself, observe the surroundings, inhale the wafts of strong coffee coming from the nearby cafés, and take a few deep breaths to get focused.

The differences will register immediately—the sound of the airport address system, the aesthetics of the signs and markings, the ethnic mix of travelers. Paris is a crossroads of movement and migration from not only Europe but its former colonies in Africa and Asia, and you'll be amazed to look up at the sign of flights arriving from Antananarivo, Madagascar; Ouagadougou, Burkina Faso; Hanoi, Vietnam; and Marrakesh, Morocco. The colorful tails of aircraft from around the world on the tarmac at Charles de Gaulle already alert you to the fact that you are far from home and that the world is a much larger place than you thought.

You'll want to feel comfortable as quickly as possible. You'll want to mix with the Parisians and take yourself to be one during your Paris stay. You don't mind being treated as a visitor, but you don't want to be shoved aside as an insensitive, ugly tourist. The best way to get yourself totally immersed in the Paris ethos is to get oriented geographically and culturally from Day One.

Paris Airports

Paris has two international airports, Charles de Gaulle (CDG), also known as Roissy because it's located in the northern suburb of Roissy about 30 miles north of Paris, and Orly (ORY), located about 20 miles south of Paris. Both are easily accessible to and from Paris by a commuter subway line called the RER, public buses, Air France buses, and taxis. Airport signs are mostly in French and English and are pretty clear.

Roissy/Charles de Gaulle Airport (CDG)

Charles de Gaulle Airport is large, expansive, and modern, and not overly intimidating. There are three principle terminals: the older and circular *Aérogare* 1, which is devoted to long-distance international flights; *Aérogare* 2, newer and user-friendly, divided into six halls or sections (2A, 2B, 2C, 2D, 2E, and 2F), and dominated by Air France and other European airline flights; and *Aérogare* T9, which is principally used for charter flights, many of which serve Canada.

Aérogare 1   If you're arriving from North America you'll probably be arriving in the morning, and often very early. As you disembark you'll follow the glass corridors and the crowd onto a long and bouncy moving sidewalk that carries you and your hand luggage toward the core of Aérogare 1 and the waiting Immigration and Passport Control lines. Non-EU (European Union) citizens must fill in a simple yellow embarkation card; you should fill this in on the airplane to save you the time and aggravation of having to procure the form at the front of the line. *Aérogare* 1 is in the shape of a large circle, with numbered satellites branching out from the core. The lines to get past the immigration inspector are often long and somewhat unruly. You will notice that the French—who love form—are not too concerned with order, and are not keen on civic education. Thus, there will be some jockeying for position in the line. Nonsmokers will be irritated to find returning Parisians already firing up for a nicotine fix, which is illegal but still not fully enforced.

You'll be tired, and waiting in a smoky line is not fun. Instead of waiting in the line in front of you, walk around the circular *Aérogare* 1 and within two minutes you'll come to the next available Passport Control point. There will be many fewer people here. Go through. You can often avoid the big rush in a big way. Don't worry, you can't get lost; all Passport Control points converge on the same descending escalators toward the exit *(sortie* [soar**tee**]*)*. Follow the signs to the *bagage* (bah-**gahj**) claim area.

Claiming Your Luggage   Your luggage emerges from below and tumbles out onto a circular conveyor belt rather quickly. First, grab yourself a free luggage cart from the stacked line. There are usually plenty, but on days in which lots of flights arrive at once, you may have a problem finding a free cart. Special luggage like animal cages, skis, oversized packages, bicycles, and so forth are brought into this area by hand on a large cart, so keep an eye peeled if you checked in anything of an unusual dimension.

If your baggage is missing or damaged, there are counters within this area for reporting this. Our experience is that trying to make claims on small damages is not worth it, just as it's rarely worth it back home. A report will be made and you may be sent to a luggage repair shop in the middle of Paris to have your American Tourister restitched. This will be a waste of time. If there is substantial damage, file a form nonetheless. You may be sent to the same shop for a replacement piece, or you may attempt to take this up with the airline upon returning. Some tourists have had success waiting to report the damage until they're back in the United States, since satisfaction was easier to obtain in the more customer-oriented U.S. offices.

With your bags, proceed to the *sortie.* Be careful: from the luggage carrousels there are two exits, sortie 14 and sortie 32. If someone is picking you up or waiting for you, make sure that you exit from the *sortie* that is indicated for your flight or you may end up waiting at the wrong spot. This happens. As you approach the sliding doors, you will spot customs officials in blue uniforms. There will be two sides and two signs. In green, meaning, keep going, is RIEN A DECLARER/Nothing to Declare. In red, meaning stop, is A DECLARER/To Declare. Chances are you'll have nothing to declare traveling into the country, so you should just ignore these people and keep walking. Do not slow down, hesitate, or make eye contact, or you might give them the chance to stop you and make a spot check of your luggage. This doesn't happen too often, but people who are too hesitant or are lugging massive packages do get stopped on occasion. It may also help to keep your passport out and take on a bored, indifferent look as a visual reminder that you needn't be bothered. In almost all cases, you won't even notice that you went through customs. Although the 2000 foot-and-mouth disease scare has created more customs-consciousness, France does not pay particular attention to passengers arriving with food, fresh produce, flowers, or even dogs and cats.

If you're coming into Paris from another EU country, there won't even be a Passport or Customs Control. You will have cleared that in your first country of entry.

Now, in the outer part of this circular terminal you'll see signs overhead in French and English for the numerous exits, parking, taxis, and buses.

Aérogare 2   The process of getting from the plane through the passport control and baggage claim area in *Aérogare* 2 is much simpler and faster than in *Aérogare* 1. The procedure is the same, but the lines are shorter and the luggage recovery tends to be quicker. There is no chance of exiting from the wrong sortie. Follow the same general procedures here as with *Aérogare* 1. American Airlines uses a round pavillion that jets out from *Aérogare* 2. Walking to and from with heavy luggage is rather inconvenient.

When exiting, the ADP Information Stand is immediately to your left and is open from 6 a.m. to 11 p.m. Phone cards can be bought in the newspaper stand to your right and left. There are also ATM machines scattered around the different halls, for your convenience.

Aérogare T9   This terminal is primarily used for charter flights. It is served by taxis and the free airport interterminal shuttle bus, which also connects to the RER station at the airport.

Lost Luggage Service   Tel. 01 48 62 10 46. Call here with questions about lost or damaged luggage.

ADP Information Stands   These Information Stands, marked in French as *Renseignements,* provide lots of useful information and assistance in English. They distribute brochures and maps in English upon request. They also provide a little-known hotel reservation service that can not only get you lodged in a choice hotel, but can also give you substantial savings of up to 50%!

Getting into Paris from Charles de Gaulle Airport Aérogare 1 or 2 Your first big decision is how to get into Paris. Here's how to solve this one.

If you don't have a lot of luggage, take the RER train. It's fast and reliable, and there are no traffic snarls.

If you do have a lot of luggage and you'd rather not incur the cost of a taxi, take the Air France bus into Paris or arrange for a pick-up service. If your hotel is near one of the Air France bus stops in Paris you may prefer this option whether you have a lot of luggage or not.

If you're in a hurry and don't mind spending some cash, take a taxi.

RER (Paris's Fast Commuter Train Network) This is the fastest and most reliable access into Paris from Charles de Gaulle Airport. Count on about 40 minutes of travel time to central Paris. If you plan to buy the highly recommended 5-zone Métro pass *(Paris Visite)*, the trip into Paris will be included.

There is direct access by foot to the RER station at the airport from Terminal 2. Follow the signs for RER. From Terminal 1, you need to take the free airport shuttle *(navette)* to the RER station, which is only five minutes away.

Trains run every 15 to 20 minutes from 5 a.m. until 11:45 p.m. and cost €7.32 per person each way. Tip: Show up with exact change and you can buy your ticket from a machine without standing in line. If you change money at the airport, make sure to ask for some euro coins. Some machines will accept your VISA or MasterCard, but we don't like risking a problem so early into the trip.

It's always best to ask your hotel in advance which RER stop you should get off at, but when in doubt, get off at Gare du Nord and either transfer to the Métro or take a taxi to your hotel. The RER stops in Paris at Gare du Nord, Châtelet–Les Halles, Cluny–La Sorbonne, Luxembourg, Port Royal, Denfert-Rochereau, and Cité Universitaire. One way of selecting a hotel is its convenience to one of these stops.

Above the platform you'll see a lit-up sign indicating which train will be the next to *départ* for Paris. The airport is the end of the line, so you can't possibly take the train the wrong way. The RER now connects with the TGV service to points north. In some cases you may be able to take the Brussels- or Amsterdam-bound train directly from the airport and not have to go into Paris. The TGV station is at the RER station called Charles de Gaulle 2.

Air France Airport Bus This is a very convenient and comfortable way to get in and out of town. It is accessible to everyone; do not be confused—

you do not need an Air France plane ticket or need to be an Air France passenger to use the Air France airport bus service. From your terminal, follow the well-marked signs for Buses to Paris. From Charles de Gaulle, take either line 2 or line 4, depending on where in Paris you'd like to be dropped off, Etoile/Porte Maillot or Gare de Lyon. All Air France buses are disabled accessible and there is a baggage handler at each stop. You do not need to prepurchase tickets; you pay onboard. Children ages 2–12 pay half-price. Call 01 41 56 89 00 for more information.

Line 2   Line 2 leaves from Terminal 2 and stops at Palais des Congrès at the Porte Maillot and at the Charles de Gaulle-Etoile RER/Métro stop (avenue Carnot exit). Service runs from 5:45 a.m. to 11 p.m. Price: €10 per person each way/€18 round-trip.

Line 4   Line 4 leaves from Terminal 1 but stops at Terminal 2 before leaving for Paris's Gare de Lyon train station (Métro: Gare de Lyon, boulevard Diderot) and Gare Montparnasse (Métro: Montparnasse, rue Commandant Mouchotte). Service runs every 30 minutes from 7 a.m. until 9:30 p.m. Price: €11 per person each way/€20 round-trip.

Roissybus   This airport bus runs between Charles de Gaulle Airport Terminal 2 and the Opéra (rue Scribe in front of the American Express office near the Place de l'Opéra; Métro: Opéra). Service is provided daily every 15 minutes between 6 a.m. and 8 p.m. and every 20 minutes between 8 p.m. and 11 p.m. Price: €7. For information about this and other RATP airport links, call 08 36 68 41 14 (€0.34 per minute).

RATP Buses (Local City Buses)   Less known to out-of-town visitors, the RATP runs two lines between Paris and Roissy/Charles de Gaulle. These are the slowest and least convenient but cheapest form of public transportation between the city and the airport. If you're traveling light, have plenty of time, or are staying close to either the Gare de l'Est or Nation, you may opt for this service.

Bus 350 leaves from the front of the Gare de l'Est.

Bus 351 leaves from Place de la Nation.

Both make local stops and take one hour and ten minutes. The trip costs six Métro tickets, which equals a total of just over €5 if you buy a *carnet* of ten tickets. Your *Paris Visite* is valid on these buses too.

Taxis   Follow the signs for taxis and line up on the sidewalk as the next available taxi pulls up to the curb. Parisians do not share taxis, and drivers do not appreciate your attempts to make a deal with the people in front or in back of you in line. Paris taxi drivers are not known for their loquaciousness or general friendliness. Few speak English. Some smoke. Others drive around with a dog in the front seat. In terms of honesty, it's not common that a driver will try to rip you off, but nonetheless, you should check that the meter only starts once you've gotten in. You should have a rough idea where your hotel is situated and not appear hopelessly dependent. Look like you know the ropes and you shouldn't have to worry about getting "taken for a ride." From Charles de Gaulle Airport to central Paris, count on the ride costing €40–45. You'll be charged €1 extra for each piece of luggage. Count on the ride taking an hour from the airport to the middle of Paris, depending on the time of day and traffic. For more details on Paris taxis, see Part Five, Getting Around Paris.

Shuttles and Pick-Up Services   Aside from hotel services and limousines, there are several companies offering regular and reliable shuttle or pick-up services. Three of the main ones are Airport Shuttle, Paris Airports Service, and Voyages à Paris—although the last isn't technically a shuttle.

Airport Shuttle operates seven days a week, year-round, and offers a guaranteed service regardless of season or demand. For €13.50 per person for a party of two or more, or €18 if you're alone, one of this company's bright blue-and-yellow eight-passenger minivans will be waiting for you at your terminal at Charles de Gaulle Airport or Orly Airport. There is no extra charge for luggage. Simply reserve ahead by phone, fax, or e-mail stating your name, airport, flight number, and time of arrival. Upon landing, but before clearing customs or claiming your baggage, you must call their toll-free telephone number (0 800 50 56 10) to let the driver know that you've arrived. This allows him to coordinate a reliable pick-up. In normal circumstances, you can expect to be at your hotel about an hour and a half after landing.

Returning home, reserve the Airport Shuttle two days before your departure by either calling the same number yourself or asking your hotel concierge to book the pick-up for you. Although Airport Shuttle promises not to make any more than three stops after yours to pick up other passengers, make sure you leave early enough to avoid close calls. Give yourself an hour and a half to get to the airport. So for a 10 a.m. flight from Charles de Gaulle, you'll want to check in between 8 and 8:30 a.m., meaning that depending on the location of your hotel and the traffic patterns, you'll need to be picked up between 6:30 and 7 a.m. You can also make reservations online at www.parisanglo.com; just click on the blue bus under Paris Services.

Paris Airports Service offers the same kind of service, but the phone lines are often busy and the voice-mail options are not clear enough to inspire confidence. Their rates, which depend on the number of passengers, start at €8 per person to or from Orly and €11 per person to or from Charles de Gaulle. Although we were unable to confirm this, some travelers speak of PAS's "pipeline pick-ups," meaning that travelers are asked to meet at a common pick-up point. They can be contacted at Tel. 08 21 800 801, fax 01 49 62 78 79, or www.parisairportservice.com.

Car Rental Follow the signs for car rental (Location de voiture). For local car rental phone numbers and a discussion of the pros and cons of renting a car in Paris, see Part Five, Getting Around Paris.

A Note on the Drive into Paris Chances are it'll be early morning when you arrive, it'll be overcast and drizzly, and your taxi driver will be grumpy. It's not your fault, but he has just spent two to three hours waiting in line for your fare. Make sure that the meter does not already show some horrendous sum like €30 before you even get going. Some tourists have reported paying three times the correct fare due to this ruse. The areas between airports and cities are often ugly, and Paris's are no exception. The drive through the north suburbs along the A1 or 13 highway from Charles de Gaulle Airport into Paris is ugly and industrial. You're likely to gasp, "This is Paris?!?"

Note: For Inter-Airport buses between Charles de Gaulle and Orly Airports, take the Air France Bus Line 3 (price: €15). Count on an hour of travel time. The Air France Airport Bus service operates an information number in French and English at Tel. 01 41 56 89 00. You can also take the RER to Gare du Nord, change to the B line of the RER, take it south in the direction of St. Remy–lès Chevreuse or Robinson, and get off at Antony. From here, take the Orlyval to Orly Airport. The trip costs €16, half-price for children ages four to ten.

Orly Airport

Orly Airport has two main terminals, Orly Sud and Orly Ouest. You'll most likely be arriving at Orly Sud. Both are equally served by ground transportation into Paris.

Getting into Paris from Orly Airport (Sud and Ouest Terminals) Your first big decision is how to get into Paris. Here's how to solve this one.

If you don't have a lot of luggage, take the RER train. It's fast and reliable, and there are no traffic snarls.

If you do have a lot of luggage and you'd rather not incur the cost of a taxi, take the Air France bus into Paris or arrange for a pick-up service. If your hotel is near one of the Air France bus stops in Paris you may prefer this option whether you have a lot of luggage or not.

If you're in a hurry and don't mind spending some cash, take a taxi.

One Paris-lover commented: "Instead of a taxi, I use the Air France bus departing Orly Sud and stopping at Orly Ouest every 15 minutes. There's a French and English video played on the 40-minute drive into town. I tried the Orlyval to the RER to the Métro once, but with luggage the bus is much easier."

RER/Orlyval Follow the signs for the RER/Orlyval. The trains are accessed directly from both terminals. The Orlyval is a fast, fully automated train offering a connection service between Orly Airport and the RER (Line B) intersection at a station called Antony. The trip takes 32 minutes to Châtelet in the center of Paris. Tip: Show up with local currency, and, if possible, enough coins to be able to buy your ticket from a machine and not have to stand in line. If you have bought the *Paris Visite* 5-zone pass, your trip into Paris is included. Follow the well-marked signs for the RER/Orlyval train toward Paris. The train stops in Paris at Cité Universitaire, Denfert-Rochereau, Port-Royal, Luxembourg, Cluny–La Sorbonne, St. Michel/Notre-Dame, Châtelet–Les Halles, and Gare du Nord.

Orlyval runs every four to seven minutes between 6 a.m. and 11 p.m., Monday through Saturday, and between 7 a.m. and 11 p.m. on Sunday. The price, including continued use of the Métro (subway), is €8.69 per person each way and half-price for children between the ages of four and ten. The round-trip price is exactly double the one-way price, so there is no advantage to buying your return portion in advance.

Air France Airport Bus For a description, see Arriving under the section on Charles de Gaulle Airport (above). From your terminal, follow the well-marked signs for Buses to Paris. From Orly Sud or Ouest, line 1 takes you to Montparnasse (in front of the Hotel Meridien, 1, rue du Commandant-Mouchotte, Métro: Montparnasse) and the Air France Terminal at the Invalides Métro station. The bus will also stop at Porte d'Orléans and Duroc Métro stations if you ask it to, but only for passengers that do not have luggage stowed underneath.

All Air France buses are disabled accessible, and there is a baggage handler at each stop. You do not need to pre-purchase tickets; you pay onboard. Children pay half-price.

Line 1 Line 1 leaves Orly Sud and Ouest every 12 minutes between 6 a.m. and 11 p.m. and costs €7.60 per person each way. Round-trip costs €13, so if you'll be using the service to get back to the airport, consider buying the round-trip ticket when you arrive, for the savings. A 24-hour information service can be called at Tel. 01 41 56 89 00.

Orlybus The RATP offers a regular Orly Airport bus service to the RER station at Denfert-Rochereau. You can get off at intermediate stops such as Jourdan Tombe Issoire and Alésia René Coty. Travel time is 30 minutes. Catch this bus at *Porte* H at *Quai* 4 in Orly Sud or *Porte* J on *Niveau* 0 in Orly Ouest. The service runs from Monday to Friday every 13 minutes from 6 a.m. to 11:30 p.m., and Saturday and Sunday every 15–20 minutes from 6 a.m. to 11:30 p.m. Cost: €5.60 per person each way. Your *Paris Visite,* 5-zone pass is valid on this service. Tickets are purchased on the bus or at the ADP window in the airport. Many travelers use this service to Den-fert-Rochereau and then take a taxi or jump on the Métro to their hotel.

Taxis   Follow the signs for taxis and wait in line on the sidewalk as taxis pull up curbside. Expect to pay €20–33, depending on your Paris location and the traffic, as well as €1 per piece of luggage. Be careful to check that the meter is started only when you get in the taxi. The best way to avoid being "taken for a ride" is to have a good idea where your hotel is situated.

Shuttles and Pick-Up Services   Aside from hotel services and limousines, there are several companies offering regular and reliable shuttle or pick-up services such as Airport Shuttle and Paris Airports Service.

Airport Shuttle operates seven days a week, year-round, and offers a guar-anteed service regardless of season or demand. For €13.50 per person for a party of two or more, or €18 if you're alone, one of this company's bright blue-and-yellow eight-passenger minivans will be waiting for you at your ter-minal at Charles de Gaulle Airport or Orly Airport. There is no extra charge for luggage. Simply reserve ahead by phone, fax, or e-mail stating your name, airport, flight number, and time of arrival. Upon landing, but before clearing customs or claiming your baggage, you must call their toll-free telephone number (0 800 50 56 10) to let the driver know that you've arrived. This allows him to coordinate a reliable pick-up. In normal circumstances, you can expect to be at your hotel about an hour and a half after landing.

Returning home, reserve the Airport Shuttle two days before your depar-ture by either calling the same number or asking your hotel concierge to book the pick-up for you. Although Airport Shuttle promises not to make any more than three stops after yours to pick up other passengers, make sure you leave early enough to avoid close calls. Give yourself an hour and a half to get to the airport. So for a 10 a.m. flight from Charles de Gaulle, you'll want to check in between 8 and 8:30 a.m., meaning that depending on the location of your hotel and the traffic patterns, you'll need to be picked up between 6:30 and 7 a.m. You can also make reservations online at www.paris-anglo.com; just click on the blue bus under Paris Services.

Paris Airports Service offers the same kind of service, but the phone lines are often busy and the voice-mail options are not clear enough to inspire confidence. Their rates, which depend on the number of passengers, start at €8 per person to or from Orly and €11 per person to or from Charles de Gaulle. Although we were unable to confirm this, some travelers speak of PAS's "pipeline pick-ups," meaning that travelers are asked to meet at a common pick-up point. They can be contacted at Tel. 08 21 80 08 01, fax 01 49 62 78 79, or www.parisairportservice.com.

Car Rental   Follow signs for car rental *(location voiture)*. For local car rental phone numbers and a discussion of the pros and cons of renting a car in Paris, see Part Five, Getting Around Paris.

Lost Luggage Service   Tel. 01 49 75 04 55. Call here with questions about lost or damaged luggage.

That First Phone Call

If you're using the Atlantic prestocked access number you purchased before leaving home, simply pick up the receiver in any telephone *cabine* and dial Tel. 0800 06 40 06, or the back-up number Tel. 01 47 67 78 77 (local access from Paris). A recording will ask you to punch in your security code followed by the number you wish to reach. For international calls, remember to start with 00 followed by the country code and city code (when applicable), and finally the telephone number. Your credit will be debited automatically with each call.

If you are calling home and have come with your AT&T, Sprint, or MCI card and PIN number, access your carrier's operator by dialing:

AT&T   Tel. 08 00 99 00 11

Sprint/Global One   Tel. 08 00 99 00 87 (You'll get a recording with instructions in English. To bill the call to your VISA card, you punch in 00. To use a prepaid calling card, punch in 01.)

MCI/World Phone   Tel. 08 00 99 00 19

If you are not using one of these cards brought from home, you'll need to purchase one or a France Telecom *carte téléphonique* (cart-te**lay**-fohw**neek**) at the newsstand or post office in the airport for use in the public pay phones (cabine téléphonique; ca**been**-te**lay**-fohw**neek**), which are everywhere. If you'll be using the phone regularly and plan on calling overseas, buy the 120-unit card for €14.75. Otherwise, buy the 50-unit card for €7.40. Note that on the 120-unit card the rate is 20% cheaper.

A word of warning: It is hard to believe, but the access numbers and instructions that your telephone operator at home gives you are often wrong or incomplete or simply outdated. For years, MCI kept giving out French prefixes that expired in 1996! It is our experience that U.S.-based telephone operators are insufficiently briefed on how to instruct customers on using their service internationally. You'll spend long periods on hold and you'll get nothing but polite "I'm sorry sir/madam (followed by gibberish)."

Don't count on making a call from a coin-operated pay phone; these have all but disappeared except in bars and cafés. Don't plan on calling home collect (PVC) either using the French operator; the practice is not widely done, the prices are high, and the procedures are confusing.

Note: if you own a GSM-equipped cell phone, it will probably work in France. Ask your provider back home before traveling with the phone. Although this may be convenient, be prepared: the roaming costs can be steep. If you travel in Europe regularly, you may prefer to buy a cell phone in France and use a pre-stocked card with it. France Telecom, SFR, and Bonygues all provide these products.

Changing Money at the Airport

If you can avoid it, aside from using an airport ATM, don't change money at the airport (or train station). Your choices are limited, the exchange rate is lower than average, and you'll be wasting time. On a day when the official exchange rate was $1 = €1.17, for instance, the Thomas Cook office at the St-Lazare train station posted rates of $1 = €1.09 for dollar-holders buying euros, and $1 = €1.25 for travelers wanting to buy dollars. On the other hand, if you arrive without a euro in your pocket, you'll need some cash to get you into the city. If you can change $100 you'll be secure for the next few hours. Situated near the exit of each airport terminal you'll find a Travelex window. This is the old Thomas Cook foreign exchange office with a face-lift. The exchange rate at the airport is not negotiable, regardless how much you change. They offer a buy back service, "Buyback Plus," for €3.80, whereby they'll buy back any unused currency at the same rate you bought them for up to 31 days later. This is only an advantage if you miscalculate how much you'll need and end up with too many euros. Remember, of course, you can use the same euros in Belgium, Holland, Luxembourg, Germany, Spain, Italy, Greece, and Portugal. As of 2001, the U.K. has not opted to join the euro. But they also offer frequent flyer miles on British Airways and Air France. To understand the posted rate card, note that the *vente* column represents at what price they are selling the currency; the *achat* column represents at what price they are buying your dollars. For a more detailed explanation, see "Changing Money" later in this chapter.

Our choice is to arrive with a minimal amount of euros and supplement this at an ATM (*guichet automatique*). There are lots of these in every hall of each airport terminal and train station. Have your PIN ready. When you do get your first bank notes, study the currency for a minute to get acquainted with its denominations.

Departing

You'll probably just want to reverse your steps to get back to the airport. Don't forget your passport and airplane tickets! Keep them in a handy but secure place. Check your information twice for the airport and terminal you are leaving from. You'll almost always leave from the airport you arrived at, but occasionally airlines operating out of both airports change schedules. Check, just to be sure. Going to the wrong airport or the wrong terminal at the right airport is no fun.

Your options for Roissy/Charles de Gaulle Airport (CDG) are Terminal 1 (CDG 1) or Terminal 2 (CDG 2A, 2B, 2C, or 2D). CDG T9 is Charles de Gaulle Terminal T9.

Your options for Orly (ORY) are Orly Sud (ORY SUD) or Orly Ouest (ORY OUEST).

Note: Several small airlines have begun flights between the United Kingdom or Ireland and the Paris regional airports Cergy-Pontoise (POX) and Beauvais (BVA). Cergy-Pontoise is on the RER A line; Beauvais requires a bus. For ground transportation, inquire with the airline or your travel agent.

Confirming Your Flight: Reaching the Airlines

Airline offices do not answer their phones around the clock like they do in North America. You either call them during working hours or call the airport information number for flight information and for direct airport telephone numbers for some airlines.

Roissy/Charles de Gaulle Traveler Information Tel. 01 48 62 12 12
Orly Airport Traveler Information Tel. 01 49 75 15 15
Flight Update Hotline (Incoming and Outgoing) Tel. 0 836 681 515 or www.adp.fr.

MAJOR AIRLINE OFFICES IN PARIS

Air France	0 802 802 802
Air Canada	01 44 50 20 20
American Airlines	0 801 872 872
British Airways	0 825 825 400
Continental Airlines	01 42 99 09 09
Delta Air Lines	0 800 354 080
Northwest Airlines	0 810 556 556
TWA	0 810 892 892
United Airlines	0 810 72 72 72
U.S. Airways	01 42 25 21 70

Getting to the Airport on Time

Every traveler has his or her own style. Some have nervous breakdowns if they aren't checked in three hours before the scheduled flight time. Others just seem to breeze in at the last minute before the flight is closed. On international flights we strongly suggest that you plan to be checked in at least 90 minutes (preferably two hours) before the scheduled flight time. If you plan on claiming a VAT refund on your purchases or visiting the duty-free shops, or you want to make sure you get good seats, plan to arrive two hours before departure time, which is what the airlines instruct. Air France and others tend to overbook their flights, and passengers arriving an hour or less before flight time are often told to "wait and see" if there is room—even when they are holding paid and confirmed tickets. It's better avoiding such stress.

As a rule, give yourself one hour and 15 minutes to reach Charles de Gaulle Airport and one hour to reach Orly Airport, regardless how you're getting there.

For a more detailed description of each of the following services, see the arrival information earlier in this chapter.

Roissy/Charles de Gaulle   To get to Roissy/Charles de Gaulle Airport from Paris, depending on the location of your hotel, the amount of luggage you are carrying, and your budget, select the means that suits you best.

RER B   RER B offers direct service to Roissy/Charles de Gaulle Airport from the following Paris stations: Gare du Nord, Châtelet–Les Halles, St. Michel/Notre-Dame, Cluny Sorbonne, Luxembourg, Port Royal, Denfert-Rochereau, and Cité Universitaire.

Trains are frequent, but count on a 15-minute wait. Travel time is around 40 minutes, depending on where you get on. As you are waiting on the platform, note that the lit sign above the platform indicates the destination of the next train and the stops it makes. Make sure you get on a train heading toward Charles de Gaulle Airport. If your *Paris Visite* 5-zone pass is still valid, then you can use it to return to the airport. Otherwise, you'll need a ticket. Trains run every 15 to 20 minutes from 5 a.m. until 11:45 p.m. and cost €7.32 per person.

Air France Airport Bus   Line 2 leaves Paris's Etoile (1, avenue Carnot) every 20 minutes from 5:45 a.m. to 11 p.m. daily, and from Porte Maillot (boulevard Gouvion Saint-Cyr) every 20 minutes from 5:50 a.m. to 11 p.m. daily. This bus services Charles de Gaulle Airport Terminals 2A, 2C, 2F, 2D, 2B, and Terminal 1. The service costs €10 one-way, €18 round-trip, and €5 for children ages 2–12. Groups of four passengers and more are entitled to a 15% discount. Ask for it.

Air France Bus line 4 leaves Paris's Montparnasse (rue du Commandant Mouchotte in front of the Meridian Hotel) and the Gare de Lyon (20 bis, boulevard Diderot) every 30 minutes from 7 a.m. to 9 p.m. This bus services Charles de Gaulle Airport Terminals 2C, 2F, 2B, 2D and Terminal 1. The cost is €11 one-way, €20 round-trip, €5.50 for children ages 2–12. For recorded information in English 24 hours a day, seven days a week, call Tel. 01 41 56 89 00.

Roissybus   This airport bus runs between Opéra (rue Scribe in front of the American Express office at the Place de l'Opéra) and Charles de Gaulle Airport Terminal 2 daily every 15 minutes between 5:45 a.m. and 11 p.m., and every 25 minutes between 10 a.m. and 11 p.m. The price is €7. Your *Paris Visite* 5-zone pass is valid for this trip. The information number is Tel. 08 36 68 41 14.

Taxis   You can either grab a taxi at a taxi stand near your hotel or you can have your hotel receptionist call a taxi for you. If a taxi is called for you, don't be surprised to see that the meter already has €4.50 to €6 on it when it arrives. If the sum seems exorbitant, don't accept the taxi. Savvy travelers note the phone number at the nearby taxi stand and call ten minutes before they want to be picked up. The amount on the meter will be considerably less. If you want to call one of the taxi companies yourself or arrange for your pick-up the night before, here is a suggested number: Tel. 08 91 70 10 10. You can pay with Visa or Mastercard for fares over €7.60. Reservations can be made up to a week in advance or as little as 15 minutes before pick-up time.

Shuttles and Drop-off Services   If you use one of the pick-up and drop-off services, call several days in advance to reserve. Always allow for an extra 30 minutes in case there is a delay, traffic, or an unforeseen problem. Allow for an extra hour to get to the airport, since the mini-buses often make a number of pick-up stops around Paris before heading to the airport. We have heard of passengers missing their planes because of such delays. Don't assume that because the service specializes in getting people to the airport, the driver will manage your schedule well.

Car Rental   Inquire with the car rental company on the procedures for returning vehicles. Upon arriving at the airport along the A1 highway, follow the signs for Voitures de Location. For early or late drop-offs, inquire about returning your car the day before your departure. See Part Five, Getting Around Paris, for car rental numbers.

Orly Airport   To get to Orly Airport (Sud and Ouest Terminals) from Paris, depending on the location of your hotel, the amount of luggage you are carrying, and your budget, select the means that suits you best.

RER/Orlyval   Buy a ticket for Orly via the Orlyval at any Métro or RER station. If your *Paris Visite* 5-zone pass is still valid you may use it to get to Orly Airport. Take the RER B train south, direction Orly, which stops in Paris at Gare du Nord, Châtelet–Les Halles, St. Michel/Notre-Dame, Cluny–La Sorbonne, Luxembourg, Port-Royal, Denfert-Rochereau, and Cité Universitaire. Get off the train at the Antony station and transfer to the Orlyval train. It will be hard to miss because the airport connection is prominently announced in French and English. The Orlyval runs every four to seven minutes between 6 a.m. and 10:30 p.m. Monday through Saturday, and between 7 a.m. and 11 p.m. on Sunday. The price is €7 per person and half-price for children between the ages of four and ten.

Air France Bus   The Line 1 bus leaves from the Air France Terminal at Invalides every 12 minutes between 5:45 a.m. and 11 p.m. It stops at

Montparnasse (in front of the Hotel Meridien, 1, rue du Commandant-Mouchotte, Métro: Montparnasse). The cost is €7.60.

Orlybus   The bus leaves from in front of the Denfert-Rochereau RER station every 13 minutes from 5:35 a.m. to 11 p.m. Monday through Friday and every 15–20 minutes on Saturdays and Sundays. You can buy tickets on the bus or use your *Paris Visite* 5-zone pass if it's still valid. The price is €5.60.

Taxis   You can either grab a taxi at a taxi stand near your hotel or you can have your hotel receptionist call a taxi for you. If a taxi is called for you, don't be surprised to see that the meter already has €4.50 to €6 on it when it arrives. If the sum is much higher than this, don't accept the taxi. Savvy travelers note the phone number at the nearby taxi stand and call ten minutes before they want to be picked up. The amount on the meter will be considerably less. If you want to call one of the taxi companies yourself or arrange for your pick-up the night before, here is a suggested number: Tel. 08 91 70 10 10. You can pay with Visa or Mastercard for fares over €7.60. Reservations can be made up to a week in advance or as little as 15 minutes before the pick-up time.

Shuttles and Drop-off Services   If you use one of the pick-up and drop-off services, call several days in advance to reserve. Always allow for an extra 30 minutes in case there is a delay, traffic, or an unforeseen problem. Allow for an extra hour to get to the airport, since the mini-buses often make a number of pick-up stops around Paris before heading to the airport. We have heard of passengers missing their planes because of such delays. Don't assume that because the service specializes in getting people to the airport, the driver will manage your schedule well.

Car Rental   When driving to Orly Airport from Paris along the A10 highway, make sure you keep to the left when the highway splits between Lyon and Orleans. If you miss the left-lane exit for Orly, you'll be stuck with a 20-minute detour to get back.

As you approach Orly Airport, you'll spot signs for the car rental companies and *Voitures de Location.* Call your rental company in advance to inquire about special drop-off instructions. See Part Five, Getting Around Paris, for car rental numbers.

Claiming Your VAT Refund on Purchases

Don't forget to claim your VAT refund on your purchases at the airport before proceeding to your gate. For detailed procedures on doing this, refer to Part Eight, Shopping in Paris. Note that VAT can only be claimed in the last country you visit within the European Union. In other words, you can't "detax" your purchases in France when leaving for England.

Arriving and Departing by Train

Train Stations

Paris has six main train stations *(les gares)*, so the first point is to make sure you know which station you're coming into and from which station you're departing. There is nothing more stressful than showing up on time for a train that leaves from another station. All Paris train stations are accessible by at least two Métro lines.

For all stations
Information and ticket sales (French) Tel. 08 36 35 35 35
Recorded train times (French) Tel. 08 36 67 68 69

Gare du Nord 75010, Métro: Gare du Nord on lines 4 and 5, RER B and D. Served by bus lines 42, 43, 46, 47, 48, and 49. This enormous neoclassical train station was designed by Jacques-Ignace Hittorf in 1863 and was crowned with statues representing the larger cities of France. As its name suggests, it serves destinations in the north of France. It is also the departure point for the Eurostar (Brussels, London) and Thalys (Brussels, Amsterdam, Cologne, Düsseldorf) train lines.

Gare de l'Est 75010, Métro: Gare de l'Est on lines 4, 5, and 7. Served by bus lines 30, 31, 32, 38, and 39. One of the more modest stations in Paris, it serves destinations in the east of France such as Nancy, Reims, and Strasbourg, as well as Switzerland and Luxembourg. An enormous *fresque* (fresco) by A. Herter illustrating French soldiers departing for the "Grande War," as WWI is called in French, is worth a look.

Gare Montparnasse 75014/75015, Métro: Gare Montparnasse on lines 4, 6, 12, and 13. Served by bus lines 91, 92, 94, 95, and 96. This station lies beneath the 209-meter Tour Montparnasse and serves destinations southwest of Paris such as Poitiers, La Rochelle, Bordeaux, Toulouse, Biarritz, and Lourdes. Organized into two areas, Montparnasse 2 is where the TGV departs from.

Gare d'Austerlitz 75005, Métro: Gare d'Austerlitz on lines 5 and 10, RER C. Served by bus lines 61 and 65. Trains leaving from this station link Spain and Portugal with France.

Gare Saint Lazare 75008, Métro: Gare Saint Lazare on lines 3, 12, and 13. Served by bus lines 20, 21, 24, 26, 27, 28, and 29. This station has been called a "factory of dreams" because of its steel-and-glass architecture. It was built by J. Litsch in 1885 and acts as the commuter hub for most of the suburbs to the west of Paris. Note the bronze sculpture of piled-up battered suitcases in front of the station. It was here that thousands of homeless and uprooted Eastern Europeans arrived at the end of World War II.

Gare de Lyon 75012, Métro: Gare de Lyon on line 1 and RER A. Served by bus lines 20 and 63. This station has been remodeled several times since its construction (1847–1852). It has had its present-day modern style since the arrival of the TGV *(train à grande vitesse)*, France's famous high-speed train. It serves destinations between Paris and the Midi (south of France), including Dijon, Lyon, Montpellier, Marseilles, and Nice. It is also the departure point for the Artesia trains linking France and Italy (you can reach Torino in 5½ hours and Milan in 6½ hours).

The Famous TGV (Train à Grande Vitesse)

These high-speed trains have been influential in recent demographic changes in France, allowing people who work in Paris to live in the less-crowded regions around the city without losing a lot of time in commuting. Travel on the TGV requires a ticket *and* a reservation *(billet avec réservation)*. For more information and to make reservations, call Tel. 08 36 35 35 35.

Train Reservations and Tickets

Any SNCF office, train station, or travel agent can sell you train tickets and reservations. Travel agents usually charge around €5–7 above the ticket price as their service fee. This is often worth it since you won't have to go to the train station or wait in lines prior to your departure. The SNCF maintains an information phone line, but you may spend a long time on hold and then the staff may not speak adequate English or may become impatient if you ask too many questions. Ask your hotel concierge if he can help you make reservations. For information: Tel. 01 53 90 20 20, Île de France; Tel. 08 36 35 35 35, Grandes Lignes.

Lockers and Other Services

All the train stations have lockers called *consigne,* which will give you 24 hours of storage. Be equipped with coins. The stations also have a storage service for suitcases and larger items, although due to tightening security measures, regulations about their use may change without notice. Definitely do not ever leave your baggage unattended; it risks being picked up by a security team and destroyed.

Disabled Facilities

See "Travelers with Disabilities" in Part Five, Getting Around Paris.

Taking the Eurostar

Getting between England and France has never been easier. The Eurostar brought Paris and London within three hours of each other via the 22-mile Eurotunnel. The Paris-London service runs between the Gare du Nord and

Waterloo Station more or less hourly between 6:30 a.m. and 9 p.m. To make reservations in Paris, call Tel. 08 36 35 35 39.

One-way tickets cost around €300 for first class and €260 for second class. Youth fares of about €69 (second class) apply for passengers between the ages of 12 and 25; fares are €45 (second class) and €75 (first class) for kids under age 12. Eurostar offers "leisure" round-trip fares starting at about €305 in first class and €213 in second class for travelers spending a Saturday night on either side, with a range of lower rates carrying more restrictions.

The ride is generally comfortable and smooth, with the 20-minute tunnel interlude passing by uneventfully. It just feels like you're traveling at night. Multilingual Eurostar attendants decked out in navy blue and yellow scarves or ties are very accommodating, and the onboard buffet car is convenient. The train has public phones as well.

Note that there is a TGV terminal at Roissy/Charles de Gaulle Airport allowing non-Paris-bound travelers heading toward the north and southeast to avoid Paris altogether.

Is It Worth Going First Class?   Not really. In terms of comfort, you don't really need the wide, reclining seat, similar to business-class airline seats, for a three-hour journey. But you might enjoy the elegant meal served at your seat which is included in your ticket price, and the executive lounges at both Waterloo Station and Gare du Nord help reduce the wear and tear of travel. But we prefer saving the cash and having a better meal later.

It's relatively easy to find special Eurostar prices on either end, commonly at discounts of up to 50% off the published price. To inquire call Tel. 08 36 35 35 39.

Arriving and Departing by Car

If you are driving into Paris, you'll feel the presence of the big city by the congestion you hit as you approach the beltway, the *périphérique*. It's generally easier to move east and west by car in Paris than north and south. Sunday evening Paris-bound traffic on the *autoroutes* is almost always jammed up. Here are our suggestions for getting into central Paris, depending on where your hotel is located:

If you're coming into Paris from the west—take the *Voie Express,* which follows the Seine on the Right Bank easterly from western Paris.

If you're coming into Paris from the east—get off the *périphérique* at Porte de Bercy and hug the Seine on the Right Bank heading west.

If you're coming into Paris from the north or south—follow the *périphérique* either east or west depending on where your hotel is and then follow directions as if you were coming in from the east or west.

Rules of the Road

All you'll need to drive in Paris is a valid U.S. driver's license and, preferably, an international driver's license (easily obtainable from any AAA office in the United States, and valid for one year). Be aware, however, that some French rules of the road will be foreign to you. Please be certain to note the following:

- *Priorité à droite.* You must yield to the car approaching from the right. This may seem illogical or dangerous when there is no stop or yield sign present, but that's the law, so be very careful to give way to traffic merging from the right.
- Do not cross a solid middle line in the road. This is taken far more seriously than in North America.
- Buckle up for safety. There is a €23 fine for driving or riding without a seatbelt.

Parking

Paris parking can be hair-raising. And you'll be amused to see how Parisian drivers can squeeze into anything. Since Parisians are taught to leave their parked cars in neutral *(point mort),* some drivers even push other parked cars forward and backward with their bumpers to make room for their vehicle. One Japanese tourist witnessed this bumper-to-bumper contact and with alarm shouted, "In Japan that would be considered an accident!"

At night around the crowded parts of town, cars will be parked on sidewalks and along the center line in the street.

If you are driving, we recommend that you use the underground parking lots marked everywhere with a large **P**. They are for the most part affordable (you can always pay with a VISA or MasterCard) and safe, and you'll save yourself a lot of time and aggravation by avoiding street parking.

Gas

There is no problem finding gasoline in Paris, but the prices will shock you, since European countries tax gasoline heavily in order to encourage people to use the excellent public transportation system and to reduce the amount of car-related pollution. Count on paying roughly the same amount for a liter (quart) as what you pay back home for a gallon. Almost all rentals require lead-free gasoline *(sans plomb).* Unleaded gasoline (95 and 98 octane) will be marked in green. Super (leaded) gasoline will be marked in blue. VISA and MasterCard are widely accepted.

Traffic

Paris traffic is reason enough not to drive. Seriously, we recommend instead that you walk, use the Métro, and take taxis when necessary—public transportation in Paris is easy to use, efficient, and inexpensive. Otherwise, plan on being stuck in traffic along the *périphérique,* around Châtelet, or on the rue de Rivoli. And traffic patterns around Etoile at the Arc de Triomphe and the Bastille, although not mean-spirited, will qualify you for sedatives. The style of driving in Paris requires that you keep moving, yield only to your right, never honk, and don't hesitate. Parisians can be aggressive and impatient but generally refrain from demonstrating real anger. It's like a game of bumper cars, hopefully, without bumping. If you do bump into someone, though, remain calm and fill in the *Constat* report you'll find in the glove compartment of your vehicle. If in doubt, do not sign anything that you cannot read or understand.

Understanding Those First Signs and Getting Directions

Your first encounter with the French language will probably occur when you need directions or instructions, so you may want to either write out the following dialogues for handy consultation or memorize a few key lines that will be useful for getting you out of the airport, into a taxi, or to your hotel, or for finding a toilet.

- *Excusez-moi. Où sont les toilettes, s'il vous plaît?*
  (Excuse-say **mwah**. Oo-**sown** lay twa-let, see voo-**play?**)
  Excuse me, where are the rest rooms, please?

- *Excusez-moi. Où est-ce que je peux trouver un taxi, s'il vous plaît?*
  (Excuse-say **mwah**. Oo-**eska** juh **puh** troo-**vay** uh **taxi**, see voo-**play?**)
  Excuse me, where can I find a taxi, please?

- *Excusez-moi. Où est-ce que je peux trouver le RER à Paris, s'il vous plaît?*
  (Excuse-say **mwah**. Oo-**eska** juh **puh** troo-**vay** luh **air-euh-air** ah Par-**ree**, see voo-**play?**)
  Excuse me, where can I find the RER to Paris, please?

- *Excusez-moi. Où est-ce que je peux acheter une carte téléphonique, s'il vous plaît?*
  (Excuse-say **mwah**. Oo-**eska** juh **puh** ahhsh-eh-**tay** oon **cart** telay fown **eek**, see voo-**play?**)
  Excuse me, where can I buy a telephone card, please?

- *Excusez-moi. Où est-ce que je peux trouver un guichet automatique, s'il vous plaît?*
  (Excuse-say **mwah**. Oo-**eska** juh **puh** troo-**vay** oon gee-**shay** auto-mat-**teek**, see voo-**play?**)
  Excuse me, where can I find an ATM, please?

Telephones, E-Mail, and Postal Services

A Prominent Word on Calling or Faxing Paris

Don't you just hate it when a guidebook gives you a foreign phone number and you have have to search all over the book for the country code! To avoid the delay and annoyance, note:

To call or fax Paris from North America, dial 011 followed by 33 for France and 1 for Paris. Note that Paris area numbers always begin with 01 and have ten digits. **When dialing from *outside* of France you drop the 0.** When dialing in France you keep the 0. So, to reach 01 48 59 66 68 from abroad, dial 011 33 148 59 66 68.

Calling Home from Your Hotel

You'd think that making a simple phone call anywhere in the world today would be easy. But most visitors end up either fumbling for the right codes to reach their friendly state-side operator or settling for the hotel's internal direct-dialing service, succumbing to the fear that you're going to get royally fleeced. The instructions you get from your local carrier on using foreign telephones are usually spotty and often completely wrong.

The good news is that calling from Paris is not like it once was and there are some real options to lighten both the emotional stress and the burden to your wallet.

First, you should know that the deregulation of the French state monopoly, France Telecom, opened up the market to every international concern as well as to the smaller and scrappy call-back companies whose ubiquitous advertisements promise huge discounts when calling North America.

Come Prepared

To be best prepared for a short stay, we strongly advise a small arsenal of communications tools: bring your usual carrier's calling card with your code and your PIN or access number, a major credit card, and, if possible, a prepaid/prestocked calling card either from your local carrier or from Atlantic (see below). You may pick up a handy France Telecom Télécarte upon arriving, which you can easily find at the airports, *tabacs* (tobacco shops), post offices, Métro stations, and newsstands *(kiosques)* marked *"Télécarte en vente ici."* (Now, there are a lot of competitive telephone cards available and they all work perfectly in any telephone booth in France; just make sure you end up with a card.)

The telephone card is inserted in almost all public telephones (except the coin-operated phones that are still found in cafés and bars) and can be easily used to make both local and international calls. The France Telecom *Télécarte*, the most readily found, comes in two main denominations, 50 units for €7.40 and 120 units for €14.75. The 120-unit card is proportionally a better deal, with 20% more calling time. If you plan to call home or your office regularly, definitely buy the bigger card. It also offers better rates (see below).

In France, calls made via France Telecom on a private line are billed in minutes. A local call costs €0.09 for the first minute, then €0.03 per minute in peak time (8 a.m. to 7 p.m.) and €0.02 in off-peak hours. From a phone booth, a call from Paris to North America between 8 a.m. to 7 p.m. costs €0.66 a minute at peak time, €0.54 off peak with a 50-unit card—or €0.35 any time. From hotel rooms, the cost may be as much as two, three, or four times the base price, depending on the number of stars and the commercial policy of the hotel. One Best Western hotel admitted to charging the equivalent of nearly €5 a minute! So beware.

To call from your room, your best bet is to call the operator of your home carrier. Access calls to your AT&T, MCI, or Sprint operators are free from hotel rooms. Most Paris hotels now offer direct access dialing, so, once you get an outside line, you can usually reach the operator of your home carrier. Otherwise, you have to ask the hotel front desk to get you an outside line.

To reach your home carrier operator:

AT&T	08 00 99 00 11
MCI/Worldcom	08 00 99 00 19
Sprint/Global One	08 00 99 00 87
Canada Direct	08 00 99 00 16 or 08 00 99 02 16

Note that in order to call the United States from Paris with a normal AT&T calling card, your home phone number will be charged a $4.50 surcharge, plus $2.29 for the first minute and $1.73 for each additional minute. Thus a ten-minute call from your hotel room may cost you between $30 and $50 if you call direct, or $22.36 with your AT&T card, but as little as €3.50 ($3.21) if you call from a public phone with a *Télécarte*. If you plan on spending more time in France or if you return regularly on business, you could ask AT&T for their global calling card by calling Tel. (800) 435-0812. With this free card there are no more surcharges, each minute is billed at $1.45, charges are made to a major credit card, and if you designate a preferred nation before leaving home you benefit from an additional 10% off.

It is generally advisable to avoid making collect calls from hotel rooms. Also, calling mobile and cell phones from hotel rooms may cost you more than dinner!

Using Parisian Telephones

The common French public telephone booth is called a *cabine téléphonique*. They are all over the place—street corners, Métro stations, train stations, and public places—and since they do not take coins, they are rarely broken. To use one you'll either need a France Telecom telephone card or the card of one of its many new competitors. You may also access a home carrier and charge your call to your home account number or debit your prepaid card at these phones, without a telephone card.

Instructions in French telephone booths are also in English, but the writing is small and the steps are not perfectly clear. When using a France Telecom card, pick up the receiver, insert your card into the slot, wait for the dial tone, then dial. To call the United States or Canada, dial 00 1, then the area code and number. To reach the United Kingdom, dial 00 44, then the city code and number.

Coins

The French used technology to combat vandalism and increase profit, replacing the coin-operated pay phone with the telephone card pay phone. Coin-operated phones are only found in cafés and bars these days and are increasingly rare. You'll need coins *(pièces de monnaie)* to make a local call. Note that you can call internationally by simply dialing 00 and then the country code and number. Many cafés have special desk-style pay phones that cost more.

Prepaid Telephone Cards

All the major U.S. carriers issue prepaid telephone cards for domestic and international use. However, getting information directly from AT&T, Sprint, or MCI is worse than pulling teeth. It took us 16 minutes on hold to find out that MCI's prepaid, unit-based cards are sold in Shell stations, Walgreens, and CVS pharmacies. Make sure that the card you buy is coded for world service. You can order a prepaid telephone from MCI equipped with a world service code by calling (800) 830-9444. The card contains call credit at the rate of $0.29/minute for calls to the U.S. placed in France, and you can purchase one using MasterCard, American Express, or Discover.

Though that's sounds like a pretty good deal, it is generally much easier and more economical to simply buy the France Telecom *carte téléphonique* when you arrive.

Ordering Prepaid Phone Cards

A number of newly created international telephone companies have sprung up over the last several years, competing directly with both the local France Telecom and the leading American carriers by offering cut-rate access from France with the use of an access code. Some allow you to order a card before arriving. Tickets to . . . (yes, that's the whole name) presells France Telecom's télécarte online at www.ticketsto.com.

Other companies offering international access at competitive prices:

Primus	0 800 010 011
AXS Telecom	0 800 761 616
Sprint/Global One	(800) 366-0707

Look for new technology that permits international telephoning via fiber optic cable, satellite, and other digital formats at a fraction of current rates.

Dialing 01 vs. 1

Note that when in Paris, all local calls begin with 01. When dialing the same number from outside of France, drop the 0. When dialing Paris from another part of France you use the 01 prefix. The numbers for the rest of France begin with 02, 03, 04, 05, and cellular phone numbers begin with 06. Toll-free numbers begin with 08 00. Be aware that any other 08 numbers will cost you anwhere from €0.02 to €0.34 a minute.

E-Mail

In terms of the number of users, France is still a ways behind the United States and other advanced countries using the Internet, but the gap is closing, and Internet use is on a sharp rise in France. If it's important for you to access your e-mail or get online from Paris, you can do so without too much difficulty. The larger hotels have business centers with Internet connections. The city also has a handful of web bars or Internet cafés from where you can send and receive e-mail (see below).

Note that online traffic is particularly heavy in the late afternoons in Paris, and depending on your connection and modem, your experience may be painfully slow.

If You Use AOL Local Dial-Up   Set your dial-up setting on your computer in Paris to dial Tel. 08 36 06 13 10. (You can waste a dollar or two and even try this from home. You must add 00 33 and drop the 0 before the 8 when dialing from the United States.) For questions or if you have any problems while you're in Paris you can visit the AOL website (www.france.aol.com) or e-mail them at franceweb@aol.com. But if you can't get online in the first place, this won't help. You can also call customer service (French only) in Paris at Tel. 08 26 02 00 07 (Monday–Saturday, 9 a.m.–10 p.m.)

Note: The operators will assure you they can speak English but will respond in English only if you are hopeless in French. And expect to find a €5/hour surcharge to your state-side AOL account.

If You Use CompuServe   Set your dial-up setting on your computer in Paris to dial Tel. 01 41 88 08 40 or Tel. 01 41 02 03 04.

If you use IBM   IBM customers should note the two Paris access numbers:

Paris La Défense (PPP/SLIP/V.34/V.90/ISDN), Tel. 01 41 99 90 22
Paris Marne-la-Vallée (PPP/SLIP/V.34/V.90/ISDN), Tel. 01 55 85 90 10

Other Access Providers   For all other Internet users, check with your access provider before traveling about how to access your mail. If you're in a web bar and you download your e-mail, you'll either want to bring a disk to save it or make sure you leave the mail on the host server. If all else fails, you can always have your modem make an international call to your access provider back home to access your mail, in which case you'll have to reset your access settings by adding 00 1 to the access number. Connecting from a hotel room is still tricky business in most establishments due to the access number you need to get an outside line. If you are traveling with your laptop and are staying in a four-star hotel, ask for a room with a direct modem connection.

Web Bars

Paris has its dose of web bars, which can be helpful for travelers wishing to send or download e-mail. Numerous hotels now have business centers that allow you to send and fetch your e-mail and use the Internet for a fee. See the chart below for your web bar choices in Paris. For word processing on Macs or PCs, call ahead. Paris now has Easyeverything, with lots of computers, Internet access, low prices, flexible hours, and support staff.

PARIS WEB BARS

Web Bar	Address	Telephone Number	Métro
Bistrot Internet (Galeries Lafayette)	40, bd. Hausmann	01 42 82 30 33	Chaussée d'Antin, RER Auber
Café Cox	15, rue des Archives	01 42 72 08 00	Hôtel de Ville
Café Orbital	13, rue de Médicis	01 43 25 76 77	Odéon
Cristal Palace	43, bd. Sébastopol	01 42 36 22 22	Châtelet
Cyber Cube	5, rue Mignon	01 53 10 30 50	Odéon
Cyber Rest.	42, av. des Champs-Elysées	01 53 83 94 50	Franklin D. Roosevelt
Easyeverything	8, rue Harpe	01 55 42 12 13	St. Michel
Gaumont Parnasse	74, bd. Montparnasse	01 43 20 71 61	Montparnasse-Bienvenüe
Multimèdia	4, rue du Quatre Septembre	01 42 60 40 81	Bourse
Net Coffee	27, rue Lacépède	01 43 36 70 46	Monge
Planet Cyber	173, rue de Vaugirard	01 45 67 71 14	Pasteur
Virgin Mégastore	52, av. des Champs-Elysées	01 49 53 50 00	Franklin D. Roosevelt
Web Bar	32, rue de Picardie	01 42 72 66 55	Temple, République
Zowezo	37, rue Fontaine	01 40 23 00 71	Blanche

Using Cell Phones in France

Other than satellite-based phones, most American portable cellular phones will not work in France, so there's little point in bringing yours. This is likely to change quickly, and several multifrequency phones are beginning to reach the market. However, phones from the United Kingdom and the rest of Europe are capable of roaming France if you have a subscription that includes this feature. To rent a cell phone in Paris, call Euro Exaphone at Tel. 01 44 09 77 78, or Rent a Cell at Tel. 01 53 93 78 00 (fax 01 53 93 78 09).

Understanding the Busy Signal

When you dial a number in France and the line is busy, you will often get a recorded message in French stating in a pleasant, feminine voice that the line is busy, and would you please stay on the line. This is the french equivalent of "call waiting." Don't get confused and hang up.

Using the French Post Office

Post offices in France are easily identifiable with their bright yellow markings and the words *La Poste*. Not unfriendly places, they'll nonetheless impress you with their agonizing slowness. Post offices also provide banking and financial services, so although all you'll want to do is send a postcard, you'll find yourself in a mob of diverse activities and a hefty line. The efficiency of the post office tends to vary from office to office, so if you find a good one, you're lucky. Some are organized like a bakery where you need to take a number to be served; others have a single-line feeding several counters. Don't be put off by the thick Plexiglas slab between you and the clerk. France is filled with such *guichets*, protecting the state worker from potential aggression, germs, or undue progress. On the whole, try to avoid *La Poste* altogether by sending postcards and simple letters either from your hotel or by purchasing stamps at any *tabac* and posting them yourself. Postcards and letters under 20 grams (one or two sheets of paper) sent within France or the European Union countries require the same €0.46 stamp, or €0.67 to the United States. For heavier letters, the rates jump to €0.70 and €1.25. Mark your letters PRIORITAIRE, and don't forget to fill in the country. Be careful when writing numbers, since the French 1 and 7 differ from the Anglo-Saxon equivalent. Smart travelers buy the prepostmarked envelopes, good for anywhere in the world. These cost €0.69 per standard envelope and €2.29 for larger envelopes with contents weighing up to 100 grams. Then, you just slip them into the *ETRANGER* slot of any yellow mailbox and off they go.

If you need to send packages, try to keep them under two kilos (4.4 pounds). Again, for small packages your best bet is the prepostmarked (*prêt-à-poster Export*) box, which for €16.77 (for up to two kilos) not only simplifies your life, but gives your package first-class status. Count on priority rate letters and packages to generally take a week to arrive at most major U.S. cities, although some letters make it in as little as five days or as much as two weeks.

You can also send faxes from post offices. The service is called *Postéclair,* and the price is about €2 per page.

Similarly, mailboxes are bright yellow and are situated mounted to buildings and on posts outside of tobacco shops (*tabac*) where stamps—not just cigarettes—are sold.

Post offices also house public telephone booths, copy machines, and often, ATMs. Most offer Internet access as well.

Here's a quirky tip: You can also change foreign currency at most post offices. Since the rates are changed weekly, you may find either horrendous rates or the best rates in town. Check carefully.

General opening hours are from 8 a.m. to 7 p.m., with the last mail going out for the day at around 6 p.m. Another good piece of info: The main Paris post office, Paris-Louvre, is open 24 hours a day. It is located at 52, rue du Louvre, 75001, Métro: Louvre; Tel. 01 40 28 76 00.

La Poste also provides Chronopost service, part of the EMS express mail courier network. To North America, count on a minimum charge of $40. Otherwise, call Federal Express or DHL for hotel or home pick-up. If you have a courier account already, your account will be charged back home at the American rates. If not, you'll need to pay in euros, in cash, at the time of pick-up.

Federal Express	Toll free, Tel. 0 800 123 800
DHL Worldwide Express	Toll free, Tel. 0 800 202 525
UPS	Toll free, Tel. 0 800 877 877

Understanding Euros—Adieu French Francs

Now that France and the other European Union countries have opted for a single currency, the euro, the monetary scene has changed. Although the euro became the official currency of France on January 1, 1999, until 2002 the French franc will continue to be widely used in everyday commerce. Progressively, you will see goods and services now quoted in the euro, whose value fluctuates but is pegged close to the U.S. dollar at 6.55F.

French francs come in bank notes of 500F, 200F, 100F, 50F, and 20F. Be careful not to confuse the 200F and 100F notes. The 500F notes are greenish and larger and thus pose no confusion. Try to avoid buying a newspaper or Métro ticket with a 500F bill. Having said that, as a practice it's good to count your change, but again discretion is advised in that counting your change translates into a lack of trust and you don't want to offend anyone.

The euro coins come in eight sizes and values: 1 euro cent, 2 euro cents, 5 euro cents, 10 euro cents, 20 euro cents, and 50 euro cents, as well as 1- and 2-euro coins. The paper bills include seven notes in denominations of 5, 10, 20, 50, 100, 200, and 500 euros.

It is essential that you ask for the rate and commission fees before you agree to exchange currency. Sometimes a heavy commission is camouflaged by an advantageous rate. Go slow and use your calculator. Remember that the more you exchange the better the rate. But again, don't change too much too soon. And, unless you have a particular objection, try to pay for your larger expenses (hotel, restaurants, gifts, etc.) with a major credit card. The exchange rates are better, you limit your risk of carrying cash, you benefit from built-in insurance, and in many cases you even win frequent flyer miles per dollar spent. In France, you'll even be able to pay for your entrance to the Louvre and your subway pass with your credit card.

Changing Money

It never fails. As unromantic as it seems, historically the exchange rate between the dollar and the local currency has always had a direct impact on the kind of experience visitors have in Paris. Obviously, the more euros you get for your dollar, the more mileage you get out of your budget. Although no tourist has ever been able to single-handedly regulate the strength of the dollar, there are tips for assuring that you spend as little time as possible— and nab as many euros as you can—when converting your green backs into the coin of the realm.

Thinking in Euros

It's hard to "feel" the value of a currency you don't think in, and it's normal that you'll want to translate every price in the currency you best under-stand. But when you think in dollars, everything will seem much more expensive than it would be "back home." As a result you'll tend to spend less, do fewer things, and it will generally place a damper on your level of enjoyment. So "think euros" when determining value. Soon, you'll be able to determine value by comparing euro prices at one place to euro prices at other place. Similarly, when it comes to changing money, compare your alternatives in euros.

ATMs

As for changing money, by far the easiest and most economical means is to use your VISA or MasterCard to pull cash out of the ubiquitous ATMs (*guichets automatiques*) found on nearly every corner. Most are connected to the Cirrus or PLUS networks, offer instructions in English, and are clearly marked. You'll need to bring along your PIN, of course. The great advantage is that money is available when you need it, the exchange rate is based on the bank-to-bank rate, the transaction fee is usually a set $2 to $5 (ask your bank before leaving), which appears on your monthly statement, and is lower than what local banks often charge in commissions. To be safe, ask your bank for a duplicate card before leaving. Should your card get gobbled by a French machine when the bank is closed, your trip won't be in jeopardy.

Hotels

The worst place to exchange money is at your hotel, where the rates are not competitive and service charges are often tacked on. Hotels are not banks and change money as an extra service. Avoid them when possible.

Local Banks

The second worst place to change money is a local bank. First, many branches do not have an exchange window, and often hang up confusing signs on their doors stating "No exchange" or "No change." When they do offer foreign currency exchange, you'll most often get killed by both the rate and the commission, which is always a percentage above a fixed minimum. The CCF bank on the Champs-Elysées is the exception where the rates are advantageous. To figure this out, bring your calculator.

Change Bureaux

Better than banks are the numerous "change" bureaus that populate the touristy areas of town, like Saint-Germain-des-Prés, the Champs-Elysées, Châtelet–Les Halles, Montparnasse . . . They are often grouped, thus you can compare. Be careful not to get confused between the attractive "selling" rate and the less attractive "buying" rate. Remember, you're buying euros; they're buying dollars, while you are selling dollars and they are selling euros. Most travelers never realize that the published rate hung up on the board outside is almost always negotiable, especially when you're cashing in larger sums, a few hundred dollars at least. Don't be afraid to ask for a better rate. Usually, by simply asking you'll obtain a few cents more per dollar, which can quickly add up to enough for another meal or a small gift.

Since the fall of the Iron Curtain, Paris has attracted its share of black-market money-changers, often from Kiev and points east. They linger around the change bureaus and offer you much better rates. There is little risk of being arrested, but caution is still advised. Some naive tourists have ended up not with euros but with fistfuls of outdated and worthless Polish *zlotych*.

The Best Street in Paris for Changing Money

Little known to visitors, there is one street near La Bourse (stock exchange) where the professional money changers, gold merchants, and coin dealers have set up shop. For small amounts of cash it might not be worth going out of your way, but for larger sums the savings will be considerable. You may save up to 10 percent per dollar and not pay a commission. The published rates are better than you'll find in the banks and change bureaux, and on larger sums you can do even better. Get off the Métro at Grands Boulevards or Bourse and check out the change shops on the rue de Vivienne.

Cash for Cash

Another way to change money in Paris is by inserting your $20, $50, or $100 bills into special ATMs that convert foreign cash automatically. The exchange rates are clearly posted and so there are no surprises. These machines are found at 66, avenue des Champs-Elysées (Métro: George V), on the boulevard Saint-Michel at the corner of rue des Ecoles near the Sorbonne (Métro: Cluny–La Sorbonne), and at other select locations.

La Poste

We often send friends to check the exchange rate in the "main" post offices of the *arrondissement* in which they are staying. The post office only changes the exchange rate once a week, so if the official rate has dropped during the week, you may even end up making money by using the post office, where there are no commissions.

American Express

An old-time fixture in Paris, the American Express office has been a meeting point and landmark since the war. Today, it plays a less important role. For Amex card holders, it still serves as a point for getting cash advances, cashing checks, buying traveler checks, and having lost or stolen cards and traveler checks replaced. It even has a cash dispenser for card holders.

American Express
11, rue Scribe, 75009
Tel. 01 47 77 77 17
Métro: Opéra or RER Auber

Banking in Paris

As a visitor, try to spend little time or no time at all in a Paris bank. Citibank has two branches in Paris and a 24-hour Citiphone hotline for Citibank customers, Tel. 01 49 05 49 05. But don't count on this for much help. You often wait a long time on hold and then get cut off. If you have a Citibank card you can withdraw cash at any ATM connected to the Cirrus network. The fee depends on the amount you withdraw. No one at Citibank will be able to tell you how much that is, but we've been promised that the ATM will flash on the screen how much you'll be debited for the operation and will ask you if you authorize this. If you lose an American-issued Citibank card in France call (00) 1 (210) 677-0065.

Getting in the Bank Door

Don't get spooked by the strange doors of all banks in France. For security purposes, banks have opted for a system whereby you must push a green button to be let in. The outer door unlocks when the green button lights up "POUSSER," meaning push. You enter into a middle chamber between two doors. The door behind you must lock before the door in front of you can open. You push a second green button that unlocks when a bank employee buzzes you in. Don't panic if you find yourself in this no-man's-land for half a minute waiting to be buzzed in. The same process occurs when you try to leave. Annoying, but bank robberies are down in France ever since.

For your information, the largest commercial banks with the most branches include:

BNP-Paribus (Banque Nationale de Paris/Paribas)
CA (Crédit Agricole)
CCF (Crédit Commercial de France)
CL (Crédit Lyonnais)
SG (Société Générale)

Getting Money Wired

If you need to have money sent to you or you need to send money to someone else, the French post office acts as an agent for Western Union Money Transfers. The system is simple. Someone contacts Western Union in the United States and wires an amount of dollars to you. By phone they give you the transaction code. You go into any French post office, say you want to pick up a Western Union Money Transfer, give them the transfer code, and they give you the equivalent amount in euros. The sender pays for the service.

Using Credit Cards

MasterCard and VISA are widely accepted in restaurants, shops, hotels, Métro ticket offices, cinemas, and even the Louvre. In France, you'll see these logos, plus a generic one CB for *Carte Bleue,* which administers VISA and MasterCard transactions. American Express is accepted less and less, and it is not advised to travel only with an Amex card. Diner's Club is accepted in many establishments. In France, credit cards have embedded chips built in and are used with a secret PIN code, meaning that users don't need to sign the purchase voucher. Your cards—with the magnetic strip on the back—require a swipe in the machine. French merchants don't always know how to do this. You may have to show them.

Traveler Checks

Hotels and large restaurants usually accept traveler checks. If you pay a hotel bill with traveler checks in U.S. dollars the funds will be converted to euros first. It's better to pay directly in euros or euro traveler checks.

Tipping

Tipping in French is *pourboire* (poor**bwar**), literally "for a drink." Parisians in general are not highly service-oriented, and it has not been drummed repeatedly into the heads of employees and clerks in this city that the customer is always king. Thus, the relationship between services rendered and tips given is not omnipresent as it is in the United States.

In fact tipping habits in Paris are simple to understand. There are, however, a few nuances involved. For a detailed discussion on tipping in restaurants see Part Seven, Dining in Paris. There are a few points that must be understood from the start though. France is not a tipping society in the way you may be accustomed to back home. A few modest but correct tips placed at the right time will be appreciated and will enhance the service you're getting and will continue to get.

Here are a few guidelines:

- The gesture of tipping in Paris should be characterized by a naturalness and the elegance of the act. If a 10% tip on a taxi ride brings the total fare of €5.50 you'd obviously give €6. This can work in your favor as well. Try in all cases to maintain a fluidity and elegance without either overpaying or underpaying too much.

- Waiters and waitresses: A service charge of between 15% and 20% is included in almost all eating circumstances. This means that the price of the service has been figured into the menu prices. It should not appear as an extra on your bill. The tip is only a small, ritual gesture of your pleasure with the person serving you. Parisians were accustomed to leaving a five- or ten-franc coin and maybe the small copper coins in the dish in which the bill is presented. It's too early to say what the new habit will be with the new currency, but most likely, Parisians will be leaving a euro coin or two on the plate. Do not leave 15% or 20% of the bill, ever. You'll only prove how easy it is to take advantage of ignorant tourists.

- Taxi rides: Give 10% or round out the sum on the meter when your driver has been efficient and you're satisfied. There is an automatic supplement for train station pick-ups, for luggage in the trunk, etc. Don't calculate the tip on this. Only calculate the tip on what's on the meter.

- Hotel porters: A euro or two for for each full-sized suitcase is standard.

- Concierges: Nothing, unless they have rendered a particular service for you.

- Hairdressers: One or two euros is fine. More if you're having it done somewhere chic.

- Tour guides: Play it by ear.

- Ushers: Traditionally, ushers in concert halls and small, independent cinemas are tipped €0.30 or so per person for showing you to your seat. This very Parisian habit is disappearing.

Things the Locals Already Know

Getting an English-Language Newspaper

Many Paris hotels of three stars and more receive at least a few copies of *The International Herald Tribune,* the *Financial Times,* or the European edition of *The Wall Street Journal.* You can find *USA Today* as well, but frankly, you're in Paris and you don't really need to know what's doing in Illinois. Smaller hotels may not offer newspapers at all. For general news, international and American news, and sports, you can find the Paris-based *IHT* at most newsstands *(kiosques)* in the city for €1.68. The Sunday *New York Times* can be found at the bookstores W. H. Smith (248, rue de Rivoli, 75001, Métro: Concorde) and Brentano's (37, avenue de l'Opéra, 75002, Métro: Opera).

For other info in English call the Paris Tourist Office at 08 36 68 31 12.

Other Paris Publications

Paris Voice   This English-language community newspaper is published in Paris monthly. Topical articles are mainly targeted to the English-language residents of Paris, but the listings of cultural events in English will certainly give you a great idea of how to spend your leisure time. Found in all the English-language bookshops and numerous pubs and restaurants.

Where Paris   A free city magazine of high-quality articles and relevant listings and local advertising distributed in 3,500 of Paris's finest hotel rooms. Includes excellent city maps.

Time Out Paris Free Guide   Each season the British publisher issues a 50-page giveaway of arts, restaurants, and nightlife highlights, distributed in hotel lobbies, train stations, etc.

Pariscope   For €0.46 you can pick up at any kiosque a thick weekly calendar of cinema, theater, exhibition, club, show, and concert listings in Paris. In French. In addition, you'll find a ten-page insert in English published by Time Out in which English-language events are covered. A great source of ideas for anglophone visitors. Comes out on Wednesdays.

L'Officiel des Spectacles   Same idea as Pariscope, but cheaper, and without the English-language supplement.

FUSAC   Free advertising supplement catering to the English-language community.

Irish Eyes   Free community magazine focused on the Irish community in Paris.

Other Free Stuff   The Galeries Lafayette and the Samaritaine supply free city and Métro maps in their stores and in many Métro stations and tourist offices.

Public Toilets

Understanding where to find and how to use public toilets removes not only pressure from your bladder but also a stressful burden from your mind. Thinking about this when you need a toilet is too late. Fortunately, Paris, the birthplace of the public *pissoir* (pees-**wahr**), offers easy, sanitary, and well-located solutions.

French law states that you have the right to enter any café and use the toilet without consuming anything. (Note: don't use the word *pissoir*.) We suggest that you ask first. *Est-ce que je peux utiliser les toilettes, s'il vous plaît?* You might feel more comfortable stopping into a café, standing at the counter, ordering a coffee (the cheapest thing on the menu), and then before it even arrives, following the sign to *les toilettes,* or asking *"Où sont les toilettes, s'il vous plaît?"*

Caution: some Parisian cafés still have the old-style Turkish toilets. These porcelain gems consist merely of a hole in the floor with two spots for your feet. For gentlemen executing Number One, there is no problem. For the uninitiated and all other scenarios, this is a bit crude and tricky in that you need to keep your coat, jacket, handbag, backpack, trouser bottoms, etc. clear of fire. Before you pull the chain sending a torrent of water down to rinse the environs, make sure you get your feet out of the way. A truly Parisian experience, and character-building to boot. You'll thoroughly enjoy your awaiting coffee when you reemerge into the day in progress.

Toilet paper, although often rough, is usually available, but experienced travelers carry paper on them as standard procedure. The more upmarket restaurants and hotels will have an attendant sitting at the entrance to the toilets behind a plate with a few coins on it. It's up to you if you feel like leaving a small tip.

The Public Toilet Compartments

In the late 1980s, the city erected hundreds of public pay toilets on the streets of Paris. These rather futuristic constructions require a coin for entry. A sliding door opens. You enter. The door shuts and locks. The cabin, which resembles a large airplane toilet, is well lit and heated. The rest is self-explanatory, other than after each use, the cabin is automatically washed, disinfected, and dried before it can be used again. Very reliable and worth the expense. There is no time limit to each visit, but if you stay in for too long you will arouse suspicions.

Uncurbed Dogs

Paris's reputation for dog excrement has outstripped contemporary reality, but the problem continues nonetheless. So, look down. Dog owners are getting a bit better, but no steep fines or sense of civil duty (pardon the pun) keep the owners of Rex (the most common dog name in France) in line. Dogs are supposed to be led to the gutter, *canivau,* in which street-cleaning water is often running. Paris enjoys a large fleet of street cleaners, often Africans, decked in green uniforms and manned with green, plastic, branchlike brooms, who direct the flow of street water and sweep the sidewalks religiously.

Doing Laundry

A quick scenario: You're perched in your favorite Hugo Boss blazer, feeling as cool as spring on the Seine; you're in Paris, of course, and you're sitting *tête-à-tête* with your favorite person on earth, snuggled at your favorite table in your favorite bistro, devouring your favorite meringue desert, an *île flottante.* And then catastrophe hits: an unctuous glob of rich and unforgiving *crème anglaise* slips from your dessert spoon and free-falls down your jacket, landing everywhere in your lap. You try the white wine myth, then salt. Nothing works; you need help. "And I was counting on wearing the same ensemble to the opera tomorrow night," you cry out in private pain. Help is not on its way.

Going to the cleaners in Paris sometimes feels more like being taken to the cleaners, and dry cleaning is still somewhat of a luxury in France. Be prepared to spend around €8 to have a single shirt, pair of pants, or pullover laundered and ironed. The verb to iron is *repasser.* T-shirts will cost you around €4.50, and socks and underwear cost about €2.60. A suit or overcoat will cost between €12 and €22—everything depends on the neighborhood. If you expect one-hour service or to get your clothes back on wire hangers or with cardboard in your shirts, you may be disappointed. Often, fresh laundry is only wrapped neatly in thin paper. This is more a question of aesthetics and practicality than anything else. Timing is often a problem with neighborhood cleaners, since many do not have "on location" cleaning and need three days to get your clothes back to you. And, of course, plenty of cleaners are shut on Mondays and are closed between noon and 2 p.m. for lunch. Ask in advance, and *do not lose your ticket.*

More and more laundromats have cropped up around the city, and this may be your best or only option. Plan on bringing a pocketful of coins. You may want to pick up your own soap. French washing machines take more time than their American counterparts, as do the dryers. In general, Parisians wash their clothes slowly and thoroughly but at lower temperatures. They do not overdry their clothes, since "cooking" your clothes too long weakens the fiber. They are more conscious of fabric fragility and expect garments to last longer. If you're used to a 25-minute wash cycle, count on twice that in Paris. Many laundromats include self-serve dry-cleaning machines, which are advantageous, especially for bulky coats and the like, but the results don't always cut the *moutarde* (mustard).

Your first stop for laundry will most likely be your hotel. Most of the larger and upscale hotels have their own in-house laundry services. The housekeeper is called the *gouvernante*. The Hôtel Meurice, for example, will press your suit in 30 minutes for about €18 or have it dry-cleaned for less than €30. If you're in a hurry, expect them to add a 30% charge. The smaller hotels almost always farm out your soiled and wrinkled garments to a nearby "pressing." Usually, clothes sent out by 9 or 10 a.m. will be back in your room by the next afternoon. If this is not fast enough, ask for the local equivalent of rush, *service express* (sairvees express), which in most cases means "same-day service," again for a supplement of 30% more. Really small hotels have no laundry services but will on occasion lend you an iron. Otherwise, it's either self-service in the sink or finding your own "pressing" or laundromat. Bring your own travel detergent.

Smoking

If you're a smoker, there's no problem—you'll feel right at home. But chances are that you're not a smoker, and thus the omnipresence of smokers and their smoke will take some adjusting to. The truth about smoking in France is that nearly 40% of the adult population refuses to kick the habit. That's over 20 million individuals. And although there is some progress in convincing smokers to reduce the amount they smoke or quit altogether, there is still great resistance to the idea. Even 30% of French doctors continue to smoke. The French love their nicotine (named after the Frenchman who imported tobacco into France, Jean Nicot) and prefer to view the act of smoking more as a source of pleasure and social accoutrement than as an addiction. You'll find it difficult to convince a Parisian smoker to stop on moral grounds, and if a smoker's smoke is bothering you in a public place, you're best off just saying so nicely and hoping for pity rather than making public gestures of intolerance. Parisians are intolerant of the American "intolerance" with smokers. Be careful; you're on their turf. Fortunately, French law now forbids smoking in all public places, airports, train stations, Métro platforms, buses, and government buildings. The bad news is that the law is by and large ignored. Even the lobby of the "nonsmoking" Ministry of Health building is cluttered with busy ashtrays and clouds of smoke.

Cafés and restaurants must offer nonsmoking sections by law, but in practice you'll find there are no such sections, or when there are, they'll be small and strategically placed, often near the toilets. Depending on the degree of nuisance that smoking presents to you, you'll have to pick and choose how best to avoid smoke or defend yourself. It often helps to sit outside if possible; at least then you've got some fresh air combating the smoker's pollution.

Very few hotels have designated "nonsmoking" rooms, but it's worth asking for one. Check our profiled hotels for smoke-free rooms.

When making restaurant reservations be sure to request "non-fumeurs" in advance. You may find that since the nonsmoking tables are few and far between that you'll have to wait longer for a table or not be able to get a reservation for the time that you wish. Again, decide in advance which is more important to you, no smoke or eating at a particular place at a particular time. Eating earlier helps the smoke situation somewhat in places that often get cramped and busy around 10 p.m. Check our list of profiled restaurants for their smoking policies.

If you do smoke and are looking for a pack, you'll be obliged to duck into a neighborhood tobacco shop (*tabac*) for your cigarettes, cigars, or pipe tobacco. In France tobacco is a state monopoly licensed exclusively to these authorized cafés. The usual price is about €3 per pack. You'll see the red leaf-shaped sign hanging above the sidewalk *tabac* sign. Also note that *tabacs* are official points of sale for postage stamps and other fiscal stamps. You'll always find a French mailbox (yellow and square and usually fixed to a wall) outside a *tabac*. As a service to customers, most restaurants and bars will have selected brands of cigarettes discreetly available at a marked-up price.

In France there are two types of tobacco available, *blonde* and *brune*. The *blonde* or refined tobacco corresponds to the cigarettes North Americans usually smoke. The *brune* is darker and harsher, the "filterless" kind that beret-wearing Frenchmen in black-and-white films smoke. France's best known brands are Gauloises and Gitanes. Otherwise, you'll find all the major international brands of cigarettes, although some smokers contend that the Marlboro they buy in Europe does not taste like the same brand back home. When you consider that the state collects about 75% of the cover price in taxes, you'll begin to understand why the government's efforts to reduce smoking in France lacks real teeth.

Health

International travelers are always nervous about getting sick while they're away. You should put these fears aside concerning your Paris trip. French doctors and hospitals are excellent, and 24-hour emergency service is readily available. There are two major hospitals in which English is the mother tongue, several English pharmacies, and plenty of English-speaking and often U.S.-trained doctors and dentists in Paris.

Tap Water

If you're hesitant about drinking the tap water *(eau du robinet)*, eliminate that thought from your mind this instant. Although Parisians drink bottled mineral water incessantly, the tap water is 100% safe.

Doctors

If you need a doctor, ask the concierge at your hotel, and he'll either inform you where the closest doctor's office is located or call the *Médecin de garde* (the neighborhood doctor on call) who'll make a house call to your hotel room. You'll quickly notice a difference in style and aesthetics, as French doctors come across as more professorial than clinical. Doctors do not dispense much medicine themselves. Nor do they administer tests or do any lab work. They'll give you a prescription *(ordonnance)* for medication or lab tests which you'll need to get filled at a local pharmacy or laboratory. A visit to the doctor's office will cost you between €20 and €30, and a house call will cost from €40 to €60. Specialists may cost twice as much.

Health Insurance

It's a good idea to ask your health insurance provider what the extent of your coverage is while traveling abroad, and what procedures to follow in the case of illness or accident while you're in France. Bring a copy of your health coverage card with you, and the phone and fax numbers of your health insurance provider in case you have a problem. You will have to pay your French doctor's bill in cash. You'll get a standardized form called a *Feuille de soins*, which you may be able to use for a reimbursement from your health insurance provider when you get home. Some hospitals accept credit cards, and the American Hospital can process some American insurance bills directly.

Hospitals

In case of emergency or a late-night illness or accident, consult with your hotel concierge first. He'll either call a doctor *(SOS Médecins* for 24-hour house calls) or, in extreme cases, the SAMU or *Pompiers* (pohm-**pyah** [fire department]), who'll rush you to the closest hospital.

SAMU	15
Police	17
Pompiers	18

The American Hospital of Paris *(Hôpital Américain de Paris)* is a famous, private hospital that employs British, American, and French doctors and is partially bilingual. F. Scott Fitzgerald, among others, spent time here in the prerenovation days drying out "on the wagon." It is much more expensive than French hospitals, but it offers excellent health care with a style that you may recognize and appreciate. You can pay with dollars and major credit cards. Those covered by Blue Cross–Blue Shield have their hospitalization covered at the American Hospital, provided they fill out the appropriate paperwork first.

The American Hospital of Paris
63, boulevard Victor Hugo
92200 Neuilly sur Seine
Tel. 01 46 41 25 25, Fax: 01 46 24 49 38
Métro: Point de Neuilly

Another hospital that employs English-speaking doctors and is noted for serving the anglophone community is:

Hertford British Hospital
3, rue Barbès
92300 Levallois Perret
Tel. 01 46 39 22 22 (24 hours)
Métro: Anatole-France

You can find a full listing of doctors at www.paris-anglo.com, and in the Paris-Anglophone directory, found in most bookstores. The two hospitals listed above can also provide names of doctors and specialists.

If Your Children Become Ill

Either get the hotel to call for a doctor or, in the case of serious illness or accident, call the SAMU or *Pompiers*. In the case of an emergency go directly to the closest of the following hospitals. These are Paris's best pediatric centers.

Hôpital Armand Trousseau
26, avenue Dr. Arnold Netter, 75012
Tel. 01 44 73 74 75

Hôpital Saint-Vincent-de-Paul
74, avenue Denfert-Rochereau, 75014
Tel. 01 40 48 81 11

Hôpital Necker
149, rue de Sèvres, 75015
Tel. 01 44 49 40 00

Dentists

If you need a dentist, ask at your hotel. Otherwise, call *SOS Dentaire* at Tel. 01 43 37 51 00. If you prefer an English-speaking dentist, you can request one.

Pharmacies

French pharmacies are not to be confused with U.S.-style drugstores. They are purely medical, and the personnel are highly trained and knowledgeable about illness and treatments. The pharmacist in Paris plays a more active role in curing his or her customers than pharmacists back home. When in doubt, ask a local pharmacist. They are even trained to identify poisonous mushrooms! Every pharmacy has a sign on its window indicating the *pharmacie de garde*, the closest pharmacy open during non-business hours. There is always one pharmacy in every area open at all times.

Pharmacie Swann
6, rue de Castiglione, 75001
Tel. 01 42 60 72 96
Métro: Concorde
Hours: 9 a.m.–7:30 p.m.
Closed Sundays, holidays.

Pharmacie Les Champs
84, avenue des Champs-Elysées
(passage des Champs), 75008
Tel. 01 45 62 02 41
Métro: George-V
Hours: 24 hours a day

Pharmacie Anglo-Américaine
37, avenue Marceau, 75116
Tel. 01 47 20 57 37
Métro: Alma-Marceau
Hours: Monday–Friday, 8:30 a.m.–7:30 p.m.; Saturday, 9 a.m.–5 p.m. Closed Sundays.

Prescriptions   It's best you bring enough prescribed medication with you to last for the duration of your trip. In case you need more medication (or you lose your pills), it's a smart idea to bring copies of your prescriptions with you when you travel. We tell people who are very uptight about being ill away from home to have their local pharmacist write out the generic names of their medications, since the same drugs in Europe may be available under a different trade name. Take the phone and fax number of your doctor and pharmacist with you too, in case you need a new prescription faxed to Paris. You may even want to leave copies of your prescriptions with your local pharmacist and inform him or her of your travel dates to Paris. In most cases, pharmacies in Paris will help you out even without a prescription *(ordonnance* [ordun-nunce]*)*.

To know precisely what to ask for in a French pharmacy, we suggest you ask your hotel concierge. Note: condoms are available in all pharmacies, in dispensers in Métro stations, and outside pharmacies. The French word for condom is *préservatif* (preh-zair-va-**teef**). Sanitary napkins are called *serviettes hygiéniques* (sir-vi**yet** eejeeyen-**neek**), and both are available in department stores and pharmacies.

Glasses and Contact Lenses

It's always smart to travel with a back-up pair of glasses or lenses. Also bring your prescription along in case you have to have new glasses made quickly. There are optometrists and eyeglass stores in every neighborhood.

Religion and Houses of Worship

Paris has its share of churches and other houses of worship, and you can find services and mass in English by contacting the following:

Emmanuel Baptist Church   56, rue des Bons Raisins, 92500 Rueil-Malmaison; Tel. 01 47 51 29 63; www.ebcparis.org. English services at 9:45 and 11 a.m., French service at 6:30 p.m.

Central Baptist Church   23, rue Beaunier, 75014; Tel. 01 46 55 04 21; Métro: Porte d'Orléans. English service at 9 a.m., French service at 10:30 a.m.

St. Michael's Church   5, rue d'Aguesseau, 75008; Tel. 01 47 42 70 88; http://saintmichaelspatis.free.fr; Métro: Condorde. Anglican services at 9:30 a.m., 11:15 a.m., and 6:30 p.m.

Trinity International Church   Hotel Orion at Paris–La Défense 8, boulevard de Neuilly, 75011; Tel. 01 43 33 04 06; www.trinity-paris.com; Métro: Esplanade La Défense. English service, 10:30 a.m.

The American Church in Paris   65, quai d'Orsay, 75007; Tel. 01 40 62 05 00; www.americanchurchinparis.org; Métro: Invalides. Protestant, interdenominational services, 9 and 11 a.m.

The American Cathedral in Paris   23, avenue George-V, 75008; Tel. 01 53 23 84 00; Métro: George-V/Alma-Marceau. Episcopalian and Anglican services, 9 and 11 a.m.

La Grande Mosquée   Place du Puits de l'Ermite, 75005; Tel. 01 45 35 97 33; Métro: Monge. Mosque.

Christian Science Church   36, boulevard Saint-Jacques, 75014; Tel. 01 47 07 26 60; Métro: Denfert-Rochereau.

Church of Jesus Christ of Latter Day Saints   5, rond-point de l'Alliiance, 78000 Versailles; Tel. 01 39 53 39 14. English service, 9:30 a.m.

St. Joseph's Roman Catholic Church   50, avenue Hoche, 75008; Tel. 01 42 27 28 56; Métro: Charles-de-Gaulle-Etoile. English services, 10 a.m. and noon.

Kehilat Gesher   10, rue de Pologne, 78100 St-Germain-en-Laye; Tel. 01 39 21 97 19; Métro: RER St-Germain-en-Laye. French-Anglophone-Jewish congregation (Reform/Conservative). Friday service, 7 p.m., alternating between St-Germain-en-Laye and Paris's 17th arrondissement. Phone for details or email Kehilatgesher@free.fr.

Travelers with Disabilities

Travelers with physical disabilities should not be discouraged from traveling to Paris, but they should be forewarned: France is far behind the United States in terms of both legislation and public awareness concerning the needs and rights of disabled persons. Traveling to and from Paris in a wheelchair or on crutches will pose some serious obstacles that are surmountable only when you're well informed and adequately prepared.

One disabled Floridian who visited Paris with his wife during the summer found that even in the big hotel chains in Paris he couldn't confirm a room with an easy-access shower. Often the smaller hotels do not have elevators large enough to accommodate wheelchairs. Public buildings do not all have ramps, and some that do still have a step or two at the top or bottom, making the access hazardous. We've asked a young French woman, Frédérique Suchet, who, following a serious fall while working in a local circus has been confined to a wheelchair since the summer of 1998, to point out some of the obstacles that disabled tourists should expect to encounter. Frédérique is launching a nonprofit organization to help change conditions in France for the physically disabled.

Despite the city's pride in restoring and maintaining its sites and monuments, Paris today remains only moderately accessible and friendly to wheelchair users. Your first worry will be how to get around in a city that is so vast, lively, and old. Your best bet is to have a car at your disposal (preferably a taxi) and be accompanied.

Make sure you notify your airline when booking and reconfirming your flight that you're in a wheelchair and you need assistance on both ends. This will activate the *service d'assistance* at the airport in Paris. Note that if you have an electric wheelchair, you should make sure that you remember to take care of the dry-cell batteries before leaving home. The liquid-electrolysis–type batteries must absolutely be emptied before boarding (emptying takes about an hour). Gel batteries pose no problem at all.

Upon arriving at either Charles de Gaulle or Orly airport, a private assistance company will greet you at the exit of the plane and accompany you through immigrations and customs and baggage claim.

The airport shuttle to the RER subway station at Charles de Gaulle is wholly accessible. The Orlyval, a totally automated train connecting Orly to central Paris via the Antony RER station, is also accessible for wheelchair users, but I strongly recommend taking a taxi to your hotel. Note that taxis are not supposed to charge you a supplement for the transport of your wheelchair.

If you're traveling by train, note that in all the TGV (fast) trains, special disabled seating is situated in first class but is open to you with a second-class ticket. Some TGVs are equipped with direct-access toilets for wheelchairs, but in others you'll have to ask a conductor for a *chaise de transfert,* a transfer chair. He's supposed to know what this is and where to find one onboard.

Every SNCF station in France has assistance service found in the *Accueil* area of the station, which will advise the destination station of your arrival. Use this. Don't forget to mark your baggage with disabled stickers and bring your disabled card with you.

The SNCF published a guide for the disabled voyager in May 1998, but the information is so generalized (disabled services provided in individual stations) and/or complicated (making reservations) that it is almost useless. The guide suggests that you look for the blue wheelchair sign both in individual stations and on SNCF timetables to locate disabled services and accessibility. We suggest that you call the following toll-free number for more up-to-date information (in French), Tel. 0 800 15 47 53; or Tel. 08 36 35 35 35 to speak with someone directly and make obligatory reservations (at least 48 hours in advance). Taxis that are accessible to the disabled can be ordered at Tel. 01 47 08 93 50 and Tel. 01 47 49 37 40. Contact *Les Compagnons du Voyage* at Tel. 01 45 83 67 77 to reserve a companion traveler and assistant anywhere in France.

The principal train stations are equipped with lifts, wheelchairs, ticket windows, toilets and telephone booths reserved for the disabled voyager. In theory, railway staff should be on hand to assist you. Certain first-class cars in the Eurostar and Thalys trains are equipped with disabled-adapted seats and toilets. Guide dogs ride for free on the Thalys, but animals are not allowed on the Eurostar because of English quarantine restrictions on all animals.

Hotels Equipped for Travelers with Disabilities

The legal norms and requirements for accessibility for disabled citizens in France are not as well respected as in the United States. Expect to find details that blatantly ignore all good sense. Regulated heights of steps are not respected, railings may be missing, and the like. The worst problem, though, is that in Paris the criteria for disabled accessibility have all been determined by nondisabled administrators.

Below is a partial list of hotels, organized by *arrondissement,* that offer rooms that have been adapted for safe use by disabled visitors. (Bathrooms, toilets, sinks, and showers conform to legal norms.) We've indicated the number of rooms available to you.

HOTELS EQUIPPED FOR TRAVELERS WITH DISABILITIES

1st arrondissement
Citadines Apart'Hotel
4, rue des Innocents
Tel. 0 825 333 332
Fax: 01 41 05 78 87
Métro: Châtelet
6 disabled-adapted rooms

Hôtel du Louvre ★★★
1, place André Malraux
Tel. 01 44 58 38 38
Fax: 01 44 58 38 01
Métro: Palais-Royal
2 disabled-adapted rooms

Novotel Paris Les Halles ★★★
8, place Marguerite de Navare
Tel. 0 825 333 332
Fax: 01 40 26 05 79
Métro: Châtelet
7 disabled-adapted rooms

2nd arrondissement
Citadines Apart'Hotel
18, rue Favart
Tel. 0 825 010 335
Fax: 01 40 15 14 50
Métro: Richelieu-Drouot
3 disabled-adapted rooms

3rd arrondissement
Tulip Inn Little Palace ★★★
4, rue Salomon de Caus
Tel. 01 42 72 08 15
Fax: 01 42 72 45 81
Métro: Réamur-Sébastopol
1 disabled-adapted room

5th arrondissement
Hôtel de L'Espérance ★★
15, rue Pascal
Tel. 01 47 07 10 99
Fax: 01 47 37 56 19
Métro: Censier-Daubenton
1 disabled-adapted room

6th arrondissement
Holiday Inn Paris St-Germain-
des-Prés ★★★
92, rue de Vaugirard

Tel. 01 49 54 87 00
Fax: 01 49 54 87 01
Métro: St-Placide
1 disabled-adapted room

Libertel Prince de Conti ★★★
8, rue Guénégaud
Tel. 01 44 07 30 40
Fax 01 44 07 36 34
Métro: Odéon
1 disabled-adapted room

7th arrondissement
Hôtel Prince ★★
66, avenue Bosquet
Tel. 01 47 05 40 90
Fax: 01 47 53 06 62
Métro: Ecole-Militaire
1 disabled-adapted room

8th arrondissement
Golden Tulip Saint-Honoré ★★★★
220, rue de Fbg. Saint-Honoré
Tel. 01 49 53 03 09
Fax 01 40 75 02 00
Métro: George-V
3 disabled-adapted rooms

Arc Elysées ★★★
45, rue de Washington
Tel. 01 45 63 69 33
Fax 01 45 63 76 25
Métro: George-V
2 disabled-adapted rooms

12th arrondissement
Citadines Apart'Hotel
14, rue de Chaligny
Tel. 0825 010 332
Fax 01 40 01 15 20
Métro: Reuilly-Diderot
3 disabled-adapted rooms

Relais Mercure Paris Bercy ★★
77, rue de Bercy
Tel. 01 53 46 50 50
Fax: 01 53 46 50 99
Métro: Bercy
7 disabled-adapted rooms

Using the Métro

A few Métro and RER stations, as well as a growing number of buses, are wheelchair-accessible. Ask at an RATP information office for the "plan pratique pour des personnes à besoins spécifiques." It can also be downloaded at www.ratp.fr: Click on "Voyager," then "Accessibilité."

Restaurants and Disabled Access

Numerous restaurants in Paris are accessible to people in wheelchairs inside and on their sidewalks and terraces. However, very few Paris restaurants are equipped with disabled-accessible toilets, with the exception of a few museum and chain hotel restaurants. Check our list of profiled restaurants in Part Seven, Dining in Paris, or call ahead for details. If it's any comfort to you, note that all McDonald's restaurants are wholly accessible.

Monuments and Disabled Access

Don't be shy about attempting to see everything. There will be some minor obstacles, but on the whole you can visit most sights. You must go up the Eiffel Tower. On a clear day be prepared to see all of Paris and 40 miles beyond. The night view is splendid. Go up the north leg of the tower *(Pilier Nord)*. You can go as far as the second level by elevator. The toilets on the ground, first, and second floors are all wheelchair friendly.

For disabled access information on Paris's main attractions and monuments, see the detailed listings of attractions in Part Six, Sightseeing and Tours.

A Useful Contact

The *Comité National Français de Liaison pour la Readaptation des Handicapés* (CNFLRH), Point Handicap, located at 236 bis, rue Tolbiac, 75013, Tel. 01 53 80 66 66, fax 01 53 80 66 67, publishes a guide (in French) concerning transportation, parking, public telephone booths, and recreational activities for disabled persons.

Traveling with Children

Traveling with children in general affords you great pleasures and joys in addition to daily problems to anticipate and solve. Visiting Paris with kids can be wonderfully gratifying and desperately frustrating if you don't plan ahead. On the positive side, Parisians are generally more tolerant than Anglo-Saxons when it comes to children. You'd never find condominium complexes in France for adults only, and you'll often see children in fancy restaurants. And, although many restaurants and hotels are not as family-oriented as you may be used to finding back home, there are lots of wonderful activities for kids, big and small, that will enchant you.

Eating Out with Kids

Restaurants are generally open for lunch between noon and 2 p.m. and between 7 p.m. and 10 p.m. for dinner. If feeding time for your kids differs from this, you'd better bring along snacks. Fast food is always an option for hungry or finicky kids, but we don't encourage this. You're in Paris! Don't rush off to one of the scores of McDonald's (known in Paris as *McDoh*) that grace this city.

Don't count on finding highchairs, paper bibs, crayons, or children's toys in restaurants. Your kids are welcome, but you had better bring along your own paraphernalia and amusements.

Meals take more time in Paris than you're probably accustomed to. You should ask for your children's food first. Kitchens do not always understand these special needs, so really insist on this, with a smile. If your five-year-old is about to pull a tantrum if she doesn't get her noodles *(les pâtes* [lay **paht**]*)*, order the noodles before you order anything else. If your child is not going to like a sauce, ask for the *pâtes nature* (nahtur). Memorize this sentence: *Excusez-moi, est-ce qu'on peut avoir les pâtes pour le petit (or la petite) maintenant, s'il vous plaît?* (Excusay **mwa**, **es**kown puh ahv**war** lay **paht** por luh peh**tee** (la peh**teet**) met**nawh**, see vou play.) You are asking, "Excuse me, may we have the noodles for the child now, please?"

Some restaurants will offer a *menu enfant*, which usually consists of a slice of ham or a *saucisse* (hot dog), *steack haché* (ground beef), french fries or pasta, an orange juice, and a yogurt or *crème caramel*. You may prefer to make up a plate from the good things you ordered.

For bigger kids, we strongly suggest that you let them explore freely. You are helping them develop their tastes and build their understanding of the world. Cuisine is a major part of this process of discovery.

There is no taboo in Paris against letting adolescents taste the wine.

Baby-sitters

Larger hotels may have a list of local baby-sitters and may even arrange for one, but we've researched the subject for you and can recommend several highly reputable and reliable baby-sitting services. You don't need a lot of phone numbers; you need a state of mind. You need to be 100% confident about leaving your little ones in a hotel in a foreign city. Regardless of the age of your kids, you'll be able to step out for dinner or dash around town on a shopping spree without worry and without *les enfants* (lay zohn-**fohn**) in tow.

The hourly rate for baby-sitters in Paris ranges from €5 to €8 per hour, with a bit more for multiple kids and late at night. The services listed here all claim to provide carefully screened, bilingual baby-sitters, who are almost all exclusively female university students. You can relax as you're sipping champagne at Maxim's because your kids will be learning French from the baby-sitter.

Ababa 8, avenue du Maine, 75015; Tel. 01 45 49 46 46. This service has roughly 500 available baby-sitters and has been in existence for nearly 15 years. If you want to be sure to speak with someone in English, call after 4 p.m. They prefer that you don't reserve before you get to Paris, since they want to make sure they get all the exact details right. The rate is €5.64 for one or two kids an hour with a two-hour minimum. €0.40 extra per additional child, plus a €10.21 agency fee. If you keep the baby-sitter later than 11 p.m., you'll need to pay her taxi fare home. You pay the baby-sitter directly in euros. No credit cards accepted.

Babysitting Service 18, rue Tronchet, 75008; Tel. 01 46 37 51 24; fax 01 42 66 52 45. Madame Marise Bloch's service has been providing baby-sitters since 1981. Her supply of about 100 young women includes English-speaking students. The hourly rate is €5.34, and there's a €9.15 agency fee. No credit cards accepted.

Kid Services 17, rue Molière, 75001; Tel. 01 42 61 90 00; fax 01 42 61 55 00; www.kidservices.fr. Since 1971 this highly professional and reliable service has been matching up their baby-sitters with parents who want some free time to themselves. With a pool of over 800 baby-sitters, Kid Services only needs to be contacted two hours before the time you need the sitter! They also claim that they'll send you a bilingual sitter if you request one. The hourly rate is €7.62 an hour for newborns up to 4 months of age, €5.50 per hour for older children, and €6.40 for a bilingual sitter. And you will have to pay the sitter for the Métro or a taxi if you keep her later than 11:30 p.m. There is no extra charge for extra kids. The agency charges you a €10.98 service fee per reservation, or an €82.17 fee for ten reservations. Kid Services is accustomed to sending their sitters to Paris hotels. When you book, give your credit card number, the names and ages of your kids, and the address of where you're staying. You can even reserve your baby-sitter before you arrive in France.

Special Parks for Kids

For detailed descriptions, times, prices, and hours, see Part Six, Sightseeing and Tours.

Aquaboulevard

4–6, rue Louis Armand, 75015. Métro: Balard, Porte de Versailles. Tel. 01 40 60 10 00, fax 01 40 60 18 39. Full price: €18.30; children under age 12: €9.15.

Jardin d'Acclimatation

Bois de Boulogne, 75016. Métro: Sablons or Porte Maillot. Tel: 01 40 67 90 82. Full price: €7.15; children under age 3: free.

Jardin Sauvage de Saint-Vincent

Rue Saint-Vincent, 75018. Métro: Lamarck-Caulaincourt. Tel. 01 43 28 47 63. Open April to October on Mondays (except school holidays) from 4 p.m. to 6 p.m.; Saturdays from 2 p.m. to 6 p.m.

Jardin du Luxembourg

Between rue Guynemer and boulevard Saint-Michel, 75006. Métro RER: Luxembourg. Free entrance.

Parc de la Villette

Cité des Sciences, Parc de la Villette Musée de la Musique, 211, avenue Jean Jaurès, 75019. Métro: Porte de la Villette. Tel. 01 40 03 75 75.

Parc Floral de Paris

Bois de Vincennes–Esplanade du Château, Route de la Pyramide, 75012. Métro: Château de Vincennes. Tel. 01 55 94 20 20. Full price: €1.52; children ages 6–17: €0.76; under age 6: free.

Theme Parks for Kids

For Disneyland Paris and Parc Asterix, See Part Six, Sightseeing and Tours.

Museums for Kids

Any museum can be a treat or a horror story for kids. The key is to set realistic expectations and let your kids help you open your eyes to new things. With a museum pass (see "Absolutely Necessary: The Museum and Monument Pass" in Part Six, Sightseeing and Tours), which allows you to come back as many times as you like, you won't feel guilty spending only a few hours in the Louvre or Musée d'Orsay at a time. We highly recommend a spin through the Egyptian section of the Louvre with kids. They can actually read hieroglyphics! The Rodin Museum has an enchanting sculpture garden, and little children love to interact with the forms. They'll imitate *The Thinker* for the rest of their lives. The Picasso Museum is filled with wonderfully inventive works of art that tend to ignite the imaginations of kids. The scale of the museum is not overly intimidating, and you can easily see everything in two hours. The Museum of African and Oceanic Art is a favorite for kids of all ages, with its expressive masks from Mali and the Niger Valley. What's really convenient is the aquarium in the basement. The lake in the Bois de Vincennes is within walking distance and is perfect for picnics. Dog lovers will enjoy the Bois in the summer, especially on Sundays. Hundreds of dog owners promenade with their setters and spaniels and very French-looking poodles. Although a bit out of the way, the museum at Le Bourget, the Paris airport that preceded Orly for commercial flights, hosts a stunning collection of French airplanes, including the first models of the Concorde, which you can climb into.

For all museum addresses, Métro stops, opening times, prices, and descriptions, see the Attraction Profiles in Part Six, Sightseeing and Tours.

Jardin des Enfants aux Halles (Labyrinth)   A true highlight for kids in Paris, the outdoor Labyrinth in the park at Les Halles is a wonderland of inventive and safe activities. Each hour a limited number of kids between ages 7–11 are allowed to move through a course of obstacles, illusions, doors, steps, tunnels, cliffs, slides, and more at their own pace, while curious (and envious) parents watch from behind the gates. There is no better way to spend an hour on a Saturday morning with your kids in Paris than at the Labyrinth.

105, rue Rambuteau, 75001; Tel. 01 45 08 07 18
Métro: Châtelet–Les Halles (exit Rambuteau)
Open Tuesday–Sunday. Times change seasonally. Closed when raining. €0.38 admission

Les Manèges and Les Guignols   You'll still find lots of great old merry-go-rounds from the 1920s and 1930s here, as well as the wonderful French tradition of taking kids to ride them after school at 4:30 p.m. or on the weekends. Classical examples are found at Châtelet–Les Halles near the top of the RER entrance, at the riverfront by the Eiffel Tower, and in the Bois de Boulogne and Bois de Vincennes.

Similarly, there is a great French tradition of taking children to the 4 p.m. matinee of the famous Guignol marionettes. Don't worry that the program is in French; your kids will understand it and love it. Check the weekly *Pariscope* or *l'Officiel des Spectacles* for locations and times.

Publications and Listings

For a listing of things to do with kids during your stay, check *Paris Voice* (found in English bookstores and at the American Church) or *Where Paris* (found in numerous Paris hotels).

Safety and Security

You've just arrived and you're concerned about what is safe to do and what isn't. Paris is a safe city and cannot be compared with any large American cities in terms of overall crime statistics. In central Paris, you can usually walk around day or night with little fear of aggression. However, Paris is a large city, and the crime rate has increased markedly over the last ten years. As in any city, women should be careful about venturing alone into unfamiliar areas. Most crime is located in the suburbs and occurs late at night in certain Métro stations and trouble spots. There are cases of muggings, sexual aggression, pickpocketing, vandalism, and car theft, but fortunately they are not common, and visitors should be prudent but not at all fearful or hesitant.

Lost and Found

Paris has a central Lost and Found Center *(Objets Trouvés* [oh-**bjay troo**-vay]*)* located at 36, rue des Morillons, 75015; Tel. 01 35 76 20 20; Métro: Convention. Open: 8:30 a.m. to 5 p.m. Call or ask your hotel to call for you if you lost something or left something in a taxi. Even stolen wallets turn up here (without the cash). Limited English.

Emergency Numbers

Here is a quick reference list of emergency numbers. Note that you may not find English-speakers at the other end of the line, so it may be necessary to have a French-speaking person call for you.

- Police: Tel. 17
- Fire: Tel. 18
- Medical Emergencies: Tel. 15
- Ambulance SAMU Service: Tel. 5 or 01 45 67 50 50
    (24-hour emergency ambulance service)
- Anti-Poison Center (24 hours a day): Tel. 01 40 05 48 48
- SOS Médecins (24-hour emergency medical house calls):
    Tel. 01 47 07 77 77/01 43 37 77 77
- SOS Cardiologues (emergency service for heart patients):
    Tel. 01 47 07 50 50
- SOS Dentaire (emergency dental help): Tel. 01 43 37 51 00
- Emergency locksmith (24 hours a day): Tel. 0 800 800 904
- Rape Crisis Hotline: Tel. 0 800 05 95 95 (toll-free)
- Eye emergencies: Tel. 01 47 07 64 64
- Pregnancy hotline: Tel. 01 45 82 13 14

Lost Credit Cards

- Eurocard/Mastercard/Mastercharge   0 800 90 23 90
- Carte Bleue or Visa Card   01 42 77 11 90
- American Express Card   01 47 77 72 00
- Diner's Club Card   01 47 62 75 75

If You're a Victim of Crime . . .

Paris is relatively safe—much safer than almost any American city. You will in all likelihood not encounter violent crime, and you should not feel insecure about walking around the city, even after dark. Having said that, Paris is a big place, and you should take certain precautions when you're out and about.

- Pickpockets exist in and around the flea markets and in certain crowded Métro stations. Make sure your money and passport are securely stored in a zipped portion of a daypack or in a secure pocket.

- Women should generally avoid riding the Métro or RER late at night (after midnight) alone.

- The area around Stalingrad Métro station can get a bit rough late at night, since this area is frequented by drug dealers and their clients. Similarly, late at night the Châtelet–Les Halles area should be approached with caution. Some of the nearby suburbs with large housing projects are ill-advised for late-night visits unless accompanied by someone who lives there.

- Parts of the Bois de Boulogne and the Bois de Vincennes become sex markets at night for prostitutes and transvestites. Although not particularly dangerous, you might not want to be mistaken for a client when you thought you were just going out for a long walk.

- If in doubt about an area, ask your concierge for his opinion before setting out.

If you are a victim of theft, call Tel. 01 43 12 23 47 (for information in English).

If your wallet is stolen, it's probable that your money and credit cards will be gone forever, but the wallet itself and other papers may turn up at Paris's central Lost and Found.

Hotel Security

Practically all of Paris's hotels are very safe, and it's rare to hear of break-ins, thefts, or attacks. Nonetheless, you should always lock your door when you're in your room, as well as when you leave it, and you should avoid leaving cash, jewelry, and obvious valuables exposed. Most hotels offer in-house safe deposit boxes for your peace of mind. Standard stuff.

Your Embassy or Consulate

You may register your local address in Paris with your Paris consulate, although very few visitors do this on short visits and it is not strictly necessary. On the other hand, if you are away during a sensitive time back home or you're in fragile health, the consulate can be helpful in locating you or contacting your family in case of an emergency.

- U.S. Consulate: 2, rue Saint-Florentin, 75001
  Métro: Concorde. Tel. 01 43 12 22 22.

- Canadian Consulate: 35, avenue Montaigne, 75008
  Métro: Franklin D. Roosevelt. Tel. 01 44 43 29 00.

- Australian Embassy: 4, rue Jean Rey, 75015
  Métro: Bir-Hakeim. Tel. 01 40 59 33 00.

- British Consulate: 9, avenue Hoche, 75008
  Métro: Charles de Gaulle-Etoile. Tel. 01 42 66 38 10

Part Five

Getting Around Paris

Visualizing the City

Paris possesses the quaint contradiction of being organized according to no specific system or grid, but at the same time it has been developed on a scale that makes aimless exploring pleasurable without the risk of getting too lost. In essence, streets can be small, mixed up, and obscure, but the city is user-friendly. You can always situate yourself in Paris by using the closest Métro stop as your mental and geographic crutch. Everything in Paris is accessible by Métro, and you should learn how to use it. The Paris Métro, the veins through which the life of the city flows, will become your best friend. Find a Métro station and you'll never be lost or too far from anything. You'll quickly get to know your Métro stop and a few local cafés, which you'll keep coming back to each day. Comfort and pleasure in Paris builds as you settle into these little routines.

Using our district maps in the Introduction, memorize the key areas of Paris and where they are in relation to each other and your hotel. This way, you'll always have your bearings, wherever you are! Memorize your closest Métro stop, the line it's on, and the *direction* (the last station on the line heading in the direction of your hotel).

Paris Pratique

We've mentioned on several occasions how to find free city and Métro maps. These will help you get around, except when you're looking for an obscure shop in the 13th *arrondissement* or a little bistro that a friend raved about in the 12th *arrondissement*. With one of these handy map books, you'll be able to track down every street in Paris and its closest Métro stop. The cover is waterproof. And, as a tourist, you'll look like a local! You can find the *Paris Pratique* in all stationery shops, most newsstands, and department stores for about €19. Michelin publishes a similar one for about €10. Trust us, this is a great value—you'll get very attached to your map book very quickly and will keep it for return journeys.

To get the shape of Paris clear in your head, think of a large egg lying on its side. The RATP public transportation authority uses the shape of the city as its logo, with the path of the Seine river forming the profile of a face.

The *arrondissements* are organized clockwise in concentric circles starting in the center of the city. The street signs are posted on the corner of buildings and most of the time indicate the *arrondissement* as well as the street.

Spotting the Eiffel Tower

"Where's the Eiffel Tower?" How often do we hear this of arriving visitors? For many, you're not really in Paris until you've spotted the world's most famous monument. Go quench the urge right away. If this is your first time in Paris, the single most dominant image in your mind is surely that of that spectacular hunk of metal. Most visitors don't feel like going to the Louvre or the Picasso Museum until they've first laid eyes on this larger-than-life icon, situated on the Left Bank of the Seine on a long and elegant garden called the Champ de Mars, in the 15th *arrondissement*. Aside from climbing it, the absolute best viewing point during the day—and especially at night—is from the terrace at the Trocadéro on the Right Bank. To get to the Eiffel Tower take either Line 6 of the Métro to the Bir-Hakeim station or Line C of the RER to the Champ-de-Mars/Tour Eiffel stop. For more information you can call 01 44 11 23 23.

Walking in Paris

The best way to experience Paris is by foot *(à pied* [ah pee-**ay**]*)*. The human scale of Paris permits you to move easily from the Latin Quarter, across the islands, into the Marais, along the rue de Rivoli, past the Louvre, along the Seine, over the Pont Neuf, and into the Saint-Germain-des-Prés area and back to your centrally located hotel without any problem at all. Pause for lunch and stop in at least once or twice for a coffee or glass of beer or wine in an inviting café.

Note: Traffic signals do not hang in the middle of intersections but are affixed to poles on the far side of intersections. Green and red have the usual universal meanings. Parisians are not a highly disciplined people, but they are not jay-walkers either. Don't cross in the middle of streets, and do not ignore street signs like New Yorkers do. Drivers are not used to irresponsible pedestrians and do not usually slow down for them.

Street Addresses

In Paris, street signs are fixed to the sides of buildings, much higher than eye-level. Traditional Parisian street signs are blue with a green trim. The *arrondissement* is often shown above the name.

With regard to street numbers, don't be surprised if odd and even numbers are not located opposite from each other on a street. Many Paris buildings have long and deep courtyards and passageways leading from the street. You'll often see numbers followed by *bis* or *ter,* like 37 bis or 104 ter, simply indicating that this address is adjacent to number 37 or 104.

Public Transportation

Public transportation in Paris is extensive, inexpensive, and safe and easy to use. Even if you've never used public transportation back home, or you're afraid you'll get lost or squeezed to death in crowds, in Paris, trust the RATP and use it—especially the Métro. The Métro will not only save you valuable time and lots of money, but it will quickly bring you to the heart of everyday Parisian life. The RATP also has an extensive public bus system with multiple lines crisscrossing the city that links neighborhoods between Métro stops. And you might also want to try the RATP-affiliated Bat-o-Bus, which hosts regular river traffic on the Seine.

The RATP has a 24-hour telephone hotline for all questions concerning rates, itineraries, and hours. To reach a human being who speaks some English call between 6 a.m. and 9 p.m. You may need to ask for an English-speaking agent. (Tel. 08 36 68 77 14). Otherwise you'll only get recorded messages in French.

The Métro

The backbone of the RATP network is the Métro, one of the world's greatest subway systems, inaugurated in 1900 with the Porte de Vincennes–Porte Maillot "Métropolitan" line—hence the name "Métro." Today the Métro includes 16 lines and a whopping 368 stations. Essentially every neighborhood in Paris is accessible by Métro. The Métro opens at 5:45 a.m. and closes around 1 a.m.—but don't cut it too close. Ask at the Métro station closest to your hotel when the last Métro runs. *(Excusez-moi, c'est quand le dernier Métro ce soir si'l vous plaît?* [Ex**cu**say **mwa**; say **cah**-wn luh dare-**nyeh** Métro suh swah, see voo **play**?]*)*

Each Métro line has an assigned number and is commonly referred to by the last stations or end of the line or *direction*. Each line is also color-coded, but with 16 different lines you'll find the numbers a better indicator. The colors help you follow a line across the map.

You'll want to pick up a map of the Métro and RER and keep it handy all the time. Free maps are available at all Métro and RER stations, as well as at the RATP information office in the massive Châtelet–Les Halles station, which acts as the central hub for the system and is the major intersection of numerous lines. You can also download a Métro map on the official RATP website at www.ratp.fr/images/pdf/plan.eng/nocpang.pdf. In addition, the Galeries Lafayette and Samaritaine department stores print and distribute millions of copies of colorful city and Métro maps, which are distributed free in their stores and at hundreds of points of contact for tourists.

MÉTRO LINES

Line 1	Château de Vincennes	La Défense
Line 2	Nation	Porte Dauphine
Line 3	Galliéni	Pont de Levallois–Bécon
Line 3bis	Porte des Lilas	Gambetta
Line 4	Porte de Clignancourt	Porte d'Orléans
Line 5	Bobigny–Pablo Picasso	Place d'Italie
Line 6	Nation	Charles de Gaulle-Etoile
Line 7	La Courneuve/Mairie d'Ivry	Villejuif/Louis Aragon
Line 7bis	Pré-Saint-Gervais	
Line 8	Créteil Préfecture	Ballard
Line 9	Mairie de Montreuil	Pont de Sèvres
Line 10	Gare d'Austerlitz	Boulogne Pont de Saint-Cloud/Porte d'Auteuil
Line 11	Mairie des Lilas	Châtelet
Line 12	Porte de la Chapelle	Mairie d'Issy
Line 13	Gabriel Péri–Asnières	Châtillon–Montrouge/Saint-Denis Basilique
Line 14	Madeleine	Bibliothèque François

MÉTRO TICKET PRICES

Single ticket, €1.30
Carnet (ten tickets), €4.65
Mobilis (one-day unlimited travel), €5.03 (1–2 zones) to €17.38 (1–8 zones)

Paris Visite Pass

| | One-Day | | Two-Day | |
	adults	children	adults	children
1–3 zones:	€8.38	€4.57	€13.72	€6.86
1–5 zones:	€16.77	€8.38	€26.68	€12.96
1–8 zones:	€23.63	€11.43	€34.30	€16.77

| | Three-Day | | Five-Day | |
	adults	children	adults	children
1–3 zones:	€18.29	€9.15	€26.68	€13.72
1–5 zones:	€37.35	€18.29	€45.73	€22.87
1–8 zones:	€42.69	€21.34	€53.36	€26.68

Children ages 4 to 11 pay half price.

Zones 1 to 3 include Paris and its nearby suburbs (La Défense, Saint-Denis Basilique, Le Bourget).

Zones 1 to 5 include Paris and the surrounding area (Versailles Castle, Charles de Gaulle and Orly Airports, and Disneyland Paris at Marne la Vallée).

Charles de Gaulle Airport (Roissy) is in Zone 5 and costs €7.62 each way.

Orly Airport is in Zone 4 and, via OrlyVal, costs €8.69 each way.

Disneyland Paris is in Zone 5; the special Disneyland Passeport offers round-trip service for €35.98 adults, €28.05 children.

Versailles is in Zone 4 and costs €3 each way.

Saint-Germain-en-Laye is in Zone 4 and costs €4 each way.

Distances in Time

To determine how long it will take you to get from one station to another, roughly count on between one and two minutes per station, and add five minutes for each change of line *(correspondance)* you need to make. The high-speed RER trains come less frequently than the Métros but are faster and stop less. You can get from the center of the city at Châtelet–Les Halles to the Arc de Triomphe in less than ten minutes by RER, which would take twice as long by Métro.

Buying Métro Tickets

Métro tickets will be one of your staple tools for navigating in Paris. You have several ticket options, depending largely on how long you are staying and how many times you think you'll be using the Métro, RER, or buses. Paris public transportation is organized into eight zones, each commanding its own fare, so a little calculating is necessary to make the best choice.

All public transportation (Métro, RER, and buses) within Paris city limits and all the Métro stops on all 16 lines (even those that go beyond the city limits) collectively constitute Zones 1 and 2 and require only one Métro ticket. Almost all of your travel, except perhaps to one of the airports or Disneyland Paris, will fall within these two zones. You can buy tickets one at a time as you go, in a packet of ten called a *carnet,* or as a special one-, two-, three-, or five-day visitors pass called the *Paris Visite.* Prices do change periodically, so they might be a little different from what is listed here, but changes will be minimal and proportional to the latest ones available.

As you can quickly calculate, it is very advantageous to buy a *Paris Visite* in many cases. Not only will you save money, you won't have to spend time in lines, and you won't have to figure out how, when, or where to get tickets. And, best of all, you won't hesitate over how or if you should go somewhere. With the pass in hand, you're more likely to use it and really explore Paris!

Note: If you plan to use the RER between either airport and Paris, or to and from Disneyland Paris, it is definitely a good deal to buy a *Paris Visite* upon arrival. If you are not going to use public transportation to and from the airport or Disneyland Paris, you might consider simply buying a carnet of ten tickets at a time.

Advantages of the *Paris Visite*

If you do opt for the *Paris Visite* you'll receive the following benefits:

Bateaux Parisiens   €15 discount on two lunches purchased. Fifty percent off second ticket when purchasing two cruises.

Canauxrama   One free canal trip ticket for every adult ticket purchased, except on weekend afternoons and public holidays.

Cité des Sciences   Admission discounted 25%.

Disneyland Paris   Discount of 10% at self-service restaurants.

Etoiles du Rex   One free movie ticket for every adult ticket purchased.

Galeries Lafayette   Discount of 10% on some items, plus free shopping bag with purchase of €30.49 or more.

Grande Arche de la Défense   One free roof ticket for every adult ticket purchased.

Paris l'Open Tour   Discount of 20% on tour tickets.

Montmartrain   One free ticket for every adult ticket purchased.

Jacquemart André Museum   One free ticket for every adult museum ticket purchased.

Louvre, Orsay, and Versailles museum boutiques   Discount of 10% on merchandise other than books (minimum €38.17 purchase).

Stade de France   One free "premiers Regards" ticket for every "premiers Regards" ticket purchased.

Tour Montparnasse   One free ticket for every adult ticket purchased.

Where to Purchase a *Paris Visite*

It's simple. Just go to almost any Métro or RER station ticket window and ask for a Paris Visite for the number of days and number of zones you wish. In many stations you'll be able to pay with your credit card too. You don't need a photo or any identification. And you can buy the card on any day and begin using it on any other day. It automatically activates the first time you insert it into the turnstile.

You can buy your card at the RER station at either airport, and you can even buy it from a ticket machine with your VISA or MasterCard, which will save you time.

How to Use the Métro

The Turnstile   The Métro is very easy to use once you've mastered the symbols employed to indicate exits, transfers, and train directions. After you've bought your tickets or a pass, you slip the green ticket into the slot in the turnstile. The machine will grab it and spit it out in another slot. You grab it and proceed through the turnstile. Keep your ticket until you exit the Métro system because you may be asked to show it while you're in transit. In the case of the RER, you'll need to reinsert the ticket to get past the turnstile at your exit, so don't lose it. If you do, you'll either have to explain, beg, jump over the turnstile, or pay a fine.

You will observe a number of people "cheating"—climbing over the turnstile, going in the exit door, or squeezing through the turnstile with another passenger (often strangers). Someone may even squeeze in behind you without asking. The RATP has *contrôleur* dragnets set up periodically throughout the system, attempting to catch or deter cheaters.

If you lose your ticket and have the bad luck of being noticed by a contrôleur, try to explain what happened. Most likely you'll gain no sympathy and have to either pay the €26 fine on the spot, or show your passport and agree to have a €23 ticket mailed to you at home in addition to the fine, with a copy sent to your consulate. If you're caught going through a turnstile together on one ticket, be ready for a whopping €38 fine for each of you.

Follow Your Direction   Métro lines are named after their endpoints, i.e., the Line 4 going north to Porte de Clignancourt is called Direction Porte de Clignancourt; the same line traveling in the opposite direction is called Direction Porte d'Orléans. Once you know which line your stop is located on, head in the direction of the last station on that line. Signs on the platform indicating direction are white.

Transferring from One Line to Another: *Correspondance*   For transferring from one line to another, orange signs on the quai (platform) marked "correspondance" indicate the path to other platform quais and other directions. This may be confusing because you sometimes need to follow the correspondance sign for your line through long corridors, moving sidewalks, and along platforms of other lines.

Make sure your direction is marked on the sign hanging above the platform at which you end up waiting. If you happen to get on a Métro going the wrong way, don't panic. Get off at the next stop and cross over to the platform marked with the correct direction.

***Sortie* (Exit)/*Access aux quais* (Entrance)**   Blue signs marked "sortie" point you in the direction of the exit, and often you'll have a choice of exits, all emerging onto different streets or different sides of the street. When meeting friends at a Métro station, make sure to specify which exit and whether you will meet underground or above ground. In every big station, you will find a *plan du quartier* (neighborhood map) on the platform, but all Métro stops have maps at the ticket office exit. When with a group, if one of you gets left behind, a good policy is to get off at the next stop and wait for your friend to arrive, and then continue on together.

A Tip—Avoid Long Transfers   If you are changing from one Métro line to another, study your options to reduce the number of changes and stops you need to make to reach your destination. If you can avoid transferring at Châtelet and Montparnasse, you may be avoiding a very long walk through an endless corridor with a moving sidewalk.

First Class

First class in the Métro was abolished under the Socialist government. You may still find some RER cars marked first class. Just ignore the numbers and sit where you'd like.

Street People/Beggars/Musicians

For years the Paris Métro has been home to an odd mix of down-and-out individuals, street musicians, beggars, Gypsies, winos, and street people (called *clochards*). Quite often you'll spot a sad-looking person sitting on the cement in the Métro with a hand-written sign stating his or her story or problem—"*J'ai faim* (I'm hungry)," "*54 ans, trois enfants, et sans travail* (54 years old, three children, and out of work)," "*SVP, donnez-moi une pièce ou deux* (Please give me a coin or two)." The growing homeless population—referred to as SDF, for *sans domicile fixe*—of Paris publishes several magazines, guide books, crossword puzzles, and even a brief history of each Métro stop which are sold on the Métro cars. Musicians play a song or two and then file through the moving Métro with a hat or cup. Recent emigrants, typically women, will sit with quiet infants for hours waiting for handouts. Others will give a desperate speech and come around looking for a few coins or restaurant ticket. These solicitations may make you a bit uncomfortable at times, but, by and large, they do not represent any danger to passengers. Don't feel intimidated or obliged to give anything. However, if you feel like helping someone, a few coins are always appreciated.

Occasionally in the past there have been small bands of Gypsy children roaming the Métro between Place de la Concorde and Etoile on Line 1 and in the train stations. They are seldom dangerous, but they are skilled pick-pockets. They encircle their prey and distract them as one of them grabs the contents of pockets and purses. Hang on to everything, and don't be afraid to shoo them away.

Getting Back to Your Hotel

If you memorize your Métro stop, you'll never get lost. We suggest that you keep a card from your hotel in your pocket in case you must ask someone for directions and your French accent is still a bit rusty.

Heads Up: Keep to Your Right

When walking through the corridors, on the escalators, and along the long moving beltways in the Métro, the rule is for slower walkers to keep to the right. People have the right to pass you to your left.

The RER

The RER *(Réseau Express Régional)* system—also run by the RATP—is the high-speed city-suburb network that in a short amount of time can zoom you across the city, out to Versailles or Saint-Germain-en-Laye, and even to Disneyland Paris. The aesthetics are very different from the Métro, since the stations are vast tunnels with deep platforms and the trains are fast and silent. Note that the Métros approach each platform from your left while most of the RER trains approach from your right. There are four lines on the RER (A, B, C, D), all forking out into numerous directions. Of course, the RER and Métro lines connect at various points, and although the RER is not designed to be used for very short distances, it makes longer distance traveling across the city or from city to suburb incredibly easy and efficient. Key junction *(correspondance)* stations are Châtelet/Les Halles, Nation, Etoile, and Auber. Don't confuse Charles de Gaulle/Etoile, where the Arc de Triomphe is located, with Roissy/Charles de Gaulle, the suburban site of the airport.

On the platform there are lit panels indicating the precise direction and list of stations the next train will be serving, as well as the expected time of arrival of the next train. All trains stop at all Paris stations. Be careful at Nation and Etoile stations not to board a train on the correct line but the wrong branch. Otherwise, you'll have to circle back and pay another fare. Note that you can go to the Château de Vincennes Métro stop with one Métro ticket, but in order to get off the RER at Vincennes you'll need an additional fare. Controllers often stake out the Vincennes RER station, catching hoards of violators in their net.

The trains have funny four-letter names that are written in lights on the front of the first car. The stopping point for both the long and short trains is indicated by fixed signs suspended over the platforms at the points where the front *(tête)* and rear *(queue)* of the train will be when it stops. This is an important thing to notice, since you could be waiting for a train on the correct platform but be 100 meters behind or in front of the train's arrival point.

Unlike the Métro, when using the RER keep your ticket handy since you'll need it to get out of the turnstile at your destination. You may use the RER like the Métro—with the exact same Métro ticket—when traveling within Paris. Other tickets are needed when going beyond the city limits. Be careful here. If you continue on past the city limits (Zones 1 and 2), your Métro ticket will not work in the exit turnstile, and you'll be forced to jump over the turnstile and risk a fine.

Here is a list of RER lines and some of their routes:

RER A1	Saint-Germain-en-Laye
RER A2	Cergy
RER A3	Boissy-Saint-Léger
RER A4	Marne La Vallée
RER B2	Robinson
RER B3	Roissy–Aéroport Charles de Gaulle
RER B4	Saint-Rémy-les-Chevreuse
RER B5	Mitry-Claye
RER C1	Montigny-Beauchamp
RER C2	Chemin d'Antony
RER C3	Argenteuil
RER C4	Dourdan
RER C5	Versailles RG
RER C6	Saint-Martin d'Etampes
RER C7	St. Quentin-en-Yvelines
RER D1	Orry-la-Ville
RER D2	Châtelet–Les Halles
RER E1	Haussman St-Lazare
RER E2	Chelles Gournay
RER E4	Villiers-sur-Marne/Le Plessis Trévise

Buses

It takes a while to get the hang of the buses and where they go. The great advantage to hopping on a bus is that you're above ground and can take in the scenery while you get where you're going.

Try using the public bus as an unofficial tour bus. There is nothing quite as glorious as sitting in the back of a city bus, unhurried, unlike the commuters, and watching the city—all included in the price of your single ticket or *Paris Visite.* The buses run on a kind of honor system. If you get on in the front, flash your carte at the driver. If you get on at the middle or back doors and you've got a single-use carte, there's nothing to do. If you are using Métro tickets, you must insert one in the validation machine located in the aisle. The machine validates your ticket and spits it back out, and you should keep it until you get off. You may be asked to show it to *contrôleurs* who periodically make spot-checks on buses. If you have a *Paris Visite* do not insert it in the machine.

Suggested Bus Routes

Balabus   On Sundays and public holidays from April through September the RATP offers a sightseeing line from 12:30 to 8 p.m. The bus runs between La Défense and the Gare de Lyon and costs a total of four Métro tickets if you stay on for the whole journey.

#63 We suggest catching this bus at Saint-Michel and riding it west, following the Left Bank of the Seine past the Latin Quarter, the Musée d'Orsay, the National Assembly, Invalides, and the view of the Louvre and Trocadéro. It then passes near the Eiffel Tower, where you should get off (Pont de l'Alma). When you're finished here, take the same #63 bus back in the other direction. The eastward route follows the Boulevard Saint-Germain past the chic Saint-Germain-des-Prés area, complete with galleries, shops, and the celebrated Café Flore, Brasserie Lipp, and Deux Magots, and continues past the Carrefour de l'Odéon. Hop off at the Roman ruins of Cluny just after you cross the Boulevard Saint-Michel, not far from where you got on.

#85 Start at Luxembourg Gardens, heading north toward the Seine. The bus will follow the Boulevard Saint-Michel past the famous fountain, across the Seine and past the golden gates of the Palais de Justice and Notre-Dame Cathedral on its way to the dead center of Paris, Châtelet. From here it veers west past the Louvre before turning right and heading toward Pigalle and Montmartre.

Most Parisian buses stop running around 9 p.m., and many do not run on Sundays. During the day most buses run every five to ten minutes. You can verify the schedules in the bus shelters along the routes.

Night Buses

For night owls who can't find a taxi, it's good to know that there are ten night buses, called the Noctambus (marked by an illuminated owl sign), which leave the center of the city and follow the major arteries out to the edges of Paris in every direction. This keeps late-night party hounds from becoming stranded. Buses leave from Boulevard Victoria between Châtelet and the Hôtel de Ville beginning at 1:30 a.m. and every hour after that. The fare is €2.30, but if you have the *Paris Visite* it covers this service as well.

Bat-o-Bus

Traveling on the Seine is scenic but slow. The RATP offers an affiliated boat service called the Bat-o-Bus, which is a shuttle running from May through September, with five stops departing every 30 minutes between the Eiffel Tower and the Hôtel de Ville. It does not take Métro tickets, nor can you use your *Paris Visite* here. For other Seine tours, refer to Part Six, Sightseeing and Tours.

Boarding points are found at:

- Port La Bourdonnais (Métro: Alma-Marceau [Line 9]; RER: Pont de l'Alma [Line C])
- Musée d'Orsay (Métro: Solférino [Line 12])
- Louvre (Métro: Palais Royale-Musée du Louvre [Line 1])

- Hôtel de Ville (Métro: Hôtel de Ville [Lines 1 or 11])
- Notre-Dame (Métro: Cité [Line 4])

For more information, call 01 44 11 33 99.

Taxis

Although Paris has one of the world's best subway systems, savvy visitors to the French capital need to master the ins and outs of *les taxis parisiens*. Taxis tend to be taxis, you're thinking, right? Well, almost. The quality of service is very uneven. You may have charming encounters with perfectly honest taxi drivers, or you may experience real grouches or worse, the ones that "take you for a ride." The best protection is knowing where you're going and being savvy.

If you're used to the frenzy of Manhattan and the competitive scuffs related to hailing cabs, chill out. In Paris, one rarely hails, whistles, flails at, or hustles cabs. Taxis are found at well-marked taxi stands scattered throughout the city. In fact, it is illegal for taxis to pick you up on the street if you're within at least 50 meters of an official taxi stand. Occasionally, you'll be able to jump into one in traffic, but this is a no-no and offenders risk heavy fines. So, you've been cautioned.

Your other option is to call a taxi, and here you have a number of choices. If you're staying somewhere other than in a hotel where taxis usually line up and you use taxis regularly, it's wise and economical to note the telephone number of your nearest taxi stand. Why? Because in Paris the meter starts turning the moment you call, not the moment you hop into the back seat! When calling one of the citywide taxi companies, Taxi Bleue or G7, for example, the dispatcher sends his or her closest available vehicle, but be prepared to find up to €8 already on the meter before the journey begins. Although this seems obnoxious, don't complain. *C'est comme ça ici.* (That's how it's done here.) However, if the meter reads an exaggerated sum, you are completely within your rights to refuse the taxi altogether and not pay.

Paris has over 20,000 taxis on its streets and drivers are strictly regulated by the police. You'll notice a small digital counter on the back ledge of each vehicle indicating how many hours this driver has been behind the wheel. Parisian taxis by law cannot *rouler* for more than ten hours a day. There are few moonlighters.

Meters start at about €2 during the day (7 a.m.–7 p.m.) and are calibrated on a base hourly rate of about €24. This rate is called Tarif A. *Naturellement,* the night rate, Tarif B (7 p.m.–7 a.m.), costs about 30% more. And Tarif C kicks in when you cross the *périphérique* (Paris's beltway) and venture into the near suburbs. The *périphérique* itself, however, is still considered part of Paris, so don't let your driver click the meter onto Tarif C too soon, an old trick.

A taxi with a white "TAXI" light on is available; darkened, and there's a passenger on board or the driver's on route to one. You'll also notice on the dome of all taxis three small colored lights, marked A, B, and C. When lit these indicate that there is a fare en route and the tariff is being applied. When taxis are off duty, drivers strap a funky black leather corset over the lights. Note that you'll never convince a Paris taxi driver to take you when he's off duty, and if his shift is almost over and you're not going his way, there is a good chance he'll turn you away. *Très Parisien ça!*

If you climb in at a train station or airport, expect a supplement. Luggage, bikes, skis, and packages that are either oversized or weigh more than five kilos (12 pounds) also cost extra. All charges and supplements are clearly noted on the inside passenger window in French and English for easy verification. Note: since the taxi driver's strike in 2000, the minimum fare (even to go one block) is €4.50.

In general, you may not climb into a taxi with a dog, but don't be alarmed to find a bored-looking schnauzer curled up on the passenger's seat next to the driver.

Some of the larger taxi fleets accept VISA and MasterCard; almost none accept checks, and forget about using U.S. cash anywhere in Paris. As for tipping, taxi drivers don't view this as an obligation, so the rule is to add on what you feel like. Two or three euros to or from either airport is fine, and a few coins following a short Paris jaunt is perfectly acceptable. Don't overdo it. Note, though, that the *fisc* (French tax authorities) automatically adds on 7% more than a driver's declared meter receipts. So a 7% tip simply covers costs. A 10% tip is always adequate and appreciated.

The real pleasure of Paris taxis, though, is the wide range of opinions, popular philosophy, and local commentary on French politics and Parisian life that many of Paris's animated chauffeurs provide free of charge!

Train Passes and Reservations

If you are certain you'll only be staying in or around Paris, you won't need to concern yourself with train passes or advance reservations. If you change your mind while you're in Paris, you can always buy a round-trip train ticket at some travel agencies or at a French Railways (SNCF) train station. If you are over 60 years old, you'll be eligible for reduced fares on the condition that you obtain a *Carte Vermeil,* which you can get for about €23 when buying your tickets in Paris. For SNCF information and reservations, call 08 36 35 35 35 (€0.35 per minute), or visit the website at www.sncf. com/indexe.htm.

If you plan on using the Paris public transportation system (yes, count on it!) and making short, day excursions from Paris, you can deal with your ground transportation when you arrive. If, however, you plan to visit London, Brussels, Florence, Barcelona, Amsterdam, or other European cities on the same trip, you'll want to look into buying a Eurail train pass before you leave the United States

The Eurail France Railpass ($210 first class, $180 second class) allows for any three days of Eurail France travel in one month, and you can purhcase up to six extra days (respectively $34 and $30 per extra day). There are discounted versions of this and most other passes for couples, youth, and seniors, as well as a pass which combines with a rental car. The Eurail Selectpass ($328–476) allows for unlimited travel on any 5, 6, 8, or 10 days within a two-month period, using the rail networks of any three adjoining Eurail countries. Other passes allow travel through a total of five or even all 17 of the Eurail countries. You can read about all these options and order tickets at www.raileurope.com or www.travel-in-france.com, or by calling (800) 4-EURAIL.

If you're considering a few days in the south of France, Normandy, Brittany, the Loire Valley, or the Alps, or a side trip to Brussels, Amsterdam, Barcelona, or Milan, for example, and you'd like to prearrange your travel schedule, you can consult the SNCF website or contact the Rail Europe Group in the United States at (800) 4-EURAIL.

Renting a Car

If you are flying into Paris and staying there, don't even think about renting a car. Even if you plan on taking side trips from Paris, you do not necessarily want or need a car. If, however, you plan on picking up a rental car in Paris and driving, for example, to the south of France or to the Alps, you might consider taking the train to your destination and arranging to pick up your car there. The SNCF has a program with Avis for car rental pick-ups at many French train stations. If you are holding discounted train tickets, you are entitled to discounts at Avis too. For details, visit the SNCF at www.sncf.com/indexe.htm or Avis at www.avis.com, or call Avis in France at Tel. 011 33 8 20 05 05 05 or in the United States at (800) 331-1084. If you want your car in Paris, consult a city map and arrange for your pick-up at a location closest to your hotel. If you're staying in central Paris and plan on driving south, avoid picking up a car at Roissy/Charles de Gaulle Airport, which is 30 miles to the north. The French car maker, Renault, has a "Eurodrive" rental or purchase program with pick-ups and drop-offs all over Europe. In the United States call (800) 221-1052 for details and prices.

If you do rent a car, make sure you reserve it before leaving home. North American rates are substantially lower than those offered in France for the exact same vehicle. To get an idea of prices and special offers, start with the international rental companies. Ask for a discount and see what they offer. Don't forget to pick up frequent flyer miles too. Then, try some of the smaller or more economical companies like Ada or AutoEurope. The Maison de la France Travel booklet lists scores of fly-and-drive services too.

Car Rental Company Contact Information

- Alamo: (800) 327-9633 (www.goalamo.com)
- Avis: (800) 331-1084 (www.avis.com)
- AutoEurope: (800) 223-5555
- Budget: (800) 472-3325 (www.drivebudget.com/home.html)
- Dollar: (800) 800-4000 (www.dollar.com)
- Enterprise: (800) 566-9249 (www.enterprise.com)
- Hertz: (800) 654-3001(www.hertz.com)
- National: (800) 227-3876 (www.nationalcar.com)
- Payless: (800) PAYLESS or (727) 321-6352 (www.paylesscar.com)
- Thrifty: (800) 367-2277 (www.thrifty.com)
- Tildon (Canada): (800) 227-7368

Here are a few of the leading car rental companies in Paris. They all have multiple pick-up points. Call the company to inquire which location is closest to your hotel.

- ADA   Tel. 01 48 78 18 08
- Autorent   Tel. 01 45 54 22 45
- Avis   Tel. 01 44 18 10 50
- Budget   Tel. 08 00 10 00 01
- Europcar   Tel. 01 42 16 80 80
- Hertz   Tel. 01 45 74 97 39

Online travel sites offering car rental deals with a Paris pick-up include the following. You may find that the negotiated rates obtainable through one of these operators is less than what you are quoted directly from a car rental company. It never hurts to give it a try!

www.auto-france.com   www.parisrental.com
www.economytravel.com   www.travnet.com
www.france.com   www.frenchexperience.com

A Tip about Price Quotes

Here's one detail to look out for. You should be quoted prices with the sales tax included, and if you're booking from home, you'll be quoted in U.S. dollars. When you go to pay with your credit card in Paris, you may find that the French Value Added Tax (VAT) of 19.6% has been tacked on to the sum you expected to pay. Make sure that you request that the sales tax (VAT) is included on your reservation voucher.

For real pros of unofficial travel, consider this. If you're already in Paris and decide that you want to rent a car for a few days, it's still better to make an international call back to the car rental company in the United States to reserve your car for a Paris pick-up—usually at one of the train stations (not the airports); once again, you'll benefit from the U.S. rates. And there's no need to mention that you're already in Paris. You can access 800 numbers from France, but they will not be toll free. To do this you must replace 800 with 880.

Chaffeured Touring

Instead of renting a car, you can rent an English-speaking driver and guide if you're willing to pay for this lovely luxury. You can stay within Paris or make an excursion out of the city. You only pay about €185 per half-day. You avoid the driving hassles, the gasoline prices, the insurance, the parking, and the stress, and you get your own guide and chauffeur included. To make a reservation, contact Voyages à Paris, Tel. 01 55 35 38 00; fax 01 42 61 00 13, or 01 42 61 21 64.

If you think you'll be needing limo service in Paris, contact:

Baron's Limo Service	Tel. 01 45 30 21 21
Executive Car Carey Limousine	Tel. 01 40 68 02 22
International Limousines	Tel. 01 40 43 92 92
Prestige Limousines	Tel. 01 42 50 81 81

Another excellent service that provides drivers, guides, and tours for both the Paris area and other regions around France is called True France, run by a talented, multi-lingual guide named Hans. True France, rue de la Roquette, 75011; Tel. 01 43 57 88 54; Fax: 06 07 02 73 74; or visit their website at www.truefrance.com.

Part Six

Sightseeing and Tours

Planning for Paris Touring

Managing your time will be your greatest challenge while visiting Paris. There is so much you'll want to see and do in this city that you'll be forced to determine your own priorities and make some hard choices. We'll attempt to help you structure your days and nights, and we'll offer some well-tested suggestions and options.

Opening and Closing Times

You should know from the start that many stores, retail businesses, and banks that are open on Saturdays are **closed on Mondays**. Closed in French is *fermé* (fair-**may**). Open is *ouvert* (oow-**vair**). And almost all the public museums are **closed on Tuesdays**. So plan accordingly, and if necessary, call ahead.

Banks, businesses, and big stores usually open at 9 a.m. (Remember that 9 a.m. is written in French as 9h, meaning 9 *heures*), and many close at lunch time for an hour or two—but usually not before 12:30 p.m. There is no set rule for this. Banks close at 4:30 p.m. (16:30h) or 5 p.m. (17h), but businesses are usually open until 6 p.m. (18h) with retail shops and stores staying open until 7 p.m. (19h). Bread stores and other food-related shops stay open even later. Boutiques may open as late as 11 a.m. If you're accustomed to having most stores open on Sundays, you may be surprised to find that French law requires most businesses to be closed on Sundays. And although hours are loosening up, don't expect too many 24-hour convenience stores in Paris. Sundays are great days, though, for museum visits, strolls in parks, rides on the Seine, and window-shopping. Many restaurants are closed on Sunday nights as well.

When the Lights Go Out

Paris's monuments, fountains, and façades glitter in the evenings, thanks to a municipal lighting system. But when do the lights go out? Monuments and fountains stay lit until midnight during the week and until 1 a.m. on weekends.

Planning Visits of Three, Five, and Seven Days

Statistically, most travelers to Paris stay for a week or less. Of course, some stay longer, and if you're lucky enough to spend ten days or two weeks in the French capital, you'll be able to pace yourself differently. We've offered some flexible itineraries for the three-day, five-day, and seven-day visit. Pace is everything. If you do not give yourself enough time to savor what you are seeing—to wander, wallow, mill around, and stroll—you will miss much of Paris's charm. You can't accomplish everything in a few tightly packed days, but you can see a lot, and the emotional strength of the experience can be powerful and indelible.

Here's a laundry list of *must* places to visit and the minimum time needed. Even if time is limited, try to get a taste of each of the following. These must sites are discussed in detail later in this chapter.

Notre-Dame Cathedral   Outside, inside, and if possible, a climb to the top. One hour.

Sainte-Chapelle and the Conciergerie   At least a half-hour.

Eiffel Tower   Stand under it, and then go up to the top. 90 minutes.

Arc de Triomphe   Stand in front of it, and then go up to the top. One hour.

The Louvre   Walk through the Cour Napoléon. Enter the museum and select a wing or two to visit. Half a day.

Musée d'Orsay   Study the façade from across the river. Spend at least two hours inside.

Orangerie   A half-hour gives you a delicious taste of some of the best art in France. If you can't get to Giverny, you can at least see a few huge panels from Monet's *Water Lily* series.

Place de la Concorde   Drive around in a taxi a few times. The mixture of lights and sculpture at night is inspiring. Stand at the foot of the obelisk where Marie Antoinette was guillotined. Fifteen minutes.

Île Saint-Louis   Walk across the island along the rue Saint-Louis en l'Île and walk back either way along the quay. One hour.

Latin Quarter   Deserves a daytime stroll and a late-night stroll with a café break and wine stop. One hour each.

Montmartre   Climb up to the Place du Tertre, visit the Sacré Coeur Basilica, rest on the steps, and take in the view. Day or night. If you have the time and energy, walk down the hill. Otherwise take the funicular. 90 minutes.

Montparnasse cafés   A glass of wine or a bowl of onion soup at La Coupole or Le Dôme will do it. Preferably at night. One hour.

Bastille   Drive around the place by taxi. Walk down the rue de la Roquette and the narrow rue de Lappe. Stop for drinks, dinner, music, dancing. From one hour to the whole evening.

Trocadéro   The view at night from the terrace is a must. Minimum 15 minutes.

Luxembourg Gardens   A leisurely stroll in the late afternoon or anytime on Sunday affords you both solace and a taste of timeless leisure Paris-style. Sit on a wrought-iron chair and rest. One hour.

Rodin Museum   You can get a delightful taste of the genius of this sculptor in an hour. A walk through the sculpture gardens is a must.

Pompidou Center   This mecca of contemporary culture and architecture should be seen. If you don't visit one of the exhibitions, at least take the escalators to the top for the view of central Paris. Hang out on the immense square in front and witness the impromptu carnival of counterculture, street music, and showmanship. One hour.

Place des Vosges   A stroll under the vaulted arcade past Victor Hugo's house represents only 30 minutes of well-spent time.

Père Lachaise Cemetery   If you can visit only one cemetery in Paris, let it be this one. Studded with two centuries of cultural luminaries and original ambience. 90 minutes. Add 30 minutes if you want to be with Jim Morrison for a while.

La Villette   An impressive expanse of diverse buildings and activities located on the northeastern edge of the city. Some of the most interesting and innovative exhibitions of art and contemporary themes are staged here. Also, the site of the Cité des Sciences museum and the Cité de la Musique, where a constant flow of high quality concerts are given. Great area for kids. Give yourself a good two hours.

Palais de Versailles   Out of town, but easy to get to by RER. Crowds can be intense, but a visit to the palace and a brisk walk in the gardens will be memorable. Half a day with travel time.

Below are suggested time-based itineraries for getting in the essential sights. Remember that much of the pleasure of being in Paris is just walking around. Leave time for that. Note that each day includes meals in two restaurants. (Consult the list of profiled restaurants in Part Seven for specific recommendations.)

Touring Paris in Three Days

Day 1   Visit Notre-Dame and Sainte-Chapelle, Île Saint-Louis, walk through the Latin Quarter, stroll through the Luxembourg Gardens and the Saint-Germain-des-Prés area. See the Eiffel Tower at night.

Day 2   Explore the Louvre, the Tuileries, and Châtelet-Les Halles, do a bit of shopping (window- or otherwise), visit the Pompidou Center, Pont Neuf, Samaritaine, Place de la Concorde, Champs-Elysées, and the Arc de Triomphe. Visit Montmartre at night.

Day 3   See the Marais, the Place des Vosges, do some shopping in the Marais, spend some quiet time at the Père Lachaise cemetery, and cap off the day with a boat ride on the Seine. Visit the Bastille area at night.

Touring Paris in Five Days

Follow the three-day itinerary above, and continue with:

Day 4   Visit the Musée d'Orsay and/or the Rodin Museum, then see Les Invalides and do some shopping at one of the grand magasins. Explore the Montparnasse area at night.

Day 5   Spend some time at the Picasso Museum, window-shopping in the Place des Victoires area, and visit the theater or opera at night.

Touring Paris in Seven Days

Follow the three- and five-day itineraries above, and continue with:

Day 6   Have fun hunting for treasures in the Flea Market or La Villette, and visit the Catacombs, the Panthéon, and the Place de la Contrescarpe (rue Mouffetard). Enjoy a concert or theater at night.

Day 7   Take a half-day side-trip to Versailles. Visit the bridges of Paris, and return to your favorite Parisian spots to say goodbye.

Tours and Guides

City Tours

If you'd like to get a quick overview of the city, you may opt for a mass-market, two-hour coach tour in a huge and modern bus that swings by many of the essential sites. There are several large companies that provide this round-the-clock service, including Paris Vision and Cityrama, a division of the Gray Lines. They seem to be busy, so either people like them or don't know better. We do not advise taking a tour with 50 or more tourists of mixed nationalities in which the guided narration is either prerecorded or multilingual. There is no better way to get bored than hearing the condensed history of Notre-Dame Cathedral squeezed into English, German, Japanese, and Italian.

However, there are some quality options available, and they provide you with a good overview of the city. Specialized Paris minivan tours are ideal for getting a deeper view of different aspects of Paris society and history:

Paris City First Excursions A variety of minibus tours for small groups ranging from €50 for a city tour to €215 for a night tour plus Moulin Rouge dinner and dance show. Book at your hotel.

Paris Vision A two-hour tour of the city; €23 for first passenger, €16 for each additional person (Tel. 01 42 60 31 25).

Other City Tours

Delta Lima Company See Paris from a different perspective. For €147 per person, you can take a helicopter tour that follows the Seine and covers Paris's major monuments. Price includes a meal (Tel. 01 40 68 01 23).

Paris L'Open Tour A more flexible option, this service allows you to get off and on the bus when and where you please. Prices vary, but a typical one-day ticket is €23 adults, €11 children age 10 and under. Tel. 01 43 46 52 06.

River Tours

Bateaux Mouches

Although the name of the most famous Seine river boat trip company, the Bateaux Mouches, has become the generic name for all Seine river excursion tours, there are a number of such companies offering river rides on a variety of large and small boats at comparable prices. With a carrying capacity of 21,000 passengers a day, the celebrated Bateaux Mouches gives the impression of being the "mastodon" of the river cruises, and you can be assured of finding a seat on board one of its 11 boats. Although it may seem like a tacky thing to do, there is nothing quite like viewing the city from the Seine. We especially love Seine cruising at night when the strong beams of light stroke the 17th-century façades of the buildings on both banks of the river. Cruise duration: 1 hour and 15 minutes.

There are lunch and dinner cruises available, but they are pricey, and besides, who wants to keep on eye on a shrimp cocktail when an illuminated Louvre is passing by? We like cruising the Seine without the distraction of eating. Daily departures are every 30 minutes by day and every 20 minutes in the evening. Boarding point: Pont de l'Alma (Métro: Alma-Marceau; RER Pont de l'Alma). For more information: Tel. 01 40 76 99 99.

Bateaux Parisiens (Seine Tours)

This company boasts a fleet of 13 boats and has more than 40 years of experience on the Seine. Guided tours in English of riverside monuments, the Eiffel Tower, Notre-Dame, and Parisian history and architecture. Bateaux Parisien's newest boat, the *Jeanne Moreau,* is about 50 meters long with a carrying capacity of 600 passengers.

Departure: Every hour (more often in the high season). Boarding points: Tour Eiffel trip, Port de la Bourdonnais (Métro: Trocadéro); Notre-Dame cruise, quai de Montebello (Métro: Saint-Michel). For more information: Tel. 01 44 11 33 44 or 01 43 26 92 55.

Canauxrama (Canal Tours)

A romantic cruise along the canal of Saint-Martin, with an explanation of Paris's historical canal lock system, its monuments, and the workers' quarter way of life.

Duration: About 3 hours. Departure: 9:45 a.m. or 2:30 p.m. Boarding points: Bassin de la Villette (5 bis, quai de la Loire 75019 Paris, Métro: Jaurès); Port de l'Arsenal (50, bd de la Bastille, 75012 Paris, Métro: Bastille). For more information: Tel. 01 42 39 15 00.

Biking and Walking Tours

Association for the Safeguard of Historical Paris   Walking tours of the historical districts of Paris, including the Père Lachaise Cemetery. Tel. 01 48 87 74 31.

Escapade Nature   A three-hour Paris bike tour costs about €22, rental included. English-speaking guides available. Tel. 01 53 17 03 18.

Mike's Bullfrog Bike Tours   Fun, diverse ways of visiting Paris, day or night, rain or shine, in English, bikes included! Forget buses, taxis, and vans—this is the way to see this city. Visit www.mikesbiketoursparis.com for prices and times. Tel. 06 09 98 08 60.

Moveable Feast Tours   Discover the city of Gertrude Stein, Colette, Josephine Baker, and others in the "Paris Is a Woman" guided walking tour every Saturday afternoon. On Thursdays, stroll down the street where the exiled Dante began to write *The Divine Comedy,* with the walk, "The Medieval Soul of Paris." And on Sundays, taste your way through French history on the "Belly of Paris" walk: discover food, restaurant, and market secrets of Paris. Tel: 06 66 92 34 12 or www.moveablefeasttours.com.

Paris à Vélo   A different way of seeing the city, with themes like "Unusual Paris" and "Paris by Night." Tel. 01 48 87 60 01.

Paris Vélo   Three-hour tour for €23. Tel. 01 43 37 59 22.

Paris Walking Tours A small company offering a variety of walking tours (such as Hemingway's Paris and the French Revolution), day excursions, and museum visits in English to Anglophones living in Paris, their visitors, French people who like to see Paris in English from an Anglo-Saxon point of view, and passing travelers who are clever enough to find them. Their guides are people who live in Paris and know Paris well, and the tours are informative but also fun. The program is available on request with tours every day, usually two or three to choose from almost all year round. Tours generally last for two hours and cost €10. No reservations are necessary. Contact Peter Caine by email only: pariswalking@compuserve.com or visit their website at www.pariswalkingtours.com.

Suggested Walking Itineraries

Tour 1—The Passages de Paris: Grands Boulevards Area
Take the Métro to the Grands Boulevards stop. Walk down the rue Montmartre, heading south toward the Seine. Just before you get to the rue Saint-Marc, at number 11, you'll find an entranceway to the **Passages des Panoramas.** Here you'll find a collection of cluttered boutiques, stamp shops, print shops, clothing stores, and *salons de thé* (tea rooms, where you drink tea and eat cakes). Turn to your right and follow the passage out to the bd. Montmartre. Cross the street and enter the **Passage Jouffroy** at number 10–12. Observe the tile motifs and the metalwork structure of the arcade. Here you'll find old bookshops, toy stores, the entrance to the **Hôtel Chopin,** and the main attraction, the **Musée Grevin,** Paris's celebrated wax museum. After making a quick left and a right turn, you'll follow the passageway to the rue de la Grange Batelière. Cross the street and enter the **Passage Verdeau** at number 6. Far less commercial, this arcade is a prime example of the architectural ideas of the mid-1800s. Lovers of old paper and postcards are advised to check out **La France Ancienne** at number 26. **Bonheur des Dames** at number 8 is perfect for needlepoint enthusiasts.

Exit on the rue du Fbg. Montmartre, turn right, and continue back to the bd. Montmartre. Turn right, and at the rue Richelieu cross the street. At number 97–99 you'll find the entrance to the **Passage des Princes,** opened in 1860 on the authority of the city planner Haussmann. This was Paris's last covered arcade. Admire the décor, the lamps, and the wrought iron. Exit on the bd. des Italiens.

Lunch at **Chartiers** on the rue du Fbg. Montmartre is a perfect way to conclude (or begin) this itinerary.

Tour 2—The Passages de Paris: Etienne-Marcel Area
Take the Métro to Etienne-Marcel. Follow the rue de Turbigo past the rue Saint-Denis, and just before reaching the bd Sébastopol, turn left at the rue de Palestro. At

number 3 on your left you'll find the entrance to the **Passage Bourg-l'Abbé**. Don't confuse it with the rue Bourg-l'Abbé, which was added afterward. Built in 1828 at the peak of arcade construction, today this passageway is rundown and ill-kept but still gives visitors a good hint of the era. Continue and cross the rue Saint-Denis. Directly across the street at 145 you'll find the beginning of the narrow **Passage du Grand-Cerf**, the tallest of all Paris arcades. Continue through the Place Goldoni and conclude on the busy and lively rue Montorgueil, a perfect spot for lunch. On the far side of Montorgueil, between the rue Mandar and the rue Léopold-Bellan, you'll find the **Passage Ben-Aïad**, formerly the Passage du Saumon, a celebrated spot for amorous transactions (which, as a result, is often locked from both sides). Take the rue Mondar and at number 8 turn right into the arcade. The passage continues on the other side of the rue Bachaumont, so don't give up too quickly.

You'll end up on the rue Bellan. Turn left and then right on the rue Montmartre, followed by a quick right on the rue d'Aboukir. At the corner of the rue du Caire enter the labyrinth-like **Passage du Caire** (Cairo) and enjoy a Middle-Eastern Paris you won't experience elsewhere. Cluttered with cut-rate clothes shops and sweatshops, it is in a state of dilapidation that masks the underlying handsomeness of Paris's largest arcade. But it's lots of fun to slum here. Exit on the rue Saint-Denis and cross the street. At number 212 you'll find the mouth of the **Passage du Ponceau**, an arcade that is dark and somber but worth a peek. At the far end, turn around and return to the rue Saint-Denis. Turn right and follow it through the impressive arches at the Porte Saint-Denis. On the other side of the arch, veer to turn right and enter **Passage du Prado** at 16, bd Saint-Denis. You'll find a lively right angle filled with wholesale clothes and barber shops. Exit on the rue du Fbg. Saint-Denis, turn right, and continue to the **Passage Brady** at number 46. You are in the heart of "immigrant" Paris, and the arcade is a busy thoroughfare of Turkish, Pakistani, and Indian restaurants, import-exporters, spice shops, and cut-rate merchandise.

Tour 3—The Passages de Paris: Louvre Area   Start at the Métro Louvre and walk north up the rue du Louvre. In front of the round building, the Bourse du Commerce, at a little square, take a sharp left onto the rue Jean-Jacques Rousseau. At number 19 you'll find the entrance to the lovely **Galerie Véro-Dodat,** built in 1826 in a neoclassical style. Note the black-and-white tiled flooring, the brass work, gold molding, and etched glass façades. Visit the art galleries, the fashion shops, and the gem of a boutique at number 23, Robert Capia's antique doll shop. Stop in at the **Café de l'E-poque** for a *café crème*.

Exit onto the rue Croix-des-Petits-Champs and turn right. At the very elegant Place des Victoires turn left on the rue des Petits-Champs. On your right, at number 4, enter the exquisite **Galerie Vivienne**, the most beautiful of Paris's arcades. Stroll along on the mosaic floor and take in the details of the arches, the lamps, and the windows until you reach the rotunda and its Empire décor. The tea shop **A Priori-Thé** is a perfect excuse to stop for a pot of Earl Grey. Fans of antique books will need more time getting to the exit on the rue Vivienne.

Turn left for a few steps and duck back into the same building at number 4. Here is the **Galerie Colbert**, the "sister enemy" of the Galerie Vivienne. It was built in 1826 to compete with the beauty and popularity of its neighbor. Soon you'll find yourself under a large rotunda, a stunning stained-glass dome. Exit to your right back onto the rue des Petits-Champs.

From here you can either cross the street and stroll in the Jardin du Palais Royal, or turn right and track down the **Passage de Choiseul** at number 40. In addition to the fashion house Kenzo, the famous theater Bouffes-Parisiens is found here.

Capping off your stroll with dinner at the nearby brasserie **Le Colbert** would be an excellent choice.

Exploring Points of Interest

Anglo Americans in Paris

The attraction of Paris for Americans is as old as the nation itself. Here is a partial list of leading American writers, artists, explorers, musicians, and politicians who have lived in Paris, followed by at least one of their Paris addresses. This can make for a fun self-crafted walking tour in itself. The best way to find these addresses is to look them up at www.pagesjaunes.fr and print the detailed street map.

Henry Adams	206, rue de Rivoli (Métro: Tuileries)
John Quincy Adams	97, rue de Richelieu (Métro: Richelieu-Drout)
Louis Armstrong	252, rue du Fbg. Saint-Honoré (Métro: Ternes)
Fred Astaire	10, place de la Concorde (Métro: Concorde)
Josephine Baker	32, rue Richer (Métro: Cadet)
James Baldwin	170, bd Saint-Germain (Métro: St-Germain-des-Prés)
P.T. Barnum	24, rue de Rivoli (Métro: St-Paul-le-Marais)
Sylvia Beach	18, rue de l'Odéon (Métro: Odéon)
Art Buchwald	52, rue de Monceau (Métro: Monceau)
William Burroughs	9, rue Gît-le-Coeur (Métro: St-Michel)
Alexander Calder	60, bd du Montparnasse (Métro: Montparnasse-Bienvenüe)
James Fenimore Cooper	59, rue Saint-Dominique (Métro: Invalides)
Harry and Caresse Crosby	2, rue Cardinale (Métro: Mabillon)
e. e. cummings	7, rue François 1er (Métro: Alma-Marceau)

John Dos Passos	45, quai de la Tournelle (Métro: St-Michel)
Isadora Duncan	25, rue de Mogador (Métro: Trinité)
Thomas Edison	23, quai de Conti (Métro: Pont-Neuf)
Dwight D. Eisenhower	133, av. des Champs-Elysées (Métro: Charles-de-Gaulle-Etoile)
T. S. Eliot	9, rue de l'Université (Métro: rue de Bac)
Duke Ellington	31, av. George V (Métro: George V)
William Faulkner	26, rue Servandoni (Métro: St-Sulpice)
Lawrence Ferlinghetti	89, rue de Vaugirard (Métro: St-Placide)
F. Scott Fitzgerald	14, rue de Tilsitt (Métro: Charles-de-Gaulle-Etoile)
Benjamin Franklin	2, rue de l'Université and 56, rue Jacob (Métro: St-Germain-des-Prés)
George Gershwin	19, av. Kléber (Métro: Kléber)
Nathaniel Hawthorne	164, rue de Rivoli (Métro: Louvre)
William Randolph Hearst	10, place de la Concorde (Métro: Concorde)
Ernest Hemingway	74, rue du Cardinal Lemoine (Métro: Place Monge) and 12, rue de l'Odéon (Métro: Odéon)
Harry Houdini	28, bd des Capucines (Métro: Opéra)
Langston Hughes	15, rue Nollete (Métro: La Fourche)
Henry James	13, rue de la Paix (Métro: Opéra)
Thomas Jefferson	30, rue de Richelieu (Métro: Palais-Royal) and 11, quai de Conti (Métro: Pont-Neuf)
Eugene Jolas	6, rue de Verneuil (Métro: Rue du Bac)
Helen Keller	7, rue de Berri (Métro: George V)
John F. Kennedy	37, quai d'Orsay (Métro: Invalides)
Jack Kerouac	28, rue Saint-André-des-Arts (Métro: St-Michel)
Charles Lindbergh	12, av. d'Iéna (Métro: Iéna)
Henry Miller	24, rue Bonaparte (Métro: St-Germain-des-Prés)
George Patton	25, av. Montaigne (Métro: Franklin D. Roosevelt)
Ezra Pound	9, rue de Beaune (Métro: RER Musée d'Orsay)
Man Ray	22, rue La Condamine (Métro: La Fourche)
Franklin D. Roosevelt	239, rue Saint-Honoré (Métro: Palais-Royale)
Teddy Roosevelt	Esplanade des Invalides (Métro: Invalides)
Gertrude Stein	27, rue de Fleurus (Métro: Rennes)
John Steinbeck	7, rue de Berri (Métro: George V)
Mark Twain	164, rue de Rivoli (Métro: Palais-Royale)
Edith Wharton	58, rue de Varenne (Métro: Varenne)
James Whistler	5, rue Corneille (Métro: Odéon)
Richard Wright	1 bis, rue de Vaugirard (Métro: RER Luxembourg)
Wilbur and Orville Wright	228, rue de Rivoli (Métro: Tuileries)

Getting the Best View: Micro and Macro

The deepest level of beauty in the Parisian cityscape is certainly in the details—the façades of buildings, the gold-leaf, the grillwork, the sculpted window frames and ornate doorways, the gargoyles, the fountains, the design of the Métro entrances, and even the style of the old park gates, tree enclosures, sewer grates, park benches, and wrought-iron trash bins. That's the beauty of the city on a small-scale level. It takes a bit of discipline for enthusiastic tourists eager to take everything in to slow down and look around some. Don't rush. Digesting the little things is as valid a way to see Paris as is quick, broad-sweeping gallivanting around the city to all the major sights.

The big picture, of course, affords visitors a unique sensation of largesse and splendor. To get a panoramic view of the city you have to be elevated. Paris has only one skyscraper, fortunately, but nevertheless there are several ways of seeing Paris from above:

- Eiffel Tower—Advantage: exciting going up
- Tour Montparnasse—Advantage: highest point in Paris
- Samaritaine 2 Roof—Advantage: you can order a beer or coffee
- Pompidou Center—Advantage: great view of Paris rooves
- Galeries Lafayette (roof)—Advantage: great break from shopping
- Institut du Monde Arabe (terrace)—Advantage: unique view of Seine and Notre Dame
- Grande Arche de La Défense—Advantage: dramatic perspective of Paris axis

Literary and Artistic Landmarks

Paris is studded with commemorative plaques marking where writers, artists, and musicians lived, worked, and died. Often the house is not marked at all. There is no better way to feel connected to history than stumbling upon Gertrude Stein's apartment or passing by the very spot Molière made his first appearance as an actor (at 12, rue Mazarine).

Bookstores

Paris is a joy for book-lovers, used and new. One of the most pleasant ways of passing time in the French capital is to *flâner* (to stroll aimlessly) from *bouquiniste* to *bouquiniste* (book stall to book stall) along the Seine on both banks between Notre-Dame and the Pont-des-Arts. These stalls, owned and run by literary Parisians and brimming with quality used books, posters, and vintage postcards, are passed on from generation to generation.

For English-language bookshops, **Shakespeare & Company** at 32, rue de la Bûcherie on the Left Bank in front of Notre-Dame is by far the most colorful. Owned and operated by legendary octogenarian George Whitman, the self-proclaimed great grandson of poet Walt Whitman, Shakespeare & Company is open from noon to midnight, seven days a week.

Three floors of great used books, first editions, and literary finds, this land-mark reeks of lore and poetry.

For a good dose of what's happening on the literary front in Paris today, a visit to Odile Helier's **Village Voice Bookshop** at 6, rue Princesse (Métro: Mabillon or Saint-Germain-des-Prés) is in order. Here local writers and the Anglo-American literary community come to hear writers and poets read and to buy their books. Another literary bookshop is the **Abbey Bookshop** at 29, rue de la Parcheminerie (Métro: Cluny-La Sorbonne), specializing in Cana-dian literature. The Right Bank's **W.H. Smith** and **Brentano's** are popular bookshops for new books, guides, newspapers, and magazines. **Librairie Galignani** at 224, rue de Rivoli (Métro: Tuileries), under the arcade in front of the Tuileries, is the oldest English-language bookstore on the continent.

The expatriate literary and art journal **Frank** is published in Paris and is found at the above bookshops and at www.readfrank.com.

Exhibitions and Galleries

For art lovers, Paris will be a feast. Aside from the rich assortment of major and minor museums, the art scene presents lots of opportunities for gallery-hopping. Although the bottom has fallen out of the Paris art market, the number of art galleries and art openings *(vernissages)* (vhere-nee-**sahj**) in Paris defies this. There are primarily three major areas with high concentra-tions of galleries:

Saint-Germain-des-Prés   Especially the streets between Place de l'Odéon and the Seine. A mixture of avant-garde, established, and the established avant-garde.

Bastille   Between Place de la Bastille and Oberkampf—follow rue de la Roquette. More innovative spaces and experimental work.

Miromesnil–Saint-Honoré   Highly established and renowned galleries showing artists of confirmed reputations and prices.

Your best bet for gallery-hopping is to pick up a copy of Paris's free gallery listings distributed in most galleries and cultural centers. To start out, we suggest a stroll down the rue de Seine, rue Dauphin, and rue Guénégaud, followed by a glass of Beaujolais at the famous watering hole for artists and culture-mongers, La Palette, situated at the corner of the rue de Seine and the tiny rue Jacques Callot.

Taking Classes

As a short-term visitor you can hardly sign up for a semester at the Sor-bonne, but you might enjoy an afternoon cooking class or a wine-tasting session. Some of you may even be up for a few hours of French conversa-tion. Here are some fine options:

Cooking

Here are two classic choices for Paris visitors interested in spending a bit time in an apron, learning the techniques of preparing and presenting French recipes. Inquire for specialized lessons in pastry cooking, sugar work, regional cuisine, and more.

Le Cordon Bleu   8, rue Léon Delhomme, 75015, Tel. 01 53 68 22 50. This classic landmark of French culinary education offers a wide array of short- and long-term courses and demonstrations.

Ritz Escoffier Ecole de Gastronomie Française   38, rue Cambon, 75001, Tel. 01 43 16 30 50. For program information, fax 01 43 16 31 50 or email ecole@ritzparis.com. Upscale and prestigious, the Ritz school has emerged as one of France's top institutions for training foreign visitors in the culinary arts. They offer a Wednesday afternoon class for kids that we highly recommend.

Wine Tasting

For classes and demonstrations covering the basics to the *grand crus*.

Centre d'Information, de Documentation et de Dégustation, Découverte du Vin   30, rue de la Sablière, 75014, Tel. 01 45 45 32 20.

French Lessons

Forcing yourself to actually practice the little bit of French you may know will be much appreciated by Parisians and will do wonders for your speaking confidence.

Berlitz France   Sponsors free conversation groups on selected evenings. Call Tel. 01 44 94 50 00 for details.

Konversando   Offers conversation classes. Call Tel. 01 47 70 21 64.

For a list of other schools, consult www.paris-anglo.com, the *Paris Voice,* or the advertising hand-out *FUSAC.*

Getting Tickets

For obtaining tickets to cultural events, try calling the Paris Convention & Visitors Bureau *(Office du Tourisme)* at Tel. 08 36 68 31 12 or going to any FNAC store, the Virgin Megastore, or the France Billet window in Carrefour and Auchan supermarkets.

Paris Façade Spotting

The best piece of advice for visitors hoping to really see Paris: look up!

There are a zillion ways of visiting a city as spectacular as the one you're presently in. Perhaps the simplest, and surely one of the most pleasurable, is simply knocking around with no fixed itinerary.

And September—especially September—is sublime for just that. The light in late summer is mellow, the broad-leafed trees along the boulevards cast deep shadows, the air takes on the scent of nostalgia, and the surfaces of Paris buildings are bathed in rich hues. As Parisians hurry back to the craze of *la rentrée* (return from summer holidays) and the hordes of tourists retreat to jobs and schools and busy schedules, you're here, free to loll in a luscious state of linger, to partake in the simple joy of dallying in the capital of style. To be "unrushed" in the midst of urban scurry is a rare brand of luxury for international travelers. So indulge.

In the Paris of your imagination you are not being led around at a furious pace; you are out-of-step and reflective, receptive to emotions. Aesthetics take on new meaning. In truth, the special quality of the place is its unique ability to celebrate your solitude or, for visiting couples or families, that heart-lifting sensation of being two against the world.

In English, the word *façade* implies superficiality and imitation. In the Parisian context, however, when it comes to façades, nothing could be less true. In fact, the outer surfaces of most of Paris's buildings are a veritable feast of substance, thrilling aesthetics, historical references, architectural vision, poetic narration, and passionate attention to detail. The buzz that you get again and again from strolling Paris's boulevards and back alleys comes from the Seurat-like composition of all its stylish touches.

Despite the aesthetics of function and practicality captured in such monumental achievements as the Pompidou Center, the Louvre Pyramid, the Grande Arche at La Défense, and the new Bibliothèque Nationale in the 13th arrondissement, the true statement of Parisian buildings is the public display of art in everything.

Even after a decade and a half of daily life in the French capital, it's precisely the design and artfulness of the common surfaces, not the magnificent monuments and memorable museums, but the pastiche of quaint little things, that keeps us nourished and visually alert. The cupolas and gargoyles, the trimmed doorways, the stylized arches, the braided cement appliqués and iron railings, the carved banisters, molded plaster balustrades, sculpted window frames, twirled cornices, ornate grillwork, layered moldings, and carved *pierre de taille* form a collective whole that translates seductively into beauty. Even the gates to the park squares, the wrought-iron trash cans, and the metal grates encircling the trees on the sidewalk reek of design.

The key to enjoying Paris's streets is having nowhere to go and nothing in particular to see. The greatest tip anyone can ever give you on how to indulge in the aesthetic orgy of Parisian street life is to look up, to alter your viewing habits and zoom in on the gilded art deco floral touches around the seven-floor apartment buildings on the Boulevard Haussmann, or the 19th-century headquarters of the old French supermarket chain Félix Potin on the corner of the rue Réaumur and the rue de Palestro, in the fashion designers' and textiles district. In fact, there's an entire Paris waiting to be revealed in the façades of buildings never mentioned in the guidebooks and tours. Most *quartiers* in all of Paris's 20 arrondissements lend themselves brilliantly to this act of inspired milling. If you love to take pictures, be sure to take your camera as you façade-spot. We recently gleaned the sidewalks in the 2nd and 3rd arrondissements and were bowled over by the carved visages on the old **Théâtre de la Gaîté** on the rue Papin just in front of the lovely Square Emile Chautemps. Nearby, the building found at **61–63 rue Réaumur** at the top of the ill-famed rue Saint-Denis is surprisingly ornate, covered in Ravier and Jacquier sculptures and a colorful art nouveau clock. Along the boulevard Saint-Martin, the façade of the **Théâtre de la Renaissance** is by Carrier-Belleuse and houses the very stage where Sarah Bernhardt played the works of Musset and Rostand. Even those who have walked past there a hundred times may have never noticed the ballet of sculpted figures on the west façade.

Walk down the boulevard de Sébastopol and wander east into the Marais district always looking up. The **Maison de Nicolas Flamel** and his wife, Pernelle, located at 51, rue Montmorency, sports its original medieval façade from 1407. Wander along the rue des Francs-Bourgeois past once-private mansions and take note of the carved doorways and turrets, brass knockers, and iron window-railings, details that dance between baroque, art deco, and neo-rococo.

When you're tired, stop in a café for a *panaché* (draft beer with lemon soda) or *café noisette* (espresso with a dash of milk), something that only residents know to ask for. Then start in again. Avoid the widest boulevards and wander knowing nothing more than your general direction. Use Métro stations as your only guideposts. The rue Saint-Dominique area around the rue Cler in the 7th arrondissement is well adapted for such façade-hunting. So are the back streets between Montparnasse and the Luxembourg Gardens in the 6th and 14th arrondissements. Ambitious walkers may opt for the hidden treasures and tucked-away *pavillons* (little houses) in the lesser-known 13th arrondissement between the Métro station Les Gobelins and Denfert-Rochereau. Some find the more proletarian side of the 17th arrondissement around La Fourche and Métro Guy-Môquet exciting to explore. And the elevated *Promenade Plantée* above the *Viaduc des Arts,* running from La Bastille eastward, affords a startling façade of mammoth neoclassical concrete nudes carved at the top of an otherwise banal building that houses the local police station at street level just behind the Gare de Lyon on the avenue Daumesnil. The less-visited but perhaps last remaining areas of authentic Parisian neighborhoods are tucked away in the 20th arrondissement around Belleville, Ménilmontant, and Gambetta. The chestnut tree–lined rue du Jourdain at Métro Jourdain (not to be confused with the Boulevard Jourdain) is a delightful spot to check out façades and begin an afternoon of aimless exploration.

Remember that the key to strolling is the absence of purpose. You are not sightseeing. You are not ticking off the monuments that are considered "musts." You are simply looking up, profoundly enjoying the surfaces while those unfortunate others push by with seemingly important things to do.

Cultural Paris

To come to Paris and not partake in its first-class spread of cultural events is like going to a five-star restaurant and not eating. Plan to eat heartily. Theater, opera, concerts, shows, dance performances, and cinema abound. Here's how to participate.

What's Going On

One of the best ways to find out what's going on in Paris is to call the Paris Visitors Center, a service of the Office du Tourisme, at Tel. 08 36 68 31 12. You'll be given the choice of hearing the information in English. Then proceed to push 1, to visit Paris; 2, to go out in Paris; 3, for fairs, congresses, and exhibitions; 4, for accommodations; 5, to organize events; 6, if you're a journalist; and 7, if you want to receive brochures. The most useful parts of the service are 1, to visit Paris, and 2, to go out in Paris, where a 30-day listing of the shows, plays, rock concerts, operas, ballets, classical concerts, and more are mentioned with dates, prices, and telephone numbers.

Absolutely Necessary: The Museum and Monument Pass

Regardless of the length of your stay, we strongly suggest that you purchase one of Paris's greatest inventions for tourists, the Museum and Monuments Pass *(Carte d'Musées et Monuments)*, which for one price affords you unlimited entry into hundreds of sites, museums, and monuments, representing a great savings of both money and time.

With the Museum Pass, there's no admission charge to pay, no waiting in lines, and no limit to the number of times you can visit any of the more than 60 museums and monuments in Paris region.

The Museum Pass is available for one, three, or five consecutive days.

Advantages to Pass Holders

- Free direct entry (no waiting) to the permanent collections. (Passes do not permit entry to temporary exhibits.)
- Unlimited visits, unlimited validity, and use of pass may begin any time after purchase.

Prices and Options

- Carte Musées and Monuments for 1 day—€12.20
- Carte Musées and Monuments for 3 days—€32
- Carte Musées and Monuments for 5 days—€44.21
- Admission into most museums and monuments for children under age 18 is free.
- Note that the pass does not include entrance into special or temporary exhibitions within the included museums or monuments.

Getting a Pass and How to Use It

You can obtain a pass at the Paris Office of Tourism at 127, av. des Champs-Elysées, 75008, Tel. 08 92 68 31 12, Métro: Charles-de-Gaulle-Etoile, or at any of the participating museums and at all major Métro stations. Some take credit cards, but be prepared to pay cash.

Clearly print your first and last name and the date of first use on the back of your card. (A brochure listing all the details is distributed with the card.)

Touring Neighborhoods

Here are thumbnail sketches of each of the main areas covered in this guide and a list of attractions you'll find in each.

- ## Latin Quarter

The Latin Quarter lies in the 5th and 6th arrondissements. Roman expansion covered the Left Bank beginning in the third century; however, the Quarter takes its name from the language of scholarship and religion centered around the famous Sorbonne since the 13th century. Several Roman vestiges remain from the second century, most notably the Thermes de Cluny (6, place Paul-Painlevé, Métro: Cluny-La Sorbonne) and the Arena of Lutèce (49, rue Monge, Métro: Place Monge). The Hôtel de Cluny, Paris's second-oldest residential building, has been the home of the Musée National du Moyen-Age (6, place Paul-Painlevé) since 1843. It boasts one of the most important collections of medieval finery, art, and architecture in the world.

The Latin Quarter's reputation as an avant-garde and rebel intellectual community dates from the 1950s and 1960s. It was the location of the first barricades erected by students in May 1968 and also the home of the hottest jazz clubs after WWII, showcasing musicians like Miles Davis and Thelonius Monk. It has since lost much of its student and avant-garde population to become a high-traffic tourist stop. And like most of these spots in Paris, prices are often inflated without a corresponding increase in quality.

- ## The Marais

Lovely, quaint, medieval, Jewish, gay—the Marais is many things to many people. One of the preferred areas of Paris for both visitors and Parisians, the Marais (meaning swamp or marshland) offers wonderful museums, private mansions, shops, cafés, galleries, boutiques, and restaurants. Narrow cobblestone streets teem with people day and night.

■ **Châtelet-Les Halles**

The heart of the city, Châtelet-Les Halles is the transportation hub for the Métro and RER. Historically, Les Halles was the central wholesale market for produce, meat, fish, and dairy goods for Paris. Today, the market has been transformed into a lively shopping district and commercial mall. The area is filled with boutiques, restaurants, bars, clubs, and slightly seedy porn shops. At the northern edge of this area, you run into the fashion district, which is bustling with stores and workshops filled with creativity and trend-setting ideas.

■ **Île Saint-Louis/Île de la Cité**

Unlike the Île de la Cité, the Île Saint-Louis's urbanization is relatively recent, dating from the 17th century. Developers joined the two islands called Notre-Dame and Île aux Vaches with two bridges and constructed hotels there between 1627 and 1664, giving the island an architectural homogeneity unusual in Paris.

■ **Saint-Germain-des-Prés**

The literary, publishing, and intellectual district, Saint-Germain-des-Prés today is upmarket and chic. Classy stores, expensive and stylish cafés that come with a load of existential baggage (see the profiles for Café de Floré and Les Deux Magots in Part Seven), this area is wonderful for milling around in, shopping, gallery-hopping, and browsing in the many bookshops. The hotels are quaint, but the prices reflect the style, design, and history of the area.

■ **Bastille/République**

The Bastille lodged itself in history and the consciousness of the French people in 1789 when six prisoners were freed from its walls, and thus began the sparks of revolution. Although the prison was quickly broken up, made into jewelry, and even part of the Pont de la Concorde, today the name continues to invoke something of the revolutionary spirit. But don't expect any of the quarter's diverse habitue to define this revolutionary spirit in the same fashion.

In other words, there's something here for everyone at all times of the day or night. Check out the rue du Faubourg-Saint-Antoine for fine furniture, antiques, and lamps. The rue de Lappe and vicinity is still attracting crowds for its dancing and bars just like at the turn of the century. Today there's even cheap tapas and a wide selection of sushi bars, Mediterranean cuisine, and a dozen other styles of restaurants from around the world presented *à la française*. Always *à la française*.

■ **Champs-Elysées/Concorde**

Less touristy, yet very close to everything. Paris nightlife has grown east from here, engulfing the Oberkampf, Belleville, and Ménilmontant areas. Large-scale elegance is easy to spot, from the dramatic square at La Concorde—complete with the Luxor obelisk, near the spot where Marie Antoinette was beheaded—along the Champs-Elysées axis to the Arc de Triomphe.

■ **Invalides/Eiffel Tower**

An elegant and expensive area of Paris, studded with government buildings, cultural centers, and some consulates. The hotels are generally of high quality, as are the restaurants, although visitors should be prepared to pay high prices. This is not an area for nightlife, but it is very pleasant, and what's missing in street life is made up in the architecture.

■ **Montparnasse**

In 1826 Victor Hugo rented an apartment on the rue Notre-Dame-des-Champs for the quarter's quiet, rural charm. Several dance halls, like the Grande Chaumière and La Closerie des Lilas, moved to Montparnasse soon after, along with a growing population of artists and intellectuals. Rousseau (the painter) followed Hugo in 1895. Up to WWI the Ecole de Paris group of artists like Modigliani and Foujita, Russian rebels Trotski and Lenin, Blaise Cendrars, Picasso, Marc Chagall, and Fernand Léger all animated the nightlife along the bd Montparnasse or at the carrefour Vavin in now-famous cafés like La Rotonde, Le Dôme, and Bal Nègre. Both world wars did little to interrupt the artistic energy gathering in this quarter, although they brought new names like Miró, Calder, Giacometti, Ernst, Kandinsky, Fitzgerald, Hemingway, Stein, and many others into the same cafés or new ones like Le Sélect and La Coupole. Many of these cafés are still around today and still draw contemporary artists and writers from all over the world. Prices are usually somewhat inflated, but the cuisine is consistently good, to say nothing of the real reason we are there: to take in the ambience and history, and picture Fitzgerald getting tipsy or Lenin and Trotski arguing and pounding red fists on the café's tables.

■ **Grands Boulevards**

In the mid-19th century, this was the place to stroll. Today, the area around this continuous beltway of wide busy boulevards is a mixture of bustling commercial life, ethnic Paris, and fascinating passageways affording visitors a glimpse of a former Paris. There is lots to discover in this part of town.

■ **Montmartre**

Montmartre (hill of martyrs) got its name after Saint-Denis was decapitated there by the Romans in 272 A.D. It was outside the Parisian city limits until 1860, and its once low-cost rent and rural charm attracted artists like Toulouse-Lautrec, Eric Satie, Picasso, Modigliani, and Apollinaire in the first part of this century. The view from Sacré Coeur is particularly impressive at night, as is the excitement found nearby in the place du Tertre. The least demanding route to the top is from Métro Anvers. Ascend rue Steinkerque and take a left on rue Tardieu until you come to the funicular car that whisks you up to Sacré Coeur for a Métro ticket.

■ **Outer Arrondissements**

Beyond these limits, Paris continues to offer visitors many points of interest. For example, ethnic Paris is at its greatest in the 10th, 13th, 18th, and 20th *arrondissements*. Don't hesitate to venture to the far edges of the city, and beyond.

Neighborhoods for the Adventurous

Chinatown   Paris's largest concentration of residents from China, Hong Kong, Cambodia, Laos, Thailand, and especially Vietnam is located in a slice of the 13th arrondissement beginning at the Place d'Italie and running between the Porte d'Italie and the Porte d'Ivry. Here you'll find hundreds of Asian restaurants and a lively offering of Chinese supermarkets dominated by the Tang brothers, the largest importers of Asian goods into France. Take the Métro to Place d'Italie and walk down the avenue de Choisy all the way to the avenue Masséna. Turn left and left again at the avenue d'Ivry. There are inexpensive restaurants everywhere. A particularly good one is Sinorama, 135, av. de Choisy (Tel. 01 53 82 09 51). Start at Métro: Porte de Choisy.

Pigalle   Between the Place de Clichy and the Métro Barbès-Rochechouart on the edge of the 18th and 9th arrondissements, Pigalle, Paris's bawdy quarter, is found. Traditionally bohemian, noted for Toulouse Lautrec's passion for the Moulin Rouge cabaret (still in full force although frequented only by tourists), today's Pigalle is dotted with flashing lights, bustling sex shops and live peep shows, and tacky window displays of leather objects and flourescent underwear. In the summer, the area is mobbed with out-of-towners and gawking tourists bussed in from Germany, Holland, and the United Kingdom. There is nothing to be afraid of here, although you should keep your valuables securely stowed. The 18th arrondissement between Barbès-Rochechouart and the Métro stop Marcadet-Poissonnière is filled with back streets inhabited by many of Paris's African residents and a host of daunting-looking but absolutely friendly restaurants with local specialties from Senegal, Cameroon, Congo, and Ivory Coast. Start at Métro: Pigalle.

Belleville   This former village on the northwest edge of the Père Lachaise Cemetery is today a lively mixture of North African, Eastern European, and Chinese residents, offering a wide range of both seedy and wonderful restaurants and bars. Paris's second Chinatown, Belleville also offers a healthy assortment of couscous restaurants. Today, as Paris's night life, bar scenes, and artistic hang-outs creep east (Bastille, Oberkampf, Ménilmontant), Belleville finds itself at the edge of some of the city's most creative funkiness. To get there, take the Métro to the Belleville stop and walk up to Ménilmontant. Start at Métro: Belleville.

Beyond the Périphérique   Although not too many visitors trek out beyond the city limits, delineated by the Périphérique beltway, some of the most interesting cultural activities now occur in these nearby urban communities: Montreuil, Saint-Denis, Bagnolet, and Malakoff.

Attraction Profiles

Paris attractions have been split into two main categories: Museums, Monuments, and Churches; and Parks, Gardens, City Squares, and Cemeteries. Following these profiles, you'll find a section describing Paris's picturesque bridges and fountains, and then a few suggestions for day trips immediately outside of Paris and environs. Our selection process is based on Paris's most interesting attractions. Additionally, knowing the way travelers travel, we wanted to make sure that each time you pass a building or monument and, quite naturally, ask yourself "What's that?" you'll be able to find the answer in this guidebook.

PARIS ATTRACTIONS BY TYPE

Attraction Name	Author's Rating	Arrondissement/Location
Cemeteries		
Cimetière de Montmartre	★★★½	18
Cimetière du Père-Lachaise	★★★★★	11
Cimetière Montparnasse	★★★★	14
Châteaus		
Château de Fontainebleau	★★★★	Fontainebleau
Château de Versailles	★★★★	Versailles
Château de Vincennes	★★	Vincennes
Churches		
Cathedrale de Notre-Dame	★★★★	4
Eglise de St. Sulpice	★★★	6
Eglise St. Eustache	★★	1
Eglise St-Germain-des-Prés	★★	6
La Basillique du Sacré-Coeur	★★★	18
La Madeleine	★★	8
Sainte-Chapelle	★★★★	4
City Squares		
Place Dauphine	★★★½	1
Place de Fürstemberg	★★★★	6
Place de la Concorde	★★★★★	8
Place des Victoires	★★★½	1 and 2
Place Vendôme	★★★★	1
Places des Vosges	★★★★½	3 and 4
Trocadéro	★★★★	16

PARIS ATTRACTIONS BY TYPE (CONTINUED)

Attraction Name	Author's Rating	Arrondissement/Location
Monuments		
Arc de Triomphe	★★★★★	8
Champs-Elysées	★★★★	8
Hôtel de Ville	★★	4
La Conciergerie	★★★	1
La Grande Arche	★★★	La Défense
La Sorbonne	★★	5
La Tour Eiffel	★★★★★	7
Mémorial de la Déportation	★★★	4
Palais Royal	★★	1
Place de la Bastille	★★★	11
Tour Montparnasse 56	★★★★★	15
Museums		
Centre George-Pompidou (Musée National d'Art Moderne)	★★★★	4
Cité des Sciences et de l'Industrie	★★★★	19
Egouts de Paris (sewers)	★★	7
Espace Montmartre– Salvador Dali	★★	18
Galeries Nationales du Grand Palais and Palais de la Découverte	★★★★	8
Giverny	★★★	Giverny
Hôtel National des Invalides	★★★	7
Institut du Monde Arabe	★★★	5
Le Louvre	★★★★★	1
Le Panthéon	★★	5
Les Catacombes	★★★★★	14
Maison de Balzac	★★★	16
Maison Victor Hugo	★★★	4
Musée Carnavalet	★★★	3
Musée Cernuschi	★★★	8
Musée Cognacq-Jay	★★	4
Musée d'Art et d'Histoire du Judaïsme	★★★	3
Musée d'Art Moderne de la Ville de Paris	★★★	16
Musée de la Mode et du Costume	★★	16
Musée de la Monnaie	★★★	6

PARIS ATTRACTIONS BY TYPE (CONTINUED)

Attraction Name	Author's Rating	Arrondissement/Location
Museums (continued)		
Musée de la Musique	★★★	19
Musée de l'Armée	★★	5
Musée de l'Homme	★★★	16
Musée de l'Orangerie	★★★★	1
Musée des Arts d'Afrique et d'Océanie	★★★	12
Musée des Arts Décoratifs	★★★	1
Musée des Beaux-Arts de la Ville de Paris	★★	8
Musée d'Orsay	★★★★★	7
Musée du Moyen ge (Thermes de Cluny)	★★★	5
Musée Eugène Delacroix	★★	6
Musée Grévin	★★★	2
Musée Jacquemart-André	★★★★	8
Musée Marmottan-Monet	★★★★	16
Musée National des Arts Asiatiques Guimet and Les Galeries du Panthéon Buddique	★★★	16
Musée Nissum de Camondo	★★	8
Musée Picasso	★★★★	3
Musée Rodin	★★★★	7
Musée Zadkine	★★★	6
Muséum National d'Histoire Naturelle	★★★★	5
Opéra Garnier	★★	9
Palais de Chaillot	★★★	16
Parks		
Bois de Boulogne	★★★★★	16
Bois de Vincennes	★★★★★	12
Jardin d'Acclimatation	★★★★	16
Jardin des Plantes	★★★★	5
Jardin du Luxembourg	★★★★★	6
Les Tuileries	★★★½	1
Parc André Citroën	★★★	15
Parc de la Villette	★★★★	19
Parc des Buttes-Chaumont	★★★★	19
Parc Monceau	★★★★	8 and 17

PARIS ATTRACTIONS BY TYPE (CONTINUED)

Attraction Name	Author's Rating	Arrondissement/Location
Parks (continued)		
Parc Montsouris	★★½	14
Parc Zoologique de Vincennes	★★★	12
Promenade Plantée and Viaduc des Arts	★★★★	12
Theme Parks		
Disneyland Paris	★★★★	Marne-La-Valée–Chessy
Parc Astérix	★★★★	Plailly

PARIS ATTRACTIONS BY LOCATION

Name	Type of Attraction	Author's Rating
1st arrondissement		
Eglise St. Eustache	Church	★★
La Conciergerie	Gothic structure and former prison	★★★
Le Louvre	Museum	★★★★★
Les Tuileries	Park	★★★½
Musée de l'Orangerie	Museum	★★★★
Musée des Arts Décoratifs	Museum of French decorative arts	★★★
Palais Royal	Architectural remnant of the French monarchy	★★
Place Dauphine	City square	★★★½
Place des Victoires	City square	★★★½
Place Vendôme	City square	★★★★
2nd arrondissement		
Musée Grévin	Wax museum	★★★
Place des Victoires	City square	★★★½
3rd arrondissement		
Musée Carnavalet	Museum on history of Paris	★★★
Musée d'Art et d'Histoire du Judaïsme	Museum of Judaica	★★★
Musée Picasso	Museum	★★★★
Places des Vosges	City square	★★★★½

PARIS ATTRACTIONS BY LOCATION (CONTINUED)

Name	Type of Attraction	Author's Rating
4th arrondissement		
Cathedrale de Notre-Dame	Gothic cathedral	★★★★
Centre George-Pompidou (Musée National d'Art Moderne)	Museum	★★★★
Hôtel de Ville	Paris's city hall	★★
Maison Victor Hugo	Historic home and museum	★★★
Mémorial de la Déportation	Memorial to French Jews deported to Nazi death camps in WWII	★★★
Musée Cognacq-Jay	Museum	★★
Places des Vosges	City square	★★★★½
Sainte-Chapelle	Collection of stained glass windows	★★★★
5th arrondissement		
Institut du Monde Arabe	Museum of Arab culture	★★★
Jardin des Plantes	Park and zoo	★★★★
La Sorbonne	University	★★
Le Panthéon	Mausoleum and museum	★★
Musée de l'Armée	Military museum	★★
Musée du Moyen Âge	Museum of Paris's Roman past	★★★
Muséum National d'Histoire Naturelle	Natural history museum	★★★★
Opéra Garnier	Opera house and museum	★★
6th arrondissement		
Eglise de St. Sulpice	Church	★★★
Eglise St-Germain-des-Prés	Church	★★
Jardin du Luxembourg	Park	★★★★★
Musée de la Monnaie	Museum of France's national mint	★★★
Musée Eugène Delacroix	Historic home and museum	★★
Musée Zadkine	Museum	★★★
Place de Fürstemberg	City square	★★★★
7th arrondissement		
Egouts de Paris (sewers)	Underground musuem	★★
Hôtel National des Invalides	Military museum	★★★
La Tour Eiffel	Monument	★★★★★
Musée d'Orsay	Best collection of impressionist and art nouveau paintings and sculptures in the world	★★★★★
Musée Rodin	Museum	★★★★

PARIS ATTRACTIONS BY LOCATION (CONTINUED)

Name	Type of Attraction	Author's Rating
8th arrondissement		
Arc de Triomphe	Roman-style monument	★★★★★
Champs-Elysées	Famous street	★★★★
Galeries Nationales du Grand Palais and Palais de la Découverte	Museum	★★★★
La Madeleine	Church and monument	★★
Musée Cernuschi	Museum of East Asian art	★★★
Musée des Beaux-Arts de la Ville de Paris	Museum	★★
Musée Jacquemart-André	Intimate, private museum	★★★★
Musée Nissum de Camondo	18th-century mansion and museum	★★
Parc Monceau	Park	★★★★
Place de la Concorde	City square	★★★★★
11th arrondissement		
Cimetière du Père-Lachaise	Cemetery	★★★★★
Place de la Bastille	Landmark	★★★
12th arrondissement		
Bois de Vincennes	Park	★★★★★
Musée des Arts d'Afrique et d'Océanie	Museum and aquarium	★★★
Parc Zoologique de Vincennes	Zoo	★★★
Promenade Plantée and Viaduc des Arts	Park	★★★★
14th arrondissement		
Cimetière Montparnasse	Cemetery	★★★★
Les Catacombes	Collection of human bones stored under the city	★★★★★
Parc Montsouris	Park	★★½
15th arrondissement		
Parc André Citroën	Park	★★★
Tour Montparnasse 56	Paris's only skyscraper	★★★★★
16th arrondissement		
Bois de Boulogne	Park	★★★★★
Jardin d'Acclimatation	Educational park	★★★★

PARIS ATTRACTIONS BY LOCATION (CONTINUED)

Name	Type of Attraction	Author's Rating
16th arrondissement		
Maison de Balzac	Historic home and museum	★★★
Musée d'Art Moderne de la Ville de Paris	Museum of 20th-century art	★★★
Musée de la Mode et du Costume	Museum of fashion and costume design	★★
Musée de l'Homme	Museum	★★★
Musée Marmottan-Monet	Museum of impressionists	★★★★
Musée National des Arts Asiatiques Guimet and Les Galeries du Panthéon Buddique	Museum of Asian art	★★★
Palais de Chaillot	Museum	★★★
Trocadéro	Best open space for viewing Eiffel Tower	★★★★
17th arrondissement		
Parc Monceau	Park	★★★★
18th arrondissement		
Cimetière de Montmartre	Cemetery	★★★½
Espace Montmartre–Salvador Dali	Museum	★★
La Basillique du Sacré-Coeur	Basilica	★★★
19th arrondissement		
Cité des Sciences et de l'Industrie	Contemporary museum	★★★★
Musée de la Musique	Museum of music	★★★
Parc de la Villette	Park and exhibition space	★★★★
Parc des Buttes-Chaumont	Park	★★★★
Sidetrips from Paris		
Château de Fontainebleau	Royal residence and gardens	★★★★
Giverny	Historic home and museum	★★★
La Grande Arche	Massive archlike building	★★★
Disneyland Paris	Theme park	★★★★
Parc Astérix	Theme park	★★★★
Château de Versailles	Royal residence and gardens	★★★★
Château de Vincennes	Château and moat	★★

Museums, Monuments, and Churches

Arc de Triomphe

Type of Attraction   Roman-style monument to the french armed forces
Location   Pl. Charles-de-Gaulle (access via underground passage), 75008
Métro   Charles-de-Gaulle-Etoile   8th arrondissement
Admission   €6.10 adults, €3.80 students (age 18–25), free for children under age 11
Hours   Daily, 10 a.m.–11 p.m. (ticket office closes at 10:30 p.m.)
Phone   01 55 37 73 77
When to Go   Lunch hour
Special Comments   European tourists usually eat lunch during lunch time, leaving the attraction less crowded
Overall Appeal by Age Group

Pre-school —	Grade School ★★★	Teens ★★★★
Young Adults ★★★★★	Over 30 ★★★★★	Seniors ★★★★★

Author's Rating   ★★★★★
How Much Time to Allow   1 hour if you go up

Description and Comments   You'll never tire of seeing the arch, circling it, approaching it from the different sides, and finally climbing to its roof. Twelve majestic avenues spoke off from this celebrated landmark, forming a star shape and thus giving the bustling intersection its name, Etoile. True to Napoléon's original wishes in 1806, the Arc de Triomphe serves as a dramatic entry point into Paris used to honor and celebrate French military campaigns. Today the arch is the focal point for official parades and ceremonies, including November 11 in remembrance of the unknown soldier laid to rest at the end of World War I. Images of German soldiers marching through the arch and occupying Paris in 1940 still haunt elderly Parisians.

Touring Tips   Don't attempt to cross the menacingly dangerous intersection to reach the arch! Take the tunnel found at the top of the Champs-Elysées. On sunny days the view from the top is spectacular. Elderly people, pregnant women, and children are permitted to take the elevator. Others walk.

Other Things to Do Nearby   Champs-Elysées.

Baccarat Boutique Museum

Type of Attraction   Museum of the famous maker of glassware and crystal
Location   30 bis, rue du Paradis, 75010
Métro   Poissonnière or Château d'Eau
Admission   €2.30
Hours   Monday–Saturday, 10 a.m.–6 p.m.
Phone   01 47 70 64 30
Website   www.baccarat.fr
When to Go   Anytime
Overall Appeal by Age Group

Pre-school —	Grade School —	Teens ★
Young Adults ★★	Over 30 ★★★	Seniors ★★★

Authors' Rating ★★
How Much Time to Allow 1 hour

Description and Comments On this street devoted to fine glassware and china, the Baccarat museum (and headquarters) has a glitter that outshines all the shops. Nowhere in Paris, or anywhere else for that matter, can you admire a crystal evening gown, the Baccarat "chandelier dress." The more useful objects on view include crystal vases, chandeliers, glasses, carafes and even liquor cabinets. This is luxury nudged beyond excess. Worth a trip if you're shopping for tableware nearby.

Touring Tips Hang on to small kids!

Other Things to Do Nearby Tour the other table and glassware shops along the rue de Paradis.

Cathedrale de Notre-Dame

Type of Attraction The most celebrated Gothic cathedral in the world
Location Île de la Cité, 6, parvis Notre-Dame, 75004
Métro RER St-Michel-Notre-Dame   4th arrondissement
Admission Free; tower, €5.35 adults, €3.80 children and students under age 25, free for children under age 6; crypt, €4.88 adults, €3.20 children age 12–25
Hours Monday–Saturday, 8 a.m.–6:45 p.m.; Sunday, 8 a.m.–12:30 p.m., 2:45–6:45 p.m. Tower: Monday–Saturday, 9:30 a.m.–6:15 p.m.; Sunday 10 a.m.–4:15 p.m. Crypt, daily, 9:30 a.m.–6 p.m.
Phone 01 43 29 83 51; crypt, 01 42 34 56 10
When to Go Midnight mass on Christmas, during any Sunday service, or for the free organ recitals on Sundays at 5:30 p.m.
Special Comments Crowded during mass but much more spiritual
Overall Appeal by Age Group

| Pre-school — | Grade School ★★ | Teens ★★★ |
| Young Adults ★★★ | Over 30 ★★★★ | Seniors ★★★★ |

Author's Rating ★★★★
How Much Time to Allow 1–1½ hours if you climb to the top; add 30 minutes if you visit the crypt

Description and Comments Welcome to Kilometer Zero, the reference point for all distances to Paris from anywhere in the country. You'll be quickly reminded of Hugo's Hunchback. Notre-Dame, built on the Île de la Cité, Paris's historical birthplace, is France's most celebrated cathedral. Initiated by Bishop Maurice de Sully in 1160, it was not completed until the 14th century. It was constructed on the site of a basilica dating from the fourth century, which was itself built on the site of a Roman temple dedicated to Jupiter. Its gothic gargoyles, facade, and carved portals make it one of the best examples of the metamorphosis from Romanesque to Gothic style in European architectural history as the original plans for Notre-Dame followed the location's preceeding edifices. The first schools in Paris were founded here, under episcopal control. Before the renovation by Viollet-le-Duc in the 19th century, Notre-Dame had become so dilapidated that animals were sheltered there by nearby inhabitants, something hard to imagine today. You must climb 386 steps to reach the top of Notre-Dame and in addition pay €5.35. The view is worth it. The last few stairs are wooden, and they take you to the massive bronze bell in the tower. On busy days, the increasingly narrow stone steps get a bit claustrophobic.

Touring Tips   In the summer months, go early to beat the crowds.

Other Things to Do Nearby   Hotel de Ville, Centre Georges-Pompidou, Marais, Latin Quarter.

Centre Georges-Pompidou (Musée National d'Art Moderne)

Type of Attraction   Innovative and lively museum and cultural center
Location   19, rue Beaubourg, 75004
Métro   Châtelet-Les Halles   4th arrondissement
Admission   Exhibitions €6.10–7.60 adults, €4.60–6.10 reduced price
Hours   Center, daily (except Tuesday), 11 a.m.–10 p.m.; Atelier Brancusi, daily, 1–7 p.m.; Museum, daily 11 a.m.–9 p.m.; Library, Monday–Friday, noon–10 p.m; Saturday and Sunday 11 a.m.–10 p.m.
Phone   01 44 78 42 11; groups 01 44 78 42 11; guided tours 01 44 78 46 25
Website   www.centrepompidou.com
When to Go   Avoid the weekends
Overall Appeal by Age Group

Pre-school —   Grade School ★★   Teens ★★★★
Young Adults ★★★★   Over 30 ★★★★   Seniors ★★★★

Author's Rating   ★★★★
How Much Time to Allow   1–2 hours

Description and Comments   This highly original landmark perfectly marries function and style. Also known as "Beaubourg" because it's located on rue Beaubourg, the Centre National d'Art et de Culture Georges-Pompidou is located in the heart of Paris and acts as a major artery between Châtelet/Les Halles and the Marais. Richard Rogers and Renzo Piano designed the controversial structure (is there anything built in Paris this century that hasn't been controversial?) in 1977. The colors of its structure represent the internal machinations (electricity, water, heat, and so on) of the building. It houses an impressive library, an enormous modern art collection, research centers, cafés, and a cinema. All this attracts more tourists and Parisians than any other monument or museum in all of France. The huge cobblestone plaza in front of the center functions as one of Paris's most popular public spaces, encouraging all sorts of pedestrians, street performers, musicians, and shoppers to linger and congregate, making it sort of the people's place.

Touring Tips   Check for openings. Visit the rooftop veranda for its unique view.

Other Things to Do Nearby   Les Halles, the Marais.

Château de Vincennes

Type of Attraction   Dramatic French château and moat
Location   Av. de Paris, 94300 Vincennes
Métro   Château de Vincennes
Admission   Long tour: €4.88 adults, €3.20 students; short tour (castle and Sainte-Chapelle): €3.80 adults, €2.30 students
Hours   Daily, 10 a.m.–6 p.m.

Phone 01 43 28 15 48

When to Go When the weather is good

Special Comments Combine visit with stroll in the Bois de Vincennes and/or zoo

Overall Appeal by Age Group

Pre-school —	Grade School ★★	Teens ★★
Young Adults ★★	Over 30 ★★	Seniors ★★

Author's Rating ★★

How Much Time to Allow 1 hour

Description and Comments At the eastern end of the Metro Line 1 you come out at the Château de Vincennes, a surprisingly impressive 17th-century château with moat and dungeon at the edge of the Bois de Vincennes. Note the 14th-century keep within the thick walls. The dungeon with its turret-encased tower was used as the inspiration for *Twenty Years After,* Alexandre Dumas's sequel to *The Three Musketeers.*

Touring Tips Wear comfortable shoes.

Other Things to Do Nearby Combine a visit to the château with a picnic or visit to the Parc Floral or Zoo.

Cité des Sciences et de l'Industrie

Type of Attraction Highly contemporary museum and public space with captivating temporary and permanent exhibitions

Location Parc de la Villette, 30, av. Corentin-Cariou, 75019

Métro Porte de la Villette   19th arrondissement

Admission €7.62 adults, €5.34 reduced price for all visitors on Saturday, free for children under age 7

Hours Tuesday–Saturday, 10 a.m.–6 p.m.; Sunday, 10 a.m.–7 p.m.

Phone 01 40 05 80 00; reservations, 01 40 05 12 12

When to Go Very early or at mealtimes to avoid crowds

Special Comments Referred to as "La Villette"

Overall Appeal by Age Group

Pre-school ★★★★	Grade School ★★★★	Teens ★★★★
Young Adults ★★★★	Over 30 ★★★★	Seniors ★★★★

Author's Rating ★★★★

How Much Time to Allow From 2 hours to a full day

Description and Comments If you're traveling with kids, make sure you spend some time at La Villette, located at the edge of Paris's 19th arrondissement. Cité des Sciences et de L'Industrie is part of a complex that occupies the former slaughterhouses of the capital and includes the Musée de la Musique (listed separately), the Zénith (a venue for pop and rock concerts), and a futuristic park. There's a full day of activities to choose from. The science museum has lots of hands-on exhibits, a planetarium, a simulator, 3D films, and permanent exhibits devoted to space, language, the environment, and technology. The Cité des Enfants is an interactive science lab for kids (3–12 years old); you can sign them up for sessions throughout the day. The Geode, a mirrored globe visible for miles, shows IMAX films, and a restored submarine just outside the museum is a great draw. Let your kids play on the gigantic wooden dragon slide.

Touring Tips   Get a schedule of activities from the information desk so you can plan your time around the planetarium shows, the inventorium science labs for kids (it's a good idea to reserve a time slot when you first arrive), the Geode films, and other activities.

Other Things to Do Nearby   The park is great for picnics or summer naps. A free open-air film festival takes place several evenings a week throughout the summer. Check the *Pariscope* for details.

Eglise St. Eustache

Type of Attraction   Major church on the Right Bank with evening concert series
Location   Rue du Jour, 75001
Métro   Châtelet-Les Halles   1st arrondissement
Admission   Free
Hours   May to October, Monday–Saturday, 8 a.m.–8 p.m.; Sunday, 8 a.m.–1 p.m., 2:30–7 p.m.; November to April, Monday–Saturday, 8 a.m.–7 p.m.; Sunday, 9 a.m.–12:30 p.m., 3–8 p.m.
Phone   01 40 26 47 99 or 01 42 36 31 05
Website   www.st-eustache.org
When to Go   Anytime
Special Comments   Sunday organ recitals at 5:30 p.m. (free)
Overall Appeal by Age Group

Pre-school —	Grade School —	Teens ★★
Young Adults ★★	Over 30 ★★	Seniors ★★

Author's Rating ★★
How Much Time to Allow   30 minutes

Description and Comments   Best known for the organ and choral music recitals of first performances of works by Berlioz and Liszt, this gothic and Renaissance church is worth a short detour when you're in the Les Halles area. Started in 1532 with Notre-Dame as the model, St. Eustace wasn't completed until 1754. Its size and central location have contributed to its importance. Cardinal Richelieu was baptized here, as was the playwright Molière, whose funeral also graced this church. Near the front, to the left of the nave, you can spot an early Rubens painting, *The Pilgrims at Emmaüs*.

Touring Tips   Take a break in the pleasant René Cassin square in front of the church. Note the huge contemporary sculpture, *Tête*.

Other Things to Do Nearby   Forum des Halles, Châtelet, rue Montorgueil quarter, Louvre.

Eglise St-Germain-des-Prés

Type of Attraction   Prominent church in the heart of the Left Bank
Location   On the corner of the bd St-Germain and rue Jacob 75006
Métro   St-Germain-des-Prés   6th arrondissement
Admission   Free
Hours   Daily, 8 a.m.–7 p.m.
Phone   01 43 25 41 71
When to Go   Crowded at services, but otherwise quiet

Special Comments Many classical music concerts are given in this church. The acoustics are only fair but the ambience is magical.

Overall Appeal by Age Group

Pre-school —	Grade School —	Teens ★★
Young Adults ★★	Over 30 ★★	Seniors ★★

Author's Rating ★★

How Much Time to Allow 30 minutes

Description and Comments At the heart of the St-Germain-des-Prés area of the Left Bank lies this impressive abbey, an integral link in the prodigious line of the Benedictine order in Europe. The order produced 24 popes, 200 cardinals, and endless saints! In French, a *pré* is a field, and it was empty amid fields that the son of Clovis began building his religious shrine. Sacked by the Normans, the church was rebuilt several times over the centuries. The tombs of Descartes and other learned Frenchmen are found here.

Touring Tips The former bohemian character of this neighborhood has been thoroughly replaced by upscale shops, hotels, and cafés. Intellectual pretensions still prevail, though.

Other Things to Do Nearby The legendary cafés of St. Germain, Les Deux Magots, Le Flore, Brasserie Lipp, the Village Voice Bookshop.

Eglise de St. Sulpice

Type of Attraction Important Left Bank church with Delacroix murals

Location 21, rue Palatine, Pl. St-Sulpice, 75006

Métro Mabillon   6th arrondissement

Admission Free

Hours Daily, 8:30 a.m.–7:30 p.m.

Phone 01 46 33 21 78

When to Go Anytime; guided tours 3 p.m. the second Sunday of every month

Special Comments F. Scott and Zelda Fitzgerald lived next door. Marcello Mastroianni's funeral services were held here.

Overall Appeal by Age Group

Pre-school —	Grade School —	Teens —
Young Adults ★★	Over 30 ★★★	Seniors ★★★★

Author's Rating ★★★

How Much Time to Allow 30 minutes

Description and Comments Aside from being an impressive 17th-century church with a massive antique facade, most visitors are motivated by the murals of Delacroix (1849–1861) found inside. It's unlikely you'll be in the church at noon on the day of the winter solstice, but if you are, don't forget to observe the ray of sunlight passing through the tiny hole in the upper window in the south transept as it strikes the designated point on the obelisk in the far transept. A religious experience! Enjoy the central "Fountain of the Cardinal Points" in the square outside, erected by Visconti in 1844.

Touring Tips Hang out on the square. The nearby cafés are excellent for star-spotting.

Other Things to Do Nearby Shopping on the rue Bonaparte, Jardin du Luxembourg.

Egouts de Paris (Sewers)

Type of Attraction Paris's sewer system is an underground museum
Location Corner of quai d'Orsay and Pont de l'Alma, 75007
Métro RER Pont de l'Alma   7th arrondissement
Admission €3.81 per person
Hours Saturday–Wednesday, 11 a.m.–6 p.m. (until 5 p.m. May through September)
Phone 01 53 68 27 81 or 01 47 05 10 29
When to Go It's never too crowded
Special Comments Read the printed descriptions in the exhibit
Overall Appeal by Age Group

Pre-school —	Grade School ★★★	Teens ★★★
Young Adults ★★	Over 30 ★★	Seniors ★★

Author's Rating ★★
How Much Time to Allow 1 hour

Description and Comments   It is fascinating to note that every Paris street address has its equivalent address underground in the Paris sewers and is accessible by footpaths, some of which are lit. The Paris sewers have a celebrated history that goes far beyond the remarkable process in which Paris water is used, filtered, cleaned, and recycled. The network empties at Archères in the northern suburbs, one of the world's largest water purification systems. Initially part of Napoléon III's engineering project for the capital, the sewer system today includes over 1,300 miles of tunnels and underground waterways that can be visited with guides by descending an ominous stairway at the foot of Pont d'Alma on the Left Bank. The tour is a bit dark and musty and although the air has been sanitized and deodorized, it's still a bit funky. But the network and its historic use during World War II for hiding French resistance fighters excites the imagination. Note, too, the massive pipes for transporting fresh water, electric power, telecommunications lines, and more recently fiber-optic cable. An unusual but very interesting and uniquely Parisian attraction.

Touring Tips Perfect for rainy days.

Other Things to Do Nearby   Eiffel Tower, Les Invalides.

Espace Montmartre–Salvador Dali

Type of Attraction Private museum dedicated to the Father of Surrealism
Location 9–11, rue Poulbot, 75018
Métro Anvers or Abbesses   18th arrondissement
Admission €5.34 adults; €3.81 students, children age 8–25, seniors; free for children under age 8
Hours Daily, 10 a.m.–6 p.m. (until 9 p.m. during July and August)
Phone 01 42 64 40 10
When to Go Early, just after opening
Special Comments Bookshop includes full range of posters and postcards of Dali's work.
Overall Appeal by Age Group

Pre-school —	Grade School —	Teens ★★
Young Adults ★★	Over 30 ★★	Seniors ★★

Author's Rating ★★
How Much Time to Allow 1 hour

Description and Comments Just steps from the flourishing tourist trap of Place du Tertre is this small museum, with 330 works by the surrealist master Salvador Dali. Voice recordings of the painter and sculptor accompany you as you wander through the collection. Dali lovers should make the trip.

Touring Tips Take a moment to enjoy the marvelous view from the tiny Place du Calvaire just in front of the museum.

Other Things to Do Nearby Join the other tourists milling about Place du Tertre; explore the quieter side streets and make your way over to the Sacré-Coeur for the view; stop by the sober Romanesque St. Pierre Church on the way.

Galeries Nationales du Grand Palais
Palais de la Découverte

Type of Attraction Leading museum complex for temporary and permanent exhibits in the realms of art and science
Location 3, av. du Général Eisenhower, 75008
Métro Champs-Elysées-Clemenceau 8th arrondissement
Admission Without prebooking: €6.86 adults (after 1 p.m.), €4.73 (Monday and reduced price); with prebooking: €7.77 adults (10 a.m.–1 p.m.), €5.64 (reduced price only on Monday)
Hours Thursday–Monday, 10 a.m.–8 p.m. (box office closes at 7:15 p.m.); Wednesday, 10 a.m.–10 p.m. (box office closes at 9:15 p.m.). For the Palais de la Découverte: Tuesday–Saturday, 9:30 a.m.–6 p.m., Sunday, 10 a.m.–7 p.m.
Phone 01 44 13 17 17; Palais de la Découverte, 01 40 74 80 00
When to Go Try not to go on Mondays
Special Comments For prebookings go to any FNAC or Virgin Megastore (Métro Franklin Roosevelt) or to the Printemps department store (Métro Havre-Caumartin). Often, there are two exhibitions happening at once, and you can buy a single ticket for the two. (Prices: without prebooking: €10.67 adults and €6.86 reduced price for students and all visitors on Monday; with prebooking: €11.59 adults and €7.77 reduced price for students and all visitors on Monday.)
Overall Appeal by Age Group

Pre-school ★	Grade School ★★★	Teens ★★★
Young Adults ★★★	Over 30 ★★★	Seniors ★★★

Author's Rating ★★★★
How Much Time to Allow 2 hours

Description and Comments This giant iron and glass structure, built for the 1900 Universal Exhibition, now has two distinct sections: the Galeries Nationales and the Palais de la Découverte. The first is the venue for blockbuster temporary exhibitions; recent shows include Cézanne, Corot, and ancient Egypt. The second houses a science museum and a completely revamped planetarium, highly recommended for anyone traveling with children. A third section used to house the FIAC art fair and the annual book fair; it is currently under renovation.

Touring Tips To avoid the long lines for the temporary shows, prepurchase entry tickets at the FNAC ticket outlets. Mornings are reserved for ticket-holders; if you haven't managed to book ahead, you can wait in line in the afternoon. The Palais de la Découverte has lost a few visitors since the Cité des Science opened at La Villette, but the new planetarium makes it worth the trip, and kids love it.

Other Things to Do Nearby Explore the gardens; admire the glitter and gold on Pont Alexandre III, built at the same time as the Grand Palais; wander up the Champs-Elysées.

Hôtel de Ville

Type of Attraction Paris's dramatic city hall with public exhibitions
Location Pl. de l'Hôtel de Ville (main public entrance, 29, rue de Rivoli), 75004
Métro Hôtel de Ville   4th arrondissement
Admission Depends on exhibitions; the city government side is closed to the public
Hours Open for tour groups and during exhibitions only
Phone 01 42 76 50 49
When to Go Exhibitions are rarely crowded; city hall offices are closed to the public
Special Comments This building acts as the backdrop in the famous black and white photograph of a returning French soldier embracing a local lass at the end of WWII.
Overall Appeal by Age Group

Pre-school —	Grade School —	Teens —
Young Adults ★★	Over 30 ★★	Seniors ★★

Author's Rating ★★
How Much Time to Allow View this building from the outside

Description and Comments Visitors should note that in French the word *hôtel* means mansion or large private building, and that every French town has its Hôtel de Ville, or City Hall. Paris's Hôtel de Ville, built between 1874 and 1882 in the neo-Renaissance style, offers a stunning facade of nearly 150 statues depicting leaders from French history and celebrated French cities. The ornate Third Republic ballroom and reception areas reflect both belle epoque and Renaissance decor, but unfortunately, unless you're invited by the mayor or happen to be in Paris on the Fête de la Patrimoine, when public buildings are opened to the public, you have no chance of seeing past the facade. The open square in front of the Hôtel de Ville is a pleasant place to rest. In the winter, the area is used to erect a Christmas manger and an ice-skating rink.

Touring Tips Use the pedestrian underpass to get across the street separating the Hotel de Ville and the Seine.

Other Things to Do Nearby BHV department store, Notre-Dame, Centre Georges-Pompidou, the Marais, Île St. Louis.

Hôtel National des Invalides

Type of Attraction France's most celebrated complex of military museums, including Napoleon's tomb
Location 6, Bd. des Invalides, 75007
Métro Latour-Maubourg, Varenne, or Invalides   7th arrondissement

Admission Free

Hours Daily, 10 a.m.–6 p.m. (open until 5 p.m. October to March)

Phone 01 44 42 37 79 or 01 45 51 95 05 (Musée de l'Armée)

When to Go As early as possible; gets crowded in the afternoons

Special Comments The dome was regilded in 1989

Overall Appeal by Age Group

Pre-school ★   Grade School ★★★   Teens ★★★

Young Adults ★★★   Over 30 ★★★   Seniors ★★★

Author's Rating ★★★

How Much Time to Allow 2 hours

Description and Comments Although the Hôtel des Invalides was built by Louis XIV in 1674 as a military hospital for aging veterans, Napoléon's spirit reigns now over this giant homage to French military might. He died in exile, but his nephew, Napoléon III, orchestrated the return of his remains to Paris in 1840 and transformed the crypt to house a grandiose tomb (there are actually six coffins, one inside the other, all placed in a red porphyry sarcophagus). Several other museums are housed in the buildings. The Army Museum is reputed to be one of the best military museums in the world. There are often school groups here, and the kids enjoy the old armor and military garb from around the world. Less well known is the Plan and Relief Museum, also a favorite with kids. It houses scale models (some up to 20 feet across) of fortified French towns and harbors, built over the last few centuries to help military leaders plan campaigns and design defense installations.

Touring Tips One ticket is valid for Napoléon's tomb, the Army Museum, and the Plan and Relief Museum. This is the place for those interested in all things military; others may want to visit the nearby Rodin Museum or stroll along the Seine.

Other Things to Do Nearby Rodin Museum.

Institut du Monde Arabe

Type of Attraction Stunning museum and exhibition center devoted to Arab culture

Location 1, rue de Fossés St-Bernard, 75005

Métro Jussieu   5th arrondissement

Admission €6.86 (for exhibitions); €3.81 (for the museum)

Hours Tuesday–Sunday, 10 a.m.–6 p.m.

Phone 01 40 51 38 38

When to Go Crowded on Sundays

Special Comments No English brochures. English guided tour available; ask for it when you buy your ticket.

Overall Appeal by Age Group

Pre-school —   Grade School ★★   Teens ★★

Young Adults ★★★   Over 30 ★★★   Seniors ★★★

Author's Rating ★★★

How Much Time to Allow 1–2 hours

Description and Comments This is a fascinating building, with exhibitions that will open your eyes to regions of the world you may not be familiar with. Not much in English.

n are married with contemporary architecture
ıce that is often overlooked by visitors. There is
the top floor with an exquisite view.

art from the ninth to nineteenth centuries, cover-
and ornaments including wood, ivory, bronze, glass,

ıe current exhibit interests you. Kids don't find this
ɔ the nearby Jardin des Plantes zoo can be mixed into
the s⌄

Other Things ⌄⌄   ⸍by Jardin des Plantes, Museum National d'Histoire
Naturelle, La Mosquée, Arène⌄ de Lutèce, Notre-Dame.

La Basilique du Sacré-Coeur

Type of Attraction Famous basilica and landmark situated at the top of Montmartre
Location 35, rue du Chevalier-de-la Barre, 75018
Métro Abbesses   18th arrondissement
Admission Basilique, free; dome and crypt, €2.29 person; crypt and dome €3.81 adults,
€1.98 children age 6–25, free for children under age 6
Hours Basilique, daily, 7 a.m.–11 p.m.; dome and crypt, daily, 9 a.m.–7 p.m.
Phone 01 53 41 89 00
Website www.sacre-coeur-montmartre.com
When to Go Crowded on the weekends and in the evenings
Special Comments Guided tours
Overall Appeal by Age Group

| Pre-school — | Grade School ★ | Teens ★★★ |
| Young Adults ★★★ | Over 30 ★★★ | Seniors ★★★ |

Author's Rating ★★★
How Much Time to Allow 1 hour

Description and Comments Visible on clear days from many corners of Paris, La
Basilique du Sacré-Coeur (Basilica of the Sacred Heart), with its unmistakable white dome,
is one of the city's most beautiful sights from both far off and up close. Located on the top
of the city at the pinnacle of Montmartre, this church was an undertaking of the French
government in 1873 at the initiative of Catholic citizens. The church was designed in a
Roman-Byzantine style by Paul Abadie, who died before seeing his plans completed. It was
concluded only in 1914 and serves as a destination for thousands of pilgrims each year.
The stained-glass windows are not the originals—those were destroyed in 1944 during
World War II. The inside of the church is kind of gloomy, but you can climb to the dome's
peak and exit along a railed area, below which all of Paris rolls out. In the summer, the area
in front of Sacré-Coeur and the steps that wind down through the Square Willette below
are usually cluttered with students, foreign backpackers, the local riffraff equipped with
beer bottles and guitars, and African vendors of cheap carvings and leatherwork.

After visiting the church, take a spin around the very touristy but nonetheless charming Place du Tertre, celebrated for its now kitschy collection of street artists and carica-

turists, postcard vendors, or postcards and cheap reproductions of Toulouse-Lautrec. The square is lined with pleasant but overpriced cafés and crêperies.

Touring Tips It gets crowded with tourists on summer nights, but no visit to Paris is complete without a hike up to Sacré-Coeur and Place du Tertre. From Métro Abesses take the funicular ride to the top for only one Métro ticket and walk down if you feel up to it.

Other Things to Do Nearby Dali Museum, Montmartre cemetery.

La Conciergerie

Type of Attraction Gothic structure and former prison
Location 1, quai de l'Horloge, 75001
Métro Cité   1st arrondissement
Admission €4.88 adults, €3.20 children age 12–25, free for children under age 12; €7.62 per person for Conciergerie and Sainte-Chapelle
Hours Daily, 9:30 a.m.–6 p.m. (April–September); 10 a.m.–5 p.m. (October–March)
Phone 01 53 73 78 50 or 01 43 54 30 0 6
When to Go Crowded during the tourist season
Special Comments Daily guided tours at 11 a.m. and 3 p.m.
Overall Appeal by Age Group
  Pre-school —   Grade School —   Teens ★★★
  Young Adults ★★★   Over 30 ★★★   Seniors ★★★
Author's Rating ★★★
How Much Time to Allow 1 hour

Description and Comments La Conciergerie will excite your imagination for medieval times with its 14th-century gothic architecture and Reign of Terror prisons. In 1793–1794, over 2,500 imprisoned men and women (including Marie Antoinette) were sent from here to be guillotined at various spots in Paris. It is said that 1,306 heads from La Conciergerie rolled in 40 days at Place de la Nation. From the outside, you should note the famous Tour de l'Horloge, which boasts the first public clock in Paris, built in 1370. It still runs! Inside, don't miss the Salle des Gens d'Armes, a masterpiece of gothic architecture. (Note that Gens d'Armes, from which comes today's gendarmes, means men-at-arms.)

Touring Tips It's pleasant to walk along the upper quais of the Seine outside the Conciergerie.

Other Things to Do Nearby Notre-Dame, Sainte-Chapelle, St. Michel, Shakespeare & Company Bookshop.

La Grande Arche

Type of Attraction Massive, archlike building at La Défense marking the western point of the longest urban axis in the world
Location 1, Parvis de la Défense, 92044 La Défense
Métro Grande Arche de la Défense, RER La Défense
Admission €6.10 adults, €4.88 children under age 18
Hours Daily, 10 a.m.–7 p.m. (box office closes at 6 p.m.)
Phone 01 49 07 27 57

Website www.grandearche.com

When to Go The earlier in the day the better

Special Comments Panoramic view of Paris, exhibitions, bookshop, restaurant, lots of modern sculptures

Overall Appeal by Age Group

Pre-school —	Grade School ★★	Teens ★★
Young Adults ★★★	Over 30 ★★★	Seniors ★★★

Author's Rating ★★★

How Much Time to Allow I hour if you go up

Description and Comments The sprawling esplanade in front of La Grande Arche and the steep but wide steps that lead up to it reflect a very different look at Paris. From the arch, you can follow the axis that lines up the Arc de Triomphe, the obelisk at Place de la Concorde, the pyramid at the Louvre, and onward to the column at the Bastille. Eight kilometers of perfect symmetry. La Défense is far from beautiful, but this outcrop of sky-scrapers, malls, office towers, and apartments comprises the heart of Paris's contemporary corporate culture.

Touring Tips You don't have to go up the Grande Arche to get a flavor of La Défense and to appreciate the view. But make sure you climb the steps at least in front of the arch.

Other Things to Do Nearby Underground shopping mall accessible from the Esplanade.

La Madeleine

Type of Attraction Church and monument whose façade is a Paris icon

Location 14, rue Surene, 75008

Métro Madeleine   8th arrondissement

Admission Free

Hours Monday–Saturday, 7 a.m.–7 p.m.; Sunday, 7 a.m.–1:30 p.m. and 3:30–7 p.m.

Phone 01 44 51 69 00

Website lesmadeleines.free.fr

When to Go Anytime

Special Comments Peering from La Madeleine, you see across the Place de la Concorde and the Seine what looks like the front door of the Assemblée Nationale, an optical effect created to give the impression of an axis between the two.

Overall Appeal by Age Group

Pre-school —	Grade School —	Teens —
Young Adults ★★★	Over 30 ★★	Seniors ★★

Author's Rating ★★

How Much Time to Allow 20 minutes if you climb the tower

Description and Comments This church, dedicated to St. Mary Magdalene, is a major landmark on the Right Bank located near the Place de la Concorde on the rue Royale joining Paris's belt of grand boulevards. This Greek temple–like structure was completed in 1842 after many years of construction and Louis XVIII's 1814 orders to turn the temple into a church. Enter the church and climb the steps of the tower for a fine view of the posh rue Royale with its swanky shops, the famous Maxim's restaurant, and the obelisk in the majestic Place de la Concorde beyond.

Touring Tips If you go on a Saturday, you may get a glimpse of a society wedding. It is said that Paris's best families marry off their daughters at La Madeleine.

Other Things to Do Nearby Outside the church is a flower market with Paris's most famous gourmet caterers, Fauchon and Hediard, respectively, across the street on opposite sides. Visit the Maille mustard shop for excellent, original gifts. The same-day, half-price theater ticket counter is also located on the square.

La Sorbonne

Type of Attraction France's oldest and most celebrated university. Symbol of knowledge and enlightenment for over seven centuries.
Location 47, rue des Ecoles, 75005
Métro Cluny-La Sorbonne   5th arrondissement
Admission Limited public access
Hours Monday–Friday, courtyards, 9 a.m.–4:30 p.m.
Phone 01 40 46 20 15
When to Go Anytime
Special Comments The Latin Quarter gets its name from the fact that students used to study Latin at the Sorbonne.
Overall Appeal by Age Group
  Pre-school —   Grade School —   Teens —
  Young Adults ★★   Over 30 ★★   Seniors ★★
Author's Rating ★★
How Much Time to Allow 30 minutes

Description and Comments The Sorbonne's reputation alone is reason to take note of this famed institution. Started in 1253 as a tiny college for poor students of theology, the Sorbonne was named after Robert de Sorbon, who came from a village in the Ardennes region. It was not until after Napoléon's rein, though, that the university grew into the institution of higher learning that it is known for. Today, the chapel, in which the tomb of Cardinal Richelieu is located, is closed to the public except for when used for concerts and exhibitions. If you want to visit the Sorbonne, you must make reservations one month in advance (Tel. 01 40 26 20 15) and confirm by mail to Mme. Bolot.

Touring Tips Read up on French educational system as a background for your tour. Take a peek into one of the lecture halls (amphitheatre).

Other Things to Do Nearby Jardin du Luxembourg, St. Michel, Thermes de Cluny. Take a break at one of the cafés on the Place de la Sorbonne.

La Tour Eiffel

Type of Attraction The world's most recognizable landmark
Location Quai Branly, Champ de Mars, 75007
Métro Bir-Hakheim/RER Champs-de-Mars Tour Eiffel; buses 42, 69, 72, 82, 87   7th arrondissement

Admission By stairs: first and second stories, €3.05; by lift: first story, €3.66 adults, €2.14 children under age 11; second story, €6.84 adults, €3.81 children under age 11; top, €9.91 adults, €5.34 children under age 11; free for children under age 3

Hours September to June 21: daily, 9:30 a.m.–11 p.m. (by lift), 9:30 a.m.–6:30 p.m. (by stairs); June 22 to August: daily, 9 a.m.–midnight (by lift or stairs)

Phone 01 44 11 23 23

Website www.tour-eiffel.fr

When to Go Try to go an hour before sunset

Special Comments Restaurants (first and second stories), souvenir shops

Overall Appeal by Age Group

Pre-school —	Grade School ★★★	Teens ★★★★★
Young Adults ★★★★★	Over 30 ★★★★★	Seniors ★★★★★

Author's Rating ★★★★★

How Much Time to Allow 1–2 hours depending on the wait and the level you wish to climb to

Description and Comments The Eiffel Tower is the superstar of Parisian monuments and most likely the world's best-known landmark. It was the largest construction in the world at 300 meters when it was inaugurated in 1889 by Gustave Eiffel to celebrate the centennial of the French Revolution. The tower exerts per square centimeter the equivalent of a person sitting in a chair, although its total weight is over 7,000 tons. Its summit sways 12 centimeters only in the wind. Built first as a temporary structure, the tower was nearly knocked down in 1910, but due to its utility in radio and telegraph broadcasting it was saved from the scrap heap. The tower was reelectrified in 1989 for its centennial and the French bicentennial and stands today at 1,051 feet. The last days of the millennium (marked by an illuminated J for *jour*) were counted down on a huge electronic clock on the tower's front.

The tower consists of three platforms at 57 meters, 115 meters, and 276 meters. Go to the top. Don't try to save money here. From the third platform, you can see up to 40 miles when it's clear, although Parisian pollution sometimes veils the view. There is only one Eiffel Tower in the world. You've come this far; go to the top. For those of you afraid of heights, it's really not so bad. The elevator ride is scarier than the view. At the top you're enmeshed in protective cable. The best conditions are at sunset. If you're interested in the tower's utilitarian side, note that it is used as a radio and television transmitter, a weather station, and an aircraft navigational point. The tower hosts the culinary landmark, the Jules Verne, on the second level, which is terribly expensive but breathtaking. Going up the tower is always memorable regardless how many times you've done it. For returning visitors, it is worth renewing the pilgrimage at least once every decade.

Touring Tips Avoid midday when the crowds are heaviest.

Other Things to Do Nearby Walk in the Champ de Mars, Trocadéro.

Le Louvre

Type of Attraction Arguably the world's most famous museum

Location 99, rue de Rivoli, 75001 (entrance through Pyramid, Cour Napoléon or Galerie du Carrousel)

Métro Palais-Royal   1st arrondissement
Admission Permanent collections: €7 adults (until 3 p.m.), €4.57 adults (after 3 p.m. and on Sunday), free for children under age 18 and on the first Sunday of the month; temporary exhibitions: admission varies
Hours Permanent collections: Thursday–Sunday, 9 a.m.–6 p.m. (box office closes at 5:15 p.m.); Monday and Wednesday, 9 a.m.–9:45 p.m. (box office closes at 9:15 p.m.); closed on Tuesday. Temporary exhibitions: Hall Napoléon: Tuesday, Thursday–Sunday, 9 a.m.–8:30 p.m. (box office closes at 8:15 p.m.); Monday, Wednesday, and holidays, 9 a.m.–9:45 p.m. (box office closes at 9:15 p.m.)
Phone 01 40 20 51 51; recorded information, 01 40 20 53 17
Website www.louvre.fr
When to Go Try to avoid going on Sunday, especially the first Sunday of each month
Special Comments Audioguides in English (€4.57). Guided tours in English. Wheelchair access. Post office, lectures, nursery.
Overall Appeal by Age Group

Pre-school ★★	Grade School ★★★	Teens ★★★★
Young Adults ★★★★★	Over 30 ★★★★★	Seniors ★★★★★

Author's Rating ★★★★★
How Much Time to Allow 4–5 hours

Description and Comments   The Louvre is definitely a five-star Parisian draw, up there with the Eiffel Tower and the Arc de Triomphe. There's no scenic view but plenty of material to nourish your spirit and soul. Although I. M. Pei's pyramid scandalized many people when it was inaugurated in 1989, innovation at the Louvre is nothing new. Indeed, the buildings have pretty much been under construction since the 12th century, when King Philippe-Auguste had a massive fortress constructed to guard the western edge of Paris. Various monarchs added wings, courtyards, and other flourishes, creating the largest royal palace in the world. In 1793, the Musée Central des Arts opened as the precursor to today's Louvre.

The collections are divided into seven departments, housed in three main sections: Sully (in the Cour Carrée), Richelieu (in the wing on the Rue de Rivoli side), and Denon (the wing alongside the Seine). Much to the surprise and relief of longtime visitors, the museum has finally managed to create a legible, straightforward map of the collections and departments, available in multiple languages. Pick one up at the central desk under the pyramid before setting off. Although most people make a beeline for the *Mona Lisa,* we'd suggest an alternative route: Start with the Sully wing and the foundations of Philippe-Auguste's medieval keep (it's a good way to keep the kids interested as well). This leads to the Louvre's newly restored Egyptian section; with over 50,000 objects, it's the largest collection of its kind outside of Cairo. From here, you have two choices: the Richelieu wing or the Denon wing. Most people will veer off to the latter because it houses the spectacular Greek collection (do not miss the *Winged Victory*) and the Roman and Etruscan antiquities. Upstairs is the best in 16th- and 17th-century Italian painting, especially in the Salle des Etats, which has the *Mona Lisa,* and a few often overlooked masterpieces by such painters as Veronese, Titian, and Caravaggio.

Most of the French painting (with the exception of large works) is in the opposite wing (Richelieu), along with the impressive Persian section, the objets d'art (usually deserted), and the Dutch and Flemish artists. Another rarely visited area is the Napoléon III apartments. If you don't have time to go to Versailles, you can get a taste of the gilded royal style in these few rooms.

Touring Tips It's helpful to do a bit of preplanning before taking on the largest museum in the world. Select an itinerary that suits your interests (or age group, if traveling with kids). The Louvre can be daunting, so for a first visit, choose just a few works of art or periods. After 3 p.m., the price drops; this still leaves plenty of time to explore the museum. If the lines are too long at the pyramid, try the underground entrance through the shopping mall—but the best way to avoid the crowds is to prepurchase a ticket at the FNAC (€7.77); they're valid any time and you can enter the museum directly through the Richelieu entrance.

Other Things to Do Nearby Have a snack or meal at the Café Marly on the court-yard's northern leg—either sit on the terrace facing the Pyramide or inside overlooking the Richelieu wing's sculptures. After exploring the Louvre, walk through the Jardin des Tuileries and collapse into one of the green metal chairs scattered throughout the park while your kids play with rented sailboats on the pond or you admire other people's kids sailing these adorable toys.

Le Panthéon

Type of Attraction Mausoleum and historic museum
Location Place du Panthéon, 75005
Métro Cardinal Lemoine or RER Luxembourg   5th arrondissement
Admission €5.34 adults, €3.51 students age 12–25 and professors, free for children under age 12
Hours April to September, daily, 9:30 a.m.–6:30 p.m. (box office closes at 5:45 p.m.); October to March, daily, 10 a.m.–5:30 p.m. (box office closes at 5 p.m.)
Phone 01 43 54 34 51 or 01 44 32 18 00
When to Go Rarely crowded
Overall Appeal by Age Group

Pre-school —	Grade School —	Teens —
Young Adults ★★	Over 30 ★★	Seniors ★★

Author's Rating ★★
How Much Time to Allow 45 minutes

Description and Comments When you spot the Panthéon you'll think of the U.S. Capitol building in Washington, D.C. Built on the highest point of the Left Bank, this attempt at the perfect marriage of Gothic and Greek architectural styles was ordered by Louis XV, after his recovery from a serious illness, in honor of St. Geneviève, the Patron Saint of Paris. Initially a church, in 1791 it became the final resting place of great men who died in the name of French liberty. Thus, here in the crypt you'll find the tombs of Voltaire, Rousseau, Zola, Mirabeau, Hugo (historians estimate that two million people attended his funeral march from the Arc de Triomphe to the Panthéon), Louis Braille (the creator of the braille system for the blind), Pierre and Marie Curie (who was the first woman to be laid to rest here), and more recently André Malraux. If you've heard of Foucault's pendulum, you'll be delighted to note that it was from the massive dome of the Panthéon that physicist Léon Foucault suspended his iron pendulum in 1851, proving that the earth rotates on its axis. (The pendulum is now in the Musée des Arts et Métiers, 60, rue Réamur, 75003, Métro: Arts et Métiers.)

Touring Tips Climb the stairs in the dome for a great view of central Paris.

Other Things to Do Nearby La Sorbonne, Jardin du Luxembourg.

Maison de Balzac

Type of Attraction Balzac's personal residence commemorating the writer's life and work
Location 47, rue Raynouard, 75016
Métro Passy 16th arrondissement
Admission €2.67 adults, €1.37 students
Hours Tuesday–Sunday, 10 a.m.–5:40 p.m.
Phone 01 42 24 56 38
When to Go Never really crowded
Special Comments This is a good example of a writer's home turned into a museum, as is common in France.
Overall Appeal by Age Group

Pre-school —	Grade School —	Teens ★★
Young Adults ★★★	Over 30 ★★★	Seniors ★★★

Author's Rating ★★★
How Much Time to Allow 1–1½ hours

Description and Comments Overwhelmed by debt and pursued by his creditors, Honoré de Balzac moved in October 1840 to this house, where he lived under a pseudonym. The seven years he spent here were incredibly productive; you can see his writing desk, where he penned some of his masterpieces (*Une tenebreuse affaire, Splendeurs et misères des courtisanes*) and corrected the entire manuscript of *La Comédie Humaine*. A great pilgrimage for writers.

Touring Tips Though once considered a boring, bourgeois neighborhood, Passy now boasts many new restaurants and great boutiques.

Other Things to Do Nearby Wander around the nearby streets, Passy Cemetery.

Maison Victor Hugo

Type of Attraction Victor Hugo's home turned into a museum to commemorate the writer and his work
Location Hôtel de Rohan-Guéméné, 6, place des Vosges, 75004
Métro St-Paul-Le Marais 4th arrondissement
Admission €4.12 adults, €2.90 students and children over age 7, free for children under age 7
Hours Tuesday–Sunday, 10 a.m.–6 p.m.
Phone 01 42 72 10 16
When to Go Avoid Sunday afternoons
Special Comments You can also admire the view of the Hôtel de Rohan-Guéméné.

Overall Appeal by Age Group

| Pre-school — | Grade School — | Teens — |
| Young Adults ★★★ | Over 30 ★★★ | Seniors ★★★ |

Author's Rating ★★★

How Much Time to Allow 1 hour including a stroll under the arcade in the Place de Vosges

Description and Comments   Victor Hugo spent 16 years, from 1832 to 1848, living and working on the second floor of this elegant house, the largest on Place des Vosges. It was here that he wrote *Les Misérables* and received famous friends, writers, and artists, including Balzac, David, and Dumas. Much of the museum's collection consists of memorabilia, books, and drawings, displayed in reconstructions of the rooms in which he and his family once lived. This is another specialist museum, great for French literature fans; others may want to explore the lovely Place des Vosges.

Touring Tips   Keep an eye out for the plaques on many of the buildings indicating famous residents or events that occurred in the Place des Vosges.

Other Things to Do Nearby   Explore the Marais or Bastille areas.

Mémorial de la Déportation

Type of Attraction   Powerful memorial to Parisians deported to the Nazi death camps
Location   Île de la Cité, Square de l'Île de France, 75004
Métro   RER St-Michel-Notre-Dame or Cité   4th arrondissement
Admission   Free
Hours   Daily, 10 a.m.–noon, 2–5 p.m. (until 6 p.m. April through September)
Phone   01 46 33 87 56
When to Go   Any time before sunset
Special Comments   This is a somber reminder of one of the darkest chapters in French and European history

Overall Appeal by Age Group

| Pre-school — | Grade School — | Teens — |
| Young Adults ★★ | Over 30 ★★★ | Seniors ★★★ |

Author's Rating ★★★

How Much Time to Allow 15 minutes

Description and Comments   After visiting Notre-Dame, take few minutes to experience one of the most somber and moving memorial monuments in the world. At the tip of the Square de l'Île de France on the eastern edge of Île de la Cité, this monument commemorates the thousands of French Jews and resistance fighters deported to the Nazi death camps in the early 1940s. Strangely housed in an underground tunnel lit by candle, on the spot where Napoléon III built the municipal morgue, this tribute is a powerful, moving experience and a strong reminder of the horrors from the days of German occupation of Paris.

Touring Tips   A visit to this memorial will sensitize you to the many plaques around town commemorating famous as well as unknown victims of Nazi aggression in Paris.

Other Things to Do Nearby   Notre-Dame, Île St. Louis, Hôtel de Ville.

Musée Carnavalet

Type of Attraction A comprehensive museum on the history of Paris
Location Hôtel Carnavalet, 23, rue Sévigné, 75003
Métro St-Paul-Le Marais   3rd arrondissement
Admission Exhibition and museum, €4.57 adults, €3.05 students
Hours Tuesday–Sunday, 10 a.m.–5:40 p.m.
Phone 01 42 72 21 13
When to Go To beat the crowds, avoid weekends.
Special Comments Paris construction continues to unearth new archeological finds, which are catalogued here.
Overall Appeal by Age Group

Pre-school —	Grade School ★	Teens ★★
Young Adults ★★	Over 30 ★★★	Seniors ★★★

Author's Rating ★★★
How Much Time to Allow 1½ hours

Description and Comments It is fitting that the museum devoted to the history of Paris be located in the former home of the Marquise de Sévigné, one of France's most famous chroniclers of day-to-day life in the city. Recently renovated, the museum encompasses two buildings; the collections are displayed chronologically, beginning with objects from Roman times through the present day. There are lots of portraits and objets d'art, but most interesting here are the reconstructions of interiors and shopfronts, including Marcel Proust's bedroom and an extravagant 20th-century ballroom.

Touring Tips An excellent museum for those interested in the history of Paris, especially its architecture and interior design; others may want to explore the streets of the Marais neighborhood instead.

Other Things to Do Nearby Place des Vosges, Musée Picasso, Musée Cognacq-Jay, stroll through the Marais area down to the rue des Rosiers (Jewish quarter).

Musée Cernuschi

Type of Attraction Gemlike museum of East Asian art and artifacts
Location 7, av. Velasquez, 75008
Métro Villiers   8th arrondissement
Admission €3.35 adults, €2.23 students, free for children under age 18; free on Sunday mornings
Hours Tuesday–Sunday, 10 a.m.–5 p.m.
Phone 01 45 63 50 75
When to Go Rarely very busy
Special Comments Wheelchair access
Overall Appeal by Age Group

Pre-school —	Grade School ★★	Teens ★★
Young Adults ★★★	Over 30 ★★★	Seniors ★★★

Author's Rating ★★★
How Much Time to Allow 1½ hours

Description and Comments   Few people explore this museum devoted to East Asian art, with work ranging from neolithic terracottas to 12th-century bronzes and some contemporary Chinese paintings, but it houses one of the most impressive collections of its kind in Europe. Like the nearby Nissim de Camondo, most of the works in this museum were put together by a single collector. Temporary exhibitions are held on the first floor. Recommended for those interested in Asian art. Others may prefer to skip it.

Other Things to Do Nearby   Parc Monceau, Musée Nissim de Camondo.

Musée Cognacq-Jay

Type of Attraction   Jewel of a private art collector's collection
Location   Hôtel Denon, 8, rue Elzévir, 75004
Métro   St-Paul-Le Marais   4th arrondissement
Admission   €3.35 adults, €2.23 students and seniors, free for children under age 18; free on Sunday mornings
Hours   Tuesday–Sunday, 10 a.m.–5:40 p.m.
Phone   01 40 27 07 21
When to Go   Anytime
Overall Appeal by Age Group

Pre-school —	Grade School —	Teens ★
Young Adults ★★	Over 30 ★★	Seniors ★★

Author's Rating   ★★
How Much Time to Allow   1 hour

Description and Comments   This museum, like the Jaquemart-André, was formed from one couple's personal collection. Louise Jay and her husband, Ernest Cognacq (founder of the Samaritaine department store), bequeathed their collection, which includes 18th-century artworks and objets d'art (paintings by Watteau, Fragonard, and Boucher, for example). It's in a lovely old building; art lovers love it, but kids and others will probably find it a bit stuffy.

Touring Tips   Coordinate with other small attractions and museums in the area.

Other Things to Do Nearby   Musée Carnavalet, Place des Vosges, Jewish Quarter.

Musée d'Art et d'Histoire du Judaïsme

Type of Attraction   Museum of Judaica, religious and historic artifacts
Location   Hôtel de Saint-Aignan, 71, rue du Temple, 75003
Métro   Hôtel de Ville   3rd arrondissement
Admission   €6.10 adults, €3.81 students, free for children under age 18
Hours   Monday–Friday, 11 a.m.–6 p.m.; Sunday, 10 a.m.–6 p.m.
Phone   01 53 01 86 53
When to Go   Avoid Sundays.
Special Comments   Wheelchair access, bookshop, library
Overall Appeal by Age Group

Pre-school —	Grade School —	Teens ★★
Young Adults ★★	Over 30 ★★★	Seniors ★★★

Author's Rating   ★★★

How Much Time to Allow I hour

Description and Comments The Musée d'Art et d'Histoire du Judaïsme has recently moved from rather dusty premises in Montmartre to new headquarters in the Marais. Created in 1948, the museum has received generous donations from artists, including lithographs by Chagall and drawings by Soutine. The collection also includes religious artifacts and a fascinating room devoted to the architecture of the synagogue, with a rare 18th-century Italian tabernacle.

Touring Tips This is a special-interest museum; if you're not passionate about Jewish art and religion, you may prefer to miss this.

Other Things to Do Nearby Explore the Marais area.

Musée d'Art Moderne de la Ville de Paris

Type of Attraction The City of Paris's museum of 20th-century art
Location Palais de Tokyo, 11, av. du Président Wilson, 75016
Métro Iéna   16th arrondissement
Admission €4.57, €3.05 (reduced price); depends on exhibitions; free on Sunday mornings and for people under age 26
Hours Tuesday–Friday 10 a.m.–7 p.m.; Saturday and Sunday, 10 a.m.–6:45 p.m. (box office closes at 6:15 p.m.)
Phone 01 53 67 40 00; recorded information, 01 40 70 11 10
When to Go Early
Special Comments Hours can change with the exhibitions. Guided tours are available; call 01 53 67 40 81.
Overall Appeal by Age Group

Pre-school —	Grade School ★	Teens ★★
Young Adults ★★	Over 30 ★★★	Seniors ★★★

Author's Rating ★★★
How Much Time to Allow 1–2 hours

Description and Comments This museum represents the major movements in avant-garde art of the twentieth century, including fauvism, cubism, surrealism, and abstraction. The museum fosters new trends in contemporary art and writing and organizes regular events. Some of the most interesting canvasses belong to the Paris School painters (Modigliani, Foujita, Chagall). Don't miss Dufy's *Fée Electricité*, "The Good Fairy Electricity," which is supposedly the world's largest painting, with 250 panels depicting the story of civilization from the ancient Greeks to the inventors of modern electricity.

Touring Tips Check for current exhibits.

Other Things to Do Nearby Trocadéro, Musée Guimet, Eiffel Tower.

Musée d'Orsay

Type of Attraction Converted train station houses the best collection of impressionist and art nouveau paintings and sculptures in the world
Location 1, rue de Bellechasse, 75007
Métro RER Musée d'Orsay   7th arrondissement

Admission €6.10 adults; €4.57 students age 18–25, seniors, all visitors on Sunday; free for children under age 18

Hours Tuesday, Wednesday, and Friday, 9 a.m.–6 p.m. (box office closes at 5:30 p.m.); Thursday, 9 a.m.–9:45 p.m. (box office closes at 9:15 p.m.); Sunday, 9 a.m.–6 p.m. (box office closes at 5:30 p.m.); closed Monday

Phone 01 45 49 48 14; recorded information, 01 45 49 11 11; prebooking, 01 49 87 54 54

Website www.musee-orsay.fr

When to Go Not on Sunday

Special Comments English audio guide, guided tours, café/restaurant, bookshop, wheelchair access. Immediate access with prebooking (call the museum 48 hours in advance; prices €7 adults, €5.49 students, seniors, and on Sunday)

Overall Appeal by Age Group

| Pre-school — | Grade School ★★★ | Teens ★★★ |
| Young Adults ★★★★ | Over 30 ★★★★★ | Seniors ★★★★★ |

Author's Rating ★★★★★

How Much Time to Allow 3 hours

Description and Comments One of Paris's most important and pleasant art museums; no visit to Paris would be complete without a few hours at the Musée d'Orsay. This museum bridges the world of art between the Louvre and the Centre Pompidou. The space is superbly organized, the light is welcoming, and the work is well exhibited. Time passes painlessly. Victor Laloux completed this large steel and glass structure in 1900. Originally a train station serving southwestern destinations in France, new electric trains, longer than their predecessors, forced its closing by 1939. It has been a museum since 1986, housing France's impressive (and impressionist) collection of paintings and sculpture from the period 1848 to 1914. The best examples of decorative and applied arts (jewelry, ceramics, furniture, and so on) are here. Organized on three levels, the first floor is devoted to the 1840–1870 period, followed by art nouveau works on the middle floor. Impressionist and postimpressionist works are on the top floor. Don't miss Renoir's *Bal du Moulin de la Galette* and Van Gogh's *Church at Auvers*. It is particularly interesting to look out from behind the famous clock face over Paris and spot Sacré-Coeur in the distance. There is also an auditorium, a restaurant, and a movie theater.

Touring Tips We strongly recommend the inexpensive buffet lunch in the museum restaurant.

Other Things to Do Nearby Les Invalides, Place de la Concorde, walk along the Seine.

Musée de l'Armée

Type of Attraction Military museum housed in Les Invalides

Location pl. des Invalides, 129, rue de Grenelle, 75007

Métro Latour-Maubourg or Varenne   7th arrondissement

Admission €5.79 adults, €4.27 children age 11–18 and students, free for children under age 12

Hours Daily, 10 a.m.–6 p.m. (box office closes at 5:30 p.m.)

Phone 01 44 42 37 72

Website www.invalides.org
When to Go Avoid Sundays
Special Comments Wheelchair access
Overall Appeal by Age Group

Pre-school — Grade School ★★ Teens
Young Adults ★★★ Over 30 ★★ Seniors ★ ,

Author's Rating ★★
How Much Time to Allow 1½ hours

Description and Comments See Hôtel des Invalides.

Touring Tips There are impressive military parades leaving from here in full regalia. Inquire for dates.

Other Things to Do Nearby Eiffel Tower, Grand Palais, Palais de la Decouverte.

Musée de l'Homme

Type of Attraction Museum
Location Palais de Chaillot, right wing, 17, pl. du Trocadéro, 75016
Métro Trocadéro 16th arrondissement
Admission €4.57 adults, €3.05 students
Hours Wednesday–Monday, 9:45 a.m.–5:15 p.m.
Phone 01 44 05 72 72
When to Go Avoid on days when there are demonstrations and rallies planned here
Overall Appeal by Age Group

Pre-school ★★ Grade School ★★★ Teens ★★★
Young Adults ★★★ Over 30 ★★★ Seniors ★★★

Author's Rating ★★★
How Much Time to Allow 1–2 hours

Description and Comments This museum traces humankind's evolution through several thematic displays, including "The Mists of Time," a chronological exhibit, and "Six Billion People," an eye-opening look at worldwide population growth. Kids like the shrunken heads, mummies, and tattoos in the anthropology section.

Touring Tips Stop for a drink or meal at the adjoining Le Totem restaurant, which looks out onto the Eiffel Tower.

Other Things to Do Nearby Consider exploring the other museums at the Palais de Chaillot.

Musée de l'Orangerie

Type of Attraction The twin building to the Jeu de Paume houses spectacular Monets
Location Jardin des Tuileries (Place de la Concorde), 75001
Métro Concorde 1st arrondissement
Admission Closed at press time (until 2002); call ahead for information
Hours Closed at press time (until 2002); call ahead for information
Phone 01 42 97 48 16
When to Go The earlier in the day, the better

Comments Wheelchair access

Appeal by Age Group

Pre-school —	Grade School ★★	Teens ★★★
Young Adults ★★★★	Over 30 ★★★★	Seniors ★★★★

Author's Rating ★★★★

How Much Time to Allow 1 hour

Description and Comments The Orangerie—named because it was used to store the orange trees in the Tuileries gardens during the winter—houses the best collection of turn-of-the-century and impressionist painters outside of the Musée d'Orsay. Amassed by Walter Guillaume, a pioneering supporter of his era's avant-garde artwork, the collection includes paintings by Soutine, Cézanne, Matisse, and Modigliani, among others. These are great reasons to visit, but most people know about the Orangerie because of Monet's famous *Water Lilies*, commissioned for the two oval rooms on the ground floor.

Other Things to Do Nearby Stroll down to the Seine, Place de la Concorde, and the Louvre.

Musée de la Mode et du Costume

Type of Attraction Impressive museum of fashions and costume design
Location Palais Galiéra, 10, av. Pierre 1er de Serbie, 75016
Métro George V   16th arrondissement
Admission €6.86 adults, €5.34 children, €3.51 students, free on Sunday mornings
Hours Tuesday–Sunday, 10 a.m.–5:40 p.m.
Phone 01 47 20 85 23
When to Go Crowds depend on the temporary exhibits
Special Comments Check listings for temporary exhibits of interest.

Overall Appeal by Age Group

Pre-school —	Grade School —	Teens —
Young Adults ★★	Over 30 ★★	Seniors ★★

Author's Rating ★★

How Much Time to Allow 1 hour

Description and Comments The Musée de la Mode et du Costume is, well, coming back into fashion, with some popular recent exhibitions. The collection of more than 100,000 items has a strong emphasis on the 19th century, but donations by contemporary designers like Balenciaga and fashion plates like Grace Kelly have updated the museum. Due to the fragility of the clothes, they are exhibited on a rotating basis, organized into shows devoted to a single designer, period, or theme. A recent, highly successful exhibit showcased wedding gowns and included some extremely whimsical works, including a beehive-shaped knit gown. A good place for fashion followers; there's also a research library, open by appointment only.

Touring Tips Unless everyone loves to look at clothes, don't take the whole family.

Other Things to Do Nearby Musée d'Art Moderne de la Ville de Paris, Trocadéro.

Musée de la Monnaie

Type of Attraction Museum of France's national mint and the history of money and currency
Location Hôtel des Monnaies, 11, Quai Conti, 75006
Métro Pont Neuf   6th arrondissement
Admission €3.05 adults; €2.25 students, all visitors on Sunday
Hours Tuesday–Friday, 11 a.m.–5:30 p.m.; Saturday and Sunday, noon–5:30 p.m.
Phone 01 40 46 55 35
Website www.monnaiedeparis.com
When to Go Rarely crowded
Special Comments Don't miss the excellent boutique where you can buy commemorative coins marking the advent of the euro.
Overall Appeal by Age Group

Pre-school ★★	Grade School ★★★	Teens ★★★
Young Adults ★★★	Over 30 ★★★	Seniors ★★★

Author's Rating ★★★
How Much Time to Allow 2 hours

Description and Comments The elegant mansion standing on the Left Bank opposite the Louvre was not built by a rich aristocrat—Louis XV commissioned the building to house the National Mint, which operated here from 1775 to 1973. This is not just a linear display of coins under glass; the curators have designed a fascinating look at all aspects of coin and currency, from its fabrication to social and political aspects. Along the way, you'll pick up some great anecdotes: Louis XVI, for example, almost managed to avoid the guillotine by fleeing Paris but was apprehended at an inn when a man recognized the royal face from the image stamped on the coins then in circulation.

Touring Tips This is an underrated museum; few travelers have it on their list to see, but it's worth the trip.

Other Things to Do Nearby Explore the bouquinistes along the Seine; the Louvre is just across the river, and you're just steps from the Saint-Germain galleries and shops.

Musée de la Musique

Type of Attraction Thoroughly enjoyable museum devoted to music and its history
Location Cité de la Musique, 221, av. Jean Jaurès, 75019
Métro Porte de Pantin   19th arrondissement
Admission €6 adults, €5 students, €7 children age 6–18
Hours Tuesday–Saturday, noon–6 p.m.; Sunday, 10 a.m.–6 p.m.
Phone 01 44 84 45 45
Website www.cite-musique.fr
When to Go Crowded on Wednesdays and Sundays. Combine with meal or drink in the Café de la Musique and either a stroll through La Villette park or a visit to one of the temporary and topical exhibits.

Overall Appeal by Age Group

Pre-school ★	Grade School ★★	Teens ★★★
Young Adults ★★★	Over 30 ★★★	Seniors ★★★

Author's Rating ★★★

How Much Time to Allow 2 hours, plus another 2 hours for picnics, exploring the park

Description and Comments This is the most recent addition to the Villette complex. It houses the museum, concert hall, research center, and Gamelan orchestra (traditional Indonesian gongs). To visit the museum, you don headsets that are activated as you move within range of the various displays. The instrument collection ranges from obscure Renaissance instruments to Frank Zappa's synthesizer. Concerts of period musical scores with old instruments are held in the concert hall.

Touring Tips La Villette is not centrally located, but do not be dissuaded. Completely worth your time and energy. Leave yourself plenty of time.

Other Things to Do Nearby The other activities at La Villette. Great for picnics.

Musée des Arts d'Afrique et d'Océanie

Type of Attraction Art and artifacts from the peoples of Africa and Oceania, plus aquarium

Location 293, av. Daumesnil, 75012

Métro Porte Dorée   12th arrondissement

Admission €4.42 adults, €3.05 for young adults age 18–25 and all visitors on Sunday, free for those under age 18

Hours Wednesday–Monday, 10 a.m.–5:30 p.m.

Phone 01 44 74 84 80

When to Go Try not to go on Wednesday; on Sunday, best hours are noon–2 p.m.

Special Comments Perfect if it's raining and you're traveling with children. Guided tour available, but only in French; no audio guide.

Overall Appeal by Age Group

Pre-school ★★★	Grade School ★★★	Teens ★★
Young Adults ★★	Over 30 ★★	Seniors ★★

Author's Rating ★★★

How Much Time to Allow 1–2 hours

Description and Comments This museum is fun for the whole family. Haunting masks from New Guinea, bark paintings, shrunken heads, and so on. Excellent examples of sub-Saharan Banda and Molo masks and dance masks from Mali and the Ivory Coast. Downstairs, don't miss the aquarium, a favorite for kids of all ages and often overlooked.

Touring Tips Bring your lunch and picnic in the nearby Bois de Vincennes, or combine the visit with a stop at the Vincennes Zoo.

Other Things to Do Nearby Bois de Vincennes, Parc Zoologique de Vincennes.

Musées des Arts Décoratifs

Type of Attraction Massive museum collection of French decorative arts

Location 107, rue de Rivoli, 75001

Métro Palais-Royal or Tuileries   1st arrondissement
Admission €5.34 adults, €3.81 students under age 25, seniors
Hours Tuesday, Thursday, Friday, 11 a.m.–6 p.m.; Wednesday, 11 a.m.–9 p.m.; Saturday and Sunday, 10 a.m.–6 p.m.
Phone 01 44 55 57 50
When to Go Popular on weekends
Special Comments Wheelchair access
Overall Appeal by Age Group

Pre-school —   Grade School ★★   Teens ★★★
Young Adults ★★★   Over 30 ★★★   Seniors ★★★

Author's Rating ★★★
How Much Time to Allow 1½ hours

Description and Comments   Situated in the Rohan wing of the Louvre along the Rue de Rivoli, this museum is recommended to those interested in interior design. Currently under renovation (until 2002), but with much of its collection still on show, the museum covers every aspect of the decorative arts in France from the Middle Ages to the present. Over 200,000 objects, from ceramics to wallpaper, jewelry, and even toys, recreate everyday life through the ages. Highlights include the period rooms, such as the reconstruction of designer Jeanne Lanvin's apartment and the art nouveau and art deco rooms. The Textile Museum and Poster Museum are also housed here. The Textile Museum presents temporary exhibits— everything from rare fabrics and accessories to avant-garde designers.

Touring Tips   Some people may find this less daunting an excursion than the megamuseum—the Louvre—next door.

Other Things to Do Nearby   The Louvre, Tuileries Gardens, Palais Royal.

Musée du Moyen Âge (Thermes de Cluny)

Type of Attraction A breathtaking reminder of Paris's Roman past
Location Thermes de Cluny, 6, pl. Paul-Painlevé, 75005
Métro Cluny-La Sorbonne   5th arrondissement
Admission €5.43; €3.96 ages 18–25, students, and all visitors on Sunday; free under age 18
Hours Wednesday–Monday, 9:15 a.m.–5:45 p.m.
Phone 01 53 73 78 00 or 01 53 73 78 30
Website www.musee-moyenage.fr
When to Go Gets crowded on weekends
Special Comments Guided tours of the Roman baths Wednesday, Saturday, and Sunday at 2 p.m.
Overall Appeal by Age Group

Pre-school —   Grade School ★★   Teens ★★
Young Adults ★★★   Over 30 ★★★   Seniors ★★★

Author's Rating ★★★
How Much Time to Allow 1–2 hours

Description and Comments   Here's one of the more interesting architectural combinations in Paris: a 15th-century palace built on the ruins of third-century Roman baths. The museum has lots of objets d'art, for those who like gilded altarpieces and crowns, but it's well worth visiting for the series of six world-famous unicorn tapestries, which hang in a specially designed circular room. Abutting the gothic-style building are the baths. The Romans knew what they were doing. The frigidarium, the best preserved of the three, remains cool even during the muggiest of Paris summers. Don't miss the King's Gallery. These are the heads that were lopped off the figures lining the facade of nearby Notre-Dame Cathedral during the French Revolution. And you can always boast back home about seeing the oldest sculpture in Paris: the Pilier des Nautes (Boatmen's Pillar), dated around AD 100.

Touring Tips   Check out the schedule of medieval music concerts held in the third-century frigidarium.

Other Things to Do Nearby   The Latin Quarter, the Sorbonne, Pantheon, St. Étienne du Mont Church.

Musée Eugène Delacroix

Type of Attraction   Delacroix's home is now a museum commemorating his life and work.

Location   6, rue Furstenberg, 75006

Métro   St-Germain-des-Prés   6th arrondissement

Admission   €3.35 adults, €2.29 seniors and students age 18–25, free for children under age 18

Hours   Wednesday–Monday, 9:30 a.m.–5 p.m. (ticket office closes at 4:30 p.m.)

Phone   01 44 41 86 50

When to Go   Rarely crowded

Special Comments   A perfect example of how artists' homes are converted into public spaces in Paris

Overall Appeal by Age Group

Pre-school —	Grade School ★	Teens ★
Young Adults ★★	Over 30 ★★	Seniors ★★

Author's Rating   ★★

How Much Time to Allow   1½ hours

Description and Comments   This is the last place Delacroix lived; he moved here to be closer the Saint-Sulpice Church, where he was working on his final public commission. Seriously ill with tuberculosis, he nonetheless was able to complete the three large murals (visible at the church). The museum contains some smaller works by the artist and copies of other major paintings in the Louvre and elsewhere. Most interesting about the museum, though, is the intimacy of the house and studio.

Touring Tips   Although the Place de Furstenberg is in the heart of Saint-Germain, it is often overlooked by tourists. It's one of the most romantic little squares in Paris and is enchanting in the evening.

Other Things to Do Nearby   Explore the Saint-Germain neighborhood.

Musée Grévin

Type of Attraction   Paris's renowned wax museum

Location   10, bd Montmartre, 75002

Métro Rue Montmartre   2nd arrondissement
Admission €14.94 adults, €9.16 children age 6–14, free children under age 6
Hours Daily, 10 a.m.–7 p.m. (box office closes at 6 p.m.)
Phone 01 47 70 85 05
Website www.musee-grevin.com
When to Go Avoid during the school holidays or weekends
Special Comments At the turn of the last century, this is where the social elite came to be amused.
Overall Appeal by Age Group

Pre-school ★★★	Grade School ★★★★	Teens ★★★★
Young Adults ★★★★	Over 30 ★★★	Seniors ★★★

Author's Rating ★★★
How Much Time to Allow 1 hour

Description and Comments This elaborately baroque Paris wax museum offers up the usual celebrities—Napoléon, President Clinton, Marilyn Monroe—along with quintessential modern-day French figures, such as the 1998 World Cup Soccer heroes Zidane and Barthez. Not everything here is fake. The bathtub in which the effigy of the stabbed Marat lies is the genuine article. Don't miss the sound and light show held in the Palais des Mirages.

Touring Tips Kids will enjoy the daily magic shows.

Other Things to Do Nearby Explore the 19th-century covered passages that crisscross this section of Paris.

Musée Jacquemart-André

Type of Attraction Sublime private art museum
Location 158, bd Haussman, 75008
Métro St-Philippe-du-Roule   8th arrondissement
Admission €7.62 adults, €5.95 for those under age 25 and students
Hours Daily, 10 a.m.–6 p.m. (ticket office closes at 5:30 p.m.)
Phone 01 45 62 11 59
Website www.musee-jacquemart-andre.com
When to Go Avoiding weekends is always smart.
Special Comments Audioguide and wheelchair access (9 a.m.–5 p.m.), but you must call in advance (01 45 62 11 59)
Overall Appeal by Age Group

Pre-school —	Grade School ★★	Teens ★★
Young Adults ★★★	Over 30 ★★★★	Seniors ★★★★

Author's Rating ★★★★
How Much Time to Allow 1–2 hours

Description and Comments For those who prefer intimate museums, this one is a gem. Recently renovated, this lavish 19th-century home was built by Nélie Jacquemart and her husband, Édouard André, to house their personal art collection, with works by Rembrandt, Titian, and Uccello, and frescoes by Tiepolo. We've heard people rate it higher than New York's Frick Collection.

Touring Tips   Be sure to visit the austere upstairs bedroom of Nélie Jacquemart.
Other Things to Do Nearby   Parc Monceau, Nissim de Camondo Museum.

Musée Jean Moulin

Type of Attraction   Museum and monument to the French Resistance of World War II
Location   23, allée de la 2e DB (Jardin Atlantique), 75015
Métro   Montparnasse   15th arrondissement
Admission   €4.50 for exhibitions, €3.40 for the Museum; €2.30 for age 25 and younger
Hours   Tuesday–Sunday, 10 a.m.–5:40 p.m.
Phone   01 40 64 39 44
When to Go   Anytime
Special Comments   This museum is attached to the Memorial for Maréchal Leclerc de Hauteclocque and the Liberation of Paris. Requires some French to appreciate.
Overall Appeal by Age Group

Pre-school —	Grade School ★	Teens ★★
Young Adults ★★	Over 30 ★★	Seniors ★★★

Authors' Rating   ★★
How Much Time to Allow   45 minutes

Description and Comments   Jean Moulin is one of France's greatest heroes and martyrs. Tortured and killed by the Germans, he refused to divulge what he knew to the enemy. A leader in the French Resistance against the occupying Nazis in World War II, Moulin's life and actions during the war are documented in this unusual but fascinating history museum, located on the rooftop garden complex above the Gare Montparnasse. If you are a war buff and appreciate old photos, newspapers, and objects from the 1940s, you'll find this rarely visited museum to be worth the effort.

Touring Tips   The same price allows you to visit the Maréchal Lecler de Hauteclocque Memorial.

Other Things to Do Nearby   Tour de Maine (Montparnasse skyscraper with 55th-floor observation deck), Montparnasse Cemetery.

Musée Marmottan-Monet

Type of Attraction   Varied collection of work by Monet and other impressionists
Location   2, rue Louis-Boilly, 75016
Métro   La Muette   16th arrondissement
Admission   €6.10 adults, €3.81 children age 8–25 and seniors, free children under age 8
Hours   Tuesday–Sunday, 10 a.m.–6 p.m.
Phone   01 44 96 50 33
Website   www.marmottan.com
When to Go   This is a good museum to save for a Tuesday, when most of the others, including the Louvre, are closed
Special Comments   Monet fans should visit this museum as well as Giverny.
Overall Appeal by Age Group

Pre-school —	Grade School ★★	Teens ★★★
Young Adults ★★★	Over 30 ★★★★	Seniors ★★★★

Author's Rating ★★★★
How Much Time to Allow 2 hours

Description and Comments What began as a personal collection devoted to Napoléonic memorabilia gradually diversified through bequests to become a pilgrimage site for Monet lovers—especially after his son Michel left 65 canvases to the museum in 1971. Housed in a lavish mansion at the edge of the Bois de Boulogne, the Marmottan has superb impressionist paintings, including Monet's *Impression,* the painting that when first shown was mocked by critics and gave a name to the Impressionist movement. Many of the works were painted at Giverny, in Normandy; the brilliant water lily paintings are in a special room downstairs. Less well known is the Wildenstein bequest, over 200 illuminated manuscripts from the 14th to the 16th century.

Touring Tips Most people come for the Monets, but the Marmottan has superb works by Gaugin, Corot, and Manet.

Other Things to Do Nearby Combine a trip to the museum with an afternoon exploring the Bois de Boulogne.

Musée National des Arts Asiatiques Guimet and Les Galeries du Panthéon Buddique

Type of Attraction One of the world's most important museums for Asian and oriental art and artifacts
Location 6, pl. d'Iéna, 75016 Paris
Métro Iéna   16th arrondissement
Admission €5.49 adults; €3.96 students, seniors, and all visitors Sunday; free for children under age 18
Hours Wednesday–Monday, 10 a.m.–6 p.m. (ticket office closes at 5:30 p.m.)
Phone 01 56 52 53 00
Website www.museeguimet.fr
When to Go Mornings; crowded on Sundays
Special Comments Newly renovated and re-opened in 2001; wheelchair access
Overall Appeal by Age Group

Pre-school —	Grade School ★★	Teens ★★
Young Adults ★★	Over 30 ★★★	Seniors ★★★

Author's Rating ★★★
How Much Time to Allow 1–2 hours

Description and Comments One of the best collections of oriental art in the world. Great selection of Buddha heads. Key works from Cambodia, Vietnam, India, and China. *The Cosmic Dance of Shiva* is a noted bronze Hindu sculpture. If you have a particular interest in Asian history and culture, a visit here is a must. Others may feel that this is a lower priority for a Paris visit.

Touring Tips Even if you don't think you're interested in oriental art, this one is really worth making an effort.

Other Things to Do Nearby Trocadéro, Musée d'Art Moderne de la Ville de Paris.

Musée Nissim de Camondo

Type of Attraction 18th-century mansion with an exquisite art collection
Location 63, rue Monceau, 75008
Métro Monceau or Villiers   8th arrondissement
Admission €4.57 adults, €3.05 children age 5–25 and seniors, free for children under age 5
Hours Wednesday–Sunday, 10 a.m.–5 p.m.
Phone 01 53 89 06 40
When to Go Rarely crowded
Overall Appeal by Age Group

Pre-school —	Grade School —	Teens ★★
Young Adults ★★	Over 30 ★★	Seniors ★★

Author's Rating ★★
How Much Time to Allow 1 hour

Description and Comments Here's another opportunity to check out how the rich lived in the 18th century, even though the mansion was built in 1914. Count Moise de Camondo was a rich banker who loved all things French and amassed a collection of rare tapestries, furniture, and porcelain. He bequeathed the mansion and the collection to the government in memory of his son Nissim, who was killed in World War I. Of interest to history buffs and interior designers, perhaps; others may have had their fill of gold-leaf, marble, and objets d'art.

Touring Tips While you're in the area, take time to explore the Parc Monceau.

Other Things to Do Nearby Saint-Alexander Nevsky Russian Orthodox Cathedral, Parc Monceau, the Musée Cernuschi.

Musée Picasso

Type of Attraction An entire museum devoted to the life and work of Pablo Picasso
Location Hôtel Salé, 5, rue de Thorigny, 75003
Métro Saint-Paul-Le Marais or Filles du Calvaire   3rd arrondissement
Admission Exhibition and museum, €4.57 adults, €3.05 children age 18–25, students, and all visitors on Sunday
Hours Wednesday–Monday, 9:30 a.m.–5:30 p.m. (open until 6 p.m. April–September)
Phone 01 42 71 25 21
When to Go Show up early to beat the crowds.
Special Comments You can also appreciate the view of the Hôtel Salé
Overall Appeal by Age Group

Pre-school —	Grade School ★	Teens ★★★
Young Adults ★★★★	Over 30 ★★★★	Seniors ★★★★

Author's Rating ★★★★
How Much Time to Allow 2 hours

Description and Comments Housed in an elegant 17th-century *hôtel particulier,* the Musée Picasso houses the largest collection of works by this superstar artist. After his death in 1973 in southern France, the French government agreed to accept artwork in lieu of estate taxes. Although the curators had first pick of the enormous collection in

Picasso's possession, they did not necessarily choose the best work; yet the 203 paintings, 158 sculptures, 88 ceramics, and over 3,000 works on paper represent every phase of his artistic life, starting from the age of 14 up until his death. The artwork is arranged chronologically, and detailed explanatory notes are provided throughout. Picasso amassed a large number of works by friends and contemporaries, and his personal collection of these, as well as his collection of primitive art, is exhibited on two floors.

Touring Tips   This is an essential visit for art lovers; younger visitors may enjoy some of Picasso's more whimsical sculptures and ceramics.

Other Things to Do Nearby   There are several other museums nearby (Carnavalet, Cognacq-Jay), but the best thing to do in this neighborhood is to simply wander through the streets, perhaps ending up for a coffee at the Place des Vosges or for a falafel in the Jewish Quarter.

Musée Rodin

Type of Attraction   Lovely museum and gardens devoted to the life and work of sculptor Auguste Rodin

Location   77, rue de Varenne, 75007 Paris

Métro   Varenne   7th arrondissement

Admission   Museum: €2.74 age 18–25, students, €4.27 over age 25, free under age 18; park: €0.76 ages 18 and over

Hours   Tuesday–Sunday, 9:30 a.m.–5:45 p.m. (open until 4:45 p.m. October through March; box office closes a half-hour earlier than museum)

Phone   01 47 05 01 34

Website   www.musee-rodin.fr

When to Go   Go early or late to miss the lines during the summer months; try not to go on Tuesday

Special Comments   English guided tours available, but expensive (€122 per person); you can use audio guides

Overall Appeal by Age Group

Pre-school ★★★	Grade School ★★★	Teens ★★★
Young Adults ★★★	Over 30 ★★★★	Seniors ★★★★

Author's Rating ★★★★

How Much Time to Allow 1–2 hours

Description and Comments   The Rodin museum, also known as the Hôtel de Biron, was created by Aubert and Gabriel in 1728 for the financier Peyrenc de Moras and then sold to the Maréchal de Biron. It was a convent until 1902 and now houses the best collection of Auguste Rodin's work found anywhere in the world. Visit both inside the hotel and outside in the gardens. Behind the hotel is a cozy café with an affordable, quality menu. All of Rodin's major works are here. A must for both the famous sculptor's fans and the newly initiated. Great photo op next to the original *Le Penseur* (The Thinker). The gardens are delightful in the spring and summer.

Touring Tips   Let the kids play in the gardens and imitate the poses of the Rodin masterpieces. A great way to open their eyes to sculpture.

Other Things to Do Nearby   Les Invalides, Assemblée Nationale, Eiffel Tower.

Musée Zadkine

Type of Attraction Private museum created from the *atelier* of painter and sculptor Zadkine
Location 100 bis, rue d'Assas, 75006
Métro Port-Royal or Notre-Dame-des-Champs   6th arrondissement
Admission €3.35 adults, €2.29 reduced
Hours Tuesday–Sunday, 10 a.m.–5:40 p.m.
Phone 01 43 26 91 90
When to Go Rarely crowded
Special Comments It's fun running into other Zadkine enthusiasts here.
Overall Appeal by Age Group

   Pre-school —   Grade School ★★   Teens ★★
   Young Adults ★★★   Over 30 ★★★   Seniors ★★★
Author's Rating ★★★
How Much Time to Allow 1–1½ hours

Description and Comments What's interesting about this museum, which includes the house and studios where the Russian sculptor Ossip Zadkine lived and worked, is that it is almost exactly as he left it at his death in 1927. Although just a few blocks from the Jardin du Luxembourg, it is secluded, quiet, and usually tourist-free. The highlight of the museum is the sculpture garden.

Touring Tips After a visit here, stroll through the Luxembourg Gardens seeking other Zadkine sculptures.

Other Things to Do Nearby Jardin du Luxembourg.

Muséum National d'Histoire Naturelle

Type of Attraction Natural history museum with a spectacular dinosaur collection
Location 36, rue Geoffroy St-Hilaire, 75005
Métro Jussieu or Gare d'Austerlitz   5th arrondissement
Admission Grande Galerie, €6.10 adults, €4.57 students, under age 16, and seniors; other pavilions, each €4.57 adults, €3.05 students, children age 4–16, seniors; zoo, €4.57 adults, €3.05 children
Hours Grande Galerie, Monday, Wednesday, Friday–Sunday, 10 a.m.–6 p.m.; Thursday, 10 a.m.–10 p.m.; other pavilions, daily, 10 a.m.–5 p.m.; zoo, daily, 9 a.m.–5 p.m.
Phone 01 40 79 30 00
Website www.mnhr.fr
When to Go Not during weekends
Special Comments Wheelchair access
Overall Appeal by Age Group

   Pre-school ★★★★   Grade School ★★★★   Teens ★★★★
   Young Adults ★★★★   Over 30 ★★★★   Seniors ★★★★
Author's Rating ★★★★
How Much Time to Allow 1–1½ hours per pavilion

Description and Comments For years, the Musée National d'Histoire Naturelle was a dusty repository for old bones and scruffy stuffed animals. In 1994, however, the museum reopened with a spectacular new arrangement: a parade of stuffed animals cuts through the center of the exhibit like a modern-day Noah's Ark, and dramatic lighting throughout showcases the many exhibits. Marine animals hang suspended in the air—the great favorite is the 54-foot-long whale skeleton. Kids under age 12 will love the discovery room, which presents fossils and the natural sciences, and teenagers can explore the various displays in the science laboratory.

Touring Tips Combine this trip with the surrounding gardens and greenhouses and a visit to the small zoo, which retains a somewhat dilapidated charm. Explore the hard-to-find Alpine Garden (closed October to February), where 2,000 different types of plants thrive in a tiny microclimate.

Other Things to Do Nearby Cross the street toward the Seine and enjoy a stroll or picnic through the Tino Rossi open-air sculpture gardens; visit the Institut du Monde Arabe; take a break on the steps of the Arènes de Lutèce, which dates to Roman times.

Opéra Garnier

Type of Attraction Paris's first and illustrious opera house
Location Palais Garnier, pl. de l'Opéra, 75009
Métro Opéra   9th arrondissement
Admission Guided tours of the opera (and museum), €4.57 adults, €3.05 students
Hours Daily, 10 a.m.–5 p.m.
Phone 08 92 69 78 68
When to Go To observe the opera house, avoid performance times
Special Comments Includes a branch of the Bibliothéque Nationale devoted to operatic history
Overall Appeal by Age Group

Pre-school —	Grade School —	Teens —
Young Adults ★★	Over 30 ★★	Seniors ★★

Author's Rating ★★
How Much Time to Allow 30 minutes

Description and Comments Whether you're an opera or ballet lover or not, and decide to attend a performance, a visit to the spectacular Opéra Garnier is well worth the time. The great staircase and the ornate chandeliers transport you into the splendors of mid-19-century Napoléon III style of architecture and decor. Named after the relatively unknown and young architect who built the house, the Opéra Garnier is considered by many to be the best monument of the Second Empire. An absolute must for visitors taking the tour is the ceiling of the main auditorium, consisting of opera-related frescos by the modern painter Marc Chagall. The cheapest seats in the house afford you the best view of the ceiling.

Touring Tips There really is an underground lake (per *Phantom of the Opera*) though most tours do not include this.

Other Things to Do Nearby La Madeleine, Grands Boulevards.

Palais de Chaillot

Type of Attraction Four art museums in one complex
Location Pl. du Trocadéro, 75016
Métro Trocadéro   16th arrondissement
Admission Different for each museum
Hours Different for each museum
Phone 01 44 05 39 10
When to Go Avoid Sundays if possible
Special Comments Check out the gardens on the sloping side of the complex.
Overall Appeal by Age Group
  Pre-school ★★★   Grade School ★★★   Teens ★★★
  Young Adults ★★★   Over 30 ★★★   Seniors ★★★
Author's Rating ★★★
How Much Time to Allow Different for each museum

Description and Comments The Palais de Chaillot, an immense winged structure built for the 1937 Universal Exhibition, houses four museums, a theater, and a cinemathèque (listed separately). Before setting foot in any of them, however, linger on the parvis (square) and gaze across the river—this is the most spectacular view of the Eiffel Tower in Paris. There's always plenty going on here: street performers, jugglers, and clowns, not to mention the inline skaters, who have colonized the lower level of the square with ramps, jumps, and other paraphernalia. Teens and younger kids can watch the entertainment for hours.

Touring Tips There are a lot of people hustling tourists here, especially in the summer; ignore them, avoid purchasing trinkets, and enjoy the view.

Other Things to Do Nearby Take your pick of one of the museums housed in the Palais; some are closed for renovation, but there's still something for everyone.

Palais Royal

Type of Attraction Regal architectural remnant of the French monarchy, perfect for strolling, sitting, sipping
Location Place du Palais Royal, 75001
Métro Palais-Royal   1st arrondissement
Admission Free
Hours Daily, dawn to dusk
Phone None
When to Go When the weather is pleasant
Special Comments Buildings are not open to public.
Overall Appeal by Age Group
  Pre-school —   Grade School —   Teens ★★
  Young Adults ★★   Over 30 ★★   Seniors ★★
Author's Rating ★★
How Much Time to Allow 30 minutes

Description and Comments An absolutely lovely thing to do is to stroll through the gardens and along the arcades of the Palais Royal. The shops along the way characterize much of the old charm of Paris with antique books, bronze, toys, maps, stamps, and musical instruments. At the southern end of the gardens you'll find yourself hopping on contemporary pillars of varying heights that decorate the space outside the highly active French Ministry of Culture on the rue de Valois, which in the 17th century had been Cardinal Richelieu's palace. Following Richelieu, the Palais Royal was bequeathed to Louis XIII. On the opposite side you'll find the illustrious Comédie Française on the Place Malraux, where Victor Hugo launched his career as a playwright, and to this day works by Molière, Corneille, Racine, de Musset, and Beaumarchais are performed. Molière enthusiasts will enjoy noting that the famed playwright lived at number 40 on the nearby rue de Richelieu; just up the street at 61, Stendahl, the novelist of *The Red and the Black,* kept his residence.

Touring Tips   Picnic in the gardens or stroll around the arcade at night after dinner. The famed gastronomical landmark, Le Grand Vefour, sits at the far end of the Palais Royal complex.

Other Things to Do Nearby   Le Louvre, Avenue de l'Opéra.

Place de la Bastille

Type of Attraction One of Paris's most celebrated landmarks
Location Place de la Bastille, 75011
Métro Bastille   11th arrondissement
Admission Free
When to Go Anytime, though it's wise to avoid demonstrations and rallies that are often scheduled here; at night, the area is teeming
Special Comments One foreign dignitary, unaware that the original prison that was "stormed" no longer stands, once asked how they fit all the prisoners into the obelisk that now stands at the center of the square.
Overall Appeal by Age Group

Pre-school —	Grade School —	Teens ★★★
Young Adults ★★★	Over 30 ★★★	Seniors ★★★

Author's Rating ★★★
How Much Time to Allow 10–20 minutes

Description and Comments   Nothing is left of the Bastille prison that was stormed on July 14, 1789, but the July Column in the center of this busy and popular intersection now marks this historic landmark. Note the golden-winged Mercuryesque statuette at the top of the column, which has emerged as a symbol of Paris. Even today the Bastille remains an important public space for large demonstrations, marches, and rallies. Every Friday around 11 p.m., hundreds of motorcyclists on bikes of all sorts and sizes use the Place de la Bastille as the meeting point and point of departure for the noisy tour of the capital en masse. A curious scene.

Touring Tips   A canal boat trip leaves the basin at the Place de la Bastille and leads you under the Place. Otherwise, plan to hang out at least once in this neighborhood as late as possible to taste Paris by night.

Other Things to Do Nearby   Opéra Bastille, Place de Vosges, Place de la Republique, Promenade Plantée.

Sainte-Chapelle

Type of Attraction One of the most masterful assemblages of stained glass windows in the world

Location 4, bd du Palais, 75001

Métro RER St-Michel-Notre-Dame   1st arrondissement

Admission €5.34 adults, €3.51 students, free for children under age 12; Saint-Chapelle and Conciergerie, €8 per person

Hours Summer: daily, 9:30 a.m.–6:30 p.m.; winter: daily 10 a.m.–5 p.m. (box office closes a half-hour before the chapel)

Phone 01 53 73 78 51

When to Go Go early to beat the crowds and avoid the lines

Special Comments Read the windows from left to right and from bottom to top.

Overall Appeal by Age Group

Pre-school —   Grade School ★★   Teens ★★

Young Adults ★★★★   Over 30 ★★★★   Seniors ★★★★

Author's Rating ★★★★

How Much Time to Allow 30 minutes

Description and Comments If you have any affection for stained glass at all, this just may be one of your Paris highlights. This Gothic chapel, built within the confines of King Louis IX's private palace, was constructed in under three years and finished in 1248. There are two superimposed chambers forming the chapel, with a spiral staircase leading to the upper chapel. Here, the glass encasing becomes brilliantly illuminated, even when the light is low. Many of the relics of the chapel were pilfered or melted down during the French Revolution, and others have been stored in nearby Notre-Dame, but the original stained glass is the oldest surviving example of its kind in Paris. Over 700 of the 1,134 scenes represented on the 6,500 square feet of glass are original. Many of the same craftsmen from the Chartres cathedral worked on these windows. The main scenario in the glass is the celebration or Passion play as foretold by the prophets and John the Baptist. History buffs will be happy to note that Richard II of England married Isabel of France here in 1396.

Touring Tips Observe the worn floor to understand the seven centuries that have passed since its construction.

Other Things to Do Nearby Notre-Dame, Latin Quarter, Conciergerie, Shakespeare & Company Bookstore.

Tour Montparnasse 56

Type of Attraction Paris's only modern skyscraper, and until recently Europe's tallest building

Location 33, av. du Maine, pl. R. Dautry, 75015

Métro Montparnasse-Bienvenüe   15th arrondissement

Admission Visit of the 56th floor: €5.79 adults, €4.57 for children under age 20 and students, €3.81 children; visit of the 56th and 59th floors: €7.01 adults, €5.34 for children under age 20 and students, €4.57 for children

Hours Daily, 9:30 a.m.–11:30 p.m. (last visit 11 p.m.)
Phone 01 53 91 06 80
Website www.tourmontparnasse56.com
When to Go Early in the day or at night
Special Comments The prices in the 56th-floor bar are as steep as the view.
Overall Appeal by Age Group
   Pre-school —   Grade School ★★★★★   Teens ★★★★★
   Young Adults ★★★★★   Over 30 ★★★★★   Seniors ★★★★★
Author's Rating ★★★★★
How Much Time to Allow 1 hour

Description and Comments On the top of Paris's sole skyscraper you are afforded a view of the city that truly is breathtaking. This is by far Paris's most underrated site. More spectacular than the view from the Eiffel Tower, from the top of the Tour Montparnasse you get to look down at the Eiffel Tower, and only from here can you visualize and really understand the scale and overall beauty of the city. Literally beneath you, the pattern and layout of the Montparnasse cemetery is revealed. The same is true for the Jardin du Luxembourg. On the 56th floor, you're in a windowed area where the view is great and there is even a small café for drinks and snacks. To get to the 59th-floor outdoor roof you need to walk up the stairs. Hold on to your hat and small kids. You're truly at the top of the city.

Touring Tips Go up only on nice days.

Other Things to Do Nearby Montparnasse cemetery.

Trocadéro (Terrace or Esplanade)

Type of Attraction One of Paris's best open spaces for viewing the Eiffel Tower, especially at night
Location Place du Trocadéro, 75016
Métro Trocadéro   16th arrondissement
Admission Free
When to Go Anytime, but late at night is spectacular
Special Comments This hill was once used by the training cadets from the Right Bank Ecole Militaire.
Overall Appeal by Age Group
   Pre-school —   Grade School ★★★★   Teens ★★★★
   Young Adults ★★★★   Over 30 ★★★★   Seniors ★★★★
Author's Rating ★★★★
How Much Time to Allow 30 minutes to 1 hour

Description and Comments Not only does Trocadéro merit a visit for the Palais de Chaillot and its Musée de l'Homme (where prehistoric predecessor to Homo sapiens, Lucy, is kept), it is by far the single best place for viewing the Eiffel Tower. Go in the daytime, and then return at night, but before midnight when the lights on the tower go out. The square here and the park below are romantic and magical. Summer evenings are especially lively with excited crowds, bongo players and African dancers, inline skaters, and lovers hanging out.

Touring Tips Don't miss a late-night visit to this viewing point.

Other Things to Do Nearby Have a drink at the Totem Restaurant, to your right as you face the Eiffel Tower.

Parks, Gardens, City Squares, and Cemeteries

Here is a complete list of Paris parks followed by a suggested list of quaint public places perfect for a rest, a picnic, a game of boules, some people-watching, and so on. Paris's open spaces and green spaces are the thoroughfare for the city's history and architecture, as well as the venues for elegant relaxation and romance. A tour of the cemeteries reveals the city's intellectual, social, and political past—no trip to Paris is complete without at least a stroll in Père Lachaise.

Note that contrary to the American concept of public park, which is participatory, in Paris uniformed guards protect the sanctity of many of these places and will not hesitate to whistle you off the grass. *Pelouse interdit* means "keep off the grass." Paris's new mayor, Bertrand Deoanoë, has relaxed this custom somewhat, but only for green spaces of more than a hectare (around 2.5 acres).

Bois de Boulogne

Type of Attraction Paris's expansive green space and woods on the western edge of the city
Location Anchoring the city's western wing along and outward from the 16th arrondissement
Métro Les Sablons
Admission Free
Hours Daily, 24 hours
When to Go Not after dark unless you know what you're looking for
Author's Rating ★★★★

Description and Comments Paris's largest (over 2,000 acres) and most diverse green space, the Bois runs for miles at the western edge of the city. In the Bois you'll find two thoroughbred race tracks (Longchamps and Auteuil); the Jardin d'Acclimatation; the National Museum of Popular Arts and Traditions; the exquisitely landscaped Parc de Bagatelle, with Japanese water garden and waterlilies and rhododendron garden; canoeing on the lakes, horseback riding, playing fields, picnic grounds, and jogging trails; the Roland Garros tennis stadium; the Pré Catelan, where Shakespeare is played in a garden planted with every flower, herb, and tree mentioned in his plays; and the Parc des Princes, Paris's most important sports stadium until the Stade de France was built for the World Cup in 1998.

Bois de Vincennes

Type of Attraction Paris's expansive green space and woods on the eastern edge of the city
Location Technically the 12th arrondissement, but outside city limits

Métro Château de Vincennes
Admission Free
Hours Daily, dawn to dusk
When to Go Best when the weather is pleasant
Author's Rating ★★★★★

Description and Comments   Paris's most significant green space on the eastern side
of the city, the Bois de Vincennes offers a broad range of attractions including picnicking,
canoe rentals, jogging, its excellent zoo, its château and dungeon, the Parc Floral, the Lac
Daumesnil, its playing field, merry-go-rounds, bike paths, and dense woods (perfect for
mushroom hunting). One of our favorite pastimes is simply walking around the Lac
Daumesnil or Lac des Minimes on a Sunday afternoon and observing Parisians as they
stroll with their kids, play soccer, and frolic with hundreds of dogs.

Champs-Elysées

Type of Attraction The most famous avenue on earth
Location Between the Place de la Concorde and the Arc de Triomphe, 75008   8th
arrondissement
Métro Concorde, Charles-de-Gaulle-Etoile, George V
Admission Free
When to Go Avoid New Year's Eve unless you want to be caught in the craze of hyster-
ical crowds popping corks, honking horns, and kissing strangers on the lips. All major
sporting victory celebrations tend to end up on the Champs-Elysées in pandemonium.
Author's Rating ★★★★

Description and Comments   The Champs-Elysées is studded with expensive stores,
cafés, movie houses, airline offices, and clubs. Originally a field flanked by the most fash-
ionable carriage path in the city, in the early 1700s rows of plane trees were planted and
the peaceful stretch was renamed the Elysian Fields, or Champs-Elysées. Over the next
century the road was lengthened to the Arc de Triomphe (Etoile) and finally all the way to
Pont Neuilly (avenue de la Grande Armée and avenue Charles-de Gaulle). In the 1800s,
fountains and gas lights were added and concerts were given in the streets. A musician
named Sax played his newly invented instrument, the saxophone, for curious listeners. The
Champs-Elysées became the symbol for the French nation, and military parades used its
wide avenue. The Germans marched through the Arc de Triomphe in 1940. This was also
the point of celebration for the liberation of Paris in 1944. The famous cycling event, Tour
de France, finishes on the Champs-Elysées, and the Paris Marathon starts here. And the
July 14 parade moves along this avenue in an air of great triumph. When a head of state is
visiting Paris, the flag of his or her country is raised with the French flag on every pole
along the Champs-Elysées. Aside from the pomp and history of this great street, today
there is little of interest in this overpriced and highly commercial area.

Cimetière de Montmartre

Type of Attraction Celebrated Parisian cemetery, resting place for cultural stars
Location 20, av. Rachel, access by stairs from rue Caulaincourt, 75018   18th
arrondissement

Métro Place de Clichy
Admission Free
Hours Monday–Saturday, 8 a.m.–6 p.m.; Sunday, 9 a.m.–6 p.m.
Phone 01 43 87 64 24
When to Go Before dark
Author's Rating ★★★½

Description and Comments   You have to like cemeteries in the first place to go out of your way to visit this one. Tucked in under an overpass at the base of Montmartre on the Clichy side, this cemetery is a pleasure to discover because few visitors make the effort—chances are it'll be deserted. As you walk across the rue Caulaincourt, the stairway to your left brings you directly into the cemetery. You'll get a kick out of stumbling on the graves of writer Emile Zola, composer Hector Berlioz, and poets Heinrich Heine and Théophile Gautier. The painter Edgar Degas and writers Alexandre Dumas and Stendahl rest here, too. More recent members of the club include the singer Dalida and the French filmmaker François Truffaut.

Cimetière du Père-Lachaise

Type of Attraction Paris's most enchanting and star-studded cemetery
Location Bd Ménilmontant, 75011, 75020,   11th arrondissement
Métro Père-Lachaise or Alexandre Dumas
Admission Free
Hours Monday–Friday, 8 a.m.–6 p.m.; Saturday, 8:30 a.m.–6 p.m.; Sunday, 9 a.m.–6 p.m.
Phone 01 43 70 70 33
When to Go Before dark; and, for now, not on Jim Morrison's birthday
Author's Rating ★★★★★

Description and Comments   A lot more people these days visit the Paris grave site of Jim Morrison than those of Victor Hugo or Frédéric Chopin. In any case, almost everyone can find a mythic hero to visit in Paris's most celebrated and atmospheric cemetery, Père Lachaise.

Tucked into the far corner of the 11th arrondissement lies a wild and hilly spread of 103 acres that is studded with stars, broken crypts, shifty cats, and a permanent guest list that will make your French teacher back home curse you with envy. Where else can you visit the resting spot of Marcel Proust, Honoré Balzac, Edith Piaf, and Oscar Wilde in the same day? Even the remains of France's most important dramatist, Molière, are within reach. (Napoléon had Molière's bones transferred to Paris's most chic cemetery at its inauguration in 1803.)

You'll love hiking up the crooked alleys and narrow paths while getting lost in French cultural history. The mythic lovers Héloïse and Abélard are here. So are the painters Corot, Daumier, Pissarro, David, Seurat, and Modigliani. The soul of Victor Hugo can be felt, and some claim that the brave voice of Maria Callas can be heard in the late afternoon. What an eclectic party: Laura Marx, Karl's daughter, is here, as well as Gertrude Stein and Alice B. Toklas. Sarah Bernhardt was buried at Père Lachaise in 1923, and in more recent days the philosopher Louis Althussar and actors Yves Montand and Simone Signoret have joined the posthumous cast.

Jim Morrison was buried in Père Lachaise in 1971; for the first decade there was no official stone, only graffiti, love letters, and empty bottles in his honor. Signs in chalk marked "Jim, This Way" led you to the cult site. Several years back, a proper tomb was erected and a visit to the grave of the lead singer of the Doors has now become an institution, the grave location having been added to the free map of the cemetery that you can ask for at any of the entrances. Most fans never realize that Morrison came to Paris to flee stardom and live as an obscure poet. After discussion of moving Morrison (his plot lease had expired in 2001), the French government has decided to immortalize the cult figure here.

One of our favorite places to get lost in Père Lachaise is at the base of Oscar Wilde's massive but reverent tomb, a stone sphinx sculpted by Jacob Epstein. Wilde lived a number of truly decadent years in the French capital, and real Wilde fanatics can even stay in the Irish writer's room at the upscale l'Hotel on the rue des Beaux Arts. The two great French pastimes, politics and sex, join here as visitors walk by the Mur des Fédérés, the wall where the last communard rebels were shot in 1871, an icon for die-hard left-wing sympathizers; and not far away, excited souls approach the life-sized statue of the 19th-century journalist Victor Noir. (Women come to touch, rub, and even lie on his prone, stone figure because it is supposed to embody amazing fertility power.)

It's doubtful that poor Père Lachaise, King Louis XIV's famed confessor, could have ever guessed what would become of his hilly parcel of land. Some tombs are marked "perpetuité," meaning the plot was paid for for eternity; otherwise, the bones are gathered up and deposited in the catacombs every 300 years.

Cimetière Montparnasse

Type of Attraction Paris's most important Left Bank cemetery
Location 3, bd Edgar Quinet, 75014   14th arrondissement
Métro Edgar Quinet or Raspail
Admission Free
Hours Monday–Friday, 8 a.m.–6 p.m.; Saturday, 8:30 a.m.–6 p.m.; Sunday, 9 a.m.–6 p.m.
Phone 01 44 10 86 50
When to Go Before dark
Author's Rating ★★★★

Description and Comments A visit to this cemetery is called for if you want to visit the grave site of the father of existentialism, Jean-Paul Sartre, or his companion, Simone de Beauvoir, whose classic work, The Second Sex, changed the way women began to see themselves. Other stars in this orderly resting place, tucked behind Montparnasse, include Samuel Beckett, Guy de Maupassant, Man Ray, and Charles Baudelaire.

Jardin d'Acclimatation

Type of Attraction Superb educational park for children in the Bois de Boulogne
Location Bd M. Barrès, Bois de Boulogne, 75016   16th arrondissement
Métro Les Sablons
Admission €1.98 per person, free for children under age 3
Hours Daily, 10 a.m.–6 p.m.
Phone 01 40 67 90 82

When to Go When the weather is good

Description and Comments   In the middle of the Bois de Boulogne you'll find a surprisingly diverse and pleasant park designed for children but also amusing and pleasant for the rest of the family. Take the tram outside the Les Sablons Métro station right to the gate of the Jardin d'Acclimatation. There is an enchanted river ride and a miniature railway that leads you around the park. You can play miniature golf, ride mini-motorcycles, attend a puppet show, or visit the Musée en Herbe, an ecological museum and workshop. Our favorite spot is the free-range petting zoo where geese roam around the snack shop while you have your lunch.

Jardin des Plantes

Type of Attraction Lovely park and zoo on the Left Bank
Location Quai St-Bernard, 75005   5th arrondissement
Métro Gare d'Austerlitz
Admission Free
Hours Daily, dawn to dusk
Phone 01 40 79 30 00
When to Go Before dark
Author's Rating ★★★★

Description and Comments   Site of Louis XIII's royal herb garden in the 1600s, today the Jardins des Plantes offers visitors a lovely respite from the urban experience without traveling far. Tucked into the eastern corner of the fifth arrondissement, this complex includes a very pleasant zoo, a botanical garden, a winter garden filled with exotic plants, and the world-renowned Grande Galerie de l'Evolution, part of the Natural History Museum, whose gallery of extinct species alone is worth a detour. Don't miss the turtles from the Seychelles Islands and the Tasmanian devil. The kids will love this. Not far from the rue Cuvier entrance, you'll find a labyrinth of paths leading to the tomb of Daubenton, a discrete gazebo hidden in the woods. This is an ideal hike or secret rendezvous spot for lovers.

Jardin du Luxembourg

Type of Attraction The most Parisian of all Paris's parks
Location Pl. Edmond Rostand or pl. Auguste-Comte, rue de Vaugirard, 75006   6th arrondissement
Métro RER Luxembourg
Admission Free
Hours Daily, dawn to dusk
When to Go Before dark; the park is locked at night
Author's Rating ★★★★★

Description and Comments   If you're in Paris for only a day, you'll want to spend a part of it in this sprawling icon of the most Parisian Paris. There is something for everyone in this park: wooden boat rentals on the pond for children, comfortable iron chairs for snoozing or reading, paths for jogging, pony rides for kids, basketball courts, a playground, a café beneath the shady trees, a perfect lawn reserved for babies under age 2, a Tuscan palace. Jardin du Luxembourg was created in 1617 by Boyeau de La Bareaudière after the wishes of Marie de Médicis. Its borders and design have been transformed through the centuries as much by its neighbors as its inhabitants, while remaining an impressive oasis of nature and tradition that easily recalls historic Paris. The garden gives the impression that it was designed by a Parisian architect rather than Mother Nature, given all the straight lines, squares, and sharp angles that cut up most of it (even the trees). But it is a nice place to take a pause from the bustling streets of Paris. The garden is also the home of the French Senate building, where tours are available. To feel Parisian quickly, come here and sit.

Les Catacombes

Type of Attraction A haunting but fascinating collection of human bones stored under the city
Location 1, pl. Denfert-Rochereau, 75014   14th arrondissement
Métro Denfert-Rochereau
Admission €5.03 adults; €3.35 for students, seniors, and those under age 25; free for children under age 7
Hours Tuesday, 11 a.m.–4 p.m.; Wednesday–Sunday, 9 a.m.–4 p.m.
Phone 01 43 22 47 63
When to Go Perfect for rainy days
Author's Rating ★★★★★

Description and Comments For some, this may be a highlight to your Paris trip. Many of the bones in Paris's public cemeteries are regularly raked out, sorted, lugged over, and stored in this maze of tunnels. You can descend into this dark world by climbing down the steep stairs at Denfert-Rochereau and visit the miles of lined-up skulls, femurs, and crossbones. Over 6 million skeletons are down here. Originally opened to the public in 1810, the walkways today are well lit and the experience isn't oppressive. What you'll soon realize, though, is that Paris has a complex infrastructure of tunnels and ancient quarries beneath its streets. Kids and strange folks manage to get down into these tunnels, and it is believed that there is an entire universe of marginal activity down there. The French underground used the catacombs and other tunnels to organize its activities against the Nazis in World War II. Some readers advise visitors to bring their own flashlights because at times the paths are very dark. Allow about 90 minutes for a full visit.

Les Tuileries

Type of Attraction The most civilized of all of Paris's park spaces
Location 1, place Concorde, 75001   1st arrondissement
Métro Concorde or Tuileries
Admission Free
Hours Summer, daily, 7:30 a.m.–9 p.m.; winter, daily, 7:30 a.m.–7: 30 p.m.
Phone 01 49 26 07 59
When to Go In pleasant weather
Author's Rating ★★★½

Description and Comments Between the Louvre and Place de la Concorde on the Right Bank, Les Tuileries roll out in perfect splendor. This stretch of park is perfect for a tranquil stroll, a picnic, or simply as a route between the Louvre and points west. It is interesting to note that in the 1600s the area was dug up for its clay, which was used to make tiles (tuiles), from which this park gets its name. In the 18th century, public concerts were held in the château at the edge of the gardens, and Mozart himself even conducted here. The gardens have recently been renovated, and a collection of bronze nudes by Maillol have been added. The terrace overlooking the Seine affords visitors a lovely view of the river and the Musée d'Orsay on the Left Bank. Evenings and nights here now host Paris's most active and open gay cruising.

From the central pathway of the gardens, you enjoy a spectacular view of the obelisk in the Place de la Concorde and farther west along the Champs-Elysées to the Arc de Triomphe. The Café Véry is a pleasant spot for a light lunch.

Parc André Citroën

Type of Attraction One of Paris's most innovative new parks
Location Rue Balard, 75015   15th arrondissement
Métro Balard or Javel
Admission Free
Hours Daily, 8:30 a.m.–7 p.m.
Phone 01 45 57 13 35 or 01 45 57 22 14
When to Go Before dark
Author's Rating ★★★

Description and Comments Not often on the itineraries of visitors, this contemporary park is worth your time if you are staying in the vicinity. Set on the site of the former Citroën car factory, which closed in the 1970s, the park now mixes marble, steel, plants, and above all water to create an unusual effect. In the Black Garden, you'll follow a circular path to an open space covered with 64 fountains, one of Paris's best-kept secrets for the hottest days of the year. Elsewhere, 100 water fountains perform a synchronized dance. The themes of the park are color-coded.

Parc de Bagatelles

Type of Attraction Park and flower gardens
Location: Route de Sèvres-à-Neuilly, route de la Reine-Marguerite, 75016
Métro & Bus Porte de Neuilly + Bus 43 or Porte Maillot + Bus 244
Admission €1 adults, €0.50 ages 6–18, free for age 6 and under
Hours Daily, 8.30 a.m.–7 p. m.
Phone 01 40 67 97 00
When to Go Springtime is particularly pleasant
Authors' Rating ★★★
How Much Time to Allow 1–2 hours

Description and Comments Perfect for a Sunday stroll, this park within a larger park is guaranteed to please nature lovers. The most spectacular flowers follow the seasons, with May highlighting the iris garden, June through October the roses, and August being prime for the water lilies. Sculptures, fountains, bridges, and other bucolic details have been placed along the way.

Parc de La Villette

Type of Attraction Highly contemporary complex of green space, exhibition areas, recreation facilities for kids, music, and cultural events
Location 211, av. Jean Jaurès, 75019   19th arrondissement
Métro Porte de Pantin or Porte de la Villette
Admission Free
Hours Daily, 24 hours
Phone 01 40 03 77 96
When to Go Depends on what you're going to do or see there
Author's Rating ★★★★

Description and Comments Although a bit out of the way, visitors to the Parc de La Villette are never disappointed, and only the adventurous tourists make the effort. This is among Paris's largest parks, and it characterizes much of the best of the city's attitudes toward art, recreation, culture, and public space. The park is divided into sectors devoted to science and industry, music, film, and topical exhibitions of first-rate quality and originality contributing to the popular culture of the city. The Canal de l'Ourcq, which dates back to Napoléon and was used to bring fresh water into the city, flows through the center of the park. On the northern side, you'll find the Cité des Sciences et de l'Industrie, along with a real submarine you can visit, a dragon sliding board, and an unmistakable 118-foot-diameter steel globe called La Géode in which an auditorium has been equipped with an 11,000-square-foot aluminum screen used for showing panoramic films with a 180° field of vision. Whatever is playing when you visit, try not to miss this experience.

On summer evenings, you can rent a reclining chair and view a classic film under the stars. Delightful. If you're going to the Cité des Sciences or the Géode, get off the Métro at Porte de la Villette. If you are going to a temporary exhibit, the Cité de la Musique, or the Zénith concert hall, get out at Porte de Pantin.

Parc des Buttes-Chaumont

Type of Attraction Rugged and beautiful park in a less-visited part of the city
Location Rue Manin, rue de Crimée, 75019   19th arrondissement
Métro Buttes de Chaumond
Admission Free
Hours Daily, dawn to dusk
When to Go Before dark
Author's Rating ★★★★

Description and Comments This is among the largest Parisian parks, English-styled and equally beautiful as romantic. Created under Napoléon III by the designer Adolphe Alphand, it is a colorful landscape about 5,000 acres large with 600,000 trees. Wandering through the park, you can find Sibylle's temple on the top of a 89-meter cliff. One of the most secluded and peaceful spots in Paris is the cascade- and stalagmite-covered cave deep within the park. Joggers love it here.

Parc Monceau

Type of Attraction Paris's most scenic *haute bourgeois* park
Location Bd de Courcelles at the Place de la République Dominicaine 75008 and 75017
8th arrondissement (borders 17th arrondissement)
Métro Courcelles
Admission Free
Hours Daily, dawn to dusk
Phone 01 42 27 08 64
When to Go In pleasant weather, before dark
Author's Rating ★★★★

Description and Comments This park epitomizes the style and elegance of old-wealth bourgeois Paris. Artistically designed with a pagoda, temple, pyramid, windmill, and ornamental pond, Parc Monceau is surrounded by some of the finest and most exclusive apartments in the city. Nearby you'll find the Musée Nissim de Camondo and the Musée Cernuschi, which you can combine with a visit to the park.

Parc Montsouris

Type of Attraction The finest park area in southern Paris
Location Bd Jourdan, 75014   14th arrondissement
Métro Porte d'Orléans, RER Cité Université
Admission Free
Hours Dawn to dusk
When to Go Before dark
Author's Rating ★★½

Description and Comments This is the finest park in the southern half of Paris. Opposite the Cité Universitaire, Parc Montsouris was designed by the famous city planner Haussmann in 1868 in an English style with an artificial lake. The tranquility of the park and its surroundings attracted numerous artists at the turn of the century, including Georges Braque and the Douanier Rousseau. Five minutes away, you'll stumble onto the Villa Seurat, a tiny dead-end alley on which Henry Miller lived in the studio of Artaud at number 18 and which he immortalized in his Tropic of Cancer. Anaïs Nin, Salvador Dali, and Soutine also lived on this quaint alley.

Parc Zoologique de Vincennes

Type of Attraction Paris's main zoo
Location Bois de Vincennes, 53, av. de St-Maurice, 75012   12th arrondissement
Métro Porte Dorée
Admission €6.10 adults, €4.60 children age 4–16
Hours April to October, daily, 9 a.m.–6:30 p.m.; November to March, daily, 9 a.m.–5:30 p.m.
Phone 01 44 75 20 10
When to Go It's crowded on the weekends and holidays. Give yourself a good three hours to see everything.
Author's Rating ★★★

Description and Comments   If you like zoos, you won't be disappointed. You'll not miss it due to its mammoth man-made rock mountain visible from miles away. Well-designed and arranged, this zoo offers over 500 mammals and 700 birds in their natural habitats. Unfortunately, one of the most famous residents, a panda, given to former president Giscard d'Estang by China, recently died at the ripe old age of 28.

Place Dauphine

Type of Attraction   A perfectly charming and peaceful square at the westerly end of the Île de la Cité
Location   Off the Pont Neuf, Île de la Cité, 75001   1st arrondissement
Métro   Pont Neuf
When to Go   At dawn when the sun's coming up over the Pont Neuf
Author's Rating   ★★★½

Description and Comments   Tucked in at the western tip of the Île de la Cité behind the Palais de Justice, this quaint and discreet square dates back to the 1500s, when it stood as a muddy and damp area in the Seine. Henri IV conceived of a triangular square between the new Pont Neuf and the Conciergerie, and Place Dauphine is the result, named in honor of the future Louis XIII. Dotted with old eating houses and legal bookshops.

Place de Fürstemberg

Type of Attraction   Paris's most charming public square
Location   6th arrondissement
Métro   St-Germain-des-Prés
When to Go   Anytime
Author's Rating   ★★★★

Description and Comments   A stroll through this tiny square in the heart of the Saint-Germain-des-Prés area transports you back to the turn of the 18th century. At number 6, you'll find the Delacroix Museum, where the Romantic painter worked and died.

Place de la Concorde

Type of Attraction   The most elegant and dramatic square in the city, and the site on which Marie-Antoinette was guillotined
Location   Where the rue de Rivoli, rue Royale, and the quai all converge, 75008   8th arrondissement
Métro   Concorde
When to Go   Driving into the Place de la Concorde at night is breathtaking, but the driving is hazardous.
Author's Rating   ★★★★

Description and Comments   This square was built under Louis XV between 1755 and 1775. In 1793 a guillotine was installed there, and in 1833 Hittorf added the obelisk that was given to France by Mehemet Ali, viceroy of Egypt. This 2,300-year-old monolith is the most striking monument at Concorde, weighing 220 tons and measuring 23 meters high. In each of the eight corners of the Place there are statues honoring the great cities of France. It's difficult to walk around the Place, and it's treacherous driving here. At night, the Place is lit up, and an air of great regal presence is felt.

Place des Victoires

Type of Attraction Classy square in the heart of the fashion district
Location Bridging 75001 and 75002   1st and 2nd arrondissements
Métro Sentier, Etienne Marcel
When to Go During shopping hours
Author's Rating ★★★½

Description and Comments In the heart of Paris's most hip fashion district lies this very handsome square. Twentieth-century sweatshops where dresses and shirts, raincoats, and jackets are sewn sit just outside the square, abutting the 17th-century elegance. At the center is a fenced-in statue of Louis XIV on a horse, unveiled in 1822.

Place des Vosges

Type of Attraction One of Paris's most elegant and royal squares
Location Bridging 75003 and 75004   3rd and 4th arrondissements
Métro St-Paul-Le-Marais
When to Go Avoid the weekend crowds
Author's Rating ★★★★½

Description and Comments One of only five prestigious *Places Royales* in Paris, Place des Vosges was created by Henri IV in 1605 and completed in 1612. It was highly frequented by the nobles of the epoch (where rich Parisians ended their squabbles through duels), then endured a period of relative dilapidation, only recently becoming once again a symbol of Parisian luxury. Today one can enjoy, besides greenery and a constant stream of the wealthy and famous, Victor Hugo's apartment (now a museum), several art galleries, and some expensive but excellent restaurants.

Place Vendôme

Type of Attraction The only Paris square that can truly be called "Ritzy"
Location 1st arrondissement
Métro Opéra or Tuileries
When to Go Anytime
Author's Rating ★★★★

Description and Comments This square in the heart of Paris's most sophisticated fashion and design-driven neighborhood captures both the classical elegance of 17th-century style and the city's cutting-edge commercial chic. At the center of the posh and stately circle Napoléon in 1810 had the bronze Austerlitz Column erected, which was cast from the cannons used at the Battle of Austerlitz in 1805. In the Commune uprising, the column was destroyed, the painter Courbet was blamed and banished, and in 1871 a replica was finally erected. You'll find a handsome collection of arches supporting noble buildings. Today, the best known is the notorious Ritz Hotel, owned by the flamboyant millionaire Muhammed Al-Fayad, owner also of Harrods in London; his son was killed in a 1997 car crash with Diana, Princess of Wales. Although somewhat stuffy these days and riddled with security measures—rumor has it that everyone entering the Place Vendôme is videotaped—you could slip in to the Ritz for a cocktail at the famed Hemingway Bar, where the writer often sat and drank. At number 12 on the square, you'll note the house that Frédéric Chopin died in. (He's buried in Père Lachaise.)

Promenade Plantée (elevated level)
Viaduc des Arts (ground level)

Type of Attraction Paris's most original and longest park space
Location Begins at the intersection of av. Daumesnil and the av. Ledru Rollin, 75012 12th arrondissement
Métro Reuilly Diderot or Bastille
Admission Free
When to Go Weekends tend to get painfully crowded
Author's Rating ★★★★ (Promenade Plantée) ★★★½ (Viaduc des Arts)

Description and Comments Typical of Parisian priorities, instead of ripping down the old train viaduct that runs between the Bastille and the eastern edge of Paris, city planners converted the vaulted archways below into shops and cafés while transforming the wide rooftop into a planted walkway with benches and rest stops. You can stroll or jog all the way to the Bois de Vincennes or stop any time along the way. A great vantage point from which to observe the facades of buildings in the 12th arrondissement.

Bridges and Fountains

Although Paris has more than 35 bridges crossing the Seine in greatly diverse sizes, styles, and materials, arching over the river between the east and west edges of the Periphèrique (the outer beltway), there are between five and ten magnificent *ponts* that possess that special magic for transforming a mundane moment into a personal epiphany. New York or London may excite your mind or body, but Paris on the Seine is a purely emotional experience.

You might have to miss the Louvre or the Arc de Triomphe this time, skip a meal at that noted five-star restaurant you've been meaning to try, or sacrifice a run out to the *marche aux puces,* but whatever your time frame may be, don't visit Paris without stopping on a bridge and playing captain to the City of Light! (Miraculously, if you're not already in love in Paris, cross almost any bridge between Pont de Sully and Pont de l'Alma in the late afternoon or early evening, and you'll find yourself taking an inventory of the heart and realizing that being alive is, well, a glorious enterprise. What other city gives you that?

A Tour of Paris by Bridge

The nice thing about visiting the bridges of Paris is that, depending on where you're staying, you can start your walking tour anywhere. You can follow the Seine east or west, descend from the street-level embankments called the *quais,* and strut along the water in either direction. Then you can climb back up to the street at the next bridge and continue on the quai. You can connect and disconnect from the buzz of city life as you please. You can use the frequent bridges to weave across the Seine, or you can keep walking for half as long as you want to be out, and then cross at the next bridge, and return on the other bank.

Let's say you begin your stroll at Notre-Dame, a perfect point of departure in that the splendid gothic cathedral not only is Paris's most central landmark but also the very point in Paris from which all distances in France are measured. From the little **Pont de l'Archevêché,** you are afforded a spectacular view of the spines and cornices of the back of Notre-Dame and its delightful park. (At the eastern tip of the Île de la Cité, depending on your mood, you may wish to wander down into the somewhat hidden but terribly moving Mémorial de la Déportation commemorating those who were sent to death camps from Paris during the German occupation.)

From the Île de la Cité, you have several attractive options. You can continue around to **Pont d'Arcole** and Hôtel de Ville, Paris's extraordinary city hall, or you can cross the pedestrian-only **Pont Saint-Louis,** which carries you over to the absolutely charming but somewhat overcrowded Île Saint-Louis. Assuming you do the latter, make sure you wait in line for a small, scrumptious ice cream cone from Paris's most celebrated *glacier,* Bertillon. Then, either return to Pont Saint-Louis to watch the ducks, the colorful *peniches,* and the lovers, or explore Île Saint-Louis. From the foot of **Pont de la Tournelle,** Parisians tend to look up at the large window seats of Claude Terrail's culinary landmark, La Tour d'Argent, where the duck you order comes with registration papers.

From Place Saint-Michel in the heart of the Latin Quarter, follow the Quai des Grands Augustins to **Pont Neuf,** one of Paris's loveliest bridges, and the oldest means of crossing the Seine, finished in 1607 under the direction of Henri IV, who is immortalized in bronze on horseback on the bridge. In 1985, the eccentric artist Christo chose this bridge to wrap in miles of cloth and decorated the crossing with 100,000 begonias. The bridge cuts across the western tip of the Île de la Cité, creating the secluded spit of land, the Square du Vert Galant, where you can sunbathe, picnic, and embrace while enjoying the most bizarre sensation of being totally alone yet wholly visible to every pair of eyes in the city. Continue on the other side of the bridge, past the massive bronze sculpture of a mounted Henri IV, and stroll through the private and shady Place Dauphine, which looks onto the majestic backside of the Palais de Justice, in which the unforgettable Sainte-Chapelle is housed.

On the Right Bank at the foot of Pont Neuf, you'll find the celebrated department store La Samaritaine. For an aerial view of the city, enter the main building of the store, on the *quai,* and take the elevator to the rooftop terrace for a drink. One of the great pleasures of this panoramic point of view is that you're in the heart of Paris.

A few hundred yards west, and you're at the **Pont des Arts,** a wooden footbridge that attracts the city's funkier and more creative souls. The bridge is in line with the ornate, gilded dome of the world-renowned Institut, founded by Mazarin as the center of France's great science and art academies. On the Right Bank the bridge joins the Louvre, and with a little imagination, takes on metaphoric value suspended between creation and history. From the footbridge, you enjoy in every direction one of Paris's most copious visual feasts. Hang out here and rethink your life. Write a poem. Hold the hand of the person you married ages ago. Think about your kids . . . or forget them for the moment.

On both banks of the Seine you'll be amused to note the tiny green bookstalls of the merchants called *bouquinistes* permanently encrusted onto the walls above the river. This literary vocation is passed from generation to generation, as it is virtually impossible to buy or rent a new space. Browse here; pick up an old copy of Eluard's poems or some art deco postcards.

Moving west, you'll strut past **Pont du Carrousel, Pont Royal,** and the innovative **Passerelle de Solférino,** one of the city's ambitious projects to join the Louvre complex with the Musée d'Orsay and create a direct liaison with the Jardin des Tuileries. The metal arch has a two-level walkway built in exotic wood, allowing pedestrians to cross the Seine here both from the river level and from the street.

Complementing the terrace in the Tuileries overlooking the Seine and an area known as the Plage de Paris, the walkway just opposite on the Left Bank—which is studded with statuary, greenery, and houseboat moorings—is a favorite meeting place for Paris's gay community.

The Bridges by Night

From **Pont de la Concorde** at night, you'll know why Paris is called the City of Light. On one end, the Assemblée Nationale is flooded in ochre tones, and the imposing structure of the Madeleine stands in the distance at the opposite end of the axis, with the sprawling Place de la Concorde glittering with wild traffic and 500 wrought-iron lamps. The etched obelisk, carried in one piece from Luxor, Egypt, towers in the center, in perfect symmetry with the Arc de Triomphe and the tip of the pyramid at the Louvre. *Magnifique* is the only word that comes to mind. And for history buffs, it was precisely here that Queen Marie Antoinette was introduced to the guillotine.

The distance between Pont de la Concorde and **Pont de l'Alma** may be a bit much for some walkers, but the quiet **Pont des Invalides** offers a very romantic view of the river, and the *Bateaux Mouche* station, at night of course, lights up the river in a dramatic way. The approach to **Pont Alexandre III** is priceless. Winged horses, cherubs, nymphs, gold-leaf swords (regilded for the 1989 bicentennial and recently repainted in gold) grace this art nouveau spectacle. Paris's most celebrated and most photographed bridge, Pont Alexandre III was built for the Universal Exhibition in 1900 and named after Russian Tsar Alexander III, who laid the first stone in 1896. The sidewalks on the bridge are wide, and there are no benches for sitting; so despite its elegance, this bridge is more for spectators than participants.

The area around the Pont de l'Alma and the bridge that passes underneath is now heavily visited by tourists, who are fascinated to see where Princess Diana lost her life and to pay homage and leave written messages. The whole area has taken on a cultish appeal in a way. At the foot of the bridge on the Right Bank, don't miss the gold-crusted flame of the Statue of Liberty. This was recast from the authentic mold used to build the original statue, which, given to the people of United States in 1812 as a gift from France, sits today at the mouth of the Hudson River in New York harbor. A small imitation greets fluvial visitors to Paris as they sail under **Pont de Grenelle.**

Movie buffs won't want to miss the experience of stalking along the gray-metal stanchions of the **Pont Bir Hakeim** in the great style of Marlon Brando, who played a grieving American in *Last Tango in Paris* and crossed that bridge repeatedly to rendezvous in amorous anonymity with an enticing Parisienne played by a young Maria Schneider.

On your way back toward the center, the Quai de la Mégisserie between Pont Neuf and Châtelet offers an amusing distraction. Aside from the extensive selection of house and garden plants, specialty shops roll out onto the sidewalks cages with live ducks and geese, rabbits, snakes, lizards, Chinese newts, and other Parisian wildlife. One always marvels at the sight of Paris street pigeons landing on the cages of their cousins in captivity.

Just on the other side of the Seine, on the Île de la Cité, you'll find a wonderful bird market (open Sunday mornings), where the collectors and clientele are often as exotic as their Gabonese parrots or albino finches.

Let the bridges be your guide. The best way to the romance of Paris is not only to cross the Seine but to stop for a while suspended between both banks.

Day Trips and Excursions

Time permitting, you must sneak away to the Palace and Gardens of Versailles or Fontainebleau, Chantilly, or Monet's Giverny, all within easy access of Paris. But first, a few words about Le Mouse.

Disneyland Paris

Type of Attraction Classic Disney fare with a hint of Europe
Location Marne-La-Vallée–Chessy
Métro RER line A (station Marne-La-Vallée–Chessy)
Admission April through October: €35.98 adults, €28.05 children under age 11; November through March: €27 adults, €23 children under age 11; free for children under age 3
Hours Daily, 9 a.m.–8 p.m. (some seasonal variation; vist www.disneylandparis.com for details)
Phone 01 60 30 60 30
Website www.disneylandparis.com
Overall Appeal by Age Group
  Pre-school ★★★★   Grade School ★★★★   Teens ★★★★
  Young Adults ★★★★   Over 30 ★★★★   Seniors ★★★★
Author's Rating ★★★★

Description and Comments We're not sure exactly why you'd come all the way to Paris to visit a Disney theme park. But if you can't get enough Disney in the States, or alternatively, you want to see what became of all those dollars you've poured into the Disney coffers, Disneyland Paris (formerly Euro Disneyland) is a short train ride away.

Disneyland Paris was opened in 1992 on a 5,000-acre tract surrounded almost exclusively by farms just 32 kilometers east of Paris. Located strategically in this vast expanse are the Disneyland Paris theme park, six resort hotels, a convention center, an elaborate campground, a nighttime entertainment complex, shopping arcades, almost thirty full-service restaurants, golf courses, several large interconnected lakes, and a transportation system consisting of four-lane highways, a train station, and a system of canals.

The theme park is a collection of adventures, rides, and shows drawn from Disney cartoons and films, and symbolized by Le Chateau de la Belle au Bois Dormant (Sleeping Beauty's Castle). The Disneyland Paris park is divided into five subareas or "lands" arranged around a central hub. The first one you encounter is Main Street, U.S.A., which connects the Disneyland Paris entrance with the central hub. Moving clockwise around the hub, the other lands are Adventureland, Frontierland, Fantasyland, and Discoveryland.

NOT TO BE MISSED AT DISNEYLAND PARIS

Frontierland	Phantom Manor
	Big Thunder Mountain
Adventureland	Pirates of the Caribbean
Fantasyland	Peter Pan's Flight
Discoverland	Star Tours
	Space Mountain
	Le Visionarium

Main Street Electrical Parade
La Parade Disney

Gathering Information   Information concerning Disneyland Paris can be obtained at the public library, through travel agencies, or by writing or calling (do not use 33-1 when calling locally):

Disneyland Paris Guest Relations
Boite Postale 100
77777 Marne-la-Vallée, Cedex 4, France
Tel. (33 1) 64 74 30 00

In the United States, call the Disney Travel Company for information at (407) 828-3232. Or visit www.disneylandparis.com.

Admission Options   One-day, two-day, and three-day admission passes are available for purchase for both adults (12 years and up) and children (3 to 11 years inclusive). All rides, shows, and attractions (except the Frontierland shooting gallery) are included in the price of admission. Multiday passes do not have to be used on consecutive days. If you are visiting Paris from the States, however, a one-day visit should suffice.

Operating Hours   It cannot be said that the Disney folks are not flexible when it comes to hours of operation for the park. They run a dozen or more different operating schedules during the year, making it advisable to call 01 64 74 30 00, locally, the day before you arrive at the theme park.

Getting to Disneyland Paris

By Métro/RER   You can reach Disneyland Paris in about an hour by taking the Paris Métro from wherever you are in the city and linking up with the RER line "A" to Marne-la-Vallée–Chessy. For detailed tips on using the Métro and RER, see Part Five: Getting Around Paris.

By Car   Disneyland Paris is just 32 kilometers (19 miles) east of Paris, right off the A4 autoroute, sometimes known as the *autoroute de l'est*. Disneyland Paris is connected to the A4 autoroute by a direct access loop. Once on the loop, follow the signs to the park. Signs for the upcoming Parc Disneyland Paris exit appear on the autoroute, in both directions, way before you reach the general area.

Château de Fontainebleau

Type of Attraction   Excursion/day trip to this royal residence and gardens
Location   77300 Fontainebleau, about 50 kilometers from Paris
Métro   Train Gare de Lyon: direction Fontainebleau (45 minutes)
Admission   Gardens: free; castle: €5.34 adults, €3.51 students, seniors, and for all visitors on Sunday; free for children under age 18
Hours   Castle: Wednesday–Monday, 9:30 a.m.–12:30 p.m., 2–5 p.m.; reduced hours September through June
Phone   01 60 71 50 70
When to Go   In pleasant weather only
Special Comments   A pleasant place for children, especially the gardens around the castle
Overall Appeal by Age Group

Pre-school ★★★ Grade School ★★★ Teens ★★★★
Young Adults ★★★★ Over 30 ★★★★ Seniors ★★★★
Author's Rating ★★★★
How Much Time to Allow Half a day

Description and Comments Revered by French kings for its proximity to great hunting, the Château de Fontainebleau makes for a delightful side trip from Paris. Located about 40 miles south of the city and accessible by train in only 45 minutes; go in the morning and picnic on the grounds of the palace, or take a hike in the famous rock formations in the nearby forest. Plan on a good 30 to 60 minutes visiting the palace, Napoléon's favorite residence. King François I turned the hunting lodge into a kingly palace and even hired the services of Italian artist Benvenuto Cellini. Note the Gallery of François I, with its impressive succession of painted panels. The ornate Louis XV staircase is one of the highlights of the tour. Of course, it's a thrill to visit the bedroom, throne room, and bathroom of Napoléon himself.

Touring Tips Bring a picnic.

Suggested Place to Eat **Table des Maréchaux,** 9, rue Grande, 77300 Fontainebleau. Tel: 01 60 39 50 50, fax: 01 64 22 20 87, e-mail: napoleon@worldonline.fr. Credit cards accepted. Elegant and quiet dining room with a pleasant terrace. Traditional French cuisine. Count on €20–25 per person.

Other Things to Do Nearby Village of Barbizon

Château de Versailles

Type of Attraction Excursions/day trip to the most spectacular royal residence and gardens in France.

Location 78000 Versailles

Métro RER C Versailles from the Rive Gauche stations (50 minutes)

Admission Gardens: free (except when the fountains are working); castle: €7.47 adults, €5.34 after 3:30 p.m., free for children under age 18; Grand and Petit Trianon: €5.03 adults, €3.05 after 3:30 p.m., free for children under age 18; Chambre du Roi: €25 adults, free for children under age 7; Musée des Carrosses (Grande Ecurie du Roi): €1.83 adults, free for children under age 18

Hours Castle: Tuesday–Sunday, 9 a.m.–5:30 p.m. (open until 6:30 p.m. in summer; ticket office closes a half-hour before castle). Grand and Petit Trianon: daily, noon–5:30 p.m. (open until 6:30 p.m. in summer; ticket office closes a half-hour before gardens). Musée des Carrosses (Grande Ecurie du Roi): March to November, Saturday and Sunday, 2–5 p.m.

Phone 01 30 84 76 18; exhibitions 01 39 67 07 73

When to Go As early as possible, preferably on weekdays

Special Comments Audioguides in English, €4.57

Overall Appeal by Age Group
Pre-school ★★★ Grade School ★★★ Teens ★★★★
Young Adults ★★★★ Over 30 ★★★★★ Seniors ★★★★★
Author's Rating ★★★★
How Much Time to Allow Half a day or full day

Description and Comments If you'll be in Paris for five days or more, schedule a trip to Versailles. Easily accessible from central Paris via RER (under an hour), the castle and its gardens are guaranteed to impress you. The summer months attract a lot of foreign visitors, so try to go early and leave early. A complete tour of the château and gardens could take up to two days, but a good appreciation of the splendor of Versailles is possible in a half a day. Start with a tour of the interior apartments. On the first floor, do not miss the Chapelle Royale with its marble altar dedicated to Saint Louis, followed by the Grands Appartements, which include the royal bedrooms, a six-room suite occupied by Louis XIV from 1673 to 1682. Other highlights include the Galerie des Glaces (Hall of Mirrors), where Louis XIV entertained foreign dignitaries. Seventeen windows and 17 glass panels with 578 mirrors illuminate the room. The hall, with its masterful view, was designed so that the last rays of sunlight each day fall here. Two major historical events subsequently transpired in this hall: the proclamation of the German Empire in 1871 and the signing of the Treaty of Versailles on June 28, 1919, marking the end to World War I. The Appartement de la Reine was Marie-Antoinette's digs, and visitors should note her rococo touches. Nineteen royal births occurred here in the queen's bedroom; among them were Louis XV and Philip V of Spain. Then, go see the Appartement du Roi, Louis XIV's apartments, which wrap around the Marble Court. This should not be confused with the king's private apartments, which Louis XV reserved for his most intimate moments. The palace also includes the first oval opera house in France, inaugurated in 1770 for the marriage of the Dauphin—the future Louis XVI—and Marie-Antoinette.

After visiting the interior, you'll be ready for some air and open space. After viewing the front gardens, head out into the elaborate space around the Latona Basin and stroll through the groves. A walk around the grand and petit canal is a lovely way to take in the grandeur and elegance of this masterpiece of French landscaping in which nature has been organized according to classical principles. Of particular interest are the Grand and Petit Trianons (30 minutes by foot from the palace) and the Hameau de la Reine (15 minutes by foot beyond the Petit Trianon).

These Country retreats from the official palace offer visitors a rare glance at a delightful thatched-roof hamlet of cottages built for Marie Antionette. A great way to escape the crowds, too!

Touring Tips Get an early start. Bring good walking shoes. Avoid tours. Call ahead for English-language tours of the private apartments.

Suggested Places to Eat **Potager du Roy,** 1, rue Mar.-Joffre, 78000 Versailles. Tel. 01 39 50 35 34, fax 01 30 21 69 30. Closed Saturday lunchtime, Sunday evening, and Monday. Credit cards accepted. Pre-war decor. The cuisine puts the accent on vegetables since the restaurant is close to the Potager du Roi (King's vegetable garden). Count on around €20 per person.

Valmont, 20, rue au Pain, 78000 Versailles. Tel. 01 39 51 39 00, fax 01 30 83 90 99. Closed Sunday evening and Monday. Credit cards accepted. A quaint and cheerful setting with Louis XVI–style chairs and paintings of Île de France landscapes. Count on €20–30 per person.

Giverny

Type of Attraction Excursions/day trip to Monet's country residence and source of inspiration

Location 99, rue Claude Monet, 27620 Giverny, one hour from Paris

Métro Train Gare St-Lazare direction Vernon

Admission Musée d'Art Américain, €5.34 adults, €3.05 students

Hours April through November, Tuesday–Sunday, 10 a.m.–6 p.m.

Phone 02 32 51 94 65 (museum)

When to Go Leave Paris early in the day; good weather only

Special Comments Bring a picnic.

Overall Appeal by Age Group

Pre-school —   Grade School —   Teens ★★★

Young Adults ★★★   Over 30 ★★★   Seniors ★★★

Author's Rating ★★★

How Much Time to Allow 4 hours

Description and Comments Fifty miles northwest of Paris on the way to Normandy, you can visit the house and gardens of impressionist painter Claude Monet, who came to Giverny in 1883 in his early 40s. This makes for a wonderful excursion in the spring and early fall. Connecting Monet's brilliant water lilies to the pond they floated in will be a spiritually fulfilling moment. Brace yourself for bucolic settings with wisteria hanging from a Japanese bridge, weeping willows, and vibrant rhododendrons. Between Monet's death in 1926 and 1977 the house and property were abandoned and fell into a decrepit state. Gerald van der Kemp, who had restored Versailles, took on the task of bringing Giverny back to its original state, with the help of generous funds from Lila Acheson Wallace of *Reader's Digest.* Today, the property is managed by the Claude Monet Foundation. The nearby American Art Museum houses works by American Impressionists.

Touring Tips If you don't have a car, you'll have to take the Paris-Rouen train from Saint Lazare station. Get off at Vernon and take a taxi to Giverny (three miles). There are bus excursions here, but you may not want to be part of a group when visiting this country setting. You can make a full day of it and go all the way to Madame Bovary's Rouen and stop at Giverny on the way back.

Parc Astérix

Type of Attraction Excursions/day trip to this Gallo-Roman theme park

Location 60000 Plailly, one hour from Paris

Métro RER B3 to Roissy/Charles de Gaulle, then take the Asterix shuttle bus to the park

Admission €28.20 adults, €20.58 children age 3–12, free for children under age 3

Hours April through October, daily, 10 a.m.–7 p.m. (attractions close at 6 p.m.)

Phone 03 44 62 34 04

Website www.parcasterix.fr

When to Go Start out early and arrive at 10 a.m.

Special Comments A perfect way to mix history and entertainment
Overall Appeal by Age Group
   Pre-school ★★★★   Grade School ★★★★   Teens ★★★★
   Young Adults ★★★   Over 30 ★★★   Seniors ★★★
Author's Rating ★★★★
How Much Time to Allow I day

Description and Comments If you want to enchant the kids, this theme park is a perfect way to combine amusement and French history and culture. An excellent alternative to Disneyland, this park is studded with the popular Roman and Gaulois cartoon characters. Historical figures are interspersed with roller coasters and other theme rides, typical Gaulois houses, and recreated streets from Paris of the Middle Ages. Ponies, camels, and horses partake in the Olympic games in the ancient arenas, and the Descente du Styx rafting ride through cascades and rapids will cool down the kids. There is a dolphin and otter show, plus other surprises. For a theme park, you'll be delighted with this original cultural attraction.

Touring Tips Go when it's gray or overcast to beat the heat and the crowds.

Part Seven

Dining in Paris

Bon Appetit!

Brace yourself. One of your greatest sources of pleasure during your days and nights in Paris will be sublimely culinary. Of course, there is a huge difference between what you eat in a simple restaurant and what is served at a restaurant *gastronomique* (gourmet, fine dining). Nonetheless, it is in the food in France at all levels that art and aesthetics, science and sustenance, meet. Indulging in Parisian cuisine requires more than tasting and swallowing; you must observe and contemplate. Parisians do nearly everything around the lunch and dinner table, so never, ever think of a long, languorous meal in Paris as a waste of time. Try not to be rushed when in a restaurant, and approach each meal as an event as important as visiting a museum or exploring a monument.

There is no better way to learn about Parisian culture, language, social attitudes, style, and aesthetics, French agriculture and geography, and Parisian habits than *à table* (ah **tahb**la), which means "at the table." Go slow, and never forget that you are in the capital of pleasure and sensual gratification, so indulge, and for at least a few days or evenings, suspend all finickyness, guilt, waistline worries, and calorie and cholesterol counting. Try to add one new culinary adventure to every meal. There are lots of common local specialties that may be wholly new to you. Keep a little notebook of your savory discoveries, like *cèpe* mushrooms or fiddle heads, periwinkles, snails, crayfish, beef muzzle, fois gras of goose . . . and, with 450 types of cheese in France, it's going to be hard to avoid a high butter-fat adventure. If you select your restaurants well and know how to handle yourself, your dining experiences in Paris will be singularly memorable . . . and enriching. If you choose badly or just go for the quick and easy solution, eating in Paris can be both overpriced and disappointing. You don't mind a splurge once in a while, but you want the meal to overwhelm you with flavor, presentation, and ambience.

While Paris is studded with great restaurants, at the same time it is also packed with all sorts of mediocre eateries, cafés, bars, bistros, brasseries, fast-food establishments, and sidewalk stands. Without some good leads, coaching, or recommendations, you'll easily find yourself unsure of where to go and what to choose. The last thing you want to end up doing is staying in your hotel or just walking across the street to the closest restaurant because it's convenient. Similarly, returning to the same place you've been before because it's comforting to stick with a known entity is a shame. Adventure, explore, take risks . . .

The sheer number of places you can eat at in Paris is certain to make you wonder how they all manage to stay in business. Well, Parisians eat out a lot, and per capita spend more money on food consumed away from home than the residents of most other European cities.

HOW PARISIANS STAY SO SLIM

- They walk more and drive less
- They eat balanced and diverse meals
- They eat less processed food with fewer additives
- They eat fewer snacks and less in between meals
- Their food contains fewer hidden fats and sugars
- They are concerned with how they look in public
- They drink more water and fewer soft drinks
- They take more time to digest
- The size of portions is connected to reality

When to Eat

The idea of eating when you're hungry isn't quite French. Custom and habit in Paris require that you be hungry when you're supposed to be dining. So, although you can always satisfy a growling stomach and yield to that pang for something *très* chocolate, keep in mind that lunch in a restaurant is served between noon and 2 p.m. and dinner is between 7:30 or 8 p.m. and 10 p.m. In Paris, being a large city, there are plenty of exceptions and alternatives for the less traditional, but by and large these should be your dining hours. Although you can always eat something in a café, do not plan on having your midday meal in a restaurant at 3 p.m. Impossible. Don't even try. Similarly, if you're used to the early-bird special at 5:30 p.m., you had better grab a snack, a coffee, and a piece of cake in a *salon de thé*—or a *chocolat chaud* (hot chocolate) at Chez Angelina, for example— to hold you over until the Parisian dinner time.

General Hours

Breakfast 7–9 a.m.   **Lunch** noon–2 p.m.   **Dinner** 8–10 p.m.

Similarly, if you want to eat something after 10 p.m., you can, but your field of choices is drastically reduced. (See Restaurant Profiles later in this chapter for late dining hours.)

The other problematic meal in the week is Sunday night dinner. Many Paris restaurants are closed on Sunday nights, but you still have to eat. (See Restaurant Profiles later in this chapter for Sunday dining.)

A Word about Toilets and Telephones

All cafés have public toilets and telephones located inside, usually at the back and often down stairs. The toilets are almost always free, but some of the larger and classier cafés may have an attendant sitting in the doorway with a suggestive plate of coins. You're guaranteed a higher level of hygiene here, and you can leave a coin or two if you wish. Paris café toilets are known for their uneven degrees of cleanliness. Most are acceptable. Some are impeccable. Others are a bit funkier and ill-equipped. It's a good rule of thumb when traveling to carry toilet paper with you as a back-up.

One of the great character-building experiences left in Paris is the Turkish toilet (more irreverently known as the "squat-and-pray"). Be prepared. Don't just turn around and leave before you give it a shot (pardon the pun). The Turkish toilet is a glorified hole in the ground. Position your feet on the porcelain platform, squat, and aim for the hole. To flush, you pull a chain which sends a torrent of water over the platform. To avoid soaking your feet, get ready to move out of the way before you yank the chain. This may seem primitive, but it's a totally hygienic, no-contact experience, and one you should not miss.

Public telephones in cafés are often coin operated, but increasing numbers of cafés have card-operated telephones.

Paris Restaurants Defined and Explained

Just because an establishment sells food doesn't—in Paris—make it a restaurant. And similarly, don't expect to be able to walk into a restaurant (even if it has something that looks like a bar) to order a drink. The bill of fare, habits, hours, and expectations are all different. A restaurant is where the tables are set, there is a menu, and you're expected to order a full meal—to eat *(manger)*. Gobbling down a sandwich is not considered eating.

Here's a run-down on the ins and outs of Paris's eating and drinking options:

Café and Café Tabac

The café in Paris is far more than a place to drink coffee, although it is that too. It is a place to rest, to read a novel or write one, to think, to meet friends, to do business, to glance over the sports page of the *Tribune,* and to hang out and people-watch. It's probable that you'll find a café that you like, maybe even a table that you'll quickly grow attached to, and you'll return periodically. The delights are endless, but there are some basic customs you absolutely need to master before you can consider yourself a "regular."

- Cafés on the main avenues and boulevards are expensive, with a simple espresso-style coffee costing over €3. The smaller cafés on the back streets are more intimate and a bit more reasonable.

- There are three different price structures in a café. In essence, it's not the drinks you are paying for, but your location. When you sit at a sidewalk table on the terrace outside, you pay top price. When you sit at an inside table, you pay slightly less. The most economical place in a café is the counter, called the *zinc* (the counters in Paris cafés are made of shiny brass-colored zinc). Here, you stand or lean, have your coffee or glass of wine, or even grab a quick sandwich. But if you want to linger, you'd be better off taking a seat.

- Don't sit at an inside table set for lunch if you only want a coffee or drink. You'll be asked to move; these tables are for dining only.

- Standing at a bar in Paris has none of the negative stigma or connotations of "hard drinking" that exists in the Anglo-Saxon world. In fact, although the French lead the world in alcohol consumption, most of this is in the form of wine drunk at meals. Drinking under age is not a real problem here, and you'll rarely see adolescents attempting to drink in public.

- If the price of drinks at a café seems overwhelmingly expensive to you, we recommend that you stop thinking in dollars! This will reduce the pain. Secondly, as one resident American travel writer puts it, "Don't think of the price of a coffee as the price of a coffee. Think of it as the cost of renting a prime piece of Paris real estate for an hour. Four dollars an hour is a bargain, plus you get a good strong espresso thrown in as well."

- You can order a simple coffee and sit for as long as you like and no one will rush you or bother you. Take your time. There will not be pressure on you to order more or get moving.

- Don't call your waiter *garçon.* That went out a generation ago and is no longer appropriate or appreciated. To get the waiter's attention, just motion with your hand or discretely say, *Pardon, monsieur* (pahr don, miss-yer).

- When your waiter brings you your coffee or drinks, he'll leave a little cash register receipt on a small plastic dish. This is your bill. Sometimes he'll leave this there until you're ready to leave. However, when he's about to go off duty he'll ask if he can *encaisser* right away. You pay him directly and he has a pouch from which he makes change. Then he'll give the slip of paper a quick little rip which means that you've paid your bill.

- As is the case with everything that you eat or drink in France, the "service" or tip is included. So, don't leave 15% on top of your bill.

- There are certain drinks you can only order at the *zinc*, such as a glass of draught lemon soda, which is used as well in a popular summer drink called a *panaché*, a blend of draft beer and lemon soda. A refreshing variation is the *Monaco*, a draft beer with grenadine syrup.

- The smoking might stun you and discourage you at first. French law requires that all cafés above a certain size have nonsmoking sections, but in reality the smokers are so much more prevalent than the nonsmokers that either there will not be a nonsmoking section, or it'll be tiny and situated in the back. You can either find a less smoky café, sit outside when the weather permits it, or endure the Parisian air quality.

- Liquid portions are measured in liters and divided into centiliters (cl.). A beer glass has a little line indicating where the 33 cl. or 50 cl. level is. Bottled beer usually comes in 33 cl. or 25 cl. bottles. It's the measured quantity in France, not the full or almost full glass that counts.

- Tip: What culinary ingredient kills the taste buds for wine? Chocolate!

Café Tabac

The *café tabac*, easily spotted with its red neon sign, is a café with a few extra features. Primarily, these establishments have been state licensed to sell cigarettes and other tobacco products to the public. Only a *café tabac* can sell tobacco products, and often you'll see lines of smokers coming out the door. The *tabac* also sells postage stamps, lottery tickets, telephone cards, street parking cards, and fiscal stamps needed for licenses, parking tickets, and other official documents. You'll always find a yellow mailbox for all your letters outside a *tabac*.

What to Order in a Café

Coffee   Frequenting a café doesn't necessarily mean you're thirsty, but nonetheless you have to order something. (To simply quench your thirst, carry a bottle of mineral water with you during your sightseeing.) Your feet will thank you for each café stop, and there is no better way to drink up the atmosphere than simply hanging out at a marble-topped café table on a Paris sidewalk. So, what to order? The most obvious choice is coffee, and it's the cheapest too. Many Americans order *café au lait* at every chance. *Café* *au lait* is usually consumed by Parisians in the morning, but you can order one whenever you like. Parisian waiters are used to this. Ask for a café crème if you want to impress them with your expertise (don't worry, it'll be made with 2% milk, not cream). A simple coffee is called *un café* or *un express (espresso* is the Italian word.) This comes in a tiny cup, half-filled or less, with a nice layer of aromatic foam on the surface, a tiny spoon, and a sugar cube in the saucer. It is not unusual to ask for a glass of water with your coffee *(un verre d'eau, s'il vous plâit)* (ahn vair **doh**, see voo **play**). If you want a bigger shot of caffeine, ask for a *double express* (**doo bl**a ex**pres**), which is served in a larger cup and costs twice as much.

There are lots of lovely little variations and nuances on how to order coffee, a few of which we'll share with you. For those who like intensely strong coffee, ask for a *café serré* (cah**fay** sai**ray** [condensed coffee]), and you'll get the same dose of caffeine in about half as much water. For those of you who don't want a big, creamy *café au lait* but do like a bit of milk in your coffee, ask for a *noisette* (nwa-**zet**), literally meaning hazelnut, because a tiny splash of milk is dropped into your espresso forming a white shape like a hazelnut.

Hot chocolate is always an option as well, and since the quality of chocolate is excellent in France, you'll most likely be pleased. But most of the big cafés today have opted for the powdered chocolate instead of the real old-fashioned melted chocolate, so be forewarned. Parisians add sugar to their hot chocolate (since it is typically made with unsweetened cocoa).

If you're used to a huge mug of coffee à la Starbucks, you can ask for a *café long* (lohng) or a *café americaine* (cahfay amair-ree-**ken**), which will have more water and be substantially weaker. Hotel coffee will be brewed, but not café style, coming out of a steam-pressured espresso machine. Note that although France and its "French roast" have a good reputation for coffee, France is not a coffee-producing nation, and the quality of café coffee is not particularly excellent. (It's strong, though.) What is excellent is the atmosphere and culture in which you can sit with your coffee.

Lastly, there is virtually no such thing as "take-out" coffee, and hardly anyone will be drinking the stuff from elongated plastic or Styrofoam containers or transportable goblets with spill-proof covers. No one in Paris drinks coffee in the street, on the subway, all morning long at their desks, or in their cars. Don't even think of it. Just take a seat and let the time roll on.

Tea   Tea drinkers—or *thé* (tay) drinkers—should know that you cannot order just a cup of tea, but have to get a little pot of tea, which you can order with either lemon or milk. Don't be furious to learn that the wedge of lemon costs extra. Parisians are not too astute on the public relations aspect of delivering value to customers. No one complains about these sorts of things. However, you can ask the waiter to add more hot water to the pot to give yourself another cup, and this is free.

Beer A highly popular drink to order in a café is a draught beer *(biere* [**bee**-yair]*)*, popularly called a *demi,* indicating the size of the glass, a half-pint. When you ask for a beer, Parisian café waiters will often seize the opportunity to try to sell you one of the more expensive beers in bottles or on tap. If you just want the basic local beer, just ask for a *biere normal* (nor-**mahl**). The French beers are all brewed in the eastern region of Alsace, including Kronenbourg and its premium beer "1664." Dutch and Belgian beers are widely served as well. If you've never had a Belgian Leffe, treat yourself to a frothy *demi.* Be prepared to have a hard time going back to Bud or Miller Lite after you've consumed a few pints of the flavorful and hearty European suds.

Cafés also serve draft beer in a pint glass called a *formidable.* The price is also formidable.

Wine You can order wine *(vin* [**vaah**-n]*)* by the glass at all cafés. The simple standard fare is called a *ballon rouge* (bah-**lown rooj**) or *ballon blanc* (bah-**lown bloh**-n), after the bulbous round glass that the house red or white wine is served in. The bar wine is drinkable, but you'd do better asking for a *ballon* of Côte du Rhone or Beaujolais (red), or Sauvignon or Sancerre (white).

Bottles of wine and champagne are also available but usually overpriced in cafés. There are, of course, wine bars, which are another story. Read on.

Apéritifs In the late afternoon and early evening, cafés come alive with regulars having an *apéritif* (ahpera **teef**) before going home for dinner. Aside from a beer or glass of wine, one of the most popular drinks in France is *kir,* white wine with a dash of *crême de cassis* (blackcurrant liqueur), a delightful cocktail. Without a doubt you should order a *kir* or two while you're in Paris. An even more delightful spin-off is the *kir royale,* in which champagne is substituted for the white wine.

Champagne You can never go wrong with a glass of champagne as an apéritif, but be prepared to pay at least €8 for a flute of the bubbly stuff. Sparkling wine from outside the Champagne appellation is called *blanc de blanc* or *crémant.*

Whiskey and Mixed Drinks Parisians drink whiskey as a before-dinner drink, and the stigma of whiskey as reserved for heavy drinkers does not exist in France. In fact, whiskey, either the good Scottish stuff or the mythic American brands, is prestigious but expensive when consumed as a cocktail. True gourmets know, too, that drinking hard liquor before a meal is a sure way to deaden the taste buds.

In the summer, you'll want to sit outside in the shade somewhere, pretend you're somewhere along the Mediterranean, and order a *pastis*. As you add an ice cube and some water to your shot of clear amber licorice-tasting liqueur, the substance goes foggy and milky. Sip this refreshing libation and slide slowly into a stupor of relaxation.

After-dinner (or lunch) drinks are called *digestifs*. Here your choices are numerous. Try a cognac or armagnac. Late in the afternoon or in the evening, you may opt to nurse one of these while you relax in a café. To feel really part of the scene, why not order a calvados (apple liqueur from Normandy) with a coffee. In the colder months, this is the best way to warm yourself up from the inside.

Syrups and Soft Drinks Parisians drink a variety of drinks in which yummy syrups are added to either sparkling water or milk. It may seem silly standing at a bar and ordering a *lait fraise* (strawberry milk) or *lait grenadine* (pomegranate milk), but it is done. Orange juice is expensive and comes in tiny bottles, and thus tends to be a disappointment for tourists. Tomato juice comes with a salt shaker and celery powder.

Vittel *menthe* is an excellent choice for a hot day. You'll be served a small bottle of Vittel spring water and a glass with a dash of mint syrup. Be careful not to order the similar *menthe à l'eau,* which is served with mint liqueur and costs twice as much.

Very popular in the warm months is the *citron pressé,* simply a lemon squeezed into a glass, served with ice cubes, packets of sugar, and a *carafe* of water, all of which you mix in your glass according to your taste.

Young French clubbers who don't drink alcohol opt for a Coke, in French referred to as a *coca*. This will not come with ice unless you ask for it. Tourists often yearn for those refreshing liquid common-denominators, Coke and Pepsi, and they are readily available in all Parisian cafés and fast-food restaurants. Coke, still basking in its reputation as a foreign status symbol, continues to be disproportionately expensive, so be prepared to pay a lot more for a Coke than for a glass of beer or wine. Tourists often make this mistake and order a Coke thinking it'll be the most common and cheapest drink on the menu. Wrong. Also, never order a Coke in a restaurant with your meal. Parisians cannot understand how Americans can drink something that has nine spoonfuls of sugar in it with a well-prepared dinner. They have a point. Diet Coke is called Coke Lite and Diet Pepsi is called Maxi Pepsi. Since we're talking about calories, to be on the safe side, bring your own artificial sweetener.

Ice Cubes Although this is changing somewhat, ice cubes *(glaçons* [glah-sown]*)* are generally not provided or easy to find unless you ask for them specifically. Parisian waiters know that Americans have a fixation on ice, so they'll be accommodating but they will probably roll their eyes too. Generally, Parisians do not require their drinks to be excessively cold or hot, believing that, aside from it being unhealthy to drink freezing cold drinks before going back out into the heat, the flavor and taste of drinks are truer when served at room temperature. Don't confuse the words *glaçons* and *glace,* the latter meaning ice cream.

Eating in Cafés

When you find yourself hungry between official French mealtimes—before noon (too early for lunch), after 2 p.m. (too late for lunch), before 7:30 p.m. (too early for dinner), or after 10 p.m. (too late for dinner), the café will be your savior. Additionally, you may not wish to take two hours to eat, spend a lot, or be obliged to consume a large amount of heavy food before strolling around the Louvre. Again, the café is your answer. You may (we stress the conditional) eat well in a café, but then again you may not. You may be wholly satisfied, but in Parisian culinary terms, this has not been a proper French meal. You may not care. And that's fine, as long as you know the difference between having something acceptable to eat in a café and having a real meal, *un repas* (uh ruh**pah**), in a Parisian restaurant. We hear a fair number of tourists claiming to have had a delicious meal in a particular café, and without sounding too pretentious, we must correct this notion. You may have had a nice salad or a tasty *plat du jour* (daily special), but you didn't dine.

At any time of day or evening you can order a *sandwich* (sahnd-**weech**), a *croque monsieur* (**crowk**-miss-**ure** [grilled cheese with ham on toast]), or often a salad. Caution: cafés also serve a lunch meal. You'll notice that tables that are set with placemats are for people who are eating. If you are stopping in for a coffee or a drink, you cannot sit at one of these spots. If you are just having a quick *sandwich* or *croque monsieur,* these spots are not for you either. A sandwich eater in Paris is not considered to be someone who is eating. You must sit at one of the "unset" café tables. Hey, don't knock it; join in.

Sandwiches and Other Light Choices   The choice of café sandwiches is almost always identical from café to café. You can choose ham *(jambon* [dzahm-**bown**]*)*, cheese *(fromage* [frohh-**maj**]*)*, *paté* (pah-**tay**), hard sausage *(saucisson sec* [saw-see-**sown** sec]*)*, or *rillettes* (ree-**yet**), a high-fat, tasty, pork spread served on a long *baguette* (bag-**get**). One tourist complained that when he asked for a piece of lettuce on his ham sandwich he was charged extra. This was not a case of lettuce extortion; the café owner just called this simple variation from the norm a *sandwich fantasie,* and the price was adjusted accordingly. Note that it's not common to make special requests, and the guy behind the counter is not going to be very accommodating. When in doubt, we recommend the *sandwich jambon avec cornichorns* ([corn-ee-**shown**], ham sandwich with vinegar pickles) And spread your *baguette* with dabs of Dijon mustard—delicious! Mustard, by the way, makes for an excellent, original, inexpensive gift.

A very Parisian sandwich is the *croque monsieur,* or its variation, *croque madame.* Simply, this is a ham sandwich topped with a slice of *gruyère* (a Swiss cheese, Emmenthal), grilled in the broiler, and eaten with a knife and fork—the *croque madame* is the same with a sunny-side-up egg sitting on top. For about €5 you may enjoy this simplest item of Paris café cuisine. Other options include a slice of quiche or one of the many variations of *tarte* (savory pie), such as the *tarte de l'oignon* (onion) or *tarte au poireau* (leek). The classic quiche lorraine is made with cheese and *lardons* (chunks of smoked bacon, sometimes fatty and studded with crunchy cartilege; Parisians just chew and swallow).

Café restaurants almost always offer a few salads too. Salads have caught on over the last ten years as more and more Parisians want to eat lighter meals at lunch. Two standard salads to choose from are the *salade Niçoise,* which is a combination of lettuce, tomato, tuna, egg, green beans, black olives, and often rice or corn, served with a vinaigrette dressing. The other is the *salade de crotin de chevre chaud,* which is a bed of lettuce on which two disks of warmed goat cheese sit—a simple delicacy. A salad, a glass of wine, a hunk of *baguette,* maybe a slice of *tarte au citron* (lemon-meringue pie), and *un express café* and *voila,* you've had a lovely and very Parisian lunch. Formerly, this would have constituted a bare-bones minimum lunch for a Parisian. A meal that is not hot is not a meal. But habits are changing. You'll start to understand this the more meals you eat in Paris.

Cafés with restaurant sections, sometimes referred to as *cafés-brasseries,* will also offer a *plat de jour* (a daily special), which may be a meat or fish dish and may be ordered without an appetizer or dessert.

Tickets Restaurants

If you see Parisians paying for lunch with little coupons, note that many companies offer this widely accepted form of payment to their employees who pay half the value—usually four or five euros.

Restaurants, Haute Cuisine, and La Gastronomie

There is no shortage of food in Paris nor fine places to wine and dine, and dining will certainly be included in your top-priority list of essential things to do along with sightseeing, museum-visiting, and shopping. If you count each day in Paris as an opportunity for essentially two great meals, you can decide on how many of those opportunities you want to turn into memorable culinary occasions. You may decide that one serious restaurant a day is plenty, and you may want to alternate visits between lunch and dinner. If you wish to try one or more of the starred, highly celebrated, and stunningly expensive restaurants, you may opt for the more reasonable lunch experience to compensate. In any case, your culinary exploits need to be somewhat planned and quantified. What is particularly fun is to mix your eating schedule with fun and informal restaurants, a few classic *brasseries,* a serious *haute cuisine* haunt or two, a stop at some interesting regional or ethnic places, combined with a stint of Parisian street-food slumming and open-air market shopping, and, weather permitting, a picnic or two in the Luxembourg Gardens or along the Seine.

We have attempted to select restaurants that offer a truly Parisian experience, where the menu is interesting and varied, the service is attentive and elegant, the décor and style reinforces the fare, and the quality-price ratio assures you great value and a memorable moment, whether it's a magical evening at one-star landmark **Jacques Cagna** or a cheap but savory lunch at the raucous proletarian eatery **Chartier.**

Paris restaurants vary in style and form, and to our way of thinking the only thing that matters is that your experiences are truly Parisian and you have a good time. The rest is merely pretense. Fortunately, there is one overriding rule in France when it comes to food: anything you do that increases your pleasure and enjoyment at the table is permissible and encouraged. We love repeating this. Anything you do that increases your pleasure and enjoyment at the table is permissable and encouraged.

Brasseries and Bistros

What's the difference? Don't be bashful; everyone asks. Today, the two types of restaurant have gotten confused and the terms are used incorrectly.

Most cafés that serve lunch have the word *brasserie* printed on their outside awning. But for history buffs brasseries were originally the late-night eating halls owned and operated by the beer makers of Alsace. The verb *brasser* in this sense means to brew. And, thus, brasseries have always been loud open spaces for informal eating and consumption of numerous kinds of brewed beer. Today they have become more like regular restaurants, but still have an eastern French flavor, are open late, and often serve *choucroute,* the regional sauerkraut dish, and other Alsatian dishes. Many were conceived in the brasserie style but postdate the era of true brasseries themselves. Some brasseries are among Paris's most celebrated and popular restaurants today, like **Bofinger, La Coupole, Chez Jenny, Brasserie Balzar, Brasserie Flo,** and **Brasserie Lipp.** Plan to eat in one. Nonsmokers should note that today you have a good chance of finding a nonsmoking table in one of these. Ask when you reserve.

The word *bistro* has been grossly corrupted over time. Although you'll read that *bistro* is a Russian word meaning hurry-up, which hungry soldiers occupying Paris screamed in Paris cafés, this is an old and tired-out story. Traditionally, a bistro was simply a modest and simple restaurant, often a small family-run restaurant with an intimate cluster of tables and good, hearty French cuisine and good but common wines. The menu was scribbled on a chalkboard because the fare changed every day. Today a bistro is often just a café in which simple dishes are also served. Due to the great charm and simplicity of this old style of establishment, restaurateurs have usurped the name for their eateries and chains. Bistro Romain is as much a bistro as Kentucky Fried Chicken is a quaint country diner. True bistros do still exist and we recommend them for their atmosphere.

Oyster Bars   At bistros and brasseries, you'll often see an impressive wet bar outside of the restaurant on the sidewalk, adorned with huge platters of crushed ice and seaweed, on which raw oysters, clams, *langôustines,* and other unidentifiable shellfish *(fruits de mer* [fwee duh **mair**]*)* are being shucked and placed by hearty men in rubber aprons. There is a lot of ritual and pageantry in ordering and eating a platter like this, and if you are a shellfish fanatic it is worth doing this once during your Paris stay. Look under the restaurant listings for *fruits de mer.*

You'll never understand all the sizes, grades, and types of oysters offered on the menu, but here are a few simple pointers.

The *creuses* are the fatter ones in the deeper, rougher shells; the *plates* are the leaner ones in the flatter, smoother shells. The pens or beds in the oyster *parcs* in which the shellfish are raised are called *claires.* In restaurants, the *creuses* and *plates* are offered on the menu in several sizes: *creuses*: *huîtres de parc* (the smallest), *fines de claires* (medium), *spéciales* (the largest); *plates*: *Belon* (small and elegant) and *Marennes* (greenish color).

When in doubt, go for six or twelve *fines de claires* for starters. White wine is a must.

Crêperies

Although France is famous for its *crêpes,* the celebrated pancake eaten both with sweet toppings and savory ones (called *galettes*) actually originates in the Brittany region. In the area around the Montparnasse train station, a community of Bretons settled long ago, and today the neighborhood is teeming with scores of *crêperies,* restaurants that specialize in *crêpes. Crêpe* enthusiast Sophie Alvacet advises visitors that although many of these eateries are just average, the **Crêperie Le Petit Josselin** on the crêpe-studded rue du Montparnasse is "divine." The lines are long on the weekends, but you can peruse the menu in English as you wait.

Crêpes per se are made with *froment* (wheat) flour and are garnished with chocolate, jam, chestnut spread, powdered sugar, nuts, and other sweet things. The *galette* is a *crêpe* in which the batter is made with *sarrazin* (buckwheat) flour and salted butter. The dark pancake is then garnished with ham, mushrooms, cheese, eggs, and a variety of other savory toppings. Don't forget that *crêpes* are washed down with bowls of Normandy *cidre*, which is more like apple wine than apple cider. Another excellent *crêperie* not in the Montparnasse Breton ghetto is **Les Étoiles.**

Le Petit Josselin   59, rue du Montparnasse, 75014; Tel. 01 43 22 91 81; Métro: Montparnasse

Les Étoiles   13, rue Princesse, 75006; Tel. 01 43 25 78 51; Métro: Mabillon or St-Germain-des-Prés

Salons de Thé

All over Paris you'll find small, informal tea rooms offering sandwiches, warm slices of savory pies, salads, and flavorful pieces of cake and *tartes aux fruits*, and, of course, a selection of teas and coffees. These are perfect places for lighter lunches and snacks. The tartes and cakes are usually displayed, so if a wedge of salmon and spinach tarte or a plate of watercress salad with fresh beets catches your eye, go for it. There are scores of delightful *salons de thé* in Paris, too numerous to note here, but we've listed two highly recommended establishments to visit if you happen to be exploring their neighborhood.

Angelina   226, rue de Rivoli, 75001; Tel. 01 42 60 82 00; Métro: Tuileries. The atmosphere is a bit old-fashioned, but this is an address not to miss. Famous for its soupy-rich hot chocolate. You can bring a sack of the dark powder home with you.

Ladurée   16, rue Royale, 75008; Tel. 01 42 60 21 79; Métro: Madeleine. A busy spot between the Place de la Concorde and the Madeleine, perfect for a coffee, tea, and *gâteau* (cake) break.

The Baguette and Boulangerie

The staple of the French table is the nightly *baguette,* regulated in weight and price by law. Each *boulangerie* (bread shop) bakes *baguettes* at least four times a day, with the first bread coming out early in the morning and the last late in the afternoon. Currently, a 250-gram *baguette* costs about €0.60. You'll notice that regular customers are accustomed to asking for the bread stick either crusty *(bien cuit)* or softer and lighter *(pas trop cuit),* and some ask for it cut in half *(coupé en deux).* A heavier *baguette* (400 grams) is called a *pain.* And a skinny *baguette,* weighing half the grams, is called a *ficelle.*

Don't be alarmed that bread is handled with bare hands and is rarely bagged, often just wrapped slightly in a twisted piece of paper and carried under the arm and in the Métro. No one has ever gotten sick from a contaminated *baguette*. The real, old-fashioned *baguette* (not really old fashioned since *baguettes* only came into fashion in the 1920s; the 18th-century French bread whose shortage provoked Marie Antoinette to foolishly proclaim "Let them eat cake!" was flat and loaflike) has been challenged by the industrially-kneaded bread stick that looks like a *baguette*, is called a *baguette,* but according to true bread-eaters, tastes nothing like the real thing. So, avoid supermarket bread and only buy your *baguettes* from your local boulangerie. With health consciousness on the rise in France, you'll now find numerous other "bio" choices—multigrain, muesli, and other breads.

Croissants

Good *croissants* (kwas-**sahn**) are great, and you'll undoubtedly munch quite a few of these quintessentially French flaky delights during your Paris stay. But you may be wondering what the difference is between the *croissants* whose ends point straight out and those whose points are turned in? Well, the straight ones are called *croissants au beurre* and are made with pure butter. They are richer and cost about €0.10 more. The crescent-shaped ones *(croissants ordinaires)* are made with margarine and offer a few less calories.

Just for the fun of it, you might be interested to know that it was a French pastry chef who created the first *croissant* for the rulers of the Ottoman Empire, shaping the light puff pastry after the crescent star of the Turkish flag. *Croissants* are eaten almost exclusively in the morning, so if you crave one in the late afternoon, you'll look a little odd and the offerings won't be as fresh as the morning's choices. *Pain au chocolat,* however, is the traditional choice for snacks for kids of all ages on their way home from school. For sweet delights to choose for all your afternoon sugar binges, see Part Eight, Shopping in Paris.

Fast Food and French Chains

You can't help but noticing that *McDo,* as the Parisians call McDonald's, is everywhere, from the Champs-Elysées to the Latin Quarter. The lines can be long and the prices are relatively steep. Even if you're tempted, stay away. There is no reason to eat here unless you are desperately homesick and need a Big Mac fix to reestablish your mental balance, in which case, we'll consider this digression to be of medicinal value and forgive you, grudgingly.

France has its own fast-food chains. They're interesting to observe, and you may even like them, but they are hard to recommend. The *McDo* knock-off is a Belgian-owend chain called Quick. Trust us, this can be missed. A few family-style restaurant chains obviously cannot compare with real cuisine, but they can come in handy when you're limited in time or are traveling as a family. There is more space, the setting is casual, the menus are well conceived and inexpensive, and the portions are generous. Here are a few other fast-food–type places that we recommend for the kids:

Bistro Romain   Known for its all-you-can-eat plates of *carpaccio* (thin slices of raw beef or salmon), french fries, or green beans and chocolate mousse, in a tacky ancient Roman décor. The kids will like it.

Léon de Bruxelles   The specialty is mussels and french fries; can be a lot of fun for those who don't get to eat massive bowls of fresh mussels all the time. Inexpensive.

Hippopotamus   Essentially a steakhouse chain; popular with younger French couples and singles. It's fine if you know you just want a piece of meat, some fries, and a beer. Each meal counts when you're on a trip, so if necessary, digress wisely.

Street Food

Each city has its own street-dining specialties, and it's amazing how a €4 detour can end up being the highlight of a trip. In the past, Parisians rarely ate while walking, but since the pace of working life in Paris has intensified in recent years, you'll now see Parisians wolfing sandwiches while strutting to the Métro. You still won't see waves of white-collar workers lined up on a wall or around a fountain outside their office buildings eating salads out of plastic take-out containers with plastic forks as you do in American cities.

Suggested Paris Street Food and Where to Find It

Crêpes You'll find *crêpe* stands in most busy areas of town, usually attached to cafés. You'll also find dozens of *crêpes* restaurants (*crêperies*) throughout the city, with a high concentration around the rue de Montparnasse (Métro Montparnasse-Bienvenüe), noted for its large Breton community.

Falafel Rue des Rosiers

Sandwich grec (gyro) Latin Quarter

Ice cream Bertillon on the Île Saint Louis. There's plenty of Häagen-Dazs and even Ben & Jerry's, but you didn't come to Paris for ice cream you could eat at home, did you?

A Gourmand's Paradise

Fauchon is simply the most famous gourmet shop in Paris. Founded in 1896, this icon of catered extravagance with products ranging from Iranian caviar to hand-picked choice lychees from Madagascar, thinly sliced *saumon fumé,* sugar work that approaches the aesthetics of fine jewelry, and much, much more, should be treated more like a gallery than a grocery store. Never walk in hungry, or you'll walk out broke, although you should try a pastry in the Fauchon café next door. In the last few years Fauchon has developed its own brand of almost everything, which it sells in its decked-out subterranean store and cafeteria. The quality is high, but the prices top everything. Across the Place Madeleine you'll find another great Parisian culinary institution, **Hediard.** Visit both.

Fauchon   26, place de la Madeleine, 75002; Tel. 01 47 42 60 11; Métro: Madeleine.

Hediard   21, place de la Madeleine, 75008; Tel: 0143 12 88 88; Metro: Madeleine.

Classic French Dishes to Try

- *andouillettes*—chitterling sausages. The A.A.A.A.A. is a marking on the menu to indicate that this sausage has been found to be of supreme quality by the Chitterling Sausage Association.

- *blanquette de veau*—pieces of veal stewed in an egg-and-cream sauce

- *cassoulet*—white bean casserole with duck, sausage, pork, or goose

- *choucroute*—Alsacian sauerkraut dish with sausage, pork, ham, and potatoes

- *coq au vin*—rooster stewed in red wine

- *lapin chasseur*—wild rabbit, often cooked with mushrooms

- *couscous*—North African dish of steamed semolina, broth, chick peas, carrots, and assorted vegetables served with grilled lamb, beef, chicken, or merguez sausage

- *magret de canard*—sliced breast of fattened duck

- *moules marinière*—mussels cooked in white wine, onions, shallots, and herbs

- *pot au feu*—boiled beef served with carrots, leeks, and turnips

- *poulet basquaise*—chicken cooked with tomatoes and sweet peppers

Ethnic Food

If you have time, you should diversify your eating experiences by going ethnic. Paris is a cosmopolitan city and a former colonial capital with large communities of immigrants from North Africa/Maghreb (Morocco, Algeria, and Tunisia), southeast Asia (Vietnam, Cambodia, and Laos), sub-Saharan West Africa (Mali, Cameroon, Senegal, Ivory Coast, Congo, and Benin), Indian Ocean (Reunion Islands, Mauritius, and Camores), and the French West Indies (Martinique and Guadeloupe). Additionally, there are many immigrants from China and Hong Kong, Turkey, Greece, Portugal, Italy, Eastern Europe, and Latin America. Lastly, there are about 100,000 permanent Anglo-American residents in Paris. All these people contribute widely to the culinary offerings of the city. In fact, you can have some of the best African and Vietnamese food in the world in Paris.

Couscous: North African Cuisine

One of Paris's greatest resources is its cultural diversity, complete with a wide range of culinary delights. Within this fabulous pastiche that makes Paris "more than French," you'll find a vibrant North African presence.

Moroccan cuisine is some of the world's finest, most flavorful, and colorful, and many of the best restaurants for *tagines* and *couscous* are right in the French capital. If you've never had *couscous,* you haven't lived fully! This typical dish, ubiquitous across the Maghreb, is a feast of steamed semolina, a rich vegetable stew with carrots, turnips, and chick peas, an assortment of grilled lamb, chicken, and spicy red sausage (veal and lamb) called *merguez.* *Tagines* are actually earthenware crocks in which broiled meat, fish, fowl and vegetables, fruit, nuts, and spices are baked and are served simmering. Meals are followed by delicious mint tea and pine nuts served in painted glasses. *Couscous* can be found in almost every Parisian neighborhood and at all prices. Here are three excellent suggestions for elegant North African dining:

Le Souk   1, rue Keller, 75011; Tel. 01 49 29 05 08; Métro: Bastille. Reservations recommended.

Mansouria   11, rue Faidherbe, 75011; Tel. 01 43 71 00 16; Métro: Bastille. Run by a noted Moroccan anthropologist, Mansouria offers elegant dining amid attractive traditional Moroccan décor. Under $35 per person; reservations recommended.

Ziryab   1, rue des Fossés St. Bernard, 75005; Tel. 01 53 10 10 16; Métro: Sully Morland. Around $40 per person; reservations recommended. Located at the top of the L'Institut de Monde Arabe, with a fabulous view overlooking the Seine.

What to Avoid: Pizza and Chinese

Unless it comes highly recommended, be wary of the glut of Italian-looking pizza restaurants and mixed Asiatic "Chinese" restaurants. Every day, Parisians eat tons of unsliced, individual-sized pizza (with a knife and fork), and Cantonese rice. There are a number of good Italian and Chinese restaurants, but there are even more mediocre ones, and Parisians don't know the luxury of top-quality cheap pizza and Chinese food. You didn't come to Paris to order Pizza Hut or Domino's (both are here). However, for a word on great Vietnamese food in Paris, see "Ethnic Food" above. For a better Chinese experience, take the Métro to Place d'Italie and walk down to the Porte d'Ivry. You're in Paris's Chinatown. You'll find a second, smaller Chinatown at Métro Belleville, where Asian restaurants are mixed in the North African Arab fare.

Vegetarian Paris

Parisians eat not only lots of meat, but a stunning variety of animals ranging from guinea hen *(pintade)* to wild baby boar *(marcassin)*. It's not all that easy to get away from meat. The good news for vegetarians is that Parisians also eat an amazing range of fresh vegetables and fruits. And the breads are excellent, the wine is impeccable, the pastries are sinfully good, the selection of fresh fish is wonderful, and the dairy products are diverse and tasty. There are 450 kinds of cheese in France. The open-air markets are ubiquitous. And there is a small number of very good vegetarian restaurants in the city. So it's not all that difficult to survive in Paris as a vegetarian. Here are a few veggie establishments.

Aquarius 54, rue de Ste-Croix-de-la-Bretonnerie, 75004; Tel. 01 48 87 48 71; Métro: Hôtel-de-Ville. Fixed menus: lunch, €11; dinner €15. Hours: Monday–Thursday, noon–10 p.m., Friday and Saturday, noon–10:30 p.m.

Entre Ciel et Terre 5, rue Hérold, 75001; Tel. 01 45 08 49 84; Métro: Sentier. Fixed menus: lunch, €13; dinner, €21. Hours: Monday–Friday, noon–3 p.m., 7:30–10 p.m. Closed in August.

La Victoire Suprême du Coeur 41, rue du Bourdonnais, 75001; Tel. 01 40 41 93 95; Métro: Châtelet–Les Halles. Fixed menus: dinner, €14; lunch, €9 (Monday–Friday), higher on weekends. Hours: Monday–Thursday, noon–2.30 p.m., 6:30–10 p.m.; Friday and Saturday, noon–2:30 p.m., 6:30–10:30 p.m. Closed two weeks in August.

Le Grenier de Notre-Dame 18, rue de la Bûcherie, 75005; Tel. 01 43 29 98 29; Métro: St-Michel. Fixed menus: €11, €21, €17. Hours: Summer daily, noon–2:30 p.m., 7:30–11:30 p.m. Winter daily, noon–2:30 p.m., 7:30–10:30 p.m.

Le Jardin des Pâtes 4, rue Lacépède, 75005; Tel. 01 43 31 50 71; Métro: Jussieu. Hours: Tuesday–Sunday, noon–2:30 p.m., 7–11 p.m.

A Word on la Viande (Meat)

The mad cow crisis followed by the foot and mouth scare helped elevate the general consciousness of meat supply and the food chain. Although red meat consumption fell off somewhat, most people are not overly worried about potential contamination. If anything, standards—already high in France—have increased. The French charolais beef will delight meat eaters.

Understanding French Restaurants

Be prepared:

- to find menus only in French. Some restaurants will have translated menus. Some dishes don't translate too well and sound far more delicious in French. It's better having the waiter strain to explain the French menu than have an English one laid out for you. Avoid all restaurants with multi-language menus depicted by little country flags.

- to spend more time at the table than you expected. Don't rush. And in any case, you'll have a hard time speeding up the service. Never leave yourself less than an hour to eat, and try to block off at least two hours for any sit-down meal. Don't be surprised to spend at least three hours when dining in a particularly fine establishment.

- to budget more money on food in France than you would for travels elsewhere, although on the whole you should find the price-quality ratio to be excellent. Hotels may be comparatively inexpensive (if you come from a large city like New York or Los Angeles), but eating well will be proportionally more expensive. The French understand the value of culinary arts, choice ingredients, and the time and imagination needed to create wonderfully tasty dishes and artful presentations, and they're ready to pay for this.

- to have less space than you might be accustomed to. Parisian restaurants are often crowded, with tables pushed up close to each other. This doesn't seem to bother the Parisians, but it may feel too close for comfort to you. And the waiters will not be very accommodating when you ask to move to a table set for four when there are only two of you. This will be true even when the dining room is empty. Two people don't get to sit at tables meant for four—that's just how it is in Paris.

- to defend yourself if you're a nonsmoker. Many, many restaurants have a hard time blocking out a nonsmoking section, especially when they are busy. If smoke is a major problem for you, be very clear when you reserve, or select a restaurant that has made a serious effort to accommodate Paris's nonsmoking minority.

- to be served water only when you ask for a *carafe d'eau* (cahrraf-**doh**). No one will be regularly topping up your water glass with a pitcher of ice water as is common in restaurants back home. And forget the ice in any case. You may order bottled water *(eau minerale* [oh min-air-**rahl**]), either sparkling *(eau gazeuse* or *pétillante* [oh gazooz or pey-tee **yahnt**]) or nonsparkling *(eau plat* [oh **plaht**]). Note that in many restaurants, other than the fancy, starred establishments, you will not have a water glass unless you ask for one, since Parisians typically use the same glass for their water and wine, alternating between the two.

- to wait forever for the check *(l'addition, s'il vous plâit* [ladisi **youn**, see voo **play**]). The waiter will only bring you the check when you ask for it. This is a matter of local politeness. You should not be rushed. You can take quite some time after you've finished your meal before you actually leave. You may order a second coffee or a *digestif* or two, while you relax, digest, talk, or smoke. Of course, in smaller restaurants, if you see another party waiting to be seated, it's polite to not overdo your lingering.

- to peruse the menu outside before deciding to go in. French law requires all eating establishments to post their menu and prices prominently outside. This gives you the chance to review the offerings and prices before committing yourself. It is very rare to see people get up and leave a restaurant once they've been seated. Try to avoid changing your mind once inside. On the other hand, if the place's atmosphere doesn't please you or the table you've been offered doesn't cut the mustard, you should feel perfectly comfortable to politely leave right away.

Tip: If you'd love to try a really expensive restaurant, consider going for lunch instead of dinner. The prices will often be considerably lower.

Message from French Restaurant Owners to American Visitors

We love your casualness, but please don't wear shorts to our restaurants. And leave rollerblades in your hotel.

Sorry that we can't feed you as early as you'd like. Some of you want dinner before we've even cleaned up from lunch!

We know there is a law in France obliging us to have nonsmoking sections, and please understand that we'll try to find a solution to *your* problem, but there are no guarantees. Nonsmokers are still very much a minority here.

We know you love *escargot,* but if you don't like kidneys or brains, please don't order *les rognons* or *cervelle!*

A Note for Nonsmokers

As we've warned nonsmokers *(les non-fumeurs* [lay **nohn-foo**-mer])in other sections in this guide, smokers reign in France, and it'll be hard doing everything you want in Paris and successfully avoiding the smoke. More and more Parisian restaurants are making an effort to accommodate nonsmokers, although the battle is still far from being won.

If Smoke Bothers You

- Try to eat either early or late in order to get a smoke-free table.
- Definitely request a table in the nonsmoking section *(zone non-fumeur)* when you reserve.
- Be willing to eat outside or on a terrace when the weather permits.
- Avoid very small restaurants where the tables are particularly crowded.
- Select restaurants from our profiles (later in this chapter) that indicate a non-smoking sensitivity.

The Paris website www.paris-anglo.com is preparing a list of smoke-free restaurants in Paris, scheduled for early 2002. Request your copy from david@paris-anglo.com.

Manners

The service you receive in a restaurant depends greatly on the way you act. In some cases, service that you would classify as poor is the result of a waiter's repeated experiences with culturally insensitive visitors. You might not understand why you can't have something prepared "your way," and they don't understand why so many Americans expect customized preparations for dishes. These are conflicting conceptions of "service." Requests that are common or every-day in the United States, like "Can I have the dressing on the side?" "Is the salmon cooked in oil or butter?" "Is it fried or broiled?" "Can I have the beef without the sauce?" or "Bring us our Cokes with the dinner," are strange and annoying to Parisian waiters. And then their disposition annoys you, which further annoys them. Try to nip these silly types of cultural misunderstandings in the bud.

How to Settle a Dispute

It doesn't happen often, but like anywhere, it can happen. If you have a problem with your food or wine, signal to the waiter or manager *(le responsable* [le rayspown**sahbl**]*)* right away. Be extremely polite and calm and explain that your steak is very tough or that your soup is cold. The situation is more unfortunate when you misunderstood what you were ordering and you are very unhappy with what is now staring up at you from your plate. *Steack tartare* is meat served raw, spiced, and cold. So is *carpaccio. Ris de veau* is sweetbreads and *cervelle* is brains.

It's better not to err from the start and only order dishes you're quite confident you'll enjoy, but if you do, the rule is simply to not eat what's on your plate. You'll have a very hard time getting any satisfaction if you eat half of it and then complain. The Parisian mindset is very different from the American one. You may be used to a "sorry that you don't like your dinner, Ma'am, would you like to choose something else?" response, but you won't find that here. We have known cases of managers taking a bite out of your steak to determine whether it's tough or not, and then defending the perfectly acceptable condition of your *entrecôte* (the French appreciate their meat a bit chewy). If you refuse a wine, again, you had better be right. Again, the best solution is simply to not consume the food or drink in question. If you don't eat it, you'll have a better chance of not being asked to pay for it. On the other hand, if in fact there is a problem with your dish—if it's cold, burned, tastes bad, is smothered in cheese when you asked for no cheese, or similar problems—in most cases it will be taken away and replaced or fixed. Don't get mad. Don't threaten. And don't break anything, even if you're dying to. Parisians respond poorly to aggression and your evening will be ruined. Calmly and politely refuse what you've been served. If the dish in question appears on your bill, calmly and politely state that it is not customary to pay for something you didn't eat. Don't be rude, but don't be bullied either. In the worst-case scenario if you are obliged to pay for a dinner that you consider to be a total rip-off (which would be highly unusual in Paris), use your credit card and contest the bill when you get home. VISA, MasterCard, American Express, and Diners Club do not want dishonest establishments to use their services.

Be careful to note the pricing on dishes that are marked on the menu "for two" *(pour deux* [pour **duh**]*)* or "for each person" *(par personne* [par pair-sun]*)*—is the price per person, or for the whole dish? Make sure that you understand and agree that the price indicated is either for each person or for the two people *before* you order it.

The Restaurant Ratings: Stars, Forks, Toques, and More

Even Parisians don't always understand the system of awarding stars and *toques* to restaurants, and we venture to guess that most, if not all, of your excellent eating experiences in Paris will be at unstarred or *untoqued* establishments. Unlike hotels, which are awarded stars according to nationally regulated standards, restaurant stars are privately awarded by the *Michelin Guide* judges, who set the bar for the culinary world until Monsieur Gault and Monsieur Millau started assigning French chefs hats (instead of stars) to the best and the brightest. The pluralistic Zagat approach to rating restaurants arrived in Paris only in 1998, and a score of other critics have applied their own numbers, letters, hats, and forks to the establishments of the world's top culinary capital. It's still largely the stars, though, that continue to maintain the highest level of international prestige.

When Michelin gives two or three stars, a restaurant has been canonized (though with one false slip of the knife a restaurant can find itself demoted and shamed). A three-starred chef like Michel Bras, who was awarded a third star for his mountaintop restaurant in Auvergne, compares his cooking to jazz "for its architecture, its fluid elegance, its silences." In other words, don't go to a three-star if you want standard, good French fare like *canard à l'orange* or *steack au poivre.* Be prepared for *gargouillou de jeunes légumes,* literally meaning a "bubbling of young vegetables." And, for the first time in history, Michelin has even awarded a Chinese restaurant three stars—and it's in Paris. Michelin's three stars indicate "exceptional cuisine worth a special journey." There are seven three-stars in Paris and only 21 in the whole of France. Michelin's two stars indicate "excellent cooking, worth a detour," and there are 22 two-stars in Paris. Michelin's one star indicates "a very good restaurant in its category"—there are 52 one-stars in Paris.

Michelin now awards a Michelin-Man-head called the "Bib Gourmand" indicating "good meals at moderate prices" (€20–27 menus), of which there are 39 in Paris. Additionally, Michelin awards forks (1–5) indicating the level of luxury and comfort the establishment offers. The more forks the more luxurious, and thus the more expensive. The key to finding the best price-to-quality ratio in gourmet restaurants is to select restaurants with the most stars and the least forks!

The Two- and Three-Star Experience

This needs some explaining. Dining in a two- or three-star establishment is a serious and formal experience. The atmosphere may feel very formal, and the service may be overly attentive for your comfort. There are theatricality and staging, manners, codes, and gestures that are combined with a refinement and cultivation of ingredients, tastes, and aesthetic presentation, all crafted to create a total effect. This may be precisely one of your main motivations for coming to Paris. Or it may feel intimidating and uncomfortable. The price, in any case, will be memorable, and only you can decide what represents good value. Reservations are always required. The website www.bestreservations.com offers a free online reservation service for the restaurants it features, many of which are starred. In Paris, the service can be accessed Monday through Saturday (except in August) from 9 a.m. to 9 p.m. by calling Tel. 01 42 25 10 10. To call from outside of France, dial Tel. 33 1 42 25 10 10.

Unstarred Restaurants

All the restaurants in Paris stocked with ambitious owners and chefs aspire for stars, but hundreds of fabulous restaurants go unstarred or *untoqued* for decades for numerous reasons, often related to décor or service, politics, or the personal ambitions of its owners. Lots of restaurants never even aim for the big league, where the stress to remain brilliant is intense, and instead live happily serving wonderful dishes night after night to a loyal clientele of locals and their friends. We've attempted to direct you to tables that you will enjoy, period. The degree of innovation needed to be starred often produces dishes that go way beyond the enjoyment level of relative debutantes in French *haute cuisine*, whereas well-executed traditional French dishes, deemed far too ordinary and mundane for the star-keepers, are likely to be highly pleasurable to you much of the time. Everyone enjoys visiting an avant-garde art exhibition once in a while, but at the end of the day, there's nothing like the Louvre! The highest level of gourmet dining applies criteria to a meal that some of you may value, but in our experience, we have observed that what most of us want from a restaurant is a lovely evening and delicious food presented with style and grace in a pleasant and friendly setting. That's what we've kept in mind when selecting restaurants to profile. For the meccas of culinary stardom, see "Crème de la Crème" below.

The Menu vs. la Carte

Even if you don't speak a word of French, you certainly know the term *à la carte,* meaning that you order freely from the menu. In Paris, no one will understand what you mean if you use this in its English context. The word for the menu in French is *la carte*. To ask for the menu, say *"Excusez-moi, est-ce que je peux voir la carte, s'il vous plaît"* (ex**cusay** m**wa**, **es**ka dze puh v**ware** lah **cart**, see voo **play**). It is easy to get confused between the English word for menu *(la carte)* and the French meaning of *le menu* (suggested fixed menu), which is the opposite of your understanding of *à la carte*. There will usually be several *menus* offered at different prices. The more expensive the *menu*, the more choices and the more complex or finer the selections it will include. A typical *menu* will have an appetizer *(entrée)*, main dish *(plat principal)*, and dessert *(dessert)*. Depending on how the *menu* is composed, wine or bottled water may or may not be included. A *menu* in fancier and finer restaurants may include an additional course, and a *menu dégustation,* which will be the top of the line, allows you to sample the best of the entire *carte.*

Many Parisian restaurants understand that not everyone wants a long, expensive, and filling meal, especially at lunch, and thus have played with marketable variations on the theme. Now, you can find *menus* that let you select either an appetizer and a main dish or just a main dish and a dessert.

Coffee is seldom included in the *menu* price, but tax and service are.

Often, restaurants will have a *menu* that is only applicable at lunchtime or during the week. It can be frustrating to read a *menu* that seems perfect, only to be told that you can't order this now.

On the whole, a *menu* often offers a good deal and a decent choice of what's best at the restaurant. You may be bothered to see a sign out front advertising the Tourist Menu at say, €12. Tourists, especially North Americans, translate this as an invitation to be gouged and think that the word *tourist* should be avoided at all costs. Although we agree that restaurants offering "tourist menus" are probably not the most charming and authentic, a tourist *menu* doesn't necessarily mean worse quality or an exploitative price. The French don't necessarily use "tourist" as a pejorative term.

When you decide which *menu* you want, you order by referring to its price, such as the €12 menu or the €20 menu. Americans sometimes hesitate here, thinking that it's gauche or tacky calling the menu by its price, but that's how it's done.

Size of Portions

Although you will eat well and never complain of going hungry, French portions are not meant to overwhelm you. Your dinner is not a Disney production. Your *blanquette de veau* is designed for one human being, and your plate of salad should not be made of three heads. The key to the French meal is balance, and the symmetry of the dinner takes into account the three principal courses. Dessert is not just a €4 add-on, it's as important as the rest of the meal. Likewise for the appetizer; it's not a routine house salad that comes with the prime rib platter. Be prepared for smaller but balanced courses. Lastly, Parisians do not confuse quantity with quality, and although they are greatly impressed by the size and value of portions in the United States, they see American portions as a marketing device, and they continue to opt for proportion and taste over size.

Cooking Instructions

When ordering red meat, you'll be asked for the *cuisson* (kwee-**sown**) of your meat. The French eat beef much rarer than their American counterparts. People generally believe that beef, to be fully appreciated, should be eaten fairly rare, and Parisian cooking instructions correspond to this practice. Since there are three main choices—rare, medium, and well done—you'd think that the French medium *(à point* [ah **pwahn**]*)* would be the same as the Yankee "medium," but no, it's usually far too rare for American tastes. Here's how to translate the differences:

United States	France
very rare	*saignant* (sen**yohn**) (bloody)
medium rare	*à point* (ah **pwahn**)
medium	between *à point* and *bien cuit* (byen **kwee**)
well done	*très bien cuit* (tray byen **kwee**)

Even with this knowledge, problems sometimes occur. Paris restaurants that are accustomed to serving American tourists and having beef regularly sent back tend to compensate for the cultural difference automatically, but not all restaurants do this. Sort it out with your waiter. If you order in French, your meat should come out according to French standards.

A Note on French Beef

If you've heard alarming stories of tainted beef in Europe and people dying from Kreutzfeld-Jacob disease, rest assured that you have little to worry about in France. Most of the problem was in Britain, and France and other countries banned British beef. French-raised beef that is fed only non-animal-content feed is marked as such. On top of this, the French *charolais* beef is one of the choicest kinds in existence.

Note that the cuts of beef in France do not resemble the cuts you're used to back home. You won't find sirloin, t-bone, prime rib, or tenderloin. What you will find is the following:

bavette	skirt steak	*entrecôte*	rib steak
steack	beef steak	*pavé*	thick slab of boneless beef
steack hachis	chopped steak		

Although you probably won't be buying and cooking meat in Paris, you should spend a few minutes in a *boucherie* (butcher shop), observing how they prepare and dress the beef, liver, lamb, veal, and chickens, ducks, rabbits, and venison. And though you won't find any in restaurants, every neighborhood has its *chevaline* shop selling prime cuts of lean horse meat.

Ordering and Tasting the Wine

If you are an experienced wine drinker, you need no introduction here. You know what to do and what you like. The rest of you may enjoy wine but aren't all that comfortable about choosing the right bottle at the right time for the right price. At good, but not special or starred restaurants, the selected house wine or carafe wine is usually a very sound and reliable choice. At lower-end establishments like pizza restaurants and cafés, the carafe or *pichet* of wine is neither good nor good value. At very elegant restaurants there will be a wine steward, a *sommelier,* whose recommendation you may solicit, but the problem here is that he may strongly advise an excellent 1987 St. Emilion at a cool €100 when you were hoping not to exceed €30 for your wine. It can then be a bit uncomfortable to say, "Oh, yes, I'm sure that's a great choice, but we'll take the 1997 Hermitage at €25." It's better to say from the start that you'd like a wine that's *"sympathique mais pas trop cher* (**sam**pa **teek** may **pah** trow **share**). *"* In other words, a pleasant but reasonably priced wine. Of course, you may want to go for some well-known names in French wines, but what's wonderful about Paris is that you can drink some lovely wines that are never exported at very affordable prices.

The tasting of the wine is customary and ceremonial. Get into it. Take your time. Sniff. Roll your glass slightly. Observe the rich burgundy or ruby tone. Take a mouthful *(gorgée)* and roll it around your tongue. Concentrate. Let the warmth of the 11-year-old Hospice de Beaune warm your cheeks. And then nod approvingly, and smile ever so slightly at your waiter and the lovely people you're dining with. Of course, if you sincerely find the wine to have a problem, or if it is too cold or not cold enough, share this information with the waiter. You're in control.

Especially in the warmer months, it's very pleasant to select a light red wine that is drunk chilled, like a Gamay, Brouilly, or Saumur, all excellent with meat or fish.

In terms of matching wines and cheeses, it is said that if you take three or more kinds of cheeses at your cheese course, the choice of wine becomes moot. No wine can be matched with more than two cheeses.

You may wish to take a wine-tasting course during your Paris stay. See "Taking Classes" in Part Six, Sightseeing and Tours.

For a selection of wine bars, see our Restaurant Profiles.

Excellent Vintages

1990, 1995, and 1996 were very good, and in many cases exceptional years for red and white Bordeaux, red and white Burgundy, and Alsacian wines. 1990 was an excellent year for Côtes-du-Rhône.

The Structure of the Meal

To successfully dine in Paris you must understand one basic concept. Cuisine in France, although a constantly evolving art form and culture in and of itself, is bound by tradition and form. Respect the basic form of the French meal and customs and you will be thoroughly delighted. Disrespect, ignore, or fiddle with the basic conventions of the meal, and you will disrupt the flow, elegance, and deliberate balance of the experience. It is this very rigidity that is at the backbone of a sustained common culture, and it is precisely this that many Americans have a hard time understanding, since their culture is a relatively new one, driven by contemporary values of change, flexibility, and mobility. As you start to feel the history that presents itself to you in the dish in front of you, the gestures with which you're being served, and the way in which the table is set, the more you'll start reflecting on your own society and self. This, from the appetizer onward, is the true beauty of international travel. So, be prepared to respect the form of a restaurant meal in Paris.

It's better to eat less often in restaurants and eat correctly than to eat more often and try to do it your way.

The meal begins with an *apéritif* or cocktail, which you may quite easily and elegantly choose to decline. On the other hand, a *kir* is a very pleasant start to a meal.

A dinner roll or bread will be set out either in a basket or on a bread plate. Usually, butter is not served with the bread in France. You may ask for butter, but Parisians don't.

Carefully review the menu and wine list and only order when you're ready. Feel free to ask your waiter for explanations. Some restaurants have English menus prepared, but it's often a good sign if they don't. If the French is a problem for you, ask about the dishes. You might wish to carry a small pocket dictionary along for the occasion. Berlitz publishes a menu reader that allows you to know that *bigorneaux* are periwinkles and *mousseau* is beef muzzle, if that's helpful. But recognize that some delicious ingredients just don't translate well if they don't exist in an English-speaking country.

Select an Entrée

Note right away how backward Anglo-Saxon habits are. Logically, the entrée is the entry into the meal, the appetizer, not the main dish as *entrée* has come to mean in English. You may decide to let your wife or husband taste your *foie gras,* and she or he may be delighted to offer you an oyster *(huître),* but if you want to avoid aggravating your waiter and ruining the service from the word go, don't order one starter for two people. "We're going to share the leek salad" will grate on the ears of your *serveur.* If you think your *serveur's* annoyance is to do with the fact that you'll be spending less money and thus he'll make a smaller tip on the meal, you're wrong. Splitting a dish simply violates the normal symmetry of a dinner. Sharing two choices is okay, but splitting one doesn't work too well.

Select a Main Dish

Don't try to have your endive salad, which is an appetizer, served at the same time as your salmon steak just because you like salad with your fish. Parisians do not eat meat very well done, but restaurants do understand the nuances here, so be very specific about how you'd like your meat cooked. For instructions on ordering meat, see "Cooking Instructions" earlier in this chapter.

The Cheese Course

In gourmet restaurants, you'll be offered a cheese course at the end of the meal but before dessert. If it's included in your menu, accept it, even if you're stuffed full. You can have a sliver of a number of fascinating cheeses which will contribute to your culinary education.

In restaurants, if the cheese plate is brought to your table for you to serve yourself, remember that you're not expected to eat everything. Take a normal slice or wedge of what you know you like, and a few tiny slivers of others so you can test them.

Remember, it is considered gauche and awkward to cut the point off any wedge of cheese like brie or camembert. Slices or wedges are cut out of the larger wheel of cheese and you should cut along one of the existing edges.

Note that cheese in France is always eaten after the main course, but before the dessert, and not as an hors d'oeuvre with white wine, as is common in North America. Cheese is considered too heavy to eat before a meal.

When do you eat the rind? Tourists have a tendency to want to cut off too much from the cheese, thinking that when in doubt, it's better not to eat the rind. The French approach would be: when in doubt, eat it. The real answer is simple. Every part of cheese is edible except the thick, hard rinds of hard cheeses like Emmenthal and *tomme de Savoie,* which won't hurt you but are not pleasant to chew or digest. Dark plastic or woven straw wrappers along the edges of soft or crumbly cheeses should obviously be removed, but everything else is fair game. The ashes *(cendres)* on fresh goat cheese are inseparable from the cheese. You may sometimes prefer removing some of the darker, funkier, and more pungent parts of very ripe cheese, but even this is wholly edible. And, in any case, do not worry, even the advanced patches of mold on some cheeses won't hurt you.

It is generally believed that the smellier the cheese, the better it is. Some classics you should try include *crottins de Chavignol* (goat cheese served warm on a bed of salad), *camembert, brie de Meaux, Pont l'Eveque, Reblochon,* and *Roquefort*. Many guidebooks list a few noted cheese shops, but we prefer to send you to the *fromagerie* or *crémerie* in the neighborhood in which you're staying or at any open-air market. Ask, point, taste. Have your local cheese merchant write down the names of the cheeses you've bought. Buy small quantities *(juste un petit peu, s'il vous plaît* [joost ah pe**tee** puh, see voa **play**]*),* and a baguette, and plan your own cheese-tasting party in your hotel room or in a park. *The French Cheeses* (D.K. Publishing) is helpful in visually orienting cheese enthusiasts.

Select a Dessert

Yes, you're having dessert. Skip tomorrow's lunch if need be, but tonight you're having a warm wedge of *tarte tatin,* caramelized apple tart, or a plate of *profiteroles,* ice cream–infused pastry puffs smothered in warm chocolate sauce. You can start your diet when you get home. Parisians feel no guilt by being self-indulgent—when "in the act" they do not consider things like calories, bank accounts, or marriage oaths—so to really get the most out of your Paris trip, shed all pangs of guilt immediately.

Coffee or Tea

Coffee and tea are usually taken after the dessert, although some Parisians ask for their coffee with their dessert. Often it'll be served along with a dish of dainty chocolates or nougat wafers, to put the icing on the cake. Following that you may just sit back and contemplate your wonderful evening, or you may feel like a snifter of Courvoisier or a shot of Calvados. If you're afraid the caffeine will keep you up at night, you can order either an *infusion* (ahn few **ze own**), a soothing herbal tea (try *verveine* or *tilleul*), or a decaffeinated espresso commonly called a *déca* (day **cah**).

The Bill . . . l'Addition

The bill will arrive when you ask for it. You may discreetly check that it's more or less what you expected, but do not be overly obvious if you are tallying up the columns. Don't take out a calculator—this is not really done. In places frequented by tourists, however, it's not a bad idea to make sure you haven't been charged €20 for the duck dish that reads €12 on the menu; but again, be tasteful, since recalculating your bill translates as "we don't trust you" to the restaurant staff. French friends or couples don't usually split the bill, and almost never divide up and pay according to what each person ordered. This is far too vulgar for the French. One person usually pays this time, the other will pay the next time. The person who invites or organizes the dinner outing is usually the person who pays. So if you suggest to French friends "why don't you have dinner with us," you should be prepared to pick up the tab that evening.

If you are paying with a credit card, you'll notice that the waiter will bring a slick little debit machine to your table and insert your card on the spot. The French people have chip-embedded smart cards and a PIN code to punch in. There is nothing to sign for them, but you'll probably still have to sign a tiny slip of paper that resembles a cash register receipt. If you are presented with the old-fashioned form where the numbers are written in by hand, make sure that you put a line through the Service/Tip line and fill in the total at the bottom. Do not add on an additional 15% or 20%, since the service was included in the price of your food. Again, for a dinner that costs you between €30 and €100 for two people, you could leave €3 or €4 extra as a gesture of appreciation. For a bill under €30, leave €2. For more expensive meals in which you were very satisfied with your service, you may leave what you like. There is really no rule here. Customarily, you leave something in cash, typically not less than a €1 coin. Don't gather up all the tiny coins in your pocket to get rid of them in this manner; that is perceived as rude. Leave something, be elegant and understated about it, and don't draw too much attention to yourself doing it. There is still an unsaid cultural value in France that money (which everyone wants anyway) is vulgar.

Doggie Bags

Attitudes are changing a bit regarding the removal of food not eaten from restaurants. In general, though, the doggie bag concept is still not an accepted Paris practice. Not that long ago we heard of a story of a tourist who asked for a doggie bag when he left a strip of sirloin on his plate. The waiter came back with a five-kilo sack of scraps from the kitchen. Parisians love their dogs, and this bag would have made at least ten pups happy. The word "to take out" or "take away" is *emporter* (omportay). In fine restaurants, you should abandon the idea totally, but if you left half a pizza or an entire plate of steamed dumplings at a restaurant in Chinatown, don't be timid. Get your goodies to go. Restaurants will not have neat and discreet bags ready for you, and if you really insist on taking something with you, they'll have to scramble in the back and find some plastic and a bag. You get the picture. Besides, delicate sauces do not travel well, so be sure you're only trying to "take out" something highly portable.

Restaurant Profiles

Here is a list of recommended restaurants selected on the basis of their quality, particular style, value, reputation, and price-quality relationship. The list is organized in alphabetical order by restaurant name. Remember that *le menu* is a fixed menu (or *prix fixe*) and *la carte* is the menu itself. A fixed menu usually consists of an appetizer, a main dish, and a dessert for a set price. This often represents a good value overall. Wine and coffee are usually extra, but not always.

Dressing for Dinner

In Paris, informal *(décontracté)* means being dressed nicely with taste and style, but not necessarily a tie and jacket for men or an evening dress for women. Informal does not mean shorts, Dallas Cowboys T-shirts, and so on. On the whole, this should be your model dress code: For gentlemen, a jacket and open-collared shirt or polo shirt is perfectly appropriate in most establishments. We are calling this look "informal nice." Being dressed up with serious suits, evening dresses, and your best jewelry is almost never required. Elegantly dressed in Paris requires a touch of understatement and a well-selected accessory. When we suggest you dress more formally, we have labeled the look "comfortably formal."

A Reminder on the Smoking Situation

Although French law requires restaurants and cafés to provide designated seating for nonsmokers, very few establishments respect the law. Small restaurants find it impossible to enforce the law and have opted to alienate a few obstinate nonsmokers rather than the large number of clients who want to smoke during and/or after the meal. Restaurants that do provide nonsmoking sections usually place these seats at the back or near windows. Ask for nonsmoking sections when you reserve.

Our Favorite Paris Restaurants

We have developed detailed profiles for the best and most interesting restaurants (in our opinion) in town. Each profile features an easily scanned heading that allows you, in just a second, to check out the restaurant's name, cuisine, overall rating, cost, quality rating, and value rating.

Cuisine   This is actually less straightforward than it sounds. A couple of years ago, for example, "pan-Asian" restaurants in Washington, D.C., were serving what was then generally described as "fusion" food—Asian ingredients with European techniques, or vice versa. Since then, there has been a pan-Asian explosion, but nearly all specialize in what would be street food

back home: noodles, skewers, dumplings, and soups. Once-general categories have become subdivided—French into bistro fare and even
Provençal, "new continental" into regional American and "eclectic"—while
others have broadened and fused: Middle Eastern and Provençal into
Mediterranean, Spanish and South American into Nuevo Latino, and so
on. In some cases, we have used the broader terms (i.e., "French") but
added descriptions to give a clearer idea of the fare. Again, though, experimentation and "fusion" are ever more common, so don't hold us, or the
chefs, to too strict a style.

Overall Rating   Our overall star rating encompasses the entire dining
experience, including style, service, and ambience in addition to the taste,
presentation, and quality of the food. Five stars is the highest rating possible and connotes the best of everything. Four-star restaurants are exceptional and three-star restaurants are well above average. Two-star restaurants
are good. One star is used to indicate an average restaurant that demon-
strates an unusual capability in some area of specialization—for example,
an otherwise unmemorable place that has great pâté de foie gras.

Cost   In the middle of the heading is an expense description that provides
a comparative sense of how much a complete meal will cost. A complete
meal for our purposes consists of an entrée with vegetable or side dish and
choice of soup or salad. Appetizers, desserts, drinks, and tips are excluded.

Inexpensive	€16 and less per person
Moderate	€16–38 per person
Expensive	Over €38 per person

Quality Rating   The food quality is rated on a scale of one to five stars, five
being the best rating attainable. The quality rating is based expressly on the
taste, freshness of ingredients, preparation, presentation, and creativity of
food served. There is no consideration of price. If you are a person who
wants the best food available and cost is not an issue, you need look no further than the quality ratings.

Value Rating   If, on the other hand, you are looking for both quality and
value, then you should check the value rating. The value ratings are defined
as follows:

★★★★★	Exceptional value; a real bargain
★★★★	Good value
★★★	Fair value; you get exactly what you pay for
★★	Somewhat overpriced
★	Significantly overpriced

Pricing   Here we supply an average price per person to eat a full meal at
the profiled restaurant. We'll also tell you if the restaurant offers prix fixe
menus (or only offers prix fixe menus), and how much they cost.

Payment   We've listed the type of payment accepted at each restaurant using the following code: AMEX equals American Express, CB equals Carte Blanche, D equals Discover, DC equals Diners Club, MC equals MasterCard, JCB equals Japan Credit Bank, and VISA is self-explanatory.

OUR FAVORITE PARIS RESTAURANTS BY LOCATION

Name	Cuisine	Overall Rating	Price Rating	Quality Rating	Value Rating
1st arrondissement					
Au Chien Qui Fume	French	★★★½	Mod	★★★½	★★★
Café Very	Garden Café/Bistro	★★★	Inexp	★★★	★★★★
Chez La Vieille	Old-Time French Bistro	★★★½	Mod	★★★★	★★★★
L'Ami Léon	Casual French Bistro	★★★½	Mod	★★★½	★★★★
L'Escargot Montorgueil	French Snails	★★★★	Exp	★★★½	★★★
L'Impasse	French Bistro	★★★½	Mod	★★★★	★★★★
Le Grand Vefour	Classic French	★★★★★	Exp	★★★★★	★★★★★
Toupary	Contemporary French	★★★★	Mod	★★★★	★★★
2nd arrondissement					
Café Drouant	French Haute Cuisine	★★★½	Mod	★★★½	★★
Café Runtz	French	★★★½	Mod	★★★½	★★★★
Le Grand Colbert	French	★★★★	Mod	★★★★	★★★★
3rd arrondissement					
Chez Jenny	Alsacian Brasserie	★★★½	Mod	★★★★	★★★
404	Moroccan	★★★½	Mod	★★★★	★★★★
L'Ambassade D'Auvergne	French Regional	★★★½	Mod	★★★★½	★★★★
L'Auberge Nicolas Flamel	Medieval/ Traditional	★★★★	Mod	★★★½	★★★★
4th arrondissement					
Bofinger	Classic Brasserie	★★★★	Mod	★★★★½	★★★
Chez Julien	Innovative French Traditional	★★★½	Exp	★★★★	★★★
Coconnas	Traditional/ Bourgeois French	★★★½	Mod	★★★½	★★★★
Dame Tartine	Salads/Sandwiches	★★★	Inexp	★★★	★★★★
L'Ambroisie	French Haute Cuisine	★★★★½	Exp	★★★★★	★★★

OUR FAVORITE PARIS RESTAURANTS BY LOCATION *(continued)*

Name	Cuisine	Overall Rating	Price Rating	Quality Rating	Value Rating
4th arrondissement (continued)					
Le Vieux Bistro	French Bistro	★★★½	Mod	★★★★½	★★★★
Les Philosophes	French	★★★½	Mod	★★★	★★★★
Pitchi Poï	Jewish/Central European	★★★★	Mod	★★★★	★★★★
5th arrondissement					
Atelier Maitre Albert	Traditional French	★★★★	Mod	★★★★	★★★★
Campagne et Provence	French Provençal	★★★½	Mod	★★★½	★★★★
Le Jardin des Pâtes	Healthy, pasta-based dishes	★★★½	Mod	★★★½	★★★★★
La Rôtisserie du Beaujolais	Country-Style Rôtisserie	★★★★	Mod	★★★★½	★★★★
La Tour d'Argent	French Culinary Landmark	★★★★	Exp	★★★★½	★★
Le Balzar	Traditional Brasserie	★★★½	Mod	★★★★	★★★★
Toutoune	French Provençal	★★★★	Mod/Exp	★★★½	★★★★
Zyriab	Gourmet Arabic	★★★★	Mod	★★★★½	★★★★
6th arrondissement					
Brasserie Lipp	French	★★½	Mod	★★½	★★★
Chez Jean-Claude Gramond	French	★★★½	Exp	★★★★½	★★★
Fish!	Mediterranean Bistro/Wine Bar	★★★★	Mod	★★★★	★★★½
Jacques Cagna	French Haute Cuisine	★★★★½	Exp	★★★★	★★★★
La Bastide Odéon	French Bistro	★★★½	Mod	★★★★½	★★★★
Roger la Grenouille	Bawdy French Bistro	★★★★	Mod	★★½	★★★
7th arrondissement					
Le Bellecour	French Bourgeois	★★★	Mod	★★★½	★★★★
Le Récamier	Traditional French	★★★	Exp	★★★★	★★★
Restaurant du Musée D'Orsay	Traditional French	★★★★	Mod	★★★	★★★★
8th arrondissement					
Café Indigo	French	★★★	Mod	★★★½	★★★★
Ladurée	French/Tea room	★★★★	Mod	★★★★½	★★★★

OUR FAVORITE PARIS RESTAURANTS BY LOCATION (continued)

Name	Cuisine	Overall Rating	Price Rating	Quality Rating	Value Rating
8th arrondissement (continued)					
Le Buddha Bar	California French	★★	Exp	★★★½	★★★
Spoon	French	★★★★	Mod	★★★★	★★★
9th arrondissement					
Chartier	French	★★★★	Inexp	★★★	★★★★★
Chez Catherine	Neighborhood Bistro	★★★★	Mod	★★★★	★★★★
Le Bistro de Gala	French/American Southwest	★★★★	Mod	★★★★½	★★★★★
10th arrondissement					
Aux Deux Canards	French Bistro	★★★★	Mod	★★★★	★★★★
Julien	Art-Nouveau Brasserie	★★★★	Mod	★★★½	★★★
11th arrondissement					
Astier	French Bistro	★★★★½	Mod	★★★★½	★★★★★
Au Trou Normand	Neighborhood Bistro	★★★	Inexp	★★★½	★★★★★
Haiku	Vegetarian/Organic	★★★½	Mod	★★★½	★★★★★
Le Villaret	Innovative French	★★★½	Mod	★★★★½	★★★★★
Les Amognes	Stylish French	★★★★	Mod	★★★★½	★★★★★
12th arrondissement					
Le Square Trousseau	French	★★★½	Mod	★★★½	★★★★
Les Zygomates	French Bistro	★★★½	Mod	★★★★	★★★★★
13th arrondissement					
Le Keryado	Bouillabaisse Bistro	★★★½	Mod	★★★★	★★★★
14th arrondissement					
La Coupole	Traditional Bohemian Brasserie	★★★★½	Mod	★★★	★★★
Les Petites Sorcières	French Bistro	★★★★	Mod	★★★★½	★★★★
Monsieur Lapin	French/Rabbit	★★★½	Mod	★★★★	★★★★4
15th arrondissement					
L'Os à Moëlle	French Bistro	★★★½	Mod	★★★★	★★★★
La Galleria Ristorante	Authentic Italian	★★★★	Mod	★★★★	★★★★
Le Père Claude	French	★★★½	Mod/Exp	★★★★	★★★★★

OUR FAVORITE PARIS RESTAURANTS BY LOCATION (continued)

Name	Cuisine	Overall Rating	Price Rating	Quality Rating	Value Rating
16th arrondissement					
Vin & Marée	Contemporary Seafood	★★★	Mod	★★★★	★★★★
18th arrondissement					
Le Moulin à Vins	Neighborhood Bistro	★★★½	Mod	★★★½	★★★★
Le Restaurant	French/African	★★★½	Inexp	★★★★	★★★★★
Rendez-Vous des Chauffeurs	Home-style French Bistro	★★★	Mod	★★★½	★★★★★
20th arrondissement					
Café Noir	Neighborhood Bistro	★★★	Mod	★★★★	★★★★★

OUR FAVORITE PARIS RESTAURANTS BY CUISINE

Name	Overall Rating	Price Rating	Quality Rating	Value Rating	Arrondis-sement
Brasserie, Alsacian					
Chez Jenny	★★★½	Mod	★★★★	★★★	3
Brasserie, Art-Nouveau					
Julien	★★★★	Mod	★★★½	★★★	10
Brasserie, Traditional					
La Coupole	★★★★½	Mod	★★★	★★★	14
Bofinger	★★★★	Mod	★★★★½	★★★	4
Le Balzar	★★★½	Mod	★★★★	★★★★	5
California French					
Le Buddha Bar	★★	Exp	★★★½	★★★	8
Country-Style Rôtisserie					
La Rôtisserie du Beaujolais	★★★★	Mod	★★★★½	★★★★	5

OUR FAVORITE PARIS RESTAURANTS BY CUISINE (continued)

Name	Overall Rating	Price Rating	Quality Rating	Value Rating	Arrondis-sement
French					
Le Grand Vefour	★★★★★	Exp	★★★★★	★★★★★	1
La Tour d'Argent	★★★★	Exp	★★★★½	★★	5
Les Amognes	★★★★	Mod	★★★★½	★★★★★	11
Le Grand Colbert	★★★★	Mod	★★★★	★★★★	2
Spoon	★★★★	Mod	★★★★	★★★	8
Toupary	★★★★	Mod	★★★★	★★★	1
Chartier	★★★★	Inexp	★★★	★★★★★	9
Chez Jean-Claude Gramond	★★★½	Exp	★★★★½	★★★	6
Le Villaret	★★★½	Mod	★★★★½	★★★★★	11
Le Père Claude	★★★½	Mod/Exp	★★★★	★★★★★	15
Au Chien Qui Fume	★★★½	Mod	★★★½	★★★	1
Café Runtz	★★★½	Mod	★★★½	★★★★	2
Le Square Trousseau	★★★½	Mod	★★★½	★★★★	12
Les Philosophes	★★★½	Mod	★★★	★★★★	4
Café Indigo	★★★	Mod	★★★½	★★★★	8
Le Bellecour	★★★	Mod	★★★½	★★★★	7
Brasserie Lipp	★★½	Mod	★★½	★★★	6
French Bistro					
Astier	★★★★½	Mod	★★★★½	★★★★★	11
Les Petites Sorcières	★★★★	Mod	★★★★½	★★★★	14
Aux Deux Canards	★★★★	Mod	★★★★	★★★★	10
Roger la Grenouille	★★★★	Mod	★★½	★★★	6
La Bastide Odéon	★★★½	Mod	★★★★½	★★★★	6
Le Vieux Bistro	★★★½	Mod	★★★★½	★★★★	4
Chez La Vieille	★★★½	Mod	★★★★	★★★★	1
Le Keryado	★★★½	Mod	★★★★	★★★★	13
Les Zygomates	★★★½	Mod	★★★★	★★★★★	12
L'Impasse	★★★½	Mod	★★★★	★★★★	1
L'Os à Moëlle	★★★½	Mod	★★★★	★★★★	15
L'Ami Léon	★★★½	Mod	★★★½	★★★★	1
Rendez-Vous des Chauffeurs	★★★	Mod	★★★½	★★★★★	18
Café Very	★★★	Inexp	★★★	★★★★	1
French Haute Cuisine					
L'Ambroisie	★★★★½	Exp	★★★★★	★★★	4
Jacques Cagna	★★★★½	Exp	★★★★	★★★★	6
Café Drouant	★★★½	Mod	★★★½	★★	2

OUR FAVORITE PARIS RESTAURANTS BY CUISINE (continued)

Name	Overall Rating	Price Rating	Quality Rating	Value Rating	Arrondis- sement
French Provençal					
Toutoune	★★★★	Mod/Exp	★★★½	★★★★	5
Campagne et Provence	★★★½	Mod	★★★½	★★★★	5
French Regional					
L'Ambassade D'Auvergne	★★★½	Mod	★★★★½	★★★★	3
French Snails					
L'Escargot Montorgueil	★★★★	Exp	★★★½	★★★	I
French Traditional					
Atelier Maitre Albert	★★★★	Mod	★★★★	★★★★	5
L'Auberge Nicolas Flamel	★★★★	Mod	★★★½	★★★★	3
Restaurant du Musée D'Orsay	★★★★	Mod	★★★	★★★★	7
Chez Julien	★★★½	Exp	★★★★	★★★	4
Coconnas	★★★½	Mod	★★★½	★★★★	4
Le Récamier	★★★	Exp	★★★★	★★★	7
French/African					
Le Restaurant	★★★½	Inexp	★★★★	★★★★★	18
French/American Southwest					
Le Bistro de Gala	★★★★	Mod	★★★★½	★★★★★	9
French/Rabbit					
Monsieur Lapin	★★★½	Mod	★★★★	★★★★	14
French/Tea room					
Ladurée	★★★★	Mod	★★★★½	★★★★	8
Gourmet Arabic					
Zyriab	★★★★	Mod	★★★★½	★★★★	5
Italian					
La Galleria Ristorante	★★★★	Mod	★★★★	★★★★	15
Jewish/Central European					
Pitchi Poï	★★★★	Mod	★★★★	★★★★	4
Mediterranean					
Fish!	★★★★	Mod	★★★★	★★★½	6
Moroccan					
404	★★★½	Mod	★★★★	★★★★	3

OUR FAVORITE PARIS RESTAURANTS BY CUISINE (continued)

Name	Overall Rating	Price Rating	Quality Rating	Value Rating	Arrondis- sement
Neighborhood Bistro					
Chez Catherine	★★★★	Mod	★★★★	★★★★	9
Le Moulin à Vins	★★★½	Mod	★★★½	★★★★	18
Café Noir	★★★	Mod	★★★★	★★★★★	20
Au Trou Normand	★★★	Inexp	★★★½	★★★★★	11
Pasta					
Le Jardin des Pâtes	★★★½	Mod	★★★½	★★★★★	5
Salads/Sandwiches					
Dame Tartine	★★★	Inexp	★★★	★★★★	4
Seafood					
Vin & Marée	★★★	Mod	★★★★	★★★★	16
Vegetarian/Organic					
Haiku	★★★½	Mod	★★★½	★★★★★	11

ASTIER ★★★★½

FRENCH BISTRO | MODERATE | QUALITY ★★★★½ | VALUE ★★★★★ |
11TH ARRONDISSEMENT

44, rue Jean-Pierre Timbaud, 75011; 01 43 57 16 35; Métro: Parmentier or Oberkampf

Customers Mixed regulars and tourists **Reservations** Required in advance for dinner **When to go** Not too late **Pricing** Prix fixe only, €19 (lunch), €23 (dinner) **Payment** VISA, MC **English spoken** Yes **Bar** None **Wine selection** 300 wines, good-quality value **Dress** Casual **Disabled access** No

Hours Monday–Friday, noon–2 p.m. and 8–11 p.m.; closed August, December 24–January 2, public holidays, second week of Easter holiday

Setting & atmosphere Upscale bistro, linen tablecloths and napkins.

House specialties Different dishes daily, about 50 specialties each year depending on season.

Summary & comments Hip Paris has been creeping steadily into the Oberkampf area, where Astier has been for years. Here, you'll feel like you're making a real find and the Paris of unpretentious local life is still attainable. This bistro is almost always packed with an active and lively crowd that looks like they eat here each week. The decor is plain; all the energy and life of the place has gone into the cuisine, which is varied, fresh, and plentiful. For the €23 menu, you get a four-course feast that you'll have to walk off later. Everyone tells you that if you go to Astier, bring your appetite. You can start off with a salad or plate of succulent white asparagus with a tangy vinaigrette. Or you could dive in right away with a pasta dish. We loved the lapin à la moutarde (rabbit served in a mustard sauce with fresh tagliatelle). There is always a fish dish or two. Astier is also renowned for its copious and yummy selection of cheeses, served on a sprawling platter. All you can eat! Whether you're already stuffed or not, you must take at least a sliver from many of the two dozen choices. But leave room, if you can, for dessert. You'll talk for days about the rich slice of chocolate fondant soaking in a puddle of coffee sauce. Others may be cowardly and opt for the cool sorbets or the fresh fruit. The wine list is extensive; ask for help.

ATELIER MAITRE ALBERT   ★★★★

TRADITIONAL FRENCH | MODERATE | QUALITY ★★★★ | VALUE ★★★★ |
5TH ARRONDISSEMENT

1, rue Maître Albert, 75005; 01 46 33 13 78; Métro: Maubert-Mutualité

Customers Mixed, but not too young; French and visitors **Reservations** Advised for dinner **When to go** Any time, but it has more atmosphere at night **Pricing** Average per person €46; prix fixe €32–43 (dinner) **Payment** VISA, MC, AMEX, travelers' checks in euros **English spoken** Yes **Bar** Yes **Wine selection** Extensive **Dress** Informal nice **Disabled access** No

Hours Monday–Saturday, noon–2 p.m., 7–10:30 p.m.

Setting & atmosphere Very quaint bar area with amusing hanging swinglike chair. A perfect spot to celebrate a special evening, for example an anniversary or an engagement. Just steps from the Seine on a medieval street on the Left Bank, this candlelit but comfortably dark venue is detached from time. For a few hours you'll think you are hidden away in a country inn. In the winter, a fireplace dating from the period of Francis I warms this exposed stone and red velour eatery.

House specialties Rotisserie, guinea fowl, quail brochettes.

Summary & comments This is one of our favorite places to eat in Paris. Not only is the food delicious and well presented, the atmosphere is seductive and romantic. The specialties include spit-roasted meats and daily catch fish.

AU CHIEN QUI FUME   ★★★½

FRENCH | MODERATE | QUALITY ★★★½ | VALUE ★★★ | 1ST ARRONDISSEMENT

33, rue du Pont-Neuf, 75001; 01 42 36 07 42; Métro: Châtelet–Les Halles

Customers Mixed, businesspeople **Reservations** Required **When to go** Anytime, even late **Pricing** Average per person €34; prix fixe €16–29 **Payment** VISA, MC, AMEX, D, DC, JCB, travelers' checks in euros **English spoken** Yes **Bar** Yes **Wine selection** 40 labels **Dress** Casual **Disabled access** No

Hours Daily, noon–2 a.m.

Setting & atmosphere Warm and inviting. If you love dogs, you'll love this quirky but famous Paris bistro, where porcelain and ceramic hounds and poodles grace the shelf space. Yes, the "Dog Who Smokes" has original character.

House specialties Fish, seafood, fricassee of poultry with morel mushrooms.

Entertainment & amenities Jazz music in the background, air conditioned on the second floor.

Summary & comments This is one of the few reliable places to eat and enjoy yourself in and around the Châtelet–Les Halles commercial wasteland, clearly not our favorite part of town for culinary discoveries. Having said that, the terrace in the summer is pleasant, although the service tends to be either too fast or too slow. This bistro is best late at night.

AU TROU NORMAND

NEIGHBORHOOD BISTRO | INEXPENSIVE | QUALITY ★★★½ | VALUE ★★★★★ |
11TH ARRONDISSEMENT

9, rue Jean-Pierre Timbaud, 75011; 01 48 05 80 23; Métro: Oberkampf

Customers Local regulars **Reservations** Not necessary **When to go** Anytime but lunch **Pricing** Average per person €55 **Payment** Cash only **English spoken** Yes **Bar** Yes **Wine selection** Especially good selection of Bordeaux **Dress** Very casual **Disabled access** No

Hours Monday–Friday, noon–2:30 p.m. and 7:30–11:30 p.m.; Saturday, 7:30–midnight; closed August

Setting & atmosphere Rough and ready, jolly Parisian bistro. Far from fancy, this really is a neighborhood canteen packed full of laborers in their shirtsleeves quaffing jugs of rough red wine. The rue Jean-Pierre Timbaud has recently been suffering from gentrification, and it's heartening to eat in a place that is still typically working-class Parisian.

House specialties Side of veal, 30 hors d'oeuvres, 2 daily specials, 12 grilled meat dishes.

Summary & comments Au Trou Normand is the place to go to experience old-fashioned Parisian dining at old-fashioned prices. Choose between a wide variety of classic starters and main courses, such as grated carrots, egg mayonnaise, and simple grilled meats. Enjoy the hustle and bustle, the friendly atmosphere, and most of all, the check.

AUX DEUX CANARDS

FRENCH BISTRO | MODERATE | QUALITY ★★★★ | VALUE ★★★★ |
10TH ARRONDISSEMENT

8, rue du Fbg Poissonnière, 75010; 01 47 70 03 23; Métro: Bonne-Nouvelle

Customers Locals and regulars **Reservations** Advised **When to go** Early evening **Pricing** Average per person €30 **Payment** VISA, MC, AMEX, DC **English spoken** Yes

Bar None **Wine selection** 30 vintage wines, and the house special Côte du Luberon at €15 **Dress** Casual **Disabled access** No

Hours Monday–Friday, noon–2:15 p.m. and 7–10:30 p.m.; Saturday, 7–10:30 p.m.; closed from July 14 to August 15

Setting & atmosphere Warm surroundings, small restaurant.

House specialties Duck with oranges, compote of rhubarb.

Summary & comments If you don't know any Parisians who can invite you round to their apartment to eat, this is the next best thing. Dinner at Aux Deux Canards feels like supper at a friend's place. The patron is a jolly chap, determined to make sure that everyone is relaxed, happy, and having a great time. His specialty, classic dinner party standby duck à l'orange, is as good as you'll find anywhere, and the warm welcome he extends is far better than you'll find in most places. If you compliment him enough and ask nicely, he might even give you the recipe.

BOFINGER   ★★★★

CLASSIC BRASSERIE | MODERATE | QUALITY ★★★★½ | VALUE ★★★ | 4TH ARRONDISSEMENT

5–7, rue de la Bastille, 75004; 01 42 72 72 82; Métro: Bastille

Customers Tourists, regulars, and oyster lovers **Reservations** Advised **When to go** Early and late **Pricing** Average per person €29; prix fixe €20 (lunch), €30 (dinner) **Payment** VISA, MC, AMEX, D, JCB, travelers' checks in euros and dollars **English spoken** Yes, menu in English **Bar** Yes **Wine selection** Bourbon, Beaujolais, Côte du Rhône, diverse cellar **Dress** Nicely dressed, relaxed **Disabled access** Yes

Hours Monday–Friday, noon–3 p.m. and 6:30 p.m.–1 a.m.; Saturday, Sunday, and holidays, noon–1 a.m.

Setting & atmosphere The decor isn't decor—it's original art deco and Belle Epoque hardware, brassware, stained glass, and carved woodwork. When you reserve, ask to sit under the cupola downstairs. Nonsmokers' requests are respected here, too. Everyone who works here is proud of the restaurant, which has been carefully restored and is a protected national monument. Regular diners reserve a small alcove upstairs, where they're not disturbed by the stream of foreign visitors. Take a peek upstairs at the dining room and the works of art. And whether you need to use the facilities or not, make sure you check out the deco men's urinal with the carved dolphin head. A true collector's item.

House specialties Oysters, foie gras, choucroute, seafood.

Summary & comments One of Paris's top brasseries, Bofinger is a feast in every sense of the word. The selection of seafood is a great kickoff. Go for a plate of chilled oysters or, if you want a sensual experience, the plateau of mixed shellfish. Take your time and learn the nuances of withdrawing the tiny bit of periwinkle with a straight pin. The foie gras is always a great starter. The meats and fish are all fresh and well prepared. Nothing overly experimental or exotic, just good French brasserie fare served with a friendly formality. If you're wondering about dessert, definitely go for the profiteroles—a chocolate delight.

Across the street, Bofinger has a simpler bistro-style sister restaurant. The food is good and the prices are a bit more moderate, but our suggestion is if you've come this far, go for the real thing. The savings are not worth the sacrifice in atmosphere.

BRASSERIE LIPP ★★½

FRENCH | MODERATE | QUALITY ★★½ | VALUE ★★★ | 6TH ARRONDISSEMENT

151, boulevard St-Germain, 75006; 01 45 48 53 91; Métro: St-Germain-des-Prés

Customers Showbiz and TV crowd, politicians, literary celebrities, tourists seeking out celebrities. **Reservations** Advised **When to go** Late **Pricing** Average per person €44 (wine included) **Payment** VISA, MC, AMEX, DC, travelers' checks in euros and dollars **English spoken** Yes **Bar** No **Wine selection** 50 vintage wines, 10 Bordeaux **Dress** Dress well, but not formal **Disabled access** No

Hours Daily, 11:30–2 a.m.; closed December 24 and 25

Setting & atmosphere A legendary brasserie for regulars, locals, television personalities, government ministers, and curious tourists, Lipp is a Saint-Germain-des-Prés landmark. The 1920s decor, tiled floors, sculpted woodwork, and etched glass characterize the period. Lipp is always bustling. You'll feel a bit crowded and rushed. But this is an authentic Paris brasserie.

House specialties Choucroute, stuffed pig's foot, fish.

Summary & comments The food is competent and plentiful, but no more. If you'd like to take part in this living tradition and aren't motivated only by the food, certainly try Lipp. Kill two birds with one stone and order the choucroute, an Alsatian dish of sauerkraut, pork, and potatoes eaten with dabs of tangy mustard and a flavorful Alsatian wine. You'll be amused (or you should be) to note that written on the menu in English is "No salad as a meal." They're not kidding. So if you aren't into respecting the integrity of the three courses (two at the least), then move on.

CAFÉ DROUANT ★★★½

FRENCH HAUTE CUISINE | EXPENSIVE | QUALITY ★★★½ | VALUE ★★ |
2ND ARRONDISSEMENT

Place Gaillon, 75002; 01 42 65 15 16; Métro: 4 Septembre

Customers Parisian intellectuals with money **Reservations** Advised **When to go** Not too late **Pricing** Prix fixe €49 (lunch), €104 (dinner) **Payment** VISA, MC, AMEX, DC, travelers' checks in euros **English spoken** Yes **Bar** Yes **Wine selection** 100 vintage wines **Dress** Casual in the café, dressed up in the restaurant **Disabled access** No

Hours Restaurant, daily, 12:15–2:30 p.m. and 7:15–10:15 p.m.; café, daily, 12:15–2:30 p.m. and 7:15 p.m.–midnight

Setting & atmosphere The café decor is in the style of the 1930s and was particularly beloved by Jean Cocteau. Soft lighting, a low rumble of conversation, well-spaced tables.

House specialties Oyster bar, selection of fish.

Summary & comments If you come to Paris with literary aspirations and a large expense account, indulge yourself in the illustrious surroundings of Drouant, the haute cuisine restaurant where the judges of France's most prestigious literary prize (Le Prix Goncourt) meet for dinner and discussion once a month. If your wallet is more struggling artist than best-seller, go for the more reasonable option in the annex, the Café Drouant. The shellfish is excellent.

CAFÉ INDIGO

FRENCH | MODERATE | QUALITY ★★★½ | VALUE ★★★★ | 8TH ARRONDISSEMENT

12, avenue George V, 75008; 01 47 20 89 56; Métro: Alma Marceau

Customers Parisians, tourists, trendy, artists **Reservations** Advised **When to go** Anytime **Pricing** Average per person €38 (wine included) **Payment** VISA, MC, AMEX, DC **English spoken** Yes **Bar** Yes **Wine selection** 35 quality vintages **Dress** Casual **Disabled access** Yes, except restroom **Hours** Daily, 8 a.m.–11:30 p.m.

Setting & atmosphere Literary/library, modern photography.

House specialties Lots of fish dishes.

Summary & comments One of a rash of trendy places near the Champs-Elysées, Café Indigo is a great place to go if you want to experience the cool factor without the pretension and bad attitude that often go hand in hand with hip. Expect a very "designed" interior, frighteningly good-looking (but very nice) staff, decent food, and a mix of "bright young things" doing lunch. This is the kind of place where you expect to be able to eavesdrop on your neighbors' frightfully glamorous and important gossip. Unfortunately, they're as likely to be discussing last night's soap opera as anything desperately chic, but they're mostly French so you can pretend. The chic menu is full of local options for those who don't want any bulges to ruin their waistlines, while the wine list boasts some decent international bottles for those who are proud of their global outlook. Café Indigo is a lot more relaxed than its more self-conscious competitors and an ideal location for a revitalizing coffee after a monstrous shopping binge.

CAFÉ NOIR

NEIGHBORHOOD BISTRO | MODERATE | QUALITY ★★★★ | VALUE ★★★★★ | 20TH ARRONDISSEMENT

15, rue Saint Blaise, 75020; 01 40 09 75 80; Métro: Porte de Bagnolet

Customers Neighborhood crowd; about three-fourths are regulars **Reservations** Advised for dinner **When to go** Early or late **Pricing** Average per person €30 (wine included) **Payment** VISA, MC **English spoken** Yes **Bar** No **Wine selection** 120 vintage wines **Dress** Casual **Disabled access** No

Hours Monday–Saturday, 7 p.m.–midnight; Sunday, noon–midnight

Setting & atmosphere Old-style (circa 1900), decked out with hanging hats, coffee pots, bric-a-brac, French and Italian movie posters, stone sculptures from the 1930–1950 period, and a lot more. It looks like an old thrift store with ancient coffee machines, antique hats, old cinema posters, and random statues everywhere.

House specialties Duck fillet cooked with lavender, thyme, honey, cinnamon, and ginger; foie gras Guerrandaise; millefeuille of artichoke and fois gras. Menu changes twice a year.

Summary & comments Café Noir is a great introduction to bric-a-brac chic. The food is lovely and fragrant with overtones of honey, thyme, and vanilla infusing most choices on the menu. Loud music, hyper-friendly waiters, and a young clientele make for a relaxed night out. This is a great place to lose your sense of time and while away the hours with a decent bottle of red wine and maybe a super Havana from behind the bar. You'll not find a lot of other out-of-town visitors here, and you're certain to have one of the most authentic Parisian evenings of your stay. It's a bit hard to find if you're not used to Paris's 20th arrondissement, but from the Porte de Bagnolet Métro station you can easily walk. You'll love the pedestrian street on which the restaurant is found.

CAFÉ RUNTZ ★★★½

FRENCH | MODERATE | QUALITY ★★★½ | VALUE ★★★★ | 2ND ARRONDISSEMENT

16, rue Favart, 75002; 01 42 96 69 86; Métro: Richelieu-Drouot

Customers Professionals, tourists, actors **Reservations** Advised **When to go** Not too late **Pricing** Average per person €35; prix fixe €17 and €22 **Payment** VISA, MC, AMEX, DC, travelers' checks in euros **English spoken** Yes **Bar** Yes **Wine selection** 70 vintages, specializes in wines from Alsace **Dress** Casual **Disabled access** Yes, except restroom

Hours Daily, 11:45 a.m.–2:30 p.m. and 6:30–11 p.m.

Setting & atmosphere Decor from Alsace, heart-shaped chairs. This elegant brasserie is a great spot for a theater supper. Little seems to have changed since its Belle Epoque heyday—the decor has been lovingly renovated to retain its turn-of-the-century look.

House specialties Sauerkraut, chicken in Riesling wine, veal in horseradish sauce, fish.

Summary & comments The friendly chef serves up hearty food from the Alsace region; remember to take a large appetite and enjoy the choucroute sauerkraut dishes with a large Alsatian beer. The specialty choucroute is the "Gourmet," which includes blood sausage, ham hocks, and thick strips of bacon, and the Strasbourg favorite, grilled ham hocks served with warm potatoes. This is hearty eating and recommended in the cooler months.

CAFÉ VÉRY ★★★

GARDEN CAFÉ/BISTRO | INEXPENSIVE | QUALITY ★★★ | VALUE ★★★★ |
1ST ARRONDISSEMENT

Jardin des Tuileries, 75001; 01 47 03 94 84; Métro: Concorde

Customers Tourists and young professionals **Reservations** No **When to go** Lunch **Pricing** Average per person €19 **Payment** VISA, MC, AMEX, travelers' checks in euros and dollars **English spoken** Yes **Bar** No **Wine selection** Bordeaux, Bourgogne, glass €2.50–5, pitcher €6–15, bottle €15–24 **Dress** Casual **Disabled access** Yes, except restrooms

Hours Daily, 9–11:30 a.m. and noon–11 p.m.

Setting & atmosphere Modern, 120 seats.

House specialties Chicken and prawns with paprika, salmon marinated with caviar. Children's menu €10.

Summary & comments There are three important things to mention about the Café Véry: location, location, and location. Although the food can be quite ordinary and the service unexceptional, it really doesn't matter because people come here for its glorious position, right in the heart of the Tuileries. There are several other eateries in the Tuileries, but le Very is where the Parisians pause for a citron pressé during their weekend stroll around Catherine de Médici's garden and is far superior in terms of both cooking and clientele to *les autres*. The terrace tables are fabulous in the summer, and in the winter the glass interior lets you feel as if you're outside without actually having to brave the temperatures. The service is a bit indifferent, especially in the summer when the place is busy.

CAMPAGNE ET PROVENCE   ★★★½

FRENCH PROVENÇAL | MODERATE | QUALITY ★★★½ | VALUE ★★★★ |
5TH ARRONDISSEMENT

25, quai de la Tournelle, 75005; 01 43 54 05; Métro: Maubert-Mutualité or Jussieu

Customers Foreign visitors, many Japanese and Americans **Reservations** Required **When to go** Great late **Pricing** Average per person €46; prix fixe €27–33 **Payment** VISA, MC **English spoken** Yes **Bar** No **Wine selection** Mostly wines from Provence **Dress** Casual chic **Disabled access** No

Hours Tuesday–Friday, 12:30–2 p.m. and 7:30–11 p.m.; Monday and Saturday, 7:30–11:30 p.m.

Setting & atmosphere This small but attractive bistro is well situated facing the Seine. Tables are tightly packed, but the atmosphere is warm and colors are reminiscent of the French countryside.

House specialties Specialties from Provence, including crab aïoli and assorted appetizers Provençale.

Summary & comments For those of you who adore the south of France or dream of going but happen to find yourself in Paris, don't fret. Here is a charming eatery that typifies Provençal cooking and hospitality. Well situated on the Left Bank quai in front of Notre-Dame, Campagne et Provence offers colorful and well-presented dishes accented with fresh vegetables and aromatic herbs.

CHARTIER ★★★★

FRENCH | INEXPENSIVE | QUALITY ★★★ | VALUE ★★★★★ | 9TH ARRONDISSEMENT

7, rue du Fbg Montmartre, 75009; 01 47 70 86 29; Métro: Rue Montmartre

Customers Tourists, neighborhood regulars **Reservations** Not accepted **When to go** Before 9 p.m. **Pricing** Average per person €14 **Payment** VISA, MC **English spoken** Some **Bar** No **Wine selection** Adequate selection of inexpensive wines, with the Cuvée Chartier (Burgundy) at €5.50 a dirt cheap, reliable choice **Dress** Casual **Disabled access** Yes

Hours Daily, 11:30 a.m.–3 p.m. and 6–10 p.m.

Setting & atmosphere At Chartier, time stopped somewhere around the turn of the century. This noisy and spacious restaurant situated behind a revolving door at the back of an indecorous alleyway near the Grands Boulevards seats you where it can, sometimes with strangers, at simple tables set with paper napkins and paper menus that change daily.

House specialties Pepper steak, beef stew (pot au feu).

Summary & comments One of Paris's most written-about restaurants, after years of operation, Chartier continues to be a favorite eatery for visitors and residents. The food is not gourmet, the service ranges from stiff and unfriendly to jocular and amusing, the prices are about as low as you'll find in the city, and the atmosphere is a perpetual time warp. The bread and water are plentiful, the carafe wine is cheap and red, and life is beautiful. Order one or many of the plain appetizers, which run from €2 to €5. It's like what eating at home might have been like if you were a working-class Parisian in the early part of the 20th century. In fact, the little wooden drawers in the walls where the restaurant's daily customers kept their linen napkins are reminders of yesteryear. The steak au poivre is good, although you must be clear if you want your meat cooked anything other than rare. It always comes out rare. We usually take the *plat du jour*, regardless of what it is. The waiters in worn-out white shirts and black bow ties write down your order on the paper tablecloth and tally it up in front of you. Chartier is fun and perfect for tight budgets.

CHEZ CATHERINE

NEIGHBORHOOD BISTRO | MODERATE | QUALITY ★★★★ | VALUE ★★★★ | 9TH ARRONDISSEMENT

65, rue de Provence, 75009; 01 45 26 72 88; Métro: Chaussée D'Antin

Customers Lunch businesspeople, dinner tourists **Reservations** Required **When to go** Early or late **Pricing** Average per person €53–60 **Payment** VISA, MC, DC **English spoken** Yes **Bar** No **Wine selection** 200 vintage wines **Dress** Informal nice **Disabled access** No

Hours Tuesday–Friday, noon–2:30 p.m. and 7:45–10 p.m.; Monday, noon–2:30 p.m.

Setting & atmosphere Chic bistro. It feels like a neighborhood restaurant yet is more than welcoming to "outsiders."

House specialties Fondue of scallops with endive, pepper steak.

Summary & comments It is no surprise that Chez Catherine's charms have been recognized by *The New York Times,* the *Herald Tribune,* and *Vogue.* This excellent little establishment has all the elements that make a fabulous, typically Parisian bistro. The classic dishes such as steak tartare are fresh and tangy, and the more innovative choices, like the bavaroise with tomatoes and crawfish tails, can be spectacular. The wine list, chosen by Catherine's wine buff of a husband, is also a real treat. Book now.

CHEZ JEAN-CLAUDE GRAMOND ★★★½

FRENCH | EXPENSIVE | QUALITY ★★★★½ | VALUE ★★★ | 6TH ARRONDISSEMENT

5, rue Fleurus, 75006; 01 42 22 28 89; Métro: St-Placide

Customers Bourgeois, well-to-do tourists, editors and writers **Reservations** Advised **When to go** Not too late **Pricing** Average per person €53 **Payment** VISA, MC **English spoken** Some **Bar** None **Wine selection** Excellent cellar, vintage 1962 wines **Dress** Comfortable **Disabled access** No

Hours Monday–Saturday, noon–3 p.m. and 7–10 p.m.; closed in August

Setting & atmosphere This small and quaint restaurant with only 25 seats serves classical French cuisine to adoring customers. They own a painting by John Wayne!

House specialties Farm chicken from the Yonne with Chablis, lamb stew, raspberry puff pastry, Grand Marnier soufflé.

Summary & comments A bit formal and stiff, the restaurant owner and staff here are adorably accommodating, and the dishes are beyond reproach. We loved the farm-raised chicken cooked in Chablis, but at these prices it was a bit hard to stomach such a hefty tab for chicken.

CHEZ JENNY ★★★½

ALSACIAN BRASSERIE | MODERATE | QUALITY ★★★★ | VALUE ★★★ |
3RD ARRONDISSEMENT

39, boulevard du Temple, 75003; 01 44 54 39 00; Métro: République

Customers Choucroute lovers, tourists **Reservations** Advised **When to go** Late **Pricing** Average per person €30; prix fixe €15–22 (dinner, wine included) **Payment** VISA, MC, AMEX, DC, JCB, travelers' checks **English spoken** Yes **Bar** No **Wine selection** 50 wines, Alsatian wine, Pays de Loire, Bordeaux **Dress** Casual to good **Disabled access** Yes, except restroom

Hours Monday–Friday, noon–11 p.m.; Saturday and Sunday, noon–1 a.m.

Setting & atmosphere Terrace and garden seating, five dining rooms, 600 seats, 1930s sculptures, a museum of inlay work. The decor is typical, brassy brasserie style.

House specialties Regional (Alsatian), choucroute, fish, and seafood.

Summary & comments Owned by the same people who own Café Flore and the Cloiserie de Lilas, Chez Jenny is worth the trip only if you order one of the Alsatian specialties, particularly choucroute, the massive platters of sauerkraut, assorted pork cuts, sausage, and potatoes. A delicious variation is the choucroute with smoked haddock served with a beurre blanc sauce. You must order a fruity bottle of Alsatian wine or a few strong mugs of beer to wash this down. The service in our experience has been competent, but not more. Less glitzy and less expensive than Brasserie Lipp, and the food is better.

CHEZ JULIEN

INNOVATIVE FRENCH TRADITIONAL | EXPENSIVE | QUALITY ★★★★ | VALUE ★★★ |
4TH ARRONDISSEMENT

1, rue Pont Louis-Philippe, 75004; 01 42 78 31 64; Métro: Pont-Marie, Hôtel de Ville

Customers 30s and up, romantics **Reservations** Advised for dinner **When to go** Late **Pricing** Average per person €46; prix fixe €24 **Payment** VISA, MC, travelers' checks in euros and dollars **English spoken** Yes **Bar** None **Wine selection** Extensive selection of wines **Dress** Informal chic **Disabled access** No

Hours Tuesday–Friday, noon–2 p.m. and 7:30–11 p.m.; Monday and Saturday, 7:30–11 p.m.

Setting & atmosphere From the outside, this charming spot is highly inviting with its ceiling from 1900 and antique decor. In the summer months you can sit outside on the terrace and enjoy an enchanting view of Saint-Gervais Church, one of the oldest churches on the Right Bank. You're sitting a stone's throw from the Seine with your back to the Marais, and time has stopped here. Quite a romantic setting.

House specialties Profiteroles of snails with tarragon sauce, veal medallions with mushrooms, scallops.

Summary & comments We've admired this gem of a restaurant for years. One of the prettiest spots in this part of the Marais, and by far the best restaurant in the area. In the warm months, the open windows and the candlelight mix with the medieval surroundings and the 17th-century decor. We strongly recommend the snails.

CHEZ LA VIEILLE

OLD-TIME FRENCH BISTRO | MODERATE | QUALITY ★★★★ | VALUE ★★★★ |
1ST ARRONDISSEMENT

37, rue de L'Arbre-Sec, 75001; 01 42 60 15 78 Métro: Louvre-Rivoli

Customers Knowledgeable tourists, Parisians, professionals **Reservations** Required **When to go** Early **Pricing** Average per person €46; prix fixe €24 **Payment** VISA, AMEX, travelers' checks in euros **English spoken** Yes **Bar** None **Wine selection** 50 quality wines from Bordeaux, Bourgogne, and other regions **Dress** Casual to dressy **Disabled access** No

Hours Monday–Wednesday, Friday, noon–2 p.m.; Thursday, noon– 2 p.m. and 8–11 p.m.

Setting & atmosphere An excellent address where savvy Parisians sit at tables next to savvy travelers. The restaurant has more history than we have space for, so ask co-owner Marie-José Cervoni to tell you who has eaten here and what they were like.

House specialties Stew, kidneys, calf's liver, terrine maison.

Summary & comments Traditional French bistro cuisine with a very friendly, casual touch. Generous portions and a copious assortment of hors d'oeuvres and terrines. Arrive hungry or you'll feel frustrated. We like the pot-au-feu when it's cold out and the calf's liver with shallots any time.

COCONNAS ★★★½

TRADITIONAL/BOURGEOIS FRENCH | MODERATE | QUALITY ★★★½ | VALUE ★★★★ |
4TH ARRONDISSEMENT

2 bis, pl. des Vosges or 16, rue de Birague, 75004; 01 42 78 58 16; Métro: St-Paul-Le Marais

Customers Parisian regulars, tourists **Reservations** Advised for dinner **When to go** Lunch or early evenings **Pricing** Average per person €38; prix fixe €23 **Payment** VISA, MC, AMEX **English spoken** Yes **Bar** None **Wine selection** Wide selection, Bordeaux, Bourgogne, Beaujolais, certain very original wines **Dress** Casual to formal **Disabled access** No

Hours Tuesday–Sunday, noon–2:30 p.m. and 7:30–10 p.m.

Setting & atmosphere Very D'Artagnan (*Three Musketeers*)—hanging lamps and red curtains. Calm.

House specialties Tarte tatin, fish with balsmaic vinegar sauce, veal cutlet with vegetables.

Summary & comments Another of Claude Terrail's collection of fine Parisian eateries, this time under an arcade on the Place des Vosges, Victor Hugo's neighborhood. The prix fixe is a good deal for trying some of the house specialties. There is a new chef in the kitchen devising some lovely new recipes. Strolling around the Place des Vosges after dinner or lunch will be one of your most enjoyable moments in Paris. In the summer, you can sit on the terrace.

DAME TARTINE ★★★

SALADS/SANDWICHES | INEXPENSIVE | QUALITY ★★★ | VALUE ★★★★ |
4TH ARRONDISSEMENT

2, rue Brisemiche, 75004; 01 42 77 32 22; Métro: Hôtel-de-Ville

Customers Hip crowd, executives, tourists **Reservations** No **When to go** Lunch **Pricing** Average per person €13 **Payment** VISA, MC **English spoken** Some; menu in multiple languages **Bar** None **Wine selection** 3 vintage Bordeaux, Jura, Burgundy **Dress** Very casual **Disabled access** Yes

Hours Daily, 11 a.m.–midnight

Setting & atmosphere The atmosphere is upbeat and young. The terrace was recently renovated.

House specialties Chicken with morels, grilled cheese with green peppercorns.

Summary & comments Okay, this is not gourmet dining, but it's good, economical, and comfortable. If you love sandwiches, you can try a few French favorites like the salmon and zucchini or the chicken with morel mushrooms. Vegetarians have plenty to chose from, too. If you don't have a lot of time before or after a film or play, this is a good bet. Groups can negotiate with the manager for discounts of 10% to 18%. Look for other Dame Tartine locations throughout the city.

FISH!   ★★★★

MEDITERRANEAN BISTRO/WINE BAR | MODERATE | QUALITY ★★★★ | VALUE ★★★½ |
6TH ARRONDISSEMENT

69, rue de Seine, 75006; 01 43 54 34 69; Métro: Odéon

Customers Loyal regulars and tourists **Reservations** Recommended for dinner **When to go** Tourists show up at 7 p.m., the Parisians turn out at 9 p.m. **Pricing** €10–15 for main dishes **Payment** VISA, MC **English spoken** Yes **Bar** Wine bar **Wine selection** Large selection; 200+ **Dress** Casual **Disabled access** No

Hours Tuesday–Saturday, noon–3 p.m. and 7–11 p.m.; Sunday, 12:30–3:30 p.m. (brunch) and 7–11 p.m. Open afternoons for wine, snacks, and sweets.

Setting & atmosphere A cozy restaurant with comfortable and lively bar.

House specialties Grilled tuna (cooked as you like) with a garlic purée and a mille-feuille of eggplant, grilled entrecote served with radicchio and potatoes in a caper sauce, mussels marinated with cumin and corriander. For dessert, a lemon-orange tarte, carmelized apples in muscat wine sauce.

Summary & comments After two years, this "boissonerie," as it is called, continues to gain popularity with both customers from the quartier and those from abroad. Recently featured in *Gourmet* and *Bon Appetit* magazines, Fish! is known for its freshness and creativity. And the quality of its wine selection. (Fish! is in conjunction with Le Dernier Gout, a wine store just around the corner.) Without leaving Paris, here you're afforded an authentic taste of the Mediterranean in a warm ambiance. The two owners are on-site, and lend a particularly cheery touch to this successful Parisian eatery. Leave room for dessert and, of course, a glass of dessert wine!

404   ★★★½

MOROCCAN | MODERATE | QUALITY ★★★★ | VALUE ★★★★ | 3RD ARRONDISSEMENT

69, rue des Gravilliers, 75003; 01 42 74 57 81; Métro: Arts et Métiers

Customers Youngish and professional **Reservations** Required **When to go** Early or late **Pricing** Average per person €23; prix fixe €14 (lunch) **Payment** VISA, MC, AMEX,

DC, JCB, travelers' checks in euros **English spoken** Yes **Bar** None **Wine selection** Tunisian, Moroccan, Algerian, six French wines from Bordeaux and Burgundy **Dress** Casual **Disabled access** No

Hours Daily, noon–3 p.m. and 7 p.m.–1 a.m.; Berber lunch, Saturday and Sunday, noon– 4 p.m.

Setting & atmosphere When it comes to atmosphere, you'll not find more or better than 404, a small but inviting Moroccan restaurant with low, crowded tables, an open kitchen, exotic North African decor, candlelight, Arab music, and the aura of spices.

House specialties Tagine, duck with oranges.

Summary & comments Dishes are rushed to you in piping hot clay pots. You don't have to go to Marrakesh to visit the Casbah! Casual and exotic perfectly describe 404, where regulars return and bring their friends. We spotted Gina Lollobrigida here not long ago. The tagines are excellent.

HAIKU   ★★★½

VEGETARIAN/ORGANIC | MODERATE | QUALITY ★★★ | VALUE ★★★★ |
11TH ARRONDISSEMENT

63, rue Jean-Pierre Timbaud, 75011; 01 56 98 11 67; Métro: Parmentier, Rue St. Maur

Customers Vegetarians and health-conscious people **Reservations** Evenings only **When to go** Quieter early in the week or before 8:30 p.m. **Pricing** Average €16–20; prix fixe lunch €19–22 **Payment** VISA, MC **English spoken** Yes **Bar** No **Wine selection** Only one red, an organic Bordeaux **Dress** Casual **Disabled access** No

Hours Monday–Friday, noon–2:30 p.m. and 7–10:30 p.m.; Saturday, 7–10:30 p.m.

Setting & atmosphere Poetic understated design, functional and intelligent decor.

House specialties 95% organic ingredients, organic chicken, pasta inspired from Japanese lamen, tofu nems.

Other recommendations Observe the chef as he cooks in front of you in this small but original restaurant.

Summary & comments Haiku's mostly vegetarian dishes combine staple macrobiotic foods and spices in surprisingly satisfying ways. The owner was trained in microbiotic cooking in Boston and Appalachia—a highly original mix for a Parisian eatery. An Indian carrot starter salad harmoniously united nuts, ginger and raisins. Homemade, whole-grain pastas can be had stir fried with veggies or as elements of soup. Fish and chicken populate the menu, too, for those seeking a meatier meal. We tried the pâte marine, noodles with hijiki seaweed, carrots and toasted sesame seeds (€10), and the fennel- and coconut-hinted tofu soup (€8.70), both of whose noodles, greens and vegetables comprised cheap and satisfying meals in themselves. A healthy and fresh apple crumble arrived with light cream and coconut garnishes. An eclectic music selection, New Age to Soul Coughing, kept us guessing about the cook's tastes, who performed his alchemy in an open-concept kitchen in full view of the sparsely-attended, Asian-accented dining room. But more vegetarians should try

Haiku: Buddha knows there's enough mediocre-to-bad veggie food being served in Paris. Accompanying Haiku's select menu is a sort of philosophical treatise extolling the virtues of its Eastern-inspired cuisine. Other than persuading visitors that a 95% organic, low-cal, low-fat, high vitamin and mineral diet guarantees good health, the Q&A sheet also quotes from *Tampopo*, the food-obsessed Japanese cult film, by reminding diners to contemplate their noodles and ask before eating, "What good will I get from this pasta?"

JACQUES CAGNA

FRENCH HAUTE CUISINE | EXPENSIVE | QUALITY ★★★★ | VALUE ★★★★ |
6TH ARRONDISSEMENT

14, rue des Grands-Augustins, 75006; 01 43 26 49 39; Métro: St-Michel

Customers Serious culinary buffs **Reservations** Required for dinner **When to go** Early dinner **Pricing** Average per person €114; prix fixe €40 (lunch), €75 (dinner) **Payment** VISA, MC, AMEX, DC, JCB, travelers' checks in euros and dollars **English spoken** Yes **Bar** None **Wine selection** An impressive list of over 800 wines **Dress** Casual chic **Disabled access** No

Hours Tuesday–Friday, noon–2 p.m. and 7:30–10:30 p.m.; Saturday and Monday, 7:30–10:30 p.m.

Setting & atmosphere *Hôtel particulier* from the seventeenth century; wooded area, one of the most beautiful collections of seventeenth-century Dutch paintings.

House specialties Fresh snails petit gris en surprise "Jacques Cagna," fillet of river fish sautéed with mushrooms and asparagus; side of suckling veal with fresh ginger and lime and old-fashioned mashed potatoes; chopped warm apple served on vanilla ice cream; hen from Houdan, the wing poached, the thigh roasted with wild mushrooms.

Summary & comments Be prepared to forfeit a chunk of change here, but you're getting the real deal. You'll love your meal, and you'll be enchanted by the flavors, the presentation, the originality of the experience, and the delightful mix of nonpretension and utmost sophistication. Bring a dictionary and note what you've eaten. You'll not remember the details by yourself. Cagna loves to surprise and to invent. He's one of Paris's best, so remember that you're paying for the art, not just the ingredients.

JULIEN

ART-NOUVEAU BRASSERIE | MODERATE | QUALITY ★★★½ | VALUE ★★★ |
10TH ARRONDISSEMENT

16, rue du Fbg St-Denis, 75010; 01 47 70 12 06; Métro: Strasbourg-St-Denis

Customers Mixed, regulars, tourists, couples, professionals **Reservations** Advised on weekends **When to go** Late **Pricing** Average per person €37; prix fixe €21 (lunch), €30 (dinner) **Payment** VISA, MC, AMEX, DC, JCB, travelers' checks in euros and dollars **English spoken** Yes **Bar** Yes **Wine selection** 30 vintage wines **Dress** Casual to dressy **Disabled access** No

Hours Daily, noon–3 p.m. and 7 p.m.–1:30 a.m.

Setting & atmosphere Beautiful stained glass, wonderful flowers, antique hats hanging from ornate hat stands, and fabulous mirrors reflecting the art nouveau splendor surrounding you set the scene for tourists and smart French people to treat themselves.

House specialties Duck liver sautéed with lentils, filet of sole, and cassoulet.

Summary & comments Part of the Flo group of restaurants, Julien is a magnificent brasserie. The formally dressed waiters whiz around at high speed, delivering competently made if slightly overpriced dishes. Its position close to several theaters makes it a good choice for a late supper.

L'AMBASSADE D'AUVERGNE ★★★½

FRENCH REGIONAL (AUVERGNE) | MODERATE | QUALITY ★★★★½ | VALUE ★★★★ |
3RD ARRONDISSEMENT

22, rue du Grenier-St-Lazare, 75003; 01 42 72 31 22; Métro: Rambuteau

Customers Mixed **Reservations** Not needed **When to go** Sundays for lunch and dinner **Pricing** Average per person €38; prix fixe €26 **Payment** VISA, MC, AMEX, JCB, travelers' checks in euros **English spoken** Yes **Bar** None **Wine selection** Wines from the Auvergne, Bordeaux, Bourgogne **Dress** Informal chic **Disabled access** No

Hours Daily, noon–2 p.m. and 7:30–10:30 p.m.

Setting & atmosphere Warm environment. The first-floor dining room is rustic and cozy.

House specialties Regional dishes. Aligot (a wonderful mix of mashed potatoes, cheese, and garlic), beef fillet from Salers.

Other recommendations Cabbage soup with Roquefort, green lentil salad, stuffed cabbage, beef.

Summary & comments Once you've eaten here, you'll swear to return every time you come back to Paris. The Auvergne is one of France's most noted regions in terms of cuisine, and here you find the best of the region. For a group of friends looking to dine together, this is a perfect spot; the two-story restaurant has special rooms for groups of ten or more. This is a good choice for Sunday dining. The andouillette sausage is famous here. We prefer eating here in the cooler months, when the hearty cuisine is most welcome. If you've never tried an Auvergnat wine, this is your chance. And of course, try the regional cheeses.

L'AMBROISIE ★★★★½

FRENCH HAUTE CUISINE | EXPENSIVE | QUALITY ★★★★★ | VALUE ★★ |
4TH ARRONDISSEMENT

9, place des Vosges, 75004; 01 42 78 51 45; Métro: St-Paul-Le Marais

Customers Fine diners **Reservations** Reserve as far in advance as possible (a minimum of 1 month), and reconfirm before showing up **When to go** Not too late **Pricing**

Average per person €183 **Payment** VISA, MC, AMEX, travelers' checks in euros **English spoken** Yes **Bar** None **Wine selection** 500–600 vintage wines **Dress** Casual chic, sober elegance **Disabled access** Some tables only

Hours Tuesday–Saturday, noon–1:30 p.m. and 8–9:30 p.m.

Setting & atmosphere The tapestries on the walls set the tone for the meal. Two extended dining rooms are very pretty and help Danièle and Bernard Pacaud accommodate the demand to eat here.

House specialties Seasonal.

Summary & comments When Bill and Hillary Clinton were in Paris, this is where French President Jacques Chirac took them to eat. It's excellent and less pretentious than some of Paris's top gastronomic addresses, but you have to be prepared for a serious meal and a hefty bill. We have only included a few gastronomic superstars, and this is one of them. Perfect elegance abounds. You're in the hands of true artists who love to please and to surprise. Let them. The young hen dish is a celebration, if you don't look up the translation for poularde. Some rave about the marjolaine of foie gras of goose with truffles and celery. A dinner here will be more than a meal; it'll be a refined cultural event.

L'AMI LÉON ★★★½

CASUAL FRENCH BISTRO | MODERATE | QUALITY ★★★½ | VALUE ★★★★ |
1ST ARRONDISSEMENT

11, rue Jean-Jacques Rousseau, 75001; 01 42 33 06 20; Métro: Louvre

Customers Regular local clientele **Reservations** Required for dinner **When to go** Anytime **Pricing** Average per person €26; prix fixe €15 **Payment** VISA, MC **English spoken** No **Bar** None **Wine selection** 20 vintage wines from Bordeaux, Beaujolais, and Burgundy **Dress** Casual **Disabled access** No

Hours Monday–Friday, noon–2 p.m. and 7:30–10 p.m.; Saturday, closed for lunch, open 7:30–10 p.m.; closed in May and August

Setting & atmosphere With only a handful of tables, this 1945 bistro is cozy and familiar.

House specialties Changes monthly. Traditional French cuisine.

Other recommendations The chef does rabbit with great skill. The turnip and olive sautéed pork dish is delicious, too.

Summary & comments The dishes here are hearty and plentiful. The menu changes regularly, so ask what's new when you reserve. If rabbit is on the menu, order it. This is a great neighborhood find on a street filled with lots of interesting shops, including the lovely Véro-Dodat passage.

L'AUBERGE NICOLAS FLAMEL ★★★★

MEDIEVAL/TRADITIONAL | MODERATE | QUALITY ★★★½ | VALUE ★★★★ |
3RD ARRONDISSEMENT

51, rue de Montmorency, 75003; 01 42 71 77 78; Métro: Rambuteau

Customers Curious tourists **Reservations** Advised **When to go** Anytime, better at night **Pricing** Average per person €27 **Payment** VISA, MC, AMEX, DC, JCB **English spoken** Yes **Bar** None **Wine selection** 190 vintage wines ranging from small vineyards to famous crus **Dress** Casual **Disabled access** No

Hours Monday–Friday, noon–2 p.m. and 8–11 p.m.; Saturday, 8–11 p.m.

Setting & atmosphere It's always a thrill to eat in Paris's oldest house. The medieval building, a historic monument, dates back to 1407. It was once an almshouse. The 17th-century interior has been preserved, and the exposed stone and massive wooden beams create a cozy atmosphere that's perfectly authentic. The restaurant is dark and candlelit, making it particularly nice in the cold months. The upstairs dining area is called the "Salon des Anges."

House specialties Traditional cuisine. Leg of lamb that takes 48 hours to prepare, chocolate cake with 78% cocoa; beinget de fois gras; caramel au porto; tiramisu.

Summary & comments The cuisine here is heavily influenced by the traditions of the Middle Ages, and the dishes are hearty and massive. In the fall and winter, try the medieval hochepot, a complex stew of succulent parts of lamb, oxtail, and pork smothered in a kilo of vegetables. The lamb is excellent. The owner, Nathan, an accountant and wine-lover who chucked profit and loss statements to serve interesting medieval cuisine, is proud of both the restaurant and the history of the setting. He speaks English, and he's usually around from 9 p.m. onward to greet guests.

L'ESCARGOT MONTORGUEIL   ★★★★

FRENCH SNAILS | EXPENSIVE | QUALITY ★★★½ | VALUE ★★★ | 1ST ARRONDISSEMENT

38, rue Montorgueil, 75001; 01 42 36 83 51; Métro: Châtelet–Les Halles

Customers Parisians, show business workers **Reservations** Highly recommended **When to go** Early **Pricing** Average per person €46; prix fixe €23 (lunch), €29 (dinner) **Payment** VISA, MC, AMEX, JCB, travelers' checks in euros **English spoken** Yes **Bar** None **Wine selection** 100 vintages **Dress** Well dressed, but not formal **Disabled access** Yes

Hours Monday and Saturday, noon–2:30 p.m. and 7–11 p.m.; Tuesday–Friday, noon–2:30 p.m. and 7–10:30 p.m.; closed one week in August, May 1, and January 1

Setting & atmosphere The rue Montorgueil is one of the most animated and festive walkways in central Paris, deserving a visit in any case. Why not combine your stroll with a meal in this very atmospheric bistro, where meats are flamed and cut in front of you? In 1832 this building became a protected historic monument, and the decor feels more like museum than restaurant. Note that there is a painting of Sarah Bernhardt here.

House specialties Snails in different butters.

Summary & comments Don't go here if it's not for snails. But do go here for snails. Many guidebooks have dropped this one from their pages, complaining of an indifferent and pretentious service and inflated reputation. If you go for the snails and a glass of wine, you'll be delighted. Try the colimacon of mixed flavors of butter. You can share the 36-snail platter, drink up the butter with bits of baguette, and call it a meal! Don't worry about the rest, and don't feel pressured to order more. If you do, though, stay with the exotic, the stuff you can't get back home, like the frogs' legs, which are bony but tasty. Look like you know what you're doing.

L'IMPASSE ★★★½

TRADITIONAL BISTRO | MODERATE | QUALITY ★★★★ | VALUE ★★★★ |
1ST ARRONDISSEMENT

4, impasse Guéménée, 75004; 01 42 72 08 45; Métro: Bastille

Customers International **Reservations** Advised for dinner, especially for the terrace **When to go** Early or late **Pricing** Average per person €34; prix fixe €23 **Payment** VISA, MC, AMEX, DC **English spoken** Yes **Bar** No **Wine selection** 100 vintage wines **Dress** Casual **Disabled access** No

Hours Monday–Friday, noon–2:30 p.m.; Monday–Saturday, 7:45 p.m.–11:30 p.m.

Setting & atmosphere Lace windows, exposed stone and beams, marble bar. Old bistro.

House specialties Foie gras, terrine of ray with mint, terrine of chanterelle mushrooms, scallops with olive oil and basil, sweetbreads. Terrine of rabbit in aspic with sherry vinegar and cucumbers, thigh of duck in vintage wine and fruit (apples, prunes, walnuts). Beef with Roquefort sauce, escargots.

Summary & comments The pleasure of dining in Paris is discovering the authentic. This is it. It's an excellent value and about as French as it gets. Discreetly situated on a quiet street, Chez Robert has a loyal local following. Definitely try the house foie gras, which is the pride of the establishment. The wine-imbibed duck thigh served with fruit is lovely. And, the gourmandise au chocolat should not be missed.

L'OS À MOËLLE ★★★½

FRENCH BISTRO | MODERATE | QUALITY ★★★★ | VALUE ★★★★ | 15TH ARRONDISSEMENT

3, rue Vasco de Gama, 75015; 01 45 57 27 27; Métro: Lourmel

Customers Locals, Anglophones **Reservations** Advised **When to go** Not too late **Pricing** Average per person €46; prix fixe €27 (lunch), €32 (dinner) **Payment** VISA, MC, travelers' checks in euros **English spoken** Yes **Bar** Yes **Wine selection** 200 vintage wines **Dress** Casual **Disabled access** Yes

Hours Tuesday–Friday, noon–2 p.m. and 7–11:30 p.m.; closed Saturday– Monday and July 6–30.

Setting & atmosphere Red booths, lovely cellar with 17 seats for dining.

House specialties Market-driven menu, soups, homemade ice cream, and rice pudding.

Summary & comments People talk of L'Os à Moëlle as a real find; it is, although it suffers from having been discovered and claimed by everyone else before you get there. The four-course menu is good value for the money, and it's reliable. It changes daily and the quality is always high. The chef, M. Faucher, is very interested in ice cream, making this a good choice of dessert and his restaurant a good place to satisfy any cravings. The only problem with the L'Os à Moëlle is that it's a little hard to get excited about as they seem to have relaxed into a winning formula. It's a steady, safe choice in a sleepy neighborhood, which is great if that's what you're looking for. If not, try elsewhere.

LA BASTIDE ODÉON ★★★½

FRENCH BISTRO | MODERATE | QUALITY ★★★★½ | VALUE ★★★★ |
6TH ARRONDISSEMENT

7, rue Corneille, 75006; 01 43 26 03 65; Métro: Odéon

Customers Before and after theater crowd, regulars **Reservations** Required for dinner, 72 hours in advance **When to go** Early is better **Pricing** Average per person €43; prix fixe €30 **Payment** VISA, MC, AMEX, travelers' checks in euros **English spoken** Yes **Bar** None **Wine selection** Rhone Valley and Mediterranean wines plus those of Southeastern France **Dress** Casual to dressy **Disabled access** No

Hours Tuesday–Saturday, 12:30–2 p.m. and 7:30–10:30 p.m.; closed three weeks in August, one week for Christmas, and January 1

Setting & atmosphere One of Paris's newer "in" restaurants, located at the side of the Théâtre de l'Odéon and a minute's walk from the Jardin du Luxembourg. Split between two floors, both have their own charm, although we recommend upstairs for nonsmokers. Paintings on cloth, classical decor.

House specialties Riviera-style Napoleon of grilled eggplant, Provençale cuisine.

Summary & comments This address has captured the art of marrying fine ingredients and traditional cuisine with contemporary tastes and mildly innovative presentations. A highlight for us was a mysteriously crafted dessert that somehow captured warm melted chocolate inside a star-shaped cake covered with a spoon of vanilla ice cream and a lacing of coffee sauce.

LA COUPOLE ★★★★½

TRADITIONAL BOHEMIAN BRASSERIE | MODERATE | QUALITY ★★★ | VALUE ★★★ |
14TH ARRONDISSEMENT

102, boulevard du Montparnasse, 75014; 01 43 20 14 20; Métro: Vavin

Customers Regulars, artists, Parisians, tourists **Reservations** Advised **When to go** Great late **Pricing** Average per person €38; prix fixe €16–21 (lunch), €29 (dinner)

Payment VISA, MC, AMEX, DC, JCB, travelers' checks in euros **Bar** Yes **Wine selection** 80 vintage wines **Dress** Relaxed **Disabled access** Yes except restroom **Hours** Daily, 8:30 a.m.–2 a.m.; continental breakfast, 8:30–10:30 a.m.

Setting & atmosphere Large open space, dance hall (downstairs), open-style bar area (reception area, 7:30 a.m.–2 a.m.).

House specialties Indian-style lamb, raw seafood platters, onion soup.

Summary & comments You can't say you know Paris until you've eaten at least twice at La Coupole. Now part of the illustrious Flo group, La Coupole has played a significant role in the life of literary and artistic Paris for a century. Immortalized by Hemingway and Fitzgerald, Kiki of Montparnasse, and the throngs of expatriate writers and artists who frequented Montparnasse and engraved Paris as the eternal mythic capital of culture and decadence, La Coupole was their faithful watering hole. The culture set—the artists, actors and theater crowd, writers, poets with some money, journalists, and out-of-town visitors—buzz into this huge and bustling brasserie day and night. The food is fine but not high-end gourmet. Perfect for a bowl of onion soup with bubbling melted Gruyère or a plate of oysters, a pepper steak, or their special, lamb curry. We like La Coupole late at night when the crowd thins out and gets increasingly eclectic and drunk. All the clichés about Paris come true at La Coupole. It's one of the French capital's few venues where being a short-term visitor makes you a quintessential Parisian. Just keep your guidebook in your pocket and your daypack under the table.

LA GALLERIA RISTORANTE ★★★★

AUTHENTIC ITALIAN | MODERATE | QUALITY ★★★★ | VALUE ★★★★ | 15TH ARRONDISSEMENT

53, avenue de la Motte Picquet, 75015; Métro: La Motte-Piquet

Customers Mixed; neighborhood crowd **Reservations** Recommended for dinner **When to go** Late **Pricing** €20–25 for main dishes **Payment** VISA, MC **English spoken** Yes **Bar** None **Wine selection** Large selection, primarily Italian **Dress** Casual **Disabled access** No

Hours Daily, 7 p.m.–midnight.

Setting & atmosphere A chic and upbeat restaurant with a lot of style.

House specialties Suberb grilled prawns. Spicy pasta dishes with fresh egglant, peppers, and mushrooms. Lightly battered calamari. Italian regional wines.

Summary & comments Newly opened Italian restaurant in the lively area around La Motte Picquet. A short walk from Les Invalides and the Eiffel Tower. Italian owner, Fabrizio Roy, will do whatever it takes to make sure you are happy. He splits his time between La Galleria and the family-run hotel in St. Bart, and he knows the art of service. The food is delicious, authentically Italian (more northern than southern), and served hot. The atmosphere is perfect for people who love style but value comfort. The Chiantis are lovely.

LA RÔTISSERIE DU BEAUJOLAIS   ★★★★

COUNTRY-STYLE RÔTISSERIE | MODERATE | QUALITY ★★★★½ | VALUE ★★★★ |
5TH ARRONDISSEMENT

19, quai de la Tournelle, 75005; 01 43 54 17 47; Métro: Cardinal Lemoine or Pont Marie

Customers Mixed, foreigners **Reservations** Required **When to go** Early or late
Pricing Average per person €38 **Payment** VISA, MC, travelers' checks in euros **English
spoken** Yes **Bar** Yes **Wine selection** Beaujolais, 7 Bordeaux, good selection of wine
from Burgundy, Côte du Rhône **Dress** Informal chic **Disabled access** No

Hours Tuesday–Saturday, noon–2:15 p.m. and 7:30–10.30 p.m.; Sunday, noon–2:30 p.m.
and 7:30–10:30 p.m.

Setting & atmosphere One of Paris's first rotisserie haunts is both sumptuous and
relaxing for a busy bistro. You're sitting on street level by the Seine with a view of the illuminated Notre-Dame. The atmosphere is warm and lively.

House specialties Rotisserie (grilled meats), beef rib steak, cassoulet, preserved duck,
coq au vin, roast pigeon.

Summary & comments Situated next to the famed La Tour d'Argent, this very reliable and très Parisian restaurant is owned and operated by octogenarian Claude Terrail,
who owns La Tour d'Argent and other Parisian restaurants, and it rarely disappoints. Fans
keep coming back. The food is excellent although straightforward, centering around the
impressive grill, which you can watch from your table. The beef entrecôte is excellent. A
lot of people rave about the smothered duck, which you can only order for two. We found
the flavor succulent but the portions a bit lacking. This is a good place to sample coq au
vin, stewed in Beaujolais. For non–beef eaters, the cod is very good, as is the fillet de ras-
casse in olive oil. Even if you're stuffed, sample the cheeses.

LA TOUR D'ARGENT   ★★★★

FRENCH CULINARY LANDMARK | EXPENSIVE | QUALITY ★★★★½ | VALUE ★★ |
5TH ARRONDISSEMENT

17, quai de la Tournelle, 75005; 01 43 54 23 31; Métro: Maubert-Mutualité

Customers International chic set and those who want to watch them **Reservations**
Required **When to go** Lunch is a better deal **Pricing** Average per person €137; prix
fixe lunch €60 **Payment** VISA, MC, AMEX, DC, JCB, travelers' checks in euros **English spoken** Yes **Bar** Yes **Wine selection** Number one wine cellar in the world according to
the *Guinness Book of Records*, over 3,000 possible choices! **Dress** Formal—do it up here!
Disabled access Yes

Hours Tuesday–Sunday, noon–1:30 p.m.; 7:30–9:30 p.m.

Setting & atmosphere Elegant and romantic, although a tad old-fashioned. Perched
above the Seine with one of the most enchanting views of Paris at night—the vaulted back

of Notre-Dame bathed in light and shadow—La Tour d'Argent is the kind of place you return to once each decade. (By the way, we've been told that the restaurant pays for lighting the cathedral!) Woody Allen dines here on every trip to Paris. The walls are speckled with autographed photographs of movie stars, singers, and heads of state who've dined here, and even the elevator that takes you up to the main dining room is covered with personal notes from Nobel Prize winners and presidents. Other notable customers included Orson Welles, Maurice Chevalier, General Dwight D. Eisenhower, and Queen Elizabeth II.

House specialties Duckling, duckling, duckling, foie gras of goose, quenelles de brochet André Terrail (founder of restaurant).

Summary & comments Clearly past its heyday, La Tour d'Argent remains on our list due to its stature, history, and mythical value. But don't get us wrong, the food remains excellent and the atmosphere is one of a kind. The place is simply more of a landmark than a culinary mecca. Famed Parisian restaurateur Claude Terrail, now in his 80s, continues to be on hand in his impeccable bow tie on most nights. His life is this glittering spot on earth; he was born on the fifth floor. The duck is this landmark's most famous dish, as each dinner comes with a card indicating the duck's registration number. From a culinary point of view, value is a point of debate. You pay for the reputation, the view, and the right to say you've dined at La Tour d'Argent. For better value, reserve for lunch when the prices are merely expensive; to take in the view at night, try sneaking a peek when you stop by to make your lunch reservations.

LADURÉE

FRENCH/TEA ROOM | MODERATE | QUALITY ★★★★½ | VALUE ★★★★ |
8TH ARRONDISSEMENT

75, av. des Champs-Elysées, 75008; 01 40 75 08 75; Métro: George V or Franklin Roosevelt

Customers Dessert lovers **Reservations** Advised **When to go** Lunch is a good deal **Pricing** Average per person €38; prix fixe €34 for 2 (lunch), €18–30 (dinner) **Payment** VISA, MC, AMEX, travelers' checks **English spoken** Yes **Bar** Yes **Wine selection** 600 vintage wines, small vineyards, grands crus **Dress** Casual **Disabled access** No

Hours Daily, 8 a.m.–1 a.m.

Setting & atmosphere Summer terrace, Napoléon III style, decorated by Jacques Garcia; 180 seats, five private dining rooms. The decor of this famous tea room matches both its clientele and its kitchen—rich, opulent, and rather grand.

House specialties Macaroon (almond and sugar cake), seasonal produce.

Summary & comments Just as you can't come to Paris and not walk down the Champs-Elysées, neither should you be able to walk past Ladurée. There is a proper restaurant as well as the tea room, but the point here is pastries, and it seems a shame to adulterate the pure pleasure with "real" food. Lots of the smart ladies who lunch here seem happy enough to stick to a salad, but we definitely recommend that you try their amazing hot chocolate and their famous macaroons. We could happily wax lyrical about the quality of Ladurée's "macaroon," otherwise known as cookie heaven, but fear that we might get carried away. Go see for yourself.

LE BALZAR   ★★★½

TRADITIONAL BRASSERIE | MODERATE | QUALITY ★★★★ | VALUE ★★★★ |
5TH ARRONDISSEMENT

49 rue des Ecoles, 75005; 01 43 54 13 67; Métro: Cluny-La Sorbonne

Customers Very Parisian, classy customers; English-speaking tourists in the summer **Reservations** Required 48 hours in advance **When to go** Early or late **Pricing** Average per person €33 **Payment** VISA, MC, AMEX, travelers' checks in euros **English spoken** Some, English menu **Bar** No **Wine selection** Large, most under €23 a bottle **Dress** Informal **Disabled access** No

Hours Daily, noon–1:30 a.m.; closed in August

Setting & atmosphere Situated right next to the Sorbonne on the rue des Ecoles, this landmark has a touch of literary and intellectual ambience. Not a very large place, and the tables fill up quickly; without reservations you're likely to wait a while. The narrow window-box of a café/bar is very pleasant for an aperitif while waiting for your table.

House specialties Veal, liver, ray fish with capers.

Summary & comments One of Paris's staple brasseries attracts Parisians and adoring Francophiles. Legend has it that Balzar, now part of the Flo group, was created by a feuding family member who controlled Brasserie Lipp. Of the two today, we prefer Balzar. For starters, try the classic herring and warm potatoes or the leek vinaigrette, followed by a steak tartare (if you like perfectly lean, seasoned raw beef) or the raie au beurre (ray fish in melted butter). To remain perfectly classic, opt for the warm caramelized apple tart (tarte tatin) for dessert or the lemon tart with powdered sugar (tarte au citron). This is eating Parisian style.

LE BELLECOUR   ★★★

FRENCH BOURGEOIS | MODERATE | QUALITY ★★★½ | VALUE ★★★★ |
7TH ARRONDISSEMENT

22, rue Surcouf, 75007; 01 45 51 46 93; Métro: Invalides

Customers Parisian wealthy and established crowd **Reservations** Required **When to go** Not too late **Pricing** Prix fixe only, €37 **Payment** VISA, MC, AMEX, D, DC, JCB, traveler's checks in euros **English spoken** Yes **Bar** None **Wine selection** 300 vintage wines **Dress** Casual **Disabled access** Yes

Hours Monday–Friday, noon–2:30 p.m. and 7:30–10 p.m.; Saturday, 7:30–10 p.m.; closed August

Setting & atmosphere Classical, tranquil, and calm; only 12 tables.

House specialties Menu changes three times a year. Warm cutlet of buckwheat and crab with a vinaigrette dressing, daurade (bream) with a purée of eggplant, roast lamb cooked in Chablis.

Summary & comments If you are up for a bit of high-society bourgeois-spotting then you will not be disappointed with Le Bellecour. This is the perfect place to watch the French middle-class residents of the seventh arrondissement over dinner. The food, like the clientele, is perfectly respectable and subtly rich. Everyone speaks in hushed tones while enjoying good value (but not cheap) Lyonnaise food and quietly complimentary wines.

LE BISTRO DE GALA

FRENCH/AMERICAN SOUTHWEST | MODERATE | QUALITY ★★★★½ | VALUE ★★★★★ |
9TH ARRONDISSEMENT

45, rue du Fbg Montmartre, 75009; 01 40 22 90 50; Métro: Le Peletier

Customers Young and creative types **Reservations** Advised **When to go** Anytime **Pricing** Average per person €28; prix fixe €34 **Payment** VISA, MC, AMEX **English spoken** Yes **Bar** None **Wine selection** Wines direct from the vineyards **Dress** Casual chic **Disabled access** Yes

Hours Monday–Friday, noon–2:30 p.m. and 7:30–11:30 p.m.; Saturday, 7–11:30 p.m.

Setting & atmosphere The owner of this charming bistro is a cinema freak whose passion for the silver screen is reflected in the film posters decorating the walls.

House specialties American Southwest dishes.

Summary & comments You can expect a warm welcome, and if you find the tardy service inherent in many Parisian restaurants irritating you won't be disappointed by the speedy act laid on here. The house specializes in cooking from the American Southwest, and the menu changes every day, depending on what's in season. This is a welcome pit stop in an area with few decent restaurants. We can't guarantee you'll find what we found, but the gazpacho de langoustine and the carpaccio de melon with ham from the Vendée were excellent and refreshing in the summer. Other memorable dishes include the artichoke and salmon fumé rémoulade, followed by the duckling ravioli with foie gras and a surprising marmite of pig's cheeks! Lots of great fish every day.

LE BUDDHA BAR

SHOWBIZ HANGOUT | EXPENSIVE | QUALITY ★★★½ | VALUE ★★★ |
8TH ARRONDISSEMENT

8, rue Boissy d'Anglas, 75008; 01 53 05 90 00 or 01 55 35 36 80; Métro: Concorde

Customers Star-gazers **Reservations** Advised for dinner **When to go** Late **Pricing** Average per person €69 **Payment** VISA, MC, AMEX, travelers' checks in euros and dollars **English spoken** Yes **Bar** Yes **Wine selection** Good **Dress** Chic and trendy **Disabled access** Yes

Hours Monday–Friday, 12:30–3 p.m. and 7:30 p.m.–2:30 a.m.; Saturday and Sunday, 7:30 p.m.–2:30 a.m.

Setting & atmosphere A Grand Buddha sits in the large dining room, the bar is in the form of a dragon, and the mezzanine sports a massive chandelier. At the Buddha Bar, you go to see and be seen, drink, and eat, in that order.

House specialties Smoked duck, pan-fried shrimp, choice of caviar, chocolate desserts.

Entertainment & amenities DJ every night.

Summary & comments The huge, imposing, gold Buddha statue is impressive, but it won't improve what's on your plate. The dishes combine a heavy Asian influence, seasoned with California chic and sprinkled with definite Frenchness. The crispy tea duck is a favorite. Otherwise, eat elsewhere and go for a drink to see what all the talk is about. Or go for a drink first and decide if you want to stay for dinner.

LE GRAND COLBERT   ★★★★

FRENCH | MODERATE | QUALITY ★★★★ | VALUE ★★★★ | 2ND ARRONDISSEMENT

2–4, rue Vivienne, 75002; 01 42 86 87 88; Métro: Bourse

Customers Parisian regulars, after theater crowd **Reservations** Advised **When to go** Early or late **Pricing** Average per person €34; prix fixe €24 **Payment** VISA, MC, AMEX, traveler's checks in euros or dollars **English spoken** Yes **Bar** Yes **Wine selection** 60 vintage wines **Dress** Casual to dressy **Disabled access** No

Hours Daily, noon–1 a. m.

Setting & atmosphere If we asked you to imagine what a traditional Parisian brasserie looks like, we reckon that this is what you'd come up with. The Belle Epoque–style building, classified as a historic monument, is really quite stunning and definitely worth a visit.

House specialties Baked crawfish in Chablis, Indian-style lamb curry, fresh cod with olive purée.

Entertainment & amenities Air conditioning, parking, wet bar, near theaters.

Summary & comments Friendly, efficient waiters serve late at Le Grand Colbert, and there's guaranteed to be something on the long menu to make your mouth water. Fans of steak tartare will not be disappointed, but if that's not your thing, then go for the excellent cod with puréed potatoes or the tasty lamb curry.

LE GRAND VEFOUR   ★★★★★

CLASSIC FRENCH | EXPENSIVE | QUALITY ★★★★★ | VALUE ★★★★★ |
1ST ARRONDISSEMENT

17, rue du Beaujolais, 75001; 01 42 96 56 27; Métro: Tuileries

Customers Wealthy diners, Parisians, curious tourists **Reservations** Advised, at least six weeks in advance **When to go** Lunch is a better deal **Pricing** Average per person

€185; prix fixe €69 **Payment** VISA, MC, AMEX, DC, JCB, travelers' checks in euros and dollars **English spoken** Yes **Bar** None **Wine selection** 600+ vintage wines **Dress** Jacket mandatory, dresses recommended **Disabled access** Yes except restrooms **Hours** Monday–Thursday, 12:30–1:45 p.m. and 7:30–9:45 p.m.; closed August, Christmas, May 1

Setting & atmosphere 19th-century style, with an 18th-century ceiling, "Café de Chartre."

House specialties Ravioli of foie gras in a truffle-laced cream. Pigeon Prince Rainier III.

Summary & comments If you are going for a serious gourmet meal and you're not sure which of Paris's culinary landmarks to choose, let us help you. If you're after the latest and the height of Paris chic, go elsewhere. If you want high visibility and pretension, go elsewhere. If you want to be treated like a duke and duchess, sit among the royal collection of art and objects, and dine in the utmost of timeless French gastronomy under the arches of the Palais Royal, reserve at Le Grand Vefour. This is the best of Paris's old wealth. Pigeon Prince Rainier III is a house specialty. Do we need to say more? Give yourself three to four hours and get a babysitter for the kids. If you don't want to spend as much time or money on one meal, try Le Grand Vefour for lunch. You'll need a siesta, though, in the afternoon.

LE JARDIN DES PÂTES ★★★½

HEALTHY CUISINE & PASTA | MODERATE | QUALITY ★★★ | VALUE ★★★★ | 5TH ARRONDISSEMENT

4, rue de Lacèpède, 75005; 01 43 31 50 71; Métro: Jussieu

Customers Health-conscious, pasta-lovers, few tourists **Reservations** Encouraged **When to go** Anytime **Pricing** Average per person €16–20, prix fixe €19 **Payment** VISA, MC **English spoken** Limited **Bar** No **Wine selection** Limited **Dress** Casual **Disabled access** No

Hours Daily, noon–2 :30 p.m. and 7–11 p.m.

Setting & atmosphere Simple, well-lit wooden tables and soft-shaded walls. Wholesome feel.

House specialties Chestnut pasta with duck, tofu and ginger.

Summary & comments After a stroll through the glorious Jardin des Plantes (don't forget the spectacular alpine garden), why not amble over to the aptly-named Jardin des Pâtes (that's "pasta garden") for a super-filling noodle feast? Here on a quiet side-street, you'll discover a small menu of homemade dishes that attract mostly locals. This is fresh pasta, too: each dish is prepared from the various organic flours the staff grinds themselves. You may not feel obligated to order a first course: ours weren't spectacular (an avocado and melon sherbet salad struck as us the wrong combination, and an ordinary chèvre-tomato-green salad cried out for fresher ingredients). Luckily, the massive portions of pasta pleased everyone at the table, stuffing us after having consumed the first course. We sampled the chestnut pasta (with duck) in a mushroom-nutmeg cream sauce (€11.80), the rice pasta with tofu and ginger (€7.17), a tomato-mozzarella-basil sauce over wide wheat fettuccini (€5.50), and noodles and scallions held in place by an omelet

(€5.95). Try a shot of Farigoule, a thyme liqueur, to finish off: guaranteed, you've never tasted a digestif so unusually luscious. With our cereal-based fake coffee, we took in a fresh cherry claufoutis, an egg-based tart bathed in cream. This isn't a place to offer many wines, but its decent prices and generous plate sizes are rare in Paris.

LE KERYADO

BOUILLABAISSE BISTRO | MODERATE | QUALITY ★★★★ | VALUE ★★★★ |
13TH ARRONDISSEMENT

32, rue de Regnault, 75013; 01 45 83 87 58; Métro: Porte d'Ivry

Customers Locals and regulars **Reservations** Advised, especially for weekends **When to go** More fun at dinner **Pricing** Average per person €23; prix fixe €9–14 (lunch), €17–23 (dinner) **Payment** VISA, MC, travelers' checks in euros **English spoken** Yes **Bar** No **Wine selection** Small selection of white wines direct from the vineyards, Côteau d'Aix en Provence €16 **Dress** Casual **Disabled access** No

Hours Monday–Saturday, noon–2:30 p.m. and 7:30–10:30 p.m.; closed three weeks in August

Setting & atmosphere Mediterranean, decked out in white and blue.

House specialties Bouillabaisse, all kinds of fish.

Summary & comments The main attraction here is the bouillabaisse, a wonderfully rich fish soup, of which they are rightfully proud and which should not be missed. The menu offers lots of choices, but we recommend that you stick to what they do best and order the soup, which comes with an amazing side platter groaning with different fish. Everything is fantastically fresh and truly delicious, and provides a great photo opportunity. It's also a lot of fun to eat—make sure you slurp your soup, attack your lobster with gusto, and smear vast quantities of rich garlicky sauce onto your croutons. An added pleasure for tourists is that this quaint restaurant is located in an obscure corner of the 13th arrondissement and is little-known to many out-of-towners and Parisians alike.

LE MOULIN À VINS

NEIGHBORHOOD BISTRO | MODERATE | QUALITY ★★★½ | VALUE ★★★★ |
18TH ARRONDISSEMENT

6, rue Burq, 75018; 01 42 52 81 27; Métro: Abbesses

Customers Young people, neighborhood crowd, foreigners **Reservations** Advised for dinner on weekends **When to go** Not too late **Pricing** Average per person €30 **Payment** VISA, MC, AMEX **English spoken** Yes **Bar** Yes **Wine selection** Extensive selection, especially Côte du Rhône and wines from Provence **Dress** Relaxed **Disabled access** No

Hours Tuesday–Saturday, 6 p.m.–2 a.m.; closed three weeks in August

Setting & atmosphere Frescos on the wall by local painters. It is always packed with locals, artists, and other Bohemian types who hang out in Montmartre.

House specialties Andouillette sausage, bean and sausage hot pot.

Entertainment & amenities Occasionally, Saturday night is accordion night, and it's very popular. Go early and prepare to sing along to Piaf classics all night.

Summary & comments This gem of a bistro nestles at the foot of the hill and is more than enough to deter you from the climb. As the name (the Wine Mill) suggests, this is a wine buff's dream, devoted to all things rouge, blanc, and rosé. The wine list, lovingly compiled by owner Dany, is wonderfully comprehensive and will satisfy both the amateur and serious wine drinker. The food lives up to the wine and can be quite delicious. This is what a night out in Paris should be like.

LE PÈRE CLAUDE   ★★★½

FRENCH | MODERATE/EXPENSIVE | QUALITY ★★★½ | VALUE ★★★ |
15TH ARRONDISSEMENT

51, avenue de la Motte-Picquet, 75015; 01 47 34 03 05, fax 01 40 56 97 84; Métro: La Motte-Picquet Grenelle

Customers Celebrities, politicians, friends of the owner **Reservations** Recommended **When to go** Late is more fun; it's packed after 9 p.m. **Pricing** Average €20 (lunch) and €30 (dinner); prix fixe €17 lunch, €24 dinner **Payment** VISA, AMEX **English spoken** Yes **Bar** Yes **Wine selection** Good **Dress** Informal to eccentric **Disabled access** No

Hours Daily, noon–2 p.m. and 7 p.m.–until

Setting & atmosphere Friendly, bright, casual elegance, memorabilia and signed photographs on the walls. A bit loud.

House specialties Home-made terrines, sautéed frog's legs, spit-roasted beef.

Summary & comments Le Père Claude is a Paris institution. This small but accessible restaurant near the Eiffel Tower and the Ecole Militaire is a favorite of politicians, stars, business magnates, and friends of the flamboyant owner who want to let their hair down. The food is good, but the atmosphere of Parisians enjoying themselves makes this dining choice worth it. A good choice for a late night dinner when you want to be in well-dressed, loud company.

LE RÉCAMIER   ★★★

TRADITIONAL FRENCH | EXPENSIVE | QUALITY ★★★★ | VALUE ★★★ |
7TH ARRONDISSEMENT

4, rue Récamier, 75007; 01 45 48 86 58; Métro: Sèvres-Babylone

Customers Publishing world, politicians, journalists (lunch); Parisians and international set (dinner) **Reservations** Advised **When to go** Early dinner **Pricing** Average per person €69 **Payment** VISA, MC, AMEX, DC, travelers' checks in euros **English spoken** Yes **Bar** Yes **Wine selection** Extensive **Dress** Dressy **Disabled access** Yes

Hours Monday–Saturday, noon–2:30 p.m. and 7:30–10:30 p.m.

Setting & atmosphere Turn-of-century style, formerly a literary salon. Le Récamier is a landmark restaurant for elected officials and leaders in the publishing industry, including best-selling authors. Political life meets intellectual life on the spacious terrace that flanks this old-time Burgundy favorite.

House specialties Regional (Burgundy) beef bourguignonne, foie gras, Châteaubriand.

Other recommendations Veal liver, salmon.

Summary & comments The menu and the decor have become rather faded, but if this is your first time to either Paris or this restaurant, this won't be a distraction from the quality and taste of the very fresh foie gras, the parsley ham from Burgundy, and the house specialty, Châteaubriand served with perfect little pommes Dauphine. The salmon and sorrel are excellent if you like the taste of the slightly sour, spinach-like plant. Otherwise, go for the beef bourguignonne or the veal liver, which is tender and served as a thick steak. Sit on the outdoor terrace or covered terrace; they're both delightful.

LE RESTAURANT   ★★★½

FRENCH/AFRICAN | INEXPENSIVE | QUALITY ★★★★ | VALUE ★★★★★ |
18TH ARRONDISSEMENT

32, rue de Véron, 75018; 01 42 23 06 22; Métro: Abbesses

Customers Young and multicultural, artists, trendy people **Reservations** Advised **When to go** Anytime **Pricing** Average per person €27; prix fixe €12 (lunch), €18 (dinner) **Payment** VISA, MC, AMEX, JCB, travelers' checks in euros **English spoken** Yes **Bar** Yes, for diners **Wine selection** Small, 70 labels **Dress** Casual **Disabled access** Yes, except restrooms

Hours Sunday–Thursday, noon–2:30 p.m. and 7:30–11:30 p.m.; Friday and Saturday, 7:30 p.m.–midnight

Setting & atmosphere Decorated in interesting bric-a-brac with lots of wood surfaces and candles. Friendly African waitresses. Lots of diverse chairs and tables of differing sizes and shapes. Music and aromas from far-off lands.

House specialties Grilled leeks, spare ribs, duckling with honey, tagine, farm chicken, daurade (bream).

Summary & comments Innovative young chef-owner Yves Peladeau cut his culinary teeth at the illustrious Le Grand Vefour before opening Le Restaurant. The food is excellent value and focuses on marrying exotic spices, reflecting Yves's African heritage, with traditional French ingredients. The menu changes frequently depending on the season and what catches the chef's eye at the market. The young patrons are happily crushed into the intimate dining room and lap up the atmosphere and the food with great enthusiasm. This is the type of place you'll want to come back to each time you're in Paris.

LE SQUARE TROUSSEAU   ★★★½

FRENCH | MODERATE | QUALITY ★★½ | VALUE ★★★ | 12TH ARRONDISSEMENT

1, rue Antoine Vollon, 75012; 01 43 43 06 00; fax 01 43 43 00 66; trousseau@club-internet. fr; Métro: Ledru-Rollin

Customers Locals and tourists **Reservations** Required **When to go** Early or late **Pricing** Average €22 (lunch), €44 (dinner); prix fixe lunch, €19–22 **Payment** VISA, MC, AMEX **English spoken** No **Bar** Yes **Wine selection** 300 references **Dress** Casual **Disabled access** No

Hours Daily, noon–2:30 p.m. and 8–11:30 p.m.

Setting & atmosphere Bistrot 1900

House specialties Fresh, market-led cooking.

Other recommendations Pave de fois de veau sauce cassis, carrots sautéed in cumin, souris d'agneau avec les petits lugumes au jus.

Summary & comments This turn-of-the-century bistro will delight you. It's so typical, you'll think it was made from a kit. But no, it's the real thing, and on top of it, Le Square Trousseau is located on a lovely square just outside the range of the throngs of tourists. If it's full, you'll be among Parisians enjoying themselves. The wines are good, but there's no reason to go beyond the house wines which are reasonable and tasty with everything from the cold cuts to the duck, beef, and fish.

LE VIEUX BISTRO ★★★½

TRADITIONAL FRENCH BISTRO | MODERATE | QUALITY ★★★★½ | VALUE ★★★★ |
4TH ARRONDISSEMENT

14, rue du Cloître Notre-Dame, 75004; 01 43 54 18 95; Métro: St-Michel or RER St-Michel-Notre-Dame

Cust on–2:30 p.m. and 7:30–11 p.m.; closed December 24 and 25

Setting & atmosphere Turn-of-the-century bistro. What we like about Le Vieux Bistro is its timelessness. Walk around Notre-Dame at night after the tourists have left the vicinity, and you get lost in the shadows and echoes of the world's most celebrated cathedral. In its shadow, you find this old-time restaurant that seems untouched by the hordes of camera-toting visitors with water bottles.

House specialties Frisée salad with bacon, beef bourguignonne (of course).

Summary & comments Everything is good here, so take your pick, but the management is quick to point out that *American Express Magazine* called their beef bourguignonne the best in the city. We can't contest that. For dessert order the tarte tatin, which is flambéed in Calvados. We like going late and then wandering around the haunting back streets of Île de la Cité.

LE VILLARET ★★★½

INNOVATIVE FRENCH | MODERATE | QUALITY ★★★★½ | VALUE ★★★★★ |
11TH ARRONDISSEMENT

13, rue Ternaux, 75011; 01 43 57 89 76; Métro: Parmentier

Customers 25 to 40s crowd, cultivated **Reservations** Advised **When to go** Late **Pricing** Average per person €40; prix fixe €23 (lunch) **Payment** VISA, MC **English spoken** Yes **Bar** No **Wine selection** Carefully selected wines from small vineyards; many under €25; 240 vintages **Dress** Casual **Disabled access** Yes, except restrooms **Hours** Monday–Tuesday, noon–2 p.m. and 7 p.m.–midnight; Wednesday–Friday, noon–2 p.m. and 7 p.m.–1 a.m.; Saturday, 7 p.m.–1 a.m.; closed in August and for Christmas

Setting & atmosphere Le Villaret is a popular spot that's always packed with a youngish crowd enjoying a noisy evening out. The tables are tightly packed together, and the volume levels can be unbearable at times. This is best left off the list when you're choosing a romantic spot for an intimate dinner, but it's a good choice with a group of raucous friends.

House specialties Prime rib of farm veal with asparagus and morels, shepherd's pie with beef jowls, warm clafouti pie with mango and coconut milk, according to season.

Entertainment & amenities Air-conditioning.

Summary & comments The menu changes daily according to what the chef finds in the market that morning and tends to be just okay rather than really good. Watch out for the steak, which is only served rare; unless you like your beef practically still mooing, this isn't the place for you. The wine list is interesting, especially the selection of "grand cru" wines, which are offered at reasonable prices.

LES AMOGNES   ★★★★

STYLISH FRENCH | MODERATE | QUALITY ★★★★½ | VALUE ★★★★★ | 11TH ARRONDISSEMENT

243, rue du Fbg. St.-Antoine, 75011; 01 43 72 73 05; Métro: Faidherbe-Chaligny

Customers Mix of locals and tourists **Reservations** Required **When to go** Early **Pricing** Average per person €46; prix fixe €28 **Payment** VISA, MC **English spoken** Yes **Bar** None **Wine selection** Excellent selections of Burgundy, Bordeaux, Côtes du Rhône; 50 vintages **Dress** Relaxed **Disabled access** No **Hours** Tuesday–Friday, noon–2 p.m. and 8–10:30 p.m.; Saturday and Monday, 8–11 p.m.; closed three weeks in August

Setting & atmosphere Beamed ceilings, stone walls, art exhibition, warm atmosphere. Tasteful and slightly trendy, but sincere. The restaurant is small; even if you have reservations, be prepared to wait for 15 minutes or so on the weekends. The tables are a bit crowded, which is normal for Paris.

House specialties Sweetbreads, marinated sardine tart; menu changes every three weeks.

Summary & comments This is the kind of place you need to be sent to. From the street, you couldn't know that one eats exceptionally well here and the chef has a citywide reputation. In fact, from outside you'll think that you copied down the address wrong. Well, it is the right place, and you won't be sorry. You'll eat as well here as at many other gastronomic restaurants in higher-rent districts where you'd pay twice as much. The tart with marinated sardines is delicious. The wine list is ample and well selected at moderate prices. Perfect for couples out for a peaceful tête-à-tête.

LES PETITES SORCIÈRES ★★★★

INTIMATE FRENCH BISTRO | MODERATE | QUALITY ★★★★½ | VALUE ★★★★ |
14TH ARRONDISSEMENT

12, rue Liancourt, 75014; 01 43 21 95 68; Métro: Denfert-Rochereau

Customers Locals and curious seekers **Reservations** Advised **When to go** Early or late **Pricing** Average per person €30; prix fixe €18 **Payment** VISA, MC **English spoken** Yes **Bar** Yes for customers **Wine selection** 40 vintage wines and wines direct from the vineyards **Dress** Casual **Disabled access** Yes except restrooms

Hours Tuesday–Friday, noon–1:45 p.m. and 8–10:30 p.m.; Saturday, 8–10:30 p.m.

Setting & atmosphere 34 seats; you're a bit crowded, but the atmosphere is pleasant and you'll feel right at home. Modern witch motif!

House specialties Strips of duck with tapenade (purée of olives).

Summary & comments A delightful small restaurant completely worth the detour. Run and operated by owner/chef Christian Teule, bistros like this are what make Paris dining so special. The menu changes all the time, depending on the mood and idea of the chef, so it's hard to tell you what you'll find. We ate here in the winter and were greeted by a savory pumpkin soup. Dishes are conceived with imagination and skill, and the tastes are crafted in fresh and innovative ways. The tapenade is delicious. Small and a bit smoky, but very Parisian in its independent and temperamental nature.

LES PHILOSOPHES ★★★★

FRENCH | MODERATE | QUALITY ★★★ | VALUE ★★★★ | 4TH ARRONDISSEMENT

28, rue Vieille-du-Temple, 75004; 01 48 87 49 64; www.cafeine.com; Métro: Hôtel-de-Ville

Customers Locals, regulars, and informed visitors **Reservations** Not required **When to go** Lunch or late night **Pricing** Average per person €20; prix fixe €13–21 **Payment** VISA, MC, travelers' checks in euros and dollars **English spoken** Yes **Bar** No **Wine selection** 25 choice wines, many directly from the vineyards, €14.50 to a whopping €555! **Dress** Informal **Disabled access**

Hours Daily, noon–1:15 a.m.

Setting & atmosphere For those of you who know the Petit Fer à Cheval bar/café/restaurant in the Marais, you know that its former owner is capable of creating excellent atmosphere for his guests. This is what Xavier Denamur has done with Les Philosophes. The large terrace is particularly pleasant in the warm months for simple but savory dining and people-watching.

House specialties Tatin à la tomate (an original creation), espresso-flavored cake.

Summary & comments If you're planning a big meal in the evening, a light lunch here is an excellent idea, and the two-course set menu allows you to select the main course and either and appetizer or dessert. We like the tomato tart and the lamb.

LES ZYGOMATES ★★★½

FRENCH BISTRO | MODERATE | QUALITY ★★★★ | VALUE ★★★★★ |
12TH ARRONDISSEMENT

7, rue de Capri, 75012; 01 40 19 93 04; Métro: Michel-Bizot

Customers Regulars and tourists **Reservations** Advised **When to go** Anytime **Pricing** Average per person €24; prix fixe €12 (lunch), €21 (dinner) **Payment** VISA, MC **English spoken** Yes **Bar** None **Wine selection** 60 vintage wines **Dress** Casual **Disabled access** Yes

Hours Monday–Friday, noon–2 p.m. and 7:30–10:45 p.m.; Saturday, 7:30–10 p.m.; closed August

Setting & atmosphere Old charcuterie; turn-of-the-last-century atmosphere; friendly.

House specialties Pig's tail with morel mushrooms, fois gras with pine nut salad.

Summary & comments It's easy to see why Les Zygomates is always busy. Low prices, friendly service, seasonal cuisine, and excellent quality make it well worth a visit. The prix fixes are always good and modestly priced. This place used to be a pork butcher's shop, and the quality of the meat dishes reflects its previous incarnation. The specialty "queue de cochon aux morilles" or pig's tail with morel mushrooms may not sound too tempting and is maybe not for the squeamish, but it is succulent and tasty and well worth the bravery involved in the choice. Make sure to leave room for the Zygomates Greedy Platter (*Assiette Gourmandes des Zygomates*), which boasts a selection of their delicious desserts.

MONSIEUR LAPIN ★★★½

FRENCH/RABBIT | MODERATE | QUALITY ★★★★ | VALUE ★★★★ |
14TH ARRONDISSEMENT

11, rue Raymond-Losserand, 75014; 01 43 20 21 39; Métro: Gaîté

Customers International **Reservations** Advised for dinner **When to go** Anytime **Pricing** Average per person €46; prix fixe €28–46 **Payment** VISA, MC **English spoken** Yes **Bar** No **Wine selection** More than 50 vintages **Dress** Casual **Disabled access** No

Hours Wednesday–Sunday, noon–2:30 p.m. and 7:30–11p.m.; Tuesday, 7:30–11 p.m.; closed August

Setting & atmosphere Intimate. Situated just behind the Montparnasse cemetery, this is a good spot for dinner after paying homage to Sartre, de Beauvoir, and friends.

House specialties Rabbit with preserved lemon, rillette of rabbit with foie gras, shrimp ravioli.

Summary & comments Monsieur Lapin (Mister Rabbit) is keen to offer you many different ways of enjoying his particular charms. If you're squeamish about our fluffy little friends, then you should avoid this place. If not, it's an address to remember. We recommend the rabbit with preserved lemons; the tartness of the fruit perfectly complements the tender meat. Desserts are standard bistro favorites and perfectly respectable.

PITCHI POÏ

JEWISH/CENTRAL EUROPEAN | MODERATE | QUALITY ★★★★ | VALUE ★★★★ |
4TH ARRONDISSEMENT

9, place du Marché-Ste-Catherine, 75004; 01 42 77 46 15; Métro: St-Paul-Le Marais

Customers Locals and New Yorkers **Reservations** Not required **When to go** Early **Pricing** Average per person €23; prix fixe €18 **Payment** VISA, MC, AMEX, JCB, travelers' checks in euros **English spoken** Yes **Bar** No **Wine selection** French wines from the Tourraine direct from the vineyards of Mr. Leclair, as well as a selection from Israel and an excellent Tokäi from Hungary **Dress** Informal **Disabled access** Yes

Hours Daily, noon–2:30 p.m. and 7:30–10:30 p.m.

Setting & atmosphere Small but comfortable dining room that feels like you're in someone's house. Art, photographs, and objects are spread around. The colorful aesthetics of the mixed plate of appetizers captures the spirit of this friendly place.

House specialties Blinis, salmon, herring, 22 kinds of vodka, smoked fish.

Summary & comments The best of Central European Jewish food is served at this excellent and original address. Most visitors interested in this kind of fare end up at the cramped and more expensive spots on the rue des Rosiers. Smart travelers stroll down there but eat here. Tired of the same good old French fare? Come here for blinis and herring, rolled cabbage, and an enlightening selection of delicious vodkas that lighten the mood. When it's nice out, eat on the spacious terrace on the Place du Marché-Ste-Catherine, a very quaint spots in the Marais. The menu has been translated into English. The service is friendly and accommodating.

RENDEZ-VOUS DES CHAUFFEURS

HOME-STYLE FRENCH BISTRO | MODERATE | QUALITY ★★★½ | VALUE ★★★★★ |
18TH ARRONDISSEMENT

11, rue des Portes-Blanches, 75018; 01 42 64 04 17 Métro: Marcadet-Poissoniers

Customers Mixture of regulars, musicians, artists, workers, and medical emergency relief workers **Reservations** Required **When to go** Before 8:30 p.m. **Pricing** Average per person €15; prix fixe €12 (lunch and until 8 p.m.) **Payment** VISA, MC, traveler's checks in euros **English spoken** Yes **Bar** No **Wine selection** Large; 50 vintages **Dress** Relaxed **Disabled access** Yes, except restroom

Hours Thursday–Tuesday, noon–2:30 p.m. and 7:30–11 p.m.

Setting & atmosphere Old-fashioned Parisian brasserie with an original wooden counter, large bar mirrors, and benches decked in checked tablecloths.

House specialties Pot au feu stew, preserved duck.

Summary & comments This small, packed canteen is a must for those who want to experience French home cooking on a budget. Nothing fancy here—from the decor to the food, everything is cheap and cheerful. Owner Jeannot spent over 20 years living in the United States, so don't worry about your rusty French—he's happy to chat in English. Though this place is definitely a traditional French restaurant, one important detail has been imported from the United States: the "early bird menu." Three hearty courses and wine are yours for €12 if you eat before 8:30 p.m. The fact that this is both an unusual concept in Paris and an extraordinary price means that it's often packed, so plan to arrive early.

RESTAURANT DU MUSÉE D'ORSAY ★★★★

TRADITIONAL FRENCH | MODERATE | QUALITY ★★★ | VALUE ★★★★ |
7TH ARRONDISSEMENT

Musée d'Orsay, 1, rue de Bellechasse (median level), 75007; 01 45 49 47 03; Métro: RER Musée d'Orsay

Customers Mostly tourists **Reservations** No **When to go** Lunch **Pricing** Average per person €30; prix fixe €14; buffet €15 (plus ticket to museum) **Payment** VISA, MC, AMEX, travelers' checks in euros **English spoken** Yes **Bar** Yes **Wine selection** Classical but small selection, Beaujolais, Bourgogne, Bordeaux **Dress** Relaxed **Disabled access** Yes

Hours Tuesday–Sunday, 11:30 a.m.–2:30 p.m.; Thursday night, 7–9:15 p.m.; tea room, daily except Thursday, 3:30–5:30 p.m.

Setting & atmosphere Much of the enjoyment of eating here is simply the fact that you're in the midst of one of France's most celebrated and stunning museums. The restaurant is in what used to be the deluxe eatery of the Hôtel de la Gare d'Orsay.

House specialties Traditional cuisine: terrines, salades, beef, duck, fish.

Entertainment & amenities There is music during tea room hours on Sundays.

Summary & comments The cuisine is traditional French, the preparations are perfectly competent, and the price is fair. One of the great tips for travelers is to tour the museum and then break here for lunch. The buffet table is lavishly supplied with salads, cheeses, and meats, and for a small price tag you'll recharge your batteries for an afternoon of more museum visiting.

ROGER LA GRENOUILLE ★★★★

BAWDY FRENCH BISTRO | MODERATE | QUALITY ★★½ | VALUE ★★★ |
6TH ARRONDISSEMENT

26–28, rue des Grands-Augustins, 75006; 01 56 24 24 34; Métro: St-Michel

Customers Fun-loving international crowd, after-work crowd, Parisians who've been coming here for years **Reservations** Required for dinner **When to go** Early or late **Pricing** Average per person €53 **Payment** VISA, MC **English spoken** Yes, with the heaviest accent on the Left Bank **Bar** Yes (2 bars) **Wine selection** Red wines from the Var, rosés, and inexpensive Burgundy **Dress** Informal **Disabled access** No

Hours Tuesday–Sunday, 7:30 p.m.–2 a.m.

Setting & atmosphere A mythic place. Tucked into a tiny courtyard on a street off the rue Saint André des Arts, behind a window display of hundreds of assorted toy frogs, this very informal joint captures Parisian 19th-century bawdiness like nowhere else. The same waitresses have been there forever and love to aggressively tease the male customers, many of whom have danced on the tables before leaving their neckties pinned to the wall. The walls are covered in irreverent love notes and small bank notes from all continents.

House specialties Frogs.

Other recommendations Coq au vin, duck with oranges.

Summary & comments Roger the Frog is a great little find that makes for great conversation for years after visiting. The food is country-style French with generous portions of coq au vin and a delicious canard à l'orange. The Burgundy house wine is very drinkable and comes in magnum bottles. You drink what you like and are charged for the part of the bottle you consume. The house prides itself on a very naughty and sexist dessert, which causes hilarious embarrassment when ordered secretly for unsuspecting women. Just tell your waitress that you want the desert special and she'll hurry one over—served with no spoon. When it's not overly crowded, Roger le Grenouille is a lot of fun. When stuffed to its gills, the service is slow and the kitchen can't keep up.

SPOON ★★★★

FRENCH | MODERATE | QUALITY ★★★★ | VALUE ★★★ | 8TH ARRONDISSEMENT

14, rue de Marignan, 75008; 01 40 76 34 44; Métro: Franklin Roosevelt

Customers Trendy, curious, tourists **Reservations** Required, 1 week in advance; for lunch, 2 weeks **When to go** Early **Pricing** Average per person €61 **Payment** VISA, MC, AMEX, DC, JCB, travelers' checks in euros and dollars **English spoken** Yes **Bar** No **Wine selection** Extensive **Dress** Creative and trendy **Disabled access** No

Hours Daily, noon–2 p.m. and 6:45–11 p.m.

Setting & atmosphere We like the fact that the walls are white by day, and purple by night; the fact that you can order a BLT with homemade ice cream for dessert and eat it out of a bizarre, angled dish; the fact that only a tenth of the wine list is French (and over half of the rest is American); and the fact that everyone is slightly bemused but definitely enjoying themselves and the food.

House specialties Meat and fish.

Summary & comments Eating at Spoon is an enjoyable if slightly surreal experience. So much has been said about this place that it's difficult not to talk in quotation marks. It is a "designer eatery" with a "celebrity chef" famed for his "gastronomic marvels" and fabulously "creative" and "innovative" menu. Hype aside, Spoon is a really great place to go to eat. Following in the trend for world food—that is, fusion of various elements, ingredients, and styles from around the globe—uber-cook Ducasse comes up with innovative taste combinations that work surprisingly well. The menu is rather avant-garde and very confusing, but the staff is happy to explain the concept.

TOUPARY   ★★★★

CONTEMPORARY FRENCH | MODERATE | QUALITY ★★★★ | VALUE ★★★ |
1ST ARRONDISSEMENT

5th floor of La Samaritaine, 2, quai du Louvre, 75001; 01 40 41 29 29; Métro: Pont-Neuf

Customers Mixed tourists, out-of-town French, and couples **Reservations** Advised **When to go** Not too early **Pricing** Average per person €54 (wine included); prix fixe €25 (lunch), €35 (dinner) **Payment** VISA, MC, AMEX, DC, travelers' checks in euros **English spoken** Yes **Bar** Yes **Wine selection** 60 vintage wines, prices vary from €25 to €260 **Dress** Tie and jacket, dress **Disabled access** Yes

Hours Monday–Saturday, 11:45 a.m.–3 p.m. and 7:30–11:30 p.m.; tea room, 3:30–6 p.m.

Setting & atmosphere Located on the fifth floor of the Samaritaine department store (main building), Toupary is a spacious and beautiful dining room with a glass panoramic view overlooking Pont Neuf and the Seine. The Eiffel Tower is seen from many of the window seats. When the beams from the passing bateaux mouches sweep by you'll know why Paris is called the City of Light. You'll pinch yourself; this is really Paris. Insist on a window table—that's half the fun. The decor is rather modern, and the presentation of dishes is on the minimalist side.

House specialties Seasonal.

Summary & comments We've heard mixed reviews of the food itself but only rave reports on the overall pleasantness of the dining experience. We've never been disappointed with the panaché of fish. Foie gras with mangos, Szechuan peppers, and cardamom is delicious. The lunch menus are excellent deals. If you go for lunch, have your coffee on the rooftop terrace of the same building. The view is breathtaking.

TOUTOUNE   ★★★★

FRENCH PROVENÇAL | MODERATE/EXPENSIVE | QUALITY ★★★½ | VALUE ★★★ |
5TH ARRONDISSEMENT

5, rue de Pontoise, 75005; 01 43 26 56 81; Métro: Maubert-Mutualité

Customers Mixed, casual **Reservations** Recommended **When to go** During the week or early **Pricing** Average €22, prix fixe €17 **Payment** VISA, MC **English spoken** Some **Bar** No **Wine selection** Adequate list of Bordeaux and Burgundy **Dress** Informal **Disabled access** No

Hours Daily, 7–10 p.m.

Setting & atmosphere French country style, patterned table clothes, wooden tables, walls painted in Provençal frescos.

House specialties Foie gras of duck with a fig compôte, shoulder of lamb, glazed truffles.

Summary & comments You don't have to go to the south of France to benefit from its culinary joys. Toutoune is a favorite with both visitors and residents of the Latin Quarter. The portions are generous, the colors are rich, and the service is friendly. Everyone sits in one roomy dining space, and it feels like you're eating in someone's country house.

VIN & MARÉE

CONTEMPORARY SEAFOOD | MODERATE | QUALITY ★★★★ | VALUE ★★★★ |
16TH ARRONDISSEMENT

183, boulevard Murat, 75016; 01 46 47 91 39; Métro: Porte de St-Cloud

Customers Regulars and locals **Reservations** Advised **When to go** Early or late **Pricing** Average per person €40–45 **Payment** VISA, MC, AMEX, DC, JCB **English spoken** Yes **Bar** None **Wine selection** Wine menu changes every 6 months **Dress** Casual to understated elegance **Disabled access** No

Hours Daily, noon–2:15 p.m. and 7:30–10:15 p.m.

Setting & atmosphere Modern. The atmosphere in this fish restaurant is bright and intelligent, filled with people who love to eat and talk and flirt playfully, surrounded by good contemporary paintings, lots of glasses of white wine, and fumes of garlic and butter.

House specialties Fish and seafood, rum-drenched cake with whipped cream.

Summary & comments At Vin & Marée, the philosophy behind the food is freshness, great quality, and low prices, which is just fine with us. There are four branches (the others in Montparnasse, near the Eiffel Tower, and at Métro Nation) that churn out good fish with heartening regularity. It looks and feels a little chain-restauranty, albeit a good-natured one trying not to be too predictable. They only serve fish, so don't come here for a meat feast. Unfortunately, the wine list is a little dull, although it does feature some perfectly respectable bottles, and they try to make it all a little more exciting by changing the list regularly. The luscious rum baba is the house specialty and an absolute must. Look like you've been there before and talk to the waitresses, and you'll have a great time.

ZYRIAB

GOURMET ARABIC | MODERATE | QUALITY ★★★★½ | VALUE ★★★★ |
5TH ARRONDISSEMENT

Institut du Monde Arabe, 1, rue des Fossés St. Bernard, 75005; 01 53 10 10 20; Métro: Jussieu

Customers Professionals (lunch), politicians, show business, international (dinner) **Reservations** Required 2–3 days in advance for lunch, 1 week for dinner **When to go** Not too late **Pricing** Average per person €46 **Payment** VISA, MC, AMEX, travelers'

checks in euros **English spoken** Yes **Bar** No **Wine selection** North African (red, rosé), Lebanese cocktails **Dress** Elegant **Disabled access** Yes

Hours Tuesday–Saturday, noon–2 p.m.; 7:30–10 p.m.; Sunday, 3–6 p.m. (tea room)

Setting & atmosphere Cultivated and formal in style, this restaurant requires that you dress up; consequently, it's not the best choice for family dining and too formal for small children. The view from the terrace over the Seine and Notre-Dame is gorgeous.

House specialties Moroccan cuisine, couscous, tagine.

Entertainment & amenities Air-conditioning. Discreet background music. Beautiful panoramic view from the terrace. Friendly, Middle Eastern–style service.

Summary & comments Although you'll probably want to concentrate on French cuisine while you're in Paris, this culinary detour will be both original and memorable. Located on the ninth floor of the Institut du Monde Arabe on the Left Bank, Zyriab is an example of the finest Franco-Arab cuisine you'll find in the world. Moroccan cuisine is some of the world's finest, and if you've not yet been initiated, Paris is the place. The food is exotic, filled with delicate nuance, colorful, and instructive. If you have to ask what a tagine is, order one (it's a type of stew cooked in a clay pot).

Part Eight

Shopping in Paris

A Browser's Paradise

When a recent poll asked what attracted Paris-bound travelers the most, the second most popular answer was shopping! Ahead of museums and restaurants, even. And it's true that although Paris shopping is not always the most economical, it is fun. The city is perpetually rejuvenating itself with the creative spirit of new boutiques. Paris windows *(les vitrines)* are a feast in themselves. The key to shopping in Paris is to know the difference between where to look and where to buy. The great thing about Paris shopping is that the activity is as much cultural as it is commercial. You actually learn a lot about contemporary and historic France by stalking its boutiques and bundling up its finest products.

You'll want to mix and match your shopping time between the five main venues for making Parisian purchases:

- the little boutiques *(petites boutiques)*
- the department stores *(grands magasins)*
- the supermarkets *(supermarchés)*
- the museum shops *(boutiques des musées nationaux)*
- the flea markets *(marchés aux puces)*

An Unofficial Suggestion

Think twice before buying. In today's global marketplace, there are fewer and fewer truly original things to buy, indigenous to a place. Many of the famed French brand names—Chanel, Yves Saint Laurent, Christian Dior, Hermès, Louis Vuitton, and others—are not only sold and distributed internationally, but their products are likely to be less expensive back home and are probably available online. We tell friends and travelers to apply the following rule.

If you can find it at home or order it online, don't buy it in Paris. If it's made in France and can only be found in France, and you like it and can afford it and can carry it home, buy it.

There are two types of great Parisian shopping: the kind in which you spend money and the kind that costs you nothing—window shopping. Observing shop windows in Paris can be like gallery hopping.

VAT Tax Refunds on Your Purchases

The sales tax in France, or VAT (value added tax—known as the TVA in French), is 19.6% of the retail price. The tax is always built into the price that you see on price tags. When goods and merchandise are purchased for export, meaning that you will be taking them out of France with you, you have the legal right to request a refund of a part of the tax. However, there are specific conditions that must be met to qualify for this refund:

- You must spend €175 or more in the same store on the same day. Your purchases are cumulative.

- You must be a resident of a country outside of the European Union.

- You must not have remained in France or in the European Union for more than six months.

- You must be aged 15 or older.

If you fulfill these criteria, tell a sales clerk in the store where you have made your purchases that you want to receive a VAT refund on your purchases. The department stores do this a thousand times a day and will instruct you on the procedures in English.

You need to show your passport and your sales receipts. You'll fill in a VAT refund form, and you'll be asked how you wish to be refunded. The easiest way is to have your credit card credited. You may also have a check sent to you or have the money deposited to a bank account.

The form you'll be given has three copies and will be accompanied by an addressed and stamped envelope. One copy is for the customs inspector at the airport, one will be sent by mail to the store issuing the refund, and the third is for your records.

Remember that you can only receive VAT refund on purchases at your final destination inside the European Union. So if you're going from Paris to London before flying back to San Francisco, you cannot claim your tax refund in Paris (but you can claim it in London).

If you are heading home from a Paris airport, present yourself to the customs office *(douane)* in order to receive your VAT refund on your purchases. This window is clearly marked in all terminals of both airports. Note that you are supposed to show the items you have purchased to the customs officer in order to successfully receive your VAT refund on them—

so do not pack them in your suitcase! If you plan to place them in your checked luggage, make sure that you receive your VAT refund before you check in. If you check your luggage first, you will not be able to benefit from the refund in that the customs police have no way of verifying that the goods are in your bags.

The lines at this window can be long, especially if there happens to be a large group of Japanese tourists on their way home in front of you. Give yourself an extra 30 minutes at the airport to comfortably allow time to receive your VAT refund.

The customs inspector will ask you for your plane ticket, your passport, your VAT refund form or forms, and the goods. He or she will stamp the threefold form, then keep one, place one in the pre-addressed envelope, and give you the third to keep. Seal the envelope and post the letter in the yellow mailbox that will be in the vicinity. As soon as the store receives their copy, proving that the goods were VAT refunded by customs, it'll process your refund, which adds up to about 15% of the 19.6% you paid. Either your credit card will be credited or you'll receive a check. One firm, Global Refund, will process your refund on the spot for a small commission. Our experience is that the credit card credit is the best and fastest means of reimbursement.

This is an excellent way of reducing your shopping costs. It is also an incentive to group your purchases in one store, since as long as your purchases are over €175 in the same store you're entitled to this sizable refund. Most clerks will mention this refund to you as soon as they realize you're a tourist (in about three seconds), but don't forget to ask for it just in case. Always keep your passport with you when you're shopping.

Customs Restrictions

Returning U.S. residents are allowed to bring back up to $400 of retail purchases per person. Canadians are allowed up to $500.

Mailing or Shipping Home Your Purchases

Department stores will ship your packages home for you and will automatically deduct the VAT even if you do not spend €175. The service is costly, though. A better bet, especially on small, not-too-heavy, and inexpensive items, is to send them yourself in preposted mailers or boxes at any post office (refer to Part Four, Arriving, Getting Oriented, and Departing). Remember that U.S. Customs strictly prohibits the importation of any food or agricultural items. So, if you're sending a strand of fresh garlic cloves to your aunt who loves to cook, you're taking a chance. Also note that the $400 duty exemption doesn't apply on packages; the rule of thumb is "personal shipments worth up to $200 and gift packages worth up to

$100" are exempt. Go to www.customs.ustreas.gov/travel/travel.htm for more information.

Using Credit Cards

You'll be pleasantly surprised at how widespread credit card use has become in Paris. Actually, all the cards you see being used in Paris are really debit cards connected to the user's bank account. The bottom line, though, is that you can pay for everything from underground parking lots to museum admissions with your plastic money. Parisians use cards for paying tolls on the highway, paying for their groceries, and paying for cinema tickets. The preferred card is called the Carte Bleue (CB), which is the French banking administration for VISA and MasterCard (although your VISA or Master-Card will be accepted widely). American Express and Diners cards are accepted widely, but not to the same extent as CB.

The major difference between the card that Parisians carry and the ones that you carry is the embedded "smart card" chip that the French invented. Parisians do not sign anything at points of purchase; their card gets slid into a cordless hot-shoe and they punch in their PIN, which the machine recognizes and verifies. The transaction is transferred electronically to the merchant's bank, and the customer's bank account is debited automatically. These same cordless machines have swipe mechanisms built in to read the magnetic strip on the back of your card. Debit card use is spreading in the United States, but be aware that even though you should be able to use your debit card anywhere in the world, this doesn't always work in practice (contact your card's company before you head for Paris, and find out if your PIN will be valid in France—sometimes you just need to be given a different PIN to enable international debit access). Smart travelers carry at least two different cards with them, in case one doesn't work.

Note that many establishments have set a policy that credit cards will only be accepted for purchases of a minimum of €15. If you beg and ask imploringly, occasionally you'll be allowed to use the card for smaller sums.

For lost or stolen cards or other problems while in France, here are your local contact numbers:

- VISA/MasterCard: Tel. 08 36 69 08 80. You'll get a voice mail recording in French. Push 2 and hold the line for an English-speaking operator.
- American Express: Tel. 01 47 77 72 00.
- Diner's Club: Tel. 01 47 62 75 75.

Returns and Refunds

Paris businesses rarely if ever give cash refunds *(remboursements)*. In fact, it's only rather recently that you could even get store credit. The familiar "customer is king" adage never really caught on in France, and although refund policies are a bit more flexible now than before, it's better to try to avoid exchanges or returns *(retours)*. Ask what the store's policy on returns and exchanges is before you buy anything. The arrival of the American clothing chain, the Gap, sort of revolutionized the concept of retail public relations in France. You can buy a sweater at the Gap on rue de Rivoli and return it for a full cash refund in Houston, Texas. *Très rare* in Paris.

Usually, if something doesn't fit or doesn't work, you'll be able to exchange it for another size or another one on the condition that you have the sales receipt and the original packaging. Be aware that French clothing sizes vary from those in North America.

Duty-Free Shops

The duty-free shops at Paris's airports do not really offer many advantages to international shoppers. Duty-free shopping for inter–European Union travelers has been abolished since the European Union is legally considered one single market. The only advantage you'll find in making duty-free purchases at the airport is the convenience, for example, of not having to lug that bottle of champagne to the airport with you that you wanted to bring back for your brother-in-law. Prices are not all that attractive. There are plenty of touristy shops in the center of Paris advertising duty-free shopping, especially around rue de Rivoli near the Louvre. The prices here for perfume, scarves, and other popular tourist items are in line with the duty free shops at the airport or better, but these gifts tend to lack imagination and personality.

Museum Gift Shops and Bookstores

One of Paris's greatest sources of interesting, original, culturally enriching, and cost-effective gifts is the museum boutique and bookstore. There are 11 boutiques in Paris offering quality reproductions of many of the museums' masterpieces. The main office for these shops is found at 49, rue Etienne Marcel, 75001, Métro: Bourse (Tel. 01 40 13 48 00). Here you'll not only find a list of all the shops, but you'll find a detailed, free brochure for all of France's national museums, and a service for reserving tickets to major exhibitions. The museum shops also enjoy online services at www.boutique.louvre.fr and www.museesdefrance.com. So if you don't have time to make your purchases before leaving, don't feel like carrying a poster on the plane, or are unsure if that Monet reproduction will fit on your kitchen wall, you can wait until you get home to order. You can also request the mail-order catalog by calling Tel. 03 44 58 44 07.

The best and most complete shops include:

Boutique Musée et Compagnie Billeterie   49, rue Etienne Marcel, 75001; Métro: Bourse; Tel. 01 40 13 49 13.

La Boutique des Musée de France Forum des Halles, Porte Berger, niveau -2, 75001; Métro: Les Halles; Tel. 01 40 39 92 21.

Galeries Nationales du Grand Palais 3, avenue du Général Eisenhower, 75008; Métro: Champs-Elysées–Clemenceau; Tel. 01 44 13 17 41.

Musée de Louvre Under the Pyramide, Palais du Louvre, 75001; Métro: Louvre; Tel. 01 40 20 53 53.

Musée d'Orsay 62, rue de Lille, 75007; Métro: Rue du Bac, RER: Musée d'Orsay; Tel. 01 40 49 47 22.

Shopping Areas and Favorite Streets

The following areas and highlighted streets in Paris offer prime shopping opportunities:

Place des Victoires/rue Etienne Marcel

A preferred hub for fashion design houses and trend-setters. Here you'll find Jean-Paul Gaultier, Adolfo Dominguez, Miki House, Kenzo, Cacharel, Esprit, Thierry Mugler, and more. Don't miss the Galerie Vivienne covered passageway, the rue Etienne Marcel, the rue du Louvre, and the rue Jean-Jacques Rousseau. The streets around the Post Office and the rue Montmartre are cluttered with wonderful, original finds.

Les Halles

In the heart of the city, Les Halles is so trendy that no guidebook can keep up with the openings and closings. There are lots of great little finds mixed in with a lot of tackiness. We prefer the little streets in the area adjacent to the multilevel indoor mall, except for the fact that inside you'll find the **FNAC** for books, CDs, and concert tickets. Check out the rue Montmartre, the rue du Jour, rue de Turbigo, the rue Pierre Lescot, and the rue Saint-Denis.

Le Marais

More old-world than Les Halles, the Marais is studded with great boutiques offering clothes, objects, art, and accessories. Stroll along the rue Vieille du Temple, rue Sainte-Croix-de-la-Bretonnerie, rue du Roi-de-Sicile, rue des Ecouffes, rue des Rosiers, rue Pavée, rue de Sévigné, Place des Vosges, and, without fail, rue des Francs-Bourgeois, one of Paris's best shopping streets.

Saint-Germain-des-Prés

Elegant, up-market shops for the very chic. Visit the rue du Bac, rue Bonaparte, rue de l-Ancienne Comédie, rue de Sèvres, boulevard Raspail, rue Jacob, rue des Saints-Pères, Cour du Commerce Saint-André, rue de

Grenelle, rue du Cherche-Midi, rue Madame, rue du Vieux-Colombier, rue du Four, rue de Rennes, rue Saint-Sulpice, rue de Seine, and, of course, the boulevard Saint-Germain. You'll find **Hugo Boss, Sonia Rykiel, Kashiyama, Miyake's "Pleats Please," Lacoste, Paule Ka, Apostrophe, La Perla,** and the cosmetics wizard, **Shu Uemura.** The area surrounding the Place Saint-Sulpice offers a wealth of great fashion and household delights.

Boulevard Haussman, rue Saint-Honoré, La Madeleine

Welcome to the top-of-the-top, the chic-of-the-chic. In this area, also referred to as the Golden Triangle, you'll find all the world's leading haute couture fashion brands as well as Paris's top department stores.

Along the boulevard Haussman you can't help but find the **Galeries Lafayette** and **Printemps.** Stroll the rue de la Paix and enter the Place Vendôme. Here, aside from the Ritz, you'll find **Guerlain, Armani,** and **Chanel.** Around the Madeleine you'll encounter **Ralph Lauren, Cerruti 1881,** and the catering meccas **Fauchon** and **Hédiard.** We like the **Maille** mustard shop on the Place for very original and affordable savory gifts. **Guy Laroche** and **Lanvin** are on the rue du Faubourg Saint-Honoré, along with **Hermès,** the makers of mythic silk scarves, and **Yves Saint Laurent** and **Christian Lacroix.** Follow along the rue Saint-Honoré, home of fashionista havens such as **Colette.** We won't stoop to say that these shops are expensive, but one visiting woman from Boston eager to buy herself a new leather jacket in Paris was shocked by the sales tax for the price on the jacket she picked out. The 19.6% tax alone was already beyond her budget.

The Champs-Elysées

The avenue is still impressive despite the repeated invasions of **Haagen Daz, McDonald's,** the **Disney Store, Virgin Megastore,** and **Planet Hollywood.** The spokes off the avenue host some of the most elegant old-money names in the fashion industry. Wander down the avenue George V and the rue François 1er. Then stroll along the avenue Montaigne, where **Valentino** and **Christian Dior** and **Nina Ricci, Chanel,** and the forever inimitable **Louis Vuitton** have set up shops and studios.

The Bastille

New and innovative fashion designers have progressively moved east. The Bastille is still the hub of the east, but the more interesting trend-setters have ventured farther east by now: Oberkampf, Nation, Ménilmontant, Montreuil . . . Start at the Bastille and follow the rue de la Roquette and the rue de Lappe, head up the rue de Charonne, and wander down alleys and lanes like the Passage Thiéré.

Passy/avenue Victor Hugo

This is an upscale shopping haven in the lively part of the 16th *arrondissement*. **Kenzo, Chipie** (rue de la Pompe), and others, such as the famous cake-maker **Lenôtre,** are here.

Department Stores

Paris department stores *(grands magasins)* are famous and historic. Only in Paris could a department store also be a registered national monument. Such is the case with **Printemps** on boulevard Haussmann, which dates back to 1865 and hosts an exquisite stained-glass dome. Even nonshoppers don't mind wandering through this Paris landmark. All the stores offer special services for international shoppers—service in English, gifts, maps, fashion shows, and, of course, shipping and VAT refund services. Both Printemps and **Galeries Lafayette** are accessible directly from the Métro. You don't even have to go out into the street. The same is true for the **BHV** next to the Hôtel de Ville and **Samaritaine** by the Pont-Neuf.

If you get to your last day in Paris and haven't bought your gifts yet, give yourself a few hours in one or several of these stores. If you group your purchases from the same store and on the same day, you will be able to benefit from a VAT refund—assuming your purchases total at least €175. See "VAT Tax Refunds on Your Purchases" above for details on the VAT refund for tourists.

BHV (Bazar de l'Hôtel de Ville)   52–64, rue de Rivoli, 75004; Tel. 01 42 74 90 00; Métro: Hôtel de Ville. Open Monday, Tuesday, Thursday, and Saturday, 9:30 a.m.–7 p.m.; Wednesday and Friday until 8:30 p.m. This department store is convenient if you're in the Marais or Latin Quarter. What's really special about the BHV is the basement, Paris's largest and most complete hardware and housewares store. Visitors have less reason to go here, but if you're imaginative you'll find all sorts of great ideas for your house and for gifts, like new handles or knobs for your doors back home or brass fittings and trim for your kitchen.

Galeries Lafayette   40, boulevard Haussmann, 75009; Tel. 01 42 82 34 56; Métro: Chaussée d'Antin or Opéra. Open Monday–Saturday, 9:30 a.m.– 7 p.m.; Thursday until 9 p.m. You can also get a haircut or a facial or have your nails done. The **Lafayette Gourmet** supermarket is not only a great place to stalk the finest produce in the city, it's a great place to buy unique culinary gifts or step up to one of ten counters for a specialty lunch.

Le Bon Marché   22 and 38, rue de Sèvres, 75007; Tel. 01 44 39 80 00; Métro: Sèvres-Babylone. Open Monday–Friday, 9:30 a.m.–7 p.m.; Thursday, 10 a.m.–9 p.m.; Saturday, 9:30 a.m.–8 p.m. This is Paris's oldest department store, and it prides itself for being the only one on the Left

Bank. A recently opened emporium of cosmetics called the **Théâtre de la beauté** has among the best selections in the city. The **Grande Epicerie** supermarket is gourmet heaven.

Printemps   64, boulevard Haussman, 75009; Tel. 01 42 82 57 87; Métro: Havre-Caumartin, RER A: Auber, RER E: Haussmann–St. Lazare. Monday–Saturday, 9:30 a.m.–7 p.m.; Thursday until 10 p.m. Fashion shows every Tuesday (year-round) and Friday (April to October) at 10 a.m.

Samaritaine   75, rue de Rivoli, 75001; Tel. 01 40 41 20 20; Métro: Pont Neuf. Open Monday–Saturday, 9:30 a.m.–7 p.m.; Thursday until 10 p.m. This Paris landmark located between Châtelet and the Louvre is spread over two buildings. The kitchenware department is particularly good. After you've finished shopping, head to the rooftop terrace of the *Magasin Principale* (the main building) You can enjoy a beer or a coffee here and take in one of the best views of the city. The great advantage to this vantage point is that you're not on something you'd like to see!

A Selection of Special Shops

The following selection of shops and boutiques combines both the most interesting of Paris content and the most innovative contemporary architecture and design. Although the Paris stores of well-known chains like Conran's and Habitat are worth visiting, we've tried to steer you into establishments unique to Paris, and to those with things to buy that you can actually carry home. Whether you're a buyer or not, after a visit to some of these boutiques you can boast of being at the cutting edge of what's new.

Alain Mikli Diffusion   74, rue des Saints-Pères, 75006; Tel. 01 45 49 40 00; Métro: St.-Germain-des-Prés. Designer eyewear, including the Starck Eyes collection of frames and sunglasses.

Art du Bureau   47, rue des Francs-Bourgeois, 75004; Tel. 01 48 87 57 97; Métro: St. Paul. Very cool and funky office interior stuff, including modular diaries and Watchpeople, Graves, Mondaine, and Milus watches.

Asphalte   35, rue Jussieu, 75005; Tel. 01 43 29 99 59; Métro: Jussieu. A strange but enticing gallery shop with a selection of good, cheap, intelligent, and original products for the home.

Avant-Scène   4, place de l'Odéon, 75006; Tel. 01 46 33 12 40; Métro: Odéon. New talent in the field of art objects. Small series of bronze pieces uniting poetry and humor.

Beauty by Et Vous   25, rue Royale, 75008; Tel. 01 47 42 31 00; Métro: Madeleine or Concorde. Chic concept store dedicated to beauty in all its forms, with three floors of fashions for women and men by Et Vous, Marc Jacobs, and other designer names, plus top of the line cosmetics and even arty videos.

Colette   213, rue Saint-Honoré, 75001; Tel. 01 55 35 33 90; Métro: Tuileries. Paris's original temple of fashion, style, design, art, and food. The goods are displayed like art in a museum. Downstairs the restaurant and water bar features a vast choice of bottled waters from around the world. www.colette.fr, www.ilovecolette.com

Comme des Garçons   54, rue du Fbg. St. Honoré, 75008; Tel. 01 53 30 27 27; Métro: St. Philippe du Roule. Rei Kawakubo's boutique of stark minimalism, black garments, and other highly original avant-garde wear, as well as her signature fragrance, Odeur 53, Eau de Toilette.

Dom   21, rue Sainte-Croix-de-la-Bretonnerie, 75004; Tel. 01 42 71 08 00; Métro: Hôtel de Ville. A huge and popular shop frequented by gay Parisians offers parodies of design objects, fake fur, heart-shaped lights, and other fun objects.

Le 18   18, rue Keller, 75011; Tel. 01 48 05 55 62; Métro: Bastille. Showcase for up and coming French designers of fashion, decorative objects, furniture, lighting, and more, in thematic displays that change regularly. On the 18th of every month at 6 p.m. is a designer show open to all.

Hermès   24, rue du Fbg. Saint-Honoré, 75008; Tel. 0140 17 47 17; Métro: Madeleine. Hermès is an institution. An emblem of virtue, history, and class. The boutique itself makes a solid statement. For a really good time, try to be here during one of Hermès's bargain basement sales (twice a year for a week each time). Watch the most demure Paris ladies scratch, bite, and kick to get their hands on Hermès scarves marked down 50% to 70% of the retail price. The sales are usually during January and July, but call first and sharpen your nails. Credit cards happily accepted.

Isabel Marant   16, rue de Charonne, 75011; Tel. 01 49 29 71 55; Métro: Ledru Rollin. A melting pot of fun and elegant clothes that strings together North Africa, India, and Paris with its own integrity.

La Quincaillerie   3–4, boulevard Saint-Germain, 75005; Tel. 01 46 33 66 71; Métro: Maubert Mutualité. Yep, door handles from all over the world.

Laguiole   1, place Sainte Opportune, 75001; Tel. 01 40 28 09 42; Métro: Les Halles. The famous Laguiole knife is exhibited and sold in a Philippe Starck–designed factory with an 18-meter-high stainless steel blade running to the ceiling.

Les Salons Shiseido du Palais Royal   142, galerie de Valois, 75001; Tel. 01 49 27 09 09; Métro: Palais Royal Musée du Louvre. A haven of sublime scents; here you find rosewood, violets, iris, and such inexplicable fragrances as "femininity of the woods." You can even have your bottles engraved with your initials.

Louis Vuitton   54, avenue Montaigne, 75008; Tel. 01 45 62 47 00; Métro: Franklin D. Roosevelt. 101, avenue des Champs-Elysées, 75008; Tel. 01 53 57 13 00; Métro: George V. 6, place St.-Germain-des-Prés, 75006; Tel. 01 45 49 62 32; Métro: St.-Germain-des-Prés. Right from the start in 1914, Vuitton was the largest travel accessory boutique on earth. This store is an immense space with the whole Vuitton line and new things you haven't seen before.

Marie Papier   26, rue Vavin, 75006; Tel. 01 43 21 63 20; Métro: Vavin. More than 400 pages of different kinds of paper, colors, textures, and formats for writing letters, cards, etc.

Paul Smith   22, boulevard Raspail, 75007; Tel. 01 42 84 15 30; Métro: Rue du Bac. Unless you come from England, you'll want to take in the art and wit of this British clothing designer in his original shop, redesigned every two weeks.

Ron Orb   39, rue Etienne Marcel, 75001; Tel. 01 40 28 09 33; Métro: Etienne Marcel. Welcome to outer space. You'll find techno shoes, jeans, and accessories here in an atmosphere of diffused lighting and new materials.

Séphora   70, avenue des Champs-Elysées, 75008; Tel. 01 53 93 22 50; Métro: George V. France's leading distributor of perfumes and cosmetics displays the entire line in a vast den of fragrances among a video wall, a perfume organ, 654 fiber-optic heads, and endless ways to experience perfume.

Smart Center Paris/Paul Doumer   27–33, avenue Paul Doumer, 75016; Tel. 01 56 91 50 00; Métro: Trocadéro. You won't be bringing home one of these very smart electric cars, but you'll love what you see. The vehicle of urban tomorrow shown in a compact tower of aesthetics and economy of space. No more exhaust or gas bills.

Swatch Megastore   104, avenue des Champs-Elysées, 75008; Tel. 01 56 69 17 00; Métro: Franklin D. Roosevelt. The company's showcase. Over 1,000 models on display with interactive capabilities! Includes limited editions designed by noted artists.

Cool Cheap Shopping

Common and everyday objects in Parisian life become unusual conversation pieces back home. We love to shop in the kitchen utensil section of the **Samaritaine** or **BHV** department stores. A globular-shaped sugar cube dispenser found on the bar counter of every Parisian café becomes a stroke of genius for gift-giving when taken out of its context.

- A knife set from the Cordon Bleu Cooking School is a perfect gift.
- A French chef's professional apron and toque pleases.

- Women's lingerie! This is a win-win situation. Men love to buy this for their wives or girlfriends. Women love to buy it for themselves. Some of the sexiest underwear and bras in the world include the labels Aubade, known for their advertisements that teach women the art of seduction; La Perla, known for its form-fitting cuts; and Chantal Thomass, whose ruffled panties are known to inspire. Your best bet is shopping for these items in the department stores where all the brand names are found.

- Children's clothes and baby clothes. Aside from the prices—which may dissuade you—children's and baby clothing in Paris is kilometers ahead of its North American counterparts. So cute, so elegant, so original, so European. The leading stores include Miki House, Du Pareil au Même, Chattawak, and Natalys.

Haute Couture: Discounted and Marked Down

The clothing in Paris is exquisite. The prices can be through the roof. If you want to come home with a haute couture souvenir, you might want to track down one of these recommended discount shops. Note that a sign on a shop window marked *Soldes* means "Sale." *Dégriffé* means marked-down. A discount is a *remise*. Generally, the sales periods in Paris are in January and July.

Anna Lowe   104, rue du Fbg. St-Honoré, 75008; Tel. 01 42 66 11 32; Métro: Champs-Elysées–Clemenceau. Dior, Gucci, Valentino, Gucci, and other names at 40–60% off the retail price. This place has been written up in the *Chicago Tribune* as the "best of the off-price shops."

Annexe des Créateurs   19 and 21, rue Godot de Mauroy, 75009; Tel. 01 42 65 46 40; Métro: Madeleine. Cocktail dresses, evening gowns, hats, and jewelry at up to 70% discounts.

Haut de Gamme Stock   9, rue Scribe, 75009; Tel. 01 40 07 10 20; Métro: Opéra. Cerruti suits, Versace, Armani, and others.

Miss "Griffes"   19, rue de Penthièvre, 75008; Tel. 01 42 65 10 00; Métro: Miromesnil. Haute couture, prêt-à-porter, and season ends from top designers. The readers of *Where Paris* magazine get a 20% discount, so read *Where Paris* in your hotel.

Open-Air Markets

Almost as gratifying and interesting as museums, Paris's open-air markets require some of your valuable time. You'll be impressed with the selection of fresh fruits and vegetables, meats, cheeses, and fish, as well as the colorful vendors that scream out their specials to attract shoppers. Although supermarkets have gained a significant amount of market share, most Parisians still rely on their local *marché* several times a week for their fresh produce. One of the fun aspects of these markets is the identification of products you don't find at home. Some visitors have a hard time with the hanging ducks and unplucked hens, the slippery eels, and the little containers of veal brains, while others are in their element. Note the variety of lettuces Parisians consume—dent-de-lion *(pissenlit)* leaves and *mâche,* the size of the artichokes, fennel, and endives, and the long thick stalks of leeks. Every season has its share of produce in season, and in Paris much joy comes from seeing the first strawberries or cherries or melons of the season.

The autumn brings with it an awesome range of wild mushrooms, *cêpes,* chanterelles, pleurotes, and bolets. In the summer you should really try some mirabelles and questches. As a tourist, you probably won't be buying fish in the market, but you'll certainly be wowed by the urchins and *tourteaux,* the mountains of mussels and the slabs of salmon and monkfish. Parisians not only eat a lot of fish, they eat a large variety of fish. Each quarter has its own fish market. Ask at your hotel for the closest one and its days of operation. Most are open either in the morning (until 1 p.m.) or in the afternoon (from 1 to 7 p.m.).

Tips for Shopping in the Open-Air Markets

There are two kinds of open-air produce markets: the permanent ones (every day) and the roving ones (several times a week at the same location).

- Vendors can be loud and impatient. You may be interested in trying a sliver of a creamy-looking cheese; they're trying to make their living and tend not to like selling tiny slivers of anything.

- Try to figure out in what dimension and denominations produce is sold. Ham, cold cuts, and pâtés are sold by the slice *(tranche),* not weight. You must indicate how many slices and how thick—don't leave this up to the vendor. And always say *"un peu moins, s'il vous plaît"* (ahn puh **mwahn,** see voo **play**)—a little less please—to compensate for their heavy-handed suggestions.

- Fruit and vegetables are usually sold by weight. A kilo of clémentines, for example, or 300 grams of champignons de Paris.

- It's not a bad idea to discreetly count your change.

- If you intend to buy a bundle of goods, remember to bring your own bag or basket.

Here are a few outstanding and particularly colorful outdoor markets:

Permanent Markets

Make sure you visit at least one or two of these permanent markets *(rues commerçantes).* Following each listing you'll find a suggested picnic spot nearby, a perfect place to taste the rewards of your marketing. Tip: Borrow a knife and fork and some extra napkins from the breakfast room at your hotel, or travel with a basic Swiss army knife or Opinel (a French all-purpose "picnic" knife—another great souvenir idea for your gourmet friends back home). Plastic cutlery is hard to come by in Paris.

Marché Montorgueil Rue Montorgueil, 2nd *arrondissement,* in the heart of Paris, Métro: Les Halles. This is the closest you can get to the old and authentic market that nearby Les Halles once was. Check out the regional products displayed as in the good old days, open daily. Picnic possibility: On the sloped garden in front of **Church Saint-Eustache.**

Marché Mouffetard Beginning at the rue de L'Epée-de-Bois in the 5th *arrondissement,* Métro: Monge. Although the street is narrow and the market is frequented by lots of visitors, the rue Mouffetard is one of Paris's great features. Don't miss this very colorful market, where you can even join in the spontaneous choir singing of traditional Parisian tunes at the corner of rue de l'Arbalète. If the weather is good, definitely plan to waste away an hour on the terrace of one of the cafés on the **Place de la Contrescarpe.** Picnic possibility: **Arènes de Lutèce** or the **Jardin des Plantes.**

Rue Cler Rue Cler beginning at the avenue de La Motte-Picquet in the 7th *arrondissement,* Métro: Ecole Militaire. Here, you're in the heart of a stylish, traditional, and wealthy neighborhood, and the street market conveys the tastes and aesthetics of the local shoppers. You'll love the fish market and the pastries. Picnic possibilities: in the Champs de Mars, under the **Eiffel Tower** or on the lawn in front of **Les Invalides.**

Rue de Levis Beginning at the boulevard des Batignolles in the 17th *arrondissement,* Métro: Villiers. The great advantage to this bustling market is that you'll feel that you're very far from anything touristy. The famed food critic Patricia Wells raves about the Belle Epoque baguettes at Couasnon Boulangerie. Picnic possibility: definitely in the **Parc Monceau.**

Rue Lepic Wonderful, lively street that climbs the hill starting at the Place Blanche next to the famous Moulin Rouge. Picnic possibility: in the **Cimetière de Montmartre.**

Roving Markets

These roving markets *(marchés volants)* are open from about 8:30 a.m. to around 1:30 p.m. on certain days only. Here is a selection to choose from.

Marché Saxe-Breteuil From the avenue de Ségur to the Place Breteuil along the avenue de Saxe, Métro: Ségur. Thursday and Saturday. Impressive open-air market in a very bourgeois neighborhood. Picnic possibility: anywhere in the middle of the avenue Breteuil or behind **Les Invalides.**

Marché Maubert At Place Maubert in the 5th *arrondissement,* Métro: Maubert-Mutualité. Tuesday, Thursday, and Saturday. A perfect spot to both shop and observe merchants, fresh produce, and local shoppers. Picnic possibility: either in the little park at the end of the rue Lagrange or along the quai by the Seine.

Marché d'Aligre   Place d'Aligre in the 12th *arrondissement,* Métro: Ledru-Rollin. This working-class neighborhood hosts a highly cosmopolitan market with some of the best prices in Paris. Open six days a week, 7:30 a.m.–12:30 p.m. (closed Monday). Picnic possibility: **Square Trousseau.**

Marché Grenelle   Along the boulevard de Grenelle beginning at the rue Lourmel and finishing at the rue du Commerce in the 15th *arrondissement,* Métro: Dupleix or La Motte-Picquet-Grenelle. Wednesday and Sunday. Lively market in a commercially vibrant area. Picnic possibility: **Place de Dupleix.**

Marché Monge   Place Monge, Métro: Monge. Wednesday, Friday, and Sunday. Excellent selection of regional ingredients and prepared recipes. Picnic possibility: take your goodies across the street and picnic in the Roman ruins, **Arènes des Lutèce.**

Marché Raspail   Along the boulevard Raspail between the rue de Rennes and the rue du Cherche-Midi, Métro: Rennes or Sèvres-Babylone. Tuesday and Friday. Picnic possibility: around the **Place Saint Sulpice** fountain.

Organic Markets

In French, "Marché Bio" stands for *biologique,* meaning organic and organically grown produce.

Batignolles   On the boulevard des Batignolles between numbers 27 and 48 in the 8th *arrondissement,* Métro: Rome or Place Clichy. Every Saturday, 9 a.m. to 2 p.m. A bit out of the way, but a large market worth exploring if you're staying in the area.

Marché Raspail   Along the boulevard Raspail between the rue de Rennes and the rue du Cherche-Midi in the 6th *arrondissement,* Métro: Rennes or Sèvres-Babylone. Saturday mornings. You'll find a joyful crowd of environmentally conscious shoppers and New Age and health-food enthusiasts.

Flea Markets

Chiner—to wander around lazily, poking around piles of *brocante* (old stuff to them—antiques to us), slumming, and strolling at a relaxed pace—in the "Marché aux Puces" is a popular Parisian weekend activity; unearth antiques and all kind of bric-à-brac as well as second-hand clothing. If you're wondering about bargaining, *marchander* (mar-shon-**day**), the answer is yes. Expect to spend about 30% less than what you're asked for at the start. On small, inexpensive items, you can manage a symbolic discount, but don't count on much. If the merchant asks €5 for a beer mug, you'll probably get it for €4 or €4.50. Here are your main choices.

Warning: Keep your money securely stashed; there are pickpockets in some of these markets, and foreign visitors make for easy prey.

Montreuil   Located at the Porte de Montreuil, this lively flea market is open every Saturday, Sunday, and Monday from 7:30 a.m. to 5 p.m. (a bit later in the summer). From the Porte de Montreuil Métro station walk over the *périphérique* and you'll stumble on a wide variety of tables and stalls of old clothes, secondhand goods, old tools, postcards, mirrors, plates, car parts, kitchenware, chairs, and similar junk or treasure, depending on your point of view. Early risers are certain to find a few collectibles to take home. Something of little value locally, like an old plaque from a Parisian café or an ashtray from Maxim's, may make for an excellent souvenir or conversation piece back home. Montreuil is known for its used clothes, so if you have the patience to mill through huge heaps of shirts and pants and ties, and you have an eye for vintage digs, you can go home with a sack of original items that cost you only a few dollars each.

Porte de Vanves   Saturday and Sunday from 8:30 a.m. to 1 p.m. Métro: Vanves. The quality of the objects—real bric-à-brac, art deco mirrors, brassware, earrings and pendants, and drawings—is superior to what's found at the other flea markets, but the prices reflect this.

Saint-Ouen   From Porte de Saint-Ouen to Porte de Clignancourt in the 18th *arrondissement,* Saturday, Sunday, and Monday from 9 a.m. to 6 p.m. Métro: Porte de Clignancourt. The oldest and most popular flea market of Paris is divided into several markets, secondhand or brand new clothing, military surplus in **Marché Malik,** antiques in **Marché Serpette,** and others. There is a full range of new and old items ranging from trinkets to luxurious antiques. You have to wade through a lot of junk to find the good stuff, and you have to arrive early if you hope to find something great at a low price.

Specialized Markets

Marché aux fleurs (Flower market)   Parisians enjoy several flower markets, open Tuesday through Saturday. Although you won't be able to carry flowers home with you, you'll enjoy the colors and varieties. The most famous markets are located at:

- Place Louis-Lépine on the Île de la Cité, 4th *arrondissement,* Monday–Saturday, 8 a.m.–7 p.m., Métro: Cité.
- Place de la Madeleine, 8th *arrondissement,* Tuesday–Sunday, 8 a.m.–7:30 p.m., Métro: Madeleine.
- Place des Ternes, 17th *arrondissement,* Tuesday–Sunday, 8 a.m.–7:30 p.m.; Métro: Ternes.

Marché aux livres (Book market)   Old (antique) books at 87, rue Brancion, 15th *arrondissement,* Saturday and Sunday, 9:30 a.m.– 6 p.m. Métro: Porte de Vanves.

Marchés aux oiseaux (Bird market)   If you really want to feel like you're in Europe, take a stroll through Paris's bird market.

- Place Louis Lépine, Île de la Cité, 4th *arrondissement.* Next to the flower market, Sunday, 8 a.m. to 7 p.m., Métro: Cité.

- Quai de la Mégisserie, 1st *arrondissement* (on the Right Bank), Métro: Châtelet. A series of pet shops open every day.

Marché aux timbres (Stamp market)   At the corner of avenue Marigny and avenue Gabriel, 8th *arrondissement,* Thursday, Saturday, Sunday, and public holidays, 10 a.m. to sunset, Métro: Champs-Elysées–Clémenceau This is where philatelists, postcard and coin collectors, and professionals and amateurs display, buy, and sell their collections.

Fabric and Cloth Markets

Carreau du Temple   Rue Perrée, 3rd *arrondissement,* Tuesday–Sunday, 9 a.m.–noon, Métro: Temple or Arts et Métiers. A traditional covered market with a Middle Eastern feel and good bargains.

Marché Saint-Pierre   2, rue Charles Nodier, 18th *arrondissement,* Tuesday–Sunday, 9 a.m.–6 p.m. Métro: Abbesses. This famous Montmartre covered market spreads out over several floors offering clothing, tapestry, bolts of African cloth, and hundreds of fabrics for curtains, pillows, and wall coverings. If you're handy with a sewing machine and you want to bring back a highly original souvenir, go out of your way to visit this market. Bring a calculator to convert lengths from meters to yards.

Great Parisian Gifts and Where to Find Them

Antiques

Antiques *(antiquités)* are a major shopping draw in Paris.

Village Saint-Paul   23–27, rue Saint-Paul, 75004; Métro: Saint-Paul. If you'd like to bring home a piece of turn-of-the-century jewelry, an art deco mirror, a carved picture frame, or something else old, a spin through the 70 shops in this one quaint location may be just what you're looking for. The prices are on the high side, but you're sure to be getting quality.

Le Louvre des Antiquaires   2, place du Palais Royal, 75001; Tel. 01 42 97 27 00; Métro: Louvre. Tuesday–Sunday, 11 a.m.–7 p.m. Closed Sunday in July and August. For high-end antiques of the finest furniture, art objects, paintings, sculptures, and old jewelry, the best address in Paris is right across the street from the Louvre. The selection is so fine that you'll think you're in the museum.

Aprons and Knives

The famous Cordon Bleu cooking school sells its own line of cooking and baking utensils, aprons, and knives, which make for great gifts for others and a good way to spoil yourself. The school is not centrally located, but it makes for a pleasant detour to one of Paris's residential neighborhoods.

Le Cordon Bleu   8, rue Léon Delhomme, 75015; Tel. 01 53 68 22 50; Métro: Vaugirard.

Bathroom Accessories

These sorts of small and unique accessories—such as knobs, vanity accoutrements, mirrors, and the like—are perfect for design-conscious bathers.

Bath Bazaar Victoires   Place des Victoires, 2, rue D'Aboukir, 75002; Tel. 01 55 34 37 17; Métro: Sentier.

Bread

France's most famous baker by far is Lionel Poilâne, whose famed sourdough loaves are flown to New York daily. Wait until your last day, and then fill in the empty space in your luggage with a Pain Poilâne. If Mr. Poilâne is around when you come in, you'll be treated to a sermon on bread that bridges poetry and philosophy.

Poilâne   8, rue du Cherche-Midi, 75006; Tel. 01 45 48 42 59; Métro: Saint-Sulpice or Sèvres-Babylone. 49, boulevard de Grenelle, 75015; Tel. 01 45 79 11 49; Métro: La Motte-Piquet-Grenelle.

Café Tables and Other Authentic Items

Among the great sources of original gifts are the shops connected to the famous cafés and restaurants. Next to La Tour d'Argent you'll find the **Comptoir Tour d'Argent.** Next to the famous caterer **Fauchon,** you'll find Fauchon's emporium of specialty goods. We like the little store next to the **Café de Flore** where you can buy placemats, espresso cups, and even wicker café chairs. An extravagant gift item is the Café de Flore "Gueridon" sidewalk café table, a 50-centimeter round table with a green enameled top and brass edges, with the center leg in black cast iron. The cost? €458, plus about €155 to ship it home. It weighs 18 kilos and is packed in three parts. The good news is that you'll get the VAT refunded and you'll have a permanent souvenir of Parisian café life right in your kitchen.

Café de Flore Boutique   26, rue Saint-Benoit, 75006; Tel. 01 45 44 33 40; Métro: St.-Germain-des-Prés.

Cheese

Any *fromagerie* will be more than adequate in supplying a broad variety of interesting cheeses. True cheese lovers, though, will want to check out Paris's most celebrated cheese shop, **Androuët,** in business since 1909:

Androuët   19, rue Daguerre, 75014; Tel. 01 43 21 19 09; Métro: Denfort Rochereau.

Note on Cheeses

Charles de Gaulle was noted as saying, "How can anyone govern a country that has over 450 kinds of cheese?" Make it a point to try as many as you can during your Paris stay. Remember that not only cow's milk is used for cheese—try some goat cheese and sheep cheese too. You should try any of the highly flavorful raw milk *(lait cru)* cheeses, since these are not exported to the United States due to U.S. agricultural regulations, and thus you won't find them at home.

Taking Cheese Home

Carrying most food product or agricultural goods into the United States is strictly forbidden. We know of a friend who was fined $50 at Newark Airport for carrying an apple off the plane. The U.S. Department of Agriculture employs dogs to sniff out your food items at Logan Airport in Boston and other international points of entry. So take this seriously. For a list of what you *can* bring back, see www.aphis.usda.gov/travel.

Children's Books in French

What a great way to initiate the kids into French. Check out the selection of illustrated books for children here. Note that the price of books in France is high, but the quality of production and the reproductions explain a lot. Parisians are used to paying more for their cultural products.

Chantelivre   13, rue de Sèvres, 75006; Tel. 01 45 48 87 90; Métro: Sèvres-Babylone.

Chocolate

You'll never go wrong bringing quality chocolate home. Consider this: American chocolate bars contain around 2% cocoa. The chocolate bars you'll find even in Paris supermarkets contain between 35% and 72% cocoa. After experiencing European chocolate, you'll have a hard time going back to Hershey's. As an experiment, try melting any American chocolate bar in a sauce pan. Watch what happens. It doesn't melt into a rich smooth sauce the way real chocolate does. A terrific gift to take back to your family and friends back home are massive French, Swiss, or Belgian chocolate bars, which you'll find in any supermarket for between €1.50 and €3.

Serious chocolate connoisseurs, though, need to be handled specially. Try one of the **Maison du Chocolat's** six locations (call for the store closest to your hotel). Note that fresh chocolate needs to be kept cool and will spoil if left out for several days.

Maison du Chocolat   225, rue du Fbg. Saint-Honoré, 75008; Tel. 01 42 27 39 44; Métro: Ternes.

Confitures

For jams, coffees, teas, biscuits, candy, and other packaged gourmet edibles, here's a delightful but pricey one-stop solution.

Lafayette Gourmet   48, boulevard Haussmann, 75009; Tel. 01 48 74 46 06; Métro: Chausée d'Antin; RER A: Auber.

Dishes

Savvy travelers boast of great finds on the rue de Paradis in the 10th *arrondissement* near Métro: Château d'Eau. The street is packed with china and porcelain shops.

Dolls and Bears

Robert Capria   24–26, Galerie Véro-Dodat, 75001; Tel. 01 42 36 25 94; Métro: Palais Royal Musée du Louvre. There's one address that is known the world over for antique dolls. This shop will enchant you.

For beautiful porcelain dolls, visit **Galerie Saint-Séverin;** or **Jeanne et Jérémy** for dolls and collector bears.

Galerie Saint-Séverin   4, rue du Petit-Pont, 75005; Tel. 01 43 25 76 14; Métro: St.-Michel.

Jeanne et Jérémy   4, rue Frédéric-Sauton, 75005; Tel. 01 46 33 54 54; Métro: Maubert-Mutualité.

Foie Gras, Escargots, Caviar, and Saumon Fumé

Again, with a very few exceptions, it's too risky carrying these luxury gourmet items with you in your luggage, since you'll risk losing the items and paying stiff fines if you're caught. Some adventurous travelers recommend wrapping these goodies in dirty laundry and placing them deep inside a huge piece of luggage. We suggest instead that you consume these things in Paris, enjoying them in context. For a good selection and easy access, you might want to shop for these items at the **Lafayette Gourmet** supermarket in the Galeries Lafayette department store. 40, boulevard Haussmann, 75009; Tel. 01 48 74 46 06. Monday–Saturday, 9 a.m.– 8 p.m.; Thursday open until 9 p.m. Métro: Chausée d'Antin; RER A: Auber.

Gold Jewelry

Tati Or has gained a lot of press attention over the last few years since the Tati chain, previously known for its bargain-basement, lower-class appeal, has gone upscale and trendy. The clothing chain now sells an impressive line of quality gold jewelry at some of the lowest prices around. A gold Eiffel Tower charm bracelet makes for a very special gift for someone.

Tati Or   132, boulevard Saint-Germain, 75006; Tel. 01 56 24 93 15; Métro: Odéon. Call for other locations.

Hardware

Here's one of our favorite suggestions. Rummage through the basement of the **BHV** department store to be able to add really original touches to your kitchen, bathroom, or office. Banal little details like molding, brass drawer handles, or cabinet hinges—very typical and ordinary in France—really stand out back home.

BHV   52–64, rue de Rivoli, 75004; Tel. 01 42 74 90 00; Métro: Hôtel de Ville.

Kitchen, Cooking, and Dining Room Supplies

Easily one of the most enjoyable moments you'll have shopping will be while rummaging through the aisles of a Parisian restaurant and culinary supply shop. Just about everything will be a potential gift. You can spend €22 for a mustard crock or oyster shucker and delight someone back home.

A. Simon   48, rue Montmartre, 75002; Tel. 01 42 33 71 65; Métro: Les Halles or Etienne Marcel.

Linen

French linen, sheets, pillow cases, and towels make excellent gifts. Your best bet is to comb the department stores for these. Why not visit **Au Bon Marché** this time? For motifs from Provence, stalk the nearby boutiques on the rue de Bonaparte in the Saint-Germain-des-Prés area.

Au Bon Marché   38, rue de Sèvres, 75007; Tel. 01 44 39 80 00; Métro: Sèvres-Babylone.

Lingerie

Ready-made lingerie and custom-made bras and panties can be found at the boutique listed below or at department stores—just think what you'll be doing to spice up your friends' lives back home!

Alice Cadolle   14, rue Cambon, 75001; Tel. 01 42 60 94 94; Métro: Concorde.

Music and French CDs

A very original gift is a CD by one of France's leading groups or singers. France produces talent in the hip-hop and rap genres particularly. One store will have everything you need and allows you to listen before purchasing.

Any FNAC will have a healthy selection, but the **FNAC Musique** stores are made to order.

FNAC Musique Bastille   Place de la Bastille, 75012; Tel. 01 43 42 04 04. Monday–Saturday, 10 a.m.– 8 p.m. Open until 10 p.m. on Wednesday and Friday nights. Métro: Bastille.

FNAC Musique Italiens   24, boulevard des Italiens, 75009; Tel. 01 48 01 02 03. Monday–Saturday, 10 a.m.–midnight. Métro: Richelieu-Drouot.

Mustard

There are real trade-offs in contemporary France. It's true that the banks and business climate often disappoint sophisticated visitors used to the no-nononsense atmosphere of New York or Tokyo, but where else besides Paris are your pickles and mustard made from the same recipe as back in 1747? It is definitely worth a few minutes to visit the **Boutique Maille,** which not only offers its full line of the finest pickles and vinegars in elegant jars, but also serves its famous mustard on tap. Fill up and take with you a hand-painted earthenware crock with Maille's tangy delight! An excellent, original gift at a modest price.

Boutique Maille   6, place de la Madeleine, 75001; Tel. 01 40 15 06 00; Métro: Madeleine.

Original Ready to Wear and More

Absinthe   74, rue Jean-Jacques Rousseau, 75001; Tel. 01 42 33 54 44. Métro: Les Halles. This is an unusual store with one-of-a-kind outfits and jewelry.

Antoine et Lili   95, quai de Valmy, 75010; Tel. Boutique: 01 40 37 41 55; www.antoineetlili.com; Garden Shop: 01 40 37 58 14; Restaurant La Cantine: 01 40 37 34 86; Métro: Gare de l'Est or Jacques Bonsergent. Women's and children's very wearable "hippie chic" fashions set in fuchsia and acid green décors. Fun jewelry, gift items, scents, crocheted slippers, etc. The Garden Shop next door offers colorful kitschy objects and furniture for home and garden. La Cantine offers simple, fresh salads, antipasti, and the like, and sells some unusual grocery items such as hemp soda, "Natural Mystic" beer, and homemade fruit sodas, syrups, and jellies. On Wednesday evenings there's a tarot card reader. Other boutique locations: 51, rue des Francs Bourgeois, 75004; Tel. 01 42 72 26 60; Métro: Saint Paul or Rambuteau. 87, rue de Seine, 75006; Tel. 01 56 24 35 81; Métro: Odéon. 7, rue de l'Alboni, 75016; Tel. 01 45 27 95 00; Métro: Passy. 90, rue des Martyrs, 75018; Tel. 01 42 58 10 22; Métro: Pigalle.

Gravity Zero   1, rue Keller, 75011; Tel. 01 43 57 97 62; www.gravity

zero.fr; Métro: Bastille. Streetwear fashion and accessories, decorative objects, and art exhibits, all by young and exclusive designers in a compact, futuristic boutique.

Pens

One of the most classic gifts coming out of France is, of course, the Montblanc fountain pen. Why not go to the source and check out the latest Meisterstück, selling for around €250 to €425. Remember, you can *détaxe* it! (That is, receive your VAT refund.)

Montblanc   60, rue du Fbg. Saint-Honoré, 75008; Tel. 01 40 06 02 93; Métro: St. Philippe du Roule.

Perfume and Fine Cosmetics

You have to think of the making of perfume and fine cosmetics as forms of high art like wine making and cheese making and other acts of high culture. To understand France and its history at the deepest level, you must think of its perfume and cosmetics not as products of vanity but as potions marking the crossroads of science and art, passion and reason, sensuality and the land. If you're just after a half-ounce of some famous fragrance available in any duty-free store in the world, you should probably shop in a duty-free store or order it on the Internet. If you're open to another type of sensual experience, then visit one of the following perfumeries and *maquillage* shops and bring along all your senses.

Guerlain   68, avenue des Champs-Elysées, 75008; Tel. 01 45 62 52 57; Métro: Franklin D. Roosevelt. Call for other locations.

L'Artisan Parfumeur   24, boulevard Raspail, 75007; Tel. 01 42 22 23 32; Métro: Rue du Bac.

Parfums Caron   34, avenue Montaigne, 75008; Tel. 01 47 23 40 82; Métro: Franklin D. Roosevelt.

Séphora   70, avenue des Champs-Elysées, 75008; Tel. 01 53 93 22 50; Métro: Franklin D. Roosevelt.

Stationery

In the digital age, paper continues to be sacred in France. There are scores of fine *papeteries* around the city, and they offer lots of inexpensive and original gifts. Here's one we like—which is perfect to deck the kids out with back-to-school items that no one has back home.

Lavrut   52, Passage Choiseul, 75002; Tel. 01 42 96 95 54; Métro: Quatre Septembre.

Trendy Clothing

agnès b.   6, rue du Jour, 75001; Tel. 01 45 08 56 56; Métro: Etienne
Marcel or Les Halles. 6, rue du Vieux Colombier, 75006; Tel. 01 44 39 02
60; Métro: St. Sulpice. 13, rue Michelet, 75006; Tel. 01 46 33 70 20;
Métro: Port Royal. 17, avenue Pierre-ler-de-Serbie, 75116; Tel. 01 47 20
22 44; Métro: Iéna. The French know that agnès b. symbolizes contemporary French style to foreigners. There's something here for women, children, and men at four shops: *femme, enfant, homme,* and *voyage* (women,
children, men, and travel).

Jean-Paul Gaultier   6, rue Vivienne, 75002; Tel. 01 42 86 05 05; Métro:
Bourse. Jean-Paul Gaultier typifies the innovation and audacity that many
associate with Paris today. Take a look for yourself! For both men and
women.

Wines and Spirits

Although you won't be able to carry large quantities with you, a few
selected bottles of wine make for either a great gift or a great way to remember your trip. Every neighborhood has a **Nicolas** wine shop, France's largest
chain (over 250 stores). The selection is broad and the prices are reasonable.
The manager will be able to direct those with no or limited wine experience
or knowledge on a suitable purchase.

Aside from wine, a bottle of old Cognac, Armagnac, or Calvados also
makes a wonderful gift. One Plymouth, Massachusetts, resident whose son
brought him a bottle of 20-year-old Calvados writes that every snifter
reminds him both of France and his son.

More serious wine tasters and collectors may wish to spend an hour at a
well-stocked showcase. Visit **Caves Augé,** 116, boulevard Haussmann,
75008; Tel. 01 45 22 16 97.

Tips for Buying Wine and Spirits

Serious wine collectors need not read this. The rest of us may find it helpful
to know that French wine with the blue metal wrapper around the cork
indicates that the wine is a mixture or blend of collected vineyards. Perfectly fine for drinking at the table, but wholly inadequate to either take
home or collect.

- The Beaujolais nouveau, which comes out every November, is fun and light to
  consume when it comes out. It is not made to age, and some Beaujolais nouveau
  will turn to vinegar in a matter of weeks. Don't bring it home unless you plan to
  drink it right away.

- Some of the best buys are smaller, lesser-known Bordeaux that are not exported
  to North America.

- The greatest amount of pleasure comes from bringing home a few bottles of a wine you've discovered at a vineyard, a tasting, or a bistro. A good bottle of red wine makes for an excellent gift and may cost you as little as €11.75 (about $10).

- It's better to buy your wines in a wine store before leaving and not rely on the duty-free shops at the airport, where the selection is limited and the prices are high. Champagne, however, is often on promotion at duty-free shops.

- An old bottle of Armagnac, Cognac, or Calvados is a great souvenir of your trip to France. When given as a gift it will endear you for life ... or at least until the last drop.

Part Nine

Exercise and Recreation

Sports and Fitness

Since many travelers today like to exercise even when they're on the road, we have researched this subject for the Paris-bound visitor. Parisians have become more fitness-conscious over the last ten years but still cannot be considered to care as much about recreation and health as they do about pleasure. International hotels have followed the American model and have tried to incorporate exercise rooms and health centers into their facilities, but these will seem to you like afterthoughts.

Although you'll probably spend more time exploring cultural Paris, you should know that the city offers plenty of resources to the athletic crowd. For all sports-related questions, there is a municipal sports hotline, **Allô-Sports** (Tel. 01 42 76 54 54).

If you need sports equipment in Paris, there are two main chains that provide everything athletes need: **Décathlon** (Tel. 01 44 54 81 30; 94, rue de Rivoli, 75004; Métro: Châtelet) and **Go Sport** (Tel. 01 40 13 73 50; 1, rue Pierre Lescot, 75001 at Les Halles; call for other locations).

For specialized sporting equipment for cycling, jogging, swimming, climbing, and camping, go to **Le Vieux Campeur** at 48, rue des Ecoles, 75005, Métro: Cluny or Saint-Michel, Tel. 01 53 10 48 48.

Jogging and Running

Paris air quality is not wonderful, between the smoking habits of the inhabitants and the diesel fumes of the buses and trucks. Additionally, although Paris is a relatively clean city, Parisians are not all that disciplined, and many wouldn't bat an eye before tossing a candy wrapper or cigarette butt onto the sidewalk. This is surprising to many tourists. The notorious problem with "uncurbed" dogs has been brought under control in many parts of the city with the introduction of 70 motorized, municipally operated vacuum cleaners that suck up a lot of the 20 tons of dog excrement that's deposited on Parisian sidewalks each day. In the less-wealthy areas of town, these machines don't seem to make the rounds quite so often.

Joggers are best advised to run in Paris streets with great caution, unlike the example of Bill Clinton who insisted on jogging through Place de la Concorde at rush hour on his state visit to France in 1996. For your safety and the future of your lungs, you may prefer to jog in one of Paris's lovely parks or in either of the two large forests at the eastern and western edges of the city, Bois de Vincennes and Bois de Boulogne. Both are easily accessible by Métro. If you love to jog, one of your most memorable jogs will be the time you spend lapping around the lake and château in the Jardin de Luxembourg in the Latin Quarter.

A Special Report for Serious Runners

One American fiction writer, marathon-runner, and long-term Paris resident, Shari Leslie Segall, who is probably the city's leading expat authority on running in Paris (she's actually written a novel on the subject), has agreed to share some of her most treasured secrets with our readers.

Where to Run   Paris is the most beautiful place in the world to run. Forget Big Sur. Forget New England in the autumn. Forget your local path where you had the epiphany that changed your life. Paris is the most beautiful place in the world to run. It is possible, in one single (relatively lengthy) straight line, moving eastward along the upper quays of the Seine from the 15th *arrondissement* to the 5th, to pass before or through—or catch a distant flash of—almost every monument, cathedral, statue, structure, and patch of nature for which Paris—and much of western civilization—is known and loved. Along this route, the river threads through its monuments like a silk cord through precious stones: the Eiffel Tower, the golden Invalides dome (don't forget to wave to Napoléon), the Place de la Concorde (don't forget a kind word for Louis and Marie—this is where they had their epiphany), Sacré Coeur staring from the far north down a split-second glimpse of rooftop, the Tuileries Gardens, the Musée d'Orsay, the Louvre and its pyramid (run through that courtyard—it's a gas!), the bridges where famous midnight mist-kissed trysts among famous figures took place during famous wars, Notre-Dâme, the Tour d'Argent restaurant, all the way (with a couple of zigzags) to the Vincennes Zoo if you have the right shoes, stamina, and sense of history.

The city is anchored in the west by the Bois de Boulogne (*bois* means woods) and in the east by the Bois de Vincennes (which is why the Paris Marathon, which partially follows a version of the above-mentioned route, includes both); it's punctuated by patches of perfect running pockets:

the **Luxembourg Gardens** (at 6 m.p.h., you'll go around the perimeter in about 11 minutes), the **Champs de Mars** under the Eiffel Tower (about 14 minutes around the perimeter at 6 m.p.h.), the **Parc Monceau** (beautiful, but kind of small—you'll need a lot of loops and patience), and the **Parc Montsouris** (ditto). For the mega-masochists among us, there's the legendary hilly **Buttes-Chaumont**.

The Best-Kept Secret: As do residents of Seattle, runners who know about the **Promenade Plantée** keep the news to themselves for fear of invasion by the uninitiated. But you've just gotta know about this. From the Opéra de la Bastille (take the steps at the corner of the avenue Daumesnil and the avenue Ledru-Rollin) to the entrance to the Bois de Vincennes (the entrance is a street or so away, so check a very recent map if you want to continue into the Bois), roughly 3.5 km (2 miles) of old railroad tracks have been turned into a sort of linear public park, which at times, as did the train, takes you giddily high above the street, dips to ground level, rolls in and out of totally tunnel-dotted greenery to an occasional residential or commercial block, which features what always seems like the first lush roses of the summer and the first russet leaves of the fall, and generally looks and feels like you made it all up and if you open your eyes it's all going to disappear. Do it. Go there. Run there. But . . . don't tell a soul!

Where to Buy Gear   As with most goods and services in Paris, with the exception of the occasional loaf of bread or bus ride, the price of running gear is so astoundingly high that you'll think they must have made a mistake. Your impulse is to go over to the nice cash-register lady and point out that there is one too many zeros on her nice price tag. Shoes, especially, can be as much as 75% more expensive than in the United States. If you need to bring a souvenir back from Paris, stick to Eiffel Tower statuettes rather than running gear.

La Boutique Marathon   26, rue Léon Jost, 75017; Tel. 01 42 67 49 44; Métro: Courcelles. Open Tuesday, Wednesday, Friday, Saturday, 10 a.m.– 7 p.m.; Thursday, 10 a.m.– 8 p.m.

Shoes, clothing, accessories, books, etc. Prices are still outrageous, but the owner is a long-time marathoner (she ran New York costumed as Wonder Woman), all the employees know their stuff, they speak enough of at least running-specific English to keep the transaction alive, they have a stock of which other Paris running stores can only dream, they cheerfully give out free running and gear-maintenance advice, and they let you take the shoes out for a test-drive around the block.

As elsewhere in the world, no running-department employees got hired because they needed a job in a chain or department store. Unless they were runners who needed a job. Running-specific chains abound (and compete with each other) in Paris, but are more often than not staffed by kids who could just as easily be stocking shelves at the local yarn-supply boutique, and whose only exercise consists of chewing gum.

What to Take Seriously

Dogs   Paris is a true love-me-love-my-dog town. (One theory is that this gives the French something to kick after having received their own kicking for the past two millennia from tribes, church, monarchy, and disagreeable civil servants.) You will probably encounter more (usually "leashless") dogs along your route (or in your park or garden of choice) than you ever have in all your years of running in your home country. The dogs will behave like dogs behave with runners anywhere else: the ones liable to get agitated will get agitated; the urbane, blasé ones will pretend not to notice you're there. The difference is, in Paris, you're the one expected to go out of your way to avoid the dog—not the other way around. And if the dog starts getting funny on you and you react accordingly (fear, aggression of your own, a comment to the owner), you're the one who's seen (and usually soundly reprimanded by the owner as well as tag-along members of the seemingly citywide dog-walking club) as the insensitive brute. All this, of course, while you're trying to keep running.

Dog droppings   They're everywhere (surprised?). They're slippery. If you swerve to avoid one you'll surely wind up plunking right into another. All this, of course, while you're trying to keep running. There is only one solution: make sure you wipe your feet before entering your hotel room.

Traffic lights   *Rouge* may mean "red" in French, but it sure doesn't seem to mean "stop." Or, "stop right away." Never assume that once the light turns green for you and red for the crossing traffic, the crossing traffic will cease moving forward. It won't; several more cars will graze your nose before anything resembling stopping takes place. Never assume that now it's relatively safe (is it ever safe?) to cross, or that there will be no other vehicular activity in your particular intersection until the light turns red for you. There will be; cars will be making right and left turns into your path from what seems like streets all the way to the suburbs. Never assume that some smart-aleck motorcyclist won't start savagely revving his engine just as you're halfway across, mortifying you into thinking that the light's changed and you're dead. He will: the smaller his bike, the louder his rev. All this, of course, while you're trying to keep running.

Pedestrians   Pedestrians are a combination of humans, dogs (who don't get out of your way), and motorists (who look for—and seize—every opportunity to get into your way), with the added attraction that they stare at you simply dumbfounded. All over the city. They stare. They have never seen a runner before. And have always known that day would come. And here it is. And you're it. And tomorrow when you pass they will never have seen a runner before again. They will always have known that day would come again. And here it will be again. If you let it get to you it will paralyze your outing. All this, of course, while you're trying to keep running.

Swimming

If you feel like going for a swim, you'll find excellent public facilities in almost every *arrondissement*. Entry is generally about €4. The **Piscine Suzanne-Berlioux** in the Forum des Halles, impressively located underground in the center of Paris, offers rink hockey, handball, basketball, volleyball, badminton, tennis, dance courses, and martial arts, in addition to its pool facilities. It is accessible to the disabled as well.

Piscine Armand-Massard   66, boulevard du Montparnasse, 75015; Tel. 01 42 76 78 15; Métro: Montparnasse; (Closed Monday).

Piscine Saint-Germain   12, rue Lobineau, 75006; Tel. 01 42 76 78 03; Métro: Mabillon; (Closed Monday).

Piscine Saint-Merri   16, rue du Renard, 75004; Tel. 0 1 42 76 78 01; Métro: Hôtel de Ville or Rambuteau; (Closed Monday); Other activities: solarium.

Piscine Suzanne-Berlioux   4, place de la Rotonde, 75001; Tel. 01 42 36 98 44; Métro: Les Halles.

Hotel Pools

A few Parisian hotels have indoor pools, but this is rare. The Ritz has a pool that'll make you feel like you're in an Otto Preminger film, but paying Ritz prices for the sake of the pool is not a great idea.

Aquaboulevard

4–6, rue Louis Armand, 75015; Tel. 01 40 60 10 00; Métro Balard, Porte de Versailles. During the summer months when the days are hot and heavy, an outing to Aquaboulevard, an elaborate complex of swimming pools, slides, and recreational facilities, may be just what's in order.

Fishing and Boating

There is some fishing in the Seine and Marne rivers, as well as in the ponds at the Bois de Vincennes and Bois de Boulogne, but considering the need for licenses and the specific equipment needed to nab a *poisson,* we advise you to limit your fishing experiences to the restaurants. You can rent canoes in the Bois de Vincennes and Bois de Boulogne.

Barques du Bois de Boulogne

These medium-sized rowing boats on Lac Inférieur fit a maximum of five people. Rental is by the hour (€9.15), a cash deposit is required, and all boats must be back by 6 p.m. This is a lovely way to cool down at the end of a summer afternoon. Tel. 01 45 25 44 01.

Hiking

There is more nature in Paris than you'd be able to discover on your own. Short side-trips from Paris place you in dense forests laden with royal history. One of the most attractive parks inside Paris is the **Buttes-Chaumont,** which has rugged hills and even a few stalactites in a cave. This is among the largest Parisian parks, arranged in the English style and equally beautiful and romantic. Created under Napoléon III by the designer Adolphe Alphand, it is a colorful landscape of roughly 5,000 acres with over half a million trees. Check out Sybille's Temple on the top of an 89-meter cliff. Take Métro Line 7bis and get off at the Buttes-Chaumont–Botzaris stop. For out-of-town excursions, see Part Six, Sightseeing and Tours.

Parks and City Squares

See the Parks section in Part Six, Sightseeing and Tours.

Tennis

Ever since Yannick Noah emerged as a national tennis hero, tennis has shed much of its bourgeois connotation in France. As a short-term tourist it is difficult to reserve tennis courts in Paris, because reservations at public courts such as those in the Luxembourg Gardens require a Paris-tennis membership card, issued only to Parisian residents. Without a reservation it is doubtful that you will find an available court. For information on the French Open, call 01 47 43 48 00 or visit www.rolandgarros.org or www.fft.fr.

Gym Clubs

Although it's possible to get a good workout in Paris, fitness *à la américaine* is a fairly new concept in France, so don't expect to find all the amenities and services that you are used to. There are several prominent gym clubs with locations all over the city offering workout rooms, saunas, whirlpools, and other equipment. Most do not offer any day or week passes, but some do, and we've found these options for tourists who can't survive a week without their dose of the StairMaster. Some hotels do have in-house exercise rooms, but many of the smaller, older, and more quaint establishments don't. In general, Parisians are not very exercise-conscious and would rather eat, drink, or go to the cinema than sweat, but there has been a wave of health clubs that have opened in the last five years. There is no word in French for fitness, so Parisians say "*le fitness*." Note that they almost never supply towels, and if they do, they're not large, and you have to pay extra, usually a euro or two. Facilities tend to be less spacious than you're perhaps accustomed to. You'll find StairMasters, treadmills, stationery bikes, and free weights in most gyms.

Many of the municipal pools have workout equipment, but access to them usually requires an additional fee. For example, the **Piscine Club Pontoise-Quartier Latin** (19, rue de Pontoise, Tel. 01 55 42 77 88, Métro: Maubert-Mutualité) costs €13/day for their well-equipped gym and about €4/day for the pool. The **American Church** (65, quai d'Orsay, Tel. 01 47 53 04 56, Métro: Invalides) offers aerobic classes Monday through Saturday.

One of the best clubs in France, **Espace Vit'Halles,** with a younger clientele and a wide variety of programs with personalized training (weight lifting, aerobics, stretching, yoga, circuit training), is centrally located.

Espace Vit'Halles   place Beaubourg, 48, rue Rambuteau, 75003; Tel. 01 42 77 21 71; Métro: Rambuteau. Entry: €15.25/day (credit cards accepted). Open: Monday–Friday, 8 a.m.–10:30 p.m.; Saturday, 10 a.m.–7 p.m.; Sunday, 10 a.m.–6 p.m.

Gymnase Club   10, place de la République, 75011; Tel. 01 47 00 69 98; Métro: République. Entry: €26/day. Many Gymnase Club instructors speak English. With 167 clubs in the Paris region this chain is one of the most convenient for short-term visitors. Avoid late afternoons when it gets congested and sweaty.

Le Ritz Health Club   15, place Vendôme, 75001; Tel. 01 43 16 30 60; Métro: Opéra. Entry: €126/day on weekdays, €153/day on weekends! You don't have to be a hotel guest to enjoy all the services offered by Le Ritz Health Club: a 16-meter pool, squash, steam bath, Jacuzzi, free weights, circuit training, exercise and yoga classes, but the day pass just might be more than you're paying for your hotel room!

Cycling

The French are serious cyclists and host the celebrated Tour de France each year. If you'd like to ride while you're in Paris, you can, although inner-city cycling is rather hazardous. There are bike lanes in the streets, but they are almost wholly disregarded. In any case, wear headgear. Cycling in the Bois de Vincennes and Bois de Boulogne in the summer is heavenly. There are seasonal bike rental shops open in both parks. And, of course, bike trips to other regions in France are known to be glorious.

Bike Rentals

In addition to renting bicycles, these businesses also service and repair them. Most of them do tours (usually just for groups; ask when you call).

Bike 'n Roller   6, rue st-Julien-le-Pauvre, 75005; Métro: St-Michel; Tel. 01 44 07 35 89. Other locations near Eiffel Tower, Invalides.

Escapade Nature   3, rue Antoine Vollon, 75012; Métro: Ledru-Rollin; Tel. 01 53 17 03 18; fax: 01 43 43 57 19. A three-hour Paris bike tour costs about €22, rental included. English-speaking guides available.

Mike's Bullfrog Bike Tours   150, avenue Emile Zola, 75015; Métro: La Motte-Piquet; Tel. 06 09 98 08 60; mikesbikesparis@hotmail.com. Fun, diverse ways of visiting Paris, day or night, rain or shine, in English, bikes included! Forget buses, taxis, and vans—this is the way to see this city. Visit www.mikesbiketoursparis.com for prices and times.

Paris à Vélo   37, boulevard Bourdon, 75004; Métro: Bastille; Tel. 01 48 87 60 01; fax: 01 48 87 61 01. Three-hour day or night tour for €28.

Paris Vélo   2, rue du Fer-à-Moulin, 75005; Métro: Censier-Daubenton; Tel. 01 43 37 59 22; fax: 01 47 07 67 45. Three-hour tour for €23.

Shipping Your Bike

For information on shipping your bike with you, call your airline. Charter companies tend to be stricter with baggage requirements and are not equipped with bike boxes. Once you get to Paris, you shouldn't have much problem transporting your bike around. Some RER lines, one Métro line, and certain trains allow bikes on board; check the Maison Roue Libre (below) for details.

For tour operators specializing in cycling trips to France, request a copy of the Maison de la France's *Easy Reference Guide to France*, on the web at www.francetourism.com or by calling Tel. (202) 659-7779. One travel service known for their quality bicycling tours in France is Progressive Travels, 224 W. Galer, Ste. C, Seattle, WA 98119 (Tel. (800) 245-2229; www.progressivetravels.com).

Note that in the summer months, the French railroad company, SNCF, rents bicycles at almost every train station in the country with interchangeable pick up and drop-off points. For information, contact the SNCF:

Maison Roue Libre
95 bis, rue Rambuteau, 75001
Tel. 01 53 46 43 77, Fax: 01 40 28 01 00

Open 9 a.m. to 7 p.m. every day, year-round. Rental prices are very reasonable (starting at €3.05/hour, €11.45/day including insurance), and guided tours with several different theme options are available for a small additional fee.

Inline Skating

The hottest Paris sport to grasp the imagination of both residents and visitors is by far inline skating. This is a fascinating, fast-paced, and original way to see the city by day and night. Fifteen years ago there were barely 10,000 "bladers" in all of France. Today you'll have a hard time going a day without seeing one, winter or summer. With the advent of roller mania, many associations and group outings have been organized to bring together practitioners of all levels and interests. If you are a beginner, several rental and instruction options are available. The **Roller Squad Institute** (Tel. 01 56 61 99 61, www.rsi.asso.fr) offers 1½-hour lessons for €13/hour every day except Monday and Friday. They organize excursions leaving from Invalides every Sunday, and from Trocadéro every Saturday. **Nomades** (37, boulevard Bourdon in the 4th, Tel. 01 44 54 07 44, Métro: Bastille) not only rents skates but offers lessons for €12.20/hour on Saturday and Sunday starting at 10 a.m. For more advanced bladers, there is the three-hour outing that leaves from Place d'Italie every Friday night at 10 p.m. Visit www.Pari-roller.com for more information. Other skate rental companies include **Bike 'n Roller** (Tel. 01 44 07 35 89) and **Franscoop** (Tel. 01 47 00 68 43).

Golf

There are approximately 50 private and public golf courses in the Paris area, although to get to them you'll need a car. But, if you can afford the greens fees, we're not worried about your ability to get to the course. Some courses require all players to purchase insurance before stepping up to the first tee. Greens fees are expensive. For course descriptions, visit www.golfeurope.com (click on France, then Île de France).

Miniature golf courses can be found in the Bois de Vincennes and Jardin d'Acclimatation.

Horseback Riding

If you feel like riding during your Paris visit, contact the **Centre Equestre de la Cartoucherie** in the Bois de Vincennes, 75012, Tel. 01 43 74 61 25. Times, prices, and conditions tend to change, so inquire well in advance.

Part Ten

Entertainment and Nightlife

Paris by Night

What to do at night? Anything you want. Paris is practically as passive or active as you choose. It's all here. Many visitors love to spend each evening at a new restaurant, tasting new wonders and discovering liquid miracles of great vintage, and then wandering back to their hotels on a late-evening stroll along cobblestone streets to an inviting, feathery bed. For others, dinner is just the beginning of a long night, since Paris's club scene only begins to crank up at midnight and regularly pulses until the first Métro just before dawn. Culturally, Paris is so rich that the problem is always saying no to things you'd love to see. Every night there are a hundred plays produced, a half-dozen operas, a dozen concerts, and two dozen extravagant shows and performances. For the literary set, there are readings. For art aficionados, a score of openings called *vernissages* await you. Paris is the capital of cinema, with hundreds of movie houses playing countless films every night. Normally you'd never think of seeing a movie in a foreign city, but in Paris, why not duck into one of the lush cinemas and get lost in a recent French film? And the bars and cafés, the people-watching, and talking, smoking, and cognac snifting. And, of course, walking the *quai* and cruising on the Seine. And finally, the greatest of the great Parisian pastimes, *draguer,* a curiously Parisian verb falling somewhere crudely between just flirting and flirting with the intent of not going home alone. Political correctness was never taken seriously among Parisians, who on the whole love to admire and be admired and enjoy being judged by their looks, their bulges, and their curves. For the unsingle set free to *draguer* in Paris, why not *draguer* your husband or wife, boyfriend or girlfriend? In Paris, public affection is as natural as a good meal, and if love is involved, it's never wrong. In Paris you can live the clichés.

The Lights of Paris

The most impressive moments you'll spend in Paris are after dark, when the sky goes black and the beams and spots illuminate the monuments and building façades. You will quickly understand why Paris is called the City of Light. Paris after 10 p.m. begins to feel like a huge, living theater or museum, and you'll begin to realize that the best thing you can do is simply drink up its beauty. Don't try to comprehend; simply feel. You may not be into poetry, but evenings in Paris when you're free to stroll are poetic.

The City by Foot

If you want to take an evening walk, start at the middle of the **Pont Neuf** and watch the barges stroke the 17th-century buildings on both banks with their strong flood lights. Cross the bridge and follow the long textured edge of the **Louvre** on the Right Bank. Duck under the archway to your left and enter into the central courtyard of the Louvre. The Pyramid at night is spectral. With your back to the Pyramid, spot the **Arc de Triomphe** in the distance as it lines up perfectly with the tip of the obelisk at Place de la Concorde. Quickly, you'll begin to feel the symmetry of the city, and the degree of artfulness that the architectures have invested in creating this beauty through the ages. Walk back to the Seine, turn left, and follow the river to Châtelet. The **Palais de Justice** and the eerie **Hôtel Dieu,** Paris's oldest hospital, will be lit up, glittering gold and iridescent blue on the Left Bank. For information about guided walking tours, see Part Six, Sightseeing and Tours.

Self-Guided Night Tour by Taxi

For a highly original experience, jump into a taxi at Châtelet and tell the driver to follow the Seine all the way to the Pont de Bercy. Indicate that you want him to take the Voie Express, which dips down to river level and swirls and turns under the bridges. The neck of the river between the **Hôtel de Ville** and the exit for the **Bastille** is enchanting as the oldest buildings on the Île Saint Louis come alive in the lights and shadows. After the Gare de Lyon, the highway will lose some of its charm as the new Paris comes into focus, with the **Ministry of Finance** building, the **Bercy Sports Stadium,** the futuristic **CinéCité** complex of movie houses on the right of the old Bercy wine village, and across the river, the four box-like towers that are now France's new **François Mitterrand National Library** (*Bibliothèque nationale).*

Have the driver cross the river and head back along the *quai* on the Left Bank. As the back of **Notre-Dame** comes into focus, you'll know why you're in Paris. Get out at St. Michel, trot down the stone steps that lead to the edge of the Seine, and continue on foot along the Left Bank until you're tired. For less than €20, you will have given yourself the tour of your life.

One variation on this tour is to stay in the taxi and continue along the Left Bank, past the **Musée d'Orsay,** with Place de la Concorde off to your right. Take the drive down along the river and don't come up until you're under the **Eiffel Tower.** Then cross over toward Trocadéro and have the driver loop you around toward the left and up to the top of Trocadéro. Get out, have your driver wait, and pinch yourself. You'll be bowled over at the awe-inspiring view of a bejeweled Eiffel Tower. If you're up for more, follow the avenue Kléber to the Arc de Triomphe and swing down the lively-at-all-hours avenue Champs-Elysées. This is the only time of day that the Champs is truly worth visiting.

Cultural Evenings

Where to Go for listings?

If you're limited to English, start with the English-language pages produced by *Time Out* in the weekly listings magazine, *Pariscope,* which comes out every Wednesday and costs a half a euro. Your hotel may supply a copy of the latest *Where Paris* in your room, which sports an excellent selection of cultural happenings during the month. If you go by one of the English-language bookstores, pubs, or the American Church, pick up the latest copy of the *Paris Voice,* a free community paper that offers cultural journalism and a copious selection of monthly events. This can be consulted beforehand online at www.parisvoice.com.

For concerts and other live performances (other than theater), drop in at the **FNAC** or **Virgin Megastore** to review their box office listings. For serious music aficionados, pick up a copy of *Le Monde de la Musique* in any kiosk. It's in French, of course, but you'll easily recognize dates, times, Chopin, *La Flûte Magique (The Magic Flute),* and similar phrases.

The theater world in Paris is thoroughly covered in a monthly tabloid called *Cadences,* found in all Paris theaters.

Music, Opera, and Dance

There are a number of informative and accurate sources for planning a musical night out in Paris. *Pariscope,* mentioned above, is one of the most comprehensive listings. It is arranged by category: classical, world music, operas, dance, jazz-rock, and *variétés* (French variety shows), and includes addresses, Métro stops, phone numbers, hours, and prices of an extensive number of Parisian musical venues. In the *Time Out* section of the same guide, you can find good advice and descriptions in English of a selected offering of concerts, festivals, and deejayed or live-performance clubs. *Nova Magazine* is a good source with a definite penchant for the Anglophone and under-30 music scenes. *The Paris Voice* gives a monthly listing of musical events and several articles or an interview on the current month's jazz events. Below are listed a number of venues that host regular events.

Classical Music

Amphithéâtre Richelieu de la Sorbonne   17, rue de la Sorbonne, 75005; Tel. 01 42 62 71 71; Métro: Cluny–La Sorbonne

Auditorium du Louvre   Louvre Museum, La Pyramide, Cour Napoléon, 75001; Tel. 01 40 20 84 00; Métro: Palais-Royal

Auditorium du Musée d'Orsay   1, rue de la Légion d'Honneur, 75007; Tel. 01 40 49 48 14; Métro: Solférino or RER Musée d'Orsay

Cité de la Musique   221, avenue Jean Jaurès, 75019; Tel. 01 44 84 45 00; reservations: 01 44 84 44 84; Métro: Porte-de-Pantin

IRCAM   1, place Igor Stravinski, 75004; Tel. 01 44 78 48 34; Métro: Rambuteau or Hôtel-de-Ville

Sainte Chapelle   4, boulevard du Palais, 75001; Tel. 01 42 50 96 18; Métro: Cité or St-Michel

Salle Pleyel   252, rue du Fbg. St-Honoré, 75008; Tel. 01 45 61 53 00; Métro: Ternes

Théâtre des Champs-Elysées   15, avenue Montaigne, 75008; Tel. 01 49 52 50 00; Métro: Alma-Marceau

Opera and Dance

Centre Pompidou   19, rue de Beaubourg, 75004; Tel. 01 44 78 12 23; Métro: Rambuteau or Hôtel-de-Ville. Tickets: €7.60–18.30. The Paris mecca for contemporary popular culture.

Châtelet-Théâtre Musical de la Ville de Paris   1, place du Châtelet, 75001; Tel. 01 40 28 28 40; Métro: Châtelet–Les Halles. Tickets: concerts and ballets €8–58, operas €11–105. Major venue for quality productions.

L'Opéra Comique   5, rue Favart, 75009; Tel. 01 42 96 12 20 (reservations); Métro: Richelieu-Drouot. Tickets: €7–57. Specializes in operettas and new productions.

Opéra Bastille   120, rue de Lyon, 75011; Tel. 08 36 69 78 68; Métro: Bastille. Tickets: operas €10–105, concerts and ballets €7–64. This controversial opera house of modern design was created by Canadian Carlos Ott. Since its first performance was given in 1989, there has been a nearly constant storm of criticism of not only its architecture, but also its acoustics and prices. Part of this reaction can be attributed to the typical slamming of anything new by Parisians. There are actually more operas performed here than at its cross-town cousin, the **Opéra Garnier.** We can't guarantee it, but there are often discounted seats available for students and the elderly 15 minutes before the curtain rises.

Opéra Palais Garnier Place de la Opéra, 75009; Tel. 08 36 69 78 68; Métro: Opéra. Tickets: operas €7–105, concerts and ballets €5–64. This is the granddaddy opera house of Paris, built during Napoléon III's empire by the then-unknown Charles Garnier. The interior is impressive, including an eclectic mix of architecture and adornment from Gobelin tapestries to a Chagallian ceiling. A large part of its season is dedicated to ballet. Access to all the public areas of the opera and its library and museum are allowed every day from 10 a.m. to 4:30 p.m. (€4.60; Tel. 01 40 01 22 63).

Théâtre de la Ville 2, place du Châtelet, 75004; Tel. 01 42 74 22 77; Métro: Châtelet–Les Halles. Tickets: €15–29. Progressive program of French and foreign productions.

Théâtre des Champs-Elysées 15, avenue Montaigne, 75008; Tel. 01 49 52 50 00; Métro: Alma-Marceau. Tickets: (€6–80). High-quality performances; a favorite recital venue.

Concert Halls

Cité de la Musique 221, avenue Jean Jaurès, 75019; Tel. 01 44 84 45 00; reservations: 01 44 84 44 84; Métro: Porte-de-Pantin. Major venue for classical, modern, contemporary, baroque, and other serious concerts. A bit far out, but worth the visit. Good and inexpensive restaurant on the premises.

L'Olympia 28, boulevard des Capucines, 75009; Tel. 01 47 42 25 49; Métro: Madeleine. Tickets: €35–47. This is one of musical Paris's hallmarks. French singers like Edith Piaf, Jacques Brel, and Yves Montand made themselves internationally famous here. Although the *chansons françaises* once dominated the Olympia's stage, more contemporary acts from a variety of backgrounds are now included.

La Cigale 120, boulevard Rochechouart, 75018; Tel. 01 49 25 81 75; Métro: Barbès-Rochechouart. Small music hall used for eclectic performances, guitarists, reggae, and others.

Le Bataclan 50, boulevard Voltaire, 75011; Tel. 01 43 14 35 35; Métro: Oberkampf. Small concert hall for both big names and emerging ones in the rock, hip hop, reggae, and other scenes.

Maison de Radio France 116, avenue du Président Kennedy, 75016; Tel. 01 56 40 15 16; Métro: Ranelagh or Passy. RER: Kennedy/Maison de Radio

France. You can attend classical concerts, operas, and performances of the Orchestre National de France, which are broadcast on France Musiques.

Palais des Congrès 2, place Porte Maillot, 75017; Tel. 01 40 68 00 05; Métro: Porte de Maillot. Large performance hall.

Palais Omnisports de Paris-Bercy 8, boulevard de Bercy, 75012; Tel. 01 43 46 12 21; Métro: Bercy. Huge and impressive stadium and hall for big groups and international acts. Note that the sloping outer walls of the stadium are covered with real grass!

Salle Gaveau 45, rue de la Boétie, 75008; Tel. 01 49 53 05 07; Métro: Miromesnil. Small and intimate music hall for chamber music and concert recitals.

Salle Pleyel 252, rue du Fbg. St.-Honoré, 75008; Tel. 01 45 61 53 00; Métro: Ternes. Medium-sized concert hall, home of the prestigious Orchestre de Paris.

Zénith 211, avenue Jean Jaurès, 75019; Tel. 01 42 40 60 00; Métro: Porte-de-Pantin. Concert hall for some of the biggest and loudest domestic and international talent.

Church Concerts

There are weekly church concerts in all of the following churches: **La Madeleine, Saint-Sulpice, Saint-Séverin, St.-Germain-des-Prés, Sainte Geneviève, Sainte Chapelle, St. Augustin,** and of course **Notre-Dame.** For more information about specific performances and times, your best bet is to check *PariScope, Where Magazine,* or *Cadences Magazine* when you arrive.

Theaters and Spectacles

Paris has 115 theaters offering French and foreign productions. Whether you speak French or not, you may choose to spend an evening at the theater. The following Paris theaters not only offer top-quality performances, they will enchant you with their style, décor, architecture, and history. For programs, details, times, and prices, consult *Pariscope* or *l'Officiel des Spectacles.*

Athénée Louis Jouvet 4, square de l'Opéra Louis Jouvet, 75009; Tel. 01 53 05 19 19; Métro: Opéra. Classic venue.

Bouffes du Nord 37 bis, boulevard de la Chapelle, 75010; Tel. 01 46 07 34 50; Métro: La Chapelle. Home of Peter Brooke's company.

Bouffes Parisiens 4, rue Monsigny, 75002; Tel. 01 42 96 92 42; Métro: Quatre Septembre or Pyramides. Comic and dramatic works.

Comédie des Champs-Elysées 15, avenue Montaigne, 75008; Tel: 01 53 23 99 19; Métro: Alma-Marceau. Classic venue.

Comédie Française   2, rue Richelieu, 75001; Tel. 01 44 58 15 15; Métro: Palais Royal. Historic landmark—Moliere's home.

Guichet-Montparnasse   15, rue du Maine, 75014; Tel. 01 43 27 88 61; Métro: Montparnasse-Bienvenüe. Small comic productions.

La Bruyère   5, rue La Bruyère, 75009; Tel: 01 48 74 76 99; Métro: St-Georges. Traditional works.

La Cartoucherie de Vincennes   route du Champ-de-Manoeuvre, 75012; Tel. 01 43 74 99 61; Aquarium de la Tempête: 01 43 28 36 36; Métro: Château-de-Vincennes. One of Paris's most innovative theaters—home of the famed Théâtre du Soleil.

La Madeleine   19, rue de Surène, 75008; Tel. 01 45 65 07 09; Métro: Madeleine. Performs mostly French classics.

Odéon Théâtre de l'Europe   1, place de l'Odéon, 75006; Tel. 01 44 41 36 36; Métro: Odéon. Major venue for contemporary European works played in original languages.

Petit Odéon   (see Odéon Théâtre de l'Europe)

Splendide Saint-Martin   48, rue du Fbg. Saint-Martin, 75010; Tel. 01 42 08 21 93; Métro: Strasbourg-Saint-Denis. Musicals, mimes, and social comedy.

Théâtre de la Bastille   76, rue de la Roquette, 75011; Tel. 01 43 57 42 14; Métro: Bastille. Contemporary theater and dance.

Théâtre de la Huchette   23, rue de la Huchette, 75005; Tel. 01 43 26 38 99; Métro: St-Michel. Small, intimate productions.

Théâtre de la Ville/Théâtre des Abbesses   2, place du Châtelet, 75004; Tel. 01 42 74 22 77; Métro: Châtelet–Les Halles. Classical French work.

Théâtre du Palais-Royal   38, rue Montpensier, 75001; Tel. 01 42 97 59 81; Métro: Palais-Royal. Classical performances.

Théâtre du Rond-Point   2 bis, avenue Franklin Roosevelt, 75008; Tel. 01 44 95 98 00; Métro: Franklin-Roosevelt. Major theater on the Champs-Elysées.

Théâtre du Vieux Colombier   21, rue du Vieux Colombier, 75006; Tel. 01 44 39 87 00; Métro: St-Sulpice. Modern and classical works.

Théâtre Mogador   25, rue Mogador, 75009; Tel. 01 53 32 32 20; Métro: Trinité. Celebrated theater for French comedies.

Théâtre National de Chaillot   1, place du Trocadéro, 75016; Tel. 01 47 27 81 15; Métro: Trocadéro. Major venue for nationally noted talent.

Théâtre National de la Colline   5, rue Malte-Brun, 75020; Tel. 01 44 62 52 52; Métro: Gambetta. Great innovative works.

Theaters for English-Speakers

Paris hosts a half-dozen small theater companies playing regularly in English. If this interests you, pick up a copy of the *Paris Voice* for listings. To get tickets, you can call the box office directly or go to the theater. Paris also has two "same-day" ticket offices offering seats at half-price.

Le Kiosque Théâtre   Place de la Madeleine; Métro: Madeleine

Parvis Montparnasse   Métro: Montparnasse. Open from Tuesday through Saturday from 12:30 to 7:45 p.m. and Sunday from 12:30 to 3:45 p.m. (It is written everywhere that these kiosks are open until 8 p.m. and 4 p.m., respectively, but this is not true; they close 15 minutes earlier!)

These kiosks accept euro checks or cash only, no credit cards. You pay half-price plus a commission of about €3 per ticket, which is still very much worth it.

Tickets to many concerts and sporting events are available from the ticket service at the **Virgin Megastore** on the Champs-Elysées, **France Billet** in the Carrefour and Auchan supermarkets, **Galeries Lafayette,** and the **FNAC** stores. You may also buy your tickets online at www.ticketnet.fr, www.france-billet.com, or www.ticketavenue.com.

Readings and Lectures

If you're interested in what's happening in the literary scene (in English) in Paris these days, the best listening post is the **Village Voice Bookshop** at 6, rue Princesse, 75007, near Métro Mabillon, Tel. 01 46 33 36 47 (www.paris-anglo.com/villagevoice). Chances are that there will be a reading on one of the evenings that you're in town. Book events are also held at the celebrated **Shakespeare & Company** at 37, rue de la Bûcherie, 75005, Métro: St-Michel, as well as the Canadian bookshop **Abbey,** around the corner. **The American Library in Paris** hosts "Evenings with an Author" on Wednesdays at 10, rue du Général Camou, 75007, Métro: RER Alma, Tel. 01 53 59 12 60. **W.H. Smith** and **Brentano's** host book signings and talks, but these bookshops may be too reminiscent of what you left back home to feel particularly Parisian or expatriate. Of course, if your French is up to snuff, there are readings and talks in French at numerous venues. Check the *Pariscope, l'Officiel des Spectacles, Zurban,* or the French daily *Libération,* whose cultural coverage is excellent. For a younger and hipper take on the culture scene, pick up the latest copy of *Nova Magazine* in any kiosk and you'll drown in the choices of cutting-edge events.

Cinema

Paris is a cinema-lover's paradise, with more movie houses than any other city in the world. (Don't forget that the Cannes Film Festival and the

Deauville Festival are in France!) On any given night, there are around 300 films to be seen in Paris. You probably won't have time or the inclination to go to the movies while you're in Paris, but if you happen to notice that there is a great French film you've been dying to see, pick one of Paris's more illustrious movie houses and enjoy both the film and this very Parisian pastime. The beautifully stylized advertisements before the film are worth the hefty admission price alone. Plan to pay between €7 and €10 per entrance, depending on the cinema and the time. For listings, check the weekly *Pariscope* or *l'Officiel des Spectacles*, on sale at all newsstands.

Be careful: If you are choosing an English-language film, make sure it is playing in VO *(version originale)*, marked next to the listing. Otherwise, you'll be watching Woody Allen dubbed into French. If it's a Swedish film in VO, it'll be in Swedish with French subtitles. If it's in VF *(version française)*, the film will be dubbed into French.

Traditionally, cinema ushers are tipped 25 to 50 eurocents per person. This custom has disappeared in almost all of the large cinemas. The smaller ones still practice the habit. You're not obliged to comply, but it'll be a bit awkward to snub the usher if she's helped you find a seat.

Film times are listed in two ways: *séances* (the times when the shorts, coming attractions, and commercials begin), and the *films* (the time that the picture actually begins, usually 10–20 minutes later). Films usually play twice each night, around 7:30 p.m. and around 10 p.m., but this obviously depends on the length of the film. For late-night showings (11 p.m.– midnight) on weekends, check *Pariscope*.

To reserve seats at selected cinemas, check the listing in *Pariscope,* and call **Allo-Ciné** at Tel. 01 40 30 30 31, followed by # and the three-digit code found under the listing.

The Red Lights of Paris

One of the great clichés that Paris cannot seem to shake is the city's nightlife proclivity for girlie shows, can-can, cabaret, and *le grand spectacle.* Much of this comes from the simple fact that there is a healthy selection of famous and flamboyant shows in this genre that are relentlessly promoted. Although the leading shows are primarily nourished by foreign visitors, tourists, and French people from the provinces, much of the continued popularity of these extravaganzas is rooted to a constant reality: The French love glamour and possess a guiltless adoration for the female body, preferably unclothed. Being outside the jurisdiction of Anglo-Saxon puritanical attitudes and the gnawing pressure to be politically correct, you may permit yourself to check out some very exciting costumes . . . and the loveliness that they conceal.

Depending on your own tastes, these shows may seem kitschy or tacky, but they can also be a lot of fun since they are larger than life. Beware, though, that these shows are relatively expensive, but promise to be unforgettable. Only you can decide if the outlay is worth it.

Here are your choices: **Crazy Horse Saloon, Paradis Latin, Folies Bergère, Lido Cabaret,** and the well-known **Moulin Rouge.** See the Nightclub Profiles later in this chapter for details.

Tips for Going Out on the Town

Dress Codes for Paris Clubs

If you see a listing for a Paris club and are wondering how to dress, here are a few suggestions to guide you.

tenue correcte = nice but not fancy; jacket for men, dress or pantsuit for women
chic = dressed up with a touch of flair
free wear = as you like
chemise et veste obligatoires = jacket and tie required
mode = stylish, fashion-conscious
folies wear = extravagant, crazy, fantasy
ouest parisien = conservative, dressy
fancy = eveningwear
le plus fou sera le mieux! = off-the-wall, bizarre

Prices and Entrance Fees (Prix de l'entrée)

According to North American standards, Paris clubs and bars are expensive, and at times, absurdly expensive. To get into a nightclub, count on spending about €15 per person on the *prix de l'entrée,* although at some clubs on some nights, women don't have to pay admission. Most clubs offer you one drink *(consommation)* with a paid entrance. The prices of mixed drinks in these places are exorbitant, however. The price of drinks in bars depends greatly on the bar, the time, and the neighborhood (see the Nightclub Profiles later in this chapter).

Sexuality

We'll just share a few thoughts here. Public affection is both prevalent and embraced (sorry about the pun) in France. Being in love (short- or long-term) in Paris is the perfect excuse for just about anything. Nudity in the advertisements on billboards on the streets and in the Métro will quickly help you understand that there is an openness and comfort level with sexuality, sensuality, the body, and its desires and functions, that we simply don't have in the United States. Even prostitution and pornography are integrated comfortably into French culture, and more specifically, into that of Paris. It might interest you to know that the controversy over former President Clinton's behavior amused Parisians to no end, since they found the puritanism of Americans and our culture's fascination with sexual "dirty laundry" to epitomize the ridiculous.

Don't be surprised when you see attractive women standing by the sides of the main avenues leading into Paris luring customers to the curb. Similarly, the **Bois de Boulogne** is famous for its variety of exotic prostitutes, male and female (and male as female), attracting clients for amorous liaisons in the suburban woods. And the dark roads through the **Bois de Vincennes** are studded in the afternoon and night with parked step vans, all of them curiously all-white, decked out with mattresses for any interested passing motorists. A stroll down the colorful and perfectly harmless rue St. Denis in the heart of Paris affords you an excellent means of safely observing the world's oldest profession in practice with typical Parisian *laissez faire.*

Gay and Lesbian Paris

Gay and lesbian travelers will be pleased to note that the gay community in Paris is large, lively, and visible. Over the last decade the Marais has emerged as a popular area for gays, with a healthy selection of gay bars, shops, and bookstores, the best of which is *Les Mots à la Bouche,* at 6, rue Sainte Croix de la Bretonnerie, 75004; Tel. 01 42 78 88 30; Métro: St Paul–Le Marias. Here you'll find both French and English-language books and publications of interest to gays and lesbians, and additional information on gay activities in Paris.

An excellent source of information is the *Guide Gai,* an annual publication, offering readers comprehensive listings of gay bars, restaurants, hotels, activities, groups, and services. Parisians in general are highly tolerant or indifferent when it comes to people's sexual preferences and activities. If you are a gay tourist in Paris, you should feel no tension or discrimination due to your sexuality. For issues concerning health and safety, there is a gay hotline called *S.O.S. Ecoute Gay* (Tel. 01 44 93 01 02), but counseling may not be available in English. **The Gay and Lesbian Center,** located at 3, rue Keller, 75011; Tel. 01 43 57 21 47; Métro: Ledru-Rollin, offers information on activities and events of interest to gay participants. For information in English on issues related to HIV and AIDS, call **FACTS,** Tel. 01 44 93 16 32; hotline Tel. 01 44 93 16 69, Monday and Wednesday, 6–10 p.m.

There are many popular gay bars in Paris. Gay visitors to Paris often praise the establishments along the rue des Archives, rue Vieille du Temple, and rue Sainte Croix Bretonnerie.

Safe Sex

It took the French some time to take the news seriously and change their habits, but on the whole campaigns for safe sex in this age of AIDS has been successful. Condoms *(préservatifs)* are widely available at subsidized prices in pharmacies and in automatic dispenser machines in hundreds of public places around the city, including Métro stations. Condoms for women *(préservatif féminin)* are also commercially available although not widely used.

OUR FAVORITE PARIS NIGHTCLUBS

Jazzy Clubs

Au Duc des Lombards
La Chapelle des Lombards
La Locomotive
Le Bilboquet
Petit Opportun

Literary Places

Café Beaubourg
Café de Flore
Closerie des Lilas
La Palette
Les Deux Magots

Hip Clubs

Batofar
China Club
Les Bains Douche
The Reservoir
Sans-Sanz

Ethno-Hip

La Favela Chic
Le Mécano Bar

Good for a Drink

Buddha Bar
Clown Bar
Harry's New York Bar
La Palette
Le Fumoir
Le Petit Fer à Cheval
Le Sancerre
Les Philosophes
Rosebud
Taverne Henri-IV

World Music

Satellit' Café

Ballroom Dancing and Salsa

Le Balajo

The Big Shows

Crazy Horse Saloon
Folies Bergére
Le Lido
Moulin Rouge

OUR FAVORITE PARIS NIGHTCLUBS BY LOCATION

Name	Description
1st arrondissement	
Au Duc Des Lombards	Jazz club and pub
Petit Opportun	Favorite Châtelet jazz club
Taverne Henri-IV	Wine bar for professionals and regulars believing in the old France

OUR FAVORITE PARIS NIGHTCLUBS BY LOCATION (continued)

Name	Description
2nd arrondissement	
Harry's New York Bar	Celebrated American cocktail bar for expats
3rd arrondissement	
Les Bains Douches	Paris's most talked-about celebrity nightclub; a place to look and be seen
4th arrondissement	
Café Beaubourg	Stylish late-night café for the culture crowd
Le Petit Fer à Cheval	Café perfect for late-night drinks and local flavor
6th arrondissement	
Café de Flore	Literary café that's quaint day or night
Closerie des Lilas	Famous literary cocktail bar, café, and restaurant
La Palette	Favorite artists and culture crowd bar and café in the heart of the gallery district
Le Bilboquet	Hip and cosmopolitan jazz club
Les Deux Magots	Famous literary café and late-night watering hole
8th arrondissement	
Buddha Bar	Late-night café and designer restaurant
Crazy Horse Saloon	Cabaret with some of the most beautiful nude women in the world
Le Lido	Top-of-the-line contemporary Parisian cabaret
9th arrondissement	
Folies Bergère	World-famous cabaret club
11th arrondissement	
Clown Bar	Historically registered wine bar filled with authentic charm
La Chapelle des Lombards	Nightclub specializing in tropical music
La Favela Chic	Brazilian bar and restaurant
Le Balajo	Classic Parisian landmark for ballroom dancing and now salsa
Le Mécano Bar	Multicultural, ethno-hip bar
The Reservoir	Popular Bastille bar/nightclub on the crawler circuit
Satellit' Café	Paris's first world music bar/club
12th arrondissement	
China Club	Stylish cocktail/jazz club, restaurant, and speakeasy with smoking room

OUR FAVORITE PARIS NIGHTCLUBS BY LOCATION (continued)	
Name	**Description**
13th arrondissement	
Batofar	Club on a barge in the Seine
14th arrondissement	
Rosebud	Relaxing and cozy cocktail bar
18th arrondissement	
La Locomotive	Celebrated rock-and-roll club from the 1960s
Le Sancerre	Late-night café and bar
Moulin Rouge	Famous Parisian cabaret of mythic proportion

Nightclub Profiles

Note on Food at the Clubs

In the profiled selection of nightlife venues, we have combined nightclubs, bars, cabarets, and late-night and special cafés. The Paris nightclub and bar scene starts late, and although food of some sort is often available, no one goes to these establishments to eat. Only when there is some particularly noteworthy culinary offering have we included information about food.

AU DUC DES LOMBARDS

JAZZ CLUB AND PUB

Who Goes There Mixed jazz lovers

42, rue des Lombards, 75001; 01 42 33 22 88; 1st arrondissement; Métro: Châtelet

Cover €18 **Prices** From €5 **Dress** Casual

Hours Daily, 7:30 p.m.–2 a.m. (3 a.m. on weekends). Concerts at 9 p.m. in winter, 9:30 p.m. in summer.

What goes on This popular jazz club offers not only great live music but also a very comfortable environment. You can even reserve tables here, something not many clubs permit. The jazz varies depending on the group, but you can count on a lot of free jazz. American pianist Bobby Few, who still plays here, introduced live music at the Duc des Lombards in the 1970s.

Setting & atmosphere Low lighting with comfortable chairs and a pleasantly subdued atmosphere.

If you go Sometimes Monday is big-band night, but the mix is always changing.

BATOFAR

NEW AND POPULAR CLUB ON A BARGE IN THE SEINE

Who Goes There Hip locals

Facing 11, quai François-Mauriac, 75013; 01 56 29 10 33;
13th arrondissement; Métro: Bibliothèque Nationale

Cover Free—€15 depending on the night **Prices** €3.50 for a beer **Dress** Casual **Food available** Basic cantine-style munchies available Tuesday–Saturday, 5–9 p.m.

Hours Daily, 9 p.m.–3 a.m. (4 a.m. on weekends)

What goes on The Batofar is the place to be in Paris. An intelligent and eclectic program is offered each month, including the best of European house, funk, electronica, and techno. Live music of all sorts. The Batofar—literally translated "lighthouse boat"—is exactly that. Completely restored with a very solid sound system, it fills up with people instead of water every night. Consistent and different.

Setting & atmosphere You're on a hot, packed, and sweaty houseboat moored on the Seine. Wild, lively, and fun.

If you go Get there early if you don't want to feel like a refugee left ashore! No credit cards accepted.

BUDDHA BAR

LATE-NIGHT CAFÉ AND DESIGNER RESTAURANT

Who Goes There Fashion, business, film crowd, and people-watchers

8, rue Boissy d'Anglas, 75008; 01 53 05 90 00; 8th arrondissement; Métro: Concorde

Cover No cover charge **Prices** Drinks start at €6 for a Coke and then skyrocket **Dress** Trendy **Food available** Bar snacks, sashimi, tempura, sushi; Chinese chicken salad

Hours Daily, noon–3 p.m. and 6 p.m.–2 a.m.

What goes on So you've got some cash to throw around, you're thinking of selling your Sony stock, and you need some Japanese advice on the matter with an enormous Buddha overlooking the conversation. This is the place for you! Excellent mixed drinks and good wine list. The food is mediocre. You'll hear beautiful modern Indian music mixed by DJ Ravin.

Setting & atmosphere Place to be seen. Over-the-top decor dominated by Buddha icon.

If you go Don't eat. Too pricey and trendy.

CAFÉ BEAUBOURG

STYLISH LATE-NIGHT CAFÉ, MEETING SPOT FOR THE CULTURE CROWD

Who Goes There Writers, publishers

100, rue Saint-Martin, 75004; 01 48 87 63 9; 4th arrondissement; Métro: Châtelet

Cover None **Prices** €3–8 **Dress** Casual **Food available** Salads, seafood, sandwiches, traditional food

Hours Daily, 8 a.m.–1 a.m. (until 2 a.m. Wednesday–Saturday)

What goes on Literary musing, networking among publishers and media mavens.

Setting & atmosphere Maybe the old cafés make you uncomfortable. Or maybe you're in Paris for the umpteenth time and need to imagine that you're in some other city. Something more urban with an international airport feel to it. Something designed to work. The Café Beaubourg, just opposite the Centre Georges-Pompidou, is a large bar on two floors. It set out to be a literary café and is. A quiet, concentrated atmosphere prevails. Many newspapers in different languages are read. A bit more expensive than the average café, but you have extra space and aren't bothered if you linger. This is one of the few cafés that serves a glass of water with each espresso and serves milk on the side when you order a crème.

If you go Weather permitting, sit on the comfortable wicker chairs outside and people watch.

CAFÉ DE FLORE

LITERARY CAFÉ THAT'S QUAINT DAY OR NIGHT

Who Goes There Regulars, tourists, intellectuals, neighbors

172, boulevard Saint-Germain-des-Prés, 75006; 01 45 48 55 26
6th arrondissement; Métro: Saint-Germain-des-Prés

Cover None **Prices** Be prepared to spend €4 for a café crème **Dress** Casual

Hours Daily, 7 a.m.–1:30 a.m.

What goes on One of the key landmarks in literary Paris, Café de Flore was founded in 1865 and named after a statue to the goddess of flowers, which no longer sits outside. If you feel like watching Saint-Germain Parisians in an original art deco setting, come to the Flore and nurse a coffee or glass or wine. The prices are high, but it's not every day that you can hang out in the digs of Apollinaire, André Breton, Picasso, and above all Jean-Paul Sartre and Simone de Beauvoir, who wrote here regularly because it was heated. The tradition continues—intellectuals, filmmakers, and philosophers stop in regularly.

Setting & atmosphere This is a café, and the setting varies depending on the time of day or night you visit. Mixed crowd of locals, intellectuals, letter-writers, hopeful literati, and foreign tourists. Art deco decor.

If you go Weather permitting, sit on the terrace, order a café crème, and plan to waste away a leisurely hour or two.

CHINA CLUB

STYLISH COCKTAIL/JAZZ CLUB, RESTAURANT, AND SPEAKEASY WITH SMOKING ROOM

Who Goes There All ages, chic and well-dressed, romantics

50, rue de Charenton, 75012; 01 43 43 82 02

12th arrondissement; Métro: Bastille or Ledru Rollin

Cover None **Prices** Small beers for €4, cocktails €5–11 **Dress** Casual chic, stylish **Specials** Nonalcoholic fresh fruit mixed drinks at €6 **Food available** 7 p.m.–12:30 a.m., refined Chinese cuisine

Hours Sunday–Thursday, 7 p.m.–2 a.m.; Friday and Saturday, 10:30 p.m.–3 a.m. (concerts), happy hour 7–9 p.m.

What goes on Classy French colonial–style Chinese restaurant with a very high-class cocktail bar upstairs and, on most evenings, a DJ down in the cellar. If you do go upstairs to the *fumoir chinois,* you'll be seduced by the lacquered walls and very discreet and dark seating. You'll quickly forget you're in Paris; you could be in Hong Kong or New York. Despite the high prices, the cocktails are among the best in town. This is not the place to go if you feel more comfortable in your jeans and T-shirt. If you're meeting your sweetie's parents for the first time, this is a good bet. Red velvet curtains, leather lounge chairs, cigar smoke . . . far too much smoke.

Setting & atmosphere This hideaway has a feel of being out of time, a mysterious place filled with elegance and intrigue. You'll think you're in a spy novel turned into a film that was shot in Shanghai in the 1930s. Charlie Chan goes Yuppie.

If you go Act like you've been there before.

CLOSERIE DES LILAS

FAMOUS LITERARY COCKTAIL BAR, CAFÉ, AND RESTAURANT

Who Goes There Intellectuals with money, ultra-chic bourgeois clan, wannabe writers, snobs, artists, and tourists

171, boulevard du Montparnasse, 75006; 01 40 51 34 50

6th arrondissement; Métro: Vavin or Port-Royal

Cover None **Prices** Small beers €5, cocktails €10–12, brasserie meals from €42 a person, restaurant meals around €73 without wine **Dress** Casual to dressy **Food available** Brasserie food all day; steak tartare, fish, salads

Hours Daily, noon–3 p.m. and 7–11:15 p.m. (restaurant); 11 a.m.–2 a.m. (bar); noon–1 a.m. (brasserie)

What goes on One of Paris's most celebrated cafés, immortalized by Hemingway's *A Moveable Feast,* in which the writer states his disapproval of the 1923 change of policy in the café obliging the waiters to shave their mustaches in order to attract a higher-class clientele. The café nonetheless was frequented religiously by the likes of Verlaine, Lenin, Baudelaire, the Symbolist poets, the Surrealists, the Dadaists, F. Scott Fitzgerald, Archibald MacLeish, and so on. According to literary café biographer, Noël Riley Fitch, it was here that James Joyce celebrated Sylvia Beach's decision to publish *Ulysses* in February 1921. So, if motivated by literary lore, come here for a drink or stay on for dinner in either the brasserie (better deal, known for its excellent steak tartare) or more formal restaurant, which is stylish but overpriced. The open-air terrace is pleasant, but the prices inhibit all but best-selling authors in today's upscale market. A drink at the elegant mahogany bar, however, by the brass plate marked "E. Hemingway" will prove to be a memorable moment. Now owned by the same management as Café de Flore.

Setting & atmosphere Superb decor that's warm and inviting. Great oak bar, studded with copper. See the engraved plaque to Hemingway. Polished wood chairs. Mosaic floors. Large piano.

If you go Eat on the brasserie side, or simply nurse a drink and take in the historical vibes.

CLOWN BAR

HISTORICALLY REGISTERED WINE BAR FILLED WITH AUTHENTIC CHARM

Who Goes There Mixed, thirties crowd, after-theater or cinema crowd

114, rue Amelot, 75011; 01 43 55 87 35; 11th arrondissement; Métro: Filles du Calvaire

Cover None **Prices** €4 for a glass of wine, €30 for dinner **Dress** Casual **Specials** Loire wines **Food available** Roast pork, blood sausage, shepherd's pie

Hours Monday–Friday, noon–2:30 p.m. and 7 p.m.–midnight; Saturday and Sunday, 7 p.m.– midnight. Closed ten days in August.

What goes on The Clown Bar is like a museum piece that should have been in Orson Welles's personal collection. Circus paraphernalia is everywhere. Good, simple food and drink are served in a laid-back but friendly style. The Bouglione Circus is just next door in the old Cirque d'Hiver, used by the Nazis to round up Jews and political prisoners during World War II. Slip inside and see the decor. Burt Lancaster made a fabulous movie here called *Trapeze*. Original and charming.

Setting & atmosphere Beautifully decorated walls with the clown motif. Very warm atmosphere. Great zinc bar. Painted tiles, starlit ceiling. Owned by an antique dealer. Staff could use a lesson in customer service.

If you go Start your evening off with a glass of recommended Loire wine.

CRAZY HORSE SALOON

CABARET WITH SOME OF THE MOST BEAUTIFUL NUDE WOMEN IN THE WORLD

Who Goes There Tourists, out-of-town visitors

12, avenue George V, 75008; 01 47 23 32 32; 8th arrondissement
Métro: George V; www.crazy-horse.fr

Cover €70–90 depending where you sit, includes two drinks **Prices** Extra drinks start at €16 **Dress** Fancy **Food available** Dinner and show at €120, uninteresting but well-prepared French and international dishes; little choice

Hours Daily, 7:30 p.m.–2 a.m.; show, Monday–Friday, 8:30 p.m. and 11 p.m.; or shows Sunday–Friday, 8:30 p.m. and 11:30 p.m., Saturday, 8 p.m., 10:15 p.m., and 12:15 a.m.

What goes on Founded in 1951, the Crazy Horse has become unique in the world of girlie show business. This French parody of an American western saloon, featuring its established "teasing" show, now hosts original acts like 12 paintings in motion, classical as well as contemporary, consisting of 20 exceptional dancers revolving in a nude rainbow of light. Each of these live "paintings" represents a sculptural and luminous masterpiece. This nude revue emphasizes the divine figure of the dancers and is undoubtedly the most beautiful and professional in the world, as per the vision of the late founder, Alain Bernardin, who proudly mounted a corps of exquisite and well-paid beauties. Drinks are served during the show, but you can easily get away with the two that come with the entrance. Fully air-conditioned. Reservations required. The show lasts an hour and a half.

Setting & atmosphere Situated between traditional burlesque and the art of upscale sleaze, you get to gawk at some impressive female bodies without feeling politically incorrect. Stage lights, red curtains, slinky costumes that come undone at the right moments characterize the room. Lots of middle-aged, well-dressed tourists and out-of-town French visitors. Famous Mounties stand out front.

If you go Take in the show but eat elsewhere.

FOLIES BERGÈRE

WORLD-FAMOUS CABARET CLUB

Who Goes There Tourists and out-of-town guests

32, rue Richer, 75009; 01 44 79 98 98; 9th arrondissement
Métro: Cadet or Grands Boulevards

Cover €14–53 depending on seats; show and dinner €100–114 **Prices** Menus starting at €18 **Dress** Dressy **Food available** Fixed menu when you opt for the dinner show

Hours Tuesday–Sunday, 7 p.m.–2 a.m.; shows at 9 p.m., Sunday at 3 p.m.; dinner from 7 p.m.

What goes on The Folies Bergère, renowned for lively burlesque entertainment, is the oldest music hall in Paris and a permanent landmark since 1886. The risqué African American singer and dancer Josephine Baker made a name for herself at this club. Today, the nudity and eroticism has been greatly toned down; if it's skin you're hoping to see beyond the feathers and glitter, you may be disappointed. It's still a good show and makes for a one-of-a-kind evening.

Setting & atmosphere This is the real thing. Large, impressive showroom and stage. Old-world ambience stuffed into a watered-down show.

If you go Don't be late. The doors shut as the show starts.

HARRY'S NEW YORK BAR

Celebrated American cocktail bar for expats

Who Goes There Anglo-Franco literary and journalist scene, businessmen

5, rue Daunou, 75002; 01 42 61 71 14; 2nd arrondissement; Métro: Opéra

Cover None **Prices** €4–13 **Dress** Respectable; loosened neckties, after-work look

Hours Daily, 10:30 a.m.–4 a.m.

What goes on You probably aren't interested in hanging out at an American bar in Paris, but this one is such a fixture on the Paris bar scene that you might want to make an exception. Established in 1911, Harry's Bar, then called New York Bar, the oldest cocktail bar in Europe, still retains much the same feel and decor. College banners on the wall, lots of dark varnished wood, and sporting photographs of regular Ernest Hemingway fishing and hunting. Allegedly the birthplace of the Bloody Mary, which regulars swear by. In fact, the experienced bar staff does an impressive job with all the cocktails (mixing exactly the right measure effortlessly). A bit pricey, but a good value nevertheless. There's a piano bar downstairs, where George Gershwin played "An American in Paris" while F. Scott Fitzgerald drank until he collapsed. Harry's enjoys a regular clientele of expats, foreign journalists, and American-loving French who have great stories and share a common feeling of belonging here. The bar is famous for its phonetic spelling of its address: "Sank Roo Doe Noo," which was created to help English-speaking customers direct taxi drivers to the bar. Founded by Harry McElhone, whose grandson, Duncan, recently died after managing the bar in the great tradition for many years. The place is legend. Stop in for a time warp and a Bloody Mary.

Setting & atmosphere Enjoy the nostalgia felt in the decor of this landmark. Varnished, dark wooden walls, a charming wooden bar and stools. Black and white photographs everywhere. Downstairs there is a second room with small bar perfect for private parties and receptions and the occasional exhibit.

If you go Go after working hours and plan to drink with the regulars. You'll get a good earful of what's going on in Paris today.

LA CHAPELLE DES LOMBARDS

NIGHTCLUB SPECIALIZING IN TROPICAL MUSIC

Who Goes There Latin, African, and West Indian dance lovers

19, rue de Lappe, 75011; 01 43 57 24 24; 11th arrondissement; Métro: Bastille

Cover €15 Thursday, €18 Friday and Saturday (with one free drink) **Prices** Drinks range from €4–11 **Dress** Dress to get past the bouncers **Specials** Latin concert on Thursday nights

Hours Wednesday–Sunday, 10:30 p.m.–dawn

What goes on For nearly two decades, this rue de Lappe mainstay has been on the circuit for a youngish dance crowd with a passion for Latin and tropical rhythms. Lots of singles come here to dance and mingle. The bouncers have been known to be overly discriminating when it comes to single men.

Setting & atmosphere Electrified atmosphere. You go here with high energy and great expectations to dance, flirt, and boogie. Very crowded.

If you go The Thursday night concert is your best bet.

LA FAVELA CHIC

BRAZILIAN BAR AND RESTAURANT

Who Goes There Hipsters and trendsetters of all colors

18, rue du Faubourg du Temple, 75011; 01 40 21 38 14

11th arrondissement; Métro: Répulique

Cover None **Prices** Drinks from €5 **Dress** Casual **Food available** Brazilian fare of unequalled quality

Hours Tuesday–Saturday, 7 p.m.–2 a.m.

What goes on La Favela Chic is one of the true trendsetters in the emerging Menil-montant area. It's a great bar and restaurant frequented by a younger crowd with a constant stream of newcomers and regulars walking in the door. Inspiring international dishes at excellent prices (€9–12), plus memorable caipirinhas (Brazilian cocktails) at €6! Their new, larger location is the former Cacherel showroom—large and industrial with lots of room for dancing.

Setting & atmosphere Very friendly atmosphere where it's easy to strike up a chat with your neighbors. The drinks are great and the flavor of the venue is better than the food.

If you go Go for a Brazilian cocktail and to hear some authentic samba.

LA LOCOMOTIVE

CELEBRATED ROCK AND ROLL CLUB FROM THE 1960s

Who Goes There Mostly 18–25 set

90, boulevard de Clichy, 75018; 01 53 41 88 88; 18th arrondissement; Métro: Blanche

Cover €11 with a drink included during the week; Sundays, free for women until midnight; €15 with a drink on Friday and Saturday **Prices** €4 for beer, €8 for cocktails **Dress** Casual, but the more rock and roll garb you can muster the better

Hours Daily, 11 p.m.–5 a.m.

What goes on A famous rock club from the 1960s, the Locomotive has been kicking up the scene in Paris for the last few years with its innovative mixes. The enormous club (by Paris standards) on three floors holds up to 2,000 guests. Almost anyone can find something to suit them here, from the harder sounds downstairs in the boiler room to house and techno upstairs.

Setting & atmosphere On three bustling levels you'll get your fill of contemporary rock music. There are bars at every corner and every intersection. Purportedly the largest club in Paris.

If you go Dress up in the style of the 1950s/1960s and head down to the bottom level for the music of the same period.

LA PALETTE

FAVORITE ARTISTS AND CULTURE CROWD BAR AND CAFÉ IN THE HEART OF THE GALLERY DISTRICT

Who Goes There An artsy crowd

43, rue de Seine, 75006; 01 43 26 68 15; 6th arrondissement; Métro: Mabillon or Odéon

Cover None **Prices** €3–5 **Dress** Casual **Food available** Salads, sandwiches, plats du jours

Hours Monday–Saturday, 8 a.m.–2 a.m; closed August and one week in winter, as well as November 1, Christmas, New Years Day, Easter Monday

What goes on This is a favorite meeting spot for painters, sculptors, photographers, gallery people, art lovers, neighbors, and Americans. Always lively and rarely pretentious, La Palette represents the best of the area. The paintings on the wall in the back depict the ageless waiters. The wines are excellent and reasonably priced. This is one of the best spots to be on midnight in November when the beaujolais nouveau is legally released. Good, traditional French food, and on warm days and evenings you can sit out on the sidewalk. Very friendly service if they know you. A bit cool if they don't. A mixed crowd of people from the galleries, the Beaux Arts nearby, and tourists.

Setting & atmosphere Totally unpretentious while being perpetually frequented by an elite culture crowd. Very Parisian. Simple decor with a room in the back for light lunches or just those wishing to hang out and drink with friends. The waiters have been there for centuries.

LE BALAJO

CLASSIC PARISIAN LANDMARK FOR BALLROOM DANCING (AND NOW SALSA)

Who Goes There Diverse crowd, depends on event

9, rue de Lappe, 75011; 01 47 00 07 87; 11th arrondissement; Métro: Bastille

Cover €15 with one drink. €8 for afternoon dancing on Thursdays and Sundays **Prices** €9 **Dress** Depends on event

Hours Wednesday, 9 p.m.–5 a.m.; Thursday, 10 p.m.–2 a.m.; Friday and Saturday, 11 p.m.– 5 a.m.; Bal-musette, Thursday and Sunday, 3–7 p.m.

What goes on A true undying rose of a club, the Balajo—literally "Joe's ball" if you want the English translation—is a fantastic old ballroom from the turn of the century. One of the few places that still caters and creates events for an older clientele in the afternoon and a younger crowd for salsa, often until sunrise. You can feel the ghost of Edith Piaf moving between the dances.

Setting & atmosphere Large dance floor with original feel from the 1930s. Tables scattered around the edges. A fascinating time-warp. You'll see elderly couples waltzing one night, or middle-agers jitterbugging, tango afficionados doing their thing, and salsa-lovers moving to the beat—all at the Balajo.

If you go Go in the afternoon to rediscover the atmosphere of a long-lost Paris. Stroll along the rue de Lappe before and after your visit.

LE BILBOQUET

HIP AND COSMOPOLITAN JAZZ CLUB

Who Goes There Thirty-somethings and up

13, rue Saint-Benoît, 75006; 01 45 48 81 84
6th arrondissement; Métro: Saint-Germain-des-Prés

Cover None **Prices** Dinners €38–53; drinks from €20 (includes show) **Dress** Casual
Food available Good and straight-forward dishes; menu changes seasonally

Hours Daily, 8 p.m.–2:45 a.m.; jazz, 10:30 p.m.–2:15 a.m; restaurant serves until midnight

What goes on Fame graced this comfortable jazz venue when the film *Paris Blues* was shot here. The club has two levels, and the jazz gigs happen upstairs, in the restaurant. The food is standard French fare and not bad, although a bit pricey. You're paying for the music, and in the end it's worth it.

Setting & atmosphere Very classy club that attracts the famed and talented crowd. Liza Minelli, David Bowie, and others are known to duck in here when in Paris. The mezzanine is lovely. The wood, copper, and brass decor adds flavor to the evening. This is one of the oldest jazz venues in Saint-Germain-des-Prés (1947).

If you go Note that the orchestra plays from 10:30 p.m. in three sets until 1 a.m. The jazz is always very classical.

LE LIDO

TOP-OF-THE-LINE CONTEMPORARY PARISIAN CABARET

Who Goes There International visitors and out-of-town guests

116 bis, avenue des Champs-Elysées, 75008; 01 40 76 56 10
8th arrondissement; Métro: George V

Cover €123–155 for dining and dancing including champagne; floor show only, €85; bar seats available at €57 **Prices** Included in cover prices **Dress** Dressy **Specials** Dining/dancing at 8 p.m.; shows at 10 p.m. and 12:15 a.m. daily **Food available** French cuisine, menu and à la carte, planned by famed chef Paul Bocuse

Hours Daily, 8 p.m.–5 a.m.

What goes on The famous Bluebell Girls, founded by Miss Bluebell as everybody calls her, are clothed in feathers and light-reflecting material and sometimes little else but the latest modern technologies (lasers and video), making for a breathtaking spectacle. The performance is timed to a second with fantastic special effects. But the Lido is also known for its top international stars (magicians, singers, dancers), who will enchant you. If the Lido claims to be a world-famous floor show, it's because it knows just how to put on a magnificent show. This world-renowned venue presents its famous international revue in a one-and-a-half-acre cabaret. As the show begins, the dining floor goes down with all the spectators, leaving the dance floor clear to become an elevated stage offering a perfect panoramic view.

Setting & atmosphere Set on the Champs-Elysées, the Lido is the most elaborate cabaret show in the world today. A fanfare of costumes, lights, glitter, music, feathers, etc., the aesthetics collectively impress and enchant, although the whole deal is a kicking cliché caught between the turn-of-the-century and the new millennium.

If you go Reserve ahead.

LE MÉCANO BAR

MULTICULTURAL, ETHNO-HIP BAR

Who Goes There 20ish and ethno-hip crowd

99, rue Oberkampf, 75011; 01 40 21 35 28; 11th arrondissement; Métro: Parmentier

Cover None **Prices** Small beers €2.50–3.50, cocktails €6 **Dress** Casual **Specials** Coconut punch **Food available** Brunch at €13; eclectic menu ranging from chicken tagine to homemade foie gras

Hours Monday–Saturday, 9 a.m.–2 a.m.; Sunday, 10 p.m.–2 a.m.

What goes on Great ambience, comfortable wooden decor, and cheap, quality drinks ... one of the best surprises in this quarter. Oberkampf is what Bastille was before they built the opera. You should certainly take a night out in this area. The bar crowd overflows into the street and the ambience is festive. At times, a philosophy café and venue for book signings and traveling exhibitions. Fun place, but it gets crazy and the service suffers.

Setting & atmosphere Former tool shop founded in 1832. Cluttered with a number of old machines. You'll love the paintings of nymphs and the car engine on the ceiling.

If you go Stop in for a beer and to soak up the local Oberkampf scene.

LE PETIT FER À CHEVAL

CAFÉ PERFECT FOR LATE-NIGHT DRINKS AND LOCAL FLAVOR

Who Goes There Mixed, regulars, visitors, late-nighters

30, rue Vieille-du-Temple, 75004; 01 42 72 47 47
4th arrondissement; Métro: Hôtel de Ville or St.-Paul

Cover None **Prices** Dinner €18 without wine **Dress** Casual **Food available** Good, simple bistro fare

Hours Daily, 9 a.m.–2 a.m.

What goes on Since the turn of the last century this has been a local bistro where one feels good about coming back day after day. Stop in to have a drink, to nibble, to talk about nothing at all and the affairs of the heart. Good selection of lesser wines and pleasing background jazz.

Setting & atmosphere We've made many friends over the years at the Petit Fer à Cheval by just putting our elbows on the horseshoe-shaped bar and keeping an open mind. The small restaurant behind the bar with its little window onto the kitchen only adds to the charm of this café. Xavier, the owner, collects art to decorate the rooms, constantly changes the wine list with nice discoveries, and keeps the staff sharp, friendly, and responsive. A classic that has survived the 1990s in fine style.

If you go Go anytime. A perfect meeting spot in the Marais.

LE SANCERRE

LATE-NIGHT CAFÉ AND BAR

Who Goes There Locals, eccentrics, very hip individuals and deadbeats

35, rue des Abesses, 75018; 01 42 58 08 20; 18th arrondissement; Métro: Abbesses

Cover None **Prices** Around €3 for drinks, €11 for meals **Dress** Casual **Specials** Plat du jour, €9 **Food available** Down to earth, simple country dishes

Hours Daily, 7 a.m.–2 a.m.

What goes on If you get fed up walking around and want a steak and French fries, some heady wine, or a choice of beers all served with a rock and roll attitude, then stop in at La Sancerre. Named after the wine and its region, La Sancerre is a large bar that is packed on weekend nights and spills out onto the terrace. A great place to inhale the real parfum of Paris while listening to the loud music of the barman's choice.

Setting & atmosphere A simple neighborhood café to start with, this place quickly gained its reputation due to the generous and open-spirited owner and his good drinks and simple dishes.

If you go Tuesday night is especially fun.

LES BAINS DOUCHES

PARIS'S MOST TALKED-ABOUT CELEBRITY NIGHTCLUB; A PLACE TO LOOK AND BE SEEN

Who Goes There Young and beautiful, glittery people

7, rue du Bourg-L'Abbé, 75003; 01 48 87 01 80 or 01 48 87 54 78
3rd arrondissement; Métro: Etienne-Marcel

Cover Monday–Friday €15.24, Saturday and Sunday €18.29 **Prices** drinks about €10; restaurant meals about €40 per person **Dress** Star-studded, fantasy **Food available** Thai restaurant inside, with full Thai repertoire

Hours Daily, 11:30 p.m.–dawn; restaurant serves 9 p.m. to midnight

What goes on David and Cathy Guetta, golden boy and wild girl of Paris nightlife, have redeveloped the feeling inside this Paris institution. Now it's a funkier and wilder club, but it's still filled with the same clientele: top models, TV people, executives, the Brat Pack, and international stars. Here they let their hair hang loose in rare style to the sounds of Superfly, Happy House, or even the Beatles. Bring a lot of cash! You better look sharp, too. The only sneakers worn here are on the DJ's feet behind the sound booth.

Setting & atmosphere Rich people and wannabe stars stop by here regularly to see each other and the real stars.

If you go If you reserve in the restaurant you'll avoid the bouncer scrutiny. The problem here is that you don't go to Les Bains to eat.

LES DEUX MAGOTS

FAMOUS LITERARY CAFÉ AND LATE-NIGHT WATERING-HOLE

Who Goes There Locals and tourists

6, place Saint-Germain-des-Prés, 75006; 01 45 48 55 25
6th arrondissement; Métro: Saint-Germain-des-Prés

Cover None **Prices** €4 for a café crème **Dress** Casual **Food available** Café fare

Hours Daily, 7:30 a.m.–1:30 a.m.; closed one week in January

What goes on Opposite from its rival, literary Café le Flore, Les Deux Magots is deliciously situated at the corner of Boulevard Saint-Germain facing the Saint-Germain church. One of Paris's most famous cafés, it was founded in 1875 and supposedly named after the two porcelain Chinese figures that remain on the center posts inside the café. The second home to many writers, artists, and cultural personalities throughout the 20th century, Les Deux Magots is noted as the café in which Picasso created cubism and Breton and Aragon drafted the surrealist manifestos. Hemingway, Sartre, de Beauvoir, and plenty of others drank and conversed here. Plan to linger for a while and let the past meet the present. The prices are absurdly high for a coffee or glass of wine, but think of it as the price to rent the space.

Setting & atmosphere Here you are in the heart of literary folklore that continues to ring true. People around you will be reading Le Monde and good books, writing in diaries, and having lively topical or philosophical discussions. The charming decor dates back to World War I. And the quality of the service has always been a point of great pride to the establishment.

If you go Nurse your drink for a while and don't be in a hurry. Or go early in the morning for a splendid Parisian breakfast on the terrace (€12).

MOULIN ROUGE

FAMOUS PARISIAN CABARET OF MYTHIC PROPORTION

Who Goes There Out-of-town visitors, tourists

82, boulevard de Clichy, 75018; 01 53 09 82 82; 18th arrondissement; Métro: Blanche

Cover Floor show €89 at 9 p.m. and €79 at 11 p.m.; show and dinner from €125, €140, €155 **Prices** Included in cover **Dress** Formal **Food available** Traditional French cuisine

Hours Daily, dinner before the show at 7 p.m.; shows begin at 9 p.m. and 11 p.m.

What goes on Its very name breathes the mythical spirit of Montmartre and the Paris of painter Toulouse-Lautrec, the frilly feminines, the French can-can dance, which is best seen here. A historic moment built on glittering spangles. The "formidable" floor show and the 100 Moulin girls will wow you. Try to count the number of times they change costume, or just sit back and enjoy the perfection of dancing and their dynamic high-kicking French can-can in voluminous skirts and petticoats. Formal dress is required.

Setting & atmosphere Exactly like you've seen it in old French films. Everything is still in place right down to the ostrich feathers that tickle your nose. A good excuse to get a dose of French can-can dancers.

If you go Reserve in advance. Not necessary to eat here as well.

PETIT OPPORTUN

FAVORITE CHÂTELET JAZZ CLUB

Who Goes There Regulars, 30 and up

15, rue Lavandières, 75001; 01 42 36 01 36; 1st arrondissement; Métro: Châtelet

Cover €12.20 includes first drink **Prices** From €4.50 **Dress** Casual

Hours Daily, bar at 9:30 p.m., concerts at 11 p.m.

What goes on This is an old standby for the Paris jazz crowd. An underground cellar, this dive boasts of its funky piano and its creative mix of local talent.

Setting & atmosphere Very friendly atmosphere in a well decorated and aesthetically pleasing cellar dating back to the 13th century.

If you go It gets very steamy, so be prepared to shed layers, even in the winter.

THE RESERVOIR

POPULAR BASTILLE BAR/NIGHTCLUB ON THE CRAWLER CIRCUIT

Who Goes There Mixed bag of bar regulars, show-biz types, and hordes of pretty women

16, rue de la Forge-Royale, 75011; 01 43 56 39 60
11th arrondissement; Métro: Faidherbe-Chaligny or Ledru-Rollin

Cover None **Prices** Beer, €4; cocktails, €8–11 **Dress** Casual **Specials** Jazz concert on Sundays **Food available** Bar food, 8 p.m.–midnight; Sunday brunch, noon–4 p.m.

Hours Daily, 8 p.m.–2 a.m., 4 a.m. on weekends. Concerts, Tuesday–Saturday, 11:30 p.m.; closed the week of August 15

What goes on Show-biz, art, and media people define their dreams and ambitions to the eclectic sounds and rhythms programmed by the host, Marcello. Saturdays feature groove. Stars often make surprise appearances.

Setting & atmosphere This transformed storehouse with a fantastic decor (a mix of stone and wood) is the place for the cool crowd in Paris to be.

If you go Go late.

ROSEBUD

A RELAXING AND COZY COCKTAIL BAR

Who Goes There 30 and up

11 bis, rue Delambre, 75014; 01 43 35 38 54; 14th arrondissement; Métro: Vavin

Cover None **Prices** Small beers €5–7, cocktails €9.45 **Dress** Casual **Specials** Excellent cocktails

Hours Daily, 7 p.m.–2 a.m.; closed August, Christmas, and New Year's

What goes on At €9.45 for a Bloody Mary, it better be bloody good! A true American cocktail bar with real bartenders that shake up a storm of iced drinks that can whittle your wallet down. Ask to see where Jean-Paul Sartre used to sit. Today, the place has that "has been" feel to it, but the way they hang onto days gone by has its own charm, and the piped-in jazz tunes are perfect for a melancholic trip to the bar. Some say this has become a haunt for middle-agers hoping not to go home alone.

Setting & atmosphere Ideal for recharging your batteries after a stressful day. Beautiful 1930s decor with bistro-style tables and filtered light.

If you go Order a cocktail and put up your feet.

SANS-SANZ

SUPER-HOT CLUB FOR THE ROWDY AND BEAUTIFUL

Who Goes There Pretty, sexy, young, party crowd

49, rue du Fbg Saint-Antoine, 75011; 01 44 75 78 78
11th arrondissement; Métro: Ledru-Rollin

Cover €3–6 **Prices** €4–10 **Dress** Casual **Food available** Yes, upstairs

Hours Daily, 9 a.m.–2 a.m.

What goes on Excellent French bar in the Bastille that's positively heaving at weekends. Other reviewers have reported a difficult door policy, but you may not notice this at all. They serve food upstairs in a more relaxed atmosphere, but this is not really a place you go to eat.

Setting & atmosphere The crowd is cosmopolitan, young, and friendly. DJs spin the disks, while the crowd enjoys the music and drinks. The bar staff have a great time dancing and banging the symbol lampshades at strategic moments in hip-hop hits. It was extremely hot even in March when Paris was cold, so could be unbearable in summer.

If you go Prepare for a full-court press of clubgoers. On the same crawl, you can check out El Barrio salsa club across the street in the direction of the Bastille.

SATELLIT' CAFÉ

PARIS'S FIRST WORLD MUSIC BAR/CLUB

Who Goes There Very mixed, world music crowd

44, rue de la Folie Méricourt, 75011; 01 47 00 48 87
11th arrondissement; Métro: Saint-Ambroise, Parmentier, or Oberkampf

Cover €8 **Prices** €6–9 **Dress** Casual **Hours** Monday–Thursday, 8 p.m.–3 a.m.; Friday and Saturday, 8 p.m.–6 a.m.

What goes on This is Paris's first world music bar, with a collection of records large enough to make a radio station green with envy. There's an excellent sound system and a faithful clientele that chooses this large bar for the quality of its expression. You'll hear talent from North Africa, Kurdistan, the French West Indies, and French gypsy groups. Check out the 24-track mixing board! There are live bands Tuesday through Thursday and a skillful DJ on the weekends.

Setting & atmosphere Friendly setting for excellent world music and a great mix of faces.

If you go Find out who's playing before you go.

TAVERNE HENRI-IV

WINE BAR FOR PROFESSIONALS AND REGULARS BELIEVING IN THE OLD FRANCE

Who Goes There Lawyers, police inspectors, judges, ministry workers, neighbors

13, place du Pont-Neuf, 75001; 01 43 54 27 90; 1st arrondissement; Métro: Pont-Neuf

Cover None **Prices** €4–9 a glass, bottles start at €15; meals at around €20 **Dress** Casual **Food available** Tartines of cheese and sausage, escargots, platters of cold-cuts

Hours Monday–Friday, noon–10 p.m.; Saturday, noon–4 p.m.; closed three weeks in August

What goes on This is a favorite old-world watering hole sitting pretty on Pont Neuf at the mouth of Place Dauphine. The owner and barman, Robert Cointepas, has been at the helm for over 40 years, serving glasses of 20 or so wines he selects himself. This is a great place to stop in the late afternoon after a day of sightseeing or shopping for a glass of wine and a taste of old France.

Setting & atmosphere The decor is rustic, and the bar is real copper.

If you go Call the owner ahead and tell him what wine you'd like to drink. He'll let your bottle breathe before you arrive.

Index

Hotel Index

Restaurant Index

Unofficial Guide to Paris **Reader Survey**

If you would like to express your opinion about Paris or this guidebook, complete the following survey and mail it to:

Unofficial Guide Reader Survey
PO Box 43673
Birmingham, AL 35243   USA

Inclusive dates of your visit: _____

Members of
your party: Person 1   Person 2   Person 3   Person 4   Person 5
Gender: M   F   M   F   M   F   M   F   M   F
Age: _____

Have you ever been to Europe before? _____
Was this your first trip to Paris? _____
On your most recent trip, where did you stay? _____

Concerning your accommodations, on a scale of 100 as best and 0 as worst, how would you rate:

The quality of your room?   The value of your room?
The quietness of your room?   The reservation process?
Staff's relations with foreigners?   Overall hotel satisfaction?

Did you use public transportation?   What kind?

Concerning public transportation, on a scale of 100 as best and 0 as worst, how would you rate:

Ease of use?   Value vs. rental cars?
Cleanliness?   Hours and areas serviced?
Airport shuttle efficiency?

Concerning your dining experiences:

Estimate the number of meals eaten in restaurants per day. _____
Approximately how much did your party spend on meals per day? _____
Favorite restaurants in Paris: _____
_____

Did you buy this guide before leaving?   while on your trip?

How did you hear about this guide? (check all that apply)

Loaned or recommended by a friend   Radio or TV
Newspaper or magazine   Bookstore salesperson
Just picked it out on my own   Library
Internet

Unofficial Guide to Paris **Reader Survey (continued)**

What other guidebooks did you use on this trip? _____

_____

_____

On a scale of 100 as best and 0 as worst, how would you rate them?

_____

_____

_____

Using the same scale, how would you rate *The Unofficial Guide(s)?*

_____

Are *Unofficial Guides* readily available at bookstores in your area? _____

Have you used other *Unofficial Guides?* _____

Which one(s)? _____

_____

_____

_____

_____

_____

Comments about your Paris trip or *The Unofficial Guide(s):*

_____

_____

_____

_____

_____

_____

_____

_____

_____

_____

_____

_____

_____

_____

_____